THE FOREVER LEADER

THE WOMANHOOD OF GOD

Volume I — THE DISCOVERY of the Science of Man
(1821 — 1888)

Volume II — THE FOUNDING of Christian Science
(1888 — 1900)

Volume III — THE FOREVER LEADER
(1901 — 1910)

THE WOMANHOOD OF GOD

Volume Three

The Forever Leader

The Life of Mary Baker Eddy (1901-1910)

Doris Grekel

Healing UNLIMITED

1999

The picture appearing on the front cover is from a photograph taken during Mary Baker Eddy's address to her students at "Pleasant View," her beloved home in Concord, New Hampshire in the Summer of 1903.
The picture of Mrs. Eddy on the rear cover is a close-up from a photograph of the famous "balcony portrait."

Cover design by David L. Keyston

First Trade Edition

Published by
Healing Unlimited
2100 Third Avenue, Suite 1901
Seattle, WA 98121
(800) 962-1464
Email: heal@ChristianScience.org
http://www.ChristianScience.org

Publisher's Cataloging-in-Publication

Grekel, Doris.
The forever leader : the life of Mary Baker Eddy (1901-1910) / Doris Grekel.
p. cm. -- (The womanhood of God ; v. 3)
Includes bibliographical references and index.
ISBN: 0-9645803-8-1

1. Eddy, Mary Baker, 1821-1910. 2. Christian Scientists--United States--Bibliography. I. Title. II. Series: Grekel, Doris. Womanhood of God ; v. 3.

BX6995.G73 289.5'092 [B]

Printed in the United States of America.

O blessed daughter of Zion, I am with thee. And none shall take my words out of thy lips. Thou art my chosen, to bear my Truth to the nations, and I will not suffer another messenger to go before thee. . . . And I will lift thee up O daughter of Zion. And I will make of thee a new nation for thy praise.

CONTENTS

CONTENTS

PREFACE

IN an early essay Mrs. Eddy said: "The church created, founded and erected on the rock against which the winds and waves prevail not, is the church triumphant, the indwelling temple of God." Mary Baker Eddy demonstrated this "indwelling temple of God" in her own life, explained it in Science and Health, and, to help her followers make this demonstration, she set forth rules in her *Manual* of The Mother's Church, "Mary Baker Eddy's Church" *(Man.* 102).

Mrs. Eddy's sojourn among mortals was devoted to wakening mankind to spiritual life; and the higher she lifted her voice, the louder did error scream lies about her and her blameless life. In one brief answer to the mountains of falsehoods she said: "Above all the fustian of either denying or asserting the personality or presence of Mary Baker Eddy, stands the eternal fact of Christian Science and the honest history of its Discoverer and Founder."

It is the author's hope that the honest history in these pages will help the earnest seeker for Truth to find and to follow the Forever Leader, and thus to "rejoice in the church triumphant."

Doris Grekel
Havilah, California

THE FOREVER LEADER

CHAPTER I

WORKING IN GOD'S VINEYARD

Those, who are willing to leave their nets or to cast them on the right side for Truth, have the opportunity now, as aforetime, to learn and to practise Christian healing. — MARY BAKER EDDY

1886-1888

THE youthful Joseph Mann had experienced a marvelous healing in November of 1886. While target practising with his brother-in-law, a bullet from a thirty-two calibre revolver had accidentally struck him in the chest and rendered him immediately unconscious. The family doctor summoned three eminent physicians and all four pronounced the wound fatal, judging that the ball had probably touched the heart. The body was growing cold and the family physician had departed when Christian Science (which the Manns had never heard of) knocked at the door of their home in Broad Brook, Connecticut and restored the young man to life and health.

Joseph and several of his brothers and sisters began the study of Science and Health right away; and the twenty-two-year-old Joseph healed many who appealed to him for help after hearing of his miraculous recovery. His healing work led him to Mrs. Eddy's Primary class in the Massachusetts Metaphysical College in the fall of 1888. Soon thereafter he began practising Christian Science in Boston where his sister Pauline joined him.

A visit to two of his brothers, Christian and Frederick in Junction City, Kansas eventuated in Frederick's moving to Boston where he, too, became a Christian Science practitioner and was often courier for Mrs. Eddy in later years. Joseph's visit also introduced another young man in Junction City to Christian Science in a roundabout way. John Salchow was too shy to ask about the copy of Science and Health he saw in the Mann brothers' house, but he quietly sent for a copy of his own. When his initial reading brought an immediate healing, he became a serious student.

At a later date a news reporter described John Salchow as a "big Swede," but his family was German, upright in character and bitter towards religion. John very casually left his Science and Health on the parlor table where it could not be missed, and after three weeks his father (who had read the book clandestinely at first) announced that "he had been a pretty hard old infidel, but he knew this woman had found the truth." When Joseph Mann came again to Junction City, this time to teach a class in Christian Science, John Salchow and his eldest sister were in attendance.

Mrs. Eddy was always interested in such resurrective experiences as that of Joseph Mann and one day questioned him about it in detail, most especially the regenerative aspect. Then she stated: "Joseph, you have had a *wonderful* experience; you were thrown violently out of the house, and picked yourself up on the outside; go not back into it."

In 1898 when young Mr. Mann learned that Mrs. Eddy needed an overseer for her Pleasant View estate, he volunteered his services; and was liberally rewarded later that same year by being included in Mrs. Eddy's last class.

Another young man came into Christian Science by a very different route. Two of Calvin C. Hill's brothers and two sisters had died of tuberculosis. Symptoms of the disease together with his fear induced Calvin in 1890 to give up business in the East and try the high, dry climate of Colorado. Two years later a fellow salesman who had been healed by reading Science and Health introduced Mr. Hill to Christian Science, but he rejected it. Refusing much of what his friend had to say for the next three years and continuing his material remedies, Calvin found his condition practically unchanged after five years in Colorado except that he was also suffering distressfully from dyspepsia. The medical help he had sought for this latter ailment had failed to relieve him, and in his distress he decided to give Christian Science a try. He went to Mrs. Frances Mack Mann in Denver and was healed in one treatment. This opened the young man's eyes and his heart to Christian Science, and he began an earnest study of Science and Health.

Shortly thereafter when his Science friend and wife were moving to Boston, Mr. Hill decided to do the same. Early in 1895 he was back on the East coast employed by a fine firm dealing in carpets and draperies in the city of Boston, where he began attending the Mother Church. He was also earnestly pursuing his study of Science and Health, but his thought had been poisoned against Mrs. Eddy by the news media. He resented the testimonies wherein grateful appreciation to the Leader was expressed, until one evening a student of Mrs. Eddy said: "You can no more separate Mrs. Eddy from Science and Health than you can Moses from the Commandments, or Jesus from the Sermon on the Mount." A second awakening took place. The young man's eyes and his heart were opened wider and he began earnestly seeking to *find* Mrs. Eddy in her writings rather than separating them from her. He also sought out other young Christian Scientists for companionship, and in time was living with Joseph Mann and his sister Pauline before their move to Pleasant View in 1898.

One Saturday morning in April, 1899, Laura E. Sargent and James A. Neal came in to John H. Pray and Sons Company in Boston where Mr. Hill was employed, to select samples of floor covering for Pleasant View. After they had left, Mr. Hill felt that something more appropriate could be found for Mrs. Eddy's home and made a quick trip to New York the next day.

The following Tuesday morning found Calvin in a back parlor at Pleasant View arranging his samples and chatting pleasantly with household members when Mrs. Eddy came in. Before that day ended he would have the most wonderful experience of his life up to that point.

When he determined that Mrs. Eddy did not like his evasive answers, he gave her a critical appraisal of some of the decorating which led at a later date to his assisting with redecorating. But at the time Mrs. Eddy's gentle reply was: "You know I do not go shopping very often so that I do not know much about the styles."

Her thoughts were always on the things of the Spirit; and after concluding the carpet business she led Mr. Hill's thought up higher on that Tuesday morning. In her study above the back parlor they conversed for a while. Then she asked him who his teacher was:

> "Well, Mrs. — Mother," I replied, "I believe I shall have to call you my teacher. I have been studying your book Science and Health and your other writings for the past four years, and if what is said to me by one of your own students or by one of your students' students is not backed up or verified by your writings I take no stock in his statements, none whatever!"
>
> Mrs. Eddy stepped forward, placed her hand on my shoulder and patted it gently, saying, "My child, my child, my child, you're safe, you're safe, you're safe!"

The Leader asked Mr. Hill many questions during that first interview and asked him if he had any questions he would like to ask her. She talked as long as he could follow her, and quietly closed the interview when she had taken him as far as he could follow. He was lifted beyond his former self and wrote of the occasion:

> As I left Pleasant View to return to the depot, after this memorable and uplifting experience, I felt as if I were walking on air. Nothing seemed real except the truth which Mrs. Eddy had affirmed and which was inscribed on the disc of my consciousness. . . .
>
> I boarded the train for Boston, and as I rode along, my thought was completely occupied with the great illumination of the reality of Spirit and the nothingness of matter. I felt that I had been lifted to the mount of transfiguration. For a number of days all I could think of, all I could hear, was what Mrs. Eddy had said to me in answer to my question, and the spiritual light which I received during that interview remained with me in all its glory.
>
> From that time I was a different man . . .

A month or so later when Mr. Hill was visiting Joseph and Pauline Mann in the cottage at Pleasant View, he had the privilege of a second interview with Mrs. Eddy, followed by a second exalting experience. This left him with a deep desire to serve the Leader and her Cause in every possible way, which began with his making purchases for her and members of her household.

Very soon Calvin Hill became courier for Mrs. Eddy carrying her messages to her Board of Directors in Boston. This led to assisting the Board, and in time he had the sole responsibility for finding helpers for the work at Pleasant View, — a never-ending task. All the work had to be done by sincere, unselfish Christian Scientists. Few were qualified, and fewer still were willing to sacrifice self to Mrs. Eddy's great Cause for any length of time. Mrs. Eddy told Calvin to go first to her own students, and said, "Get one who loves to work for the Cause and is willing to take up the cross for it as I have done." Many were eager to go to Pleasant View, but very few knew what it was to "take up the cross."

In prospective workers Mr. Hill looked for qualities of love, orderliness, promptness, alertness, accuracy, truthfulness, fidelity, consecration, and humility. In one of his interviews with Mrs. Eddy on the subject he said, "Mother, in looking for helpers for you, I am not trying to find a pleasant personality. I am looking for a quality of thought that reflects the great revelation you have given to the world." Mr. Hill was a good judge of character, but he was amazed at Mrs. Eddy's ability in this area, and wrote of it:

> In her personal interviews with prospective helpers, I have known many cases in which she clearly discerned their thought and character at the first meeting. . . . Mrs. Eddy knew immediately whether or not a person could qualify for membership in her household. There was never any question about it. I learned that she was always right,

> whatever I myself may have thought about the adaptability of a candidate. As I saw her great intuition and wisdom manifested again and again I came to the conviction that her judgment was as near perfection as is possible in this world.

The Leader felt that Pauline Mann had the necessary qualifications and soon invited her to serve in the house. August Mann, another brother, and his wife Amanda moved into the cottage with Joseph, and August became Mrs. Eddy's coachman. By the beginning of the century Joseph, too, had been invited into the house to serve as assistant secretary and metaphysical worker.

The lawsuits launched by Josephine Woodbury in August of 1899 had been dragging on for a year and a half and were a great burden for the Leader to bear. One suit was against Mrs. Eddy, one against her directors, one against her trustees, and others against other prominent men working for the cause in Boston. Mrs. Eddy wanted each suit handled individually knowing that that would cause each defendant to work more diligently and give her some much needed support. They instead, no doubt through fear, wanted to unite all of the actions (feeling a security in numbers) and to let the church bear the burden and the expense, which threw the total burden and responsibility onto Mrs. Eddy's overburdened shoulders.

John Salchow in Junction City had an interesting dream about this time involving Mrs. Eddy and a boat he owned. It seemed he was instructed to get his boat ready because Mrs. Eddy wanted to go out in it, but, dreamlike, his much-enlarged boat was filled with people all vying for positions to see the Leader. Dutifully, John was willing merely to serve and went to the stern cabin to handle the rudder, but found his dutifulness rewarded when the door swung open a few inches and gave him a good view of Mrs. Eddy walking toward the boat with a parcel in her hand:

> It seemed as if the burden of the whole universe was on her shoulders and as if she would be crushed before she took another step, but still she came on, her eyes looking upward and beyond the world. It was the most sad and heartrending sight I had ever seen. When she reached the spot where the man had spoken to me she caught sight of me through the opening in the door. It seemed then as if the whole scene changed, her burdens fell away and she came tripping directly to the door of the cabin. Without noticing anyone else, she handed the parcel to me (it was a copy of Science and Health) with the words "To our faithful boy," and then turned and walked away.

At a later date when John Salchow was serving Mrs. Eddy at Pleasant View he felt that his dream had been fulfilled when she

GENERAL FRANK S. STREETER
Mrs. Eddy's Concord Attorney

presented him with a copy of Science and Health inscribed to her "faithful John," — although he had never told her about his dream.

But in January of 1901 "the burden of the whole universe was on her shoulders" and she often felt "as if she would be crushed before she took another step." January 4 was a day in point. A lengthy conference with her lawyers, General Frank S. Streeter and Samuel J. Elder, took place at Pleasant View. Three of her Boston officials were present, — two directors, Joseph Armstrong and William B. Johnson, and editor Judge Septimus J. Hanna.

Streeter and Elder were not Christian Scientists, and more than once she had a good deal of difficulty in persuading them to pursue the course God was directing her to take. Prior to now her students had endeavored to follow her spiritual guidance, but on this day that was not the case. They sat mute, obviously siding with the lawyers on the issue of bringing the action to New Hampshire rather than keeping it as much as possible in Boston.

Mrs. Eddy's talented new student, Judge Clarkson, had been unable to see that Mrs. Eddy was just as God-guided in meeting the exigencies of a lawsuit as she was in writing Science and Health. Being unable to convince her that it was essential to let the *men* take the lead without her dictation, he had chemicalized and resigned his post, but his persuasive arguments which could not move the Leader had greatly affected the *men* who were her older students and officials of her Boston organization. They were no help to the Leader and gave her no support as her lawyers argued at great length. Even though she finally prevailed and in time the wisdom of her way was seen and admitted, on that Friday afternoon she felt very nearly overcome. The next day, January 5, she wrote to Judge Ewing in Chicago:

> O that you had been here. I felt so alone. Judge H., Mr. A. and Mr. J. sat with the lawyers in my room, hours — the latter cutting my heart out, the former speechless. I felt as if I were in the presence of headsmen waiting to take me to the scaffold. Why O why are the declining years of a life like mine so haunted, hounded, soulless, unpitied. God only knows!

When she asked Joseph Mann to recommend someone who would "stand" if brought to Pleasant View to help with the work, he thought immediately of John Salchow in Junction City. A little later when John received a letter asking him to come to Pleasant View, he dropped everything and was on his way to Concord within two hours. Although his work was largely out of doors, maintenance, repair, handyman, etc., John found it easier to *stand* than did Joseph Mann in the heat of the battle. The first time Mrs. Eddy saw John she said, "Who is that working in my garden?" Mr. Mann responded, "That is the new man you asked me to get for you." Obviously the Leader read John Salchow's character, for she said to Mr. Mann: "I admire his unspoilable integrity."

Six other students were summoned to Pleasant View in January of 1901. Miss Mary Stewart of Des Moines, Iowa, who had been in Mrs. Eddy's last class in Christian Science Hall in 1898, received a telegram from Mrs. Eddy asking her to come at once. When she arrived in Concord she found five other Scientists at Christian Science Hall and learned that they had been summoned to do some preliminary work on the lawsuits in progress against Mrs. Eddy and some of her chosen officials. The five students had been interviewed by Mrs. Eddy that afternoon, but having a greater distance to travel Miss Stewart had arrived a day later.

That evening a messenger came from Mrs. Eddy with an invitation to call on her the next day, and with the message: "Tell her that her prompt obedience to the call will ensure to her life, health, and heaven."

The interview the next day seemed to Miss Stewart like a foretaste of heaven. Mrs. Eddy talked earnestly about the welfare of the Cause, and told how error tried to separate some of her older students from her. She emphasized healing and the importance of giving much time and consecration to the work of healing, adding, "I cannot help healing." Then:

> . . . "The worst evil is to go to a bed of sickness and say: God is All. God is Love. You are not sick." She spoke with scorn of such statements made coldly and superficially, and indicated that that sort of practice sometimes amounted to neglect of a case and brought criticism from physicians, saying: "If I were a physician I would have made the same criticisms, and they would have been just. How I decry such practice!" Then with a light in her eyes and filled with the power of Spirit she said, "Mother would say, Arise and walk!"

As Mrs. Eddy told Miss Stewart about the malicious efforts of evil against her, relating some of the attempts to break up her household, to break up the ranks, to separate her students from her, her face was illumined with the Christ-consciousness. To Mary Stewart her look and attitude declared her God-given dominion, and the threats of evil seemed so absurd, impudent, and impossible that she laughed aloud. Instantly Mrs. Eddy said: "If you take it that way, perhaps you could stand. Yes, you can — and having done all, stand."

Mrs. Eddy directed the work of the six students summoned to work specifically for the lawsuit. Mary Stewart recorded:

> During the time the group of Scientists were working together it was evident that Mrs. Eddy was constantly listening for God's direction. She sent us instructions about how to work then told us to wait; then again came definite instructions. Ever did she exemplify her words in *Miscellaneous Writings,* "With armor on, I continue the march, command and countermand."

One of the instructions Mrs. Eddy sent to this group of workers was as follows:

> LAW SUIT — Woodbury Case. God governs it. Justice, Truth and Love govern it, and nothing else can or does affect it in the least. I have faith in God. I know that faith as a grain of mustard seed does remove mountains. I have no faith in evil. I know that it cannot do anything. It is nothing. God is All. The wrath of man shall praise Him and the remainder of wrath shalt Thou restrain. All things work together for good to them who love the Lord.

On the seventeenth of January Mrs. Eddy notified her directors that she had commissioned Edward A. Kimball of Chicago, whom she had called to Pleasant View, to represent her in all that pertained to the Woodbury case. Judge Hanna responded to this message on January 19:

> I am glad Mr. Kimball is here. We need his fresh, strong thought, and I hope he will remain until it is over. He is not fagged out as are the rest of us. . . .

The working students had already improved the situation in Boston, for Hanna also wrote in his letter: "I see also a strong need of greater reliance on the Gospel and less on human law for success in the case." In Miss Stewart's reminiscence:

> When that part of the work for which this group had been called was accomplished, she directed us to return to our homes. She wrote: "I deeply thank you for your Christlikeness in coming and going at the word. Our Master did just this. I have done it for thirty years."

Other students were called to work for the case at a later date. But Mr. Kimball who came in January stayed on till the case was over, and then continued in Boston for further vital work for the Cause.

CHAPTER II

UNENDING ATTACKS

I have endured all shame and blame . . . and I have lived these down. — MARY BAKER EDDY

1901

EMPEROR William of Germany made a hasty trip to England in the first month of the new century requesting that his arrival be given no official notice. He was rushing to the bedside of his beloved grandmother, Queen Victoria, who passed away Tuesday evening, January 22. The press reported:

> When the word was sent out that the Queen was dying, her grandson, Emperor William of Germany, was one of the first to hasten to her bedside. He desired that no official notice be taken of his arrival, as he wished to be received merely as a grandson. His unaffected love for the Queen and sorrow for her loss, has endeared the Emperor to the hearts of the British people, and won for him the enhanced regard of all persons who loved the English queen.

All the world lamented the loss of the much-loved British monarch. Mrs. Eddy wrote from Pleasant View to her church in Boston:

> January 27, 1901
>
> Mr. Benjamin Johnson, C.S.B., Clerk
>
> Beloved Student: — I deem it proper that the Mother Church in Boston, Massachusetts, the first church of Christian Science known on earth, should, upon this solemn occasion congregate. That a special meeting of the First Members convene for the sacred purpose of expressing our deep sympathy with the bereaved nation, its loss and the world's loss, in the sudden departure of the late lamented Victoria, Queen of Great Britain, and Empress of India, — long honored, revered, beloved. "God save the Queen" is heard no more in England, but this shout of love lives on in the hearts of millions.
>
> With love,
>
> Mary Baker G. Eddy

The meeting was held on January 31 where resolutions of deepest sympathy were adopted and conveyed to the British government. At the suggestion of Mr. Ormond Higman of Canada, the American and British flags were flown at half mast at Pleasant View on February 2, the day of Victoria's funeral.

Newspapers around the world devoted much space to Queen Victoria, her life, her reign, her husband, her children, — especially her oldest son Albert Edward who was now King Edward VII.

On this side of the Atlantic events of great moment were transpiring, although few were truly interested in them, and perhaps only one in all the world was aware of their import. The momentous question first came to public notice in January of 1895 right after the dedication of the Mother Church in Boston. Mrs. Laura Lathrop gave a statement to reporters which caused them to request an interview with Mrs. Eddy to answer whether she was the second Christ. Mrs. Eddy preferred to answer the query in writing which she did telegraphing her response to the *New York Herald* on February 4, 1895 *(Pul.* 74). Her answer was very similar to that of Jesus in Matthew: "Why callest thou me good? there is none good but one." This satisfied friend and foe alike, but it did not silence the issue.

Mrs. Eddy's Communion Address to the Mother Church in 1899 *(My.* 124), which she has titled "Purification of the Church," stated that "the doom of the Babylonish woman, referred to in Revelation, is being fulfilled." Mrs. Josephine Woodbury saw herself as the Babylonish woman despite Mrs. Eddy's repeated efforts to rouse her from this dream. Mrs. Woodbury also saw, far more clearly than most, that Mrs. Eddy's life of purity was the fulfillment of the prophecy in Revelation of the Woman, God-crowned. This was the main accusation against Mrs. Eddy that Josephine Woodbury poured into mortal thought with scorn, — that Mrs. Eddy considered herself the Woman of the Apocalypse.

The impurity in mortal consciousness picked up Mrs. Woodbury's scorn and hurled it about. One minister in Raleigh, North Carolina, in a sermon attacking Mrs. Eddy and Christian Science late in 1900 stated: "Add to this the doctrine that Mrs. Eddy herself is the highest expression of the divine idea in the human form, surpassing Jesus as he surpassed Moses, and you have in brief the doctrine of Christian Science."

There was more truth than fiction in the minister's words, but the right thing at the wrong time ceases to be right. The world was not ready for this revelation. Only spiritualized thought can perceive spirituality. So the refutation of the attack by Alfred Farlow (Publication Committee) stated: "This is as far from Christian Science as night from day, and there is nothing in the writings of

Mrs. Eddy to warrant such assumption. Mrs. Eddy claims absolutely nothing for her personality except that she is 'the Discoverer and Founder of Christian Science.'"

Farlow was right about her claiming nothing for her *personality*; however, the paragraphs interpreting the parable of the woman leavening the three measures of meal had been in the chapter "Science, Theology, Medicine" in Science and Health since the fiftieth edition in 1891. The second paragraph then as now stated:

> Did not this parable point a moral with a prophecy, foretelling the second appearing *in the flesh** of the Christ, Truth, hidden in sacred secrecy from the visible world?

At the time of the Woodbury lawsuit that passage in Science and Health was changed to read "on the flesh" in place of "in the flesh." Christ's second appearing needed to be hidden a little longer "from the visible world." It also needed to be protected from its friends as much as from its foes. Their zealous enthusiasm would no doubt rouse the world's antagonism and jeopardize the Cause and the court case. Many a battle had been lost for lack of wisdom or discretion on the part of her own soldiers.

Mrs. Eddy's spiritual identity as the second coming of the Christ had been *revealed* to two of her disciples, Ira Oscar Knapp and Septimus J. Hanna, and they had shared it with many others. But now they were the two who most needed to guard everything they said in order to protect this divine revelation from being torn asunder.

What all had to meet every day was the unending attacks emanating from Mrs. Woodbury, and Mrs. Eddy seemed to be the only one undeceived by the malicious lies on every front. One very sad instance had occurred in 1899 and involved the enthusiastic new convert to Christian Science, Col. Oliver Sabin. He had begun devoting his publication, the *Washington News Letter,* to the promotion of Christian Science. Not only was malicious malpractice aimed at Sabin to poison his thought against Mrs. Eddy and her Cause, but a similar malpractice was directed to the First Members to poison their thought against Col. Sabin. Sadly, the First Members did not refute the wicked suggestions, and when Oliver Sabin applied for membership, his application was rejected. When Mrs. Eddy learned of it she tried to patch up the fissure and save this new student, as her letter to him clearly indicates:

> It comes to me that I ought to inform you of how I heard the first ill word of you. It came thus:
>
> I knew you had applied for church membership, but on reading the

*Emphasis added.

list of new members missed your name. Wrote to my church to know why — received no reply, and then wrote to a person that you had written to me was your *friend* to learn of him. The answer shocked me. I commenced doing what I could for you all and the result I enclose herewith.

I see it is one person that is moving in all this to harm you and become a contributor to your paper and to revenge for being excommunicated from probation in our church after I had done all in my power to reform her and she had confessed to me her crime yet not one half her guilt — and I had at last to withdraw my support from her. She claims to have been my favorite, — that was her *tale.* She never was one I could love, but I helped her all the same.

Her next move will be to cause you to admit into your paper articles not genuine and to pass them as such. *Beware.*

God help you,
Mother

Though she wrote "she never was one I could love," the Leader gave more *true* love to Mrs. Woodbury than did all the world combined, as is evident in a letter Mrs. Woodbury wrote on March 11, 1895:

Do you know — way off in that pure realm where you dwell, that the sharpest sting I feel, — is the awful sense of what your disappointment in me is? You say there is a promise of joy ahead if I will trust the dear Mother to guide me, and if I try to do right steadily, but can that Love prevent me from bearing this anguish of regret even to the end? . . . Even now when you know I ought to bear every pang alone without a hint of help from you — and bear it all and without complaint you come with your soft wing and bear me up lest I fail utterly. You know I could have borne rebuke better than this letting out of your love upon me.

In her letter to Oliver Sabin Mrs. Eddy had probably included the By-law "Alertness to Duty" *(Man.* 42). That is what she had done at that time and is most likely what was referred to in her sentence: "I commenced doing what I could for you all and the result I enclose herewith." But Col. Sabin had no understanding of malicious animal magnetism, and the damage had been done.

Evil always attributes its own wicked ways to the righteous (or endeavors so to do), and that was the thrust of Josephine Woodbury's attacks against Christian Scientists which were being spread all over the country. An editorial in Austin, Texas stated in part: "Christian Scientists contend there is no limit to their influence . . . Their efforts to coerce the Surrogate by their mental treatment illustrates a phase or side of Eddyism to which little attention has been paid. . . . Eddyism is precisely the same thing as voodooism, and the followers of the new cult, like those of the older one, believe that they can injure as well as aid, can punish enemies as well as reward friends."

An answer from a local Scientist refuting all the misstatements with quotations from Science and Health was published in the Austin *Daily Tribune.* The writer exonerated the *Tribune* by noting that their editorial "Christian Scientists in Court" was largely quoted from the *New York Times.*

The *Times'* article quoted was in relation to the Brush will case then going on in New York City. Miss Helen C. Brush had bequeathed about seventy-five thousand dollars to Mrs. Stetson's church, First Church of Christ, Scientist, New York City. Two members of Miss Brush's family contested the will, although the other members desired the provisions to be carried out.

An article entitled "Christian Science Healing Explained and Defended" was written especially for the *New York Sunday Journal* by Mrs. Eddy "in answer to charges made in the famous Brush will contest in the New York Court." The first half of the lengthy article appears in *Miscellany* (pp. 219-222) with the exception of these paragraphs:

> That a law suit was contemplated or in progress before Surrogate Fitzgerald in New York City was unknown to me until very recently, having read a report of it through the press.
>
> *I have never issued orders of any sort relative to the presiding Surrogate in the Brush case.*
>
> What is alleged to be Miss Brush's statement, namely, "It is impossible for me to die," simply reiterated the declarations of our Lord, who said, "If a man keep my saying, he shall never see death;" and "Daughter, be of good comfort; thy faith hath made thee whole; go in peace." The great Master knew that faith in God, who is our Life, is not insanity, whereas lack of charity may be a species of insanity.

The second half of this article was quotations from Science and Health which are well worth studying for elucidation on "healing explained and defended." They are pages 113:9-25; 143:5-12; 153:16-154:9; 157:8-158:23; and 98:15-21.

All of the foregoing quotations in the 1901 Science and Health are essentially the same in the latest edition. However, the closing paragraph in the article for the *New York Journal* was changed from the one in Science and Health (p. 98) to close the article thus:

> Beyond the frail premises of human hypotheses, above the loosening grasp of creeds, the demonstrations of Christian Science stand revealed as practical science. Divine metaphysics is Christ Jesus' revelation of Truth and Love, for which he labored and suffered,

then left a legacy to mankind, and which remains the divine standard for the understanding and practice of every man.

The court battle over Miss Brush's will was a fierce one aimed mainly at ridiculing and destroying Christian Science and the Leader's most prominent disciple, Augusta Stetson. It was a miniature (if not an unrecognized part) of the Woodbury case in Boston, attempting to eliminate Mrs. Eddy's strongest helper by accusing her of fraud, and attempting to discredit her cause by alleging that Christian Scientists were insane. The noted alienist, Dr. Allan McLane Hamilton was called to testify, and was asked:

> "Do you say that a person who believes in the power of God, operating through a human agent to cure disease without material means, suffers from delusions?"
>
> "Yes," he answered, "most decidedly."

The New York World telegraphed the substance of Dr. Hamilton's testimony to Mrs. Eddy in Concord and requested a reply. Mrs. Eddy's response *(My.* 301) appeared in the *New York World* of February 24, 1901:

> Concord, N. H. February 22
>
> To the Editor of *The World.*
>
> Is faith in divine metaphysics insanity?
>
> All sin is insanity, but healing the sick is *not* sin. There is a universal insanity which mistakes fable for fact throughout the entire testimony of the material senses. Those unfortunate people who are committed to insane asylums are only so many well-defined instances of the baneful effects of illusion on mortal minds and bodies.
>
> The supposition that we can correct insanity by the use of drugs is in itself a species of insanity. A drug cannot of itself go to the brain or affect cerebral conditions in any manner whatever. Drugs cannot remove inflammation, restore disordered functions, or destroy disease without the aid of mind.
>
> If mind be absent from the body, drugs can produce no curative effect upon it. Mind must be, is, the vehicle of all modes of healing disease and of producing disease. Through the mandate of mind or according to his belief, a man can be helped or he can be killed by a drug; but mind, not matter, produces the result in either case.
>
> Neither life nor death, health nor disease, can be produced on a corpse whence mind has departed. This self-evident fact is proof that mind is the cause of all effect made manifest through so-called matter. The general craze is that matter masters mind; the specific insanity is that brain, matter, is insane.
>
> Mary Baker G. Eddy

This court trial resulted in a victory for the Christian Scientists. In his lengthy decision published in the *Christian Science Journal* of October, 1901 (Vol. 19, pp. 455-467) Surrogate Fitzgerald stated:

> So far as concerns Mrs. Stetson ...I am convinced that she was entirely innocent of the fraud that has been sought to be fastened upon her.

On the twenty-eighth of February Mrs. Stetson wrote in a letter to one of her students:

> The Brush will case has been a fierce mental battle, from which I have emerged with the proof of honesty and truth written in the history of the courts. I am weary, but have no time to rest from active *duty.* My hands are torn, but I have no time to bind them up. The dear Love must heal them, while I go to others, and pour in oil and heal the broken-hearted. I must forget self and labor for others ...

Mrs. Stetson was so occupied with battles of her own that she was little aware of the intensity of the attacks Mrs. Eddy was having to meet. In his home in Vermont Foster Eddy was reading the newspaper accounts of the lawsuit against his adopted mother, and wrote her on February 28 of his loyal support, also stating: "Be careful, dear One! you are surrounded by vipers! shake them off and put your whole trust in God!" In February Calvin Frye recorded in his diary:

> Mrs. Eddy said at supper table today, ... "If I do not live to see this lawsuit of W's finished, I can say this: Calvin has helped me to live many years."

Mrs. Eddy was daily directing the mental workers in her home with Watches such as this one of February 15 preserved by Lewis Strang:

> Mother sends you this message: Rise up and defeat the evil one in the gates. The hour of deliverance is at hand and all must do their *duty* as Christian Scientists to defeat the evil that tries to find entrance here. Love, Mind, Truth rule this and every hour. *Error* is not met by prayer alone, but by *fasting.*

While rising up "to defeat the evil that tries to find entrance here" and instructing and inspiring her students to do the same, the Leader was daily watching over her flock and her Cause, guiding, guarding, directing, encouraging, mothering. In January she had had the First Members turn over their powers to the Board of

Directors. On March 7 a new by-law was published: "Each Church of Christ, Scientist, shall have its own form of government. No conference of churches shall be held . . ." Later this was titled "Local Self-government" *(Man.* 70). On March 18 young Bliss Knapp was made a First Member at Mrs. Eddy's request. The twenty-first of March saw an amended by-law for those whose teachers have left them; also, "Something New" — all churches from this date are requested to read the Scientific Statement of Being and I John 3:1-3 at the close of service. On the same date the following message went out to all the field:

> Beloved brethren all over our land and in every land accept Mother's Spring greeting while
>
> The bird of hope is singing,
> A lightsome lay, a cooing call,
> And in her heart is beating
> A love for all —
> "'Tis peace not power I seek,
> 'Tis meet that man be meek."

On April 4 the Leader wrote a message to Second Church, Chicago *(My.* 191), while the Watch for her household mental workers that day was:

> Watchfulness is the word of this hour of trial for our Cause. Keep apart from the Sunday students in our midst who trample His divine Word under foot all week and expect forgiveness on the Sabbath. Their reward awaits them.

A message to Second Church, New York, was written on April 5 *(My.* 201); a thank you for Easter gifts on April 13; and on April 25 her "Word to the Wise" *(My.* 223) was published in the *Sentinel.*

While all this and much more was going on Mrs. Woodbury was working just as assiduously pouring "wormwood into the waters — the disturbed human mind — to drown the strong swimmer struggling for the shore, — aiming for Truth, — and if possible, to poison such as drink of the living water." As the court date drew nearer Josephine Woodbury and her attorney Frederick Peabody held repeated conferences with students who had deserted and betrayed their Leader, from Richard Kennedy to William G. Nixon to Judge Clarkson, — and at the same time Mrs. Woodbury intensified her bombardment of the Leader with poisonous and deadly suggestions. On the seventeenth of April Calvin Frye wrote to Mr. Kimball of the effect this malicious mental malpractice had on Mrs. Eddy:

> She is literally living in agony from day to day waiting to have this case called up and disposed of, and W. is pouring in her hot shot declaring she cannot live through the ordeal.

Despite the agony and intensity of her suffering the Leader kept at her post continuing with her work, guiding her flock. At that time she was writing her *Message to The Mother Church for 1901.* She also called upon the metaphysical workers in her home to support her in her work. Calvin Frye and Clara Shannon were veterans in this department and had been through many a battle with their Leader, — but this was a new experience for Joseph Mann.

One day when the *Message for 1901* was about half finished, Clara *felt* the insidious wickedness that was striking at Mrs. Eddy's life and was doing her utmost to counteract it:

> Miss Shannon was keeping her Watch in another room, and Calvin Frye and Joseph Mann were with Mother, who was having a struggle as Miss Shannon knew. She could hear the two men talking with Mother, and Miss Shannon was praying to God, sometimes on her knees, for Life and strength, Truth and Love to be manifest there, for Miss Shannon felt something awful was approaching mentally.
>
> Finally, the sound of the men's voices ceased. Miss Shannon said she *heard* that *silence;* it was the most awful sound she had ever heard. She went into Mother's room, and there lay Calvin Frye and Joseph Mann stretched on the floor, flat on their faces. Then she looked at Mother; her head had dropped, her jaw dropped, and *every sign* of *death.*
>
> Miss Shannon shouted truth at her, shook her, called her, quoted the book Science and Health, reminded her that *Mother had written this book!* Finally, consciousness began to return, and Miss Shannon told her to stand on her feet, and putting her hands under Mother's arm-pits, held her up, — a dead weight. Finally and suddenly Mother *laughed!*
>
> Miss Shannon looked up and gave thanks when she heard this, and asked what the laugh meant. Mother said, "Your face! If you could see your face, you would laugh too."

Mrs. Eddy picked up her pad of paper and continued her writing as if nothing had happened which was not as easy for Clara Shannon to do. She returned to her room across the hall, but left the door ajar and kept looking in on Mother quietly. After two or three times Mrs. Eddy rebuked her saying sharply: "Go and handle your fear! You are afraid I shall have another attack. Go and handle your own fear!"

In her earnest intensiveness Miss Shannon had become unconscious of the "unconscious" men on the floor and knew not when they recovered and departed.

When the *Message* was completed Mrs. Eddy said to Miss Shannon, "Oh what a lot of love it took to do that! The mesmerists did not want the world to have that Message, but Love meant it to be given." She also told Clara that the 1901 Message was Christian Science in a nutshell.

But before completing her Message she had another concern. Joseph Mann had disappeared. He wrote later that he had been driven to distraction by his inability to meet the demands made upon him. Joseph had sought refuge in his brother's home in Boston. When Mrs. Eddy did not find him at Christian Science Hall in Concord she asked Mrs. Baker to find him for her. On May 1 Joseph wrote to Mrs. Eddy:

> I felt I must hide myself a few days, and so Mrs. Baker found me in brother's quiet home. God bless you and I thank you for sending Mrs. Baker to have me come back. . . . I could at once see how I could be helpful at the cottage at this time, however sad my failures at the house have been, for though I have kept it from you, dear mother, the cottage and August, in his general management, have needed my constant support.

On the envelope to this letter Mrs. Eddy penned the words, "Sad! Sad!" but to Joseph she wrote:

> Mother was glad when you returned and would have run out and met you if she were used to running.
>
> Now be happy in the memory of what a good son you have been to mother, think of how many times you have comforted her and how you came to Concord only to help her. After Jesus' temptation in the wilderness angels ministered unto him. Remain near me (if you are willing) and if you are in the Cottage I can call for you in need.

CHAPTER III

"THE HOLY ONE OF GOD"

O blessed daughter of Zion, I am with thee. And none shall take my words out of thy lips. Thou art my chosen, to bear my Truth to the nations, and I will not suffer another messenger to go before thee.

1901

JOSEPH Clarke had no notion of the burdens Mrs. Eddy was carrying the last few days in April while he was in Concord endeavoring to get an interview with her. This well-known reporter from the *New York Herald* finally managed through Alfred Farlow to gain an audience at Pleasant View on April 30, and his ensuing article *(My.* 341-346) appeared in the *Herald* the next day, May 1. An interesting excerpt from a statement by Mrs. Eddy in a second article by Clarke in the *New York Herald* of May 5 was published by the Committee on General Welfare in 1920:

> The problem is not so much as to the form of the government as to providing an authority that will ever keep its spirit true to the Christian Science doctrine, — a monitor more than a master. I have made rigid by-laws for the government of the Church, and every one has been necessary, but they need to be administered in gentleness and forbearance as well as in firmness with the erring. I have always been motherly to my Church, instead of dictatorial, as has been falsely said.

Further statements by Mrs. Eddy which Clarke included in his May 5 article are as follows:

> Woman has the finer spiritual nature. She more readily takes the impress of Christian Science. If, as you say (I leave all statistics to the publication department), there are 13,000 women, against 5,000 men, out of a book total of 18,000, it shows that their minds are more receptive; their enthusiasm greater at the beginning of a struggle, but

> in the strength of man lies the power of carrying it on.
>
> I look on man as the designate of the Word, but, to my view, the idea of race is superior to the idea of sex. Indeed, may we not look forward to a human condition, when perfection is nearer, wherein neither male nor female shall be known, and the race may reproduce itself otherwise than now? . . .
>
> We are not indifferent to forms of government, but we support the best in each. A church to be universal must in many things be neutral about forms of government and at the same time support what is right to support.
>
> When all men are one in the Church of Christ, the perfection of life and the perfection of government under the application of the Golden Rule will come. It will all be simple, natural, without clash or combat, all over the world in a divine brotherhood.

In his first article Clarke quoted Mrs. Eddy as saying:

> I have even been spoken of as a Christ, but to my understanding of Christ that is impossible. If we say that the sun stands for God, then all his rays collectively stand for Christ, and each separate ray for men and women. God the Father is greater than Christ, but Christ is "one with the Father," and so the mystery is scientifically explained. There can be but one Christ.

Though this message was pertinent to Mrs. Woodbury's accusations, it was not the one that caught the world's attention. Surely Mrs. Eddy knew that the world's curiosity would be roused by her statement: "You would ask, perhaps, whether my successor will be a woman or a man. I can answer that. It will be a man." Herbert Eustace has interpreted her reason for this statement:

> In making her statement referring to her successor, "the man," Mrs. Eddy well knew what would be the reaction of the human mind — a torrent of curiosity asking, "Who is it, where is he, etc.?" That was exactly what she desired to have, a large wide-awake audience ready prepared to hear her answer to that very question, "Who is the man?" and she wanted her answer to go home in such a way that it could never again be asked. So, in due time, May 16th, 1901, she gave that answer to the largest distributors of news in the world, the Associated Press.

Her answer is familiar to every serious student of Christian Science today, and on the sixteenth of May in 1901 it was flashed round the world as fast as the media of that day could manage it. All over this planet people read eagerly:

> I did say that a man would be my future successor. By this I did not

mean Mr. Alfred Farlow nor any other man today on earth.
Science and Health makes it plain to all Christian Scientists that the manhood and womanhood of God have already been revealed in a degree through Christ Jesus and Christian Science, his two witnesses. What remains to lead on the centuries and reveal my successor, is man in the image and likeness of the Father-Mother God, man the generic term for mankind.

Is not Mrs. Eddy saying plainly that she can have no human successor for the "womanhood of God [has] already been revealed"? When *Christ and Christmas* was published she explained that "Christian Unity" (the one and only circular illustration) was intended to "foretell the typical appearing of the womanhood, as well as the manhood of God, our divine Father and Mother." This picture tells us even more. It bespeaks the fulfillment of Jeremiah's prophecy: "the Lord hath created a new thing in the earth. A woman shall compass a man." Mrs. Eddy knew this full well else she would never have had the light surrounding the woman's head brighter than that around the head of the man.

None but the pure in heart can see God or recognize the Christ. But the "unclean spirit" is more *aware* of its destroyer than are the children of light. In Jesus' time it used a man to say: "Let us alone; what have we to do with thee, thou Jesus of Nazareth? I know thee who thou art, the Holy One of God." But in 1901 the serpent that was aware of its destroyer had become the great red dragon, using Mrs. Woodbury in its effort to destroy the womanhood of God, Mary Baker Eddy, "the Holy One of God."

When "unclean spirits" cried unto Jesus "saying, Thou art the Son of God . . . he straitly charged them that they should not make him known." The Christ idea must enter the human heart silently in order to do its leavening work. Even though the Christ idea *must* be recognized, that was not the time. Nor was May of 1901 the time.

God had revealed Mary Baker Eddy's identity as Christ's second coming to Septimus J. Hanna in the spring of 1898, and Judge Hanna had written an editorial about it at that time. When he sent the proof to Mrs. Eddy for her approval she responded:

> The time has not yet come in which to say the wonderful things you have written in proof read by me today, unless you qualify it.
> Now you may hold your ground as therein, but do not say blandly that I represent the second appearing of Christ. That assertion will array mortal mind against us, and M.A.M. has been putting it into your mind to say it, and the infinite Love has inspired *you to say it.*

Her letter a few days later indicated unqualified approval in the words, "Your vision article is too grand, *true,* to be tampered with."

"The manhood and womanhood of God have already been revealed . . ."

CHRISTIAN UNITY
From *Christ and Christmas*

However, only the general part, not the heart of Hanna's editorial was published in July of 1898.

Mrs. Eddy had felt in '98 that "the time [had] not yet come in which to say . . . that [she represented] the second appearing of Christ." Mortal mind would have been arrayed against her, and against Hanna, too. Now, in 1901, with ire aroused, mortal mind would rip them both to shreds, — or endeavor so to do, — were that assertion made public. It was endeavoring to do just that through Mrs. Woodbury. Judge Hanna was exhausted, and Mrs. Eddy had a daily battle to maintain her sense of human life, as Clara Shannon, Calvin Frye, and Joseph Mann well knew. As much as the world needed to know the complete identity of its Saviour, this truth must be hidden a little longer, must be protected for the progress of the Cause and for the prosecution of the pending lawsuit.

The time had come, however, when her students must learn to distinguish between the human Mary Baker Eddy and the Christ which she manifested. Science and Health was leading the Christian to stop deifying Jesus, and teaching the Scientist to learn to differentiate between Jesus and the Christ, between the human and the divine. Now they *must* learn to do the same with their Leader. Sinaitic detonations from Pleasant View had shaken her "men in Boston" causing William P. McKenzie to write to his fiancee, Daisette Stocking: "One thing we shall have to cease forever, and that is the superstitious worship of a personal Leader." McKenzie had accepted what Miss Stocking had told him, — that Mrs. Eddy was the second appearing of Christ and was greater than Jesus because woman is higher than man, — but his acceptance was human belief rather than spiritual understanding. As a result he had indulged in superstitious worship of personality, as had many others, and this must be abolished.

Mr. Kimball was the Leader's conciliator. He undertood her God-given place, but he did not worship a human personality. This enabled him to accept her decisions (which some thought arbitrary) without murmuring, while at the same time pouring oil on the disturbed waters in Boston. Ira Knapp and Judge Hanna, whose understanding of Mrs. Eddy's identity was unshakeable, needed to be most careful to speak discreetly. Mr. Kimball was a great help to all, but no doubt to those two especially; nonetheless, it was thought wise that the Hannas be sent away from Boston for a very welcome vacation.

Mrs. Woodbury's specific charge was that Mrs. Eddy's remarks about the Babylonish woman in her Communion Address in 1899 *(My.* 125:29) were referring to her, and she was asking one hundred fifty thousand dollars in damages. Her suit also claimed that Mrs. Eddy claimed to be the woman of the Apocalypse and that Science and Health was inspired.

Christian Scientists alone (and not many of them) have an understanding of the woman of the Apocalypse. And Mrs. Eddy's astute attorneys, who were fine men, were not Christian Scientists. To their understanding they were working for a dedicated human personality named Mary Baker Eddy. It has been recorded that in answer to their questions she wrote them stating that "a white-haired old lady could not be the woman of the Apocalypse":

> Mrs. Eddy's lawyers took the position that the charge made by Mrs. Woodbury concerning the woman of the Apocalypse and that Science and Health was inspired was not germane to the case . . . [and] brought a demurrer suit for the purpose of eliminating those two items . . .

A demurrer admits that a claim may be true but is not germane to the point at issue. The judge was convinced and ordered those two items removed from the Bill of Complaint. The entire action, however, was the deadly attempt of malicious mind to destroy God's chosen witness. Even Attorney Elder saw that "the *only* mark they are aiming at" is Mrs. Eddy as the Discoverer and Founder of Christian Science.

The case came to trial in Judge Bell's courtroom in Boston on May 29. Even though the issue of the woman of the Apocalypse had been eliminated from the case, the plaintiff did not drop it.

Mrs. Eddy had impressed her disciples with the fact that she did *not teach* her spiritual identity, and that they must refrain from trying to do so. This revelation *must* come from God, not man. There is little doubt that Edward Kimball and Ira Knapp discussed this issue, including the fact that the woman of the Apocalypse is a divine idea. And also the fact that the public saw Mrs. Eddy as just one mortal among mortals. Consequently Mr. Knapp was able to answer the questions put to him on the stand at the same level at which they were asked:

> Peabody: Mr. Knapp, did you know that it was a part of the belief of the people to whom that message was being read, that the author of the message was, herself, a person referred to in the Book of Revelation?
> Knapp: I did not.
> Peabody: Didn't you then know it to be a part of Mrs. Eddy's teaching, and the belief of the people assembled in the church of that day, that she is what the Book of Revelation calls the "woman clothed with the sun . . .?"
> Knapp: I do not know.
> Peabody: Did you then know that that was the belief of the other

Christian Scientists present?
Knapp: No sir; I did not.

It is obvious that Mr. Knapp had to differentiate between the human personality of Mary Baker Eddy and her spiritual identity in his own mind in order to "render unto Caesar the things that are Caesar's." Despite the enemy's attack on Mrs. Eddy "the earth helped the woman." After only one day of court proceedings Mr. Kimball wrote to her in Concord:

> Only one like myself who is on the inside of the whole history can understand how thoroughly Peabody was beaten yesterday on the generalship of the case. All of his hopes and threats to the effect that they would expose Christian Science and reveal its unfavorable workings were utterly shattered yesterday because the court ruled over and over again that all of those outside matters had no relation to the issue in hand at all. Peabody was in a state of almost constant discomfiture. . . . He has none of the sympathy of the Jury and our lawyers have secured it at once. I do not think the case will last more than ten days.

As it turned out it lasted less than ten days. One of the Scientists Mrs. Eddy called to Boston to work during the proceedings was Mrs. Stetson from New York. Two days after the trial ended she wrote home to one of her students:

> Hotel Touraine, Boston, Massachusetts
> June 7, 1901
>
> My beloved Student, —
>
> I have been so constantly occupied with the work on this trial, that I have felt it wise not to write or think outside of it if possible, and I know that so far as I could, I must leave my students to do their own work. So I have had no care for them. The victory has come at last. We have demonstrated the *powerlessness* of hypnotism, witchcraft and mental diabolism to overthrow the Cause of Christian Science and the work of our beloved Leader, Mrs. Eddy. We have realized enough of Truth and Love to nullify the seeming power of the foe. Now we can say understandingly, "The accuser of our brethren is cast down . . . unto the earth."
>
> What has the enemy not tried to do all these years to injure our Leader and me! In a letter written by Mrs. Eddy to me are these words: "The lies that are told about me or what I say of you are not worth your notice nor mine." I thank God that I have been able to stand until error uncovered and destroyed itself. The error was made so unreal that instead of three weeks, which the Judge gave for the trial, it was over in four days. The enemy was conquered as soon as we rose in a body to spiritual understanding and realized the allness of God and the nothingness of evil. . . .

After four days of testimony for the plaintiff Peabody rested his case. Mrs. Eddy's attorneys made a motion for a directed verdict without presenting any of the extensive evidence they had accumulated, but on the declaration that Peabody had not proved his case. The judge concurred and instructed the jury to bring in a verdict in favor of Mrs. Eddy, which was done on Wednesday, June 5.

The whole point of the trial had been to subject the Woman, God-crowned to the ridicule of the world, and the press was not averse to such scandalous publicity. On June 8 the *Boston Journal** reported:

> It was for the purpose of making clear the attitude of Rev. Mary Baker Eddy . . . regarding certain points that came out in the testimony submitted by plaintiff . . . that a *Boston Journal* reporter asked Mrs. Eddy for a statement.

Mrs. Eddy referred the matter to Edward A. Kimball; and now it was essential that Mr. Kimball be just as cautious and discreet with his answers as he had encouraged Ira Knapp and others to be on the witness stand. If he was not, they would still lose the case for God's chosen witness even though the verdict had already been rendered in Mrs. Eddy's favor. It might be well for us to ask ourselves if we could have done as well in Mr. Kimball's place:

> Mr. Kimball said: —
>
> "Mrs. Eddy does not wish to make any statement relative to this subject. She has solemnly declared from the first that she did not refer to the plaintiff when writing about the Babylonish woman and the only dignified and consistent course open to her is to rest peacefully on that declaration and let others contend, if they will."
>
> "What about the statement that Christian Scientists regard her as being infallible?"
>
> "Mrs. Eddy does not believe or teach or want any one else to believe or teach, that she is infallible. She and we believe in the infallibility of God only."
>
> "Does she think that she is the 'woman clothed with the sun' spoken of in Revelation?"
>
> "She does not. She does not teach or want any one to teach that . . ."
>
> "Why did not the witnesses explain what your belief is about Mrs. Eddy?"
>
> "Because there is no formulated belief on the subject . . ."
>
> "To whom did your people think the message referred?"
>
> "I do not know. I can only say that I have never yet talked with any one who said he thought it meant a person."

Though this trial was lost by Josephine Woodbury, the venomous serpent still used this poor woman in its continued attempt to

*See Appendix A.

destroy God's chosen witness. Mrs. Eddy knew that the effective mental work, and especially her *Message of 1901,* had won a battle, but the war was raging on. She wrote to Mr. Tomlinson in mid-June regarding the mental work that had been done:

> This has been the lever of Truth that has shown on the press and the field, and my message turned the tide to a flow. What I mean is, that nobody *sees* the moves of the enemy or knows when he *feels* them, unless I talk, talk, talk; and this is a mental period and mental malpractice holds the signs of the times, that the students must discern, or our Cause will be held back centuries by it. In this *direction* I *am alone* and few *notice* what I say, or believe it.

Rev. Tomlinson was soon to experience the "moves of the enemy." Peabody spent the next quarter of a century endeavoring to destroy Mrs. Eddy, and even though Mrs. Woodbury remained more or less in the background, for several years she directed malicious wicked malpractice for the same purpose. As Mrs. Eddy had said in her message *('01* p. 19) "The whole world needs to know that the milder forms of animal magnetism and hypnotism are yielding to its aggressive features."

Mrs. Eddy on the other hand went right on fulfilling her own description of her life and work written after Judge Clarkson had deserted her: "Behold a woman! — the almond blossom upon her head, busy hands and pen, never leaving the post of duty, but week after week, month after month, and year after year, toiling, watching, praying, and sending forth messages of God's dear love over all the earth." And now she had plans for another major project to be sent "over all the earth."

CHAPTER IV

COMMUNION SEASON—1901

Our first communion in the new century finds Christian Science more extended, more rapidly advancing, better appreciated, than ever before, and nearer the whole world's acceptance.

— MARY BAKER EDDY

1901

IT was announced that the Annual Meeting of the Mother Church was postponed from June until autumn in 1901. On May 16 a notice stated that Communion Sunday would be June 16 instead of the second Sunday in June. And on May 30 another notice said: "Owing to circumstances the Communion Service . . . of The Mother Church [has] been postponed until further notice." The circumstances, though not mentioned, were of course the lawsuit that was still going on.

A great many people had come to Boston for the Communion season who had to return to their homes before that happy event, which was next announced for July 7 and then pushed back to Sunday, June 23 when the lawsuit ended after only four days in court. Many visiting Scientists who had come long distances, — from Ireland, from Scotland, from Italy, etc. — stayed on for Communion Sunday. Others remained for an additional reason. Mlle. Demarez from Paris, France, the Earl and Countess of Dunmore and two of their daughters from London, and Mrs. Sara Pike Conger (wife of the American minister to China) from Pekin, were among the eighty-one Scientists who had come to attend the Normal Class of the Board of Education of the Massachusetts Metaphysical College which had originally been scheduled to convene Monday, June 3, but which also had been postponed. When the class convened later in June there were members from twenty-one states plus Canada, Scotland, England, France, and China.

One interesting member of the class was a Methodist minister from Brooklyn, New York. Rev. Severin E. Simonsen had first been introduced to Christian Science in 1886 about the time of Joseph Mann's dramatic healing. Simonsen, too, had had an outstanding healing in 1886, but it had taken him the better part of fourteen years to reach the third river — "Hiddekel ... Divine Science ... *acknowledged*"* (S.& H. 588).

Rev. Simonsen had a devoted wife and two small children and was a dedicated young minister in La Crosse, Wisconsin early in 1886 when his health utterly failed him. Several doctors told him there was no hope and gave him but two or three months to live, but he rejected Christian Science when presented. However, when he felt his life was slipping away, as a last resort he visited a Christian Science practitioner (as secretly as possible), and found the next day to be a glorious one for him. He soon realized that he was totally healed. This caused him to begin reading Science and Health, which in turn enabled him to meet the illnesses of his growing family, including a beautiful healing a few years later of himself and his oldest son of a severe attack of scarlet fever. Because the press and ministers in general were rather solidly opposed to Christian Science he confined his healing work to his own family except in a few extreme cases such as the following:

> I well remember calling one evening on a family to see their little son who was very ill. When I arrived the doctor had just left, and the father told me the physician had given the boy up, advising them he could not live through the night; ... everything had been done for the child that could be done. He said he would call in the morning ... and bring the boy's death certificate.
>
> ... I said to myself, "Come what may, I will tell these good people what had healed me." I did so. They forthwith appealed to me to do something for their child. I treated him in Christian Science and he was completely healed in one treatment. When the doctor arrived with the boy's "death certificate" the following morning, he found the lad well, and up and dressed.

In 1892 Rev. Simonsen was transferred to Brooklyn, New York, where he was very happy in the most successful pastorate of his career. But as time went on he began struggling with a mental conflict between the Christian Science he was learning and demonstrating and the theology he was preaching. About this time one of their seven children was stricken with an illness which the father seemed unable to meet. Severin and his wife Mary Elizabeth, who were at one in all their decisions, agreed to send for an M.D., — a specialist, to treat the child. They were not surprised at the physician's failure, but they did feel free then to call for Christian Science help.

*Emphasis added.

The first practitioner failed to reach the cause; and the second (recommended by his future primary teacher) asked him many probing questions before she agreed to take the case, and even then only on the condition that the father was to take treatment along with the son. The true healing was of the conflict in the good minister's thought, and as his understanding of Science progressed he saw that the Truth would take him out of the Methodist Church. Giving up the security of his position and the Ministers' Aid Society was an alarming prospect to Rev. Simonsen who by then had a wife and seven young children to support and no savings to fall back upon. But the practitioner said, "Do you not think that God is just as able to support you and yours in Christian Science as He is in Methodism?"

The Simonsens did decide to put their pursuit of Truth uppermost and applied for class instruction. The teacher, who was with Mrs. Eddy a great deal, said she would not accept him without first consulting the Leader. When Mrs. Eddy was apprised of the situation she said, "Yes, take Mr. Simonsen, but handle him without gloves." This "handling" caused Mr. Simonsen to see that as an honest man he *must* take his stand for Christian Science.

So it was that at the close of the old century and the beginning of the new there were a great many news items about the Methodist minister who was leaving his position in order to practise Christian Science. An April *Sentinel* reprinted much of the story, and in May Mrs. Eddy had her Board of Directors extend to Rev. Simonsen an invitation to attend the Normal Class in June. Mrs. Stetson, his primary teacher, told the Leader about Simonsen's family and financial situation and suggested it would be lovely if he were given a free tuition card, to which Mrs. Eddy replied: "Please keep your hands off of Mr. Simonsen and let me handle his case." Her words to Mrs. Stetson regarding this case fell in the same category as did those she had written to Mr. Kimball near the end of the lawsuit:

> I have found you *wise, watchful, vigilant* —but none can see what I see; hence the wisdom of faith in me.

Mrs. Eddy was elevating not only Rev. Simonsen, but the entire Christian ministry, which is most evident in Simonsen's words:

> The fact that I had to pay my own tuition the same as any other student, was a great blessing to me, greater than might appear on the surface. As a clergyman I had been the recipient of many special favors ... in the form of donations, half-fare rates ... special discounts, etc. This sort of thing had had the tendency to cultivate in the minds of the clergy the idea that they were a special class,

entitled to special favors and privileges along every line. *It was not elevating in the least** . . . In Christian Science this had all changed. Now I, too, could play the part of a real man, and pay my own way in full as did other men. It was a splendid thing for me, and I was more deeply grateful to God and Mrs. Eddy than words can express when I walked up the aisle of the Mother Church and paid my tuition in full.

The teacher (in whom Mrs. Eddy was well pleased) who had taught all of the normal classes since the reopening of the College in 1899 was Edward A. Kimball. Both he and Mrs. Eddy were fully occupied with the Woodbury case as June dawned, but when the Normal Class convened June 20, 1901, Mr. Kimball was the teacher. Rev. Simonsen wrote:

> I have sat for months in class rooms listening to learned professors and able teachers, but I never supposed it to be possible for any human being to teach and unfold to his students, in the short space of two weeks, all that Mr. Kimball imparted to us . . . His teachings were deep and comprehensive. To me he left nothing to be desired. His style was simple, clear, logical, convincing and illuminating.
>
> He was thoroughly imbued with the great Truth he unfolded. He seemed to sense the need of each student. With it all he was so humble and unassuming. Loyal to our Leader, he unfolded to us her God-given place . . .

This last point is of utmost importance. Mr. Kimball was the most outstanding teacher of Christian Science in the movement, second only to Mrs. Eddy; and for that reason he became a target for animal magnetism. Many fine students of Science succumbed to the suggestions of malicious mind in condemning Mr. Kimball and his teaching. These malicious suggestions never pointed to Mr. Kimball's *teaching* about the Leader's God-given place, but always centered upon the conciliatory interview he had given to the press following the Woodbury trial. That interview was for public consumption and was an expedient to protect and hide the divine idea from the unprepared thought as was Mrs. Eddy's rewording in Science and Health at that time from "the second appearing *in* the flesh" to "the second appearing *on* the flesh." Simonsen's appreciation of Mr. Kimball continues:

> At last I had found a teacher who was able to answer without begging from or evading any of the many important questions which he was called upon to answer. No wonder Mrs. Eddy loved him and deeply appreciated his understanding and correct teaching, his wise counselling, and the inspiration he instilled in all who came in contact with him . . .

*Emphasis added.

Mrs. Eddy knew of the attacks of malicious mind against Mr. Kimball and his teaching. She was well aware of the constant suggestions of animal magnetism which most of her students accepted unwittingly. But one incident was an eye-opener for Calvin C. Hill:

> One day when I was with Mrs. Eddy she rang for her personal maid and requested that she bring some article to her. The maid returned, bringing something totally different from what Mrs. Eddy had asked for. Mrs. Eddy looked at her earnestly and said, "Dear, that isn't what I told you to bring; I told you to bring [naming the article], and I told you where to find it. Now please get it."
>
> Turning to me Mrs. Eddy remarked, as I recall her words, "That is what animal magnetism does to the members of my household, and they will say, 'Mother sometimes forgets!'" . . . shortly after I left her I met this same maid in the hall, and she said to me, "Mother sometimes forgets what she asks for!"

Malicious animal magnetism, sometimes appearing as the glister of the world, endeavored to keep students from a deep dedication to Christian Science. Lewis Strang recorded this Watch on the ninth of June in 1901:

> Truth declared heals the sick. Prove this and help the Cause at once. Students asleep M.A.M. has already handled. Know that your Leader cannot be deprived of the helpers she needs by the glister of the world. Mind is All. Divine Love rules this hour. *Know this.*

The Leader was always seeking earnest workers for her great Cause as well as teachable helpers who could serve both her and the Cause at Pleasant View. She greatly appreciated Kimball's evaluation of the students in his Normal Class which he wrote her on the first of July. "One of the best students of the second generation that I know of," he wrote of Mr. Bicknell Young of Chicago, adding that he could be a help in Boston. And of Professor Hermann Hering from Baltimore he said, "Please keep him in mind. He is splendid — because he has felt the very touch of God and has been born again." He felt that Lord Dunmore's grasp of Science was less than his wonderful enthusiasm for it. He was most pleased with George Kinter of Buffalo of whom he wrote:

> A splendid man . . . a genuine, kind, strong, generous fellow who is too grand in general to be small or mean in particular — sensible, business-like, effective. Would be a good man for you to have in Boston.

Of Rev. Simonsen he said, he "is a grand man, fine looking,

benevolent, honest, upright, manly, gentle, humble, teachable." He had many fine things to say about John Willis including that "he is naturally spiritually minded," but he also stated that "his grasp of C.S. is on the intellectual side," and "he clings much to the idea that the good (?) of mortal mind is ... worthy to coalesce with Science."

Rev. Simonsen was much impressed with the simplicity of the Communion service in the Mother Church on Sunday, June 23. The Mother's *Message* was read by John Reeder. This Message which she had said is "Christian Science in a nutshell," she also named "Infinite Personality" when naming her messages, and added, "My best." The reading of it took one and one-half hours making the total service two hours long, but the three services planned could not accommodate the people, — so a fourth was added.

The following day a great many of the visiting Scientists, reported to be as many as seventeen hundred, made a trip to Concord to visit the Leader's home town for a day. On that Monday afternoon an announcement from Boston spread like wildfire among the visitors, that Mrs. Eddy had invited her church members to visit Pleasant View on Tuesday, June 25. Immediately between a thousand and seventeen hundred people who had come for the day were seeking overnight accommodations in Concord, which quickly filled every hotel and depleted every store of toothbrushes and other toilet articles. Concordians, many of whom had never done so before, generously opened their homes to absorb this tidal wave, — a hospitality which was much appreciated and gratefully acknowledged.

Tuesday morning at ten o'clock the gates of Pleasant View were opened to visitors and from then until evening close to three thousand Christian Scientists plus reporters from several papers strolled about the lawns and walks. The railroad ran three special trains of ten cars each in addition to its regular service from Boston.

The visitors enjoyed the lovely, spacious grounds, but of course all were hoping for a glimpse of Mrs. Eddy. She gratified their hope shortly before her daily carriage drive. The *Boston Globe* reported:

> Mary Baker G. Eddy walked out upon the balcony, far above the heads of her people, at just 1:55. Her step was firm. Her manner was impressive. Her movement was graceful ...

She smiled graciously and spoke very briefly. The next day, June 26, the *New York Journal* published this message:

> Please say through the *New York Journal* to the Christian Scientists of New York City and of the world at large that I was happy to

receive the call of about three thousand believers of my faith in this city . . .

I am especially desirous that it should be understood that this was no festal occasion, no formal church ceremonial, but simply my acquiescence in the request of my church members that they might see the Mother of Christian Science.

The brevity of my remarks today was due to a desire on my part that the important sentiments uttered in my annual message to the Church last Sunday should not be confused with other issues, but should be emphasized in the minds of all present here today.

Mary Baker G. Eddy

Only those closest to Mrs. Eddy had any idea what these pilgrimages to her home cost the Leader, but the crowds were orderly and reverent. Many felt greatly blessed and inspired; and the Mother's whole life was devoted to blessing her children. The *Journal's* closing words about the occasion were: "It will remain always a sweet memory to all who were present."

CHAPTER V

GOD'S MESSENGER

Behold a greater than Solomon is here. — JESUS

1901

WILLIAM Dana Orcutt, John Wilson's protege and successor and Mrs. Eddy's printer, wrote her in 1901 that he was making a trip to Europe and asked whether she had any business she would like to discuss with him prior to his departure. She answered immediately in the affirmative and asked him to come to Pleasant View at his convenience.

Mr. Orcutt was impressed with how little Mrs. Eddy had changed since his first visit to Pleasant View nearly a decade earlier. And he was doubly impressed by the vastness of the project she outlined to him. After discussing his pending trip she enquired as to the date of his return, considering it thoughtfully for a moment. Then she said: "That will fit in perfectly with my plans. When you return I shall need your assistance." She told him she was working on a major revision of Science and Health which would require a resetting of the entire book with a new problem in typography to solve because she planned to number the lines. As soon as the plates were completed Mr. Conant was to begin work on a comprehensive concordance to replace the index. The magnitude of her project astonished the young man. In his reminiscences of *Mary Baker Eddy and Her Books* he reviewed her unparalleled accomplishments up to 1900 and then stated:

> When I consider the sum total of her known labors during that period, I cannot avoid asking myself what other man or woman in all history ever equalled this record. To me this is an unanswerable challenge, yet all this was but a prelude to even more astonishing accomplishments still to come!

Her project was the most ambitious on his agenda, and he knew nothing of *other* projects she was working on including the Mother Church Extension and the gathering of material for her autobiographical *Footprints Fadeless.*

Her students were contemplating the purchase of the four-story brick Hotel Brookline in August, 1901, which stood where the Extension now stands. But in September Mrs. Eddy advised them not to purchase this or any other properties until the church had more funds.

Chosen students were collecting material from the past for her autobiographical project. Irving C. Tomlinson had written to Mrs. Eddy's sister-in-law, Mary Ann Baker, and received a lengthy response from her dated August 20, 1901, in which she said:

> At this time when so much is being said in public most appreciatively of the Rev. Mary Baker G. Eddy . . . and also somewhat that is untruthful, absurd, and wholly unchristian, I desire to make the following statement:
>
> First I will say that I am not a Christian Scientist . . .
>
> Mrs. Eddy's character is above reproach. No libelous words can touch it, no foe can assail it. Hidden in God it shall shine and reflecting Him, its brilliancy will be seen long after she who labors ceases her work for ultimate rest. Her large and extensive work, with her unprecedented following, has called forth malignant utterances. so utterly false they should not go unchallenged. . . .

One of the utterly false, malignant utterances had been heard at Tremont Temple on the first of August and most likely caused Mrs. Eddy to collect refuting testimony. This was a lecture by Frederick Peabody titled "A Complete Expose of Eddyism or Christian Science."

But Mrs. Eddy forged ahead despite such attacks. She had outlined her idea for a concordance to Science and Health to Albert Conant who worked out the plan for its production. She also employed Mr. Conant to do this work, but he could not implement his plan until the revision of Science and Health was completed.

The last major revision of the textbook had been the fiftieth edition in 1890. She had sought the assistance of a student on that revision, but his efforts had not been successful; which had caused her to start anew and do all the work herself. This time, however, she had two fine scholarly students to assist her. Though temporarily disenchanted with her leadership in the heat of the Woodbury controversy, William P. McKenzie had come through the ordeal with renewed faith in the Leader and became one of her able assistants in this undertaking. The other was her competent, ever-faithful Edward A. Kimball. But this project was to begin in the fall.

In midsummer, July 10, Mrs. Eddy wrote a message to Third Church of Chicago which Mr. Kimball read at their dedication services on Sunday, July 14:

> *Beloved Brethren:* — May this church find God all instead of part, and reflect His goodness and power. Behold, how good and how pleasant it is for brethren to dwell together in unity!
>
> Mary Baker G. Eddy

The Christian Scientists in Chicago had a remarkable and exemplary sense of unity, but when Mrs. Stetson endeavored to adopt their methods Mrs. Eddy quickly stopped her. The Leader *knew* that this unity must be mental and spiritual, rather than organizational, in order to endure. For that very reason, she had written a new by-law the previous winter which had been published in the *Sentinel* of March 7, 1901, as follows:

> **Church By-Laws**
>
> This is the denominational rule of Christian Science. Each Church of Christ, Scientist, shall have its own form of government. No conference of churches shall be held except the annual conference at the Mother Church in Boston in June of each year. Let *individual** intercourse and fellowship be among the churches and that love continue whereby the brethren may encourage and strengthen one another.

But, as Mrs. Eddy had written to Mr. Kimball, "none can see what I see." Not only did the Chicago students not *see* what she saw about *self*-government, they evidently did not even see (and surely did not implement) what she wrote about it and about no conference of churches. At their dedication services the following was stated:

> We return our sincere acknowledgments to the Christian Scientists of Chicago and vicinity who have furnished the means that has enabled us today to present this building as a proper setting for the teaching of Divine Science in the measure that it comes to us. The body that has made this aid efficient is the Conference Committee of the Churches of Christ, Scientist, of Chicago. It is composed of the officers and Readers of the various churches and the lecturers resident in the city. Its general oversight and guidance exercised in building these churches has been generous, wise, and business-like. . . .

Such actions, though having the outward appearance of success and progress, caused the weak to lean upon the strong, as the Leader well knew. Her every action and instruction tended toward

*Emphasis added.

self-development which caused the weak to *become* strong. This was most obvious in her treatment of Rev. Simonsen and his Normal Class tuition.

In August Rev. and Mrs. Simonsen were delighted to receive an invitation to attend the Concord State Fair as Mrs. Eddy's guests. She had purchased one hundred tickets, largely for the First Members of her Church, and invited Scientists to attend on Governor's Day, August 28.

The previous day, August 27, had been designated as Children's Day when all children were admitted free of charge. An interesting feature of that day was repeated in succeeding years. Mrs. Eddy had given out word that she would provide a pair of shoes to all children who needed them, and a representative of William E. Thompson's Shoe Store gave out over two hundred tickets, each to be redeemed for a pair of shoes. Many Scientists are aware of this act of charity on Mrs. Eddy's part, but few are aware of the occurrence in Mr. Thompson's shoe store earlier that year which induced her to this action.

All of the papers reported Mrs. Eddy's appearance at the fair on Wednesday, August 28. One paragraph from the *Boston Globe* reported:

> It was a great day, but perhaps the man on whom the sun shone with the greatest splendor was Norin, the high diver, whom Mrs. Eddy came more especially to see.
>
> She saw his act last year and was much impressed by it and she expressed a desire to see it again this year. Her desire was granted and Norin was consequently the observed of all observers today as he climbed the dizzy heights of his rude scaffold and plunged into the tank of water eighty-seven feet below.

What the *Globe* reporter did not know about Oscar Norin was that Mrs. Eddy had invited him to come to see her at Pleasant View following his performance which she watched with interest. The interest of the crowd was on Mrs. Eddy as her landau was seen to enter the grounds promptly at 2:45 P.M. Calvin Frye was on the box with the driver and Judge and Mrs. Ewing were in the carriage with Mrs. Eddy. Following an official welcome, her carriage advanced to a point opposite the high diving scaffold:

> Norin quickly appeared, climbed about ten feet to a spring board and turned a back somerset into the water. He then kept going higher and higher, diving each time, until finally he reached the topmost point and made his great flight through the air, graceful and steady, into the tank with a loud splash.

Immediately Mrs. Eddy's carriage turned about and departed slowly as she waved to the thousands who were waving to her. The reporter described her attire, said she "looked well and cheerful," and added: "From the press stand she appeared to be in good spirits, although she did not manifest any particular enthusiasm in what she saw." Perhaps she was contemplating what she had perceived about Mr. Oscar Norin.

Both Clara Shannon and Mrs. Ewing have passed on records of Mr. Norin's visit at Pleasant View. Mrs. Eddy first questioned him about his diving and then talked to him in a "heavenly way for some time" according to Clara Shannon, until "one could see by the expression of his face how enlightened he was." Then Mrs. Eddy said:

> "You are able to dive because you have overcome fear." He said, "Yes," he had no fear whatever, he had practised for a long time taking a higher and higher dive till he could do it without fear. Then Mrs. Eddy said: "Use that overcoming of fear on your eyes." The man had dark glasses on and said: "Well, I damaged one eye so that the eyeball had to be taken out, and this is why I wear the glasses, because the eye is unpleasant to look at."

They were sitting in the library at the time of this interview and Clara Shannon said:

> . . . as she talked to him I could see and feel that his fear was removed, and his thought was full of hope and joy, although he did not then realize the blessing he had received.

The cabman who drove Mr. Norin to the station told them a day or two later that Mr. Norin had taken off his dark glasses when he got to the station, and that he had two perfect eyes — the missing eye had been restored. That is what Mrs. Eddy had been doing while others were enjoying the diversions of the fair.

On Thursday, August 29, Rev. and Mrs. Simonsen visited Mrs. Eddy at Pleasant View at her invitation. It was the first time they had met the Leader, and Rev. Simonsen said of the occasion:

> I was most singularly impressed with the purity and beauty of her countenance . . . But to me the most striking attraction was her wonderful eyes, the like of which I have never seen in all my experience of contact with people; they expressed volumes. It is beyond my power to describe how they responded to, and in various ways portrayed the sacred subject she would at the moment be discussing. You realized that she reflected the Christ mind so fully that she discerned without effort your mental state; but it did not disturb you. The sense that came to you was her desire not to injure, but to help

DANIEL
By Briton Riviere

and save . . .

Following this visit the Leader had both Mr. and Mrs. Simonsen elected First Members of her Church, and during the visit she gave them wonderfully helpful instruction — never to be forgotten. She also showed them many of the treasured gifts from her students including paintings hanging on the walls. As they stood admiring her "Banner," which is a life-size painting of "The Good Shepherd" with his flock, the Leader said: "See how perfectly happy and contented they all seem? No crowding or pushing for place or position. They are all glad and willing to leave their future in the hands of their Shepherd."

She told the Simonsens that she prized Briton Riviere's steel etchings of Daniel in the lions' den very highly. They were all looking at Daniel in the lions' den on her wall, and Rev. Simonsen recalled:

> As we stood before this most interesting picture she gave us a very entertaining and instructive explanation, not only of Daniel, but of the seven lions. Then she went on and told us that when error seemed to press her exceptionally hard, she would leave her work for a few minutes and come and stand before this picture, and study anew the calm and loving manner in which Daniel looked steadfastly to God and God only. He paid no heed to the lions or seeming danger, letting his dear heavenly Father care for the ferocious beasts and keep them at a safe distance. With new and fresh courage, she said, she would return to her work, with a heart full of joy and gratitude for His protecting care.

Before this visit with the Leader, Rev. Simonsen had wondered at the devotion of her faithful followers, but it was clear to him after he had come "in contact with this great heart of love." From that time he never ceased giving thanks for this Christly leader and her marvelous mission. He wrote in his book *From the Methodist Pulpit Into Christian Science:*

> I know of no words adequate to express fully my gratitude to God for this noble and wonderful woman, who was good enough, pure enough, unselfish enough, and intelligent enough to receive this revelation of divine Science, and to record it in such language as to make plain to the benighted understanding of mankind the way of God's full salvation through Christ.

DANIEL ANSWERS THE KING
By Briton Riviere

CHAPTER VI

WORK, WORK, WORK

O the amount that I see to be done for all, before Christian Science is established on the Rock 'gainst which the billows beat in vain!

— MARY BAKER EDDY

1901

NO doubt the workers in Mrs. Eddy's home who were aware of Mr. Norin's healing were inspired in their own healing work. Mrs. Eddy strengthened their resolve in this Watch of September 4 preserved by Lewis Strang:

> Healing alone built this Cause and will not be lost if hearts open to His Truth and Love sustain the hands of those appointed to voice God in this age. Form in service means nothing; only healing can build His temple in the wilderness. How Mother longs, prays to hear of more healing in the service of divine Love!

More and better healing is accomplished when more time and thought is devoted to sustaining "the hands of those appointed to voice God in this age." While a *few* devoted students were aware of Mrs. Eddy's healing works that never ceased, and were dedicated to improving their own work in this area, a great *many* Scientists were interested in her appearance at the fair and in her place of residence. Just so, thousands had visited Pleasant View, but very few knew that it was a well-managed farm. A short article from the *Concord Monitor* during the 1901 harvest season gives us an inkling of the diversification of Mrs. Eddy's interests:

> **Harvesting on the Rev. Mary Baker Eddy Place**
> Few of the many visitors to Concord, who enjoy so much the charming drive out tc Pleasant View, with its macadamized road, well-kept lawns, flowers, and shrubbery, imagine that the Rev. Mary Baker Eddy has one of the best-equipped model farms in New Eng-

> land. This is under the careful management of Mr. August Mann, and it would well pay any one interested in agriculture to look over Pleasant View's farm machinery and pattern after its methods. One of the latest acquisitions is an Adriance Rear Discharge Reaper and Binder, working in the twenty-acre field of rye, which handles the six-foot grain with perfect ease, though badly lodged in places. It is a great favorite with the farmer. The large grass crop at Pleasant View is handled by a six-foot Adriance Buckeye Mower and New Yorker Rakes, and while the territory mowed over is not so large, the crops are very heavy. They have a full equipment of plowing and pulverizing machinery including New Yorker Disk and Loam Smoothing Harrows. One should not forget the dairy at Pleasant View. It is fully supplied with cream separators, churns, and butter workers of the latest improved patterns, in fact, every department of the estate of the modest owner is looked after with great care.

Mrs. Eddy supervised *all* of the work that was done at Pleasant View and made all of the decisions, but most of her work was done in her own study, and much of it while seated in her favorite armchair.

Calvin Hill was often in Mrs. Eddy's study after his first visit in the spring of 1899. On one visit he noted how badly worn was her armchair and determined to surprise her with a new one. After getting exact measurements and having a reproduction made, he exchanged the new chair for the old one while Mrs. Eddy was out on her drive one day. With his gift he left a letter of appreciation and gratitude stating that his "only desire is that it may give you the comfort that it does me the joy in giving it."

Mrs. Eddy was delighted with his considerate action, and in her letter of thanks enclosed a "card complimentary" to the next Normal Class to be held in June, 1902. In addition, in 1901 she had Mr. Hill made a First Member of her Church.

Another student who was often in Mrs. Eddy's private rooms was John Salchow. Many a time John was called upon for some repair job or another, and he went quietly about his work. Quite often Mrs. Eddy talked to him freely, but on occasion he worked for hours in her presence and never a word was spoken. John wrote in his reminiscences:

> She frequently told me that I never disturbed her, that when I came in she could feel my presence without knowing that I was near, and that sometimes, when she had been suffering, my thought helped to lift her out of it. I can never begin to tell the joy with which such words filled me.

John was an *honest* seeker for Truth, "an Israelite indeed in whom [was] no guile." The earnest, conscientious thought and service of her "faithful John" was a refreshing oasis in a desert of ambitious worldliness.

The ambitious worldliness which seemed ubiquitous at times was trying indeed, but the mindless malice her pioneering work had uncovered was deadly. She had published in her *Historical Sketch* in 1886:

> If any honest Christian Scientist can be deceived into thinking that it is chance, not direction by malicious minds which are at work, — that ignorance instead of sin is what he has to meet at all times, — this error prevents him from understanding enough of the question to ensure his own defence, and leaves him in the power of Animal Magnetism . . .
>
> Ceaseless toil, self-renunciation, and Love have cleared the pathway for Christian Science. I have learned all that I have written through experience and persecution. . . .
>
> When you denounce sin you begin to remove it; for its denunciation must precede its destruction. God is Good, hence Goodness is the Life of all men. Its opposite named Evil, is a conspiracy against man's Life and Goodness.

All the world witnessed the conspiracy named Evil, not chance, but "direction by malicious minds . . . at work," on the sixth of September. Crowds had come to a public reception at the Pan-American Exposition in Buffalo, New York, to shake hands with President McKinley. Leon Czolgosz *alias* Fred Nieman, who appeared to have an injured right hand, stood in the long line, and as he shook the president's hand with his left hand he shot him with a 32 calibre revolver concealed in the handkerchief on his "injured" right hand. All the world was stunned by this malevolence.

This act of violence may have prompted Mrs. Eddy's next action, or perhaps it just hastened it. She had executed a trust deed on February 12, 1898, conveying Pleasant View and all the personal property thereon to Calvin A. Frye. On September 5, 1901, Calvin had transferred Pleasant View back to Mrs. Eddy. It was the next day that President McKinley was shot, and the following Friday, September 13, Irving C. Tomlinson, his sister Mary Tomlinson, Myron Pratt, and Alvin B. Cross came to Pleasant View to sign their names following this paragraph on a legal document:

> Signed, sealed and declared by the above named Mary Baker G. Eddy as and for her last will and testament, in the presence of us, who, at her request, in her presence, and in the presence of each other, have subscribed our names as witnesses hereto.*

*See Appendix B.

The next day, September 14, Pres. McKinley died, although the initial reports had been hopeful of his recovery. The Christian churches in the land held memorial services on September 19. At the Mother Church in Boston Mrs. Eddy's "Tribute to President McKinley" *(My.* 291) was read, as was her letter written to Mrs. McKinley *(My.* 290) on the day her husband passed away. The prestigious *Harper's Weekly* stated:

> All the preachers preached on President McKinley; all the editors wrote about him. . . . Thousands . . . said about the same things, . . . Mrs. Eddy . . . issued two utterances . . . Both of these discourses are seemly and kind, but they are materially different from the writings of any one else. Reciting the praises of the dead President, Mrs. Eddy says: "May his history waken a tone of truth that shall reverberate, renew euphony, emphasize humane power, and bear its banner into the vast forever." No one else said anything like that. [Mrs.] Eddy's style is a personal asset. Her sentences usually have the considerable literary merit of being unexpected. Her letter to Mrs. McKinley was short, sympathetic, religious, and very much to the point. Her position in the country as the head and chief spokesman of an important religious body is very curious and highly interesting.

A few days later the *Boston Journal* asked Mrs. Eddy the question: "Why did Christians of every sect in the United States fail in their prayers to save the life of our late lamented President?" Her answer *(My.* 292) was published with the date line, Concord, N.H., September 25, under the caption "Mrs. Eddy Explains." Perhaps the most significant sentence in her explanation was: "Had prayer so fervently offered possessed no opposing element, and his recovery been regarded wholly contingent on the power of God, the power of divine Love to overrule the purposes of hate, and the law of Spirit to control matter, the result would have been scientific and the patient would have recovered."

Early in October Mrs. Eddy's thought turned to Benny in Waterbury, Vermont, and she wrote him a tender letter. He responded on October 22, beginning his letter:

> My most blessed Mother:
> Your letter came in due time, and it was so sweet and precious, just like you. . . .

Many issues of the *Sentinel* contained a notice of an Obstetric Class to be taught by Dr. Baker which was to convene October 21, and an unusual notice appeared in the *Sentinel* of October 31. It stated simply:

Reading Room in Concord, N. H.

First Church of Christ, Scientist, in Concord, N. H. has closed its Reading Room at Christian Science Hall. This room will hereafter be used for private purposes. The Christian Science literature, however, will be for sale there as formerly. This action upon the part of the church is taken with the approval of Mrs. Eddy.

Was there too much socializing and too little studying in the Reading Room nearest Mrs. Eddy's home? Or was this action related to the following notice which appeared three weeks later?

Take Notice

All gifts by mail, express, or that are handed to the porter at my door without cards, and have not come from persons with whom I am acquainted, — will be returned to the office whence they came, or rejected at my door. Recent attempts of third parties to scandalize me through the friendly means aforesaid, have occasioned this notice. Mary Baker G. Eddy

* * *

NUMBERING THE LINES

1902 Revision of Science and Health — 226th Edition

MRS. Eddy's first concern was the protection of her work, and the work at hand right now was the major revision of Science and Health. By mid-November her revising was essentially completed and she was ready for the assistance of the two students she had chosen to help with this project, Edward A. Kimball and William P. McKenzie.

Mr. Kimball had returned to his home in Chicago in July in which city he delivered an address at the dedication of Third Church, on July 14. In September he resumed lecturing, with an extremely heavy schedule in October and early November. McKenzie lectured in Barre, Vermont on November 14, but very soon thereafter the two men were back in Massachusetts working on Science and Health. Mrs. Eddy sent the changes she wanted them to work on, and Mr. Kimball wrote her their working procedure on the twenty-second of November:

> First I take the copy and study it with a view of detecting any necessary changes. Then Mr. McKenzie takes it and goes over the punctuation and corrects the quotations. After that we go over it together and discuss all changes of every kind and possibly make

more and finally each one goes over the complete copy by himself.

A completed passage was sent to Mrs. Eddy for her scientific scrutiny and final decision. More than one passage came back for further work, but all in all the task of these two able writers progressed rapidly. Mr. Kimball went over to Cambridge every day where they worked together in McKenzie's study, and the manuscript was ready for the printer by the time William Orcutt returned from Europe.

Mr. Orcutt was a little disappointed to find that his conferences were not to be with Mrs. Eddy, but with one of her lieutenants he had not met before, William P. McKenzie. As it turned out Orcutt and McKenzie were very compatible and their work together on the 1902 revision of Science and Health proved to be the beginning of a lifelong friendship. Mr. Orcutt later wrote of this period:

> As he and I went over the manuscript together, it became evident that hours of concentrated thought had gone into its revision. Mr. McKenzie pointed out to me that not less than half the pages contained corrections — a word here, a rearranged sentence there, a deletion, or an elaboration — never a change of thought, but finally expressing the author's mature judgment in making the meaning clearer . . .

The first problem to be decided by Orcutt and McKenzie was the numbering of the lines. McKenzie first thought every line should be numbered and Orcutt thought every fifth line. Then both agreed on every third line. Orcutt wrote:

> Mr. McKenzie suggested taking the three experimental pages to Mrs. Eddy. I told him that she always preferred a definite suggestion rather than alternative choices.
>
> "Put the proofs in your pocket," I said, "but show her the one you and I prefer, holding the other proofs in reserve. I don't think she will ask for them."

And that is exactly what happened. Mrs. Eddy studied the proof carefully, approved it, and went on to other details.

Her emendations and additions were not all that Mrs. Eddy sent to Mr. Kimball and Mr. McKenzie. She also sent them a large number of testimonials of healings effected solely by reading Science and Health which had been published in the *Journal* or the *Sentinel.* From this collection the two men were to make selections and plan the arrangement for the final chapter Mrs. Eddy had outlined to them and entitled "Fruitage." The first presentation of Fruitage in 1902 was 101 pages as was the last in 1910. It began on page 600 and ended the book on page 700, making it the longest chapter.

The second longest chapter was Chapter XII, "Christian Science Practice" which had been increased from 79 to 81 pages. Even though half the pages had changes and there were a good many additions, about half the chapters remained the same length. The other half were increased by one or two pages with the exception of Chapter VII "Physiology" which was decreased by three pages.

Perhaps the most significant change second to the numbering of the lines was the rearrangement of the order of the first eleven chapters in this up-coming edition which would be the 226th edition or 226th thousand copies. The following shows this rearrangement:

1901 Edition	**Chapter**	**226th Edition — 1902**
Science, Theology, Medicine	I	Prayer
Physiology	II	Atonement and Eucharist
Footsteps of Truth	III	Marriage
Creation	IV	Christian Science and Spiritualism
Science of Being	V	Animal Magnetism
Christian Science and Spiritualism	VI	Science, Theology, Medicine
Marriage	VII	Physiology
Animal Magnetism	VIII	Footsteps of Truth
Some Objections Answered	IX	Creation
Prayer	X	Science of Being
Atonement and Eucharist	XI	Some Objections Answered

It would appear that Thomas W. Hatten was a third student helping with this revision of Science and Health. Hatten had been in Mrs. Eddy's last Primary Class in March of 1889 and had been in the publishing office since his move to Boston in 1892. Over the years he became very dear to the Leader who wrote him these words of encouragement on April 20, 1897:

My Precious Child:

Do not be troubled like Martha of old over anything, do not be disheartened over failure, when at heart you are as faithful as Abraham. We are all to be tried and proved, as by fire. Now darling, there is but one Mind. No other mind exists and therefore an evil so-called mind cannot, *does not* affect you or your business. Keep the first commandment, sacredly and know there is but one Mind. Keep the ten commandments, do not let your affections rest for a moment in forbidden directions, but, dear one, have but one God, one affection, one peace. The senses that lie are nonsense. There is no sensation in wrong directions . . .

Thomas Hatten became one of the trustees of the Publishing Society in September of 1898 when Edward P. Bates resigned. In November of 1901, Mrs. Eddy called Mr. Hatten to Pleasant View where he served until the 226th edition was published in January of 1902.

It was in the January 30 *Sentinel* of 1902 that the first announcement appeared in only four lines as follows:

> **NEW EDITION OF SCIENCE AND HEALTH**
> "Science and Health with Key to the Scriptures," printed from new plates, with lines numbered, and with important revisions by the author, is now ready for distribution.

The February 6 *Sentinel* and March *Journal* contained Judge Hanna's editorial about "The New Edition of Science and Health." Each week a notice appeared for the new edition "with lines numbered," and it was announced that the next *Quarterly* would contain double references from Science and Health to acommodate both those who had the old edition and those who had the 226th or later editions. Some students numbered the lines of their old textbooks with pencil, but all serious students acquired the new edition in time.

CHAPTER VII

SLOW STEPS FORWARD

I have learned all that I have written through experience and persecution. — MARY BAKER EDDY

MRS. Eddy had learned from experience that every truth she uttered and every step she took would be resisted by even her most devout and devoted students. As early as 1878 when Mrs. Eddy made a statement of absolute Truth at a meeting of her small band of followers, Clara Choate recalled "that small company seemed like a battlefield between Truth and error." "Even dear Dr. Eddy in his quiet, patient manner and tender voice ... [tried] to enter a conciliatory compromise ... But Mrs. Eddy heroically stood her ground." And one student "almost in temper, with apparent disgust coldly left the meeting."

Could her students only have *obeyed* and *followed* their Leader, their progress would have been a marvel to cause all the world to wonder. But instead the Leader had defection after defection from her ranks, because her Truth antagonized the error her students would cling to. In 1893 she had written to Mr. Kimball, "I have learned from bitter experience that the head instructed before the heart is ready, costs me and our Cause dangerous difficulties and sore defeats." One of her bitter experiences occurred in 1888 when most of her students in Boston left in a body forsaking both the Truth they had been proclaiming and their Leader. Mrs. Eddy said at that time to her faithful William B. Johnson that:

> she found it difficult to sleep at night because so many wonderful things, — ways, means, and results at which the world would marvel, — kept coming to her. ... but she did not dare utter one word of them, because the revelation might shake the faith of even the few loyal students ...

Mrs. Eddy was immediate in following God's direction, but she had learned to introduce progressive steps or changes as gradually as possible in the effort to keep her followers at least facing in the right direction. It is altogether possible that Mind had directed her to discontinue the teaching of obstetrics following the Normal and Obstetric classes in the summer of 1900. But pursuing a gradual course, she had her church amend a by-law to read: "Beginning with the year 1901, the term for teaching obstetrics commences six months after the close of the college term."

A number of *Sentinels* and *Journals* announced that the 1901 obstetric class would convene October 21 and that "application must be made to Alfred E. Baker." In October the notices also stated, *"Any one* having a degree of C.S.B. or C.S.D., may become an applicant for the obstetric class, which convenes October 21, 1901. This includes the 1901 June class." Neither the *Sentinel* nor the *Journal* gave a report of the class nor any indication whether it was held.

Early in 1902 a notice in the *Sentinel* stated: "Article XXXIV, of said Church Manual has been repealed." At that date Article XXXIV was titled Obstetrics, and all four sections dealt with its teaching. At the same time Article XXXI (now XXVIII) which had read:

> Section 1. There shall be a Board of Education, under the auspices of the Massachusetts Metaphysical College, consisting of four members, a president, a vice-president, a teacher of Christian Science, and a teacher of obstetrics.

was amended to read: "Board of Education . . . consisting of three members [eliminating the teacher of obstetrics] . . . Obstetrics is not Science, and will not be taught."

Another issue which arose in 1901 had received this gradual treatment. When there was agitation for public debating about Christian Science the Leader wrote "A Word to the Wise" *(My.* 223) in which she said: "Avoid for the immediate present public debating clubs." But for ears that could not hear she also included the following in the same issue of the *Sentinel:*

> **Church By-law**
>
> The Christian Science Board of Directors shall elect annually, subject to the approval or the disapproval of the Pastor Emeritus, a "Committee on Debate," consisting of not less than four members. A member of this Church shall not debate on Christian Science in public debating assemblies, who is not a member of this Committee.

What a circuitous route she had to take to *lead* her dull disciples to see that debating was not a proper method for presenting Christian Science!

Irving C. Tomlinson had been involved with the mental work on the Woodbury trial. He was also the First Reader in the church nearest Mrs. Eddy's home, in Concord. And now the tail of the serpent endeavored to cast this earnest student down.

Mrs. Jennie A. Spead had attended the Concord church for several months when she consulted Rev. Tomlinson as a Christian Science practitioner in November of 1899. Two years later in the fall of 1901 she was claiming that Mr. Tomlinson "did not use reasonable skill and care, and that the plaintiff thereby suffered damage."

Mrs. Eddy's Concord attorney Gen. Frank S. Streeter and his junior partner Allen Hollis represented Mr. Tomlinson and said in their statement for the defence:

> From the time of Mrs. Spead's first attack until Mr. Tomlinson's services were first requested, she was under the general care of Dr. McMurphy. This term of treatment amounts to six hundred sixty days.
>
> Mr. Tomlinson treated her four days. She paid him one dollar, and now wants this jury to award her damages in the sum of six thousand dollars . . .

Mr. Streeter also said in his argument:

> Why was this suit brought? Was it brought for damages or for making an attack on a religion which today has one million followers?
>
> The attack is an attack upon the theory that disease may be cured by prayer. . . .
>
> The fundamental thing which Mr. Tomlinson taught [Mrs. Spead] was that he relied solely on the power of God, sought by prayer, to effect relief . . .
>
> In my belief this woman is no more a factor in this litigation than is the gilded dome of the state house a factor in making our laws. This is an assault on the Christian religion. . . .
>
> You will be asked to say that prayer is fraud. . . . Mr. Tomlinson's proposition is that the power of God can cure sickness through prayer. I don't envy the condition of mind of men who stand up and say it is a lie. That the power of God can't heal. . . . Is this man a cheat because he believes that prayer will cure the sick? Then you have got to declare against the Christian ministers who stand in the pulpits in these United States. . . .

The trial at the October term of the Superior Court in Concord was not unlike the accusations of "the rabbis, who crucified Jesus and called him a 'deceiver'" *('01.* 9). Nonetheless it resulted in a disagreement of the jury which left the case just where it started.

Mrs. Eddy turned to the thousand other things demanding her attention and directed Rev. Tomlinson to do the same. But the fact that this case was still pending could have been one of the reasons for the decision to have Tomlinson and his sister occupy the residential portion of Christian Science Hall where Dr. Baker and his wife had lived since 1898.

One of the many letters the Leader wrote during the closing month of 1901 was to George Kinter in Buffalo, New York on December 2. Her words to him have helped many a student:

> Trust your God, our God, in divine Science. There is no other way than for us to *trust always.* This I have proven consistently for forty years. Can you, will you, do the same, my beloved student? Remember this, and live continually in the thought and attitude of trust, confident expectation of good. Nothing else can do for you what this can.

On December 21 she wrote two letters to her Boston board, the first "To the Watchers *who are Mistaken":*

> Beloved students:
> Disband your meeting today and never meet again to do what is not carried out *scientifically.* Each one do the work of daily duty. Each one realize the allness of God, good, and that there is no opposite evil. Do not meet together to discuss or to direct the prayers of Scientists unless *I* call you together. Each one pray daily and not ask amiss. I have known of the discord before of prayer that is amiss. You all can know that newspaper men will not publish aught against Christian Science. Please *know this* — and also know that you can do this separately as well as together.
> With love, Mother M. B. Eddy

> Beloved Student:
> I forgot to say this: Take up nobody personally but let your prayer be impersonal and God will bless the right.
> With love, Mother
>
> Do not think of me or my affairs. Let God do this and you invoke a general blessing.

She was having to say to these students what she had written to Mr. Kimball the previous spring: "none can see what I see, hence the wisdom of faith in me;" plus the instruction she had given in her message in June *('01.* 20), "The Christian Scientist is alone with his own being and with the reality of things."

A statement received in December was from her first student Hiram Crafts, and was added to the collection of letters, statements, and documents for her autobiographical sketch. Several letters written in January of 1902 by her directors and other students were added to this collection; however, the following letter written by Mrs. Eddy to Augusta Stetson on January 8 of the new year was not related to that project:

> My Beloved Student:
>
> You have sent me a beautiful teajacket. . . . I am sorry to give you so much trouble, even though I have little else all my time. Now dear one, remember you cannot be swamped or harmed by M.A.M. God, *good,* is your life, health, hope, salvation. Then what is there left to harm you? God knows all about our every need and will build your church edifice, if you do not make it a "skyscraper." But the divine Mind makes the human meek, and lowly in spirit, binds up all wounds and heals the sick and weary ones. You are healed, and every trial of your faith in good makes you stronger and better, if you improve this lesson from Love.
>
> You are able to judge of the interest of your church. Let not a single element of discord outside or inside trouble you. Do right and Love will bless you. There is no harm in doing rightly before a *stated time,* meeting, or assembly. My whole heart thanks you for your childlike care of my wardrobe and God will bless your every good deed. Be happy in well doing, be happy this and every year.
>
> Mary Baker Eddy

Mrs. Stetson, more than any other individual, helped Mrs. Eddy with her wardrobe. Many, many of Mrs. Eddy's letters to Augusta expressed thanks for her care in this area or for some particular item of apparel.

Mrs. Eddy's ability to turn her whole attention from one topic to another was phenomenal. As soon as the plates for the revision of Science and Health had been cast, establishing the numbered lines, she had had Mr. Conant start his final work on the Concordance. Early in 1902 she called Albert F. Conant and William Dana Orcutt to Pleasant View for a conference requesting the latter to please bring his drawings of his new type. Mr. Orcutt was delighted. This was his pet project, though totally unrelated to the work at hand. When Mrs. Eddy received Mr. Orcutt at Pleasant View she said:

> I hope Mr. McKenzie has made it clear to you how pleased I am with the new edition. . . . Today we have to talk about the Concordance. In making that book, you will be dealing with Mr. Conant, who will join us in half an hour — but first I want to hear about your new type.

Then she gave her undivided interest and attention to the topics nearest William Dana's heart. In half an hour Mr. Conant was summoned and the conversation turned to the Concordance easily and naturally. Orcutt wrote:

> Her ability to change from one topic to another with such consummate ease continued to amaze me. The earlier subject was not left

hanging in the air but was completely finished, at least for the time being. When that topic came to be taken up again, Mrs. Eddy would make the contact with perfect accuracy, and would carry on from the previous point as if the discussion had never been interrupted.

Mr. Conant presented their plan for the Concordance to Mr. Orcutt with only an occasional comment from Mrs. Eddy. When she was satisfied that it had been presented *exactly* as she wished it, the conference was terminated.

The Leader's attention may have turned next to the autobiographical material she had been collecting, for a copyright was applied for on February 12. On February 13, 1902, a copyright was issued for *Footprints Fadeless* by Mary Baker G. Eddy published by Joseph Armstrong. Most probably it was *not* published at that time for she wrote of *Footprints Fadeless* to William D. McCrackan in 1902 stating that it was a record of her early history; but she did not want it known as yet that she had written it. Her *Footprints* as well as her identity needed to be hidden a little longer from the world. When future generations would seek to find the footprints of the Revelator to this age, they would rejoice in her dedication and the words she chose to preface her text of *Footprints Fadeless:*

TO
The patient, glad toilers in the vineyard of our
Lord, I lovingly dedicate my *Footprints.*
— Mary Baker Eddy

Footprints, that perhaps another,
Sailing o'er life's solemn main,
A forlorn and shipwrecked brother,
Seeing, shall take heart again.
Longfellow — *A Psalm of Life*

Oh sometimes gleams upon our sight,
Through present wrongs, the eternal Right;
And step by step, since time began,
We see the steady gain of man.
Whittier — *Old and New*

* * *

On January 22, 1902 Mrs. Eddy wrote "To Whom It May Concern" *(My.* 223:11-19) which she had published in both the *Sentinel* and the *Journal* together with a by-law for the lecturers which was adopted January 28. This by-law read in part:

> It is the duty of the Board of Lectureship to include in each lecture a true and just reply to public topics condemning Christian Science, and bear true testimony to the facts pertaining to the life and character of our Pastor Emeritus.

Mr. Tomlinson was also the victim of attempted character assassination and understood the importance of refuting these attacks against the Leader. So he was a help in this area as her letter to her directors on January 25 regarding this by-law indicates:

> Nothing could injure our Cause more than the general silence that prevails on the topic of your Leader's character. This silence is causing the press to publish Peabody's lies, for it looks as if the Board of Lectureship was ashamed to speak in defence of your Leader, or has nothing to say in her behalf! Pass this By-law and publish it in the next Sentinel, and I will write to the members of the Board to do their duty, and Mr. Tomlinson will also write to the Board on this subject.

None of the students at the turn of the century could differentiate between the Christian Science Movement and the organization. Mrs. Eddy was ever and always teaching the importance of *healing* over all else while the students became more and more interested and involved in organizing churches and building buildings. When she first brought Ezra Buswell to Concord she endeavored, unsuccessfully, to impress him with the fact that she did *not* want a church, but healing in Concord. Soon after Tomlinson began reading at the Concord church she wrote him at length on the subject. Part of her letter written in April, 1899 stated:

> I am becoming in need of rest and peace to an extent beyond what you see. I have a problem to work out that you will not have for *many* years. If you and others give me not sufficient chance to do it, the Science is not demonstrated. I did not want a church so near me as Concord. I have all I should do for mine in Boston. But Mr. Buswell started the Sunday service without my proposing it and then ran out. Could get no place or hall fit to use. Then to save dishonor to our Cause, I got the Hall. My next step to organize was influenced by others that I do not name. Now I see the care is increased that I need diminished and if there were no Sunday services [but] healers here, I sincerely believe it would be better for me and the world. I seem to be beyond this organized work. I have had my experience and it worries me more than all else. If only I had what time I could work to give to writing, it would do more good than I can tell. God governs me. When I sent for Mr. B. I told him I did not want a church or Sunday services which lead to it, but *healing done where I was.** This was God's first order, and in thirty-three years I have not yielded to depart from His first order without being driven back to take it up.

*Emphasis added.

The Leader was leading in the true Way while endeavoring to *show* this way to her true followers, but they could not see it. Hence her words: "I seem to be beyond this organized work. I have had my experience and it worries me more than all else."

It is probable that she tried to make this same point with Dr. Baker and his wife when they first came to Concord. The point was, not that healing should be first and church organization second, but that her followers should turn first and *only* to healing, and *away* from the organization of churches. In January of 1902 Mr. Tomlinson recorded in his diary that Mrs. Eddy said: "I do not believe in much organization in church. The churches are over-organized."

But she did something much more emphatic at this same time in directing Dr. and Mrs. Baker to follow in the way she was leading. In February the Bakers moved from Christian Science Hall in Concord, New Hampshire to Brookline, Massachusetts. Both Alfred and Anna Baker were listed in the March, 1902 *Journal* as practitioners in Brookline; and on the twenty-fifth of February the directors passed the by-law Mrs. Eddy sent to them (as one of their private by-laws). But they did not understand it. Mrs. Eddy's letter stated:

> No member of the Mother Church shall form a church organization or erect a church edifice in Brookline, Mass., until a By-law shall be passed, permitting such organization or edifice. . . .
>
> Do not publish the By-law relative to the church in Brookline, but should you ever hear of any movement looking toward a church organization or edifice there, then notify the parties of the By-law.

There was a good deal of speculation as to her purpose for this by-law, but there was *no* understanding. Perhaps Gilbert Carpenter (though he speculated as did all the others) came closest in his statement: "One point is certain. Mrs. Eddy did not make any moves from the standpoint of human opinion. Acting under inspiration, she did not gauge a situation according to its present appearance, but saw into the future, and took care of that which the human mind knew nothing about."

Perhaps the Leader's action was for our generation. As her *followers* we must consider the facts that she was *not* a member of her church, that she did not *attend* church, and that she rarely allowed her household to *attend* church. Her true church was a daily and an hourly affair, not a material organization, and "this *organized* work . . . worries me more than all else." It is clearly seen that in 1902 the Leader is *pushing* some of her closest students *out* of organization, no doubt with the hope that church would become a daily and an hourly animus in their experience even as it was in that of their Leader. She was pushing the Bakers out of organization, but not out of the Mother Church. How, oh how, could she teach her students the difference between true church and material organization! A "watch" for her mental workers on March 25 points to this problem. Henrietta Chanfrau recorded:

> Mother asks you: Drop all patients and take for your one unworthy patient The Mother Church of Christian Science which needs healing from its sins this day.

The previous day, March 24, the Leader had had Carol Norton made a circuit lecturer which meant that he would be lecturing in any of the states plus Canada. Judge Ewing was the only one who had done this heretofore with the exception of Judge Clarkson's brief experience in Christ's work. The Leader may have been thinking of Clarkson's departure and the sad experience before this disciple when she wrote in her *Message for 1901:*

> What Jesus' disciples of old experienced, his followers of today will prove, namely, that a departure from the direct line in Christ costs a return under difficulties; darkness, doubt, and unrequited toil will beset all their returning footsteps.

This paragraph ends with, "Only a firm foundation in Truth can give a fearless wing and a sure reward." One's foundation in Truth was not firm if it lacked a true understanding and appreciation of the Revelator to this age. This was doubly important for the lecturers and was a concern for Mrs. Eddy as the April 10 "watch" preserved by Henrietta Chanfrau implies:

> Work for lecturers. A city that is set upon a hill cannot be hid, and the life of their Leader must be shown as it *is.* Never did I neglect Jesus in my sermons in the first days of Christian Science; now they must not forget me. The scandalous attacks on the Discoverer and Founder of Christian Science will stop if the *truth* about her be shown to the world.

Judge Ewing had done better than most in showing this *truth* to the (new) world, and now he would be taking it to the old world in the very first overseas lecture tour.

In her Easter message to the Concord church *(My.* 155) Mrs. Eddy began by saying: "Allow me to thank you for lending to me your good Church-leader, Rev. I. C. Tomlinson, a few days in the week, and on the seventh day cheering him with your earnest attention." This close association with the Leader gave Tomlinson a good deal of growth, and his work saw fruition in his lawsuit with a verdict in his favor on April 15. A few days earlier he had written the following letter:

Pleasant View, Concord, N. H.

To the Christian Scientists of Baltimore, Md.

Dearly Beloved Brethren: — Our Mother in Israel asks me to reply to your glad letters containing the joyful news of the spirit of Unity manifest in her Baltimore children. When your Easter anthems reached her she called us to her to hear the good news. And as she read to us your Christian correspondence, which so rejoiced her mother heart, tears of gladness glistened in her eyes.

These signs of the risen Christ, betoken the coming fulfilment of our great Master's prayer, "That they all may be one; as thou, Father, art in me, and I in thee, that they also may be one in us, that the world may believe that thou hast sent me."

Our revered Mother wishes these beloved students to know that their obedience has brought her much joy.

Your brother in divine Love,
Irving C. Tomlinson

A rift in the Baltimore church five years earlier had caused one faction to separate and start Second Church. There were sincere students in both churches, but working in true unity is something few have accomplished even today. The mental workers in Mrs. Eddy's home came closer to this accomplishment than have any others in all history, but even they fell far short of what the Leader envisioned.

Very possibly the unity manifested in Baltimore in the spring of 1902 was one of the results of the Leader's contacts with Emilie Hergenroeder of that city. The result the world saw was the beautiful portrait the artist produced under Mrs. Eddy's direction.

The Leader's letter to the artist on the seventeenth of April stated:

> I can never express my full appreciation of the loving care which prompted the dear church in Baltimore to give a portrait of me to the world. I have often wondered, when thinking of the indifference that other churches have shown on this point, which does concern the history of Christian Science at present, and will in the future more than today.

Those who are concerned today about the history of Christian Science are indeed grateful to the Baltimore church and to Emilie Hergenroeder for giving to the world this visible record of our Leader's appearance in 1902.

MARY BAKER EDDY
Original painting by Emilie Hergenroeder of Baltimore, Maryland

CHAPTER VIII

CHRISTIAN SCIENCE ABROAD AND AT HOME

Healing is the best sermon, healing is the best lecture, and the entire demonstration of Christian Science. The sinner and the sick healed are our best witnesses. — MARY BAKER EDDY

1902

OVER two thousand people gathered at Queen's Hall, London on Tuesday, May 6 to hear a lecture by the Hon. William G. Ewing. One peculiar account in *The* (London) *Onlooker* was entitled, "Being the Impressions of an Unbeliever." In capsule the "unbeliever" stated:

> The date is graven on the tablets of my memory . . . I believe now that the speaker believed he had a message to deliver and that his message was true. It may be true; it may be false. But he believed in it with his whole heart and soul — or he is the most marvelous and magnetic actor that has ever faced the public gaze.
>
> This is an admittedly impressionist sketch . . . of one who went to jeer, but who found that the jeer died upon his lips.

Very soon glowing reports of this and Judge Ewing's other lectures in Great Britain were pouring into Boston along with many grateful letters of appreciation.

Edward A. Kimball received a very different and unexpected letter in May. It was from Mrs. Eddy, and in it she asked him to "be prepared to take the position of Editor of the Journal." At the end of December Kimball and McKenzie had completed their work on the revision of Science and Health and Mr. Kimball had resumed a very heavy lecturing schedule with often a lecture each day and on occasion two lectures in one day. He expected to be back in Boston in June to teach the Normal Class of the Massachusetts Metaphysical College, but he had not expected to continue in Boston.

In writing of Jesus' experience in her *Message to The Mother Church for 1902* (p. 18) the Leader was writing also of her own experience:

> The constant spectacle of sin thrust upon the pure sense of the immaculate Jesus made him a man of sorrows. He lived when mortals looked ignorantly, as now, on the might of divine power manifested through man; only to mock, wonder, and perish. Sad to say, the cowardice and self-seeking of his disciples helped crown with thorns the life of him who broke not the bruised reed and quenched not the smoking flax, — who caused not the feeble to fall, nor spared through false pity the consuming tares.

The cowardice and self-seeking of the woman's disciples had prolonged the Woodbury trial and increased the cost tremendously; which trial was won only legally, for the malicious lies had proliferated ever since. She seemed to have but one student who could be counted upon to use good judgment, who could represent her satisfactorily, who could say or do the tactful and proper thing without her constant supervision, — and that one was Edward A. Kimball. She needed Mr. Kimball every place. And under Mind's direction that is where she kept him, helping God's cause on *every* front.

Septimus J. Hanna was earnest, dedicated, and very well liked, but his editing had caused Mrs. Eddy and/or her attorneys concern on more than one occasion in the past several months until the Leader felt she must have more help than he was giving her. It is altogether possible that she also was removing Hanna from his positions in Boston for another reason. Infinite Love had revealed to Hanna the Leader's spiritual identity as the Second Coming of the Christ, and he had been unfaithful to his own revelation when he had failed to support his Leader during the Woodbury trial.

Early in June Mrs. Eddy wrote to Mr. Kimball: "I must have an advocate . . . the cause must have an advocate, in those at the head of our publications [who will] not *dodge* when they should fire and not fire when it is unwise." She had decided that the editorship was not Mr. Kimball's place, but asked him what he thought about making Archibald McLellan editor-in-chief. Mr. Kimball replied on June 3:

> I grieve much because Judge Hanna has failed to meet your views and the needs, but if there is to be a change, I am indeed inclined to think . . . McLellan would be as good as any.

Five days later Mrs. Eddy wrote to Mr. McLellan whom she had not met:

Dear Student:

I am today in receipt of your telegram to Mr. Kimball. I would gladly confer with you on the subject of becoming editor- in-chief of the Christian Science Journal and Christian Science Sentinel, but as I am situated now it seems quite impossible. You are aware that an editor should be reliable in word and deed, adroit, wise, apt in discerning the public need, in rebuking the private evil and unselfish in doing it.

Cowardice, deceit, will without wisdom, have imposed on me tasks incredible. It is wise to protect as far as possible a Leader, instead of putting her to the front in every battle, laying her on the altar and saving themselves. I have now no relatives to defend me and my age requires some consideration after thirty-six years of constant conflict.

I have helped Judge Hanna to the advantageous positions he occupies — but he forgets this. I request the editor of our periodicals to send the proofs to me of special articles they write about me and to head no articles "Defence of Mrs. Eddy"! My history is enough for that. For the sake of our cause I ofttimes change orders and veer like a weather-vane. A direction that is right under existing circumstances may change the next hour for circumstances alter cases, then I countermand my order and it works well.

Mr. Kimball's recommendation of you is very satisfactory. May I name you for Editor-in-Chief of the Christian Science Journal and Christian Science Sentinel? Please wire yes or no.

There may have been one more reason that Mind was telling the Leader to remove Judge Hanna from Boston, — the need for a progressive by-law for her church. Hanna had been the First Reader of the Mother Church for seven years and its pastor prior to the inception of Readers. Before the end of May Mrs. Eddy had her directors publish a by-law amendment stating that "Every third year the Mother Church shall elect new Readers." Judge Hanna stepped aside graciously from both the readership and editorship, perhaps truly grateful for the rest. Mrs. Eddy had him appointed immediately to the Board of Lectureship. Soon the Hannas moved to Colorado to serve in the western section.

While the directors were concerned with replacements for Hanna's positions, Mr. Kimball was teaching the 1902 Normal class. One of the students in this class was Calvin C. Hill. Another was Rev. Simonsen's wife, Mary E. Simonsen. A young couple, Bessie and Herbert Eustace, traveled from California to attend the class which Herbert called "one of the most joyous and enlightening experiences that has come to me." He wrote of this experience:

Those who knew Mr. Kimball know what a profound and analytical thinker he was. In that class truths that were dimly stirring in the depths of my own aroused thought were elucidated — truths which with their logical sequences meant genuine Christian Science, truths that meant the *"clear, correct teaching of Christian Science,"* rather than faith and belief in it.

Mr. Eustace also stated that their main reason for wanting to attend the class was to learn more about handling malicious mind. He was impressed by the following, and doubly so when he considered that the message was sent "to a body of Scientists who had gathered from the 'ends of the earth' with the sole intention of later teaching classes, themselves":

> I remember Mr. Kimball brought a message to the class directly from Mrs. Eddy. The message was, that the only *excuse* for holding any class, was to show how evil was to be handled, quietly without publishing it broadcast. That was the one purpose. It was not for anything else.

The graduates of this class attended a meeting of all the Normal Class graduates (1899 through 1902) at the Mother Church on Monday, June 16. The day before had been Communion Sunday, but the communion service had not been held in the Mother Church. Because large crowds were expected from far and wide, a morning and an afternoon service were held in Mechanics Hall. The reports estimated that twelve thousand people attended including a contingent from Germany.

* * *

CHRISTIAN SCIENCE IN GERMANY

> *Germany will be the first European nation to accept Christian Science. Their love of God, their profound religious character, their deep faith, and strong intellectual qualities make them particularly receptive to Christian Science.* — MARY BAKER EDDY

IN the winter of 1896-97 an American woman wintering in Dresden for the enjoyment of the German music and art, was also studying Science and Health and interesting her acquaintances there in its message. After returning to New York she convinced Laura Lathrop that a worker should be sent to Dresden, and Mrs. Lathrop sent Frances Thurber Seal to this outpost, over the latter's protests.

Mrs. Seal knew no German, had limited (borrowed) funds, and had been studying Science little over a year when she set sail for Germany in December of 1897. But she had the feeling that God was sending her on this mission. God indeed inspired her healing work and directed every action of her daily life, which direction unexpectedly brought her back to New York and to the 1899 Normal class in Boston. Also, unexpectedly the Board of Education awarded Mrs. Seal a certificate to teach and requested that she go to Berlin, the German capital, to establish Christian Science there. So the summer of 1899 found Mrs. Seal in Berlin. Her healing work was more than remarkable; it was stupendous! Her patients never said they came for treatment, but that they had come to be healed by the Christ healing. Most of them spoke no English, so after beginning English services, Mrs. Seal had her first German student in Berlin, Frau Bruno, translate the lesson and:

> she and I read it. I practised with her several hours each week. Through constant prayer and the consecrated study of the English Lesson, in addition to the coaching by her, I was soon able to understand the translated word and read it so that it was not only satisfactory to the people, but brought out much healing. This was pure demonstration, as I had never studied German, having had to give all my time to studying Christian Science and to the healing work.

The healing work plus all the work connected with the services kept Mrs. Seal busy night and day until she began feeling a sense of depletion. In her words:

> I had been so constantly busy many hours of each day, that, while I read some of the books and studied the Sunday Lesson, it seemed difficult to lose myself and lay aside the problems of the practice and the Church long enough to go into the mountain to refresh my thought, . . . After a time there came to me a sense of barrenness, together with spiritual hunger that could be appeased only by deep draughts of Truth . . .

This situation caused Mrs. Seal to plan a quiet day for study only, asking a lady who came for healing for her mother to please come the next morning. All that day and far into the night Mrs. Seal walked and talked with God; and she was still on the mountaintop the next morning when the two women arrived. In fact, her elevated thought remained in Love, and she did not even hear the claims they told her. In parting, the mother said that if God would let her look once upon her daughter's face she would be willing to die; to which Mrs. Seal responded that God would let her look upon her daughter's face and live. Then she bade them good morning and did not think of them again.

The younger woman led her mother to the street car and placed her in a seat where she looked out the window at the street and trees and flowers:

> She spoke of what she saw, then her daughter screamed and told the people that her mother had not been able to see for many years.

The mother had been totally blind for many of her sixty-seven years, "had suffered many things of many physicians," and had finally been told that there was no hope of recovering her sight. In one Christian Science treatment her sight was restored. Mrs. Seal was almost as overwhelmed as were they:

> It must have been a thrilling experience for the people on that street car, for both mother and daughter talked, telling of her past affliction, and that God had healed her. No words could describe the awe that filled my thought in the presence of this demonstration of the Christ power.
>
> Our weekly testimony meeting took place on the following evening, and everyone who had been on that street car attended this service. The seats were all filled and the people stood in the hall and adjoining rooms. . . .

In May of 1901 First Church of Christ, Scientist, Berlin, sent greeting to the Mother Church. Their progress report was intended for the Annual Meeting, but as there was no Annual Meeting in 1901, it was published in the *Sentinel:*

> In October, 1900, we organized a church under the laws of Germany. The police department treated us with the greatest courtesy. They asked for a copy of our regulations, creed, etc., to place on file. I sent them one of the printed slips, with the tenets of the Mother Church . . . so our tenets form a part of the official records of this Empire. . . . Our English congregation averages about fifty, the German congregation averages seventy- five on Sunday and from one hundred to one hundred fifty at the week meetings. It is difficult for the Germans to obtain release from their state church . . . A German who is not confirmed cannot sign a legal contract, according to present laws. . . . Much healing work is being done. Many earnest seekers come to inquire about this wonderful revelation of Truth; for these strong, earnest thinkers . . . are reaching out for a demonstrable Christianity.

And then the persecution began! The Emperor issued orders for the police to stop the meetings, get rid of the American woman and exterminate the teaching. For several months Mrs. Seal could scarcely find a place to lay her head, let alone receive patients or hold meetings. Few fell away even though the surveillance was extreme. If a patient was confined to his bed a detective was stationed in the house in the hope that the patient might die and Mrs. Seal be arrested on criminal charges. In one extreme case a woman was told she could not live twenty-four hours without an operation which she refused to have. Her husband fearfully went for Mrs. Seal, and the physician notified the police who sent a detective to stay until the woman died:

> She recovered within a few days, and the detective who had watched the case came to the services as soon as the official surveillance was withdrawn.

The *Sentinel* of February 27, 1902, stated in an article entitled "Christian Science in Germany":

> Much has recently been said in the newspapers concerning opposition to the spread of Christian Science in Germany. The dispatches are to the effect that the Emperor of Germany has intervened to prevent its further inroads into Court circles. It has also, it would seem, been discussed in the Reichstag.

According to this article a member of the Reichstag stated that Christian Science should be suppressed in Germany as it had been in the United States, — which gives us a picture of the unfavorable treatment Christian Science was receiving from the press in 1902. But, as Mrs. Eddy had written many years earlier: "God is responsible for the mission of those whom He has anointed."

Bible scholars, who have devoted themselves to tracing and locating the twelve tribes of Israel, state that Finland is the tribe of Issachar. They quote Finland's president at a time of invasion in the twentieth century as stating to his people: "Sons of Issachar, Arise!" These scholars say that Denmark is the tribe of Dan, and Germany is the tribe of Judah.

Germany, like Judah, was always strong, and seemed to fulfil Jacob's prophecy: "Judah, thou art he whom thy brethren shall praise; thy hand shall be in the neck of thine enemies; thy father's children shall bow down before thee." But there is more to Jacob's prophecy for Judah, which Germany also seems to have fulfilled: "The sceptre shall not depart from Judah, nor a lawgiver from between his feet, until Shiloh come."

If we find Shiloh in a current dictionary it may say: a park in Tennessee; a battle in the Civil War; or an ancient village in Palestine. However, if we use the *Key* to the Scriptures that Mrs. Eddy has given us we find that Shiloh means tranquil, and is an epithet for the Messiah. It comes from a primary root meaning: "to be *tranquil,* i.e., *secure* or *successful:* — be happy, prosper, be in safety." When the Children of Israel (Christ's offspring) understand and demonstrate Science, are they not tranquil, secure, successful? Does not Science teach one to be happy, prosper, be in safety? Christian Science is truly the coming of Shiloh. The "safety" that inheres in Shiloh was manifested in Mrs. Seal's experience at the time of the persecution:

> Germany had a law which provided that any foreigner could be sent out of the country on three days' notice without being given any reason. If the person sent away wished to know the reason he could learn it only through an inquiry made by his government. Many people who knew this wondered that they did not avail themselves of this law to get rid of me. There could be but one reason . . . that God had sent me there and sustained me . . .

The newspapers carried many articles traducing Mrs. Seal, calling her an American swindler; but not one of her students lost faith. During the months of constant harassment every case was healed. And the Cause prospered:

> The young workers took the simpler cases and did much healing, while the more difficult cases were left to me. I, too, was a young worker, for I had known Christian Science only three or four years at this period, hence there could be no question that Christ did the work. The human workers were equipped only with love and obedience. As time went on and the early students gained in experience, they also took so-called fatal cases, such as tuberculosis, cancer, blindness, etc., and all were healed. There were no failures.

In the spring of 1902 the work was progressing beautifully and the persecution was a thing of the past. In a spirit of rejoicing Mrs. Seal and some of her students crossed the ocean to attend the Communion service of the Mother Church. When Mrs. Seal heard Mrs. Eddy's *Message to The Mother Church for 1902* she felt that the Leader's heart had spoken directly to hers in the words: "Beloved brethren, another year of God's loving providence for His people in times of persecution has marked the history of Christian Science. . . . Evil, though combined with formidable conspiracy, is made to glorify God."

The following week found these students from Germany visiting in Concord. At the Wednesday evening meeting of June 25 Mrs. Seal, Frau Friedrich, and Baroness von Beschwitz all gave testimonies of the work in Germany. The *Concord Monitor* reported these and other testimonies at the overflowing meeting, but it did not know of another meeting of far more importance to Mrs. Seal. Frances Thurber Seal was, in fact, overwhelmed by this meeting, for on her second day in Concord Mrs. Eddy came to visit her, — an honor she had never even dreamed of.

> She told me that she was engaged in a most important work, the completion of the government of the Mother Church, and she had found it necessary to declare that she would not receive any visitors during this summer, so she could not invite me to her home but must come to me.

Mrs. Seal could not understand why she should be so honored, and when she asked the reason Mrs. Eddy replied: "I could not let you go away without taking your dear hands in mine, and looking into your brave eyes and saying, 'Thank you.' " "Thank me, Mother. For what?" asked Mrs. Seal. "For being brave and true, for facing error courageously and standing with Truth," replied the Leader. Mrs. Seal wrote:

> I had not known that she knew aught of conditions in Germany, but she said, "I know always what my children are doing, and of Truth's progress and triumph."

The Leader expressed her joy at their victory and likened their persecution to that of the early Christians. She also said that God would reward their faithfulness, and that the demonstration that their courage and loyalty brought about would strengthen many in years to come. She sent her loving greetings to the workers in Germany who had stood with Mrs. Seal:

> This loving recognition of our work and tender benediction upon it sent me back to my German home and field with joy unspeakable. I had indeed found a Mother in Israel, one who knew the pains of her children, watched over them and with them, and rewarded them with her blessing.

The Leader had known about the persecution in Germany, but she had given no visible aid or support. She had let Mrs. Seal "stand or fall by her own demonstration," and she had *stood.* From this time on Mrs. Eddy frequently sent messages to strengthen and encourage their work. No doubt she also knew that Shiloh had come to Germany, and the balance of Jacob's prophecy was being fulfilled: "The sceptre shall not depart from Judah . . . until Shiloh come; unto him shall the gathering of the people be." Him, Shiloh, is Christian Science.

CHAPTER IX

EXTENDING THE MOTHER'S CHURCH

The next deed you have made, have it read, "Mary Baker G. Eddy's Church, The First Church of Christ, Scientist," in the deed.
— MARY BAKER EDDY

1902

WEDNESDAY, June 18, 1902 the Annual Meeting of The Mother Church was held at Mechanics' Hall. The meeting was opened by the retiring president, John B. Willis. The clerk read the announcement of officers for the coming year: *President,* John W. Reeder; *Clerk,* William B. Johnson; *Treasurer,* Stephen A. Chase; *First Reader,* Hermann S. Hering; *Second Reader,* Ella E. Williams. In previous years the only change had been in the office of president, but pursuant to the recent rotation in office by-law, this announcement included new readers.

Professor Hermann S. Hering, of Baltimore, Maryland, taught electrical engineering at Johns Hopkins University for eight years prior to his full-time devotion to the work of Christian Science in 1899. Mrs. Ella E. Williams was one of Mrs. Eddy's students and had been practising in Chelsea, Massachusetts for many years.

Following the treasurer's report Mr. Kimball introduced a motion, seconded by Judge Ewing, which was by far the most interesting thing to the field and to the general public. That was a pledge to contribute two million dollars for the erection of a larger auditorium for the Mother Church *(My.* 7-8). Some of Mr. Kimball's words, like many of Mrs. Eddy's, are somewhat enigmatical:

> Our denomination is palpably outgrowing the institutional end thereof. We need to keep pace with our own growth and progress.

The Mother Church officials had long been looking toward enlarging and expanding the Mother Church complex while the Leader was ever endeavoring to teach them wisdom and economy. The previous September she had written to the clerk:

> Have the Board of Directors do as they think best on the purchase of real estate. If I have written in favor of the Church getting in debt, it was because I did not understand the situation. Do not consult me again on purchasing Church property. I decline to give any further attention to it. You know the Church By-laws. Act in accordance with them.

The day following this letter she had received a letter and map from Mr. Johnson and had written again:

> Your map and letter explain what is to be purchased. I do not believe in getting in debt, especially on church property. . . . compulsory giving is not my idea of church charity. Let the church consider all that I have done for it, and give without being asked. Cancel their account with God is my advice to the church officers . . . I consider it a silly expenditure to build a church that costs what ours does to run it. . . . I think now you better look after m.a.m. before acting.

ANNUAL MEETING AT MECHANICS HALL
June 18, 1902

The Board of Directors did not at that time purchase the Hotel Brookline, which was adjacent to the publishing society buildings, but they got a member of the church, Mr. Arthur Bingham, to buy it for them. It may have been Mrs. Eddy's statement, "I consider it a silly expenditure to build a church that costs what ours does to run it," that caused Mr. Bingham to become fearful over his purchase. Or it may have been the publication in early November, 1901 of:

CHURCH BY-LAW
Finance Committee

Art. XVIII., Sect. 4 — There shall be a Committee on Finance which shall consist of three First Members of this Church in good standing therewith. Its members shall be appointed annually by the Christian Science Board of Directors and with the consent of the Pastor Emeritus. They shall hold quarterly meetings, and keep themselves thoroughly informed as to the real estate owned by this Church, and the amount of funds received by the Treasurer of the Mother Church, who is individually responsible for said fund. They shall attend to having the books of the Church Treasurer, audited annually, by an honest, competent accountant.

Prior to paying all bills against the Church, the Treasurer of this Church shall submit the same to said committee for examination, — and the committee shall decide thereupon by a unanimous vote, and their endorsement of the bills shall render them payable.

The books are to be audited on May first, and shown to the Pastor Emeritus on May fifteenth.

If it be found that the Church funds have not been properly managed, it shall be the duty of the Church, namely the Board of Directors and the Treasurer, to be individually responsible for the performance of their several offices satisfactorily, and for the proper distribution of the funds of which they are the custodians.

Whatever the cause of Bingham's fearfulness, he approached the directors about taking the hotel off his hands. They were not yet ready financially, so they asked Gilbert C. Carpenter to assume the burden, and he indicated his willingness to do so.

Mrs. Eddy has said that the *Manual* sprang from the logic of events, and it is altogether possible that the Finance Committee by-law was partially for the protection of Stephen A, Chase. It was about this time that the other directors were criticizing Mr. Chase and thinking of removing him from office. Mrs. Eddy told Calvin Hill about the dispute and asked his opinion. Mr. Hill defended Mr. Chase. Mrs. Eddy striking the palm of one hand with the clenched fist of the other, said, "I would bank my life on Stephen A. Chase."

At this point Mrs. Eddy gave Mr. Hill some verbal messages for the

> Directors. After he had delivered these messages, he said to the Directors, "Now I am going to say something more to you which Mrs. Eddy voiced to me personally." He then related what had been said about Mr. Chase. The Directors looked rather serious, but Mr. Chase jumped out of his chair and walked around the room all smiles.

The questioning of Mr. Chase was probably in relation to all the money he was handling as treasurer of the Mother Church. A news clipping from the Fall River, Massachusetts (Mr. Chase's home) *Daily Globe* of December 12, 1902 gives an explanation:

> Over a period of time many letters containing money sent to Stephen A. Chase, treasurer of The Mother Church, were lost. Finally two postal inspectors, according to the despatch, investigated the loss by using decoy letters. The validity of Mr. Chase's complaint was proved when five out of thirteen decoy letters were stolen.

In the spring of 1902 when the directors were giving their thought to acquiring more land and building larger buildings Mrs. Eddy was occupied with "a most important work, the completion of the *government* of the Mother Church," as she said to Mrs. Seal. Already there were rumors here and there in the field, and particularly in Boston, that Mrs. Eddy was too old to continue running such an extensive organization. Every time she took a progressive step it caused a great stir, a good deal of reaction; and not infrequently such reaction occasioned a good deal of suffering for the Leader. Nonetheless she knew she was chosen of God to found her church for all time according to His direction, and she hesitated not at whatever step God revealed to her.

The new rotation in office by-law which had caused Judge Hanna to retire had caused a great stir and a good deal of questioning of Mrs. Eddy's wisdom and ability. This was nothing new. From the beginning her students had often felt that they could run things better than she could, but now they added the belief of old age to their arguments against her. Mr. Carpenter, who was on the scene at the time, said in retrospect:

> Today . . . it is evident that she was fully capable of fulfilling whatever she was called upon to do, and did it scientifically and correctly. Every move she made, every precedent she laid down, was right and necessary; but at this time — 1902 — many students were assailed by doubt as to her ability to carry on. We have instances where those closest to her, often distrusted her wisdom, and felt that she was ruining the prosperity of her Cause by some of the moves she made.
>
> As the Cause grew to world-wide proportions, the question arose as to whether this frail woman in Concord could continue to be its head,

and to run it successfully. Could she possibly know enough about what was going on, to handle all the details as they should be handled?

It was very true that Mrs. Eddy needed a great deal more help than her lieutenants gave her, but she was far more aware of what was "going on" than any of them could even imagine. On May 16 she wrote to her directors: "O how I wish you could see what I see before us in the history of the churches, unless a change takes place."

In the hope that a change might take place she was bringing new workers to Boston. There had been correspondence for the past year regarding bringing Archibald McLellan, a Chicago attorney, to Boston to be the business manager of the Publishing Society, but in the spring of 1902 it was decided that he would become the editor-in-chief of the *Journal* and *Sentinel.* In addition, Mrs. Eddy had asked Stephen A. Chase to resign from the Board of Directors although he was to remain the treasurer of the Mother Church.

Arthur P. DeCamp was a very successful, wealthy business man who was dedicated to Christian Science. He had attended the Normal Class taught by Mr. Kimball under the Board of Education in January of 1899. Later that year, at Dr. Baker's suggestion, Mr. DeCamp had bought controlling interest in the *Concord Patriot* (newspaper) in an effort to aid Mrs. Eddy and Christian Science. When the Finance Committee was established in the fall of 1901 Mr. DeCamp was one of its members. Now, in June of 1902 the Leader decided to make Mr. DeCamp one of her directors, a position he assumed on the nineteenth of June. A few days earlier she had written to the other directors:

> With lone and dreary foresight of my tasks I look on this hour unless you help me more in helping new officers know what is best to do and how to do it. But you must help in this, or give up your office on our Board, for I cannot and I shall not do it alone.

In this same letter she had said that Mr. Bingham was to be president, but evidently the directors had second thoughts about his election. It was about this time that Gilbert Carpenter bought the Hotel Brookline from Mr. Bingham, which business Mr. Carpenter operated for the next two years until the directors were ready for the property.

Mr. DeCamp was untried; the other dirctors were often asleep to the import of the moment. Few, if any, of Mrs. Eddy's followers could feel the depth of her words: "With lone and dreary foresight of my tasks I look on this hour . . ." Perhaps Edward A. Kimball came closest to an appreciative understanding of her labors and her position, but animal magnetism endeavored to rob her of his help. He wrote her that he could not stay in Boston because of the attacks of illness. She responded to his letter on July 3:

> There is no *liver,* no pneumogastric nerve and no nerves, no solar plexus. Then *stand,* having done all, *stand* on *this Rock.* There is no matter, no *substance* but *Spirit.* Stand there, know it, draw all other physical conclusions from this one *all Truth.* Stay in Boston and vicinity always if you please. I know you can master it, the lie, there as well as elsewhere. To run before a lie is to accept its terms. This works like running before the enemy in battle. You will be followed, pursued, till you face about, *trust* in *God* and stand on *Spirit* denying and facing and fighting all claims of matter and mortal mind, both one. I and you have grown to be honored by God with entrance into this department of learning.

If Mr. Kimball had responded when Mrs. Eddy had invited him to serve at Pleasant View, it would have been a great boon to him and to the Christian Science movement, but the Leader told Nemi Robertson that he was not happy over her invitation, and "I knew then what he had to meet, and I let him go to meet it. It was up to him to know how much he had to meet it *with.* God gave him an opportunity to work here, but he made his choice."

When God gave such opportunities they were rarely repeated. When Mrs. Eddy asked Nemi Robertson to serve in her home, the same animal magnetism misled her into thinking she could not accept because of personal problems. She asked Mrs. Eddy to allow her to come later, but the invitation was not extended a second time.

Perhaps it was Mr. Kimball's awakening to this lost opportunity that caused him to dwell a great deal upon opportunity in his teaching and lecturing. When Mrs. Eddy had seen that he was not happy about serving at Pleasant View she let him go, and she "knew then what he had to meet." What did he have to meet? Was it the belief of male superiority? Many men *and women* who are earnest students of Christian Science have not *yet* learned much about man and woman and the "different demands of their united spheres" (S.& H. 59); nor that "One infinite God, good . . . equalizes the sexes."(S.& H. 340) And this belief of male supremacy was very generally accepted as fact in Mrs. Eddy's time. Even dear Mr. Carpenter, who acknowledges and proclaims Mrs. Eddy's unerring wisdom, interprets a passage from one of her early poems as follows:

From the darkness of the night,
Into morning's golden light,
Sisters — labor on;

> Mrs. Eddy has said nothing about the masculine side. Yet suddenly she refers to the feminine, just as if at this time there were no men in the Christian Science movement. One reason is that the masculine element does not need to be told that it is a worker, and that it is the demonstration of wisdom that carries on. It is the feminine nature that needs quickening.

At the time this poem was written one man after another upon whom Mrs. Eddy had placed leadership in her cause had failed her. The defection of James Howard in the fall of 1881 brought about a change. The Leader left her flock and left their leading to four of the women in her church, one of whom, Julia Bartlett, was the recipient of this stirring poem along with the instruction, "To be read today in meeting."

In the second half of the *twentieth* century when the author read a particularly stirring poem to an appreciative friend, a Christian Scientist, his response was: "You mean to tell me a *woman* wrote that!" The belief of the Adam does not yield easily. Whether or not this was what Mr. Kimball had to meet at the turn of the century, he did meet the physical attack on his health in the summer of 1902 and remained in Boston for a time. Mrs. Eddy wrote him again in July:

> I only wish you could stay with us and be on the Board of Directors, but knowing the cost to you I wait on God to see His deliverance. Did you know what I have had to do in every direction, no one ready to help, the Board of Directors asleep, H[anna] ill, nothing ready; and now new officers to train for use, I old, and God my only helper — then the lesson would be learned by you before it is learned.

Did she mean by this last statement that if he could understand and appreciate her experience "then the lesson would be learned" before he had sharp experiences of his own to teach it to him? Mr. Kimball responded: "I am not wise enough to see my own way and shall do what you tell me is wise for me to do." It would appear that the Leader had him remain in Boston for only a short time, probably to assist with McLellan's training, for, as she had written Kimball earlier, "men generally are more ready to yield to a man than a woman." This statement may be less true today, but Gilbert Carpeneter wrote of that period: "When Mrs. Eddy had to assume full responsibility for a matter, the fact that she was a woman in itself was enough to create doubt in the minds of students, and she became the object or victim of such doubt."

On the tenth of July Mrs. Eddy wrote to Archibald McLellan:

> Beloved Student,
> You show a good record surely but I chose you before seeing it.
> We are waiting to welcome you in Boston at the earliest possible date.
> My kind regards to Mrs. McLellan for concluding in our behalf.
> With love to you both.

Mrs. Eddy was at work constantly on two fronts. First and foremost she was pointing the way to Zion, — "spiritual foundation and superstructure;" and on this front she was *demonstrating* every precept and every step of "the way." Secondly, she was reaching down to her followers, to each student, at his own level of understanding, all the while constantly giving to the world information, answers to questions, and gems of wisdom. Her message on the twenty-first of July was in the second category:

> *To the members of the Mother Church* — I am bankrupt in thanks to you, my beloved brethren, who at our last Annual Meeting pledged yourselves with startling grace to contribute any part of two millions of dollars towards the purchase of more land for its site, and to enlarge our church edifice in Boston ...

A second missive from her pen on the same date was also reaching down to her students to calm the tempest, the reaction, to the three year term for readers. Her message was entitled "Afterglow" *(My.* 250), and stated in part:

> I rest peacefully in knowing that the impulsion of this action in the Mother Church was from above. So I have faith that whatever is done in this direction by the branch churches will be blest. The Readers who have filled this sacred office many years, have beyond it duties and attainments beckoning them. What these are I cannot yet say. The great Master saith: "What I do thou knowest not now; but thou shalt know hereafter."

It is interesting to study the Leader's words about the duties and attainments beckoning beyond (church organization?). She very obviously knows what these further duties are and says, "*thou* shalt know hereafter," but "*I* cannot *yet* say."

On the other hand, she was *always* saying to her students that *healing* is first and foremost. A letter to her "darling Augusta" (Stetson) in New York in the summer of 1902 said this once again:

> My Precious Student:
> I want you to give most of your time to healing. This department of C.S. is the one in which no student has equalled me. It is the one to which every student should aspire more than to any other. It is the

one most vacant at present.

. . . O, how I wish my best students would strive most to attain the standard of Scientific healing!

I pray daily for all the members of my church and hope and pray they will lead in healing the sick, more than in teaching or church making. Why? Because, my darling student, healing is the foundation of Christian Science. A poor healer can never be a good teacher. . . .

Mrs. Stetson was more dedicated and successful than almost any other student, but she was also much like an over-zealous mother. She guarded, guided, protected, and assisted her students, whereas the Leader knew that each fledgling *must* try his own wings. In August Mrs. Eddy said in a letter to William D. McCrackan, C.O.P. for New York: "Mrs. Stetson manages her students not as I do students, and to herself I thunder the law and gospel on this subject, but it must not be made public, lest the unity of our Churches be broken and thus our prestige and power in the right direction be hindered."

Another message the Leader gave to the world in the summer of 1902 was "The Signs of the Times" in the *Concord Monitor (My.* 266) in which she stated: "It is undoubtedly true that Christian Science is destined to become the one and the only religion and therapeutics on this planet." And a worldly message to her church stated:

To the Committee
Beloved Students:

I cannot, much as I love and desire to see my church — I cannot immediately after our sacred sacrament meet them on the Fair Grounds in Concord; and think it wise to leave this subject *this year* as I have left it in my Message. With love,

Mother
M. B. Eddy

Omitting the heart and meaning of her message the "Committee," late in August, published this

Special Notice

To forestall any possible disappointment for those who may be planning to attend the New Hampshire State Fair next week, we are authorized to say that our Leader will not find it convenient to be present.

Before the summer was over she was warning her directors once more about taking on debt, this time with a telegram followed by a letter:

(Telegram) I do not think it advisable to take that land it would be too heavy a burden. M. B. Eddy

Beloved Students:

I saw your sketch of the lot of land, or site for the Publishing House, and admired it — but when I learned of the price, I took not two minutes to decide as to purchasing it.

We cannot prosper on a wrong premise. We take the *Bible* for *our guide,* and find in it this Scripture: "Owe no man." A slight sum of indebtedness with a speedy prospect of payment would not break the spirit of that Scripture, but so large a one does. Why? Because it involves a material thinking and acting and taking thought that is not advantageous to spiritual growth. The Scripture saith, "Take no thought for the morrow."

A third message on this subject was sent to William B. Johnson: "Tell the Christian Science Board of Directors to pray three times daily that they cannot be made to waste or to deplete the funds of The Mother Church."

The students thought that they were building up the Cause of Christian Science with their extensive plans for acquiring land and building impressive buildings, while the Leader knew that she was providing for the future of her Movement with the completion of the government of the Mother Church in her *Manual.* The dangers she saw besetting her great life work were set forth in a "Watch" recorded by Lewis Strang on the fifth of September:

One Mind controls this and every hour. When the Discoverer of Christian Science in this age must deal with *sinning,* so-called Christian Scientists, those who *know* their Leader as she *is* must be *awake* to the delusions of M.A.M. that would make Jerusalem a waste and desert place. Take up those transgressors in our midst who would undo the work of their Leader. Love is All. One Mind. Dear one, Mother knows your heart is active in His service. Waken to the need of this hour that those who would set aside the Manual of The Mother Church with its *just* By-laws see the sinfulness of their ways.

CHAPTER X

THAT IDEA ON EARTH

When the Discoverer of Christian Science in this age must deal with ***sinning,*** *so-called Christian Scientists, those who* ***know*** *their Leader as she* ***is*** *must be* ***awake*** *to the declarations of M.A.M. that would make Jerusalem a waste and desert place.*
— MARY BAKER EDDY

1902

TOGETHER with all the new officers in Boston that needed much help in their new positions, the Leader also had new students coming to serve at Pleasant View in the summer of 1902. She needed assistance in training all these newcomers, and she did receive a little help from one of her students in New York City. Mrs. Stetson was often in Mrs. Eddy's home and she knew a great deal about the routine at Pleasant View and how demanding was the service to the Leader. This enabled her to write the following letter which was helpful to her student who had been called to serve at Pleasant View, as well as to Mrs. Eddy:

June 8, 1902

My dear D . . .

. . . I am so glad that you are appreciating the great privilege of serving our beloved Leader and Mother in Israel, and I pray that you will keep in the one Mind, that she may be helped in her wardrobe, which should be perfect, comfortable, and harmonious, the expression of spiritual thought. I am sure you will give her your whole attention, and will be careful that your thoughts are right, that you may not disturb her with a discordant tone. We are all so earthy, and she is so heavenly. She is so patient and loving with us, else we could not stand.

I know that you will get time to read and commune with God, and handle every suggestion of error that would take you into chaos. I have taught you by precept and example to conquer error, and to love all. You have had a wonderful blessing in going to Mother and her household. I know you will strive to be worthy.

Give my love to dear Clara, Laura, and Pamelia, my beloved sisters, and to dear Mr. Frye, who is one of the best men on earth today, because he has guarded our darling Leader all these years. Remember me kindly to Mr. Mann and his wife.

I do not send love to Mother, for I would not ask you to trouble her, and I am now writing her. She knows that I love her better than all the world, and there is nothing that I would not do for her, but I do not ask the dear ones to trouble her with a message.

Now dear, dear D . . . , watch and work, and pray. Do all carefully, and be sure that you make everything comfortable for our dear Leader. Make all to suit her. She knows what she wants, and if you study to please her, you can.

Love to you, dear. Now *know* that you can make everything exactly as she wants it; there is no power but Mind, and Mind governs you. Love will help you.

Ever lovingly,
Always yours,
Augusta E. Stetson

It is probable that Mr. Kimball remained in Boston through July and August to launch Mr. McLellan in his new duties. The day after Kimball resumed lecturing early in September, Mrs. Eddy wrote a letter to Mr. McLellan about "the first mistake that I have seen in the Sentinel since the present editorial corps have conducted it." Her letters to the new editor-in-chief continued, often daily, from then on. Judge Hanna was preparing his first lecture, and the Leader's letter to him on August 26 included this advice:

Whoever opens most the eyes of the children of men to see aright and to understand aright that IDEA ON EARTH that has best and clearest reflected by word or deed the divine Principle of man and the universe, will accomplish most for himself and mankind in the direction of all that is good and true.

Hanna's first lecture was in Dayton, Ohio on the seventh of September, and he repeated it in many other cities and towns. No doubt he sent reports to Mrs. Eddy and asked her for advice. She wrote him early in October:

I can do you most good by pointing the path, showing the scenes behind the curtain. The united plans of the evildoers is to cause the beginners either in lecturing or teaching or in our periodicals to keep Mrs. Eddy as she *is* (What God knows of her and revealed to Christ Jesus) out of sight; and to keep her as she is *not* (just another white-haired old lady) constantly before the public. This kills two birds with one stone. It darkens the spiritual sense of students and misguides the public. Why? Because it misstates the idea of divine Principle that you are trying to demonstrate and hides it from the sense of the people.

Keeping the truth of her character before the public will help the students, and do more than all else for the Cause. Christianity in its purity was lost by defaming or killing its defenders. Do not let this period repeat this mistake. The truth in regard to your Leader heals the sick and saves the sinner. The lie has just the opposite effect, and the evil one that leads all evil in this matter knows this more clearly than do the Christian Scientists in general.

The Leader seemed to be the only one concerned with the "united plans of the evildoers" and with their incessant attempts to reverse her work. But she knew that in time every Scientist would have to meet the hypnotic attacks of animal magnetism. By the fall of 1902 she had added a paragraph to Science and Health on page 442 with the marginal heading "Christ the great physician":

Neither animal magnetism nor hypnotism enters into the practice of Christian Science, in which truth cannot be reversed, but the reverse of error is true. An improved belief cannot retrograde. When Christ changes a belief of sin or of sickness into a better belief, then belief melts into spiritual understanding, and sin, disease, and death disappear. Christ, Truth, gives mortals temporary food and clothing until the material, transformed with the ideal, disappears, and man is clothed and fed spiritually.

It was on the twenty-eighth of September in 1900 that the Leader had written to William P. McKenzie: "I have travailed in soul for the dear students in Germany and have built up a theory for their relief that I want made practical by our Publishing Society in Boston." In this same letter she had stated: "Please bring this request of mine to your Board at once and act upon it . . ." However it was nearly two years later, and after Archibald McLellan had become editor-in-chief, that any action was taken. Mr. Kimball was also a party to the action. In fact, it is very likely that he was the prime mover, having been made aware by the Leader of how remiss her officials had been in this area. If Mr. Kimball induced McLellan to make the German publication his first item of interest along with the *Journal* and *Sentinel,* as it would appear that he did, he surely helped the newcomer to find favor in the Leader's eyes.

In mid-September she was sending her new editor advice, suggestions, corrections almost daily, — such as, "I would like to have a woman on your list of editors . . ." and, "Always avoid if possible using Principle in any other sense than God." Early in November she commended McLellan for a fine editorial and for not mentioning specifically the court case in New York. She thought at first to give this editorial wide circulation, but decided instead to write her own, "Wherefore?" *(My.* 226), which was published November 27 and in which she *was* specific, stating in the penultimate paragraph:

> The sinner may sneer at this beatitude, for "the fool hath said in his heart, No God." It is known that the good young student, Mr. Lathrop, after he was prosecuted for practising Christian Science, finished healing the cases of diphtheria that he had on hand. Statistics show that this Science cures a larger per cent of malignant diseases than does *materia medica.*

About this same time she sent a hand-written note to Mr. McLellan approving his management of the *Sentinel* in the words: "That little newspaper you are making an angel visitant and intellectual guest that blesses and feeds the hungry. God bless you."

If one of her new officers was filling his position satisfactorily, another was not able to do so. Arthur DeCamp had an interview with Mrs. Eddy at Pleasant View on November 20. The next day she wrote to the directors:

> Since my interview with Mr. A. P. DeCamp yesterday, almost the reverse of what was then deemed right relative to the Church Building has come to my thought, and I must accept it as God given, and report it in this letter as follows:
>
> Do not commence to build the addition to the Mother Church until after the Annual Meeting next June. Allow Mr. S. A. Chase to perform his part ... Have the Directors and Finance Committee cooperate according to the Church By-laws. By all means let the Church Building Fund remain with Mr. Chase and continue him as the custodian of this fund.
>
> I ask the Directors to repeat to Mr. DeCamp the manner in which the funds for our first church were lost and let that be a warning.
>
> Relative to the discipline and excommunication of offending members, I have only this to say: Confine yourselves strictly to the By-laws of the Mother Church and be merciful and just according to the Golden Rule.
>
> ... The information I received yesterday about the offending members has shown me the wisdom of restoring the By-law as it read on discipline and excommunication.

Once again the "united plans of the evildoers" seemed to be directing her directors, and the one *most* susceptible to this malicous mental malpractice was the one who had not been under the Leader's direct guidance over the past several years, Mr. DeCamp. Two days later she wrote her directors again:

> . . . This is the cyclone hour with our cause when my weather vane must veer with the wind in order to indicate the right course. What seems best today, tomorrow may make not best. Be strong and clear in your convictions that God, not m.a.m., is influencing your actions. In order to be this, you must surely pray daily that God, good, divine Love — your only Mind — be followed, be loved, be lived by you.

"This is the cyclone hour!"; and the only one who knew the meaning of that statement was Mrs. Eddy. She said at this time to Nemi Robertson, who had been in her last class in 1898 and who visited at Pleasant View on several occasions: "One God, one Mind. All is Truth, Life and Love. This is the path, straight and narrow, leading to the Father's secret reward. You must follow every step of the way. I alone know what this means." This verbal message to Miss Robertson was elucidated by the further written message from the Leader:

> Many minds are at work at this instant to stop our work for humanity and for the Cause. But their efforts will fail. Why? Because God speaks to me as He has spoken from the earliest days when He guided me to the founding of this Cause. He speaks, and I must follow. This is my cross. How I wish I could explain to you what this means.

Another message from the Leader in November of 1902 directing a student in his mental work for the Cause was to Lewis Strang. It said in part:

> The Cause of Christian Science needs *healing.* Do you know what this means? . . . The future will bear witness that the Church established foursquare rests on foundations of Love which cannot be taken away. Christian Scientists will one day know the wisdom of their Leader and Mother in Israel.

Earlier in the month she had written to her directors on the issue of discipline and excommunication, amending the by-law so as to require the consent of the Pastor Emeritus for the latter:

> It is just that my old church shall not become the victim of m.a.m. without my interference in its behalf. I see what you do not in these cases of discipline. If I were to have the students that break faith all excommunicated without sufficient effort on my part and on yours to save them, how many members think you would be left in it?
>
> . . . God give you the wisdom to obey the Golden Rule and bless you, is the prayer of mother. . . .
>
> N.B. Remember your church by-laws and that my communications to you are not to be named to anyone outside of your meetings.

One of the effects of the "many minds . . . at work" to stop the progress of Mrs. Eddy's cause was the disciplining and planned excommunication of one of her oldest students, — the faithful, honest Capt. Eastaman. It is said that she called the captain to Pleasant View for a long talk and then sent him to the directors with a letter stating that he was one of her best students and was to be reinstated. Her letter of December 4 was to but two of the directors, Messrs. Johnson and Armstrong:

> Be of good cheer. God has shown me the way out of it. Meantime restore Capt. Eastaman to the First Membership . . .
>
> . . . I feel that God alone has shown me just what to tell you. "Knowest thou not the way to come unto me?" . . .
>
> N.B. Remember Woodbury blames me . . . I have asked in a letter today, Mr. DeCamp to resign his place on the Board . . . Tell Knapp he must not work against it, for I see what he does not. It is hard for me to have this to do, but it must be done.

Mr. DeCamp tendered his resignation the next day, December 5. The Leader's letter of December 8 told her directors to elect Stephen A. Chase to the Board, but it also sounded as if she had previously told them to elect Thomas Hatten to fill the vacancy which they had not done. Her instructions regarding reinstating Capt. Eastaman went on to say:

> This lying about my student and causing him and his innocent wife so much suffering, is one of the deepest plots laid since my prosecution for repeating the Revelation of St. John. What has occurred since Mr. DeCamp was here shows me that I am right in what I say on this subject.
>
> God is guiding me as I act. . . .

Mrs. Woodbury never ceased her persecution of the Revelator to this age. She had beguiled the astute and scholarly Mr. Wiggin (with whom she had worked on the *Christian Science Journal* in early years) and drawn him into her camp. She had reversed the earnest protestations of the new student, Oliver Sabin. Mrs. Woodbury and Capt. Eastaman had both been members of Mrs. Eddy's class in December of 1884. Perhaps Josephine Woodbury was now endeavoring to separate the captain from his leader, and the directors had been unwittingly aiding this plot. Frederick Peabody, though he may have been a willing accomplice, was the mouthpiece for Mrs. Woodbury's lies about the Leader. And it is altogether possible that her malicous mental malpractice was directed to a more prominent public figure.

Mark Twain had come forth with ridicule of Christian Science in

Cosmopolitan magazine in 1899 when Mrs. Woodbury had launched her legal attack against Mrs. Eddy and her officials. Now, once again, Mr. Twain was attacking Christian Science, and this may have been one of the things that had "occurred since Mr. DeCamp was" at Pleasant View. The first of four articles by the famous author, deriding Mrs. Eddy and Christian Science, appeared in the December issue of *North American Review.* A good deal of corespondence ensued, particularly between Alfred Farlow in Boston and William D. McCrackan in New York. Once again Archibald McLellan came up with something right for the Leader. On December 11 she wrote him:

> Your kind letter was a "cup of cold water in His name." I *thank* you for it. Few on earth minister to my needs, many, or think that I have any. . . .

One of the *few* who did minister to the needs of the Leader was her faithful Augusta in New York. This willing assistance, fidelity, and loyalty on Mrs. Stetson's part caused Mrs. Eddy on more than one occasion to tell her "obedient child" that she was chosen of God. The Leader's words were echoed in a letter Augusta wrote to one of her own beloved students in December of 1902:

> Your fidelity to Principle reveals much to me. I am reluctant to believe that I have attained to the Christliness you accord me. I feel at times that I am the *least* of the apostles, and then God seems to speak to me through my beloved Leader, Mrs. Eddy, or through you, or some other loyal, faithful student, and tells me that I am a chosen vessel. I think my mission and the *cup* and *cross* are hidden from me, or I could not so fearlessly go on to conquer the foe — mortal mind. I am more grateful than words can express for my dear students. I could weep when I think how I sometimes have to apply the rod — rebuke to error — only to save, or awaken the dreamer. God will never forsake me, and I shall not always have to drag around the dead bodies of luke warm and material students in my effort to save them until I almost faint and fall. The sifting has begun. I am waiting on God. He will bring it to pass in his own time and way. . . .

Very possibly Mrs. Eddy had said to Augusta Stetson what has also been recorded by other of her students, viz.: "There are many members of my church who should not be, and sometime there will be a sifting in my church."

One of the members of Mrs. Eddy's church who would survive the sifting was Mrs. Pamelia J. Leonard. Mrs. Leonard first studied with Mrs. Eddy in 1886 and had been an earnest, dedicated worker ever since. She was often called to serve in the Leader's home for short periods, and was at Pleasant View to help train newcomers in the summer of 1902. It was in August while Pamelia was at Pleasant View that Mrs. Eddy had Frank H. Leonard made a First Member of her church. Many people were very happy when Mrs. Leonard returned to her home in Brooklyn, New York in December. Mrs. Eddy received a grateful letter from Pamelia Leonard's students very shortly thereafter:

> December 18, 1902
>
> *Beloved Teacher and Leader:* — Your student, Mrs. P. J. Leonard, on her return to Brooklyn delivered to her students here, your inspiring word, that the healing must now be brought out, as proof of Christian Science.
>
> This has awakened the students to a renewed sense of love and gratitude for the revelation of Christian Science and for your unselfish work in uplifting mankind, and destroying sin and suffering.
>
> This fresh message of healing comes so near to the Christmas tide that we hail it as a precious Christmas gift, and send to you our love and gratitude and Christmas greeting. . . .

The Leader's letter to William B. Johnson the second week in December could also have been viewed as a Christmas gift. She said therein:

> What do you say to putting . . . your son on the Board of Trustees? . . .
>
> You know him and his adaptability to such a position better than I do and I leave the decision to you. If you think he is ready for it, put him there. . . .

Evidently Mr. Johnson did not think that William Lyman was ready for the position, for Mrs. Eddy's letter to Mr. Johnson, Sr. two days later instructed:

> Within find the names of the Building and Finance Committee. Please say to Mr. Whitcomb that Mother wants him to be appointed as builder of the new Mother Church. In view of this fact you say to him that you think it would look better for him to resign as a member of the Finance Committee and ask him if he is willing to do so. . . . Please appoint the following on the Building Committee and the Finance Committee.

Building Committee	Finance Committee
Mr. Carpenter of Prov., R.I.	Leon Abbott, esq.
Mr. E. P. Bates of Boston and	Calvin C. Hill and
Thomas W. Hatten	William L. Johnson

A letter to William B. Johnson on December 19 was a lesson for him and for several others:

> You say, "When shall we learn the way?" I reply, When you have *all faith* in *Truth,* hence no faith in error. Gain this point, overcome evil with the good by knowing that good is *supreme* — is the master of so-called evil. Work mentally with this consciousness and you will overcome evil just as I have done so many years, and carried on a cause in the midst of all opposition, to such heights of success.
>
> True, I am battle-stained; but I still love and give orders that are blessed and foil the enemy.
>
> Read this letter to the C.S. Board of Directors and let your noble son study it. . . .
>
> N.B. Naming persons in prayer, is the fight between beasts. Overcoming their evil and lies with good, and Truth in your prayers is *C.S.*

"True, I am battle-stained" — that was a part of the Leader's founding work the field knew nothing of. "Showing the scenes behind the curtain" is a great help to the advanced Scientist, but it is not for the neophyte or the general public. It was her constant words of wisdom, inspiration, and blessing showered upon the whole world that maintained her cause and blessed all mankind. Mr. McLellan felt blessed when he received this Christmas letter from the Leader:

> Xmas 1902
>
> Beloved Student,
>
> You will accept my thanks, and present them with overflow to the signers of your "Grace be with you." May the God of our fathers bless you all with His presence and power divine, give you many more Christ-days, and joyful years and time well spent. Then may we all meet — where no partings are — with the spiritual unction and self conscious approval of "Well done good and faithful."
>
> With love,
Mother
Mary Baker G. Eddy

CHAPTER XI

THE CHURCH NOT MADE WITH HANDS

Only healing can build His temple in the wilderness.
— MARY BAKER EDDY

MRS. Seal's mission to Germany had begun in December, 1897. She went first to Dresden arriving on a Friday evening. Sunday morning had found her in the room of a young American lady who had a copy of Science and Health and was happy to meet someone who could tell her more about Christian Science. The two women were reading the lesson together when there was a rap on the door:

> . . . another American lady entered, saying that she was looking for a Christian Scientist. She stated that she was a cousin of Mark Twain, and had witnessed the healing of his daughter from tuberculosis through the ministrations of Christian Science many years before.

It is sad that from this promising introduction Mark Twain should have sunk so low as to ridicule and traduce God's witness to this age.

The wicked attacks on Mrs. Eddy had hounded her footsteps since Kennedy had first initiated them in 1871. Following the Woodbury lawsuit they had intensified. In his vicious attack on August 1, 1901, among many unkind and untrue remarks, Peabody had called Mrs. Eddy "the most audacious and most successful adventuress, the most mercenary and calculating charlatan, the most vindictive, relentless and cruel woman the enlightened centuries had produced."

"Agree with thine adversary *quickly* whiles thou art in the way with him." *Quickly* is the key word in this instruction to come to agreement with the adversary, but in this case that was not done. The directors did not notify the Leader of this attack, and Alfred Farlow wrote an ineffective refutation of Peabody's lies. The right moment for answering had passed before Mrs. Eddy learned of

Frederick Peabody's lecture. On December 3, 1901, she had written to William D. McCrackan:

> I cannot quite forgive my students for depriving me of that golden opportunity to have answered the libel of Peabody's. Only a page of reply would have shown him a liar. All he said could be met by dates and proof of its falsehood. I could have written it not in reply but simply stated the facts and not called him a liar, but left the reader of them to know that he was. But it was over a week after his lecture before I was told of it, and then it was too late. If Farlow had written nothing on that subject and let his silence speak, it would have been decent. As it was, the whine he sent out was all the enemy wanted.

Alfred Farlow kept a constant stream of gentle corrections of misstatements of Christian Science in the public press, but his gentle manner and knowledge of facts had not been sufficient for this malicious character assassination. Perhaps this situation had been the impetus behind Mrs. Eddy's *Footprints Fadeless.* It may also have caused the changed marginal heading on page 560 in Science and Health. This paragraph had formerly borne the heading "Human botany." In the 1902 revision the marginal heading reads: "True estimate of God's messenger." This heading points to the true import of the paragraph:

> . . . This goal is never reached while we . . . entertain a false estimate of anyone whom God has appointed to voice His Word. Again, without a correct sense of its highest visible idea, we can never understand the divine Principle.

Now, at the beginning of 1903 the Leader was again faced with vicious attacks against her blameless character. This time Mrs. Eddy wrote a letter to the *New York Herald (My.* 302) which was published with the title: "Mrs. Eddy Replies to Mark Twain." A letter to the editor of the *Boston Journal* signed by "One Who is Not a Christian Scientist, but Who Believes in Fair Play" assesses the two authors:

> Mark Twain's greatest misfortune is that he feels compelled to sustain his reputation as a wit, a humorist, a very funny fellow.
>
> . . . One need only to read, side by side, in the *Boston Journal* of the other day, extracts from the magazine article written by Mark Twain, and a criticism of the same by Mrs. Eddy; the one flippant, inconsequent, so-called wit; the other dignified, reverent, and patient, to form a very fair opinion concerning the spirituality of the two writers.
>
> If Christian Science has never cured one single case of disease its teachings to do right, to love and trust God, and to love one's neigh-

> bor as one's self are sufficient to make a tremendous power for good among us — to exempt it from ill-mannered, snarling attacks, and to entitle it at least to tolerant welcome if not to our active support.

Such public support was greatly appreciated, but one brief sentence from the revelator will ring down the centuries. Mrs. Eddy wrote to Farlow shortly after Mark Twain's first article appeared:

> I advise you to take no notice of Mark Twain's effusion of folly and falsehood. Time tells all stories true.

It has been intimated that Mrs. Eddy's early directors followed her instructions blindly, but that is not the case. They were not unlike many other students, in that very often their personal opinions differed from what Mrs. Eddy told them on a subject, and quite often they thought she was wrong. Gilbert Carpenter, who knew both Mrs. Eddy and the directors has said, "in those early days, students did not hesitate to go contrary to her wishes, when they had a strong conviction that she was mistaken. . . . the Directors . . . did not function under coercion or blind obedience."

In December Mrs. Eddy had sent her directors the names of those she wanted on the Finance Committee, which members were duly appointed. Young William Lyman Johnson did very well in his new position and had the advantage of working very closely with his father. Calvin C. Hill remained a member of this committee continuously from this time until he passed away in 1943.

The Building Committee did not fare quite so well. Early in the new year, and very shortly after the formation of the Building Committee with the appointment of Thomas Hatten, Gilbert C. Carpenter, and Edward P. Bates, Joseph Armstrong came to Mr. Carpenter with a request. He wanted Carpenter to ask Mr. Bates to resign from the committee, one of his reasons being that Mr. Bates was unpopular with a clique in Boston. Had Mr. Carpenter known at the time that Mrs. Eddy had made the appointments, he probably would have hesitated to comply. But he did not know. He did, however, say to Mr. Armstrong: "Suppose Mrs. Eddy does not like it?" Joseph Armstrong was willing to bear the burden of the Leader's disapproval, so Gilbert Carpenter did the directors' bidding, and Mr. Bates was replaced with Calvin Hill.

Mrs. Eddy wanted her students to use initiative, but they were so often wrong, — motivated by erring, human judgment, — that time and again she had to rebuke. The Leader did not *tell* her students what to do. She tried to open their eyes and their understanding so that they would see the right course for themselves. Absolute obedience to Principle is essential, but it must be with spiritual understanding. *Blind* obedience does not lead to salvation. In a great many of her letters the Leader tells her directors what she thinks should be done and then tells them to do what they think is right. She knew that very often the action they took might not be right, but that their present understanding was not elevated enough to discern the right even when she stated it.

She did have the hope that future generations who had known no God apart from Father-Mother God, Principle, Mind, Soul, Spirit, Life, Truth, and Love would perceive Principle in all being and see the wisdom, rightness, and consistency of all her actions and instructions. And she knew from her own experience that these enlightened students would be the prime targets of the prince of this world. While her devoted followers in 1903 were concerned with building the excelsior extension of the Mother Church, made with hands, the Leader was building her church not made with hands, eternal in the heavens, for a future generation which would have outgrown material organization. The church built with hands was soon to be seen in Boston. But the church not made with hands was to be hidden in the *Manual of the Mother Church*. To this end she was working diligently on a new edition of the *Manual.*

On February 5 Mrs. Eddy sent some new by-laws to her directors asking them to convene immediately and vote on them. One of these by-laws added a fifth member to the board of directors. In the same letter she nominated Archibald McLellan for the position, stating: "I have watched him and so far he has been right on all important subjects." William Lyman Johnson says that Mrs. Eddy was very disappointed with McLellan's work as editor and expressed the desire to his father that someone else might be found for the position. William B.'s response was that the directors could help him if she would give him another chance. William Lyman has written:

> His election to the Directorate came about as follows. Mrs. Eddy realized that Mr. McLellan was not fulfilling her hopes. He did not seem to be a vital factor in the work of the headquarters, and she discovered that certain persons were giving him advice instead of looking to her or to the Board of Directors, then made up of her veteran students . . . She called William B. Johnson and asked him how Mr. McLellan could be helped. He suggested that the Board of Directors needed more than ever the advice of one who knew something of legal matters, and that if Mr. McLellan were to be helped in his editorial work it was necessary for him to be in closer touch with the Directors so that he could better understand her labors. Mrs. Eddy considered the matter . . .

and her letter of February 5 followed. The directors acted immediately and on February 7, 1903 Mr. McLellan was made the fifth director. In fact, he was made the chairman of the Board of Directors succeeding Ira Oscar Knapp, "and the old Board members, with their new chairman, went forward with the erection of the extension," according to Mr. Knapp's son.

Their first order of business was finalizing the acquisition of land for the new building. As always the Leader's thought embraced the church not made with hands, as one of her letters before the end of February so clearly tells:

February 27, 1903

Christian Science Board of Directors
Beloved Students:

I am not a lawyer, and do not sufficiently comprehend the legal trend of the copy you enclosed to me to suggest changes therein. Upon one point, however, I feel competent to advise, namely: Never abandon the By-laws nor the denominational government of the Mother Church. If I am not personally with you, the Word of God, and my instructions in the By-laws have led you hitherto and will remain to guide you safely on, and the teachings of St. Paul are as useful today as when they were first written.

The present and future prosperity of the Cause of Christian Science is largely due to the By-laws and government of "The First Church of Christ, Scientist" in Boston. None but myself can know, as I know, the importance of the combined sentiment of this Church remaining steadfast in supporting its present By-laws. Each of these many By-laws has met and mastered, or forestalled some contingency, some imminent peril, and will continue to do so. Its By-laws have preserved the sweet unity of this large church, that has perhaps the most members and combined influence of any other church in our country. Many times a single By-law has cost me long nights of prayer and struggle, but it has won the victory over some sin and saved the walls of Zion from being torn down by disloyal students. We have proven that "in unity there is strength."

With love, as ever,
Mary Baker G. Eddy

N.B. I request that you put this letter upon our church records.
M.B.E.

"Never abandon the By-laws"! The By-laws of Mary Baker Eddy's Church are from God, and so they are like the ten laws God gave to Moses. They are *never* outgrown: they are to be fulfilled. God used His servant Moses to instruct the children of men. He used His son, Jesus, to enlighten mankind, and the son called himself the "door." Love used Her daughter, Mary Baker Eddy, to focus Her light upon the way in Science, and the daughter called herself the "window." On the nineteenth of February in 1903 Mrs. Eddy wrote in a letter:

> . . . Divine Love knows that love is light, even that light which is the Life of man. Divine Love knows His window and knows that it gives light, not darkness, and is the means of love's entrance into the hearts of men. The wonder is that aught can make God's window seem to be what it is not. It was the doubt and ignorance of what Jesus was and did for all mankind, that shut out and still shuts out the light of Love. What if the window does offend the sense with the objects it reveals and the path it points out! It is Love's window and Love's revelation to mankind. The good gaze at last with gratitude and joy on what they had not seen, but now see through the window that disturbed the senses but pointed the way in Science.

A letter to the Leader which was published in the *Sentinel* of February 26 set another building project in motion. It was from the First Reader of the Concord church, Irving C. Tomlinson. Rev. Tomlinson's closing paragraph stated:

> Our Sunday congregations, even in this wintry weather, fill our little hall. We are even now in need of larger quarters, and unless other arrangements are made before next summer people will be turned away.

Now the Mother's thought would turn to her children in Concord even as it had when she first supplied them with Christian Science Hall several years earlier. She was always reaching out to do for others. Once Mrs. Eddy said to Clara Shannon and Laura Sargent that "she thought she had discovered the way to eternal Life, and that was, whenever she wanted to do something for herself, to put self aside, and do something for others; just to learn to be unselfed." Perhaps the most unselfed people in the whole world second to the Leader were those few who served her long and faithfully at Pleasant View, — most notably Calvin A. Frye and Laura E. Sargent. Clara Shannon, too, had served in Mrs. Eddy's home since 1894, but early in 1903 Clara's mother passed away in Montreal, Canada, and Clara felt the need of returning there, and then to London to look after her affairs in her native England. After leaving Pleasant View Miss Shannon said: "Dear Mother has taught me much in this short time, which will help me forever and help me to help others." As soon as she was settled in London she began at once to practise Christian Science. No one could take Clara's place, but in the spring of 1903 Mrs. Eddy called her student Lida Fitzpatrick to Pleasant View as well as the youthful John Carroll Lathrop who had recently been prosecuted in New York courts for practising Christian Science healing.

If March was saddened by Clara's departure, it was cheered by a harmonious chord from another direction. There had been a good deal of discord in the church over the music and musicians, which had greatly affected the Leader's beautiful, healing poems. On March 3 she was able to write to her directors:

> Your request to hear my Hymns that are set to music by Mr. Johnson again sung in the Mother Church cheers my advancing years.
>
> That tones liked or disliked should rule in or out of our church words like those in my Hymns, has been a sad experience for me; and I rejoice that the Christian spirit is calling these words back to remembrance. One of the wealthiest and most devout members of this church has recently requested me to have my Hymns sung more frequently in The Mother Church. It would be a good thing to have one of my hymns read and sung about every Sunday. It would spiritualize the thought of your audience and this is more needed in the church than aught else can be.

The wealthy, devout member who requested Mrs. Eddy to have her hymns sung more frequently was Mary Beecher Longyear. Mrs. Eddy's answer to Mrs. Longyear was dated March 4:

> Beloved Student:
>
> Your dear letter is received. First will say, I stopped the singing of my two hymns because the music set to them offended certain members of the church. Now I have received your good will on restoring these hymns, also a request that they be sung again in church, and this request comes from our Directors! one of whom has bitterly opposed hearing the music that came with them. I thank God, thank you, and others for this unification in our church.

On the eleventh of March the Leader wrote one further word to the directors on this subject: "Be ye governed by your own convictions and wisdom in the use of my hymns." However, the last two sentences in her letter of March 3 practically became an unwritten by-law for them. One still hears dissension over Mrs. Eddy's hymns, but never from those who have felt their healing power. Her inspired words cannot be sung or heard too often for those hungering after righteousness.

Another occurrence that cheered the Mother's heart in early March involved Calvin Hill. He told her that he was leaving business in order to devote all his time to the Cause. She wrote him on March 2:

> Beloved Student:
>
> I am glad that you have left all, left but nothing for something, and this something *is All.*
>
> God bless your brave, honest intent with its fullest fruition.

There are the sick, the halt, the blind to be healed. Is not this enough to be able to accomplish? Were I to name that which is most needed to be done of all else on earth, I should say heal the sick, cleanse the spotted despoiled mortal; and then you are being made whole and happy, and this is thine, "Well done good and faithful," enter thou into all worldly worth and the joy of thy Lord, the recompence of rightness. Again, God bless you, dear one, and guide your footsteps.

Here again the Leader is building her church universal and triumphant, the church not made with hands, by naming "that which is most needed to be done of all else on earth." She could not help thinking of the mania for building beautiful edifices which had become paramount throughout the field. How she longed for just one student who would leave all else for this higher attainment of *healing.* Even her darling Augusta in New York City had been devoting much of her time and effort for nearly four years to erecting a beautiful edifice that would seat twenty-two hundred people, and to meeting the cost of one million two hundred fifty thousand dollars for building this magnificent structure. A few days after her letter to Calvin Hill Mrs. Eddy wrote to Augusta Stetson:

March 13, 1903

My precious Student:

I have longed to hear from you of your spiritual growth, — to have you write of your healing, of your great growth in demonstration, whereof you would cite the works that prove it. O Augusta, I pray to God that you will leave all for this highest attainment on the scale of human life — *outward, onward, upward.* Unless my students do reach a higher position in this line of light, their sun will *set.*

This I know, as certainly as I know that C.S. is C.S. and that healing the sick and reforming the sinner demonstrate Christian Science and nothing else *can, does.*

Beloved child, will you not address yourself to gaining this height of holiness? Nothing is so much needed for your own happiness and distinguishment, and for the success of our Cause and for the glory of leading on and up the human race, as this one demonstration. By it I got the attention of the world. My words and writings, sermons and students or adherents could not, did not do it. But my wonderful *healing* did it. I had hoped that you would have followed in these footsteps. Dear, dear Augusta, begin today. Leave all for this.

Lovingly thine *own,*
Mary B. Eddy

CHAPTER XII

DEEDS AND TRUSTS

O how I wish you could see what I see before us in the history of the churches. — MARY BAKER EDDY

1903

IT would appear that both Mrs. Eddy and her veteran directors were aware that the fifth director did not have the same status as the other four. It would also appear that Archibald McLellan, who had not yet met Mrs. Eddy, made an unexpected and uninvited visit to Pleasant View to complain about his inferior position, on the eighteenth of March or thereabouts, for the Leader wrote to him on March 19:

> I require no apology. I was delighted to meet you and intended to invite you and Mrs. McLellan to P.V. when we get over the present purchase of land in Boston. I reminded the Directors of this intent and my inability to meet you that day and told them to tell you. My son from the far West was waiting at the Eagle Hotel to see me, hence my situation. . . .
> N.B. I regret that your name cannot appear as a member of the C.S. Board of Directors in their deeds. I have twice urged this question but Mr. Elder finds it cannot be legally so.

It is most probable that Mrs. Eddy "urged this question" with Mr. Elder, and possibly with General Streeter too, *before* she sent her by-law amendment stating: "The Christian Science Board of Directors shall consist of five members." It is also possible that God had spoken to her through Genesis 14, which is the battle of the four kings with the five kings. In this battle the brethren of Abram (whose name was changed to Abraham) were taken captive; and Abram (Abraham: Fidelity [S&H 579]) "pursued them unto Dan" (Dan: Animal magnetism; so-called mortal mind controlling mortal mind [S&H 583]). "And he brought back all the goods, and also brought again his brother Lot, and his goods, . . . and Melchizedek king of Salem . . . blessed him and said, Blessed be Abram of the most high God, possessor of heaven and earth." Fidelity is the way. At one time Mrs. Eddy told Calvin Frye that he was placed in the front ranks of Christian Scientists. Calvin said: "I know it, but I do not understand why it should be so." The Leader responded: "Because of your faithfulness . . ."

The battle of the four kings against the five kings *in Boston* erupted in the courts after both Mrs. Eddy and Mr. McLellan were no longer present. The directors dismissed John V. Dittemore from the Board on March 17, 1919, and he sued to be replaced. The court found in favor of Mr. Dittemore because, of the three members who met and voted his dismissal, one was Edward A. Merritt who had succeeded to McLellan's position (making him the *fifth* director), and the court determined that the vote of the fifth director did not count. Voiding Mr. Merritt's vote left the vote standing at two to two, a tie, and according to the findings of the court Mr. Dittemore had not been dismissed.

Mrs. Eddy may have foreseen such proceedings, but it is certain that no one else did in March of 1903. The main concern of the directors was "the present purchase of land in Boston," and in this regard Mrs. Eddy had written them on March 9:

> I hereby request that it be named in the deed of land, that the same inscription which is on the outside of the present church edifice shall be placed on the new church. Also I request that according to page 108, clause No. 3 of the old deed, as published in our Manual, you add to the deeds of land the following clause: No new Tenet or By-law shall be adopted by this church, and no Tenet or By-law shall be amended or annulled without the written consent of Mary Baker G. Eddy, the author of our textbook, Science and Health with Key to the Scriptures.
>
> My dear Students, I *foresee* that if you add to your deed the aforesaid clause, it will save you sad experience. It will tend to keep out of our church disloyal students, and to preserve the loyalty of those who are members thereof.

The legal member of the board, Mr. McLellan, may have suggested the addition of the phrase "during her natural life," for in her letter of March 10 with the "No" underlined, she wrote: "During her natural life. *No.*" Once again her followers were acquiring deeds to the land upon which to erect the edifice made with hands while the Leader was laying the foundation for the structure "not made with hands, eternal in the heavens."

The land the directors were acquiring was essentially triangular in shape bounded by St. Paul, Norway, and Falmouth Streets. The point where Norway and Falmouth Streets meet is the original Mother Church. The deed of trust for that parcel of land is in the *Manual,* page 128. The deeds for the nine other parcels which complete the block all contain the further trusts specified in Mrs. Eddy's letter of March 9. They also contain the words "Executive Members," for early in 1903 the designation "First Members" was changed to "Executive Members." One of the nine deeds is included in the *Manual* on page 136. The last parcel was acquired on March 30. The *Boston Globe* stated:

> The last parcel in the block bounded by Falmouth, Norway, and St. Paul Streets, in the shape of a triangle, has passed to the ownership of the Christian Science Church . . . In the purchase of this parcel which is known as the Hotel Brookline, a four story brick building also in the shape of a triangle, from Gilbert C. Carpenter, it gives to the above society the ownership of the entire block.
>
> During the past two weeks considerable activity has been going on in property on these streets . . .
>
> Just what use the society will make of the property has not been stated . . . No block is so well situated for church purposes as this one, being in a fine part of the city.

Before this last purchase was recorded Mrs. Eddy had written to Joseph Armstrong specifying another foundation stone in her "church universal and triumphant."

> March 22, 1903
>
> Beloved Student:
>
> One thing in my haste was forgotten, namely, the designation of The First Church of Christ, Scientist as *my church.*
>
> The question will be, is, asked whose church is it? We cannot say it is Mr. Hering's or the Board of Director's church, for it surely is not. It was my church in the beginning as much as Mrs. Stetson's church is hers. We must be orderly in these things or it will lead to difficulties that you do not see, but *I do see them.*
>
> Now, dear one, I entrust you with this secret; do not disappoint me. The next deed you have made, have it read, "Mary Baker G. Eddy's Church, The First Church of Christ, Scientist," in the deed. *Remember this.* Consult with Elder on it and keep it from other ears and tongues. Ask Elder if this can not be done in your next deed? Write me his answer.

Mr. Elder obviously said that it could be done, for, though most of the deeds were already recorded, the next one, which was from the Carpenters, included the words: "the Executive Members of 'Mary Baker G. Eddy's Church, The First Church of Christ, Scientist'."* This stipulation was further emphasized with a by-law ti-

*See Metcalf deed in Manual, page 137.

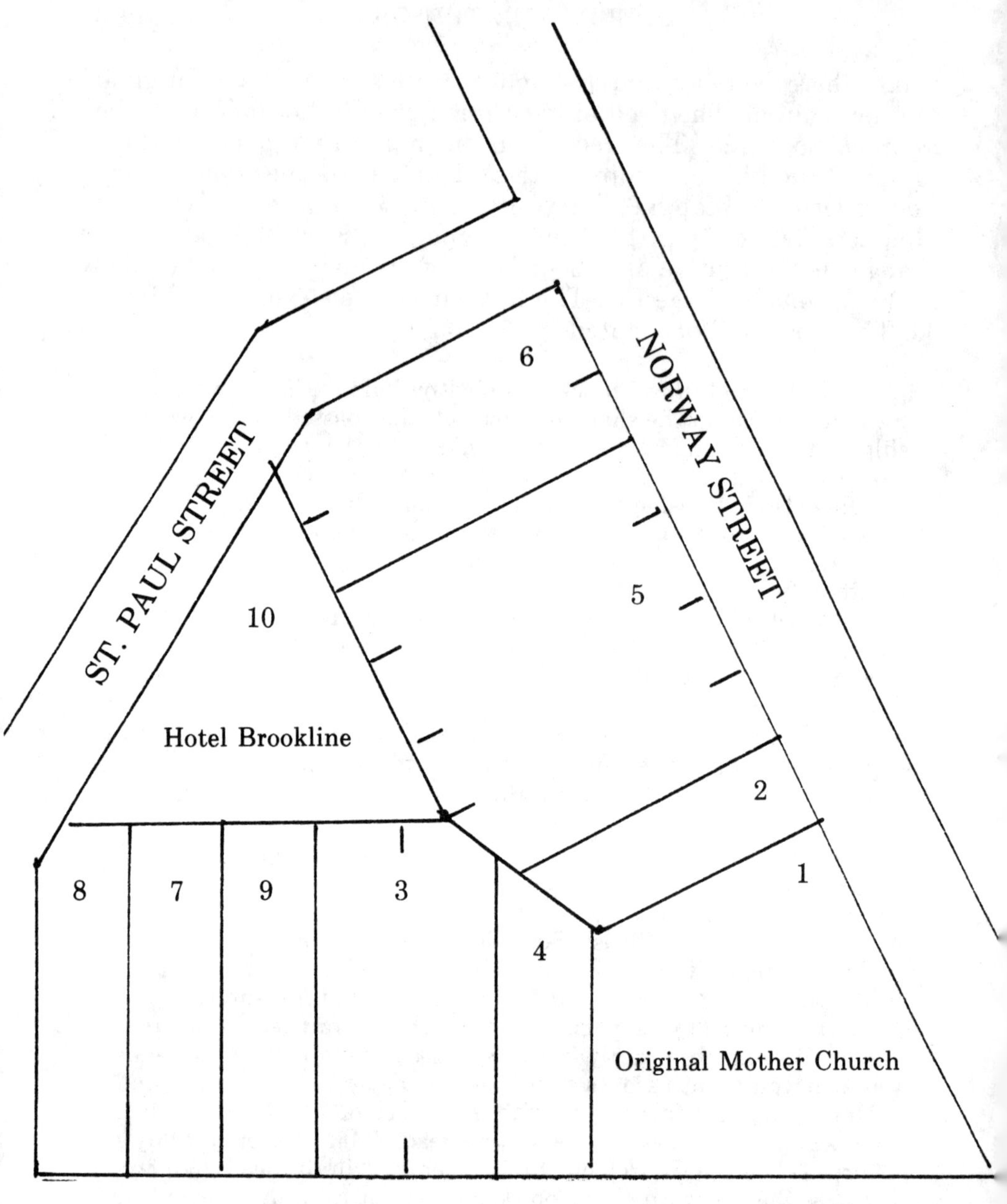

The ten parcels of land on which the Mother Church and Extension are built. They are numbered according to the order in which they were deeded to the Board of Directors.

tled **Designation of Deeds,** Article XXXIV, Section 2 *(Man.* 102).

The first *Manual* published in 1903 was the twenty-eighth edition which was also the first *Manual* providing for a five member Board of Directors. This by-law also included the double check that the Leader held over her directors and which she had first included in the tenth edition of the *Manual in* 1899. (Several editions had included a Section titled **Tenth Edition the Authority.)** The twenty-eighth edition states:

> **Directors.** Sect. 4 The Christian Science Board of Directors shall consist of five members. *They shall not fill a vacancy occurring on that Board, except the candidate is approved by the Pastor Emeritus** and the remaining members of the Board. *This By-law can neither be amended nor annulled, except by the written consent of Mrs. Eddy, the Pastor Emeritus.**

The twenty-eighth edition had no sooner been published than new by-laws were required in relation to the land deeds for the erection of the extension of "Mary Baker G. Eddy's Church." Every great spiritual discovery had gone through three stages and had been lost to the world by the time the third stage was complete. The three stages are: persecution, popularity, and organization. Mrs. Eddy's discovery had survived the persecution and was enjoying unprecedented prosperity. In fact, it was a youthful giant frightening those who chose to cling to the ways of the world and to orthodox beliefs. Organization was necessary to direct the steps of this young giant, but only the Leader saw the perils of organization. And none but the Leader could *foresee* or even believe that her great discovery would become nothing but lifeless words unless the perils of organization could be overcome. To this end she worked unceasingly, but this was a part of the Leader's great mission that few if any of her students were aware of, and that not one of them understood. She wrote to a student in 1903: "O the amount that I see to be done for all, before Christian Science is established on the Rock 'gainst which the billows beat in vain. . . . My labors are harder now than ever before." So the Leader labored on, and much of her work at this time was with her *Manual.* But what all the world saw on the first of April was the new publication, *Der Christian Science Herald* in the German language. Thanks poured in from Germany and from many other places including the following from California:

> . . . having resided in the United States for nearly thirty years, I thought myself so familiar with the English language that the Ger-

*Emphasis added.

> man Publication would be of no real benefit to me. The first appearance of our new periodical, however, dispelled this illusion, and I found that sentences which have been read over many times in the English, never appealed to my thought as when read in my mother tongue . . .

A practitioner in Saratoga Springs, New York, wrote of sending her patient home with *Der Herald* to a very sick husband who had been in bed several days, and of finding him completely healed of rupture and cold the following Sunday. Mrs. Seal wrote from Berlin:

> The first number of *Der Christian Science Herald* came to us this week, and at our Wednesday evening meeting it was suggested by one of our German members that a vote of thanks be sent to our Leader, whose untiring love has made this possible, and to her faithful workers at headquarters.
>
> The need for literature with which to feed the hungry hearts has seemed very great . . . The loving faith of these dear people who have been coming to the meetings month after month, and some of them year after year, to drink in all of Truth that they could glean from the reading, has been touching beyond expression. . . . Those who could do so have studied English, but not all of them could do that . . . Ours is indeed a happy church and congregation, and expressions of thankfulness are coming from all parts of Germany. . . .

Augusta Stetson's visit on the eleventh of April brought a ray of sunshine to the Leader's busy schedule. During their conversation she invited Augusta's church to Pleasant View during the coming Communion season, but amended the invitation in a note that evening:

> My precious Student:
>
> I said two things to you today that I must recall before I sleep. One was in reference to W. — the other to our next Communion. Let God deal with her, and promise me that you will not name my reference to her today — will you?
>
> Also I invited you and your dear church to come here at our next Communion season, but I meant that if my Church come generally, to be sure that you, *dear* one, and your church shall come also. I want my Church to act in *unity* and each one to prefer another, and to love one another even as I have loved them.
>
> Darling, I love to think of your cheerful face that I saw today — to think of you as *happy* and *prosperous.* O may *God bless you* dear, and crown your life with His Love.
>
> Ever tenderly, lovingly thine,
>
> M. B. Eddy

On the first of April Calvin Frye's salary was raised from $1000 per year to $100 per month. This was probably in accordance with the new by-law, **Opportunity for Serving the Leader,** which would appear in the next (twenty-ninth) edition of the *Manual.* This by-law provides for calling students to serve at Pleasant View, and the closing sentence read:

> These assistants of the Pastor Emeritus shall be paid semi-annually at the rate of twelve hundred dollars yearly, in addition to rent, board, and traveling fare for the round trip.

In 1903 twelve hundred dollars *without* room and board was double the annual salary of a great many people. Even the directors of the Mother Church were paid much less. In January, 1903, Art. VI, Sect. 1 of the *Manual* stated: "The salary of each member of this Board shall at present be seven hundred dollars per annum."

In April when she first sent the new by-law to the directors for their approval and to be included in the new *Manual,* she wrote them:

> When a nation defends itself against wrong it is sometimes driven to accomplish this ... through its army.
>
> Our cause needs defence and its principal *fort* needs fortification. I now call soldiers to supply this need, defend this fort, and the officer working within it for her Church, the field, and the world.
>
> When a nation needs more soldiers it necessarily drafts them. I have come to this necessary call for Christian Scientists to hold our fort in God's service. I gladly pay them for their service and give mine; my only sigh is that these soldiers of the cross have not been *volunteers.*

The Leader knew that Pleasant View, which she sometimes called Fort Besieged, needed fortification. She knew that this "principal *fort*" and "the officer working within it" needed the defence of seasoned, dedicated "soldiers of the cross." But early in May, and before this by-law was published or the defences strengthened, the fort and the officer within suffered a severe attack weakening the soldiers she did have. A few days later she changed the by-law and wrote her directors again:

> ... some of the students went away from me in my sorest hour of need, and I regret to say it, apparently *heartless* in my dire necessity. This has at times grieved me almost to death.
>
> ... Also before I changed the By-law I deeply pondered the example of our great Wayshower when calling his students and compelling them to leave all for him, and his call was without conditions,

> imperative. ... This By-law may be the hobby of my foes and be criticised by my friends, but such has been the case with all of my movements in the first stages of the history of Christian Science. ... I am watching and praying that I do just His bidding and "hurt not the oil and the wine."

It is possible that the change she made was the addition of the sentence: "A member who leaves her in less time without her consent or who is discharged shall be dropped from the Church." But that was not the sentence that caused a great stir in the field!

Theoretically the men in the Christian Science ranks had recognized the equality of male and female even though the nation as a whole had not. "The error of the ages is preaching without practice" (S&H 241); and evidently that is what a good many male Scientists were doing. What else could account for the amendment to this by-law which later changed it to read:

> Male members ... shall be paid semi-annually at the rate of twelve hundred dollars yearly in addition to rent and board. Female members shall receive one thousand dollars annually with rent and board.

This issue of unequal salary was finally resolved in the seventy-third edition of the *Manual* in 1908: "Members thus serving the Leader shall be paid semi-annually at the rate of one thousand dollars yearly in addition to rent and board."

CHAPTER XIII

EXPLORING THE WAY

Ceaseless toil, self-renunciation, and Love have cleared the pathway for Christian Science. — MARY BAKER EDDY

1903

AFTER Clara Shannon's departure the Leader wrote to a number of her older students, and some came to Pleasant View for interviews. This probably occasioned a good deal of speculation in the field as to who would be called to Pleasant View. And the speculation surely caused Mrs. Eddy's article of April 20 entitled "Significant Questions" *(My.* 228), which appeared in the April 25 *Sentinel:*

> Who shall be greatest? The great Master said: "He that is least in the kingdom of heaven" — that is, he who hath in his heart in the least the kingdom of heaven, the reign of holiness, shall be greatest.
>
> Who shall inherit the earth? ...
>
> Who shall dwell in Thy Holy Hill? ...
>
> Who shall be called to Pleasant View? ...
>
> It is true, that loyal Christian Scientists called to the home of the Discoverer and Founder of Christian Science, can acquire in one year the Science that otherwise might cost them a half century. ...

Mrs. Lida Fitzpatrick first turned to Christian Science for help in 1887. She had been in Mrs. Eddy's Normal class in the Massachusetts Metaphysical College in 1888, and had been healing and teaching in Cleveland, Ohio ever since. Now she was the first new soldier to be enlisted at the fort. It was 3:30 on the afternoon of May 3 that she arrived at Pleasant View to stay to serve the Leader, and to "acquire in one year the Science that might otherwise cost ... a half century."

Occasionally Mrs. Eddy remarked to her household that some day her followers must know what it had cost her to found Christian Science. The price she paid was total self-sacrifice. She had told one of her early classes of her unselfish love for all mankind when she said: "I could annul the effects of the malpractitioners on myself with my own understanding, but I allowed it to work on myself without meeting it, until I discovered a method for my students to use to overcome it through argument." One day in the spring of 1902 she had told Calvin Frye, Clara Shannon, and Irving C. Tomlinson that she used no argument when she began healing. According to Calvin's diary:

> . . . when she began to teach students to heal she had to work all sorts of ways to start them from their standpoint, for she could not start them from hers, for they could not understand [it] and were not ready to do as she did. But when she dropped down to their methods of arguments she began to fear, and the error began to appear real to her . . .

After Judas' betrayal, when Jesus told Peter to put up his sword, he said: "Thinkest thou that I cannot now pray to my Father, and he shall presently give me more than twelve legions of angels? But how then shall the scriptures be fulfilled . . . ?" Mary Baker Eddy, too, was God's chosen witness fulfilling the Scriptures. Her mission was not to save herself, but to find the way of salvation for all. It was clear to her that fear and the seeming reality of disease and error were what all her followers *must* overcome, so she stayed down on their level seeking to find a way by which they could meet the incessant attacks of malicious mind. This was her cross, and she suffered untold agony on this cross many long years. She wrote once to an early student: "I know, my dear student, the way is the way of our Master, full of crosses and crowns. I have more to meet than my students, so much more, you cannot conceive of my cup."

The night of May 3 was one of the crosses in her experience, and it was a malicious attack upon her life and her citadel. It was probably the first lesson for Lida Fitzpatrick at Pleasant View, and a hard one. At 11:30 P.M. Mrs. Eddy suffered a sudden attack. The four practitioners in the house were unable to relieve her of the severe pain, so she sent for Rev. Tomlinson. But he, too, gave her no help. It has been written that on other occasions Calvin Frye had suggested that she call in her cousin, Dr. Ezekiel Morrill, for a medical diagnosis, to which she had never consented. For many years Clara Shannon, whom the Leader described as strong, courageous, and faithful, had been working in the home with her other students, and every challenge had been met and overcome. Now, without the help of Clara's strength and courage to fortify them, they did not overcome their own fear and became discouraged. So the Leader in agonizing pain finally consentd to a medical diagnosis and to their calling Ezekiel Morrill. He, however, was out of town, and his father, Dr. Alpheus Morrill was sick and could not come. They then sent for Dr. Conn, who came at 2:15 A.M., but found the pain so intense and slow to respond that he called in Dr. Stillings for consultation. The doctors diagnosed her suffering as renal calculi (kidney stones). After they left at 4 A.M. she was a little relieved and at 5 A.M. slept for an hour. According to Calvin Frye's diary paroxysms of pain continued the next day, and "she called in Dr. E. Morrill and he gave her an hypodermic injection." If this is a true account of the situation the lulling of the pain enabled her to handle her own case; but there is some room for doubt. Portions of Mr. Frye's diary including this May 3 episode, fell into enemy hands — hands of those who published wicked lies about Mary Baker Eddy and Christian Science. Could his entries have been tampered with?

The Leader was *never* wrong in her diagnosis of disease, and there were times when Mind spoke as clearly to some of her followers. But that was not the case with the workers in her home in the early hours of May 4. Following the medical diagnosis, her students proceeded to work from their standpoint with greater confidence. The Leader knew it was unscientific and she knew the danger as stated in the textbook on page 161:

> The ordinary practitioner, examining bodily symptoms, telling the patient that he is sick, and treating the case according to his physical diagnosis, would naturally induce the very disease he is trying to cure . . .

But she also saw that the physical diagnosis had alleviated the fear of her students somewhat and given them direction in their work. Since the fiftieth edition in 1891 there had been in Science and Health a sentence which reads: "If Christian Scientists ever fail to receive aid from other Scientists, — their brethren upon whom they may call, — God will still guide them into the right use of temporary and eternal means."

This concession to *materia medica* was a "temporary means" she had not considered before. It was a new departure in "the way" she was exploring for her followers, and she gave it a good deal of thought. A week later she sent a new by-law to the directors which read:

> If a member of this Church has a patient whom he does not heal, and whose case he cannot fully diagnose, he may consult with an M.D. on the anatomy involved.

This by-law was written to allow students such help if they felt the need for it, but the balance of the Section *(Man.* 47) gives the Leader's feelings: "And it shall be the privilege of a Christian Scientist to confer with an M.D. on Ontology, or the Science of being." A few weeks later the lesson for the students in her home included: "God is All; you do not have to delve into matter, the body, to know how things are. Spirit shows us things as they are.

"Keep your thought up there; this will heal; it is all that is necessary. When you are 'on the house top, do not go down into the house to take anything out.'"

It is most likely that she discussed this point with her teacher in the Board of Education, Edward A. Kimball, whose teaching she wholly approved and endorsed. The following has been recorded in Mr. Kimball's *Teaching and Addresses:*

> Christian Science is the great physician, and Truth will diagnose the case for you, and you need not consult the doctor-books nor an M.D. We are bound to win in this continual effort in the right direction. The more error talks, the more it insists on its claims, the more it is a liar, and it knows it is a liar, and cannot deceive the Truth, and I am governed by Truth.

While the Leader was working to strengthen scientific *healing,* the Christian Scientists in Concord were working on building their church, as this May 6 news item describes:

> Through the generous gift of the Reverend Mary Baker Eddy the Christian Scientists of Concord, N. H. are to have one of the finest church structures in the Granite State. The plans for this edifice were presented at a largely attended church meeting tonight, and work will begin upon the new structure in the near future. The gift of Mrs. Eddy includes the desirable lot of land now occupied by Christian Science Hall in the heart of the city at the corner of State and School Streets, and is without doubt one of the finest locations in Concord for a church building. . . .
>
> The church will be built of the same beautiful Concord granite of which the National Library Building in Washington is constructed. This is in accord with the expressed wish of Mrs. Eddy made known in her original deed of trust first announced in the *Concord Monitor* of March 19, 1898. In response to an inquiry from the editor of that paper Mrs. Eddy made the following statement: —
>
> "On January 31, 1898, I gave a deed of trust to three individuals which conveyed to them the sum of $100,000 to be appropriated in building a granite church edifice for First Church of Christ, Scientist in this city." . . .
>
> The architecture will be Gothic, and in keeping with modern ideas of a church building. It is intended that the pews of the church will

> seat one thousand.
>
> The trustees of the Building Fund, Fred N. Ladd, Josiah E. Dwight, and J. Wesley Plummer, will have charge of the construction of the new edifice. Francis Richmond Allen and Charles Collins of Boston have been employed as architects. . . .

On May 11 the Leader wrote that her church would receive no annual Message this year, that the crumbs and *monads* "already given out" would "feed the hungry" and that even "the fragments gathered therefrom should waken the sleeper" *(My.* 133). However, the next month she did send a letter to her church.

Lida Fitzpatrick's Divinity Course notes began on May 13 and included: "You do not have to argue; KNOW. Know God and His idea, and not argue about sin. It was years before I argued." Lida's May 13 entry ended with: "A year is a short time for a Divinity Class."

On the same day Mrs. Eddy returned the proofs for the next (twenty- ninth) edition of the *Manual* to William McKenzie. Young Mr. McKenzie and Daisette Stocking (both of whom were in Mrs. Eddy's last class in 1898) had married in August of 1901 and now had a baby boy. In her letter accompanying the *Manual* proofs the Leader wrote: "Give my love to your wife, kiss the baby for me and know I love it — but I pity it for the inheritance it has to overcome." Of course "the inheritance it has to overcome" is the same we all have to overcome, — that is, the first death told of in Revelation, the belief of being born mortally. This overcoming may have been in the Leader's thought a few days later when Lida Fitzpatrick recorded her words: "I know what is coming. I dare not tell you what I know . . . You will know some day."

May 14, the day after returning the proofs for the *Manual,* Mrs. Eddy wrote to Edward A. Kimball:

> Each day since your letter came I have endeavored to answer it, but unexpected care, or work, or a *belief* has prevented it. . . . I know not what a day may bring forth. I have accomplished a *great* amount for the present and future of our cause since I saw you.

The next day, May 15, she wrote to Mr. Kimball again:

> I write these lines simply to thank you deeply for your dear letter that is a balm for wounds that *you* never inflicted — and in evidence of my unfaltering faith in *YOU.*
>
> Whatever else befalls I shall never look for your downfall in Christian Science nor a lack of heartfelt fidelity to your Teacher and its Founder.
>
> God bless you and make your exit from sense to Soul, from earth to

Heaven *here,* gentle.

That same day the Leader turned her thought in another direction. Mr. Conant and his staff had completed their work on the Concordance to Science and Health. It had not been an easy task to *complete,* for with each new edition — which came frequently by 1903 — there were changes. In April Mr. Conant had written asking if she had made her "last change of Science and Health." Her response on April 22 stated:

> My "last changes of Science and Health" may continue so long as I read the book! But I will stop now and you may finish the Concordance immediately. Owing to the fact that this book should unfold in proportion as my thought grasps the spiritual idea more clearly so as to voice it more simply and thus settle many queries — I have wished I had not commenced a Concordance, but had had an index attached to Science and Health.

Difficult as it was for the Leader in her future revision, there is not a student today who is not grateful that she "commenced a Concordance." She did stop revising (temporarily) in April so that Mr. Conant could complete his work, and on May 15 she completed the *last* step by writing the Preface. All was ready for Mr. Orcutt to begin the printing.

Even though the Leader had given Christian Science Hall and the land on which it stood plus one hundred thousand dollars to the Concord Scientists for their church edifice, she looked upon it as a concession to their state of consciousness even as was the new bylaw regarding medical diagnosis. To the students in her home she said on the twenty-first of May:

> The true Science — divine Science — will be lost sight of again unless we arouse ourselves. This demonstrating to make matter build up is not Science. The building up of churches, the writing of articles and the speaking in public is the old way of building up a cause. The way I brought this Cause into sight was through HEALING; and now these other things would come in and hide it just as was done in the time of Jesus. . . .
>
> We must show the difference between Christian Science healing and quackery.
>
> Healing is demonstration; nothing else is. . . . through the healing this Science was brought to notice. It is lost sight of and must be regained. . . .

But those in the field thought the new Concord church was Mrs. Eddy's special church, and they began showering her with letters and gifts. Her Card written May 24 was just the first of many such notes of thanks:

> From the overflow of my heart I hereby send to the Christian Scientists at Boston, Mass., *thanks* for their desirable gift of additional land whereon to build the edifice of First Church of Christ, Scientist, Concord, N. H., and to First Church of Christ, Scientist, New York City for the sum of one thousand dollars to said Church.

Mary E. Speakman had been assistant editor of the *Sentinel* and *Journal* since the summer of 1902, and it has been recorded that when the Sentinel arrived at Pleasant View Mrs. Eddy always read her editorials first. In May Miss Speakman's correction of a mistake was published. She had violated a rule of the Publishing Society (now appearing in *Miscellany* 130:21). She may have been dismissed, or she may have received a rebuke and resigned in reaction as had Julia Field-King several years earlier, — whichever, she was replaced a few weeks later by Mrs. Annie M. Knott. About the same time in May the Leader commended Archibald McLellan for his editorial in the May 16 *Sentinel,* part of which was later included in *Miscellany,* page 11. Her letter to McLellan included the statement: "I have been so occupied with the *Manual* have not written sooner." An article by Mr. Kimball in the May 16 *Sentinel* said:

> . . . Mrs. Eddy has been constantly at her post during all the storms that have surged against her for a generation. She has been the one of all the world who has encountered the full force of antagonism. We know, too, that during these years she has not tried to guide us by forced marches, but has waited for us to grow into readiness for each step, and we know that in all this time she has never urged upon us a step that did not result in our welfare.

Kimball's appreciative article, "By Way of Reminder," stressed the fact that *now* was the time to support the Mother Church. Mrs. Eddy's article, "Now and Then" *(My.* 12) which appeared two weeks later began with this theme that *"now* is the accepted time." To the students her article pertained to the building of the extension of the Mother Church, but the Leader's thought and words were ever embracing the spiritual "structure of Truth and Love" (S&H 583):

> . . . to build a temple the spiritual spire of which will reach the stars with divine overtures, holy harmony, reverberating through all cycles of systems and spheres.

This certainly refers to her "church universal and triumphant," her church not made with hands. What else could reverberate "through all cycles of systems and spheres"? The Divinity Course in her home far more than the structure of stone in Boston was building this "spiritual spire . . . which will reach the stars."

The main thing Mrs. Eddy was teaching her students at Pleasant View was how to watch. What is watching? It is watching every thought that comes to consciousness and making every thought conform to the laws of God. Gilbert Carpenter wrote:

> In the home of Mary Baker Eddy, the Discoverer and Founder of Christian Science, those whom she called mental workers were instructed to sit quietly in their rooms and watch and pray, usually for an hour at a time. These periods she called *watches,* after the Master's query, "Could ye not watch with me one hour?"
>
> It was her custom to furnish these workers with written texts or outlines of thought which she expected them to amplify.
>
> . . . the mental workers in her home learned to take the fragmentary outlines which she furnished them daily, and to use them as mental "primers" — as water is used to prime a pump and to start the well flowing — to open a flood of spiritual and inspirational thought that truly was reflected from God.

In addition to the written outlines the Leader gave verbal instructions to the workers in her household. On the twenty-sixth of May she said: "If you take up arsenic you will hit it in most of the cases in 1903."

On that day the conversation was on drought, and Mrs. Eddy, missing Clara Shannon, said: "Clara could bring the clouds and the rain." Then she gave them a beautiful lesson on rain, which was followed by several others on weather on subsequent days. On May 30 Lida Fitzpatrick recorded: "There was a nice quiet rain all night and Mrs. Eddy said we brought the rain; this broke the thought of drought."

On May 31 the Leader told her students: "I never argued until I began teaching students and had to meet the thought where it stood. . . . I have been made the way-shower." Her words which would elevate their work were: "Now drop arguing and hold to God. I used to do my healing with — 'God is All.'" It was the twenty-ninth of May when she told them that no one else would ever have as much to meet as she had. Mrs. Fitzpatrick recorded the Leader's words:

> I am only a windowpane through which the light comes. You are helping yourselves more than you help me, for I am *helping* you; the Discoverer has to discover the way to meet these things; you will not have that to do; you are *learning* NOW how to meet them; I have had to discover it.

CHAPTER XIV

COME TO ZION

An editor should be reliable in word and deed, adroit, wise, apt in discerning the public need, in rebuking the private evil and unselfish in doing it. — MARY BAKER EDDY

1903

ON May 30 when Mrs. Eddy's article "Now and Then" appeared in the *Sentinel,* an article appeared in the *Literary Digest* of the same date which attributed the origin of Christian Science to Ralph Waldo Emerson. Immediately Mrs. Eddy wrote a refutation *(My.* 304) which was published in the *Boston Journal* on Monday, June 8, with the title **Mrs. Eddy Corrects a Misstatement.** A good deal of discussion ensued in the public press which caused Mrs. Eddy hastily to write a second article which, without proofreading, she immediately sent on to her editor with this note:

> I appeal to you in my need and for our cause. Will you examine this that I have not time now to look over, make it right where it is wrong, punctuate it, take it to Farlow and see that he puts it through the best papers in Boston, N. Y. City, and into the Associated Press. In great haste.
>
> With love,
> M. B. Eddy

Mr. McLellan did her bidding, and what is titled "A Plea for Justice" in *Miscellany* (p. 305) was published widely. The second paragraph begins:

> Far be it from me to tread on the ashes of the dead or to dissever any unity that may exist between Christian Science and the philosophy of a great and good man, for such was Ralph Waldo Emerson . . .

And the enemy used the *New York Sun* to strike at the Woman. The *Sun* changed her word *dissever* to *discover* which totally changed the meaning. The Leader wrote her editor on June 18:

> I see the need of arming and fortifying against the enemy as never before. Publish that article of mine published in the New York Sun that for "dissever" printed "discover" . . . and comment *sharply* on such an abuse . . . Again the enemy can fire and will through the Press but they cannot *heal* who lie. If we beat in this battle it must be through demonstrating above *their ability.* I started this great work and woke the people by demonstration, not words but works. Our periodicals must have more Testimonials in them. The Sentinel is of late a Shakespeare without a Hamlet. Three pages of testimonials are the least to have in the Sentinel. Healing is the best sermon, healing is the best lecture, and the entire demonstration of C. S. The sinner and the sick healed are our best witnesses.

At that date the *Sentinel* was a publication of sixteen pages including the front and back covers, so three pages was a large portion of the copy. McLellan did increase the space devoted to testimonials in future issues; however, he did a very poor job of correcting the *Sun's* abuse. As soon as she received the proof for the next issue, the Leader wrote him again:

> The Sentinel must not be issued with the present arrangement of the reply to an *insult* to your Leader, to her students and our cause! It is tame, and the Editor assumes as Editor no responsibility of thought on such a matter of importance — even in his editorial.
>
> Place my article as I wrote it, — first, then follow it with the N. Y. Sun's shameful publication of it.
>
> Make the heading a sharp allusion to said word that he supplied and not as *my order!* but the proper indignation of the editors of the Christian Science periodicals; and make it in a way that will not invoke discussion but *stop* it. Get Mr. Willis to prepare if need be and hand this letter to him. In great haste and with love.
>
> M. B. Eddy

The editor-in-chief had expressed no indignation at the insult to the Leader, hence her suggestion that he turn the matter over to John B. Willis, Assistant Editor. Sad to say, the *Sentinel* was already printed with Mrs. Eddy's article not as she wrote it, but copying "the New York Sun's shameful publication of it." This was followed by McLellan's "tame" comments and editorial. Mrs. Eddy's letter to her editor gives us a much clearer picture on this issue than do the files of the *Christian Science Sentinel.* It also shows how her officials failed to uphold the Leader and her work. Most of the time all of the upholding fell upon her own shoulders.

CHRISTIAN SCIENCE HALL
Concord, New Hampshire

A brighter note was heard in Concord while this was going on in the press. The final meeting at Christian Science Hall held on June 3 was very largely attended, and there was a natural regret at the thought of parting with this dear, historic building, this beautiful hall which had been a headquarters for Scientists from all lands. All hearts were cheered by the announcement that other churches in Concord had offered them temporary shelter for their meetings during the course of construction on their new edifice. The *Concord Evening Monitor* stated:

"The Unitarian Church has extended the privileges of their beautiful edifice so long as it shall be needed. This permission has been accepted . . ." The continuity of the Christian Science meetings in Concord was appreciated and of public interest. But the practice of Christian Science in Concord which was not seen was expressed in a letter from the Leader to the First Reader, Rev. Tomlinson shortly after their last meeting in Christian Science Hall: "I ask that you and your sister and all the practical, good Christian Scientists in Concord each day twice take up in prayer the solemn subject that no accident nor harm shall come to those employed on our Church building."

A by-law had been amended earlier in the year changing Communion in the Mother Church to the last Sunday in June, which meant that it would be June 28 in 1903. Extensive preparations were being made for this annual event. The most significant and far-reaching occurrence of this Communion season was the first appearance of a new volume added to the literature of Christian Science. Among the announcements for all the meetings and various activities in the *Sentinel* of June 27 was the following:

THE NEW CONCORDANCE

A Complete Concordance to Science and Health with Key to the Scriptures is now ready for delivery . . .

In the excitement of Communion Week it is possible that the great importance of this new volume was somewhat overlooked at its first appearance. But its inestimable value, immediately recognized by the scholar, was soon seen by all real students.

Several issues of the *Sentinel* contained announcements that Mechanics Hall would be headquarters for all the visiting Scientists in Boston for a week beginning Thursday, June 25. The Executive Members (formerly First Members) met in the Mother Church on Saturday morning, June 27, and the next day three communion services were held at Mechanics Hall. Although Mrs.Eddy had announced that there would be no Message to her Church this year, she did send them a short message *(My.* 133). She also sent these instructions regarding this message:

. . . It is *multum in parvo,* so I take the liberty to say it is at the mercy of the reader. The style of reading needs to be conversational. . . . I want you to select the best reader you can find to read my short Message; one whose voice is *ample,* articulation distinct, and whose emphasis, pause, tone is according to conversation, — to the laws of *understanding* his subject and making it clear to the hearer.

The man selected to read her short message was the First Reader, Professor Hermann S. Hering. Let us hope that he read it with more understanding than the typesetter for the *Sentinel* who put "lessons" instead of "lessens" in her closing lines:

Truth happifies life in hamlet or town;
Life lessens all pride — its pomp and its frown —
Love comes to our tears like soft summer shower,
To beautify, bless, and inspire man's power.

Near the close of the communion service Prof. Hering read the Leader's Message which began: "My beloved Brethren — I have a secret to tell you . . ." All were interested in her secret, and all were delighted a short time later to receive an invitation to visit the Leader at Pleasant View the next day. All who could possibly do so availed themselves of the invitation, for ten thousand or more made the trip to Concord on Monday, June 29. The *Boston Evening News* editorialized:

Boston is used to conventions and big gatherings. Possibly for that reason the feat of the Christian Scientists in filling Mechanics Hall three times on one Sunday for a strictly religious service has not attracted undue attention.

But even Boston is not accustomed to seeing seven or eight thousand people arrange within eight hours for an all day excursion, have tickets printed and issued and special trains engaged inside that time, and actually be on their way before the invitation to go was twenty-four hours old.

That is something that usually follows weeks, even months, of careful planning, and yet the Christian Scientists did it in hours. Moreover, everything went as smoothly as if the details had been worked out by rule and rote. Not even a railroad official lost his temper, and there was not the semblance of an accident reported.

The vast gathering was handled, both in Boston and in Concord, by the volunteer ushers of the church. They did the policing and the directing. The people themselves did the rest.

Whatever one may think of Christian Science, whatever he may think of this visit to Concord, which outsiders persist in terming a "pilgrimage" and which insiders say was nothing of the sort, its success as a mere exhibition of how a crowd can be handled and can handle itself is sufficient to classify it among the extraordinary events of the moment. . . .

Aside from the satisfaction of seeing Mrs. Eddy and hearing her speak, the characteristic of the Concord visit which most seemed to please and impress the Christian Scientists was the hospitality with which they were received by Concord itself.

The city . . . [threw] open to them its doors — even the doors of its clubs and private residences.

A conspicuous leader in this particular was the Wonolancet Club, whose spacious house in the heart of the city was placed absolutely at the disposal of the Scientists. . . .

To how many promiscuous gatherings of excursionists from all over the world would the Wonolancet Club care to throw open its home without restraint? . . .

We all have our little weaknesses, and Christian Scientists may have theirs. But it would appear from a candid examination of their case that they also have some qualities which are worth almost anyone's emulation.

At least they know how to conduct themselves like ladies and gentlemen when they go on excursions, and that of itself is a bit of a virtue.

More than one newspaper reporter was greatly impressed by the gathering of ten thousand people on the lawns of Pleasant View. Frank W. Gale, a practitioner and teacher from California, was one of the many busy men directing the people and carriages as they arrived.

One of those arriving was an accomplished and well-known photographer from Concord, Mr. W. G. C. Kimball. Mrs. Eddy was his friend, and though she could not spare time for photographers, she gave Mr. Kimball her permission to take her picture if he could do so without inconveniencing her, which he had done on several occasions. Mr. Kimball had asked on this occasion if he might photograph Mrs. Eddy on the balcony. At first she had declined, but then said if he would stand at a distance and not distract the visitors he might take a photograph.

Mary Baker Eddy speaking from her balcony at Pleasant View to 10,000 people gathered below on June 29, 1903.

The reporter from the *Boston Herald* wrote:

> By noon the thousands who had come from Boston, and others who had journeyed to Concord from other points, awaited admittance.
>
> Shortly before 1:30 P.M. the gates opening on the street were thrown back and the crowd passed through, seeking the places nearest to the east balcony, from which Mrs. Eddy was to address her guests. The time for her appearance had been set at 1:30 P.M.

It was just a little before 1:30 when one of her corresponding secretaries, young John Carroll Lathrop from New York City, entered the Leader's room to ask her a question. She invited him to remain in her room and listen to her address through the open window, and then called her maid to put on her wrap and bonnet. The *Herald* reporter wrote: "When Mrs. Eddy came out on the balcony her appearance created a profound impression." John Lathrop said: "A multitude of joyous, upturned faces greeted their dear Leader in a stillness indescribable." Mayhap Mr. Lathrop was reminded of the passage, "And I, if I be lifted up . . . will draw all men unto me." According to the *Herald:*

> Mrs. Eddy looked over the throng for a moment, advanced to the front of the balcony and with hands folded in front of her began to speak. Her words came clear and distinct . . .

Mr. Kimball took his photograph. John Lathrop said that he was later informed that every word was heard as she spoke slowly and distinctly:

> *Beloved Brethren:* — Welcome home to your home in my heart. Welcome to Pleasant View, but not to varying views. I would present a gift to you today only that this gift is already yours, God hath given it to all mankind. It is His coin, His currency, it hath His image and superscription. This gift is a passage of Scripture, it is my sacred motto, and reads thus: "Trust in the Lord, and do good; so shalt thou dwell in the land, and verily thou shalt be fed. Delight thyself also in the Lord; and He shall give thee the desire of thine heart. Commit thy way unto the Lord; trust also in Him; and He shall bring it to pass. He shall bring forth thy righteousness as the light, and thy judgment as the noonday."
>
> Beloved, some of you have come long distances to kneel with us in sacred silence in blest communion — unity of faith, understanding, prayer, and praise — and to return in joy, bearing your sheaves with you. In parting I repeat to these dear members of my church: *Trust in Truth, and have no other trusts.*

With emotion manifest on her face she looked smilingly upon the thousands of upturned faces and waving them goodbye passed within. Her face was radiantly happy as her maid removed her wrap and bonnet. She sat down in her big chair, folded her hands, and said: "Wasn't it a wonderful occasion?"

Then she asked John: "What are they doing?" He looked out the window and told her they were having silent prayer, to which she responded: "We will pray, too."

"Now what are they doing?" she asked. Someone had started singing, "Shepherd show me how to go," which spread quickly to the farthest corners until the strains were swelled by ten thousand voices singing in unison.

The Communion Hymn was also sung, and the Lord's prayer repeated. After repeating the Scientific Statement of Being from Science and Health the throng began to disperse quietly.

Then Mrs. Eddy said to John: "Now I will see what God says about it." As she did on every occasion every day, she picked up her Bible and opened it at random. And God said to her: "And the ransomed of the Lord shall return, and come to Zion with songs and everlasting joy upon their heads: they shall obtain joy and gladness, and sorrow and sighing shall flee away."

"See how God is always with me," she said to John. "That verse I will add to my address." So when her brief address was printed in the *Sentinel* it ended with the verse from Isaiah, preceded with the Leader's words: "Today is fulfilled the prophecy of Isaiah."

Mr. Kimball was not expecting much because of his poor vantage point when he photographed Mrs. Eddy on her balcony. When he developed the film it was just about what he expected, — so he tossed it among the discards.

At a later date when going through his discards before disposing of them, Kimball again discarded the balcony scene, then took one more look and decided to enlarge it. And, lo — the BALCONY PORTRAIT!

Many years later Rev. Irving C. Tomlinson and his wife visited Mr. Kimball at his studio. As the photographer told them the story of this famous picture he said: "It was lucky I didn't throw it away, for the 'Balcony Portrait' has brought me more business than all the others put together."

THE BALCONY PORTRAIT

Mary Baker Eddy speaking to 10,000 Christian Scientists gathered at Pleasant View on June 29, 1903. Taken at a distance by photographer W. G. C. Kimball.

CHAPTER XV

"THE STRUCTURE OF TRUTH AND LOVE"

The future will bear witness that the Church established four-square rests on foundations of Love which cannot be taken away. Christian Scientists will one day know the wisdom of their Leader and Mother in Israel. — MARY BAKER EDDY

1903

THE visit to Pleasant View on June 29 was the high light of Communion Week, but it was not the end. That night in Boston Alfred Farlow met with all the visiting Committees on Publication. Tuesday, June 30 the Annual Meeting was held at Mechanics Hall at 2 P.M. The next morning at 9 A.M. at the Mother Church Edward A. Kimball met with all the Normal Class Graduates of the Board of Education. That night the closing meeting of Communion Week was the Wednesday Evening Testimonial Meeting. Mechanics Hall was packed with an estimated eight thousand people with every seat taken and hundreds standing. At least two thousand more attended the overflow meeting in Exhibition Hall conducted by Edward A. Kimball. Testimonials from all over the world made a most fitting closing to a very active week.

There were more events of import to Scientists to come in July, but the most important to George Kinter came on July 7. It was a letter from Mrs. Eddy. The Kinters had been interviewed in regard to having Mr. Kinter serve at Pleasant View and also in regard to Mrs. Kinter's willingness to have him do so. They were both waiting and hoping for this message from the Leader:

> Yes, come at once. Mr. Frye has written you for me as to what to bring with you. God is leading you into a blessed privilege, a wonderful opportunity. May He in His infinite mercy grant that you be kept right, sound in mind and body, free from the a.m., "The sin that doth so easily beset us." Notify me immediately upon your arrival in Concord.

The *Sentinel* of July 11 announced the laying of the corner stone of the Concord church on July 16 at two o'clock, and ended with "A cordial invitation is extended to all." Mrs. Stetson was at the Hotel Touraine in Boston on July 15 planning to attend the ceremony the next day as were hundreds of other Scientists. But the editors and directors were chagrined by a letter Mrs. Eddy had written them the day before, July 14:

> Are you asleep on so important a subject as to make the laying of our Church Corner Stone in Concord a desecration, instead of a quiet, solemn, brief ceremony? You who profess to know there is *no matter* to elevate the usual material ceremony above all precedent.
>
> Not over fifty persons shall be present on that occasion with my consent.
>
> With love and all the patience God would give me for such *sin,* such *folly,* such a waste of time and money only to obey M.A.M. and make sport for our enemies.
>
> N.B. I had not seen your notice in our publications till today.

The Leader was not writing this letter just for her directors of that day and for her church in Concord. She was writing it to the members of her forever Church to remind them always to do their work in sacred secrecy (in their closet) and to give as little time and attention as possible to "material ceremony." But to bring the lesson home on this occasion she requested that the corner stone be laid at 12:30 instead of the announced 2 P.M. The article in the *Sentinel* telling of the event said that fewer than one hundred were there, and "But for the expressed desire of Mrs. Eddy the attendance would have been very large, as people from various parts of the country, to the number of two or three thousand had arranged to be present." This article also stated:

> The church of Gothic architecture, will be eighty feet wide and one hundred twenty feet deep and will seat one thousand people comfortably. It will be built entirely of Concord granite. A handsome tower over one hundred feet high, and three beautiful entrances will adorn the front. . . . the builder is Mr. E. Noyes Whitcomb of Boston.

The message from the Leader which was read on that day *(My.* 158) said in part:

> This day is the natal hour of my lone earth life; and for all mankind today hath its gloom and glory: . . .
>
> The burden of proof that Christian Science is Science rests on Christian Scientists. The letter without the spirit is dead; it is the Spirit that heals the sick and the sinner — that makes the heart tender, faithful, true. Most men and women talk well, and some

practise what they say.

She sent a letter to William P. McKenzie with this same message about this same time:

> I have much to tell. One thing is — unless there is less teaching, less church making, and better *healing,* and more of it — our denomination will sink into the slough of past sects in having a religion of the letter without the spirit — of doctrine without demonstration.

On the natal day of her "lone earth life" the Leader wrote to the Executive Members of her church her "heartfelt acknowledgment of their beautiful gift," a loving-cup *(My.* 347). On July 20 she received the following note from the editor of the *Concord Monitor,* George H. Moses:

> *My Dear Mrs. Eddy:* — In case you care to make any public comment upon the death of Pope Leo XIII, which occurred at Rome this afternoon, the *Monitor* would be pleased to become the vehicle to transmit your tribute to the public.

Mrs. Eddy responded immediately to this "sad, sudden announcement" *(My.* 294). She also sent a reprimand to her directors because they did not have the bells of the Mother Church join in tolling with the others in Boston at the time of Pope Leo's funeral.

The leader in the *Sentinel* of August 8 was an article by Joseph Mann entitled "Seventeen Years a Witness," which was a lovely tribute to Mrs. Eddy. Joseph recounted early experiences and stated he had been at Pleasant View nearly six years:

> six years of extraordinary opportunity to practise in my own everyday life such a sense of honesty, absolute justice, and fidelity to Truth, as the world outside of Christian Science little dreams of, and of which even Christian Scientists outside of Pleasant View have more of the letter than of the spirit, as they would see if they judged themselves by the standard of the natural daily conduct of their Leader . . .

Joseph had fled from this exacting standard on more than one occasion, and it would appear that he may have done so once again, for on August 16 Mrs. Eddy wrote to Mr. McLellan:

> Please inform me what day Mr. Joseph Mann called for his manuscript that he sent to you for publication. He is off on a vacation and hence my inquiry of another and I need to know the date.

The date of a codicil to her will was November 7, 1903, and the first provision began:

> 1. I hereby revoke the bequest in paragraph numbered 5 of my said will, to Joseph G. Mann of the right to occupy with Calvin A. Frye my homestead premises known as "Pleasant View" during the lifetime of the said Mann ...

Joseph probably knew neither of the bequest nor of its revocation when he retired from Pleasant View in 1904 and became a busy practitioner and teacher in Connecticut.

* * *

THE MANUAL

> *Knowing this, that the law is not made for a righteous man, but for the lawless and disobedient* ... — PAUL

THE Leader may have hoped to have her new revision of the *Manual* ready for delivery for Communion week along with the *Concordance to Science and Health,* but it did not appear then, nor in July. On August 17 she wrote to her board of directors:

> I give you direct orders to bring out our Manual and not to delay one other day. I know the Manual is right. God tells me to have it published as it is. You have adopted the By-laws; now delay no longer to put it in book form.
>
> Nothing whatever but malicious mortal mind is now causing delay.

The Leader had labored long over this revision, and the directors were happy to be able to tell her that it was now available and that Mr. McLellan's editorial entitled "The Revised Church Manual" was already in print in the latest *Sentinel.* Her editor had written therein:

> Recently the By-laws have been thoroughly revised by their author and as revised they are now published in the twenty-ninth edition of the Church Manual ... This edition presents many changes in the By-laws ...
>
> This revision of the Manual has engaged the attention of our Leader for some considerable time, and but few may know of the great care and labor she has bestowed upon this important work ...

In recognition of her toil, the directors offered to pay her for all her work on the new *Manual.* She thanked them graciously but stated that she could not begin to accept money from her church:

> What I do for it no one but myself knows nor could do. . . . This task nothing can compensate but the joy of saving [the Children of Israel]. All the money in the world could not prompt me to do it and sometimes I almost think my human life will be the price of my incessant struggle, care and perplexity.

The 1903 *Manual* saw many additions and changes including **Opportunity for Serving the Leader** and **The Title of Mother Changed** *(Man.* 64): "In the year nineteen hundred and three and after, owing to the public misunderstanding of this name, it is the duty of Christian Scientists to drop the word *mother* and to substitute Leader already used in our periodicals." The Leader was still fondly called Mother by her household, and her Christliness continues to mother all mankind. She will ever be the Mother in Israel, but to Christian Scientists she became their Leader.

One of the few who knew "of the great care and labor she has bestowed upon this important work" was Clara Shannon, for this revision had begun while Miss Shannon was still at Pleasant View. In March of 1903 Mrs. Eddy had been working on it most diligently, — especially upon the legal aspects, — and Clara's recollections and notes were probably of this period:

> . . . when making some by-laws which were needed she said, "This church Manual is God's law as much so as the Ten Commandments and the Sermon on the Mount. It is God's law and will be acknowledged as law by law." And she smiled and looked up from her writing and said, "I mean by the laws of our State, even if it has to go to the Higher Courts." . . . She finished up, both at the beginning and the end of what she was saying with the words, "Now remember what I say."

Miss Shannon also wrote in her notes: "I've forgotten while listening to her if the word was 'Higher' or 'Highest.' "

The *Manual* "will be acknowledged as law *by law!"* Ordinarily church by-laws are voluntary laws strictly protected from any interference by legal civil authority. But the Constitution of the United States which provided such religious liberty for Americans could also protect "Mary Baker Eddy's Church." It had protected her great discovery enabling her to publish it and to teach it to others despite opposition and persecution. She had released many a sufferer from the belief that he was physically controlled by and subject to the organs of a material body, by *knowing* that All is Mind, there is no matter. All kinds of organic ailments, diseases, and malfunctions had been healed in Christian Science.

And now she was releasing her followers from a larger sense that they were mentally controlled by and subject to the organs of a material body politic. To Mrs. Eddy nothing was material, — neither her church nor any of the steps she took in founding her church upon the rock. She said to the students in her home in the summer of 1903: "Each one must work out of matter for it is wrong in every way . . ." A little later her lesson included: "The earth is spiritual — not material . . . The material senses are lies; the spiritual sense is the real. The spiritual sense *destroys* the material." And her lesson of August 11 was: "Humility is the door, honesty is the way, and spirituality is the summit." The church she was striving to protect was not a material organization. It was the church she had described in an essay several years earlier: "The church created, founded and erected on the rock against which the winds and waves prevail not, is the church triumphant, the indwelling temple of God". While the members of The Mother Church thought they were acquiring material land upon which to erect a magnificent material edifice, the Leader was turning constantly to God to protect her church and to build it upon a wholly spiritual foundation. And God showed her the way to protect her life work from the peril of the third stage, — organization, which had nullified every other great spiritual movement.

The first protective legal step was embraced in her letter of March 9, 1903 to her directors: "I hereby request that it be named in the deed of land, that the same inscription which is on the outside of the present church edifice be placed on the new church." The inscription on the original Mother Church states:

INSCRIPTION ON ORIGINAL MOTHER CHURCH

The second legal step was in the same letter: "Also I request that . . . you add to the deeds of land the following clause: No new Tenet or By-law shall be adopted by this church, and no Tenet or By-law shall be amended or annulled without the written consent of Mary Baker G. Eddy, the author of our textbook, Science and Health with Key to the Scriptures." One of the deeds of land including these two stipulations is included in the *Manual* (pp. 136-138).

The deeds to the ten parcels of property upon which The Mother Church and Extension are built are strictly *legal* documents of ownership and restriction and are therefore entitled to the legal protection of the courts of the United States of America which means the protection of our Constitution. And now one more step would bring her Church Manual under the same Constitutional protection so that at some future day it would be "acknowledged as law by law." That step was to include as the last by-law in the *Manual* (p. 105) the same stipulation that was in the legal land deeds, viz., that no by-law shall be adopted, amended, or annulled without the written consent of Mary Baker Eddy.

Mrs. Eddy knew that legality would annul her stipulations; but she also knew that spirituality would cause Christian Scientists to endeavor to follow their Leader in every particular, — and nothing but spirituality could save her movement from the perils of organization.

None but the Leader saw any of this in 1903, but when the twenty-ninth edition of the *Manual* was published letters of appreciation began pouring in. Perhaps the title of her response *(My.* 229) was in anticipation of the time that they would understand what they were praising:

MENTAL DIGESTION

> . . . Heaps upon heaps of praise confront me, and for what? That which I said in my heart would never be needed, — namely, laws of limitation for a Christian Scientist. . . . Notwithstanding the sacrilegious moth of time, eternity awaits our Church Manual, which will . . . stand when those [ministries aggressive and active] have passed to rest.
>
> . . . Its rules apply . . . to one and all equally. Of this I am sure, that each Rule and By-law in this Manual will increase the spirituality of him who obeys it . . .

* * *

CALVIN A. FRYE

JOSEPH Mann, who worked closely with Calvin Frye for more than six years, described him in a letter to William Lyman Johnson:

> Mr. Frye was a man big enough to do his own thinking, that is, he did not reach conclusions by comparing notes with others, nor even by consulting with himself; for he had within himself a very appreciable element of that good old-fashioned Christian spirit which consulted God. . . . He was no soft-gloved theorist, but a horny-handed metaphysician; an obedient servant of God . . .

John Salchow wrote of Calvin Frye in his reminiscences of life at Pleasant View, that he "was full of fun and usually entered into almost any kind of a good joke;" and Laura Sargent, wide-eyed and serious, was at times the victim of their joking.

A reporter who came to Pleasant View a little later described Calvin Frye as "a very pleasant-faced man, with hair slightly tinged with gray and with a short gray moustache. Delightful of manners, easy, and graceful."

One day in 1902 Mrs. Eddy had said: "When Mr. Frye is himself, he can accomplish the work of fifty men in mental practice, but he is liable the very next day to be off again." But she greatly appreciated Calvin's faithful service and remarked to more than one student that she didn't know how he accomplished all that he did.

August 16, 1903 marked the day that Calvin Frye had been serving the Leader continuously for twenty-one years. Mrs. Eddy presented him with a gift of appreciation, a check for one thousand dollars. She also wrote to her directors suggesting that they reward his dedicated service, stating in her letter that Mr. Frye —

> has stood by my side to help *our Cause 21 years,* . . . He has done more practical work in my behalf . . . than any other Student.

The directors passed the message on to the Executive Members, and about three weeks later, on September 12, a gift from the Executive Members in recognition of his twenty-one years of service to Mrs. Eddy was delivered to Mr. Frye at Pleasant View. It was a beautiful, large mahogany roll-top desk and chair with which Mr. Frye was greatly pleased.

Calvin Frye was the one individual who was the closest to Mrs. Eddy for the longest period of time. In that position he came under heavier fire from the enemy than did any other person aside from the Leader herself.

CALVIN A. FRYE

The first loss Mrs. Eddy had experienced on the field of battle had been the death of her dear husband Asa Gilbert Eddy in 1882. She had never lost a case from the time of her discovery sixteen years earlier, and she had not really taken hold of Gilbert's case for he had assured her that he could handle it himself. The loss was a great blow to her, but it also pointed up the deadliness of the enemy's attacks constantly aimed at her and those closest to her and most prominent in her cause. All of her employees who were Christian Scientists had to learn to meet malicious animal magnetism for their own protection, for the protection of Pleasant View, and for the furtherance of Christian Science. Considering that she had a large number of employees and that Pleasant View was "Fort Besieged" for seventeen years, it is no small miracle that *no one* ever died at Pleasant View.

Calvin Frye suffered a number of deadly attacks, and on more than one occasion several of the students in the home witnessed Mrs. Eddy's work in bringing him back from death. John Salchow and his sister, who was also working at Pleasant View, were the only two witnesses to one such occurrence in 1903. Whether it was as serious as the other attacks is not known, but Miss Salchow thought it was, for she was the one who found Calvin slumped over his desk, and she was sure that he was dead. Mrs. Eddy was summoned immediately, and as John and his sister watched, the Leader brought Calvin back to consciousness in about five minutes. Of course these repeated venomous attacks were aimed at the Womanhood of God, but because Calvin Frye was always standing in front of her, endeavoring to the best of his ability to protect her, he often was the one that received the deadly blows. Mrs. Eddy knew Calvin's devotion and dedication and had said to him one day in 1902: "During the last twenty years you have done more good than any one else on earth except myself." The world owes a great debt to Calvin A. Frye.

* * *

EDWARD ANCEL KIMBALL

EDWARD Ancel Kimball was raised in Buffalo, New York, and as a young man became very successful in business in Chicago. Early in the 1880's, though not yet forty years of age, he began suffering distressfully from ill-health. Seeking relief from the medical schools for several years and finding none, the Kimballs embarked upon a world wide search for some specialist who could lead them to health, for Mrs. Kimball, too, was failing under the strain. But they had not gone far when Mr. Kimball's weakened condition caused them to abandon the quest and return to the United States. A sister who met their boat in New York told them about the healing of another sister through a new metaphysical science. That was the Kimballs' introduction to Christian Science in 1887.

Mrs. Kate Kimball was healed very quickly. Edward did not respond as immediately, but he persevered until he, too, had regained his health. When Mr. Kimball applied for admission to Mrs. Eddy's next Primary class in March of 1888 he was rejected, for the class was full, but once again he persevered until Mrs. Eddy finally wired: "Well — come." So both Kate and Edward Kimball were members of Mrs. Eddy's Primary class in March, 1888. They also attended the last class she taught in the college in 1889, and were both invited to be members of the Leader's final class taught in Christian Science Hall in Concord in 1898.

None of the Leader's students reached the heights that she attained or had her broad vision and understanding. Perhaps Calvin A. Frye was the closest to her in many ways, but the student who was intellectually and metaphysically closest to the Leader was Edward A. Kimball. Bicknell Young was greatly impressed by his depth of character —

> which had a certain majestic kindliness all its own, for Mr. Kimball not only had a great intellect but a great heart as well. One of his striking characteristics was the power of analysis, which in his case amounted to genius.
>
> ... naturally dignified in appearance and manner, Mr. Kimball was the most approachable of men. His native ability and breadth of vision set him apart ...
>
> His executive ability, judgment and resourcefulness were invaluable to the movement ...
>
> He could deliver extemporaneously a lecture that might have been printed practically without alteration.

Mrs. Eddy was well aware of Mr. Kimball's ability and sterling qualities, the most important of which was his absolute devotion to the cause of Christian Science and to its Founder. She had appointed Mr. Kimball chairman of the Board of Lectureship when it was formed in 1898. She had made him the Normal Teacher when the Board of Education was established in 1899. In the fall of 1899 she had transferred all her copyrights to Mr. Kimball. There was a further transfer in 1903 when the copyrights of the new revision of Science and Health and of the Concordance were also assigned to Mr. Kimball. Mr. and Mrs. Kimball travelled often from Chicago to Pleasant View, for Mrs. Eddy frequently summoned them to confer with her.

Mrs. Eddy was the primary target of the enemy's unceasing attacks, and her closest students were always in the line of fire if not targets themselves. This is very obvious in Calvin Frye's experience. Mr. Kimball, too, was in the line of fire and had much to meet.

Young students tend to think that everything is easier for advanced students. In one sense this is true, because as one advances he learns the importance of *quickly,* in agreeing "with thine adversary quickly." But the serious student soon learns that working out the problem of being is not unlike a course in mathematics. Each new page has new problems and those in the back of the book are commensurate with the student's increasing ability.

As early as 1895 Mr. Kimball and Mrs. Ewing (both outstandingly successful practitioners) had discussed the attacks upon their own health which had to be met. At the first opportunity Mr. Kimball discussed this with Mrs. Eddy and wrote Mrs. Ewing the Leader's words which were that "we would all be tested and that we might be glad that our temptations came in the way of sickness rather than sin."

At a later date he suffered such an acute attack that he wrote a fearful, despairing letter to Mrs. Eddy. She responded immediately "casting out evils" and ending her letter with the words: "I and you have grown to be honored by God with entrance into this department of learning."

William Lyman Johnson wrote: "In about 1901 statements were put forth that . . . young active blood was needed that would bring into the work the most modern type of business methods." Some of the animus back of such statements was merely ignorance, but some was a lust for place and power. By 1902 this had grown to a questioning of Mrs. Eddy's ability to such an extent that the rebellions in her church in 1881 and again in 1888 would have been repeated had it not been for the *Manual.* This aggressive element was trying once more to oust the Leader from her movement, but she had learned from past experiences how to protect her work from the destruction of mortal mind. In her words:

> I finally said, there will have to be laws to put a *stop* to this (mortal mind) work. Then I wrote the *Manual.* I never had a Church until I had the *Manual.*

A dedicated practitioner whose mother was an active worker at this time told us that in 1902 the field was ready to put both Mrs. Eddy and Mr. Kimball out of the organization. There was no more foundation to the whisperings against Mr. Kimball than there was to those against Mrs. Eddy, and it was always animal magnetism. It is very probable that Mrs. Eddy had foreseen this and had forewarned Mr. Kimball even as she had done with Edward P. Bates. If you remember, after Mr. Bates had completed the building of the Mother Church she called him to Pleasant View and said: "Are you prepared for the treatment you will receive? . . . You came here in answer to prayer. . . . you followed my demonstration and the church is finished; — but they will hate you for helping Mother. . . . They will shun you; they will try to ruin you morally, physically, financially and spiritually." Mr. Bates said he had ample proof of this within a few weeks; and it was probably this same hatred using good Christian Scientists that put Mr. Bates off the Building Committee for the Extension after Mrs. Eddy had appointed him. The most hatred and revenge was vented upon the students who helped Mother most.

All the dedicated teachers in the field taught to the best of their ability, including the two that Mrs. Eddy had selected to replace her in the Massachusetts Metaphysical College. But the requirement was beyond their understanding; hence the Leader's words: "I have never yet had a student who has reached this ability to teach; it includes more than they understand." In Mr. Kimball she had at last found a teacher who could begin to approximate her teaching, and so, of course, he had continued to be the one and only Normal Teacher on the Board of Education. And by 1902 Mr. Kimball and his teaching were both under fire along with the Leader, — targets of the hatred and revenge of malicious animal magnetism aimed at those who helped the Leader most.

God had guided Mrs. Eddy in writing the *Manual* to protect her cause against the animal magnetism which would take it over and cast her out. The by-laws put her position and her authority upon an unshakeable foundation. So by 1902 when m.a.m. would try once again to oust her from her own church, she had the necessary laws for her protection. But she had to do something to protect Mr. Kimball and his teaching.

At the communion season in 1901 and 1902 the *Sentinel* and *Journal* both included reports of the Normal class of the Board of Education taught by Edward A. Kimball. But there was no such report in 1903, because there was no Normal class. That was the first step the Leader took to meet this situation, — that is, she discontinued the Normal classes. There was, however, a meeting of the Normal graduates of the Board of Education (all of whom had been taught by Mr. Kimball) on July 1, during Communion week. Later in July Mr. Kimball wrote to Mrs. Eddy about the opposition of some of the older teachers to the newer ones that he had taught.

The Leader's second step to calm the waters was the formation of the General Association of Teachers which was to meet annually. Before their first meeting, which was held in the Mother Church on Monday, October 26 at 9 A.M., this by-law amendment was published in the *Sentinel:*

> The session of the General Association of Teachers may be held two days, closing daily not later than 6 P.M. The main topics for discussion are, *unity of action,* strict conformity to the Mother Church By-laws and to the contents of the chapter on "Teaching Christian Science" contained in Science and Health.

This call for *unity* was emphasized, and it was reemphasized in the message the Leader sent to them *(My.* 251) at their meeting in 1903:

> I call you mine, for all is thine and mine. . . . You have convened only to convince yourselves of this grand verity; namely, the unity in Christian Science. Cherish steadfastly this fact.

A letter written to Augusta Stetson on October 25 ended with: "I hope the Teachers' Association will be harmonious and my rules for their best interest will be unitedly adopted and followed."

Late in the summer of 1903 Mr. McLellan had written Mrs. Eddy at some length about all his editorial problems. Her reply of August 29 began:

> I deeply sympathize with you in all you wrote. I would quickly, joyfully give you a rule for each need wherewith to supply it, but God alone can do this and He will do it. Ask for wisdom of Him, the divine Love and you will receive it and as ye pray *believe* and it shall be done unto you are the words of our Master.

A few weeks later, on the eighteenth of October she extended the following invitation to Mr. McLellan:

> Beloved Student,
>
> You being a member of the C.S. Board of Directors and our Editor, I extend to you an invitation to attend the annual meeting of the Teachers' Association this month.

Mind had not directed the Leader to discontinue either the Board of Education or Mr. Kimball's teaching, so she had him teach a class in October, but designated it a Primary class. She also invited Mr. and Mrs. McLellan to attend the *next* class Mr. Kimball would teach under the Board of Education which was scheduled to begin December 1. Before this class began Mr. Kimball wrote the Leader and she responded on November 26:

> My honored and *beloved* Student:
> Do not think that I doubt your loyalty and *strict* fidelity. O no far from it! . . . I think, owing to the one you name in this last letter, that it is best for you not to locate at present in Boston, and for sake of Truth to teach in the Board but two classes annually. This is better than more would be at present. Our cause demands *better* healers; and if less teaching classes is enjoined more practitioners will be fitted by the book to heal. I see the need of a healer to be as excluded from other work in Christian Science as for the M.D. Who would look for a successful M.D. who was a lawyer or that was a teacher by profession and practising teaching? A jack at all trades is good for none is an old adage. I am sorely disappointed in the demonstration of C.S. and it must improve or our cause will float into theory and we will not "show our faith by our works." A chatterer of C.S. is never a healer.

Some of the members of the December class in addition to the McLellans were Judge Ewing, Judge and Mrs. Clifford P. Smith, Bliss Knapp, and Mr. and Mrs. William Rathvon. The teacher related an interesting experience to this class which was a help to them in their own work. He said that:

> Soon after he issued invitations to a college class, he began to feel a pain in the back, which he handled as a pain in the back for three days consecutively, but unsuccessfully. Then he demanded the intelligence God gave him, by which he could know instantaneously whatever he needed to know. Right away it occurred to him that several hundred disappointed ones, realizing that their applications to the Board of Education had been turned down, were beginning to express themselves quite freely towards the teacher, with thoughts of resentment, hurt feelings, anger, and malicious criticism, disappointed ambition, and the like. Well, when he began to protect himself from projected anger, resentment, hate, and so forth, that pain in the back stopped right away.

Mr. Kimball's students loved him dearly, and so did his Teacher. But she knew that the field in general was seething with jealousy and resentment that was largely unvoiced but that would break forth with fury if she was not there to hold it in check. Something more must be done for this beloved student's protection. God led her to extend the step she had already initiated with a by-law:

> ARTICLE XXII. NO MORE STUDENTS. Sect. 7. The Board of Education will receive no more students in the Normal class for three years from this date, December 8, 1903.

CHAPTER XVI

THE SPIRE WHICH REACHES HEAVEN

The Church is that institution, which affords proof of its utility and is found elevating the race ... — MARY BAKER EDDY

Institution: A textbook. — WEBSTER

1903

THE work of a dedicated student in New Bern, North Carolina came to fruition in the fall of 1903. The lies of a calumniator regarding the life of Mary Baker Glover and her husband George Washington Glover in North and South Carolina in the 1840's had led Mary Hatch Harrison to discover the facts for herself. The historical records she uncovered were published in the *Wilmington Dispatch* of October 24, 1903. Then Miss Harrison's letter and related historical data *(My.* 329) were published in the Christian Science periodicals in November and December. Mrs. Eddy's instructions to Calvin Frye resulted in this letter to Irving C. Tomlinson:

> Dear Brother Tomlinson:
> Mrs. Eddy says please select the Christian Science literature that should go into the box in the cornerstone for the church at New Bern, N. C., and request Mr. Armstrong to send it to them, and for him to send the bill for same to Mrs. Eddy.

A news item in the *New Bern Journal* a few weeks later stated:

> The Christian Scientists of this city are in receipt of a rich New Year's gift from Mrs. Mary Baker G. Eddy, the great Leader of the Scientists.
> The gift was three thousand dollars which is to be used in the erection of the Scientists' new church in New Bern. ...

On the seventeenth of October Henrietta Chanfrau recorded a

watch in which Mrs. Eddy said: "When will blind eyes see their Leader as she is?" At this same time, while Miss Harrison was working in North Carolina, Mrs. Stetson and her students were working diligently in New York for the dedication of their new edifice. On October 22 Mrs. Eddy wrote to Mrs. Stetson:

> I have taken deep thought on the subject of your telegram and as I understand it, God gave me the answer that I have sent herewith to your church . . .

The answer which the Leader sent to First Church, New York read as follows:

> My beloved brethren:
> What if your church edifice in the far future be desecrated and used by others? Then your inscription "to the glory of God" would be a stumbling block. I advise you not to engrave that assertion on stone but write it on your hearts, and demonstrate it in your glorious lives; let it be at present a silent desire and God will reward the prayer. A declaration before a preparation of the heart is a hindrance to advancement. The Scriptures say, "The preparation of the heart and the answer of the tongue is *from* the *Lord.*" . . .

The churches were blessed by the Leader's messages of guidance and instruction sent to her faithful followers. It would seem that malicious animal magnetism was seeking always to separate these followers from their Leader as is evident in this notice from Mrs. Eddy dated November 13:

> Take Notice
> I hereby notify the public that scurrilous letters purporting to bear my signature — letters of evil intent — that I never wrote, never caused to be written, and never saw until they were given to me by the individuals to whom they were superscribed, are constantly being circulated. But those who know me, know that I never wrote them.

The November *Sentinel* in which this notice was published also contained the following written on the same date by Calvin Frye:

> Counterfeit Letters
> I learn that letters have been received by persons, purporting to bear my signature, making complaint against them; one of those declares I had consulted a lawyer for Mrs. Eddy on what I complained of. I never had consulted a lawyer relative to the subject named. I never wrote those letters nor knew anything about them until said parties sent one of those counterfeit letters for me to

examine.

The denial of such falsehood was but the first step and was followed by this lesson of November 17 preserved by Lewis Strang:

> To my Household at Pleasant View: The rules of this house do not permit of evil being spoken, thought or heard. Love rules this and every hour. M.a.m. is without power, powerless. Darkness is nothing. Mind is All, God is All and His voice is heard in all places. God judges and His judgment is sound and righteous. Know this now and every hour. . . . no malicious animal magnetism to lie or hear a lie. God reigns and loveth whom He chasteneth. No work is done until I say it is and no student will forsake his post in any moment. God is Love, Love is All. Truth reigns.

Later in November the Leader sent a message to First Church in New York City *(My.* 193) for the dedication of their beautiful $1,250,000 edifice on November 29. Perhaps her second paragraph pointed toward the future she foresaw for Mrs. Stetson and her church:

> The letter of your work dies, as do all things material, but the spirit of it is immortal. Remember that a temple but foreshadows the idea of God, the "house not made with hands, eternal in the heavens," while a silent, grand man or woman, healing sickness and destroying sin, builds that which reaches heaven. . . .

Also in November the New York Central Christian Science Reading Room Association opened a Central Reading Room under the auspices of representatives from Second, Third, Fourth, and Fifth churches of New York. This brought a great deal of criticism upon Mrs. Stetson and upon First Church which was conspicuously absent from the joint venture. The critics had no way of knowing that Mrs. Eddy had written to Mrs. Stetson on October 25:

> I did not get your last letter in time to reply before you left N.Y. — to your question on selling my books down town in your city. That movement would be unwise in many ways and would not prosper, abandon such a thought. You have fulfilled the By-law in our Church relation to a Reading Room: and it only remains for you to carry on your Reading Room and for the down towners to unite and have a Reading Room that is centrally located. This is what must be done.

The Leader was intentionally separating her beloved Augusta and causing her to stand alone. Often it was not easy for Mrs. Stetson to do this. It is possible that the joint venture Reading Room was her idea in the first place, but her obedience to the

Leader was instant and unquestioning.

Ever and always the Leader was pointing to *healing* as her true church. And she was *always* demonstrating this true church in all of her affairs. One such healing in 1903 was that of a seminary student, E. N. Lamour. As acting pastor of the Methodist Episcopal church at Bow, New Hampshire, young Mr. Lamour sent out an appeal for funds to repair their church building. The response to this appeal which he received from Mrs. Eddy was not at first appreciated. She had offered to contribute fifty dollars toward a bell if they could raise the balance of the cost, — an expense and project they had not even considered. However, others soon pledged the difference which amounted to ninety-five dollars, and Mrs. Eddy was so notified. Her response this time, a check for one hundred dollars, confused the young pastor who called at Pleasant View to learn her intentions.

She explained that fifty dollars was toward the bell and the other fifty dollars was for repairs. And he explained, in answer to her query, that he could not see a thing without the heavy glasses he was wearing. When he got home from Pleasant View that day, he found that he could not read a thing, — until he took his glasses off! A half century later his wife wrote that from the time of his visit with Mrs. Eddy in 1903, Mr. Lamour's eyesight was perfect and remained so for the rest of his life.

On December 3, 1903, Mrs. Eddy answered the telegram from Mrs. Stetson and her church officers in which they presented her with their new edifice. In declining this munificent gift *(My.* 194) Mrs. Eddy said that she would "gratefully accept the spirit of it." One more letter from the Leader to Mrs. Stetson in December said: "My precious Student: Read S.& H., page 576 and read through that chapter." Could this have been one more effort to turn this student away from the temple made with hands? Page 576 in Science and Health states: "There was no temple, — that is, no material structure in which to worship God, for He must be worshipped in spirit and in love." Her true church was embodied in her textbook. To Mr. McLellan she wrote in December: "Advertise always on this circular Science and Health with Key to the Scriptures." This could probably apply to most if not all of the leaflets they published.

The gift of a beautiful otter robe brought the Leader "warmth without weight" on her daily drives, and she thanked the donor graciously:

Dec. 6, 1903

Mr. Carpenter, C.S.B.
Beloved Student:

Each day when sitting under the warmth of the fine fur robe you gave me I say, What a nice thing it is, would that the good giver of it knew how comfortable it makes me and I will write it to him. This is my thanks to such a soul as thine who loves to do good. God bless you with the heavenly robe of righteousness and its sweet rewards.

Sincerely yours,
Mary Baker Eddy

A December news item about the ground occupied by New Harlem in New York City included this dispatch from Mary Baker Eddy to the *New York Herald:*

Over an article on the above subject published in the *World,* November 27, you said: "The followers of Mrs. Eddy plan to establish a New Jerusalem here." Allow me to state I knew nothing of the Harlem movement until recently when receiving a book written on the subject. Said book I have not read, and am not at all concerned in the history of New Harlem, or the building of a new Jerusalem, since, as I apprehend it, the New Jerusalem "cometh down from heaven," and is not an outcome of litigation. Christian Scientists are not, to my knowledge, interested in locating heaven, but in finding it within themselves.

Part of the lesson for the workers at Pleasant View on December 7 was: "What we most need is wisdom. . . . God is Father and Mother — one; the Christ reflects the male and female Principle — one — not two. The end of the belief in male and female as two, will be when woman stops child-bearing." And on December 17 she told them: "It was not the material cross that killed Jesus, but it was the desertion of his students that killed him."

During Christmas week the *Concord Evening Monitor* reported:

At the Unitarian Church on Sunday a Christmas gift of three hundred dollars from Mrs. Mary Baker G. Eddy was announced and was acknowledged by a rising vote of thanks. During the erection of their new church the Christian Scientists of this city have been worshipping in the Unitarian edifice.

The Leader's Christmas lesson to her household workers in 1903 was:

Let us take "heart" as a token of our Christmas; the great heart of Christ; it is the palpitating presence encircling the universe; it is the only intelligence, and that is what? Love. Could there be anything greater?

A few days before this, on December 21, Mrs. Eddy had executed a new deed for the two lots on which the publishing rooms stood and which would soon be used for the Extension of the Mother Church. This new deed contained the further trusts regarding "no new tenet or by-law" and also the wording "Mary Baker G. Eddy's Church etc." Perhaps these "commandments" were in her thought when she wrote a Christmas letter to her Board of Directors:

December 27, 1903

My beloved Students:

May this dear Christmas season be to you a Christ risen, a morn, the break of day. There is nothing jubilant attached to the birth of a mortal— that suffers and pays the penalty of his parents' misconception of man and of God's creation. But there is a joy unutterable in knowing that Christ had no birth, no death, and that we may find in Christ, in the true sense of being, life apart from birth, sorrow, sin and death. O may your eyes not be holden, but may you discern spiritually what is our Redeemer.

I thank you, dear ones, for your kind remembrance of me — the most lone and perhaps the most loved and hated of earth! May you watch and pray that you keep the Commandments, and live the Sermon in the Mount this coming year. Watch, too, that you keep the *commandments* that experience has compelled to be written for your guidance and the safety of Christian Science in our Church Manual.

CHAPTER XVII

CONSTANCY

I pray daily for all the members of my church and hope and pray they will lead in healing the sick, more than in teaching or church making. — MARY BAKER EDDY

1904

THE genesis of the change in teaching Christian Science can be seen in Mrs. Eddy's letter to Edward A. Kimball of November 26, 1903 wherein she had written: "Our cause demands *better healers;* and if less teaching classes is enjoined more practitioners will be fitted by the book to heal." By January she was thinking in terms of rotation in office for the teacher of the Board of Education; however, the Board of Education was only one of the many things demanding the Leader's attention at the dawn of 1904. She may have written to other students as she did to Augusta Stetson on the first day of the new year:

> My beloved Student:
> On this first day of the New Year, I send you my love and prayers for the divine Love's rich blessings to enfold you in the arms of His protective wisdom and guidance.
> Ever yours tenderly,

On January 8 she wrote to her Trustee, William P. McKenzie, of her Publishing Society:

> I gave my C.S. Journal to the Publishing Society on the grounds that it should be well conducted etc. Now I ask you to see that we have more that is understandable and interesting to the general public ... No matter about the cost of it, but I insist that such writers as Judge Jones, M. K. Kains, Mr. Samuel Greenwood, Mrs. Mims of Atlanta, Edward A. Kimball, Rev. Vosburgh etc. be employed and paid as contributors to our periodicals and *constant* contributions be had from them.

On a Saturday in January the Leader called Mr. Kimball to Pleasant View and told him about her idea for rotation in office for the teacher of the Board of Education. He wrote her the next week:

> Three years ago you told me that you were very desirous of getting Judge Hanna out of office and out of Boston. . . . I resolved that if I ever got the slightest hint of the kind concerning myself I would make short work of it by speedily getting out of the way.
>
> The problem which you had with Judge Hanna was solved by a by-law which terminated his official tenure and precluded by means of the 3 year rule the possibility of his continuance.
>
> Last Saturday, you told me you were going to put into effect the same rule concerning the teacher of the Board of Education and I construe this as a possible hint to me. . . . Considering our educational system which is in great need of uniformity and stability, I hardly think you would provide for frequent changes in the teaching, except because of unusual stress.
>
> The annals of the race make no mention of anyone whose tasks were so severe, so continuous and complex as yours are. . . . I greatly long for your peace, for the more tranquil flow of your life, and I want you to know, my dear dear friend, that there is not an atom of disposition on my part to stand in the way. You do not need to take any unusual or radical step on my account, dear Mother. I know what it means to ascend the cross and have the nails driven into me. The one who craves position, power or emolument in the Cause of Christian Science is mad. There is nothing that I want except a chance to pray and repent. . . . Your ways are higher than mine and I do not clearly see the way. . . .

The Leader seldom told her students *why* she took the steps she took. She followed the direction from God, sometimes not knowing herself until afterward why she was directed to take a certain course. Even when she did know, she *never* tried to explain her actions to her students, knowing that those who cared enough to trace her footsteps would find out her reasons for themselves in due time. Her ways were higher than those of her students. Those endeavoring to make their own ways higher can appreciate the words she wrote to one of her secretaries on January 21: "I have no hope in earthly ways and means; God has pointed my path higher. O for the eagle's wings, the power divine, to mount to Thee!"

Many of the lessons Mrs. Eddy gave to her household in January were on watching and learning what *watching* means. A letter to Augusta Stetson on January 20 could have been in response to the Leader's message from God when she opened her Bible that morning; it was a "watch" message to Augusta:

> Do you recognize the need you have to watch and pray that your

true sense of God and of His anointed be not taken away from you? Read Jesus' words to Peter when he said "Satan desired" so and so. Watch darling, that you be not demoralized as some others are to forget your duty to me who has laid herself on the altar and all of this world — for you and for all — to serve Christ and to drink his cup for the salvation of the race. May God in His dear Love hold you in His arms, show you the way and enable you to see the temptation and to overcome it — is the prayer of her who loves you and who cannot lose her love for you through temptation.

Mrs. Stetson was not the only student who received messages to "watch," and often the "watches" sent to her best and most earnest and dedicated students were requests to work on some specific problem. She wrote to Hannah Larminie that the Cause would have been lost if such watches had not been kept in Boston. The righteous prayers the Leader sent to several students she denominated "watch prayers" in accordance with Jesus' instructions: "And what I say unto you I say unto all, Watch" (Mark 13:37). "And this know, that if the goodman of the house had known what hour the thief would come, he would have watched, and not have suffered his house to be broken through" (Luke 12:39). The chosen students in Boston who worked thus for the cause were called Watchers, and following is a watch prayer they were using early in 1904:

THE PRAYER OF THE WATCHERS — The effect of this prayer *is not reversed.* God, good reigns; there is *no other mind.*

Love reigns; there is no envy no revenge.

All things are working together for good to those that love good.

We do love good, God, and He gives us all our thoughts, and governs all our acts.

The divine Love preserves our Life and health, and they cannot be taken from Christian Scientists, and Christian Scientists cannot be made sinful.

We love God and God loves us and is guiding us every moment.

This prayer cannot be reversed.

This prayer bears fruit after its own kind, it does good, and blesses us and all others.

(Charge them not to change, add to, or diminish this prayer. Something is out of tune. This will be a chord.)

This watch prayer together with the instruction for the watchers was sent to William B. Johnson, but its use was discontinued on March 6 because another of her officials in Boston was managing the watchers to some extent which she said must not be done.

On the third of March Mrs. Eddy had executed another deed covering two of the parcels of land on which the Extension was to be built. This deed included the further trusts regarding "no new tenet or by-law" and "Mary Baker G. Eddy's Church" already included in some of the other deeds. In addition it included this further stipulation:

> Nothing in this deed contained shall *ever** be construed as a waiver or as permitting a modification in any degree of any of the trusts and conditions as the same are now established and exist under and by virtue of the deeds above described. I do further declare that nothing herein contained shall ever be construed as a waiver or as permitting a modification in any degree of the further trusts set forth in deed of Albert Metcalf to Ira O. Knapp and others dated March 19, 1903 . . .

The Leader was giving much thought to the *future* of her church. But she was also required to give her attention to its present status. At the time of the building of the original Mother Church mortal man was determined that the Founder should neither buy nor sell nor *build* without the mark of the beast. But God led her in the wording of her deed of trust to bind mortal man. During the controversy that ensued she wrote to Aususta Stetson:

> It is just awful that the Trustees have not started to build our Church. The land I conveyed for the *perpetual* use of this Church is now valued at 20,000 dollars! God has so arranged this conveyance that while the enemy saith "none shall buy or sell that hath not the mark of the beast" — He saith none shall *sell* that hath the mark of the *lamb!* And this is the poser to future speculation over my lot and the church building that troubles the builder.

A fierce battle was waged, and one of her trustees left in wrath, but the spiritual foundation was firm and stood fast. And every step of the building of the edifice was a demonstration. Now, in 1904, these founding footsteps in stone needed further protection, for it would appear that the architects were entertaining the idea of tearing down the original Mother Church edifice in their plans for the Extension. On March 18 the Leader sent this message to Henrietta Chanfrau:

> . . . take up the architects that God may open their eyes to the terrible sin they contemplate. The Mother Church is founded on *Truth* and cannot be removed nor taken down. Mother knows days and nights of anguished prayer that none know aught of, lest the sheepfold be taken down wherein the lambs are sheltered. Weary in days of trial but freshened in His service, she waits till all unworthy ones come neath the shadow of His wing.

In addition to having students work for the architects, the Mother felt it necessary to protect her Mother Church edifice erected in

*Emphasis added.

1894 with a by-law *(Man.* 103) which was published in the *Sentinel* early in March. On March 11 when Mrs. Eddy was occupied with these church concerns, Calvin Frye answered an urgent but sad letter from Rev. Tomlinson regarding a case of death:

> if the case was under my care I should make careful examination to find out if there is not a faint *trace of life there,* before removing the remains, by the employment of an expert because the case was peculiar. . . .

The case was that of Mrs. Mary Munroe who had first studied with Mrs. Eddy more than twenty years earlier and had been an earnest worker in the cause ever since. She and her husband had purchased one of the lots of land for the Extension and held it until the directors were ready for it. At the time of her passing away in 1904 Mrs. Munroe was a member of the most vital of the Committees, the Bible Lesson Committee. The Leader sent to her editor a Song *(Po.* 3) which she had written many years earlier, for publication in the next *Journal:*

CONSTANCY

WHEN starlight blends with morning's hue,
I miss thee as the flower the dew!
When noonday's length'ning shadows flee,
I think of thee, I think of thee!

With evening, memories reappear —
I watch thy chair, and wish thee here;
Till sleep sets drooping fancy free
To dream of thee, to dream of thee!

Since first we met, in weal or woe
It hath been thus; and must be so
Till bursting bonds our spirits part
And Love divine doth fill my heart.

Mrs. Eddy was very appreciative of Mr. Frye and all the work he did for her and the cause. In her lesson to her household on February 16 she had said:

> . . . We *say* Spirit is All and then when we have to take our choice between Spirit and the flesh we cry, the flesh, the flesh. God is coming very near to us; is making demands upon us. Mr. Frye made his choice twenty-one years ago and since then has been having his experience, and if he should pass now would waken to glorified being. . . .

In a notebook she kept, Mrs. Eddy wrote: "March 12, 1904, I gave as a present to Calvin A. Frye 5,000 dollars . . . Mary B. G. Eddy." On the same day Calvin recorded in his diary: "Mrs. Eddy presented me today with a check for $5000, saying, when she handed it to me, 'This is a love-gift, Calvin.'"

But neither Calvin nor any other student had the wisdom and perspicacity of the Leader. On the twelfth of January she had written to Bliss Knapp that she wanted him to become a lecturer. Bliss had graduated from Harvard three years before and had what he described as "an extreme case of bashfulness." Calvin Frye warned Mrs. Eddy that it was a mistake to place one so young and timid and fearful on the Board of Lectureship, but she knew better. Although she did not know what would transpire before his appointment on May 5.

At the age of twenty Carol Norton had been healed of a serious illness by one Christian Science treatment, and almost as immediately had left a thriving business to devote himself to the study and practice of Christian Science. He was only 27 years of age when the Board of Lectureship was formed in 1898 and Mrs. Eddy appointed him one of the five first lecturers. He was a successful, popular lecturer and had covered a good deal of territory on his tours, speaking to large audiences and small from Maine to California and also up into Canada. Mr. Norton was in Chicago early in April when news came to Boston that he had died suddenly. Mrs. Eddy wrote to Mr. McLellan:

> Have a short, true, impressive obituary in your next issues of our weekly and monthly, of our beloved student, friend, brother, Carol Norton.

Sister thoughts to the "song" she had published so recently for Mrs. Munroe came to the Leader, and she wrote this poem *(Po.* 25) which was published in the *Sentinel* of May 21:

FLOWERS

Mirrors of morn
Whence the dewdrop is born,
Soft tints of the rainbow and skies —
Sisters of song,
What a shadowy throng
Around you in memory rise!

Far do ye flee,
From your green bowers free,
Fair floral apostles of love,
Sweetly to shed

Fragrance fresh round the dead,
And breath of the living above.

Flowers for the brave —
Be he monarch or slave,
Whose heart bore its grief and is still!
Flowers for the kind —
Aye, the Christians who wind
Wreaths for the triumphs o'er ill!

This was probably written for Carol Norton's sweet wife of only three years who was doubly bereaved, for she had lost her baby very shortly before the loss of her husband. But the Leader did more for the stricken young widow. She sent for Mrs. Norton that she might comfort her. In later years Elizabeth Norton recalled that meeting at Pleasant View:

> I shall never forget the first time I talked with her. She had sent for me to call upon her. On entering the room she extended her hand and asked me to be seated. I walked across the room and sat down in a chair. Mrs. Eddy very deliberately arranged her dress and sat down on a sofa. She looked at me so tenderly and patting the sofa beside herself, she said, "You are too far away from Mother, darling." I immediately went to her. She took me in her arms and kissed me. She was not afraid to express her love humanly, and I did not mistake it, for I learned then and there that divine Love must be expressed humanly in order to heal the broken-hearted. Oh, let us all learn to love as did this precious Christ-idea. Let us love her because she first loved us by teaching us that Life is Love and Love is Life. She is our Mother in Israel and is still saying to us all, "You are too far away from Mother, darling."

The Mother in Israel sent a letter of instruction to her board of directors on April 9 in which she said:

> I recommend that you fill the vacancy on Lesson Committee with Mrs. Knott. She will have time apart from her office as Assistant Editor to fill this office of our late lamented sister. For lecturer to take the place of the dear departed Mr. Norton, I name Mr. Clarence A. Buskirk of Princeton, Ind. . . .
>
> Watch the field; it needs watching. . . . There is not time for the new teacher in the Board of Education to get up a class in May next. Write Mr. Kimball that he must teach this class. . . .

But neither Mr. Kimball nor any other teacher taught a Board of Education class in May, for the Leader's attention was demanded by another issue and she needed Mr. Kimball's help in that direction.

Following the World's Parliament of Religions at the World's Fair in Chicago in 1893 opposition from other Christian denominations intensified. Mrs. Eddy had written in one of her letters at that time:

> The Catholic priests call at my door and demand to know if I have any Catholic help. All the help of that kind I have had they take away from me. It would seem since the World's Fair that they are afraid of the power of Christian Scientists and would exterminate the Leader.

In April of 1904 Mrs. Eddy received a letter from the Pope in Rome asking her to have her followers stop teaching *"his subjects"* Christian Science. He also stated that he was sending his emissary to see her. The Mother in Israel called *her* emissary, Edward A. Kimball, to Pleasant View and instructed him for his mission to New York, which was to intercept the Roman Catholic Cardinal when he arrived in that city and to dispose of the issue there.

The settling of the issue was the new by-law the Leader wrote *(Man.* 87) which appeared in the *Sentinel* of April 30: "Neither the Pastor Emeritus nor a member of this Church shall teach Roman Catholics Christian Science, except it be with the written consent of the authority of their Church."

We have covered only a tithe of the issues demanding the Leader's attention early in 1904. Everything the Mother in Israel said or did was challenged and lied about by the world. The serpent was *ever* at the heel of the Woman. One minor issue was a McNeil ancestor.

When Mrs. Eddy first wrote her autobiographical *Retrospection and Introspection,* it began with "Voices Not Our Own," which is now the eighth page; and it continued that way through several editions for several years. The seven pages about her family and ancestors was a later addition, perhaps to refute the lies heaped upon her and her background. She sent the following, which was published in the March 12, 1904 *Sentinel* to Editor McLellan telling him to sign his name if agreeable and send no more proof:

> A Correction
>
> Some years ago a relative of our Leader and Teacher, the Rev. Mary Baker G. Eddy, a member of the McNeil family from which Mrs. Eddy descended, reported that the Right Hon. Sir John McNeill, G.C.B. of Edinburgh, Scotland, was her ancestor.
>
> The source of information seemed to be authentic, and the statement was accepted and used in good faith by writers on Mrs. Eddy's genealogy. Mrs. Eddy has had this matter carefully investigated and

having obtained no positive proof that the Right Hon. Sir John McNeill was her ancestor, she requests that all others writing upon her biography shall in future observe this correction.

General John McNeil, who is known as the hero of Lundy's Lane, was a relative on Mrs. Eddy's father's side of the Baker family. And he was the brother of President Pierce's mother. This is probably the line of McNeils to which Mrs. Eddy belongs. Mrs. Eddy herself has no special interest in these subjects.

Archibald McLellan

It is interesting to note that though Mrs. Eddy wrote the above to appease the challenges of the world, she did *not* change her statement regarding her Macneill ancestry in *Retrospection and Introspection.* The world would keep the Woman always answering its challenges and lies ever endeavoring to keep her away from God's work if it could. A month before the McNeil question she had written McLellan on another issue:

> In this instance you had better take no notice of those clippings from newspapers and thus stop the matter. A reply will invite new charges or attempts to vindicate those already made.

But later the same day she wrote him again: "I enclose your article so that you can publish it if the newspapers keep up firing. It is well prepared and you may have to use it."

For nearly a decade thousands of people had visited and or attended Mrs. Eddy's church in Boston. During that same period a handful of people had found her "structure of Truth and Love" at Pleasant View, — the hub of the wheel, the center of all spiritual activity. This center of spiritual activity was her true church and was not found in the beautiful edifice in Boston or any other city. At a later date Mrs. Eddy said to her household at Pleasant View: "There is one thing needed all over the field and which is only supplied here, and might not be supplied in the field in centuries . . . " Pleasant View was a citadel safeguarding her spiritual church. In 1903 Mrs. Eddy had begun making the *Manual* her citadel for the safeguarding of her spiritual church in future generations, and on March 11 in 1904 her last deed stating that "nothing . . . shall ever be construed as a waiver or as permitting a modification in any degree" was recorded. This deed also tied these restrictions to the deed from Metcalf to Knapp etal in the *Manual.*

Mrs. Eddy knew that Calvin Frye and the others named in her will could not continue Pleasant View as she ran it. Now that the *Manual* was her citadel for the future she could release the future of Pleasant View which she did on May 14 with another codicil to her will.*

*Mary Baker Eddy's will in Appendix B.

One of the new by-laws in the spring of 1904 was intended to keep Christian Scientists spreading the gospel to all the world rather than talking only to one another. When a group of New York businessmen formed a New York Christian Science Lunch Club which invited prominent Scientists to address their luncheon meetings, Mrs. Eddy wrote to the Lathrops, John and his mother Laura: "If you go into clubs you go out of the church in spirit." This was followed by a by-law (Article XXVI) in the April 23 *Sentinel* titled:

> CHURCH ORGANIZATION AMPLE. Sect. 14. Members of the Mother Church shall not be made members of clubs or organizations, the Free Masons excepted, which exclude either sex or are not named in the Manual of the Mother Church. God separates the tares and the wheat to garner the latter in His storehouse.

A card published three weeks later stated:

> Thanking the courteous Christian Science lunchers for their respectful attention to our denominational By-law on clubs and organizations, I beg to say: Said By-law prohibits neither informal meetings nor luncheons and select, invited guests.
>
> Mary B. G. Eddy
>
> May 6, 1904

This new by-law caused a good deal of consternation together with a great many resignations, causing Mrs. Eddy to issue this further notice:

> I beg to inform my beloved members of the Mother Church that the By-law in Article XXVI of its Manual does not require members of the benevolent and progressive organizations, such as the Free Masons, Odd Fellows, temperance societies, and those of similar cult, to resign their membership. It specifies in plain English that after individuals become members of our Church, they shall not *thereafter* "be made" members of clubs or other organizations not named in its Manual, and wherefore? Because our religious denomination demands the faithful attention and labor of its members in all philanthropic, therapeutic, and progressive Christian work for the human race, and relies upon the adequate, scientific Source and resource therefor.

The press remarked freely and usually quite critically upon everything that Mrs. Eddy said or did. But upon this by-law there was a good deal of favorable press comment, — the following from the *Topeka Daily Herald:*

> Viewed wholly from the standpoint of church management this

> ruling makes an interesting study. At a time when the orthodox churches of this country have had a very hard time to make any pronounced growth, the Christian Science church has in a little over thirty years secured one million adherents and built some of the most valuable church property in existence. That its material growth and development are due more to the wisdom of Mrs. Eddy than to any other cause is very generally conceded. As a church builder, she has proven herself to be a genius. For this reason any new method adopted by the church of which she is the accepted head becomes of interest to those who seek the cause for retarded growth in other churches.

In May Mr. Johnson wrote to Mrs. Eddy asking permission to resume the "watch prayer" that had been discontinued on March 6. He stated that since its discontinuance the death rate of church members had been very high. Mrs. Eddy stated in her response:

> Have the "Watchers" use that prayer so long as it works well. I find that the law of mesmerism that relies on *reversing* the effect of Truth, is sometimes forgotten and in this case it does not work well. . . . Please have the dear "Watchers" resume the prayer you sent to me at once and charge them to let no one know it but yourself.

Mr. Carpenter, who preserved this record, added an interesting comment: "It will always be helpful to know that in those early days a few watchers working in the one Mind could help to destroy the fear of death for the entire organization, as long as they handled the claim of reversal."

There was no Board of Education class held in May of 1904, but there was a very interesting notice in the *Sentinel* of May 14 entitled "Christian Science Board of Education," Which also appeared in the June *Journal.* The first paragraph has been reprinted in *Miscellany* beginning on page 246 line 30. The closing paragraph reads:

> The long term of the incumbent teacher in the Board of Education, Mr. Edward A. Kimball, C.S.D., expires in June next, when he retires crowned with honors — his Teacher and Leader loving him, his students praising him, and the race benefited by his labors. May his successor go and do likewise.

By this statement the Leader was solidifying the status of Mr. Kimball and his teaching for all time to come. But the future of her Board of Education was still undecided.

CHAPTER XVIII

BUILD ON THE ROCK

I have put on paper enough to reveal criminal magnetism and to meet its developments for time to come. — MARY BAKER EDDY

1904

IN 1900 a by-law in the *Manual* had stated: "The Communion shall be observed by this Church anually on the Sunday following the second Monday in June". In 1901 the Woodbury lawsuit had caused the date of Communion Sunday to be changed several times before it was finally held on June 23. In 1902 it was again on the Sunday following the second Monday; but in 1903 the by-law was changed to make Communion Sunday the last Sunday in June.

Communion season was looked upon by many as the most important event of the year. It was always a difficult time for the Leader, — perhaps because so much worldly thought was focused upon her. Or perhaps malicious thoughts were intentionally directed against her and her followers at the time that thousands of Christian Scientists congregated in Boston. Whatever the reason, the Leader was directed to change the date on short notice, which she did on more than one occasion. In time, the *Manual* stated that annual meetings were to be held the Tuesday following Communion Sunday in June, but no mention at all was made regarding which Sunday was to be Communion Sunday. Obviously flexibility was a necessity at this busy season. In 1904 there was a further attempt to lessen the busy-ness of communion season. A notice in the April *Journal* had stated:

> Many inquiries regarding the Communion and Annual Meeting of the Mother Church are being received, therefore it seems best to announce to all that a general gathering such as has taken place in past years is not contemplated this year. When our church edifice is built then you can better afford the cost of coming. . . .

On the seventh of June Mrs. Eddy wrote the following which may be related to the news clippings she had told Mr. McLellan to ignore a few months earlier:

> THE MENTAL MURDERERS
>
> Their published boast, in 1903, that Mary Baker G. Eddy would never again meet with her church is not fulfilled. She deems it wise for her church not to visit her home at each Communion season. Also, the less ceremony we include in our worship the better. Hence I hereby notify my beloved brethren that I shall not attend the church dedications, but, as usual, remain at home working and praying for the prosperity of Zion.
>
> The mental assassins are in God's hands, and He will uncover their crimes and punish them in His own good time and way. Let us obey Jesus' command, to bless our enemies, and do good to them that despitefully use us. Mary B. G. Eddy
>
> Pleasant View, Concord, N. H., June 7, 1904

The foregoing was published in the *Sentinel* of June 11 and in the July, 1904 *Christian Science Journal*. Perhaps the public boast of the mental murderers had something to do with changing the date of Communion Sunday in 1904; but whatever the reason, it was not held on the last Sunday, but on June 12, the second Sunday in June. Just before communion season the Leader wrote a most interesting letter to Mr. McLellan:

> June 1, 1904
>
> Beloved Editor: In your excellent article "The Question of Omnipotence" [C.S.S. 5/21/04] you contradict your assertions. Pardon me, but reread it and you will find you wrote that evil is not "something that enjoys, *suffers* or is real." Then again you speak of evil "as a mirage that *misleads* the traveler."
>
> Who is the traveler that is *misled* and must suffer for it? who but the evil so-called, and does not evil destroy itself through its own lie, namely a belief in evil, sin, *suffering* and death? Yes it does, in belief, and to sever it from this doom would be an evil of itself.

Another letter of import was written on the same day, — this one to Augusta Stetson and her church. The first time the Leader saw Mrs. Stetson in 1884 she had said to her: "You are going to do a great work in Christian Science." In a letter in 1891 Mrs. Eddy wrote to Augusta: Oh dearest, precious child, how much you have done and will yet do for our cause, none knows but me." In 1904 still none but the Mother knew what Augusta would yet do for the cause of Christian Science, but her letter of June 1 *(My.* 165) thanking the New York church for their gift to the Concord church, was elevating and fortifying Mrs. Stetson for this mission:

> ... goodness identifies man with universal good. Thus may each member of this church rise above the oft-repeated inquiry, What am I? to the scientific response: I am able to impart truth, health, and happiness, and this is my rock of salvation and my reason for existing.
>
> ... God grant that this church is rapidly nearing the maximum of might, — the means that build to the heavens, — that it has indeed found and felt the infinite source where is *all,* and from which it can help its neighbor. Then efforts to be great will never end in anarchy but will continue with divine approbation. ...
>
> Religions may waste away, but the fittest survives, and so long as we have the right ideal, life is worth living and God takes care of our life.

These words would be a great comfort to Mrs. Stetson in her days of trial, but in June of 1904 she was looking forward, as were thousands of other Scientists, to the communion season in Boston. The Leader's communion message to her church was little more than: "Already I have said to you all that you are able to bear now," followed by the words of the excellent hymn:

I love to tell the story,
Of unseen things above, ...

Those who had been disappointed by the Leader's notice of discontinuing the visits to Pleasant View were somewhat recompensed by her letter of June 11 which was received during the progress of the first service and read at the close of each of the Communion services:

> *Beloved Students:* The new Concord church is so nearly completed that I think you would enjoy seeing it. Therefore I hereby invite all my church communicants who attend this communion, to come to Concord, and view this beautiful structure, at two o'clock in the afternoon, Monday, June 13, 1904.

At two o'clock on Monday afternoon Mrs. Eddy graciously acknowledged the silent greeting of her assembled students as her carriage drove past, stopping on North State Street. There she was greeted by Edward P. Bates, president of the Mother Church. She presented him with a small gift for her church and spoke a few words to all those within hearing distance.

Concord's reception of all the Christian Scientists was as cordial as it had been the year before, and Mrs. Eddy wrote a letter of appreciaton to the local newspapers *(My.* 173). But very shortly thereafter she published a rebuke to some Christian Scientists in the form of a new by-law entitled:

> ARTICLE XXVI. THOU SHALT NOT STEAL. Sect. 15 Neither a

Christian Scientist, his student or his patient, nor a member of the Mother Church shall daily and continuously haunt Mrs. Eddy's drive by meeting her once or more every day when she goes out — on penalty of being disciplined and dealt with justly by her church. Mrs. Eddy objects to said intrusion, inasmuch as she desires one hour for herself. And she who for forty years had "borne the burden and heat of the day," should be allowed this. The only exception to this By-law is on public occasions, when she has the privilege of seeing others and being seen

How the Leader loved and appreciated her few faithful students who never obtruded themselves upon her or her time. On July 4, when the nation was celebrating Independence Day, Mrs. Eddy wrote to Augusta Stetson:

Darling, my darling Student:

I have only time enough now to say your precious letter has healed my wound that was bleeding before I received your own words on this subject.

I know the *evil one* is trying to turn you against me and so discourage me and injure you more than aught else could do. But God will save you and by adhering to His lonely, present highest idea of love, you will hold to its Principle and be safe. O! I thank Him, *love Him* and love *my Augusta.*

Lovingly and everlastingly,

The directors of the Mother Church had profited from Mrs. Eddy's rebuke a year earlier at the time the corner stone for the Concord church was laid, and the laying of the corner stone for the Extension was done essentially in "sacred secrecy" on Saturday, July 16 *(My.* 16). The next day was the dedication of the Concord church. The termination of visits to Pleasant View had been stated in Mrs. Eddy's brief message to the Mother Church on Communion Sunday in these words: *"My Beloved Brethren:* As you are not expecting an invitation to visit Concord at each successive Communion season, I shall not disappoint any hope of your receiving it. My heart goes out to you as ever in daily desire that the Giver of all good transform you into His own image and likeness." An announcement *(My.* 163) read at each service of the Concord dedication reiterated this message:

Not having the time to receive all the beloved ones who have so kindly come to the dedication of this church, I must not allow myself the pleasure of receiving any of them. I always try to be just, if not generous; and I cannot show my love for them in social ways without neglecting the sacred demands on my time and attention for labors which I think do them more good.

Lovingly, M. B. G. Eddy

BICKNELL YOUNG
During his musical career in Chicago prior to his introduction to Christian Science

In 1903 Mrs. Eddy had had Bicknell Young appointed to the Board of Lectureship, and now in the summer of 1904 she chose him to read her message *(My.* 159) at the Concord church dedication on Sunday, July 17. His reading made her words memorable to those present; and the publication of her words in the periodicals gave them to the field and made them even more memorable:

> . . . I send to you the throbbing of every pulse of my desire for the ripening and rich fruit of this branch of his vine . . .
>
> At this period the greatest man or woman on earth stands at the vestibule of Christian Science . . .
>
> . . . To live so as to keep human consciousness in constant relation with the divine, the spiritual, and the eternal, is to individualize infinite power; and this is Christian Science. . . .
>
> I am asked, "Is there a hell?" Yes there is a hell . . . The advanced psychist knows that this hell is mental, not material, and that the

> Christian has no part in it. Only the makers of hell burn in their fire.
> ... A small group of wise thinkers is better than a wilderness of dullards and stronger than the might of empires. Unity is spiritual cooperation ...

This message inspired the whole field. One earnest student wrote in appreciation: "Single sentences in your address to the Concord church contain enough inspiration for a life work." The Leader also said in this address:

> We read in Holy Writ: "This man began to build, and was not able to finish." This was spoken derisively. But the love that rebukes praises also, and methinks the same wisdom which spake thus in olden time would say to the builder of the Christian Scientists' church edifice in Concord: "Well done, good and faithful."

"The builder of the Christian Scientists' church edifice in Concord" was Mr. E. Noyes Whitcomb, who was also the builder of The Mother Church Extension, which building was now in progress. It is altogether possible that this praise was intended as a loving rebuke to Mr. Whitcomb and all others involved in the deception. Or it may be that God inspired His anointed to write this message to meet a situation she was not yet aware of. Her own words could substantiate this latter possibility:

> Whatever I have discovered, understood and taught of Truth, I have never known beforehand its why or wherefore. It has always come into my thoughts and gone forth in words or deeds, before God's dear purpose in it and the fruits it would bear were fully revealed to me. I have always been called in spiritual paths to walk by faith and not by sight, to abide in the senses of God and not body for insight and action.

Whether or not she was aware of the deception on dedication day, God was speaking through her to the builder. Mrs. Eddy had given the site plus one hundred thousand dollars to build a church in Concord. The field had voluntarily contributed approximately eighty thousand dollars more toward its building, embellishing, and furnishing. But those in charge had not observed Mrs. Eddy's instructions on indebtedness, and Mr. Whitcomb had personally gone into debt nearly seventy-five thousand dollars for added architectural features. So in effect, and contrary to the rule in Christian Science, the Concord church was not debt free when it was dedicated.

Those responsible had endeavored to keep this fact from Mrs. Eddy, and perhaps they did so temporarily. On other occasions when her lieutenants went against her instructions or known wishes and endeavored to conceal that fact, she had written such terse remarks as: "It is not wise to try to deceive me." In this case she said nothing, even when it was "fully revealed to" her, as undoubtedly it was.

The main lesson for the student today is to learn the meaning and importance of obedience. At a later date the Leader said to her household: "If the work had been done in the time of Jesus, it would not have to be done now; but the disciples did not do their part; they were not obedient to him; they questioned what he was doing." Were not the Woman's disciples just as disobedient and questioning as were those of Jesus?

On the twenty-first of July the Leader wrote another letter to her "darling Augusta," part of which has circulated throughout the field:

> Repeat the following affirmations silently several times each day not with strained anxiety to get something out of them, but trying calmly to realize the meaning of the words:
> God is All; there is no evil.
> All is harmony; there is no discord.
> All is health; there is no sickness.
> All is Spirit; there is no matter.
> All is joy; there is no sorrow.
> All is Truth; there is no falsehood.
> All is faith; there is no fear.
> All is Life; there is no death.
> All is Love; there is no hate.

The Leader knew that the evil one or one evil would endeavor to nullify the provisions she had made for her church in the deeds and in the *Manual,* so she mentioned this point in a letter to her directors on July 25, along with a reminder of the true church:

> . . . May our God who is Spirit be worshipped by you in spirit, and the house you are about to erect be built on the Rock of ages; while you, my dearest ones, are rearing in your consciousness a "temple not built with hands" — and consecrated alone to the One- and-All apart from all material considerations. . . .
>
> Meantime let me *warn* you to have the architect and builder of the new Mother Church decide early upon the best and most artistic and seeable part of the building for the outside inscription; else the evil one may give you trouble on this particular point.

The "evil one" had already given them trouble on another point, and a crucial one, — the financing. At the beginning of the year when they were just getting under way, the building fund was in a healthy state for that stage, when they

> received a letter from a friend in another city, saying that he had just been informed — and his informant claimed to have good authority for the statement — that the entire amount required to complete The Mother Church building fund had been paid in; consequently further payments or subscriptions were not desired.

An editorial in the January 2 *Sentinel* called this a "subtle lie with which to ensnare a generous and loyal people," for probably less than one-fourth of the total amount required had been paid in. Nonetheless this "subtle lie" did affect the building fund until finally the financial situation was presented in the *Sentinel* of July 2. In August, Treasurer Stephen A. Chase received contributions from the church in Colorado Springs together with a letter which read in part:

> On July 6 last our building committee was in session. It had met to pass finally upon the plans selected for our local church, and which were to be submitted at our business meeting of July 7.
>
> The *Sentinel* of July 2 had just been received. The condition of The Mother Church Building Fund as therein set forth was earnestly considered, and it did not seem right that we should build under such conditions, — conditions that were a complete surprise to us.
>
> The result was a joint meeting with our Board of Directors and Trustees, when it was decided to submit the selected plan, blue prints, and report on our proposed building, then read the article in the *Sentinel* of July 2 already referred to, and leave the whole matter to the church.
>
> This was done, with the result that the members unanimously postponed our building, discharged the building committee, released all pledges to our fund, and earnestly advised that the sums so released be turned into The Mother Church Building Fund.
>
> While under consideration many beautiful expressions of gratitude and loyalty to our dear Leader were voiced and not one dissentient or disappointed word uttered or, we believe, thought.
>
> As a church and individually, we are truly grateful for this opportunity, — we deem it a privilege of which we joyfully avail ourselves, — and we do want to be a branch bearing fruit meet for our Leader's approval and our true growth.

Mrs. Eddy was deeply touched when Mr. Chase sent this letter on to her, and she answered it on September 1 *(My.* 19), closing her letter of appreciation and blessing with Jesus' words: "Verily I say unto you, Wheresoever this gospel shall be preached throughout the whole world, this also that she hath done shall be spoken of for a memorial of her" (Mark 14:9).

CHAPTER XIX

BETTER HEALERS

Healing the sick and reforming the sinner demonstrate Christian Science and nothing else ***can, does.*** — MARY BAKER EDDY

1904

THE unselfish loyalty of the church in Colorado Springs which brought forth the Leader's unending recognition was a reflection of the unselfish thought of the student most responsible for this branch church, Ella Peck Sweet. The church's action may have been a surprise as well as a joy to Mrs. Sweet in the summer of 1904, for she was not in Colorado at that time but was at Pleasant View, one of the mental workers in Mrs. Eddy's household.

ELLA PECK SWEET

MRS. Ella Peck Sweet had learned from her devoted mother to turn to God for guidance, but she was a frail, sickly child and continued to suffer from ill health for many years. When Mr. Sweet moved his family to Buffalo Springs, Colorado in 1880 it was with the hope that Mrs. Sweet would find the mountain climate beneficial, which had proved a frustrated hope. By the fall of 1885 at the age of 47 her physical condition was so critical that she went to Denver to live out her final days. But Mrs. Sweet did not find the end she anticipated in Denver that October. Instead she found a new beginning through the renewing of an old acquaintance.

Mrs. Sweet had first met Mary M. Hall when Mrs. Hall was living on a ranch some twenty or thirty miles from Buffalo Springs prior to her move to Denver. In Denver in 1883 Mrs. Hall had become blind and lame, and in the spring of 1885 embarked for New York, with two of her daughters, in search of medical aid. En route the trio found Christian Science in Chicago and Mrs. Hall went to Roger Sherman for treatment. Roger and his parents were the pioneers who simply had found the textbook and begun healing. In September, four months later, Denver was all astir when Mrs. Hall returned completely healed. She and her twenty-two year old daughter Minnie had had primary class instruction from Roger Sherman's father, Bradford Sherman, while in Chicago, and back in Denver they were overwhelmed with patients, — at times as many as one hundred in a day.

One of Minnie's patients was her friend Mrs. Sweet who was healed quickly and completely and who began an earnest study of Science and Health. The interest was so great in Denver in the fall of 1885 that Bradford Sherman was summoned for help. Ella Peck Sweet was a member of the first of the two classes Mr. Sherman taught in the Hall's home in December.

When Mrs. Sweet returned to her own home, the news of her healing spread rapidly and she was soon healing throughout the area as she had been healed.

The next fall, 1886, Mrs. Eddy invited Mrs. Sweet to attend her Normal class at the Massachusetts Metaphysical College. But alas! Mrs. Sweet had been doing all her healing work freely and had no funds for this progressive step. Mrs. Eddy told her to be prepared the following year. When the call came again in October, 1887, Mrs. Sweet was ready with the necessary funds and with eager anticipation.

In the classroom the Teacher was delighted when she called upon Mrs. Sweet to define animal magnetism and Mrs. Sweet answered: "Animal magnetism is the sum total of all error, and that in itself nothing until you attach belief to it." Mrs. Eddy clapped her hands and said, "Well answered!"

Following her course at the college Mrs. Sweet expanded her "missionary work" responding to calls within a hundred mile radius of Buffalo Springs. She taught classes in Colorado Springs, Pueblo, Canon City, and Denver, and was instrumental in founding the church in Canon City and especially the one in Colorado Springs.

At the time of the building of the original Mother Church in 1893 the Leader invited a number of her students each to contribute one thousand dollars to the building fund. In the 1890's that amount was more than the annual income of a great many people in the United States. Few of those selected could easily afford such a contribution, but the Leader had chosen strong, dedicated, conscientious workers, one of whom was Ella Peck Sweet. In retrospect Mrs. Sweet said:

> It was only by entire reliance on divine Mind that I was enabled to

> reply to Mrs. Eddy that I would accept her invitation. Such a sum of money had never been in my hands. Infinite resources seemed at once opened to me, and at the appointed time the amount was mine to send, and my gratitude for this great proof of Love's supply was unbounded.

The Sweets were living in Denver in June of 1904 when a telegram arrived one Saturday asking Mrs. Sweet to meet with the Board of Directors in Boston the following Tuesday. Within three hours she had made the necessary arrangements and boarded a train for Boston. Her promptness caused William B. Johnson to remark that she must have had her shoes on her feet and her staff in her hand. She was truly a minute man for the cause and for the Leader.

That Tuesday afternoon in an interview at Pleasant View Mrs. Eddy questioned Mrs. Sweet about her work and her family and then asked her if she could come to live at Pleasant View for a while. Following a trip home to arrange her affairs Mrs. Sweet returned to Pleasant View. Newspapers in both Denver and Colorado Springs commented upon the honor conferred upon Mrs. Sweet in being called to Concord.

Very soon after her arrival Mrs. Sweet visited the Concord church which was nearing completion and injured herself when she slipped on a board. She and other members of the household at Pleasant View worked to meet the situation without success. When Mrs. Eddy asked some of them what was wrong with Mrs. Sweet, they said she was all right, and Mrs. Eddy said, "She is not all right." She then asked Mrs. Sweet what was wrong, and Ella replied that it was being met, to which Mrs. Eddy responded, "It is not being met." When the Leader asked Mrs. Sweet how she was working, the latter said she was knowing there was no accident in Mind. To this Mrs. Eddy replied: "That would not heal you. You were brought here to help me. You are one of my best workers."

> She then pointed out that the only trouble was an argument to interfere with her usefulness to the Leader. By the time Mrs. Eddy finished talking to her, Mrs. Sweet was healed. Mrs. Eddy said to her, "I will say for your comfort that if you were brought here with every bone broken in your whole body, you would respond to my treatment."

Mrs. Sweet had been at Pleasant View two or three months when the *Sentinel* of September 10 published the letter from First Church of Christ, Scientist, Colorado Springs along with Mrs. Eddy's response. In that same September 10 *Sentinel* was this brief news item about a triennial meeting:

The Sixth International Zoological Congress, in session at Berne, Switzerland, has accepted an invitation to hold the next Congress, in 1907, in Boston.

Triennial meetings were something that were also in the Leader's thought. Several years earlier she had adopted them for her National Christian Scientist Association before discontinuing their meetings altogether. She had taken the first step toward triennial normal classes in December, 1903, when she wrote the by-law "NO MORE STUDENTS." Now an amended by-law in the September *Journal* took another step in this direction: "The Board of Education has two classes annually, a Primary and a Normal class, each not exceeding thirty pupils. But no Normal Classes are to be taught before December 8, 1906." She may have considered Mr. Kimball's last Board of Education class in December, 1903, as a normal class, although it was later designated as primary.

Christian Science was spreading by leaps and bounds in 1904, but the field did not need more teaching. What it needed was consecrated application of what had already been taught. Mrs. Eddy wrote to one of her students: "I gave so much to your class — my last class — and *so little* has been done with it." Perhaps she had seen the necessity for curtailing the teaching of Christian Science when she had written to Mr. Kimball nearly a year earlier: "Our Cause demands *better healers;* and if less teaching classes is enjoined, more practitioners will be fitted by the book to heal." Now she was limiting the number of classes and of pupils, but she was introducing this change for teachers and teaching gradually as she had been forced to do on so many other issues, lest her followers chemicalize and resist completely. Her lieutenants who thought she was always changing her mind were unaware that she was leading them one small step at a time to accept an advanced concept which they would rebel against if taken in one decisive step. To those who could understand, Mrs. Eddy said, "Often I sent out an angel (a new by-law) and it would come back bruised and bleeding, and I'd have to take it in and cherish it until the Field was ready for it." At one time a *Manual* with new by-laws had been printed but at the Leader's direction withheld from distribution. Mr. Kimball was at Pleasant View on the Saturday that the new *Manual* was put on sale, and he said he never saw such a thunder and lightning storm as besieged Pleasant View that day (and which proved to be but local). Mrs. Eddy pointed out the window to the storm and said to Mr. Kimball: "This is mortal mind's answer to my *Manual.*" The amended by-law in the September *Journal* in 1904 restricted not only the Board of Education but also primary teachers to fewer and smaller classes:

Apart from the Board of Education, the teachers of Christian Science shall teach but one class yearly, which class shall consist of not more than thirty pupils.

There may have been pressure from Pleasant View to get this September *Journal* with its curtailing message out promptly, for Mrs. Eddy's secretary George Kinter wrote to the Publishing Society at the end of August:

Accept our sincere thanks and most cordial congratulations upon the prompt delivery of the September Journal. Every body from the Leader down was pleased to get it so early.

Another letter from Kinter to the trustees of the Publishing Society in September stated:

our Leader directs that you may make the change at the head of the Editorial page, as proposed, provided you do not make any change in the present form of the cover of the Journal.

One of Mrs. Eddy's letters of October 3 reveals how much Augusta Stetson helped her:

I sent to you a 20 dollar gold piece, *not* as *money,* for that can neither express nor pay for your kindness in helping me to outside wear or apparel. It was simply saying, *"You* keep the *Golden Rule* in this way; and my gratitude is golden beyond words." Did you get that? Can I do more for you in any way than I am doing? As for work, I cannot, for I have more to do now than I ought to or can attend to; but I can advise or instruct when you need it.

Darling, I need teajackets, two at least for the cool weather and have but *one!* I herewith send cloth for one and you can send samples and I will select the sample for another. . . .

Herewith please find my old waist for a measure guide. Have the teajackets plain and *nice fitting* — smooth but loose around the hips and in front and not very long below the waist line. Those Miss Moulton sends hang in folds and a foot below the waist. I will not wear them anymore.

Darling, *rise* each hour. Now is the resurrection morn and I want Augusta to be my Mary.

Her closing paragraph deeply affected Mrs. Stetson for the rest of her years. Fifteen years earlier Mrs. Eddy had written to this "precious Student":

Your dear letters are a great reward to my tired life . . . For this I thank God and *you!* After one quarter of a century I have gotten such

> as you, a few noble, faithful students.
>
> . . . Do you not see that when you do as I request how you prove your ability to do what you had before doubted and how everything goes well if my directions are followed?
>
> Yes, darling, you are learning this and growing like a sweet, fat, promising baby, like a beautiful sapling, like the reeds by the river, like the child, Jesus.

Unlike the majority of the Leader's students and followers, Mrs. Stetson was instant in following her Teacher's directions: and everything had gone very well for her. Gilbert Carpenter said of Mrs. Stetson: "she was a brilliant woman with a recognized ability and understanding of leadership far greater than any other student I ever knew outside of our Leader. . . . Mrs. Stetson had the finest church in the Field, she had the wealthiest and most socially prominent students in New York among her congregation and association. . . . Her students who were business men advised her in her investments so that she might be prosperous and live in elegance."

And envy and jealousy had set in against Mrs. Stetson even as with Edward P. Bates and Edward A. Kimball. But *every* student who helped the Leader most or followed closest in her footsteps came under such attacks. And the dear students who indulged in the gossip and slander were unaware that they were being handled by the age old problem of who shall be greatest.

Mrs. Seal whose healing work in Germany was so outstanding, was another whose very success brought much criticism upon her. In a letter to Mr. McKenzie in October, 1904, Mr. Kinter said: "When I was coming through Boston last fall, en route to Concord, I asked at the Publishing Office about Mrs. Seal, being in need of her address, but was given a most decidedly cool impression of her standing, you know, innuendo, and arched eyebrows." This attitude was never from the Leader who, on more than one occasion gave words of warning, encouragement or comfort to those students who helped the Mother most and whose accomplishments brought the envy in others to the surface. Another letter in October to her helpful Augusta said:

> The hood is very nice now; your love and faithfulness have again triumphed. God bless, guide, perfect my precious child; and He will, inasmuch as you minister to me in temporal things divine Love will lead you into the eternal. Giving, we receive, and the measure ye mete shall be measured to you again, even though you have to wait as long as I have waited to prove this, and in some things and ways of this world's approval. Accept my deepest love and *thanks.*

CHAPTER XX

GOD'S GIVER

My published works are teachers and healers. My private life is given to a servitude the fruit of which all mankind may share.
— MARY BAKER EDDY

1904

A STEP stressing healing was launched in October and was given as a problem to the Board of Trustees of the Publishing Society to solve. Kinter's letter from Pleasant View to the chairman of the board, William P. McKenzie stated:

> There is a matter of considerable import, to which I beg to invite the attention of your board, viz: the names in our Journal directory. As I understand it, the directory is intended as a book of reference to those seeking help, of reliable Christian Science Practitioners, persons able and ready to heal the sick, and whose first calling is the healing work.
>
> It is well known that there are many names of persons recorded in said register, who not only never do any healing, but who intend not to, and whose time and energy are wholly mortgaged in other matters; furthermore the Journal has become top-heavy, and something must be done, to make room for more reading matter . . .
>
> P.S. I will venture to hint that if the program is not already unchangeably made up for the coming Teachers' meeting, that would be a suitable place to discuss the subject, as it is really in the hands of the Teachers.

"The coming Teachers' meeting," the second annual meeting of the General Association of Teachers, was to be held in Chicago on October 24 and 25. Young Bliss Knapp had just been notified that he had been made a member of this association although he was not yet a teacher. Mrs. Stetson wrote from Chicago to her students the day before the meeting:

> I am waiting on God — no one yet knows anything that is to be done. All are very happy, and the Association will give a power to the body, as all these old soldiers (teachers), battle-scarred but strong, take a firmer hold upon the infinite, and press forward to the end of all error. I pray that you all may feel the pulse of the great heart of Love, and that you will rise into newness of life and see the reward of your efforts for self-abnegation, consecration, divine love and unity. Oh! watch with your Christ. Protect your Christ-child, your spiritual consciousness, or Herod, mortal so-called mind, will destroy it.
>
> Choose to walk with God, and trust God to care for you. Learn to lose with God. Lose your *material* sense of yourselves and of others — lose your trust in *material* ways and means to an end, — lose your sensuous appetites and tastes, and see that God is substance, who supplies our material needs until He is found to be our only support.
>
> Be not murmurers in the wilderness, nor cry for the "quail" and "garlic." I pray that you will be circumspect and never repeat to the unbelievers what sacrifices of personal sense and self you make to reach eternal Life, and your oneness with Principle. They would not understand your consecration, and could not see your reward in love, peace, and joy. . . .
>
> How few are ready to grow gradually out of the human into the divine. If we are ready, we should not reprove another who is not able to run so fast as we the race for immortality, nor offend him by repeating our victories over material sense. . . . God bless each of you, my dear students, and may I bring you fresh inspiration . . . from this meeting . . .

Mrs. Stetson did not yet know anything that was to be done, but some of the others did, one of whom was Herbert W. Eustace, a teacher from San Jose, California. Mr. Eustace addressed the Association on the theme of obedience to the Discoverer, Founder, and Leader of Christian Science — an obedience which to make this army of workers impregnable, he said must be unbounded, unswerving, unqualified, and unconditional.

On the first day of their meeting, which was largely attended by members from practically every state in the Union, a despatch of greeting was sent to the Leader expressing recognition and appreciation and ending with:

> We love you, but your abundant reward rests in the full fruitage of the divine declaration, "Inasmuch as ye have done it unto one of the least of these my brethren, ye have done it unto me." Dutifully awaiting any communication you may desire to make to the Association we are
>
> Sincerely your students,

All of these students were *called* to do God's work, and a few of them were *chosen.* Many are called, few are chosen, and a very few are *sent.* Jesus told his disciples that the Father had sent him. Mrs. Eddy told the same thing to her disciples, but hid it from the worldly, when she published in *Christ and Christmas:* "In tender mercy, Spirit sped A loyal ray." Now this "loyal ray" said it again to these called and chosen students who were awaiting a communication from her. In her response on October 25 *(My.* 253) their Leader stated simply:

> I thank you. Jesus said, "The world hath not known Thee: but I have known Thee, and these have known that Thou hast sent me."

The problem which Mrs. Eddy had given to her trustees was most probably put before the Teachers' Association as suggested. It is also probable that the issue was intended to cause these thinkers to place healing above teaching in their work as Mrs. Eddy was always endeavoring to do. It is also a possibility that the message in a 1904 letter to her directors found its way to this meeting:

> We want the right teaching of C.S. or *none at all.* I am so disappointed in my students in this respect I have no words to utter myself. . . . It absolutely disgusts me to hear them babble the letter and after that fail in proving what they say! It is high time that they stop talking science or . . . prove their words true.

In the summer she had voiced this disappointment to Nemi Robertson who enjoyed a longer than usual visit with the Leader at Pleasant View. She told her never to be satisfied until she healed with one treatment — or not more than three. She then told Miss Robertson a number of her own instantaneous healings and ended by saying: "Divine Love alone can heal and to know that God is All covers the whole ground." As she said this to Miss Robertson "she seemed transfigured and glorified. It was wonderful." But the Leader's disappointment with the healing work caused Nemi Robertson to write her a comforting letter, to which Mrs. Eddy responded on August 13:

> Your letter I do not understand, but I know your tenderness, and trust it will help you on. You mistake, dear one, in thinking I am sad! I am the very opposite — am filled with gladness and gratitude for the unsurpassed prosperity of Christian Science.
>
> It was only when naming the need of more and better healers in the field that my face expressed my disappointment. Do not think I am not the happiest of the happy, for I am, and I should be, but address yourself and fellow students to leave behind the fashions and foibles and pride and vanity of the world, and to *demonstrate* Chris-

> tian Science. Teaching, and church-making and leading, will never demonstrate what is taught.

In the fall of 1904 there were nearly fifteen pages of advertisements for Christian Science institutes all across the United States as well as Canada and Germany, and many of the owners of these institutes were the teachers attending this meeting of the General Association of Teachers in Chicago. Perhaps the fact that the Board of Education did not advertise was brought up. Perhaps they discussed the by-law entitled "Healing Better than Teaching." Whatever the reason, following the meeting a number of teachers withdrew their Institute advertisements from the pages of the *Journal.* A month later the trustees proposed omitting *all* institute advertisements beginning in January. Mrs. Eddy told her secretary, George Kinter:

> Answer for me that I say do what they, the Trustees, think is best on this subject. I like their decision.

Mr. Kimball's successor as the teacher for the Board of Education was Eugene H. Greene of Providence, Rhode Island, and he approached his new position with trepidation. A week or two after the meeting in Chicago Mr. Greene wrote Mrs. Eddy that he still felt unready and unworthy for this position. At the convening of his first Board of Education class early in December he wrote the Leader:

> I appreciate far clearer than ever before what it has cost you to bring this spiritual idea to humanity. I am grateful for the help you are imparting to me. I am conscious of such a spiritual lack and need I can only ask constantly for divine strength and guidance.

This Primary class sent a letter and telegram to Mrs. Eddy at Pleasant View. One sentence in her reply *(My.* 253) has meant much to many students: "We understand best that which begins in ourselves and by education brightens into birth."

Following the Teachers' Meeting in Chicago, Mrs. Stetson met with the members of her New York Christian Science Institute. The main item on their agenda was a telegram to the Leader, part of which read:

> We reconsecrate ourselves that we may demonstrate the spiritual cooperation which is the unity to which your wise leadership calls us. Our earnest aim is to reach your exalted ideals of purity and power.

The Leader caused their telegram to be published in both the

Sentinel and *Journal* together with her reply which read: "Accept my thanks and loving congratulation. Jesus said, 'My sheep hear my voice and I know them, and they follow me.'"

On the last day in October Editor McLellan wrote Mrs. Eddy:

> The enclosed letters from Mr. McCartney and Mr. Miller of Philadelphia, testify to the wisdom of all your steps in connection with "Bohemia." I thank you for having used me in this matter. If it seems best to you I shall comply with Mr. McCartney's request.

Bohemia was intended as a masterpiece. It was a huge volume produced by the International League of Press Clubs which was published in the summer of 1904. This collection of able American journalism was augmented by articles expressly prepared for this publication by men of distinction, — presidents, ex-presidents, kings, admirals, etc. One of the "men" of distinction — the few specially selected contributors — was a woman, Mary Baker Eddy. When James McCartney had proposed an "official presentation" of Mrs. Eddy's especially made volumes of the book, she had declined graciously. An account of their delivery to Pleasant View by special messenger was published in the *Concord Monitor* which account included:

> It is a notable fact that Mrs. Eddy's is the only contribution in the book which deals with other than a literary or personal theme, and this will be taken as another indication of the widening scope of her recognition and influence . . .

Mrs. Eddy's contribution as well as all of her steps relating thereto was one of her charities, — a giving of her precious time to the demands of the world. The world, of course, did not see it as a charity, for it knew not the value of the Woman's time. But one of the editors of *Bohemia* did get an unforgettable lesson regarding the worth of Mrs. Eddy's every minute.

Arthur Talmadge Abernathy had come in contact with Mrs. Eddy in his editorial capacity, and at a later date made an impromptu social call at Pleasant View when he found himself in Concord with free time. In response to his message asking for an interview, the busy Leader sent down her message on a card: "I am very busy. I would rather give you a thousand dollars than a minute of my time." In a light, jesting mood Mr. Abernathy returned the card with the penned note: "My initials are A.T.A."

A. T. A. Abernathy may have expected to be received, but he was not expecting what he *did* receive which left him stunned and somewhat ashamed. As he was leaving the house a messenger handed him Mrs. Eddy's engraved card, "With compliments of" in Mrs. Eddy's handwriting above her name. Her handwriting was also on the accompanying check made out to Mr. Abernathy for one thousand dollars.

The demands upon the Leader's time and money were numerous and continuous. Though she guarded the former as zealously as possible, she was very generous with the latter responding with donations to unending solicitations. Her generosity endeared a great many hearts to her, if not to her cause, but the stream of requests and demands increased to a flood. On November 18 she wrote "Charity and Invalids" *(My.* 231) and sent it to her editor. Her article began:

> Mrs. Eddy endeavors to bestow her charities for such purposes only as God indicates. Giving merely in compliance with solicitations or petitions from strangers, incurs the liability of working in wrong directions. As a rule, she has suffered most from those whom she has labored much to benefit — also from the undeserving poor to whom she has given large sums of money, worse than wasted. She has, therefore, finally resolved to spend no more time or money in such uncertain, unfortunate investments. . . .

"Charity and Invalids" was published in the *Sentinels* of November 26 and December 3, and was not only notification to the field, but a guide to her followers. Her contributions to the endeavors of others never ceased, but perhaps this notice reduced the flood of solicitations. At any rate it was a guide for her secretaries who opened the hundreds of letters addressed to Mrs. Eddy which found their way to Pleasant View.

A notice that appeared in the *Sentinel* of November 5 was entitled "Holiday Gifts," and began: "The holidays are coming, and I trow you are awaiting on behalf of your Leader the loving liberty of their license."

The world has never had a giver of gifts that could equal Mary Baker Eddy. She gave to the world not only her great discovery of the Science of being, but every moment of her time for its establishment in the hearts of all who would accept this pearl priceless. In addition she was constantly giving charming (and often costly) gifts to her helpers, such as one she sent to Calvin C. Hill in 1904 — a small reproduction of a photograph of herself accompanied by a twenty dollar gold piece and the message: "Accept my golden gift as the symbol of your Golden Rule of life."

Mr. Hill was superintendant of the Mother Church Sunday School in 1904 and may have been one of the many who caused Mr. McLellan to write to the Leader early in November:

> We receive a great many requests for the republication of your article regarding the Sunday School work entitled, "What We Can Do for the Children," which appeared in the October, 1895 JOURNAL. If you see that the republication of this article is desirable at the present time, will you kindly give me permission to republish it in the SENTINEL?

Mrs. Eddy penned on McLellan's letter: "Beloved Student: Publish the above article as often as is best to do so." This was followed by incorporating the essence of her article into the *Manual* as bylaws for the Sunday School. The December *Journal* published an appreciative letter from the Mother Church Sunday School Superintendant Calvin Hill alongside the Leader's cryptic reply:

> Good deeds overdone numerically, or bad deeds, are remedied by reading the *Manual.*

The gifts from Mrs. Eddy that all her students treasured most in the years to come were her letters of concern, comfort, and reassurance. One day in 1904 she wrote to her secretary, George Kinter, who was briefly confined to his room struggling with a problem:

> God is nearer than ever before to you. Divine Love *holds you up.* You cannot fall. His arms are around you. If you would like to have your dear wife with you just now be sure and send for her.

In her notice "Holiday Gifts" this giver of gifts asked her followers to "Bring all your tithes into His storehouse, and what you would expend for presents to her, please add to your givings to The Mother Church building fund, and let this suffice for her rich portion in due season."

Another request the Leader made near the end of 1904 was almost a gift. She asked Mr. Johnson's son, William Lyman, in a letter dated December 2 to write music for her hymns "Christ My Refuge" (O'er waiting harpstrings of the mind) and "Feed My Sheep" (Shepherd show me how to go). Both of young Mr. Johnson's arrangements appeared in the next revision of the hymnal.

In mid-December the Leader wrote to her faithful Augusta in New York:

> December 17, 1904
>
> My darling Student:
>
> I have tried to reply sooner, but I could not. Do not doubt my *love* for you, my faith in you, and my faithful rebuke if need be. Above all, dear one, know that God knows your good works and will reward them, that He loves you and her whom He has called loves you just as

tenderly in giving you His rod or His staff and by them both — His rod and support — you cannot doubt His care and love for you, my precious one. Now be of good cheer, be not afraid for such are God's proofs to all His own, that they are His and *none can* pluck them out of His hands.

Your explanation is so comforting to me that I thank Him and you for it with tears of joy. . . .

M.A.M. is busy at this wicked moment now that my works are being better appreciated. But where is the Christianity that C.S. brings to all who understand it, the Golden Rule that governs it and should, must govern all who live Christian Science?

I thank God for your good works and love you more and more.

The last *Sentinel* in December, 1904, contained an article Mrs. Eddy had written for the *Boston Globe* — "How Strife May Be Stilled" *(My.* 278). One sentence therein should be a guide to the whole world: "Governments have no right to engraft into civilization the burlesque of uncivil economics." She closed her article with the solution for all wars in one sentence:

God is Father, infinite, and this great truth, when understood in its divine metaphysics, will establish the brotherhood of man, end wars, and demonstrate "on earth peace, good will toward men."

CHAPTER XXI

"BREAK EARTH'S STUPID REST"

Mortal mind must waken to spiritual life before it cares to solve the problem of being, hence the author's experience; but when that awakening comes, existence will be on a new standpoint.

— MARY BAKER EDDY

1905

THE building of the Mother Church Extension was progressing as the new year dawned in 1905. But the real extension of the Mother's Church was the Divinity course that was taught in her home at Pleasant View. Few students were qualified for this advanced teaching, and even among those few many thought they were not taught the course because Mrs. Eddy did not assemble them in a classroom and say, "This is the Divinity Course."

The Divinity course was putting into practice what every sincere, dedicated, consecrated student of Science already knows; that is, to turn to infinite Mind for absolutely everything every minute of every day. Whether he knew it or not Gilbert Carpenter was describing the Divinity course when he said:

> I can assert with conviction that Mrs. Eddy's home was the only place where I ever saw a perfectly consistent application of scientific demonstration in all matters. She made it a requirement that we must demonstrate all the material experiences of ordinary daily life and strive to see God back of everything, no matter how insignificant an incident might seem.
>
> . . . the minutiae of life, which one is almost tempted to neglect, the questions of eating, sleeping, the commonplace daily necessities, are of the utmost importance from the spiritual standpoint, because they are the deep-rooted beliefs which bind man to dependence on matter. Thus, we perceive the deep spiritual insight of our Leader in her insistence on demonstration in the non-essentials. She saw that, although they appeared trifling to material sense, they represented the most important mile-stones of the students . . . that will eventu-

ally win man that goal of freedom — freedom to depend wholly upon God.

Practising twenty-four hours a day is the most demanding, exacting, and exalting experience anyone can have. It is what Mrs. Eddy demanded of herself. It is also what she desired and required of those in her household without stating it in words. If they did not see and understand what was required, telling them would do no good.

From the beginning of the Adam dream the omnipotence and glory of God had been forgotten and the world had been lulled to sleep by animal magnetism. The Woman's great mission was to "break earth's stupid rest." But, alas! even the dear, chosen students in her home were so glamoured by animal magnetism that they often saw the Leader's requirements as exacting and demanding rather than exalting. And this necessitated many lessons on animal magnetism. Most students had to be frightened by its aggressive features before they were willing to be awakened. They preferred to remain in the dream so long as it was pleasant.

One day while Mrs. Ella Peck Sweet was at Pleasant View the Leader asked her to repeat the definition of animal magnetism she had given in the classroom in 1887. Mrs. Sweet declared, just as she had in the classroom, "Animal magnetism is the sum total of all error, and that in itself nothing until you attach belief to it." Once again the Leader clapped her hands in approval just as she had done seventeen years earlier.

Mrs. Sweet was no longer at Pleasant View in January of 1905. Her arrangement had been to return to her home in Denver for Thanksgiving. Mr. Kinter would soon be returning to his home, already having stayed several months beyond the specified one year. Mrs. Eddy called the clerk of the Mother Church, William B. Johnson, one of her directors, to Pleasant View temporarily until she found one qualified to come for the full year term. In mid-January she was writing to one of her disciples, Mary Beecher Longyear, regarding an ambitious project this student had proposed:

January 15, 1905

My Mary and my disciple:

God is moving on the face of the waters of your thought and His creations will appear.

I propose that the institution you found be called Sanatorium, also that it be for teaching surgery, training nurses, teaching cooking, and healing the sick. Also that it be a resort for invalids without homes or relatives available in time of need; where they can go and recruit, etc.

You who are so capable of financial operations can arrange all without my suggestion.

Our cause demands a wider circle of means for the ends of philanthropy and charity, and better qualifications for practical purposes. This latter lack in students of Christian Science is a great hindrance to our cause and it must be met and mastered. The students need to be qualified so that under the fire of mortal mind they can stand, and "having done all to stand" (St. Paul).

Special Notice of the Present

Let none but yourself into this movement or *know of it* now. Do not rely on me at all for I have not a half hour to spare, or a moment some days, and God with you is your majority. Keep your thoughts away from me lest they bring too much of this world with them and, dear one, this would surely not help you. I want this work done wholly apart from me.

It was probably in Janaury — it was a cold winter night early in 1905 shortly before George Kinter returned to his home — that a very dramatic experience occurred.

The household had retired for the night when Mrs. Eddy rang for Mr. Frye, which was not unusual, for she often worked day and night. But when the summons was unanswered she rang for Mr. Kinter, who dashed through Mr. Frye's room as a shortcut, and told Mrs. Eddy immediately that Mr. Frye was sitting in a chair in his room looking as if he were in a coma. Mrs. Eddy sent George back to rouse Mr. Frye and rang for Laura Sargent.

When Mr. Kinter reported that there was no sign of life, that Calvin's body was stone cold and stiff with no perceptible pulse or breath, Mrs. Eddy got up from bed and went quickly to him. Bending over the sitting figure she began making bold, audible declarations of truth.

The house was icy cold and Mrs. Eddy was in her nightdress, but she was oblivious of the protests of Laura Sargent and George Kinter as she told Calvin to "wake up and be the man God made!" For over an hour she continued to call him, unaware of what the others were doing for *her.* They wrapped her in a double blanket, and as she bent over Frye's form in a half-stooping position Mr. Kinter supported her. Though she was unaware of their help, Mr. Kinter's back was aching an hour later when Calvin moved slightly and began to murmur: "Don't call me back. . . . Let me go. . . . I am so tired."

The Leader refuted those suggestions saying she most certainly would continue to call him back from that dream-state — that he loved life and its activities too well to fall asleep, that he was freed from the thralldom of hypnotism and alive to God, his Saviour from sin and death.

Half an hour later Calvin was completely recovered and everybody went back to bed. No one mentioned the incident, and life went on as usual the next day at Pleasant View, although George Kinter did record the event in his reminiscences.

The twenty-eighth of January saw a portent of things to come. Calvin Frye recorded in his diary that at 4:30 P.M. a messenger named Harding arrived from Washington, D.C. bearing a lengthy letter from her son George W. Glover — a letter "in which Glover virtually accuses her of not being competent to conduct her own business." That evening Mrs. Eddy said to Calvin: "I am going to give George some history about you and let him know how faithful you have been to me." The historian wonders, With whom was George Glover visiting in Washington, D.C.?

Mr. Frye asked Gilbert Carpenter to come to Concord on January 30 to discuss finding a suitable maid for Mrs. Eddy. But it would appear that the Leader had more than the maid in mind when she talked with Mr. and Mrs. Carpenter that day.

GILBERT C. CARPENTER

IT was 1894 when Mr. and Mrs. Carpenter became interested in Christian Science, a time when the emerging Christian Science churches either had pastors or did their own thing. Some held Sunday School for adults. Mr. Carpenter said: "When I first attended services in Providence, Rhode Island, they consisted wholly of an informal discussion of the lesson in the Quarterly led by Eugene H. Greene."

It was four years later in May of 1898 that the Carpenters wrote Mrs. Eddy what Gilbert had found and unfolded in researching the word eddy. The Leader responded to Mrs. Carpenter on May 22, 1898:

> My dear Mrs. Carpenter:
>
> Your kind letter at hand. The interpretation is quite noticeable in some directions. God grant that I be found not wanting in the direction that runs Heavenward. The stream of our lives meets with much resistance, but there is a hope beyond earth's ebb and flow. May you and all find the shoreless sea where Life is infinite, and all that seems to be and is not, is swallowed up in the reality of Life and Love.
>
> With thanks and love,
>
> Mary Baker Eddy

The Carpenters were sincere young students who idealized the Revelator to this age and knew nothing about animal magnetism. They wrote to Mrs. Eddy on July 20, 1900:

Providence, R.I.

Beloved Mother:

It has been in the thought of some of your loved little ones in this city to send to you some permanent expression of their love and appreciation. Now that the world is getting more and more to realize the freedom that you have brought to it, would it be to your liking to have us erect a flag pole at "Pleasant View" one hundred feet high, with a flag that could be seen by the dwellers at Concord, the pole surmounted by a woman's head and shoulders supported by two eagles' wings?

If this our pleasure should be yours, would Concord Day, "Old Home Week," be too soon to expect to unfurl the flag to the breeze?

Our courage to write this letter came from opening the Bible to Jeremiah 51:27, "Set ye up a standard in the land . . . " If you should feel that this plan or any of its details are not just what you would like to see brought out at "Pleasant View" it would be our pleasure to express our thought some other way, for, dear Mother, our hearts are full and it is our prayer to be found worthy to touch the hem of your garment.

Lovingly your children,
Mr. and Mrs. Gilbert C. Carpenter

In later years when Gilbert had crossed swords with animal magnetism and learned that Pleasant View was "Fort Besieged" as long as the Leader was there, he knew how immature his suggestion had been. But it is sad that those who "bought" Pleasant View under the terms of Mrs. Eddy's will did not follow through with this rare gift at that time and set "up a standard in the land," as Mrs. Eddy's answer implied could be done:

July 25th, 1900

Beloved Students:

Your dear letter would have been answered sooner but for innumerable duties to be done.

Your conception in design is very fine, your proposed gift is a rare one, grand, and illustrative. But, my dear friends, so little is the world up to, or near, your thought it would be a pearl cast before swine. And you know, Jesus saith, that such is trampled upon. I think that now is not the time for the erection of such a storied flag pole. If I should at any future time sell P.V. to a student he could have that erected properly; but I have not the sense that it is best to be done while I occupy the place. With grateful appreciation of your high thought, and dear desire to do this for me I close. May our God give you joy for contemplating it. Give the dear grand students who thought of it with you my love and thanks. May the wings of the eagle be thine to mount upwards in Christian Science, and divine Love be and abide with you.

With love, mother
Mary Baker Eddy

In 1901 Mrs. Eddy had Mr. Carpenter elected a First Member of the Mother Church. And in 1902 she had him appointed to the building committee of the Mother Church Extension. At about this same time Mr. Carpenter became aware through Mr. Mann that Mrs. Eddy's sleigh was in need of new bells, which he hastened to supply. The salutation on Mrs. Eddy's letter of thanks is noteworthy:

December 21, 1902

Mr. Gilbert C. Carpenter, Christian Scientist
Beloved Student:

You will please accept my warm thanks for the pretty sleigh bells you sent to me. I love to hear their silver tones over the snow, and think of your kindness to contribute to mother's one hour cheery vacation from the desk. May the coming Christmas bring you additional joy and advancing footsteps outward, onward, upward, is the prayer of mother.

Ever yours, M.B.G. Eddy

P.S. I had the pleasure of learning of your acceptance of the place on our Church Bil. Comm. and was greatly pleased therefore. Again M.B.E.

It was probably some time in 1903 that Mr. Carpenter had his first interview with Mrs. Eddy. She had called him to Pleasant View to talk with him regarding his securing a new carriage for her. Afterward, when he recorded the interview, he wrote: "I found that in the course of a half hour's talk, she had answered every question on Christian Science that had been troubling me over a period of two years — yet I had not voiced one of them."

It was arranged that Mr. Carpenter would have a carriage built for Mrs. Eddy according to her specifications. After selecting a firm in Taunton, he and Mrs. Carpenter journeyed there every day for many weeks supervising every detail. On the day it was finally delivered Mrs. Eddy exclaimed, "Isn't it a dandy!"

This lovely carriage was probably the one that was delivered in 1904 and gave August Mann and John Salchow a problem to solve. It may have been after her first drive when descending from the carriage her heel caught in the openwork pattern of the new iron steps. The Leader's direction to correct the situation caused August Mann to order new steps immediately and to take the unsatisfactory ones to a carriage building firm to be adjusted for temporary use. Two hours later the original steps had been spoiled beyond use, and when the new ones arrived they proved to be duplicates of the openwork steps. John Salchow wrote:

> Such instances as this had early shown me that error was always trying to tell those who worked for Mrs. Eddy that they could not carry out her instructions. She herself talked with me and taught me how to resist these arguments and to meet the belief of reversal. . . . I had learned to be awake to the error and to protect myself against it. After her few talks with me, I saw that if I did not meet the arguments that I could not do what was expected of me I would fail Mrs. Eddy and be of no use to her; so I never questioned her instructions but did my best to carry them out.

On this occasion he told August to start a fire in the forge. (John had been interested in iron work since boyhood and had set up a small forge at Pleasant View.) Then, almost to his amazement, he came upon a piece of iron almost exactly the right size, lying upon a little piece of lawn that was mowed regularly each week. It was not unlike the silver in the fish's mouth. John Salchow wrote:

> Where it had come from I do not know, for I had never seen such a piece of iron around the place before. But there it was, just as if it had been deliberately placed there for me. I had chisels and tools of my own and was able to cut the iron to just the size to fit inside the rim of the steps. . . . when completed it made a perfect step.

Minnie McDonald, Victoria Sargent's daughter, who served at both Pleasant View and Chestnut Hill once said to John Salchow: "If Mother told you to hang a lantern on the moon, you'd try it;" to which John responded: "Well, if she told me to do it, there would be a way to do it!"

Anything that was done for Mrs. Eddy as a spiritual demonstration was always satisfactory. But few students turned first to God in their efforts to help their Leader. And very few Christian Scientists had any idea that the Discoverer and Founder ever needed any help. They imagined that her life was one of serene bliss. A student had to be wakened from this beautiful dream and his eyes opened to the attempts of evil to destroy the Christ-idea before he understood how to work effectually.

The time had come for the awakening of Mr. and Mrs. Carpenter. It was the first time they had been invited to Pleasant View for a visit, and little did they expect that they were to be jolted by the aggressive features of animal magnetism on that lovely day.

Mrs. Eddy arranged the seating placing one on each side of her on

THE CHRISTIAN SCIENCE BANNER
"His Banner over me was Love."

the sofa. She held their hands in hers, and then she told them the story of Dr. Eddy's being arrested for murder. Such sinister motives had never entered the thoughts of these young people, and the uncoverings in this long, dark episode seemed horrible to them; but it caused them to ponder ever afterwards, and it began their awakening. At the close of the visit Mrs. Eddy apologized for spending the whole time in telling about such an incident and told them they must come again soon:

> Before she would let us go, she insisted that we see her banner picturing a shepherd carrying a lamb, with the quotation from the Song of Solomon, "His banner over me was love." She said, "I have carried the little lambs in my arms just like that."

Little did the Carpenters realize that she had been carrying *them* in her arms that very day while opening their eyes to the insidiousness of evil.

It was in the spring of 1904 that Mr. Carpenter became aware that Mrs. Eddy was in need of a new team of horses. An article in the *Boston Journal* stated:

> Mrs. Mary Baker Eddy would not have the finest pair of carriage horses in America. She said when she looked such a pair over, "They are a pair of devils sent to kill me." The team had been selected by J. M. Osborne of Paris, Ky., who had instructions to buy the best team of carriage horses in the United States. Mrs. Eddy made the expression quoted in a letter to T. L. L. Temple of Texarkana, Ark., who had sent her the team as a gift. The team consisted of the blue ribbon winners Tattersal and Eckersall. They cost Mr. Temple $10,000, and Mr. Osborne accompanied the horses to the home of Mrs. Eddy and tried to persuade her to ride behind them. They remained in her stables but a few days, when she had them shipped back to the donor, and Mr. Temple is using them on his carriage.

Mr. Osborne may have been one of the committees that had been searching the country for a suitable pair of horses for Mrs. Eddy. Her old span had misbehaved too often to be kept much longer, and her directors had appointed more than one such committee. Mr. Carpenter discussed the situation with August Mann, and the imminence of the need caused him to join the search. He spent the next thirty days visiting sales stables and every other possible source, — all to no avail.

> Then one morning I realized that I had spent thirty days fruitlessly . . .
>
> I proceeded, therefore, to wake myself up mentally by realizing

that God has a pair of horses for this dear one who loves and trusts Him and who has sacrificed her human all in the effort to establish His kingdom on earth. I then declared that it was time my dull eyes were opened to see this fact manifested. . . .

On the way to my office I saw a pair of horses harnessed to a carriage. I recognized those horses as the manifestation of my demonstration for our Leader as plainly as if I had raised them from colts.

The owner said the horses were not for sale, but on April 5, 1904, Mr. Carpenter had a bill of sale making him the owner of Princess and Dolly. The next morning August Mann came to approve the pair and soon thereafter Mr. Carpenter arranged for their shipment to Concord.

On her daily drive one of her old span misbehaved once more and Mrs. Eddy said to Mr. Mann, "I cannot drive with these horses any longer; do you know where I can get another pair?" August responded delightedly, "Yes, Mother, they are in the stable," — for Princess and Dolly had just arrived at Pleasant View the day before. However, Mrs. Eddy would not even look at the horses until she had sent for Mr. Carpenter and heard his story, following which she said, "Then you demonstrated them?" When he assured her that he had, she said, "Then I can keep them."

May 10, 1904

Mr. Gilbert C. Carpenter
Christian Scientist,
Beloved Student:

I am told by Mr. Mann and Mr. Frye that you have made the gift to me of one of the finest spans of horses I ever owned. I did not look for such largess! It seemed enough that you should search and find them for me. I feel bankrupt in thanks. Words cannot express my gratitude to you. It is the dearest, the best, the most needed gift I ever received. What shall I do to repay you? I can only say, call on me in an hour of need and I will try to help thee. Give my love to Mrs. Carpenter. I deeply enjoyed my few minutes with you both.

Ever gratefully, lovingly, your leader
Mary Baker Eddy

In his response Mr. Carpenter wrote:

. . . the offer of a sheltering harbor if my faith should fail, more than compensates for the little the foresight of your household has put in my way to do for you. Should I devote my life and all my substance to help make your life more comfortable during its earthly sojourn, I should still be your debtor. My week's stay at Pleasant View taught me more practical Christian Science than is accorded to most of humanity and for this I desire to return thanks. That you should have taken your priceless time to have seen us personally has touched me deeply and will never be forgotten, but only makes the demands more imperative to demonstrate more of Christian Science.

On the thirtieth of January in 1905 Mrs. Eddy talked with Mr. and Mrs. Carpenter at Pleasant View on the subject of finding a suitable maid for her. Mr. Carpenter said: "If we are good enough God will show me some one for your helper." A little later in the conversation he said, "It is a privilege to suffer for Christ," and Mrs. Eddy asked him if he was willing to leave his business, his family and all to come and serve her. He promptly answered, "Yes." When she asked about his family he told her he had three children, the eldest eight-year-old Gilbert, Jr. and the youngest a two-year-old toddler.

Next the Leader asked Mr. Carpenter: "Would you be willing to let your wife come and serve me for one year?" He answered unhesitatingly and unreservedly, "Yes!" Mrs. Eddy then talked with Mrs. Carpenter who agreed to come in two days provided her babe could be allowed to come occasionally to see her. As it turned out, when the call came a few weeks later Mrs. Carpenter was pregnant with their fourth child, so it was Mr. Carpenter who went to Pleasant View for a year.

CHAPTER XXII

LIFE AT PLEASANT VIEW

When Christian Scientists come to Pleasant View, I demand of them that they leave their belongings and take up the cross.
— MARY BAKER EDDY

1905

ON the ninth of February Mrs. Eddy contributed a short article entitled "Heaven" *(My.* 267) to the *New York American* in response to an invitation received from that publication. In a notebook she kept she wrote on the same date: "Mrs. Sibyl O'Brien of the *Boston Herald* sought me to contribute to a symposium in that paper." She acquiesced to this request also with "Prevention and Cure of Divorce" *(My.* 268) which appeared in the *Boston Herald* on Sunday, March 5. First she poses the question:

> The frequency of divorce shows that the imperative nature of the marriage relation is losing ground, — hence that some fundamental error is engrafted on it. What is this error?

Her answer, "Christ's plan of salvation from divorce," will stand for all time and leads unto life eternal.

But while the Woman was teaching and *demonstrating* eternal life, the mental murderers were again striking at her human sense of life with a recent report sent through the press that Mrs. Eddy had died of pneumonia three or four months ago. After keeping the story alive for quite some time, the *New York Herald* sent a reporter to Concord to see Mrs. Eddy personally. For one who readily gave one thousand dollars rather than one minute of her time, this was a trying demand. It was probably William B. Johnson who answered the door when the man from the *Herald* arrived. In the reporter's words:

> In a few minutes the door opened and an elderly man, in clerical

garb, bade me enter. I entered the vestibule and then the hallway. It was bright and withal homelike and comfortable in its oaken finishings.

I was ushered into the cosily but not extravagantly furnished parlor at the right. My host invited me to be seated, and drawing up a chair faced me. He did not say so, but I knew he wanted to know about my mission. No, I was not speaking with Mr. Frye. I asked his name, but it was not given me.

As the two men sat talking another man entered:

It was Mr. Frye, a very pleasant-faced man, with hair slightly tinged with gray and with a short gray moustache. Delightful of manners, easy and graceful, Mr. Frye has a bright, smiling eye.

He greeted me cheerfully and said that he had read my letter to Mrs. Eddy and that she would see me in her library for a few minutes. . . .

Following this brief interview Mrs. Eddy wrote to the editor of the *New York Herald* on that Saturday:

A representative of the *Herald* called today to inform me of the rumor that I had deceased some three months ago. This is an oft-repeated falsehood. I granted him a moment's interview, hoping you would refute this rumor in the next edition of your paper. I am in my usual good health, drive out every day, and attend to my regular business.

The reporter's story appeared in the *New York Herald* of Sunday, March 5. He said of Mrs. Eddy:

As Mrs. Eddy spoke her face lighted sweetly, a motherly expression, and the brightness of the large, full eyes bespoke the owner's mental activity. Her tall figure was exquisitely gowned in black silk of becoming modish cut. Her welcome was cordial, but withal I could not but feel the exigencies of my quest for facts had not been without their exactions in thus compelling Mrs. Eddy to stand before me to prove that she still lived. But her grace and charm softened the difficulty and hardship of that visit and I left Pleasant View with a mind filled with peculiar thoughts.

Mrs. Eddy still lives and apparently is enjoying the normal health of one of her years.

The Leader wrote Mr. Farlow that the article would help to refute the rumor, but a few days later she wrote him again to "Please say and do no more on this silly subject of my decease." But there were times when the world's hatred constantly endeavoring to destroy her seemed almost overwhelming. It took more than faith to sustain her and enable her to face the wicked lies and malice in the storm she sensed was coming. She did not see a glad pathway ahead in the poem she wrote on March 16:

WHITHER

Father, did'st not Thou the dark wave treading
Lift from despair the struggler with the sea?
And heed'st Thou not the scalding tear man's shedding,
And know'st Thou not the pathway glad and free?

The weight of anguish which they blindly bind
On earth, the bitter searing to the core of love;
This crushing out of health and peace, mankind —
Thou all, Thou infinite — dost doom above.

Oft mortal sense is darkened unto death
(The Stygian shadow of a world of glee);
The old foundations of an early faith
Sunk from beneath man, whither shall he flee?

To Love divine, whose kindling mighty rays
Brighten the horoscope of crumbling creeds,
Dawn Truth delightful, crowned with endless days,
And Science ripe in prayer, in word, and deeds.

Love divine uplifted her beyond reach of the enemy's fire, and she in turn was uplifting her children with the same divine Love. On March 10 she wrote to Calvin Hill in appreciation:

You are more than a hill — you are a mountain, and the dwelling place of tenderness, unselfishness, Soul. The silver dish you sent me is very convenient to keep my lunch warm. Will you let me pay for it? I feel badly to have you expend your money for me. It is all I need and just what I do need to have you care for my needs, just as you are doing. God bless you, dear one, fill you with victory over the falsities of human thought and with sweet peace and rest from all fear. *Love* casts out fear.

On March 15 she said in a helpful letter to Laura Lathrop:

The body and you are not one. You are not in the body, talking to it, and it cannot talk of itself. You are spiritual, not material; you are my good, faithful, follower of Christ — the image of God. Indeed, you are this idea and have no strife with the flesh. You reflect God, and His image is like unto Spirit, not matter. The flesh has no connection with you. Realize this, and you are master of the situation.

And to her Augusta she wrote:

> My *precious Student:*
> Yes, you are conscious of God's care and love; and that I will stand by you, will warn and comfort you and help you onward and upward. Be patient, humble, loving, full of faith and good works and all will be well with thee.

Augusta did not yet know how straight, and narrow, and singular the path onward and upward is. But the Leader knew, and was constantly guiding and leading this student to be separate, as her closing paragraph shows:

> Be of good cheer, darling, you are supported by a strong arm, — your students are loyal. Now take my advice. Do not counteract any movement for churches or for the unity of two in one — even if it seems best to do so. But let the students learn from experience, and God direct them. *You are entrenched,* and had better be left out than mixed with what cannot mix. So be wise and wait on God and He will direct thy path.

Later in March she wrote to Augusta again:

> Darling, my darling Augusta:
> Do not name a season dress for me now. I am submerged in work for the field and cannot attend to being fitted now.
> I am going to send you a little remembrance of me as soon as I can attend to it.

The Leader was submerged in work for the field and she was also very busy at home. George Kinter had returned to his home fairly early in the year. William B. Johnson returned to his home in Boston on March 16, the day that Gilbert Carpenter came to Pleasant View to spend a year. Mr. Carpenter made a decision when he embarked upon this year of service to the Leader. That was the decision not to take the time to treat himself while he was in her employ. He reasoned that if he did, error might keep him constantly employed in maintaining his own physical well-being to the neglect of his work for the Leader and the Cause. He saw himself as "a channel through which the unbroken power of infinite good flows out to the universe;" and only when thought turns to self is there an interruption of this power, producing illness — stagnation, inflammation, etc. He tested this unfoldment the first time he was tempted with illness:

> I sat down by the window and let my thought go out in prayer to all

> the sufferers in the world in hospitals; in sick rooms; those condemned under the classification incurable; those without knowledge of the presence of God to care for them; to bring them the truth that there is no incurable disease and that, even though they did not know it, they do *have* a heavenly Father who is the great Physician, who "healeth all thy diseases." I let my thought issue forth to all who needed God, with the true realization of the God that is all-presence, all-power and Love. When I returned from this mental journey, I found myself well. . . . During the year I was at Pleasant View, this divine mode of effort, which I believe was God-inspired, never failed me.

Mrs. Eddy was an enigma to most of her students much of the time, but Mr. Carpenter spent the ensuing fifty years endeavoring to understand the baffling experiences that others chose to ignore, bury out of sight, or whisper about behind closed doors. The record of his soliloquies and probings has given us a picture of life at Pleasant View.

One of the first things the Leader asked each newcomer to her home was, "Do you want to go to church?" If the answer was, "Yes," she explained that it was a mistake for a mature student such as those in her home to think they could *get* something from going to church. Their work was so much broader, on such an advanced spiritual plane, and, under her guidance, so much more vital in spreading the gospel of Truth, that the desire to attend church was a return to old theology. She impressed upon them that it was their business to uphold the church, not vice versa. One dear teacher has said: "If you go to church, be sure to take it with you."

The days at Pleasant View did not vary. Sunday was no different from any other day. The main work was the mental work which Mrs. Eddy termed watches in which everyone participated including the Leader. There were three regular daily watches of one hour each which in 1905 were the morning Watch Hour from 9 to 10 A.M., the afternoon Watch Hour from 3 to 4 P.M., and the evening watch from 8 to 9 P.M. Each mental worker had an additional watch of his own in which he worked alone for an hour. There were times when all worked uninterruptedly to meet some exigency, but this was the exception and the foregoing was the general routine.

Mr. Carpenter has outlined a typical day at Pleasant View in 1905 from a secretary's point of view. Breakfast was at 7:30. The assistant secretary sorted the morning mail separating all that the secretaries could answer from that needing the Leader's attention. They learned to assume responsibility and not to usurp her valuable time for needless details. When they needed help Mr. Frye made final decisions.

Either Mr. Frye or Mrs. Eddy wrote out instructions for the

morning watch at nine o'clock. At ten o'clock work on the mail continued, and at 10:45 that which had been set aside for Mrs. Eddy's attention was taken to her. Dinner was at noon, and Mrs. Eddy's was taken to her in her study, although she came downstairs for most of the other meals.

Her daily drive was usually at 1 P.M. and at least an hour long. This was a busy hour for all the household, for they endeavored to clean all the rooms — particularly Mrs. Eddy's — and have all in readiness when she returned. She usually rested for half an hour after her drive, then spent the afternoon, first with the Watch Hour, then reading, answering, or dictating answers to, letters.

Supper was at six, following which she occasionally called the students for a period of quiet conversation. More often she called only one student to attend to some business at hand. At times she might dictate an article. At one time she dictated some of her early history to Mr. Carpenter.

The evening Watch Hour for all the household was from 8 till 9 P.M. Mr. Carpenter's additional watch was from 11 P.M. till midnight. At the evening watch Mrs. Eddy went out on the porch and sat in the swing as Mr. Carpenter has recorded:

> Every night she sat on the upper porch in her swing from eight until nine, at which time she retired. Just before leaving for her room she might call me to come to her swing to say good night. I always felt that she devoted this hour to a general outpouring of spiritual good to humanity, because the sweetness of her thought stood out so vividly when she said good night, that it never failed to bring tears to my eyes. It seemed more than I could stand. A peace, a love, a strength and calm emanated from her thought to such a degree that human sense could hardly endure it.

Another student who received training in the Divinity Course at this time was a well known lecturer. Dr. Fluno was a member of Mrs. Eddy's household during part of the year that Mr. Carpenter was there.

DR. FRANCIS J. FLUNO, C.S.D.

FRANCIS J. Fluno, M.D. was a practising physician when he first heard of Christian Science in the summer of 1885. In November of that year both he and his wife were members of Mrs. Eddy's Primary class in the college. Almost immediately Dr. Fluno entered upon the practice of Christian Science in Lexington, Kentucky.

In February of 1887 Dr. Fluno again attended the Metaphysical College, this time as a member of Mrs. Eddy's Normal class which convened February 7.

The following year, 1888, the Flunos moved to San Francisco, locating permanently in Oakland, California in 1889.

Soon after the formation of the Board of Lectureship in 1898 Dr. Fluno was appointed to that Board, lecturing first in the far western United States, and later throughout much of the world. The first lecture in Hawaii and the first in Africa were both given by Dr. Fluno. No doubt being a member of Mrs. Eddy's household strengthened him in his work. He was not a young man at this time, and young Gilbert Carpenter was impressed by the doctor's words. Mr. Carpenter recorded:

> An interesting incident I recall is, that when he was seventy years old, he sent Mrs. Eddy three lectures for her approval. She turned down one of them, declaring that the public was not ready for it. She said that he might give it in twenty years. The question assailed him as to whether he would be lecturing when he was *ninety* years old, but he did not doubt. He gave the lecture as Mrs. Eddy directed him. It was called "Christian Science: Pure Metaphysics," and was printed in pamphlet form in 1917.

In 1905 at Pleasant View when Mr. Carpenter had been there only about three weeks, he got a lesson in the Divinity Course which was quite a surprise to him. Mrs. Eddy called him and asked him to work for her. At the time he did not know that all the mental workers who were newcomers to Pleasant View got this same assignment after they had been there about three weeks. After thirty years of pondering he wrote:

> The main value of the effort to help our Leader would have been lost, had there been the slightest suggestion that she was asking for such help for any other reason than that she needed it. But after thirty years of pondering the problem, I am reaching the conclusion that perhaps she did not need the help, but requested it for the sake of the growth of the student who was to give it.

There is no doubt that the world's resistance to and hatred of the highest manifestation of womanhood ever to appear on this planet caused the Woman a great deal of physical suffering which she was endeavoring to train students to meet and overcome. But the training went on in the *Divinity Course* in her home whether she was experiencing physical suffering or not. After thirty years of pondering and probing Mr. Carpenter began to suspect that this was the case:

> At times she would call me in the middle of the night to come to her to help her audibly. Yet I think she was far more interested in determining my mental status and in training me, than she was in receiving such help. One reason for this conclusion is the fact that she listened carefully to every scientific argument I used, and was alert to correct me for the slightest deviation — all of which was unlike a person in such great need that they could not help themselves metaphysically. . . .
>
> As I argued, she followed me, ready to correct me if I made one misstatement. No matter how badly off she seemed to be, her thought was alert and ready to detect one false declaration.

Many of the mental workers who went through this training program in the Leader's home believed that their work for her was the important thing, and they well knew each time they were called whether it was a success or a failure, for she told them. Little did they know what the Leader was doing for them and for the world. They went back to the field far better prepared to meet the malicious animal magnetism that would attempt to drown the Cause of Christian Science, and many of them thought and said that they were never taught the Divinity Course.

CHAPTER XXIII

DETERMINED REPORTERS

The truth in regard to your Leader heals the sick and saves the sinner. — MARY BAKER EDDY

1905

THE daily mail at Pleasant View kept several secretaries busy, their first task each day being to decide what needed Mrs. Eddy's attention. The correspondence from her churches and students all over the world had to be sifted, while the constant stream of missives from her lieutenants in Boston — directors, trustees, and editor always had priority.

There was a good deal of correspondence early in 1905 regarding changes in the *Journal.* The April issue would begin volume twenty-three with a new dress. In February Mr. Johnson had written from Pleasant View to Mr. McKenzie that Mrs. Eddy would send a list of contributors and some suggestions before publication of the April number. Also that she was returning their samples having marked her preference, but would like a lighter shade of green for the cover. A little later she approved the color and lettering but did not care for the faddish edges, stating, "the shabby, uneven top, bottom and sides I do not like."

On April 2 she wrote Mr. McLellan that this month's *Journal* was fine, the only imperfection being too many testimonies, "24 pages . . . are too much like patent medicine suggestions." This April 2 letter also stated:

> Please present my compliments to the Publishing Society for their loving sense of my little poem; and for $100 which I certainly do not desire for the service rendered, but greatly prize the courtesy that prompted it. You must not repeat it, but give me the pleasure to know what you think of my old age versification.

This was no doubt for "Whither" *(My.* 350) which was the leader in the April *Journal,* but it is not likely that her ambitious, young editor felt the poem's depth and meaning. Today it continues to lift the "weight of anguish" from her disciples who feel overburdened by "the Stygian shadow of a world of glee," as it surely lifted the Leader above the shafts of the mental assassins to Love divine in the spring of 1905. On April 26 she wrote to Calvin Hill:

> The first thing I do in the morning when I awake is to declare I shall have no other mind before divine Mind, and become conscious of this; and then adhere to it throughout the entire day, and then the evil cannot touch me. I have done it, but am a poor specimen of preservation. But the greatest miracle of the age is that I am alive.

An appreciative letter from Mrs. Mims commenting upon Mrs. Eddy's article on "Divorce" caused the Leader to write her editor in April to please publish Mrs. Mims' letter along with these comments:

> On reading the above letter from our distinguished lecturer and beloved student I was reminded of the following Scripture "For as Jonas was a sign unto the Ninevites, so shall also the Son of man be to this generation. The queen of the south shall rise up in the judgment with the men of this generation, and condemn them; for she came from the utmost parts of the earth to hear the wisdom of Solomon; and, behold, a greater than Solomon is here." Luke 11: 30,31.

The Leader wrote to churches in Brooklyn, Pittsburg, and St. Louis *(My.* 196) in April, but her letter to Third Church, London *(My.* 205) on April 28 is of special interest.

There had been an epidemic of letters from students of Science at this time all of which had been withheld from Mrs. Eddy by her secretaries. Several referred to a distinguishable portrait of Mrs. Eddy in the shadows on the full moon asking if this had spiritual significance. One from Providence told of a practitioner's taking a group of students to a reading room to view a portrait of Jesus which in a certain light resembled Mrs. Eddy. Mr. Carpenter knew that these and similar letters relating to such phenomena (many of which had come from England) had not been seen by Mrs. Eddy; yet, when she dictated the letter to Third Church, London, to Gilbert Carpenter, one short paragraph stated:

> Seeing a man in the moon or seeing a person in the picture of Jesus, or believing that you see an individual who has passed through the shadow called death, is not seeing the spiritual idea of God; but it is seeing a human belief, which is far from the fact that portrays Life,

Truth, Love.

One of the issues that her secretaries endeavored to handle without disturbing the Leader was the constant stream of requests from reporters for interviews with Mrs. Eddy. They turned down all such requests and did their best to shield her from this invasion, but in the spring of 1905 one persistent reporter from the *Boston Herald* would not give up. Her name was Mrs. Sibyl Wilbur O'Brien.

SIBYL WILBUR

SIBYL Wilbur's mother was a Congregationalist and her father was a Quaker, but both died before Sibyl had finished school, so she left her New York home to live with Methodist relatives in the midwest where she attended a Methodist university in St. Paul. Her journalistic career which began in Minneapolis with society editing, took her next to Washington, D.C. where she met and married a gay young Irishman named O'Brien and joined the Catholic church.

In her reporting she covered all areas from working and weeping with striking miners to lunching, teaing, and dining with celebrities, all of which she termed an apprenticeship to her next step, foreign correspondence: — "Embassies and Spring salons in Paris, Ballets, racing and Parliament, teas on the embankment in London." This worldly success had been Miss Wilbur's life for fifteen years. Now at age thirty-five she had her own *feuilleton* in the *Boston Herald,* — her own page to fill each Sunday with topics of her own choice. In less than a year in Boston she had interviewed a great many New England dignitaries including prominent speakers at Harvard University, the aged Queen of the Back Bay, Julia Ward Howe, and a great many others. Miss Wilbur soon learned that the toast of Boston snobbishness: "To the great state of Massachusetts, home of the sacred cod, where the Lowells speak only with Cabots, and the Cabots speak only with God"; was growing old, but some Boston intellectuals, the wits, were extending it to a woman in Concord, New Hampshire, which caught her interest. They said this woman lived in seclusion, spoke only with God, and had learned a strange language which none but herself and some of her followers could understand.

Miss Wilbur had not been in Boston long enough to know much about Christian Science activities in that metropolis, but her interest was aroused and she suggested to her editor the name of Mrs. Eddy of Concord for one of her Sunday topics. He laughed tolerantly as he responded: "That might be interesting to some people and tiresome to more, but you won't get anywhere with it. She is a recluse, probably an invalid, or this seclusion may be a pose. Her representatives guard her like the Pope in the Vatican."

"And who are her representatives?" "Her principal spokesman is Alfred Farlow. . . . Every time we mention the subject of Christian Science in a news way, he appears with a correction, and he is so suave and persistent we have to insert the correction. It's a nuisance, because we never seem to say things right." After a good deal more conversation he said of course they would print an interview with Mrs. Eddy if she should get it, "But you won't get it."

Miss Wilbur's next step was to call on Alfred Farlow for a letter of introduction. She found his office in very modest quarters on Huntington Avenue and very convenient to where she lived just across the square. On this visit she asked him if Christian Science did not mean mind over matter and was astonished by his reply: "No, Miss Wilbur, Christian Science says there is no matter. That is just how ridiculous we are in the eyes of the world. Matter is a state of mortal mind. In reality, all is Spirit." He smiled kindly and they sat in silence, for as an interviewer she had learned not to argue, but she was thinking: "no matter indeed, when we live and move and have our being in matter!" As the conversation resumed she felt Mr. Farlow's attitude was that of a sympathetic teacher with an intelligent child. She did not gain the letter she sought, but was invited to return whenever there was something more she wished to discuss.

About this time God moved in Miss Wilbur's life with what she described as:

> . . . a struggle and sharp experience which changed the aspect of my world. After a long night of sorrow I heard one Sunday morning the bells of the new Old South across the square and said aloud, "God, let me do something for women who are alone."

As she voiced this prayer to God a vision of the Woman in Concord came before her eyes and all doubt of the Woman's noble cause dropped away from this worldly journalist. In ensuing visits with Mr. Farlow she began learning a little about Spirit and matter, but her main purpose still was an interview with Mrs. Eddy. Several visits and about two months later Mr. Farlow told her one day that Mr. Armstrong, a Director of the Church, was coming to see her with a message from Mrs.Eddy. When he came:

> . . . he looked observingly around my study and somewhat scrutinizingly at me, I thought, and I looking at this bearded man . . . rugged, honest, earnest . . . said to myself: "Here is St. Peter, I do believe, come to my abode, greatly humble and humbly great. And what has

he for me?"

He had a letter from Mrs. Eddy and a copy of Science and Health, and a signed photograph. He said very little, refused to be seated, and departed leaving a current of fresh air that came as from another world; a world much different from smug and busy Boston, Back Bay mansions or even classic Harvard.

The letter from the Leader that Joseph Armstrong bore said:

March 25, 1905

Dear Madam:

You will excuse me since I must be uniform in declining the honor of calls from newspaper reporters. Christian Science cannot be carried on in certain worldly ways. Accept my thanks and this book. Please read page 464, paragraph 1.

Sincerely yours,
Mary Baker Eddy

Miss Wilbur immediately read paragraph 1 on page 464, and this gracious refusal caused her to ponder her own motives. She determined to read Science and Health and set down all her questions and criticisms, and began carrying the book, covered, everywhere she went, reading on trains and streetcars. The book answered many of the first foolish questions on her list which were crossed off as more mature questions were added.

Several weeks had elapsed when Miss Wilbur arose a little late one Sunday morning, took in her morning papers and saw screaming headlines in the *New York Herald* about Mrs. Eddy. The story depicted Mrs. Eddy as a hopeless invalid, unbalanced if not insane, and her followers as duped by those who kept the Leader drugged and helpless. Amazed and indignant that America's greatest newspaper would flash such an outrage to the world, she phoned Mr. Farlow, then with his assent dashed across Copley Square to his office.

She found him unbelievably calm and composed and asked breathlessly if he hadn't seen the morning's *New York Herald.* When he said he had, she said, "You have seen the papers, you know what has happened?" His calm reply was: "I have seen the papers. Nothing has happened." Miss Wilbur expostulated a little longer, then burst into tears, and Mr. Farlow gently told her to sit down and compose herself:

I sat down, wept a little longer, dried my eyes and looked at him. He was leaning back composedly in his chair, no longer smiling, but gazing at me seriously, questioningly. Presently he said, "One might think you loved Mrs. Eddy. Do you?"

> "I don't know. How can I know? I am thinking of her church, her great book, her noble work for humanity. They want to make it all ridiculous, make her a foolish, silly old woman, a lunatic. This beloved Christian woman all right-minded people must at least respect. Yes, I love her and I want to help her."

Miss Wilbur could not accept Mr. Farlow's assurrance that nothing had happened to Mrs. Eddy. She said she knew that newspaper and that it would print the story in its Paris Herald, in London and in Rome, — would stop at nothing and would keep it up until someone outside the Christian Science church answered them. To which Mr. Farlow responded, "Perhaps you will be that someone." Then he offered to send her list of questions to Mrs. Eddy at Pleasant View. But Miss Wilbur declared emphatically that *now* was the time to go to Pleasant View and she was going with or without a letter of introduction.

When she told her decision to her editor he said she would fare no better than the *New York Herald* reporters who had prowled the grounds and photographed Mrs. Eddy being helped into her carriage, but had not been admitted to the house. Before the week was out, however, Mr. Farlow gave her a letter of introduction to Calvin Frye, though not to Mrs. Eddy, and Saturday morning found Miss Wilbur on her way to Concord.

It was afternoon when she arrived at the gate of Pleasant View where she dismissed her carriage, and only a few minutes later when she was in the library conversing with Mr. Frye who was very busy and a little annoyed. At his insistence that Mrs. Eddy was very busy and would not grant an interview she replied that she would wait in Concord until Mrs. Eddy was free to see her:

> If Mrs. Eddy is ill, I will not wait; if Mrs. Eddy is not ill I shall wait with what patience I can find, knowing that you will eventually understand that my business is serious.

After considering, Mr. Frye said that he could not persuade Mrs. Eddy but would give her the message and hoped her decision would be favorable. Laura Sargent then showed Miss Wilbur around the lower floor introducing her to several in the household; then introduced her to their steward, August Mann, who would show her all about the grounds. Two or three hours later after she had seen the stables and carriage house, the horses and Mrs. Eddy's several carriages, plus the cow barn and adorable Jersey heifers, and the hot house, Mr. Frye came down to tell Mr. Mann to send the carriage to the door to drive Miss Wilbur back to her hotel. He also bore the message that Mrs. Eddy would send her word tomorrow when she could come to see her.

The next day, Sunday, May 21, August Mann came to tell her that Mrs. Eddy would see her for a few minutes at one o'clock. A little before one as she approached the door a ripple of laughter and soft piano music greeted her ear. A few minutes later in the parlor she again met Mrs. Sargent and a young man (at the piano) she had not seen the day before, Assistant Secretary Gilbert Carpenter. Mrs. Eddy had asked them, and also Mrs. Pamelia Leonard, to show her the treasures in the house.

To Mr. Carpenter Miss Wilbur seemed a typical reporter, keen, intelligent, aggressive. She appeared determined not to miss anything, even turning the pictures on the wall. Before he had finished showing her the various gifts Mrs. Eddy had received, a maid came to say, "Mrs. Eddy will see you now."

When she entered her study on the upper floor Mrs. Eddy was standing looking out the window. In a moment she turned, approached and extended her hand as she welcomed Miss Wilbur cordially, speaking her name. Then she said, "All this fuss to see poor little me." Miss Wilbur answered, "I feel greatly honored at the privilege granted."

"But why should you, my dear child? Why do so many people wish to see me?"

There were so many things Miss Wilbur had wanted to tell Mrs. Eddy, — that an evil power was threatening her, etc., — but she found she could not speak. In a melodiously sweet voice, Mrs. Eddy continued: "All that I ask of the world now is that it grant me time, time to assimilate myself to God." Again Miss Wilbur could not reply.

"Are you satisfied, now that you have met me personally, and now that I have acceded to all your requests?" To this she replied, "I am satisfied."

A few minutes later back in the parlor she sat down quickly, closed her eyes and clasped her hands over her heart. Mr. Carpenter asked if she would like to see the rooms she had not yet inspected, and she answered, "No, I want to go. Why didn't somebody prepare me? I didn't suppose there was any living being like that on earth." Pointing to her heart she added: "It affects me right here." Many a student had felt what Sibyl Wilbur experienced that day. Julia Bartlett wrote:

> I could not come into her presence without feeling an uplift and the love and purity of her thought. I have seen students come from her room so softened and chastened and in tears saying they never saw such love.

From the time of this meeting on May 21 Sibyl Wilbur was dedicated to defending Mrs. Eddy. At a later meeting the Leader put her hands on Miss Wilbur's shoulders and said: "You are doing for me what I cannot do for myself; may we gather flowers together in the fields of eternity."

CHAPTER XXIV

A CHANGE OF SCHEDULE

Thou through thy commandments hast made me wiser than mine enemies: for they are ever with me. — PSALMS

1905

THE day following Sibyl Wilbur's visit, May 22, Alfred Farlow wrote to Gilbert Carpenter:

> Mrs. O'Brien was just in. I think she is the happiest woman on the earth. She was altogether overcome by her interview with Mrs. Eddy and thinks she is the most wonderful woman she ever saw.

Mrs. Eddy was very pleased with Mrs. O'Brien, and sent the following card to the *Boston Herald:*

> A Card
>
> My recent interview of a few moments with Sibyl Wilbur of *The Boston Herald* was prolific. I confess to having yielded reluctantly to meet the occasion for quieting the billows of public opinion, while constantly signalling it as to my course and hoped-for haven. But what a grand, calm call was hers, what a short time it took for us to talk when touched by the truth of an honest purpose! By speaking less and feeling more we parted reciprocally blest. Will Miss Wilbur accept my thanks for her kind courtesy, for leaving me with not one hour less in which to put my mite with hers into the vast treasure-troves of eternity, to draw the interest on deposits gained from minutes, till we receive the principal whereof God keeps account? May she, because of her goodness, broaden her wide range of usefulness; and I, work on to widen mine into paths of peace; till the burden and heat of the day are done, the eventide is past, and bird and blossom awake in the sunshine.
>
> MARY BAKER EDDY
>
> May 24, 1905

This card was published in the *Boston Herald* when Miss Wilbur's interview appeared two or three weeks later. *One* reporter was reporting the truth, but it was quite obvious that others were embarked upon collecting slanderous and false testimony. Several months earlier rumor had reached Alfred Farlow that S. S. McClure, owner of *McClure's Magazine* and McClure Syndicate was planning a muckraking campaign against Mrs. Eddy and Christian Science. Farlow had written to Kinter that the journalist Mrs. Georgine Milmine Welles, with whom he had had pleasant dealings in the past, had been turned against Mrs. Eddy.

In May while Mr. Farlow was concerned about *McClure's Magazine* the Leader was busy with the many aspects of her church. A short message to the May Primary Class of the Board of Education (*My.* 254) was written on May 6. In the *Sentinel* of May 6 she published an amended by-law:

> Article XXVIII [Presently Art. XXIII]. THE MOTHER CHURCH AND BRANCH CHURCHES. LOCAL SELF-GOVERNMENT. Sect. 1
>
> The First Church of Christ, Scientist, in Boston, Mass., shall assume no general official control of other churches of this denomination; and it shall be officially controlled by no other church. This is the denominational rule of Christian Science. Each Church of Christ, Scientist, shall have its own form of government. . . .

The big boarded enclosure behind the little Mother Church in Back Bay Boston was beginning to draw interest and attention. It was also beginning to draw fire from the enemy, and as usual Mrs. Eddy was the prime target. When such attacks caused her severe physical pain she called upon the mental workers in her home to help her, and she expected to receive *immediate* help from them, even as all did from her treatment. At times her students *were* able to help her. On one occasion several years earlier when all in the house had failed, they called A. E. Baker to Pleasant View. Mrs. Eddy opened Science and Health and read three paragraphs which helped her (beginning 312:14) and asked Dr. Baker to read them. He called her attention to the last two lines:

> Therefore God, even thy God, hath anointed thee
> With the oil of gladness above thy fellows.

He then told her of his interest in the last chapter of II Thessalonians which she read, and then immediately exclaimed: "I have got back my God." She was relieved, and rested on that occasion.

But on many occasions the fear of inadequacy in the thoughts of her students eclipsed the help they were trying to give, and the

Leader was obliged to do all her own work. This was no doubt the reason for the paragraph she sent to her directors in May, 1905 to be added to the next edition of Science and Health. The paragraph she had so recently referred Sibyl Wilbur to on page 464 immediately precedes this new paragraph, also on page 464:

> If from an injury or from any cause, a Christian Scientist were seized with pain so violent that he could not treat himself mentally, — and the Scientists had failed to relieve him, — the sufferer could call a surgeon, who would give him a hypodermic injection, then, when the belief of pain was lulled, he could handle his own case mentally. Thus it is that we "prove all things; [and] hold fast that which is good."

The position of this paragraph sandwiched between two paragraphs of the Founder's experience, tells us that it was an expedient of her experience and not a part of the practice of Christian Science. She was leaving a complete account of all her footsteps for the guidance of her children. We have no record that she did call a surgeon for a hypodermic injection in May of 1905, but we can conjecture that she suffered pain so violent that it caused her to provide this expedient for any of her followers who found themselves in such an extreme situation. But the true practice of Christian Science is instantaneous healing which the leader reiterated to Mrs. Stetson in her letter of May 25:

> Darling:
>
> I have little *time* to write my best beloved even.
>
> I was delighted that you were called to bind up the broken hearted — but O, what an opportunity for honoring our Cause by *healing* the man! What I need for help in my life-labor more than all else on earth is — a *healer* such as I were when practising. I beg and pray that you become that.
>
> Yes, I would resign the Readership for three years and this will give you a much better chance to gain that one point, an instantaneous healer of all manner of diseases. I was that, and you should be. Our great Master was that and called upon his followers to do likewise. You can be this and must be in order to be a Christian Scientist. Now address yourself to this duty of yours. Watch, pray, labor, and have **faith,** — *know* that you can be what God demands you to be — and *now are* — His image and likeness — reflecting God, the one and only Healer, reflecting Good, Life, Truth, Love.
>
> Lovingly yours,
> M. B. Eddy

The Leader's message to Lewis Strang two days later again stresses the importance of *healing* above all else:

> One Mind demonstrated *handles* serpents, casts out demons of sense with power of Truth. When will Christian Scientists learn that *blab* never made a single demonstration in building up this Cause? How Mother longs, prays, hopes for *healing* in Truth and Love!

If all Scientists would strive above all else to be instantaneous healers, the attacks of the enemy would be met and mastered, but as it was, under attack, the Leader was left virtually alone to meet the deadly blows of malicious animal magnetism against her life and her cause. Her life was "hid with Christ in God," but her cause suffered a severe blow in May with the sudden death of Mr. E. Noyes Whitcomb, builder of the Mother Church Extension. It is recorded in *Collectanea* that "Mrs. Eddy was indignant when she learned that the Whitcomb family had worked for their father three days after he had passed on to bring him back. She said, 'What! You kept that dear man in the vestibule three days?' " The June *Journal* said of Mr. Whitcomb:

> Our Leader has spoken of him as "one of the noblest, most lovely, and best of men" . . .
>
> He first became known to Christian Scientists in 1894, through his work as one of the contractors for the Mother Church edifice, then in course of erection, but he has become most widely known to them as builder of the church in Concord . . . and as builder of the new edifice now in course of construction for The Mother Church in Boston.
>
> Mr. Whitcomb . . . was elected an Executive Member, December 28, 1901 . . .

Joseph Armstrong may have been unconscious of the subtle fear that took lodgement in his thought, but it did not escape detection by the Leader. Following a subsequent visit Mrs. Eddy wrote to Joseph: "I read in your mind what startled me! . . . You must meet and break the spell of m.a.m. to ruin you and *you can."* Her letter caused Mr. Armstrong concern which caused her to write him again two days later that she was:

> sorry if I gave you a single unnecessary care for yourself. But since the death of Mr. Whitcomb — when I see the image of an evil one in the mind of any one it startles me! But this should not alarm you. . . . Because you have met and mastered this before you can again and *always can* for God is all and there is no other mind.

Joseph Armstrong's care, as was that of the other directors, was almost totally absorbed by the building of the church in Boston. The original plan had called for completion of the Extension of The Mother Church in June, 1907, but the magnitude of the plans of the enemy in opposition to this visible progress caused the Leader to alter her strategy. She asked her directors to dedicate the Extension in June, 1906, — that is, to complete the building a *year* sooner than originally called for. When the directors consulted with the architect and builder they were told that was an absolute impossibility. They next consulted other eminent men in the building profession only to hear the same verdict — that their request was humanly impossible.

At this point the directors ceased asking for *human* opinions and turned to God. Their directions came from God's messenger to this age and if she required it, it was possible of achievement. Their work was to break mortal mind's resistance to the accomplishment in their own consciousness. Soon after they began working rightly, the builder said that he thought it might be done. The architect's chief assistant was directing the work, and he, too, soon conceded that it was possible. But the architect was adamant and unyielding.

Mr. Charles Brigham was a fine architect who had produced a magnificent plan for the Extension, but he was not a Christian Scientist and could not remove the limitation from his thought. He was also suffering from illness, and his physician ordered him to take a trip to the Bermuda Islands for his health about this time which left his assistant in complete charge. From then on the speed of progress on the building increased, but there still remained two year's work to be accomplished in one year of time.

A second step the Leader took was published as a notice from the Board of Directors in the *Sentinel* of May 27:

> In view of the fact that a general attendance of the members of The Mother Church at the Communion and Annual Meeting in Boston entails the expenditure of a large amount of money, and the further fact that it is important that the Building Fund of The Mother Church should be completed as early as possible, it has been decided to omit this year the usual large gathering in Boston, and to ask the members to contribute to the Building Fund the amount which they would have expended in such an event . . .

The time this move saved was far more important in the Leader's eyes than was the money consideration, but mortal mind tends to measure everything in terms of dollars and cents.

Another step the Leader took at this time in 1905 was to awaken students to the mental methods employed by the enemy. She had her secretary Gilbert Carpenter write to Mr. Johnson's son, William Lyman, to make a research into mediumship, clairvoyance, animal magnetism, and modern hypnotism. This he did in the Boston Public Library and the Boston Medical Library, working evenings (after closing hours) in the Clerk's office in the Mother Church. When he wrote his extensive findings to Mrs. Eddy she had Mr. Carpenter write her thanks and "well done" to young Mr. Johnson.

It was June 11 when Sibyl Wilbur's article* appeared in the *Boston Herald:*

> I have seen Mrs. Mary Baker G. Eddy. ...
>
> Mrs. Eddy is alive and well ...
>
> The secret of Pleasant View is no secret at all. ...
>
> ... Mrs. Eddy [spoke] in a voice which had the sweetness of a silver chime about it ... there was force and decision in every word so gently uttered. The force was like a command from a mind accustomed to be obeyed. ...
>
> My last glimpse of her was as she stood there, erect as youth, dominating in expression, and yet gentle, flowerlike, and very lovable. Her last gesture was a wave of her uplifted hand. ...
>
> I left with her secretaries the outline of an interview which Mrs. Eddy agrees to look over at her leisure. ...

Miss Wilbur's article closed with her list of questions each followed by Mrs. Eddy's answer which to many was simply either Yes or No. When republished in the *Sentinel* of June 17 the article was followed by this note:

> *Nota Bene:* Miss Wilbur's courteous and correct explanation of the so-called secret of my isolation from the world leaves one feature, and the main one, to be mentioned.
>
> My seclusion is not at all on account of my age, but solely from lack of time in which to accomplish what I do for humanity, and have the moments left in which to regale myself with the sweet intercourse of society.
>
> My first and forever message is one and eternal, and I shall reiterate it this year, *next year,* and so forth.
>
> MARY BAKER EDDY
>
> June 16, 1905

*See Appendix C.

CHAPTER XXV

OUR MOTHER IN ISRAEL

All the people need to love and adopt Christian Science is a true sense of its founder. In proportion as they have found it will our Cause advance. — MARY BAKER EDDY

1905

COMMUNION season in Boston in the summer of 1905 was a good deal quieter than it had been in previous years with a greatly reduced number of visitors from other states. The Leader's message *(My.* 279) sent to the annual meeting of her church on Tuesday, June 13, reflected an issue that was dominating the news of the day:

> To My Church
>
> *Dearly Beloved:* — I request that every member of The Mother Church of Christ, Scientist, in Boston, pray each day for the amicable settlement of the war between Russia and Japan, and pray that God bless that great nation and those islands of the sea with peace and prosperity.

The three-year term of the readers of The Mother Church had ended and the names of the new readers were announced, — William D. McCrackan, First Reader, and Mrs. Laura Conant, Second Reader. The position that Mr. McCrackan would vacate when he moved to Boston, Committee on Publication for New York, was filled by Mr. Cornell Wilson. The retiring first reader of The Mother Church, Prof. Hermann Hering was requested by Mrs. Eddy to become first reader for the Concord church.

Though the meetings during communion week in 1905 were considerably smaller than in former years, there were still many Christian Scientists from many different locations that attended the Wednesday evening meetings of both The Mother Church and the Concord church. A testimony given by one of these visitors at the Concord church that Wednesday evening, June 14, was of the utmost interest to all. It was given by the wife of General C. C. Allen of Los Angeles, California. Mrs. Allen was a member of Second Church, Los Angeles, and spoke substantially as follows:

> Two years ago I had a man come to my house to repair some window shades in the parlor. When he had finished his work I asked him to come to my study. I left him in my room for a time, and when I returned he said, "I see that you are a Christian Scientist," because he saw my literature in the room. Then he said, "I was healed by the Discoverer and Founder of Christian Science, Mrs. Mary Baker Eddy." I said, "I want you to tell me all about it." Then he gave me these facts: About eighteen years ago, while living in Boston, I fell from the third story of a building on which I was working, to the pavement. My leg was broken in three places. I was taken to a hospital, where they tried to help me. They said that the leg was so bad that it would have to be amputated. I said, "No, I would rather die." They permitted it to heal as best it might, and as a result I had to wear an iron shoe eight or nine inches high. I was called to Mrs. Eddy's home on Commonwealth Avenue, in Boston, to do some light work. Mrs. Eddy came into the room where I was busy, and observing my condition, kindly remarked, "I suppose you expect to get out of this some time." I answered, "No; all that can be done for me has been done, and I can now manage to get around with a cane." Mrs. Eddy said, "Sit down and I will treat you." When she finished the treatment she said, "You go home and take off that iron shoe, and give your leg a chance to straighten out." I went home and did as I was told, and now I am so well that, so far as I know, one leg is as good as the other.

The Discoverer and Founder who never ceased such immediate proofs of the truth and practicability of her great discovery was little understood and often gossiped about by those nearest to her. On this same June 14 she said in a letter to her editor, Archibald McLellan: "What you may hear of me can give you little idea of what you should know — or what is true of me." What he "should know" and what is true of the Discoverer and Founder of Christian Science is what every Christian Scientist should know, — that Mary Baker Eddy is God's chosen witness and just as much the manifestation of the Christ as is her brother, Jesus. Jesus' revelation to John was not fulfilled until the advent of Mary Baker Eddy. And Jesus rejoiced to see her day: "and he saw it, and was glad." The Leader tried repeatedly to give this message to her students, but they were dull of hearing, so very often her words were not unlike those of Jesus:

> John 8:49 I honour my Father, and ye do dishonour me. . . .
> 54 If I honour myself my honour is nothing: it is my Father that honoureth me; of whom ye say, that he is your God;

> 55 Yet ye have not known him; but I know him: and if I should say, I know him not, I shall be a liar like unto you: but I know him, and keep his saying.

Laura Sargent was one of the very few students who faithfully served the Leader year after year, who anguished when Mrs. Eddy anguished and rejoiced when she rejoiced. One day in June Laura had cause for rejoicing. Mary Beecher Longyear had been invited to Pleasant View where she enjoyed an hour's visit with Mrs. Eddy, which the Leader also enjoyed, for this student never brought her problems nor came asking favors. Following the visit Laura said to Mrs. Longyear: "What in the world were you talking about that made Mother laugh so heartily? I haven't heard her laugh like that since I don't know when!"

Another student who faithfully served, *obeyed,* and followed her Leader was Augusta Stetson. A June 14 letter to Augusta said:

> I am in great need of summer suits of clothing; two dresses, and two teajackets. Will you send me samples for these? O, how good you are to me! What can I do to pay you, tell me dearest one? You are all the student that I can depend upon to clothe me, and inasmuch as you have done it to me, ye have done it unto the Father, said Jesus.

In June of 1905 Mrs. Eddy became the recipient of the first copy (numbered No. 1) of *The Book of the Presidents,* "a rare volume, which has received the highest praise." This collection of biographies of presidents included a few other outstanding Americans, four of whom were women, one of whom was Mary Baker Eddy. The Leader had commissioned Edward Everett Norwood to make the arrangements for the inclusion of the requested Christian Science manuscripts. In this capacity he had had a confrontation with the editor, Congressman Charles H. Grosvenor (from Ohio), in which he had had to defend Mrs. Eddy most vigorously. When Mrs. Eddy learned of it she sent Mr. Norwood a twenty dollar goldpiece with this note:

> Please accept this symbol of my thanks to you for obedience to Golden Rule, and great kindness to me.

The heirloom edition of one thousand copies at $1000 each was offered to one thousand specially selected "representative citizens of the United States of America, who stand at the head of their respective vocations." *The Boston Herald* of June 26 stated:

> The place and importance accorded to Mrs. Eddy is in full keeping with the distinguished character of this great work. . . . Accompany-

ing her written history is a beautiful engraved portrait . . . There are also fine photogravures of her present home estate, Pleasant View, her former home in Lynn, where she wrote the Christian Science textbook, Science and Health; First Church of Christ, Scientist, of Concord, N. H., Mrs. Eddy's munificent gift to the Concord Scientists, and Mrs. Eddy's house on Commonwealth Avenue in Boston.

The biography of Mrs. Eddy is a just and discriminating article by Judge Septimus J. Hanna . . . the special feature of this great work is the remarkable letter by the Discoverer and Founder of Christian Science . . . In this letter, Mrs. Eddy, in a few clear statements presents the fundamentals of Christian Science in a way as convincing as it is forceful.

The distinguished place accorded to Mrs. Eddy is another of the many evidences of the widening sphere of her spiritual ministry, and emphasizes the patent fact of her growing influence among the intelligent and cultured classes of this and foreign lands.

The few clear statements in Mrs. Eddy's brief letter which she had written September 17, 1904 said:

Upheld by divine Love man can make himself perfect, but he must not attempt this too rapidly with his neighbor. To so live as to keep consciousness in constant relation to God, is to individualize infinite power, — and this is Christian Science.

On the twenty-seventh of June "a spiritual foresight of the nation's drama presented itself" to our Leader's consciousness. She saw that the United States of America which had *always* stood *alone* was being manipulated to get involved in international affairs, the entangling alliances of which the Father of our country, George Washington, had warned us to beware. Immediately she wrote to the Israelites, her children, a word of guidance *(My.* 280) which was published in the next issue of the *Sentinel:*

"HEAR, O ISRAEL: THE LORD OUR GOD IS ONE LORD"

I now request that the members of my church cease special prayer for the peace of nations, and cease in full faith that God does not hear our prayers only because of oft speaking, but that He will bless all the inhabitants of the earth, and none can stay His hand nor say unto Him, What doest Thou? Out of His allness He must bless all with His own truth and love.

This request evoked a great deal of comment from the public press, and caused Mrs. Eddy to send "An Explanation" *(My.* 280) to the *Boston Herald* which appeared in that paper on July 13. In her "explanation" she stated that "a spiritual foresight . . . awakened a wiser want, even to know how to pray . . ." Jesus' foresight caused him to weep over Jerusalem, and Mrs. Eddy's foresight caused her to weep for America, but she also taught her students how to combat the wickedness that caused the downfall of Jerusalem, — the same wickedness that was plotting the downfall of America. When Jesus wept over Jerusalem he said: "If thou hadst known ... the things which belong unto thy peace! but now they are hid from thine eyes." If they had only understood peace! Was not this the same thing Jeremiah saw when he said: "They have healed also the hurt of the daughter of my people slightly, saying, Peace, peace, when there is no peace." On July 16 Mrs. Eddy gave a new watch prayer to the students in her home:

> Beloved Students at Pleasant View: Handle electricity of mortal mind; no arsenical poison, no belief of nerves. Love governs all. One Mind, one Truth. God is All-in-all. Jesus knew the hour of temptation and *wept,* but he also knew the power of Love supreme over all the errors of sense. No lie *stands* in the presence of Truth. No theosophy, black magic. No destructive electricity. "He commanded and it stood fast." God, good, is All. (Take this up every morning and evening until I tell you to change your prayers.)

Events of the ensuing few weeks give a fuller explanation of Mrs. Eddy's foresight. The treaty of Portsmouth was signed on August 5 in Portsmouth, New Hampshire. The people rejoiced at the announcement of peace, and the press around the world lauded President (Theodore) Roosevelt for his part in the negotiations. Was God's chosen witness, the Founder of Christian Science, the only one who saw that this was an abrogation of our United States Constitution? When the *Boston Globe* requested a statement from her she responded with a message *(My.* 281) which was very graciously worded, but the pith of it was:

> The treaty of Portsmouth is *not** an executive power ... I believe strictly in the Monroe doctrine, in our Constitution, and in the laws of God.

Mr. Carpenter was the secretary who transmitted this message one hot summer evening:

> I can recall one hot August night going down into the city to telephone a newspaper article to Alfred Farlow in order that it might appear in the *Boston Globe* the next day. The article was written by Mrs. Eddy in answer to a request for her to issue some pronouncement on the establishment of peace in the war between Russia and Japan.

Mrs. Eddy permitted no telephones at Pleasant View, so all

*Emphasis added.

phone calls had to be made from public phones in Concord. No one complained about this inconvenience because they knew how much it meant to Mrs. Eddy's peace of mind. Mr. Carpenter evaluated it in this way:

> When a spiritual leader reaches the point where he or she recognizes that the outpouring of spiritual thought is of the utmost importance to the world, higher than any demand the world might claim to have, then anything that might interrupt that continuity of spiritual thought is something to be avoided if possible. Mrs. Eddy knew that a telephone could easily become the medium through which a connection might be established with many whose thought would be barred from the home through all other channels.

Barring mortal mind's entrance by telephone was but one small effort toward making Pleasant View the heaven on earth the Leader knew as present reality. Henry David Thoreau had caught glorious glimpses of this spiritual reality. He wrote in his journal on May 23, 1854:

> . . . There was a time when the beauty and the music were all within, and I sat and listened to my thoughts, and there was a song in them. . . . I sat and listened by the hour to a positive though faint and distant music, not sung by any bird, nor vibrating any earthly harp. When you walked with a joy which knew not its own origin. When you were an organ of which the world was but one poor broken pipe. I lay on the rocks, foundered like a harp on the seashore, that knows not how it is dealt with. You sat on the earth as on a raft, listening to music that was not of the earth, but which ruled and arranged it. . . .

This music and joy, this beauty of holiness were ever a part of the life of God's chosen witness. She spent all her years endeavoring to open men's eyes to the present reality of this omniscient power.

The discord among Christian Scientists over the music for her hymns had caused the Leader to write in her *Message for 1900:* "Once I was passionately fond of material music, but jarring elements among musicians weaned me from this love and wedded me to spiritual music, the music of Soul." She predicted to Mr. Carpenter that the time would come when man would not listen to music if the thought of the musician was sensual or hateful, for it would be jarring to those who are advancing spiritually. She also told Mr. Carpenter a little, but very little, about "spiritual music, the music of Soul," when she told him that there were times in the early morning, and sometimes in the night when she was awakened by strains of beautiful music which the human ear could not hear.

CHAPTER XXVI

HER REBUKE WAS FEARFUL

You cannot add to the contents of a vessel already full.
— MARY BAKER EDDY

1905

A CARD from Mrs. Eddy in the July 8 *Sentinel* and August *Journal* thanked Mrs. Stetson and the practitioners in her Reading Room for exquisite gifts for the Mother's room in the Concord church which included a solid silver service with the inscription on the silver cup, "A cup of cold water in his name." But Mrs. Eddy's letter of July 2 to Augusta and the practitioners said even more:

> Dearly beloved:
> Words fail me, they are insufficient to tell my gratitude for your remembrance of me. I love you — I deeply appreciate your love for me, and your magnificent gifts for my room in Church, the silver ice set, and gilt onyx table. More than a cup of cold water in his name, even, is the love that overflows it all — that you feel and constantly demonstrate for me. Darlings, it blesses you, it blesses me, and the whole world! Your love reflects the divine Love which heals the sick, conquers sin and the sinner.
> Here let me assure you that I never said or thought I should remove female students from their sacred office of Reader in our churches.
> The evil one or one evil, is ramified just now in attempts, but God, good, is *all* and you have nothing to fear since evil is nothing and you are a great something in God's dear sight. He will uphold you with the right arm of His righteousness. I pray for you daily. God loves you and I love, and you are the sheep of His pasture. Rest my darling Augusta, in peace. God is with you.
> Ever lovingly thine own,
> Mary Baker Eddy

A personal letter to Augusta written on the same day preceded this letter of thanks:

> My precious darling,
> I thank you for the beautiful summer gowns, but O, I am so occupied with other work I cannot have them fixed at present. Do not fear what man can do unto you when you are doing good and this you are doing constantly. I l*ove* you. The students know I never speak a word against you and you must not believe that I do. God will reward you for all you have done for me and this is indeed much. I will thank you and yours in a letter soon for your last most exquisite gifts for my room in Concord Church. With a pen overflowing I stop.
> Lovingly *ever* thine *own,*
> M. B. Eddy

Mrs. Stetson seemed to be the only student who gave the Leader much help with her clothing which was really of great importance, because, though Mrs. Eddy cared very little about style, she was constantly subject to public scrutiny. She wrote to Augusta again on July 9:

> My dearest one:
> Your dear letter is so comforting to me. No one but you cares specially for my clothes or comfort. Will you send me at once something cooler than I now have to wear in the carriage. All that I now have are not right. Shawls *trouble* me getting in and out. I want something adjusted to the carriage, a sort of loose jacket made of silk and lined, simply lined, *not wadded,* the sleeves loose at the wrists and made for *coolness, not heavy.* No matter about the *fashion.* I want it for comfort. Excuse erasures and haste.

It was July 18 that Mrs. Eddy wrote "Signs of the Times" *(My.* 235), a sign, or message, that few Christian Scientists have heeded to this day:

> Are you a Christian Scientist? I am. Do you adopt as truth the above statements? I do. Then why this meaningless commemoration of birthdays, since there are none?

God spoke to His chosen witness constantly through the pages of the Bible. She turned to it daily for His word on every issue confronting her or every topic under discussion. And through the Leader He also spoke to her students. Mrs. Eddy frequently called the mental workers in her home to her study for a morning lesson. Those present for such a lesson on the morning of August 9 were Calvin Frye, Mrs. Julia Prescott, Laura Sargent, Mrs. M. V. Blain, Gilbert C. Carpenter, and Mrs. Grace Greene. She said to them that morning that the moral atmosphere of Pleasant View was just perfect, that there was not a Judas thought in it. But she added "there is yet a lack and I should not be a faithful teacher if I did not tell you this." She waited for one to ask what this lack is, but no one spoke up. She deplored this lack of inquiry, but told them that the lack in the perfect moral atmosphere was a lack of spirituality. Then she opened her Bible at random as she was wont to do and God spoke to these students:

> John 4:10 Jesus answered and said unto her, If thou knewest the gift of God, and who it is that saith to thee, Give me to drink; thou wouldst have asked of him, and he would have given thee living water.

The Leader always had so much more to give than her students seemed capable of receiving. One day when her student, Emilie B. Hulin was at Pleasant View, Mrs. Eddy said to Mrs. Hulin and Mrs. Sargent: "Girls, would you like me to talk absolute Christian Science to you?" They answered eagerly in the affirmative, but though they were both the sincerest and best of students neither could understand a word she said.

The materiality in the thought of all her followers caused the great gulf between the Leader and her students, and also accounted for their lack of comprehension. Nothing can be added to a vessel that is already full, hence the constant necessity for rebukes to empty her students' minds of their *human* sense of goodness and accomplishment. If the self-satisfied *human sense* was not first driven out, the spirituality she poured out upon them simply rolled off and was lost. But those who could endure the emptying process gained more spiritward than have any others in all the history of the world.

Perhaps the student who helped her most, gained the most, and was also under the rod more than any other, was Calvin Frye. This was no doubt why she could say of him: "When Mr. Frye is himself, he can accomplish the work of fifty men in mental practice." But he was not always himself, and as with all students there were times when the suggestions of mortal mind seemed very real and overpowering. Such was the case one night in August. Just as Mrs. Eddy retired at nine P.M. she asked Calvin to talk with her. He believed he could not and left her without a comforting word. He knew his action was a deadly blow to the Leader and recorded in his diary:

> I gave the alarm and called others to her rescue. They watched with her the rest of the night and I was allowed to go to my room . . .

The next day Calvin was much improved, and the following day wrote in his diary: "Mrs. Eddy [and] I both gained our normal condition again." During such periods of trial the students in the home worked conscientiously to give back to the Leader a portion of the Truth she had so generously bestowed upon them and was daily giving to all the world.

Mrs. Eddy's life was a life of giving, not only in her healing and teaching but in every other way. When she learned the condition of Mr. Whitcomb's estate she stepped in and purchased a very expensive parcel of land in Brookline solely for the assistance of the Whitcomb family, which transaction is described in the following letters:

August 16, 1905

Dear Madam:

We are acting as counsel for Mrs. Whitcomb, the administratrix of the late E. Noyes Whitcomb, in settling her husband's estate, and we desire personally to thank you for relieving the estate from very serious embarassment by taking title to the Brookline land which Mr. Whitcomb just prior to his death had contracted to purchase. . . .

Yours very truly,
Nay and Abbott

— — —

August 19, 1905

My dear Sirs:

Your favor of the 16th inst. was duly received; please accept my deep appreciation and gratitude for your kindness and professional skill.

I well know that the dear Whitcomb family held no legal claim against me for debt; and yet, the moral demand remains with every Christian Scientist to comfort such as mourn. Let us trust that no sinister consciousness will trample on this priceless pearl. The bereaved family are members of my Church, and the sudden loss of a husband and father, one of the very best of men, strongly appealed to me, otherwise, I could have ill afforded so great an undertaking and expense. It is far better to do unto others as we would have them do to us than fail to obey a single precept of our Lord.

Most sincerely yours,
Mary B. G. Eddy

It *was* a great undertaking and expense. The *Boston Herald* reported that the property had a total valuation of $69,000 "but the price paid was considerably in excess of this." The *Herald* also reported that Mrs. Eddy had purchased the property for the purpose of building a residence for herself. This news item caused reporters to seek confirmation from Mrs. Eddy. Her answer to their query published in the *Concord Monitor* said: "Nothing of the kind is contemplated. I purchased the lot to save some Christian Scientists from meeting a financial disaster." This action by Mrs. Eddy helped the Whitcomb family, but it did not take care of the indebtedness upon the Concord church, a problem yet to be solved.

The *Concord Monitor* made note of another of Mrs. Eddy's charities in the summer of 1905. That was her annual distribution of shoes to needy and deserving children through her almoner William E. Thompson at the Concord State Fair.

As always the serpent was at the Woman's heel. It has been stated that Richard Kennedy inherited the house belonging to Sarah Bagley in Amesbury, Massachusetts. In the summer of 1905 a news dispatch from Amesbury reported the death of Miss Bagley along with the statement that she had taught the Rev. Mary Baker G. Eddy "her first lessons in the healing art." Once again the Leader had to issue a refutation in which she stated that she had taught her first student in 1867 quite some time before she ever met Miss Bagley and that Miss Bagley was a Spiritualist when she had known her.

A less insidious attack was the questioning as to why Mrs. Eddy did not attend the State Fair. And once again the Leader answered:

> Why does not Mrs. Eddy attend our State Fair? This question would not naturally be asked concerning another lady of my years and everyday life, but being up we answer it. Because I have lost all pleasure in such entertainments by having found so much else in moral and spiritual directions that demand my entire time and attention, that I deem it my duty and privilege to abstain from all else.
>
> The managers of our State Fair have my good wishes.

On the eleventh of September Mrs. Eddy visited the new Concord church for the first time. Part of the article in the *Concord Daily Patriot* describing her visit stated:

> Mrs. Eddy entered the church by the southeast door, which admitted her to the room prepared for her use in the edifice which the Scientists call "Our Leader's room," . . . Her artistic sense took in at a glance the beautiful circles of light falling in pendants like grape clusters, the delicate pale green upholstery, embroidered silk drapery, the highly polished Indiana oak floor, and the lighting, done by means of numerous incandescent bulbs deftly hidden in the corniced moulding of the room . . .
>
> After spending some time here, Mrs. Eddy visited the public Reading Room, which is kept open every weekday from 2 to 5 P.M. Thence she entered the church proper, and after a general survey took a seat in one of the carved upholstered pews, to view deliberately the magnificent transept windows, the grand gift of First Church of

> Christ, Scientist, of New York City, placed in position last week. . . .
> The organ engaged her attention, and called forth encomiums; the graceful lines of the massive roof-timbers, the fine natural finish of the Indiana oak comprising the entire woodwork, the interlocking noiseless rubber floor tiling, the harmony of coloring and arrangement of the entire auditorium, were all noted and favorably commented upon with much joy.

It was the following evening as she sat in her swing on the upper porch that Mr. Carpenter learned how Mrs. Eddy effortlessly thought and spoke in poetry rather than prose. He recorded her words that September 12 evening:

> Guide us gently, God,
> Through the cloud
> Or on the sod;
> Be our everlasting stay,
> Night or day.

On another occasion another student recorded her words: "Father, teach me how to still the clamoring of sense, and fill my place as listener, that I may hear Thy voice and grow to understand Thy Word, and so become Thy messenger. Then teach me how to banish pride and stubborn will that I may be Thy representative — with no false sense of human zeal, that every word may bless and heal, when I Thy message give." Had more of the Leader's words been recorded, we could fill a book with their poetry like this:

> Father, teach me how to still
> The clamoring of sense, and fill
> My place as listener,
> That I may hear Thy voice and grow
> To understand Thy Word, and so
> Become Thy messenger.
>
> Then teach me how to banish pride
> And stubborn will that I may be
> Thy representative —
> With no false sense of human zeal,
> That every word may bless and heal,
> When I Thy message give.

The September 16 *Sentinel* in 1905 brought a rebuke to the editor and a correction from the Leader's pen.

When the wealthy young man came to the Master asking what he could do to inherit eternal life, Jesus beheld his goodness and "loved him." But his unequivocal answer, which stands for all time, saddened the sincere young man and caused him to turn away "grieved: for he had great possessions" (Mark 10:22). What did he turn away from? The demand to dispossess himself of *all* he had, to take up the cross, and follow Christ.

The best of students today are no different from that young man. They will agree to take up the cross and to follow the Christ, but they will not or can not let go of their material possessions. When Lydia Hall was serving in the Leader's home, Mrs. Eddy one day told her to sell everything and come and live with her. Lydia —

> made no reply, but was very sad at heart over the prospect and the great sacrifice it would mean. In a few moments Mrs. Eddy called her to her and said, "No, you need not do it."

The manifestation of the Fatherhood of God said to his disciples, and to the world, "How hardly shall they that have riches enter into the kingdom of God!" But the manifestation of God's Motherhood spent all her years endeavoring to lead her "rich" children one small step at a time toward the kingdom of God.

Some of those who are very rich can measure their wealth in money. Others can measure their wealth in terms of worldly knowledge and education which is even more difficult to part with. The Leader did not require that such students give up their doctorates or other titles of honor or the recognition the world had bestowed upon them, but she did demand that they give up the material knowledge such titles implied. Jesus let the sincere young man depart grieved because he could not separate himself from his wealth. Mrs. Eddy endeavored through rebukes to separate her sincere students from the material "wealth" that controlled them. Two students who had much of the world's learning to their credit (and hindering their progress toward eternal Life) were John Buckley Willis and his wife Ella Lance Willis.

Dr. Willis, who was Ella Lance, M.D. before she found Christian Science, had spent a year in Mrs. Eddy's home at Pleasant View in 1904 at the same time Ella Peck Sweet was there. And Ella Willis had smarted under a good many rebukes during that year. John Willis, Second Editor, was the author of the offending article in the *Sentinel* of September 16 which Mrs. Eddy had received at Pleasant View by Friday, September 15. She wrote to Editor McLellan that day:

> Beloved Student:
> It has become my duty to say to you that Mr. Willis' article in this week's Sentinel mistakes C. S. and will tend to mislead its readers. All the factions in our denomination have commenced in just this way. I had great occasion to rebuke his wife while she was with me

and I fear that she is misguiding his thought but in a recent answer to my letter his reply was good and gave me hope and I said this in my answer to him. But now I am again shocked by his article in this week's Sentinel.

His article is in line with the "evil one" viz. to scare folks with truth and to content them in error. In substance it directly contradicts the sayings of Jesus "go tell thy brother his fault," "Why do ye not understand my speech? Even because ye cannot hear my word. Ye are of your father the devil" "He that covereth iniquity shall not prosper" etc. etc.

Also it is the very opposite, of the teaching in Science and Health which says "To put down the claim of sin you must detect it, remove the mask, point out the illusion, and thus get the victory over sin, and prove its unreality." etc . . .

This letter is confidential and written that you may see how to help him and save him from the leading of the enemy to which he and his wife seem to be blind. No more such misteaching as his last article must be allowed to appear in our periodicals.

Lovingly yours,
Mary Baker Eddy

"All the factions in our denomination have commenced in just this way." The factions comprised those students who did not want to handle animal magnetism. They wanted the truth of being without divesting themselves of their favorite errors, and derided Mrs. Eddy for making much of animal magnetism when it was really nothing.

John says, "For this purpose the Son of God was manifested, that he might destroy the works of the devil." And in Jesus' day the "faction" said: "Let us alone; what have we to do with thee, thou Jesus of Nazareth? art thou come to destroy us? . . . And Jesus rebuked him, saying, Hold thy peace, and come out of him. And when the unclean spirit had torn him, and cried with a loud voice, he came out of him."

For this purpose the Daughter of God was manifested, that she might teach how to destroy the works of the devil by uncovering and handling animal magnetism. And she was as severe as her brother Jesus in rebuking the evil that handled her students. Many of them were torn by the "unclean spirit" which "cried with a loud voice" before departing and leaving them receptive to Truth. Many others clung to the error saying that Mrs. Eddy made much ado about nothing. John Willis was drawing very close to this latter category in his editorial "Watching *versus* Watching Out" part of which stated:

> If we fail to know the claims of evil for what they are — the nothingness of illusion — and enlarge upon the incidents of their

seeming, we are likely to exhibit that frightened and frightening bewareness which can but lead others to think that, despite our declaration "There is no evil," we are very decidedly and old-fashionedly fearful lest this "nothingness" unexpectedly smite us. . . .

The contrast between a calm watchfulness and a perturbed "watching out" is too distinct to escape the notice of an observing world. Watchfulness means thoughtful forelooking from the citadel of conscious adequacy. "Watching out" describes a timid endeavor to ward off an unrecognized but presumably impending ill.

He who watches rightly minimizes the manifestations of evil, is quiet and confident; he who is striving to watch out talks much of the possibilities of error, explains, multiplies, and doubts as to the outcome. The one knows the lions are chained, and goes forward with freedom and inward rejoicing; the other peoples the air with dragons and indulges in a strained and elaborate caution. . . .

Although the field in general was unaware of it, this was a very pointed criticism of the Leader. Mr. Carpenter said that many in the household felt that when Mrs. Eddy "had a difficulty of the flesh she . . . stirred up everybody unnecessarily." He analyzed this agitation as follows:

Scientifically understood, the very phases of Mrs. Eddy's experience that might seem foreign to a patient, loving, Christian nature, teach lessons which are invaluable, and no more merit criticism as failures to live up to her own teachings than do the sweeping strokes of the swimmer which he uses to produce progress, as compared with a calm floating on the surface, which is peaceful to be sure, but it is not productive of any results. Whenever Mrs. Eddy felt . . . thought slowing up spiritually she began to thrash the waters of mortal mind in order that she might start a renewal or progress, a thing which she invariably accomplished.

Very few, if any, of the Leader's students understood her rebukes nor her necessity for rebuking. And they were such children in the Truth that she could no more explain this to them than can a mother explain her actions to a three-year-old child. But unlike the three-year-old, who never criticizes nor judges its loving mother, many of the Children of Israel judged and criticized their Mother most severely causing much gossip and whispering. Gilbert Carpenter spent the next half century endeavoring to fathom his experiences at Pleasant View, and he wrote of those who judged their Leader:

It is an interesting commentary on human blindness that any of Mrs. Eddy's household should have felt that although they had a great love for her and an appreciation for what was unquestionably

> good in her life and teaching, it required more or less tolerance on their part to overlook Mrs. Eddy's own impatience and to ignore her lack of appreciation and even criticism of what was done for her through their love and effort. To some, her rebuke seemed the voice of animal magnetism. They felt that in coming to Pleasant View they had come face to face at close range with the real Mrs. Eddy, and the idol was found to have feet of clay.

It was the calm, patient, tolerance of students blinded by animal magnetism that was one of the hardest things for the Leader to penetrate. She well knew that "whom the Lord loveth he chasteneth, and scourgeth every son whom he receiveth" (Heb. 12:6). But at times the good effect of her chastening rebukes was nullified by self- justification, which clung tenaciously to its own human sense of good, saw feet of clay on God's Revelator to this age, — and didn't see the dragon at all.

In his editorial Mr. Willis shows no understanding of the great red dragon. He thought that the lion was chained. Mrs. Eddy *knew* that the angel which "laid hold on the dragon, that old serpent, which is the Devil and Satan, and bound him a thousand years" was Science and Health. She also knew that the "thousand years" of the dragon's being bound by the Truth of being in human experience, expired with the uncovering of animal magnetism. "And when the thousand years are expired, Satan shall be loosed out of his prison, And shall go out to deceive the nations ... to gather them together to battle ... And they ... compassed the camp of the saints about, and the beloved city" (Rev. 20).

Who is watching to warn and defend the "camp of the saints" "and the beloved city"? At times the Mother in Israel felt as if she was the only one watching. On September 18 she wrote an article entitled "Watching *versus* Watching Out" *(My.* 232) which began with: "The above is the caption of an article in the *Sentinel* of September 16, 1905, that needs to be corrected." This correction appeared in the *Sentinel* of September 23. On September 28 she wrote McLellan:

> I hereby request that the article forthcoming relative to my article and to Mr. Willis' shall be *brief* and apologetic, it shall not be explanatory, this is not requisite. Why? Because in the words of Jesus, "Why do ye not understand my speech? Even because ye cannot hear my word." A little child does not understand the sayings or doings of his mother hence my positive position on this point and the good that will result from it, or the evil that would follow the opposite course. The student is no more capable of explaining my sayings or my life than the student in the first two rules of arithmetic is of explaining or commenting on problems in Euclid. With the

> student one extreme is apt to follow another; for example, I requested you not to pirate my works in our periodicals; thence followed *no* quotations from my works, when it should be otherwise for an occasional quotation therefrom to seal a sentiment is sometimes needed.
>
> The article should have appeared in this issue of the Sentinel.
>
> Please let these directions be ample and so close all future comments on *my* writings that is injurious.

The next day the Leader wrote McLellan on this subject once again:

> . . . This is what I now beg to have done. Tell Mr. Willis for me that I desire him not to refer in writing to "Watching vs. Watching Out" again. When I requested him to give us a few words on that subject like those he had written to me in his letter, I did not desire a long article or anything but his kind apology. It is too late now to bring it up. Ask him to please drop the subject — it has done its work all over the field.
>
> N.B. What I have said in this letter for Mr. W. you will please also to accept as to yourself. Unless you say in your nice way a brief word for my article as editor in chief and have no session upon it.

McLellan did write "An Apology" in his "nice way" which appeared in the September 30 *Sentinel:*

> We regret that the article "Watching *versus* Watching Out," which appeared in the Sentinel of September 16 and was corrected by Mrs. Eddy in last week's issue, should have found a place in our columns. It is the duty of the Editor and his associates rigidly to guard our columns against the intrusion of any article or statement which misstates the teachings of Christian Science and its textbook, "Science and Health with Key to the Scriptures" by Mary Baker G. Eddy. That this duty was not performed in this instance is deplored by the editorial staff, and it is but proper that this apology should be made.
>
> It is fortunate for Christian Scientists that our Leader is watchful over our Cause, and alert to detect and correct the errors which creep into the work of her followers. For this loving care and watchfulness and for her prompt and satisfying correction of this erroneous article she has our thanks.

It is possible that the Leader's rebuke of the evil using the Willises left them torn; but surely they profited from this rebuke, for they both continued to be earnest workers, and Mr. Willis continued in his position as second editor, although he still had another rebuking session on this issue in store for him.

CHAPTER XXVII

HOLD FIRE ON YOUR LEADER

If thou knewest the gift of God, and who it is that saith to thee, Give me to drink; thou wouldst have asked of him, and he would have given thee living water. — JESUS

1905

AS the Extension of The Mother Church began to make an impression on the Boston skyline, interest in Christian Science increased. About this time in a memorandum Mrs. Eddy said:

> Although there has been no special organized effort at propagandism in this direction, the growth of the cause of Christian Science seems too rapid to be healthful. As a means for remedying this abnormal condition let there be no proselyting from churches of other denominations for Christian Science teaching. While not prohibiting Christian Science healing to such as are needing and request it, let it not be urged upon them beyond their individual growth in this direction. This accords with the Golden Rule.

The thoughts about teaching may have been for the upcoming meeting of the General Association of Teachers which was to meet in New York City in 1905. A letter to the Leader from Augusta Stetson on September 8 said:

> . . . I grieve when I see that some of the dear ones have to turn back and walk a while longer with their idols.
>
> . . . It is a marvel that among so many, so few are found who are able to run the race *continuously.* If you have anything you would like me to do at the meeting of the Association of Teachers, please tell me. We have no idea where they intend to meet in our city, but God is guiding, and He will put His children in the right place. It is not so much a matter of consequence what environment they will have, as whether we meet in love and unity and spiritual cooperation.

May I be worthy to wash the feet of the disciples.
With devoted love and gratitude, and loyal obedience.

It is possible that "some of the dear ones" who had to "walk a while longer with their idols," together with the immature thought of newcomers to the ranks, were tending to pull the organization back to outgrown ways, which could account for the Leader's message to Lewis Strang on September 22:

> The Cause of Christian Science is founded on Principle, not person. Loyal students of the Scriptures and Science and Health *know* that when the Discoverer and Founder of Christian Science appointed these Books as the *only preachers* in our churches, God was leading this Cause as surely as He led the Children of Israel in the desert.

A few days later, on September 26, she wrote to Augusta in New York:

> My precious Student:
> I was delighted to read in the N. Y. American your dear church and students reference to my love of you. But I have hesitated on account of your attack on the street (by that mad man) to refer to you again publicly lest I might thereby endanger your safety.
> Did you read what else was published in that same article?
> Will you in time attend to getting me an Autumn bonnet? Or have you too much to meet to aid me? O no, I can hear you say. God bless my darling Augusta. Be most careful to do nothing in secret that you would not have seen openly for the world is not up to understanding the motive behind the act.

It was in the fall of 1903 that Mrs. Stetson's church, First Church, New York City, was dedicated, and now in 1905 her students were taking on a new building project, — a home for their teacher. On the second of October Mrs. Stetson received a letter from Mrs. Eddy in which she said:

> Am glad to hear that you are to have a home. You deserve it, and your Father is rich, and will not deprive you of one good thing, but will add continually to your storehouse of blessings: everything belongs to God, then it is yours *now,* as His reflection, for there is no debt in divine Love.

On October 4 the Leader wrote Augusta again:

> My darling Student:
> Your letter was a feast for my hungry heart. You, dear one, little

> know what an effort I have to make in order to keep the students awake to the subtlety of M.A.M. O! I am so happy that *you* are *saved.* Now *watch.* See how stealthily she got you to class her with you and *all my* students in that article! And see what a boon has been given through our Pub. Com. of the amendment of it as I published it. Give my *thanks* and *love* to your dear students for what they did to *honor you.*
>
> You asked what I meant by "doing nothing in secret that you would not do openly"? This was my meaning. To keep your thoughts aright in God's sight. It is one of my greatest struggles to guard the unseen consciousness so that the visible shall always bless myself *and others.*
>
> God bless my precious Augusta — my faithful helper in worldly necessities. Send the bill for my bonnet. Is it for both Autumn and winter?

The day following this letter to Augusta the directors and editors arrived at Pleasant View having been summoned by a telegram from the Leader. It was 2 P.M. on October 5 when Messrs. Knapp, Johnson, Chase, Armstrong, McLellan, Willis, and Mrs. Annie Knott were shown into Mrs. Eddy's study where they took seats in the semicircle of chairs which had been arranged for them in front of the chair in the corner where Mrs. Eddy usually sat.

She first greeted them and then asked each director individually whether he read the *Journal* and *Sentinel* carefully. Each said that he did but perhaps not as carefully as he ought. Then, very gravely, she said she wanted them to read them with the utmost care to assist her in protecting the periodicals from erroneous statements the editors may have missed.

At this point she picked up the latest issue of the *Sentinel,* September 30, and read: "a diseased body is not acceptable to God;" with no indication whether she approved or disapproved. She asked each in turn whether he considered that statement scientific. The last to be asked was Mrs. Knott who responded that she had stumbled over it twice but had decided to let it go through.

After a brief pause the Leader said in unforgettable tones: "Then you are the one to blame. You are my student, are you not? . . . Did I ever teach you anything like this?"

All were beginning to realize that a serious mistake had been made, and she said to them strongly: "Now, will you any of you tell me whether God has any more use for a well body than for a sick one?" Is the image and likeness of God physical? She referred them to Science and Health 313:12-19; and asked them to study daily 295:5-24.

This may have been the *reason* she called all her directors and editors together, and it may have been the *pretext* for what came next as she turned, probably to Mr. Willis, and said: "You sometimes believe, do you not, that you can see as well through a brick wall as through a window?" He answered respectfully that he hoped he did not, but she replied that what he wrote would make it appear as if he did. Then with great humility and splendid dignity she referred to herself as the transparency through which the light of Truth had come to this age.

She turned next to the false concept of Jesus which sometimes crept into the pages of the *Sentinel* and *Journal,* and said very forcefully to the editors: "I do not want to see any more of those namby pamby concepts of Jesus go out through our periodicals to mislead people as to what he actually taught." After quoting some of Jesus' severe rebukes and denunciations she said, "If I had said such severe things about those who have opposed Christian Science as he did to his opponents, I would have been put to death long ago."

It was nearly 4 P.M. before they were dismissed, and Mrs. Knott was able to write in retrospect: "I was deeply grieved to have caused our Leader disappointment, indeed sorrow, [but] a rebuke from her was worth much more than the praise of others, and I took it gratefully." It is to be hoped that Mr. Willis took the rebuke directed to him as gratefully, but it would appear that Mrs. Eddy was not sure of this.

On October 7 the Leader responded to a letter from Editor McLellan which was probably an apology for publishing the article with the unscientific sentence:

> I did not intend to condemn the article of Mr. Chadwick for it was good — but only that line I pointed out. Had I been the poor editor-in-chief of our papers I should have erased that line and published the article. . . . this is an editor's privilege that whatever contradicts his doctrine and a science he can erase or correct and should do so.

On October 10 she wrote to Mr. McLellan again:

> I thank you deeply for our last Journal. I believe that it is the best one that has been issued. If you would suggest to Mr. Willis to make his interesting articles more simple or comprehensible to the average reader, it might do him good. . . .

In 1901 John Buckley Willis had been a member of the Normal Class of the Board of Education. Following the class Mr. Kimball had written an evaluation of the students to Mrs. Eddy and had said at that time of Mr. Willis:

At this stage his grasp of C.S. is on the intellectual side although he is naturally spiritually minded.

He has not demonstrated much and his chief drawback lies in the fact that he clings much to the idea that the good (?) of mortal mind is very admirable and worthy to coalesce with Science. Mr. Willis will progress rapidly as soon as he learns that what the world calls wisdom is foolishness with God.

I like him very much and have great hope concerning him but no student in this class has needed such constant attention on my part or needed as much argument in order to yield and be satisfied.

The Leader never rejected a demanding thought or a "doubting Thomas" if he was a sincere seeker. She knew that both Willis and his wife had "great possessions" that they could not easily part with, and she had labored with them long. John had been put on the Bible Lesson Committee even before he was appointed Associate Editor. Ella was a teacher and had spent a year in the Leader's home at Pleasant View; but John's criticism of the Leader in his editorial showed an unyielding resistance to her leadership. If she still felt this resistance in the interview at Pleasant View on October 5, that could well account for her next publication in the *Sentinel* of October 21, — a new by-law:

PUBLICATIONS UNJUST [Now Article XI, Sect. 10] Should a member of The Mother Church publish, or cause to be published, an article that is false, or unjust, — hence injurious to Christian Science, or to its Leader, — upon complaint thereof, by another member, and the Board of Directors finding the offence has been committed, the offender shall be suspended for not less than three years from his or her office in this Church and from its membership.

On the twenty-third of October William B. Johnson was in New York City for the meeting of the General Association of Teachers which was being held in the edifice of First Church, New York. Probably the Association's first order of business was to send a telegram to the Leader, for Mrs. Eddy responded on that day with this telegram to William B. Johnson:

Thanks for the telegram. Hand in hand, heart with heart take step forward, march and hold fire on your Leader. God bless you. Lovingly, Mary Baker Eddy

The next day, October 24, the Leader wrote to Augusta:

My precious Student:

If you knew how *directly God inspired* me to write that telegram to the Teachers' Association — you would thank Him for it, and your Leader through whom He has spoken, and written what is for your salvation. If you heed this warning, you will master your would-be destroyers; if you do not, they will master your understanding of the Way, the Truth, the Life.

The malpractice implied in the words "hold fire on your Leader," and Mrs. Eddy's letter of warning were not lost on Augusta, which is evident in the Leader's letter to her on October 31:

My precious Student:

Your quick, spirited letter came duly. Accept my thanks. But dear one, The Golden Rule must guide all your acts. Thirty years ago and over, I taught the Old Testament rules or laws of defence. But now I no longer teach the law, but the Gospel in this line, even the rule of our blessed Lord, viz. Love your enemies, and return good for evil. And, thank God, I practise these rules daily and hourly leaving the punishment for mental malpractice alone in His hands, who cannot fail in justice, or mercy or wisdom.

You, dear one, will be guided by God and do His will in all things and ways, if you trust alone in Him and love and obey His appointed and anointed. Jesus said: "Inasmuch as ye do it unto me, ye have done it unto my Father." May God bless and guide and *protect* you.

Lovingly, faithfully thine,

Mary B. G. Eddy

CHAPTER XXVIII

GIFTS AND GIVERS

We lose nothing by giving. God pays back a scientific giver.
— MARY BAKER EDDY

1905

A LETTER to the Leader from her editor-in-chief on the last day of October stated in part: "I am planning to get into this week's Sentinel the newspaper account of Judge Ewing's lecture in Concord, and especially Mayor Corning's fine tribute to you and to your work." In answering his question as to which local newspaper account she preferred, Mrs. Eddy added:

> One thing I regret viz. the space *too fully* used in speaking of me if it were so. The mayor is a noble man. I never met him. But Judge Ewing is the soul of eloquence but I wish all our lecturers would conform themselves mostly to explain the healing of Christian Science.

On November 14 the Leader graciously responded to an invitation from the First Congregational Church in Concord to be present at the observance of their one hundred seventy-fifth anniversary. Included with her letter of regret *(My.* 174) was her check for five hundred dollars "to aid in repairing your church building."

Another gift given by the Leader in November was a beautiful scarfpin — a large lustrous pearl surrounded by diamonds. This note to Mr. Carpenter accompanied the gift:

> Beloved Gilbert C.S.
>
> Please accept this little gift as a symbol of the priceless divine Love, and my gratitude to you.
>
> Mary Baker Eddy
> Nov. 9, 1905

Gilbert was overwhelmed as his note of thanks reveals:

Precious Mother:
Mr. Frye has just handed me the beautiful pin and its message of love. It has overwhelmed me to think of your giving to me more, after so freely inviting me and all to share with you the *Pearl of great price,* that sacred acquirement of self-sacrifice. I can only say, t*hank you.* But I can see in this type, your pure selfhood set in a crown of stars, and by wearing this on my heart, keep a watch over the spiritual idea, through which *nothing that worketh evil or that maketh a lie* can enter.

Your child, Gilbert

The recipient of another gift from Mrs. Eddy in 1905 was Calvin C. Hill who received from the Leader a beautiful gold locket set with a solitary diamond. Inside the locket was a lovely, sober picture of the Leader. Artists and photographers had a difficult time portraying Mrs. Eddy as she was, because her main quality was spirituality which was so far beyond their comprehension that its beauty eluded them.

Mrs. Stetson also was probably the recipient of a gift from Mrs. Eddy toward the end of 1905 as this letter of November 25 implies:

Darling, my darling Augusta:
Do not name a season dress for me now. I am submerged in work for the field and cannot attend to being fitted now.
I am going to send you a little remembrance of me as soon as I can attend to it.

An editorial in the *Sentinel* of November 25 suggested that this Thanksgiving season was an "appropriate time for completing the building fund" of The Mother Church. Many churches made a special effort to do so, and Mrs. Stetson's letter in this regard was published in the *Sentinel* in December:

December 6, 1905

My Precious Leader:
I am writing just to tell you of my ever-increasing love for you, and of my constant efforts to follow and obey you and your teachings. I am trying to demonstrate Christian Science and praying for grace and love to endure to the end. Our church is most prosperous in Truth. The healing is being demonstrated, and many are rejoicing in the health and peace which they find in Science and Health. Grateful and loving disciples call you blessed, and thank God. On Thanksgiving Day we contributed twenty-two thousand dollars to The Mother Church. It has all been paid in, I believe, and will be sent to Mr. Chase. This makes eighty-four thousand which our church has con-

tributed, and we want to make it one hundred thousand dollars if necessary. We have not more than four men in our large membership who can be called rich. All give all they can, and rejoice in the privilege and the sacrifice which test their faith and trust in infinite Love. It is joy to give to the Cause, and particularly to the dear mother vine. I long to do more for you and to be worthy of your dear love.

Ever your faithful, obedient child,
AUGUSTA E. STETSON

Another letter which the Leader had published was written on the same day and came from Herbert W. Eustace's church in San Jose, California:

The members of this little branch church do not send you the enclosed invitation to the dedication of their church edifice, with any anticipation that you can either be present in person or with us in thought, but simply to add, if possible, an iota of joy to gladden your tireless labor in its never-ceasing effort for others, by a positive proof that your work has not been in vain, else this edifice would not be.

We know that all we have, we owe to your faithful love and labor for mankind. We understand that it is not words you require from your followers so much as works, and this branch has endeavored to live up to this requirement.

During the past year, besides completing our own church edifice, at a cost including the ground of about forty thousand dollars, we have been enabled to forward to the Treasurer of The Mother Church over eighteen thousand dollars. This with what we previously had sent makes almost twenty-four thousand dollars for which our church holds receipts. We know this will please you, for this branch numbers only one hundred and three members.

Our Reading Room is now selling your glorious work, Science and Health, at the rate of a copy every other day, more than double the sales of last year.

The sick are being healed and the sinful regenerated through the reading and studying of this wonderful book. For this we are deeply grateful to our heavenly Father, divine Love, and our hearts never cease to go out in deepest affection to you, our beloved Leader — an affection we are striving to manifest through a more loving obedience.

The Leader received so many petitions for her largess, that letters of grateful giving and loving obedience such as Augusta's and this one from San Jose were a joy to the Mother's heart. And her response to the San Jose church *(My.* 197) was a gift far greater than all the lockets and scarfpins she gave. It helped to sustain Mr. Eustace in later days of trial, and it reinforced his conviction that her "far Western students, the Christian Scientists," were not deviating from Principle nor erring in interpreting her teaching and instructions. None of this had entered Mr. Eustace's thought at this date, but it may have been in the Leader's thought when she wrote:

> December 13, 1905
>
> *Beloved Students:*
>
> Words are inadequate to express my deep appreciation of your labor and success in completing and dedicating your church edifice, and of the great hearts and ready hands of our far Western students, the Christian Scientists.
>
> Comparing such students with those whose words are but the substitute for works, we learn that the translucent atmosphere of the former must illumine the midnight of the latter, else Christian Science will disappear from among mortals.
>
> I thank divine Love for the hope set before us in the Word and in the doers thereof, "for of such is the kingdom of heaven."
>
> Gratefully, lovingly,
> Mary Baker Eddy

Sue Harper Mims treasured a letter she received from the Leader at this time. It was written on November 27, and one treasured sentence from that epistle reads: "That which you impart either impoverishes or enriches being."

A letter of November 29 to McLellan endeavored to resolve some of the controversy in the building of the Extension:

> I think your salary named for Mr. Hill is all right. Perhaps you had better have a less number of picture windows. I think you had for there are so many in the first building.
>
> Please let Mr. Beman decide this question as well as all other relative to our church extension. If he had not built it as it is I would not have decided to have it remain thus but I like it as he has it now. . . .

Mr. S. S. Beman, an architect from Chicago, was the assistant architect who had been in charge since architect Brigham had been sent to the Bermudas for his health. But the architects needed more metaphysical support to assure that the temple they were erecting was God's temple. The Leader sent this message to one of the workers, Lewis Strang, on December 13:

> I have this day asked you by word sent by Mr. Frye to take up for M.A.M. the architects of The First Church of Christ, Scientist, Boston. If *sinning* so-called Christian Scientists would listen to their Mother, this work would have been done to the glory of divine Mind and the confusion of those enemies of Christ, Truth, working *within* the gates of this Cause. When Rev. McKenzie was here, Mother told

him of the need which she felt was so great then, but minds many and earthly cares turn many from His table of Love.

The *New York World* asked Mrs. Eddy to contribute to a symposium entitled "The Significance of Christmas" which was to be published on Sunday, December 10. Her contribution *(My.* 259), which she dictated to her associate secretary, Gilbert Carpenter, ended with:

There is but one Jesus Christ on record. Christ is incorporeal. Neither the you nor the I in the flesh can be or is Christ.

An editorial note in the same issue of the *World* said:

Card from Mrs. Mary Baker G. Eddy:
No person of prominence in the country has been more sought after for magazine and newspaper articles than Mary Baker G. Eddy, the Discoverer and Founder of Christian Science. In recent years she has almost uniformly refused requests of this kind.
This year, however, she consented to write an article for the ... Christmas section of today's *World.* A subsequent letter from Mrs. Eddy to the editor of the *World,* possibly explains why she is averse to writing for publication. Her statement is as follows: *Nota Bene:* I hereby certify that counterfeit letters frequently follow my contributions to newspapers, letters representing the opposite of my views, feelings, and nature, the contents of which are so subtle that I expose this lawlessness to save those to whom they are addressed from being misinformed.

In "The Significance of Christmas" Mrs. Eddy said: "mere merry-making or needless gift-giving is not that in which human capacities find the most appropriate and proper exercise." There was a good deal more on this point in the next issue of the *Sentinel* (December 16) which also reprinted the *World's* article. The first was "A Question" by Mrs. Eddy which is titled "Principle or Person?" in *Miscellany* (p. 233). At an earlier date she had said that telegrams were less time consuming than were gifts, but now she was overwhelmed with telegrams and had to write: "I cannot watch and pray while reading telegrams; they only cloud the clear sky, and they give the appearance of personal worship which Christian Science annuls."

This "Question" was followed by a by-law, Duty to God *(Man.* 67). And this notice dated December 21 appeared in the next *Journal:*

Take Notice

Members of our Church that have not read the By-law, "Duty to

> God," in the issue of our *Sentinel* of December 16, 1905, are not amenable for disobeying it until they have read it, but they will be thereafter.
>
> Mary Baker G. Eddy

On December 28 the Leader wrote one last (1905) word on Christmas titled "Christmas for the Children" *(My.* 261), wherein she stated that the "juvenile joy" provided by the "wisdom of their elders who seek wisdom of God" should continue as it is with one exception:

> the children should not be taught to believe that Santa Claus has aught to do with this pastime. A deceit or falsehood is never wise.

The Board of Education Primary class which was held in December sent a message to the Leader on December 13. This message and the Leader's reply *(My.* 254) appeared in the *Sentinel* of December 23.

A December 15 letter from the Manchester, England church saying that they had just sponsored a lecture by Mr. Bicknell Young, also said: "Your loving gift of Christian Science, made yet more priceless by your selfless labors and constant prayers for all, has welded a bond of union between us 'in the old country' and you 'in the new' which nothing can sever . . ." The Leader's words of appreciation included:

> Neither space nor time can separate genuine Christian Scientists. "Behold, how good and how pleasant it is for brethren to dwell together in unity."

The Leader also sent for publication a letter from Electra Scribner in Tombstone, Arizona. Her response to this "student's student" stated:

> The above letter is redolent with love, and the embroidered bedspread is the most beautiful thing of the kind I ever saw. But more than all else of earth is your joy-inspiring recital of the good being done in your midst by Christian Science and your faithful labors.

Some of the students in remote places did better at times than some at Pleasant View. Mrs. Eddy did not explain to those in her household how they failed, but gave them the teaching that would enable them to figure it out for themselves if they made the effort to do so. Mr. Carpenter wrote:

> For instance when she gave me the privilege of carrying her tray to

her room at noon, and then replaced me at the end of ten days, it took twenty-five years for me to come to an understanding of just how I failed her. It was not the food, but the thought back of it, that caused the food to be acceptable to her or not. I am convinced that she hoped I might make the demonstration to put back of that food the thought that would make it acceptable to her, by ruling out all belief in a so-called human mind. This error-mind in any student was the enemy of Mrs. Eddy's spirituality which all of the students were pledged to help her to maintain and sustain.

Minnie Weygandt was a wonderful cook. She was also devoted to Mrs. Eddy and eager to serve her. But, as many another student who said each day that "All is infinite Mind and its infinite manifestation," she had not accepted that fact as present reality. To Minnie the food she cooked each day was matter, and sometimes this belief of materiality overpowered the food. At such times the Leader returned the meal untouched, which was very distressing to Minnie. She began preparing a complete second meal which she called the "in-case" dinner. In case Mrs. Eddy refused the first meal Minnie had another to send up. No doubt it was Minnie's concern and love that often caused the Leader to eat the "in-case" meal. Minnie's work would have been considerably lessened if she could have turned to Mind for the cooking. The Leader tried to open blind eyes in this regard with instructions such as this one to Lewis Strang: "Treat Minnie daily for spoiling the simple food she cooks for me." At the end of 1905 Minnie was feeling exhausted and ill from much work, and the Leader wrote to her:

December 31, 1905

My dear Minnie:

You have been a long time at work without a vacation and now you can have one and get well and rested. True, *you do not* need this for God, divine Mind, rests you and heals you; matter cannot do this, and the Scripture bids us to come to Christ, Truth, and find rest in these words of Christ, "Come unto me, all ye that are weary and heavy laden, and I will give you rest. For my yoke is easy, and my burden is light." Working for the good of others is not hard work, it is a burden that is light. You have worked for me to help me many years and it has not hurt you for it cannot. Doing good helps us all; it has carried my life on forty years and it will sustain yours. Do not feel you must come back to work till you *believe you are rested* and able to do so.

With love,
M. B. G. Eddy

Do not *think* of *me;* keep your mind fixed on God. Take no thought about my food. It only wastes thought to dwell on matter.

The last sentence was the key to Minnie's problem if she could only have seen it.

The Leader had sent many inspiring, elevating, loving messages to the field and to the world this December, and malpractitioners were sending to her the suggestion that she would not live to see the new year. New Year's eve was very discordant for her because of this mental suggestion, and Calvin Frye wrote in his diary:

> . . . I took a strong stand that she would live to see 1906 and declared I would sit up and watch and work until the New Year comes in and defeat the purpose of m.a.m. . . .

By 10:45 P.M. the enemy had been routed, and Mrs. Eddy told Calvin to drop the work and retire. Calvin Frye, too, was a giver. He gave his whole life to helping his Leader in her great labor of establishing Christian Science upon this planet. Are we as faithful in helping, protecting, and defending our Leader today as Calvin was in 1905?

CHAPTER XXIX

RESISTANCE

Often I sent out an angel (a new by-law) and it would come back bruised and bleeding, and I'd have to take it in and cherish it until the Field was ready for it. — MARY BAKER EDDY

1906

THE first *Journal* in 1906 contained an interesting letter to the Leader from Bad Sachsa am Harz, Hermannklause, Deutschland:

About a year ago I asked you to allow "Science and Health with Key to the Scriptures" to be translated into German, and though my wish is, and ever will be, the same, I have seen since then how wise it was of you not yet to give that permission. I admire your wisdom, and I am waiting silently and patiently, knowing that the right time will be revealed to you, I am full of joy to have become now a member of The Mother Church, full of thanks to belong to the great brotherhood of Scientists, and do see in you a wise and beloved Leader. In thinking of you there is always the one thought coming to me, that by you "Love is reflected in love." My desire is to do the same, to give up self-will and to do nothing but the will of my Father, to overcome personality, and to be nothing but "reflection." This is the goal which I am wanting to reach, and I think that in striving for it I can best prove my gratitude to you, for what you have done and are doing for me and mankind.

I am, dear Mrs. Eddy, yours in reverence and love,

Countess Fanny Von Moltke

The Leader's loving reply came from God as was so often the case, through the pages of the Bible:

I thank you for your excellent letter, and reply in the words of Scripture: —

"The meek will he guide in judgment: and the meek will he teach his way. All the paths of the Lord are mercy and truth unto such as keep his covenant." "Endeavoring to keep the unity of the Spirit in the bond of peace." "Unto the upright there ariseth light in the darkness." "For as a prince hast thou power with God and with men, and hast prevailed."

In the first *Sentinel* in 1906, January 6, was a quotation from Phillips Brooks:

> God has not given us vast learning to solve all the problems, or unfailing wisdom to direct all the wanderings of our brothers' lives; but He has given to every one of us the power to be spiritual, and by our spirituality to lift and enlarge and enlighten the lives we touch.

Beneath that quotation in her copy of that January 6 issue Mrs. Eddy penned: "The secret of my life is in the above."

In January Mrs. Sarah Pike Conger, wife of the American minister to China, received a letter from Hong Kong telling about the beginning of public Christian Science services in China. Soon thereafter Mrs. Eddy received a letter from Miss Maurine Campbell regarding work in China which caused her to write to Mrs. Conger:

> Beloved Student:
>
> Since ever receiving your card I have desired to write to you; and now after what Miss Campbell has written I hasten to reply. Her report of the success of Christian Science in benighted China, when regarded on one side only, is cheering, but to look at both sides of the great question of introducing Christian Science into a heathen nation gives it quite another aspect. I believe that all our great Master's sayings are practical and scientific. If the Dowager Empress could hold her nation, there would be no danger in teaching Christian Science in her country. But a war on religion in China would be more fatal than the Boxers' rebellion. Silent prayer in and for a heathen nation is just what is needed. But to teach and to demonstrate Christian Science before the minds of the people are prepared for it, and when the laws are against it, is fraught with danger. The dear Countess Von Moltke has come to see that your text-book, Science and Health, cannot be translated at present, not even in Germany.
>
> Give my kind regards to our much respected Minister, your husband, and give my love to Miss Campbell.
>
> Please to pardon (if it needs forgiveness) my frankness in this letter, and know that it proceeds from the best motives.
>
> Lovingly yours,
>
> Mary Baker Eddy

While the Leader was directing Christian Science work all over the world few were *consistently* helping the Leader or following her *direction.* Too often Scientists became involved in their own projects or their own ideas for the promotion of Christian Science. It appears that is what happened to her Committee on Publication in January. Calvin Frye recorded in his diary:

> Great discord over Alfred Farlow classifying works on Christian Science in libraries. Mrs. Eddy feared it would give the enemy chance for a libel suit at law. . . .

On January 8 Gilbert Carpenter wrote the following letter to Mr. Farlow at Mrs. Eddy's dictation:

> My dear Student:
> Your report on libraries in N. Y. City received. Thank you deeply for having instituted this important work on reform; it is much needed. I have not the time to inform myself on this subject sufficiently to suggest other than what you are already attempting. May God prosper and speed your undertaking. Have no lawsuits about this.
>
> With love, yours,
> Mary Baker Eddy
>
> I called a halt to inquire as to results before writing you. Litigation must not attend this work.
> N. B. In Church Manual see page 34, Art. 6, Sec. 1, on your duty as a member of my Church and show your plans to its Directors for their approval before you execute them. M.B.E.
> W — seals those papers that report me done (?) as Leader, all over the country. You wrong me and your correction is not read by thousands and injures our Cause in the eyes of thousands, every time you allow such lies about me to be published and if you cannot or will not stop doing this, you are unfit for the General Pub. Com. and will be removed. Eddy

All of Mrs. Eddy's lieutenants needed stern rebukes such as this from time to time to stop them from doing the work of animal magnetism and to keep them doing the work for the cause in the world as the Leader outlined it. However, this letter of rebuke was never sent to Mr. Farlow. Instead she called him to Pleasant View for an interview.

The enemy was always attacking Mrs. Eddy's leadership and her life. It also attacked the lives of her workers at Pleasant View, but they were unconscious of this because they were kept constantly at work for God. The Truth and Love their Leader poured into their thoughts was an impervious armor. Only the Leader understood the deadly thrusts of evil against her and her household. After many years of analysis Mr. Carpenter began to comprehend the situation and wrote:

> Think what it would have meant, had some student fallen violently ill and passed on in the home of the greatest healer . . . in this age! It never happened at Pleasant View, although it was a constant threat. And it was our Leader's wisdom that was responsible for this protection of her home.

The Leader knew when any particular student was under attack and assigned other students to help him or her. Calvin Frye wrote in his diary on January 11: "Mrs. Eddy says I was under the spell of m.a.m. all day today and she could not by mild methods waken me." It may have been January of 1906 Mr. Carpenter was recalling when he wrote:

> . . . during one of the general Watch Hours, Mrs. Eddy sent the following directions written in her handwriting, covering work for Calvin Frye, who was in need of help at that time: "No arsenical or mercurial rheumatism or neuralgia; no effect of arsenic on the nerves, stomach or liver. No relapse nor return of these beliefs. It does him good to work for me. This with all else God gives use in argument for F."

Mr. Carpenter also said regarding the scientific correctness of Mrs. Eddy's diagnosis:

> Mrs. Eddy could tell from Mr. Frye's symptoms of depression and unconsciousness that mortal mind was affecting him like a poison. Hence she was able to point out the remedy . . . while I was at Pleasant View, I saw her bring him back from what seemed death after all of her students had failed . . .

Gilbert was not at Pleasant View much longer. His year was up on March 16, 1906, and on the morning he left Mrs. Eddy said to him in the presence of the other students: "Gilbert, it is like taking my heart out to let you go. During the year that you have been here you have not committed a single moral offence!"

Before Gilbert's departure another earnest student had joined the Pleasant View household as Associate Secretary.

* * *

LEWIS CLINTON STRANG

LEWIS CLINTON STRANG

LEWIS C. Strang, a New Englander, graduated from Boston University in 1892. He was well established as an editorial writer and drama critic before he became interested in Christian Science, and was listed in *Who's Who in America* as a dramatic critic. Several of the books he authored were mentioned in that biographical sketch.

Mr. Strang's serious interest in Christian Science began in 1901, and from that year he preserved many messages from Mrs. Eddy. He became a permanent member of the household at Pleasant View in January of 1906 where he was Associate Secretary for about the next fifteen months.

Mr. Strang may have arrived just about the time the cook returned from a two week vacation or while she was staying in the Pleasant View cottage. Minnie's thought had grown so worldly while she was away that its discordance caused Mrs. Eddy to send her to the cottage to stay until she was fully recovered.

On January 17 Mrs. Eddy was jolted by a discordant note from Chicago. She was accustomed to shocks when things were running smoothly, but it was nonetheless disturbing. Calvin Frye recorded in his diary:

> Mrs. Eddy was much disturbed today from a letter about discord in the Chicago churches because of By-law in our Manual forbidding church conferences, etc.

As always the Leader acted immediately, and on the same day wrote the following letter to her directors, endeavoring to lessen the reaction to the change in a newly issued *Manual:*

> Beloved disciples:
>
> The six churches of our denomination in Chicago are in need of help out of confusion in acting on church matters without conferring together on said matters.
>
> For this purpose I propose the enclosed amendment.
>
> To prevent a difficulty *caused* by a *conference,* I sent this article to you years ago, and it did prevent all troubles at that time; but now a change comes over the spirit of their dream and they write us that they must meet and confer or tumble one on to another in acting. I struggled too hard to plant Christian Science on a Rock in Chicago to let the worms, or the gates of hell prevail against it, hence this amendment for you to act upon. I am sorry to trouble you, Mr. Armstrong, with these changes in your *new edition* of our Manual, but as fate has it whenever you issue one, — I have noted this. I am

used to all sorts of shocks when getting on well, but can pity others who are in my predicament.

The amendment to meet the Chicago situation (which is now Art. XXIII, Sec. 1) was published in a January *Sentinel* and the February *Journal.* The pertinent sentence read:

> No conference of churches shall be held, except the annual conference of The Mother Church, unless it be when our churches located in the same state convene in unity and love to confer on a statute of said state, or to confer harmoniously and agree on individual unity and action of the churches in said state.

The Leader found it necessary to concede to the demand for conferring, but she made no concession to majority rule or group action. She is inflexible in her insistence upon *individual* action.

Mrs. Eddy had also been giving thought to the institution Mary Beecher Longyear had proposed a year earlier. She wrote to Mrs. Longyear on January 21:

> Since reading your letters, pondering the subject of an institute or Sanatorium and studying our Manual, I see it is not best for you to take the initiative in this matter. It properly belongs to the Christian Science Board of Directors to do that, for thereby we shall avoid much confusion in the future. So please drop the matter.

Calvin Frye was a greater help to the Leader than was any other of her students. In 1906 he had been by her side every day for twenty-four years, and when Calvin was not himself Mrs. Eddy suffered. On the night of January 25 discord and suffering caused the Leader to have three of the students, Laura Sargent, Julia Prescott, and Gilbert Carpenter to keep unity watches every three hours throughout the night. Probably Lewis Strang was not yet trained for such work, and perhaps Calvin Frye was not himself. The next afternoon, according to Calvin's diary, Mrs. Eddy told him that he had gained his natural, strong, clear sense of Christian Science, and she thanked God for it.

A fine tribute, "Our Debt to Christian Science," by Rev. F. N. Riale of Chicago appeared in *The Westminster (*Philadelphia, Pa.), accompanied by the editor's comment: "If anything in this old world needs interpretation it is the facts of Christian Science. The greatest fact is Mrs. Eddy's book. But no one can interpret that. It is non-interpretable. It is like Sau Abrah's garments, 'Just the same on one side as on the other' — just the same interpreted as not interpreted; nonsense either way." This was reprinted in the *Sentinel* of February 10 along with Mrs. Eddy's comments. The Leader was unperturbed when she read the editor's caption, and smiled as she said:

> That editor hit the nail on the nonsense, and broke his fingers, poor man! He could not interpret the nonsense, no sense, of evil, not knowing the all sense of good; if he could, it would heal his fingers.

Lewis Strang's talent and experience as an editorial writer (He had been leading editorial writer on the *Washington*[D.C.] *Times* in 1904.) were a great help to Mrs. Eddy. He was often able to write letters on her behalf that she would have had to dictate to most others. The following letter to George H. Lounsbery in Chicago was written on February 23:

> Dear Brother:
>
> At the request of our beloved Leader, I am writing you in reply to your letter of Feb. 18. ... You say in your letter: —
>
> "We recently organized our work into four groups of classes, one for the study of the Commandments, one for the Lord's Prayer and its Spiritual Interpretation, one for the Beatitudes, and one for the Lesson work."
>
> Our Leader bids me ask you this question: Would you feed a babe on milk or on meat? Of course you will answer milk. Our Leader would have the Sunday School officials and teachers in all fields keep this necessity constantly before them in their work with the children. She would have them wise, for wisdom is essential in every line of Christian Science endeavor.
>
> When our Leader gave the By-law on "Subjects for Lessons" in the Sunday School, it was not her intention to limit Sunday School instruction to the routine of memorizing the letter of the designated portions of the Scripture. She meant that the children should be taught the *meaning* of the Ten Commandments, the Lord's Prayer and its Spiritual Interpretation, and the Beatitudes. These spiritual fundamentals should be so set forth by means of practical illustrations and everyday examples of love, obedience, and good, that the child will catch their spirit, understand them, and as a result be interested in them.
>
> This work, you will readily perceive, requires consecrated and intelligent effort on the part of all connected with the Sunday School. It means the demonstration of that love which does things. To teach a child the words, "Thou shalt have no other gods before me," is a comparatively easy task. To teach a child the meaning of that commandment so thoroughly that he can and will prove in his living that he actually has no other gods before good, is the grand privilege of the Christian Science Sunday School teacher.
>
> Yours in Truth,
>
> Lewis C. Strang, Associate Secretary

All eyes were focused upon the new Mother Church in Boston, and the directors were working uninterruptedly for its completion by June. When they wrote the Leader that they were planning to inscribe "The First Church of Christ, Scientist" upon the major or tenor bell of the chime, she proposed an amplification. So according to her proposal the inscription on the tenor bell reads:

The First Church of Christ Scientist
in Boston, Massachusetts
1906
Founded on Love

Lest her students forget the "greater part," the Leader gave this word of warning which Lewis Strang recorded on February 20:

> The Directors of The First Church of Christ, Scientist, must work in this hour that the dedication of the earthly tabernacle in the wilderness be accomplished sure this year. For this reason Mother places upon all loyal students this word of warning — healing the sick and sinful is the greater part and all must join in this work, who wish not to see this Cause go down.

The earthly tabernacle was for that time, but the Mother's "word of warning" was for "all loyal students" for all time.

The Leader kept in touch with her youthful lecturer, Bliss Knapp. In her letter of February 27 to him she said: "Your mother looked for the hour of your demonstrated wisdom and growth in Christian Science and with me, rejoices in it."

Rev. James J. Rome, who was listed in the *Journal* as a Christian Science practitioner in Boston, was asked by the directors on March 25 if he would do some night watching at the new church building. Mr. Rome assented readily, and on his first nightly tour he assumed that communion would be postponed till the end of summer since the building could not possibly be completed sooner. But he was jolted awake (as his interesting letter *[My.* 60-62] states) by an announcement in the April 14 *Sentinel* that the extension would be dedicated on June 10.

An amended by-law in the April 7 *Sentinel* foretold the discontinuance of the General Association of Teachers. The beginning of this step at this date was the announcement that their meetings "shall be held biennially."

Miss Caroline Foss was a student of Laura Lathrop in New York, where Miss Foss was a listed practitioner. In April when Caroline was called to Pleasant View she was given the special task and privilege of being Mrs. Eddy's personal maid. One experience that was helpful to her at that time has helped many another student since then. That was the making of Mrs. Eddy's bed. Laura Sargent told Caroline Foss that no one seemed to be able to make the bed to satisfy Mrs. Eddy so that she rested comfortably:

> As Miss Foss was working to smooth out the lumps in the feather mattress, she thought, "This bed belongs to God. I am making it up for Him, and not for any personality. He sent me here to do it so I can do it right." There never was one complaint from Mrs. Eddy, during the whole time Miss Foss was there as to the condition of the bed. But she confessed that among her many duties, the bed making was the only one she really tried to demonstrate consistently.

Caroline Foss received her share of rebukes from the Leader as did every student at Pleasant View with the exception of John Salchow. Mr. Carpenter recorded that John Salchow served the Leader faithfully for fourteen consecutive years and during all that time she rebuked him but once. It has been said that John was so devasted by the one rebuke Mrs. Eddy gave him, that she never gave him another. This circumstance alone is proof (if mortal mind needs proof) that the Leader's rebukes were *never* for the work done or not done, but *always* for the development and progress of the student. However in 1906 none of the students knew this, and all of the students who served in her home were surprised and sometimes shocked to learn how "fussy," exacting, and demanding the Leader was. They often thought that she made everything as difficult for them as she could, which she did, because she was endeavoring to *force* them to turn to God, divine Mind, for *everything,* as she did. How many students, even today, turn to Mind *first?* Are not most satisfied with a *human* sense of good and accomplishment? It is this human sense of accomplishment and good that is the greatest stumbling block to the student's progress Spiritward.

The Divinity course at Pleasant View was not to teach the students *about* divinity nor how to *become* divine. It was to waken them to the reality of their own divinity and unlimited potential which was already a present fact. But this *wakening* was not an easy task. it took sharp rebukes of their humanhood and seemingly impossible demands upon them to jolt them out of a complacent sense of *human* good. Even then, many a student left the Leader's home only to cherish his bruised and battered sense of humanity and to whisper about the Leader's unreasonableness. It became official policy to ignore and bury out of sight these invaluable lessons that were so largely misunderstood.

But there were a few who pondered deeply the rebukes they

received and lessons they learned. We can thank God for Mr. Carpenter who devoted all his years to pondering and endeavoring to unravel what he called the "mystery of Mrs. Eddy's life." He may not have known that she was God's chosen witness on this planet, but he did discover the key to unraveling what others had considered her inexplicable behaviour. When Mr. Carpenter accepted the premise that Mrs. Eddy was always right and for that reason not to be criticized in any degree, the "mystery" of her life began to unfold to him. He began to see that had she explained the reason for some of her requests and demands, the effect would have been lost.

In the spring of 1906 Caroline Foss and Lewis Strang were receiving some of the lessons that Gilbert Carpenter had received a year earlier. One of these lessons was being called to work for Mrs. Eddy in the night. Few students ever knew how often the Leader worked day and night. But after thirty years of pondering Mr. Carpenter came to the conclusion that when she called upon new students to treat her audibly it was mainly for that student's training and not because she needed help. In his words:

> When Mrs. Eddy called upon me to help her audibly at night during my stay in her home, I had to feel that her harmony and rest through the night depended wholly on my demonstration. Otherwise I would not have worked as I did. Had I believed that she gave me that task merely to train me — as I now believe . . . I would not have been so zealous, as careful, or eager as I was, nor would I have put into the work the extreme unction that I did.

By endeavoring to understand and *explain* what was in essence the Divinity course at Pleasant View, Mr. Carpenter has enabled earnest, loyal students *today* to take the Divinity course in Mrs. Eddy's home.

CHAPTER XXX

AWAKE THOU THAT SLEEPEST!

It will be indeed sweet at its first taste, when it heals you; but murmur not over Truth if you find its digestion bitter.
— MARY BAKER EDDY

IT was about 1902 when a Chicago physician, Dr. Edmund F. Burton, who had been using morphine for nearly a year to subdue the symptoms of consumption, was advised by two of his colleagues that his only chance for life was to move to Arizona. Dr. Burton wrote:

> When I went to Arizona I tried to stop the drug, but found that I had a well-founded opium habit, and that when I attempted to break it, which I did several times, the lung trouble became too serious to be borne. Thus the habit increased, as it always does. I had been a moderate drinker, but became less moderate in the use of alcohol, and soon began to use cocaine to alleviate both the effects of the morphine and for throat symptoms. To make a long and miserable story as short as possible, these three things — alcohol, morphine, and cocaine — became my food and drink.
>
> After some time in Arizona I went to Southern California — to Pasadena. Here I sought the aid of a hypnotist to enable me to free myself from these habits, and found this method ineffectual. After this experience the quantity of the three things that I was taking was enormously increased, until toward the end I was taking such quantities of morphine and cocaine as no one has ever recovered from, so far as I know. I became entirely demented and a menace to those about me.

In the spring of 1905 when Dr. Burton had been unconscious for forty-eight hours, five of his fellow physicians held consultation and told Mrs. Burton he could not live three or four weeks and arranged that he be sent to the State asylum the next day. On this dark day, April 19, 1905, a friend induced Mrs. Burton to allow a Christian Science practitioner to call, — which he did, spending three hours with her husband. Dr. Burton says:

> I have no memory of his coming or of his going, but he left me asleep, and I woke on the following morning free from all these habits, normal in brain and nerves, hungry, energetic, clear-headed, and happy. I knew the moment that I awoke that something had happened to me, and that whatever had done it, I was free from the awful things that had bound me. But I did not know what it was that had done it until I was told.
>
> ... From that moment I have never felt the slightest appetite for an opiate, cocaine, or alcohol in any form, have never felt any symptoms of lung trouble, and have been mentally sound and clear. Nor was there a moment of convalescence. My bowel condition was normal. ... My nerves were steady and quiet. I read quietly and with understanding, for the greater part of the morning, a book which took a great deal of mental concentration to understand, the like of which I had not been able to do for months. I drove my automobile half the afternoon, also a thing I had not been able to do for some time. ...

April 20, 1905, was a great turning point in Dr. Burton's life. A year later at 5:13 A.M. on Wednesday morning, April 18, 1906, a severe earthquake rocked California causing San Francisco to suffer one of the worst disasters in United States history. Overturned stoves and gas lamps plus broken electric wires and gas mains caused explosions and raging fires which could not be checked because of broken water lines. For three days the fires raged, and on the second day Dr. Burton was asked to assist in the surgical work at the San Francisco Emergency Hospital. This was April 20, exactly one year from the day of his miraculous recovery. He responded to the call for help and:

> ... for three weeks I stood on my feet and operated for about sixteen hours a day. This was my last surgery and coming after a year of study of Christian Science, decided me as to my future course.

As the news of the catastrophe spread across the country, earthquake relief funds sprang up. The following appeared in the *Concord Patriot:*

> Concord will do its full share in the work of relieving the suffering people of San Francisco. This was made evident last night at a meeting called by the Commercial club to systematize the work of relief. ...
>
> At first the idea was expressed that two thousand dollars would be about all that Concord could afford to give to the fund [but] ... Mr. M. Meehan changed the aspect of affairs by presenting the following letter:

April 23, 1906

Dear Sir:

Enclosed herewith is check for one thousand dollars, my contribution to the local fund for the relief of the San Francisco sufferers. You will please turn the same over to the treasurer of the committee.

Very truly,
Mary Baker Eddy

Following the reading of Mrs. Eddy's letter the local citizens determined to endeavor to raise five thousand dollars for the relief fund. About the same time the Concordians were meeting, a Christian Scientist in California was writing this letter:

April 25, 1906

Dear Mrs. Eddy:

I was instructed by the Board of Directors of First Church of Christ, Scientist, San Jose, Cal., on the evening of the day of the earthquake, after we had held our regular Wednesday evening meeting, to wire you that none of the Scientists in this community had received any bodily injury, and that our new church was practically untouched by the terrible disaster, but it has been impossible to send any satisfactory telegram, hence this letter.

We were obliged to hold our service by candle-light, for all electric and gas lines were cut off. It would indeed have gladdened your heart to have heard the testimonies given that night, and to have listened to the grateful thanks offered to our loving Father for the precious gift to mankind of Science and Health, and its loved author — you, our dear Leader — whereby peace, comfort, and assurance had been granted to each one, to sustain him throughout the trying ordeal. On Sunday no services were allowed in the city limits, and in consequence we held our service in a schoolroom outside the city. . . .

It will please you to know that telegrams offering assistance have been received from Scientists in distant cities. . . . We were glad to be able to say to all these loving offers, that we did not need anything; and this we understand is equally true of our brethren in San Francisco, Oakland, and neighboring towns. . . .

[A young business man who has lately come into an understanding of Christian Science] was buried for three hours under a mass of debris, through the collapse of a hotel; his mouth and nose were almost stopped up with mortar, and his body was crushed into a seemingly impossible space. He told me that while confined in this position, he saw more clearly than ever before the truth taught by Christian Science, that the mortal concept of himself was not the real self at all, that the real self was ever free, and was so right then. He was finally rescued uninjured, and one of the physicians who was on hand to render any assistance possible, told me that he could not understand how any "living soul could have been rescued from such a place."

Faithfully yours,
Herbert W. Eustace

Dr. Burton's surgical work for three weeks following the earthquake and fire decided him as to his future career. He spent the ensuing year in the study of Christian Science and then began its practice. In January of 1915 Senator John D. Work of California used Dr. Burton's letter of testimony in the United States Senate in opposing a bill for a Federal Department of Health. Dr. Burton's letter said:

> I was most enthusiastic in the practice of surgery and was a Pharisee of the Pharisees as to its virtues. I gave it up only after being most thoroughly convinced that there was something better. I have learned to my entire satisfaction, knowing both sides of the question, that Christian Science is a science, and not only that, but also that it is an advanced step — and a long one — beyond medicine and surgery, and that time will prove this to the whole world. . . .

Following San Francisco's experience earthquakes and disasters were on every tongue for weeks, and it was important that Christian Scientists reverse this trend. In mid-May the Leader sent these instructions to her Board of Directors:

> Consider this, my proposition: that you require some of the best Christian Scientists in Boston and vicinity to pray once each day that no thought of earthquake, tornado or destructive lightning enter thought to harm it, but that He who reigns in the heavens and watches over the earth saves from all harm. Again let me say, pray not on *hire* but the demand of love to God and man.

This "proposition" no doubt freed the thoughts of the directors to pursue the main item on their agenda at that time which was the completion of the Extension in the specified time. They had already announced in the April 14 *Sentinel* that it was to be dedicated on communion Sunday, June 10. In that same issue of the *Sentinel* the Leader had published a Card *(My.* 25) saying she would not be present *"in propria persona"* at the dedication.

As the magnificent Mother Church was nearing completion the Leader knew only too well the dangers besetting the pathway of the students, and that popularity and pride would cause them to worship church edifices. Lewis Strang did a splendid job of presenting the danger in a letter to the Editor of the *Sentinel* on April 21. This letter *(My.* v-vii) was published in the *Sentinel* of April 28 under the title "Lest We Forget." Perhaps the most significant paragraph reads:

> Strive it ever so hard, The Church of Christ, Scientist, can never do for its Leader what its Leader has done for this church; but its

members can so protect their own thoughts that they are not unwittingly made to deprive their Leader of her rightful place as the revelator to this age of the immortal truths testified to by Jesus and the prophets.

When the Leader selected Mr. Strang's letter for the Foreword in *First Church of Christ, Scientist, and Miscellany* was she not reminding us once again not to let her great revelation be engulfed by and buried in the organization:

"Lord God of Hosts, be with us yet;
Lest we forget — lest we forget!"

"Lest We Forget" and a letter from Mrs. Eddy which had also appeared in the April 28 *Sentinel* were both republished in the May *Journal.* The Leader's letter to her Board of Directors *(My.* 26) thanked them for "the largest sum of money that I have ever received from my church." It also stated:

The enclosed notice I submit to you, and trust that you will see, as I foresee, the need of it. Now is the time to *throttle the lie* that students worship me or that I claim their homage.

Gratitude and appreciation, not homage, are the avenues for understanding both Mrs. Eddy and Christian Science. The Notice *(My.* 27) she sent for publication read:

To the Beloved Members of my Church, The Mother Church, The First Church of Christ, Scientist, in Boston: — Divine Love bids me to say: Assemble not at the residence of your Pastor Emeritus at or about the time of our annual meeting and communion service, for the divine and not the human should engage our attention at this sacred season of prayer and praise.

In April the Leader invited Mr. Carpenter to return to Pleasant View with his wife for a visit. On the morning of April 27 Mrs. Eddy opened her Bible at random as was her custom and gave them a lesson on the passage God gave her. That morning she opened to Luke 9:56, "For the Son of man is not come to destroy men's lives, but to save them." Mrs. Carpenter wrote down the Leader's words as she recalled them on the train on their way home:

What is the Son of man? He is the idea of God, the consciousness of Truth. If you had children, you would make them obey. You would find some way to make them mind, and if you couldn't do it any other way, you would punish them. If you wanted to get a man out of a house, would you make it comfortable for him? No, you would make it uncomfortable. You would pull down the chimneys and take out the windows. Now we have got to get out of this house (mortal habitation). What holds us in it, pleasure or pain? The pleasures of sense hold us, not the pains of sense. I've got to get out of this old woman and you, Mrs. Carpenter, have got to get out of this young woman. Is this mortal existence real? No. Is there any mortal man? No. It is only the Adam-dream. Is it real, then? No. Then, is there any pain? No. Then we are out of it *now.* Is there any creation apart from God? No. Then, is he the father of children? No. Can he be the father of a lie? No. Has a lie a father? No. Then, is there any lie?

The Daughter of man is not come to destroy men's lives, but to save them. All her words were to *waken* them from the Adam-dream, the belief in a material creation, to see the reality of spiritual being here and now. All wanted to be healed of pain — of human disease and discord, but none wanted to be healed of pleasure — of human ease and harmony. Hence the Leader's thankless task. But some in her home were elevated into more spiritual latitudes as can be seen in Mr. Carpenter's words:

Many of the students did not relish having their human harmony invaded and shaken up, and they rebelled as much as they dared. Others were obedient and thoughtful, and yielded to the greater wisdom of their Leader. They were the ones in whom she was able to accomplish the healing of human harmony, so that they gained a taste of divine harmony; and who would willingly go back to the deadening condition of the false peace of mesmerism after they had been touched by and experienced the soul-satisfying divine harmony, which Mrs. Eddy's rebuking and healing of human harmony brought out in them.

About the time of the Carpenter's visit Calvin Frye received a letter inquiring:

Has Mrs. Eddy given out any orders recently — or at any time — that Christian Science practitioners are not to take Roman Catholic patients or give them any of her writings? . . . I doubt the truth of any such report, as it is not consistent with Christian Science teaching, but for the satisfaction of others I think it is my duty to inquire at headquarters about the matter. . . .

This letter, together with Mr. Frye's answer of May 4, was published in the *Sentinel* under the title "A Question Answered":

In reply to your question "Has Mrs. Eddy given out any order recently — or at any time — that Christian Science practitioners are

> not to take Roman Catholic patients or give them any of her writings?" will say: Mrs. Eddy has issued no such orders. She takes no patients, but through her writings gladly helps all those who will receive her help.

This may have elicited protests from representatives of the Roman Catholic church, because a by-law amendment was published before the end of June which said:

> Neither the Pastor Emeritus of The Mother Church nor Christian Scientists shall treat or teach Roman Catholics except with the written consent of the authorities of their church. Teaching and healing are separate departments. If you cannot heal without teaching said patients, abstain from doing either.

Less than a month after the publication of this amendment, Mind clarified the issue for all time, and Mrs. Eddy changed the by-law to the present reading in the *Manual* (p. 87) Article XXVII, Sect. 4.

A Sunday School superintendent in Indiana wrote an appreciative letter to the Leader on May 10 describing their work in Indianapolis. One paragraph of her letter stated:

> Once, when the chapter [for study] was Matthew 2, a young mother said, "My child has never heard the word death, so I did not read about Herod's killing of the children." It seemed to me to attempt such a course was impracticable and really suggested by fear; that instead the child needed the protection of the spiritual explanation.

This brought forth from the Leader's pen "Inconsistency" *(My.* 235), in which she states the impossibility of teaching the truth of life without using the word death. She asks the gentle, devoted mother: "Can I teach my child the correct numeration of numbers and never name a cipher?"

Milk for babes, and meat for men. Eugene H. Greene was soon to teach the Board of Education class in the Metaphysical College, and Mrs. Eddy wrote him on May 31:

> One thing I forgot to name is this: Teach your class that the pleasures of sense material are to be overcome as well as its pains. Hence the Scripture, "None but the pure in heart can see God." The sexual element is not *natural,* if nature is God, and it certainly *is God,* for matter is not God, and material sense has no law and no gospel on its side. Even eating is a "suffer it to be so now." Sometime we shall all learn this. Let us begin now to learn it, and to practise it.

CHAPTER XXXI

DEDICATING THE EARTHLY TABERNACLE

Remember that a temple but foreshadows the idea of God, the "house not made with hands, eternal in the heavens," while a silent, grand man or woman healing sickness and destroying sin, builds that which reaches heaven. — MARY BAKER EDDY

1906

ALL the field thrilled to the notice Stephen A. Chase wrote on the second of June *(My.* 27). The *Boston Globe* wrote it up this way:

> "Please do not send us any more money — we have enough!"
> Briefly that is the notice which Stephen A. Chase, treasurer of the building fund of the new Christian Science temple, sent forth . . .
> . . . when they erected the first church in Boston twelve years ago . . . it was found necessary to issue a similar notice . . .
> If you ask a Christian Scientist how they do it, the reply will be in the form of a quotation from Science and Health (p. 494) "Divine Love always has met and always will meet every human need."

By early June all the Boston newspapers were reporting on the size, beauty, and architectural details of the beautiful new Mother Church Extension as well as all of the activities and pending activities connected therewith. The *Boston Post* said:

> Never before has the city been more frequented by members of the titled aristocracy of the old world than it is now. From all the centers of Europe there are streaming into town lords and ladies who come to attend the dedication of the new church for Christian Scientists.

A few days later the *Boston Transcript* reported:

> Special trains and extra sections of trains are due to arrive in

> Boston tonight, bearing the first instalments of the crowds of Christian Scientists from the central and western sections of this country. Those from abroad and from the far West to a large degree are already in Boston. . . .

Extensive newspaper coverage was given to the dedication of The Mother Church Extension. The reporter from the *Boston Herald* expressed a feeling and a truth which was felt by many:

> . . . there have been church ceremonies that appealed more to the eye, but the impressiveness of this lay in its very simplicity; its grandeur sprang from the complete unanimity of thought and of purpose. There was something emanating from the thousands who worshipped under the dome of the great edifice whose formal opening they had gathered to observe, that appealed to and fired the imagination. A comparatively new religion launching upon a new era, assuming an altogether different status before the world.

The reports from Boston were reprinted and repeated in every town and hamlet in the United States and in cities all over the world. Even scoffers were impressed as this article from the *Norfolk* (Neb.) *Tribune* implies:

> To those who seem to see no good in Christian Science, it must stagger their faith not a little to read the account of the dedication of the vast temple located in the heart of the city of Boston, the supposed fountain of knowledge and seat of learning of America; the spectacle of thirty thousand people assembling to gain admission to the temple shows an enthusiasm for Christian Science seldom witnessed anywhere in the world on any occasion; and this occurred in staid old Boston, and the fact was heralded in flaming headlines in the leading newspapers of the world. According to the despatches, that assembly was not a gathering of "the vulgar throng;" the intelligence and wisdom of the country were there. There certainly must be something more than a fad in Christian Science, which was placed upon a far higher pedestal by that demonstration than it ever occupied before.

The world saw the architectural splendor and the thousands who came to witness the dedication of this marvel, but the heart and soul of the occasion was the Leader's message, "Choose Ye" *(My.* 3):

> . . . The Scripture reads: "He that taketh not his cross, and followeth after me, is not worthy of me." On this basis, how many are following the Way-shower? We follow Truth only as we follow truly, meekly, patiently, spiritually, blessing saint and sinner with the leaven of divine Love which woman has put into Christendom and medicine.

> . . . It will be found that, instead of opposing, such an individual subserves the interests of both medical faculty and Christianity, and they thrive together, learning that Mind-power is good will towards men.
>
> . . . The modest edifice of The Mother Church of Christ, Scientist, began with the cross; . . . Its crowning ultimate rises to a mental monument, a superstructure high above the work of men's hands, even the outcome of their hearts . . .

Her words were for a future generation. The Christian Scientists in 1906 were rejoicing in the structure which *was* "the work of men's hands," which the *Boston Post* called "a marvel of architectural beauty," and which was receiving the world's acclaim.

The *Post* also remarked about its "enormous size" stating: "But one church in the country exceeds it in seating capacity." Notwithstanding this fact, it was necessary to hold a second session to accommodate all the members who were there to attend the annual meeting on Tuesday, June 12.

On this day when Christian Scientists from around the world were rejoicing over and in their new edifice, another man was quietly contemplating what he saw as "marvelous beyond all imagining." Samuel Putnam Bancroft, who had been in a class Mrs. Eddy had taught in 1870 when she was still Mary B. Glover, had attended the dedication service and could not help but reminisce about the early days. The letter he wrote to Mrs. Eddy *(My.* 58) on June 12 was subsequently published in the *Sentinel* with the caption "A Contrast of Forty Years." Though Mr. Bancroft, whom Mrs. Eddy had affectionately called Putney in those early days, had not remained an active Christian Scientist, he had remained faithful, and he signed his letter "Respectfully and faithfully yours."

The thing that most attracted public attention, aside from the building itself and the six services to accommodate the thirty thousand who came to see it dedicated, was the Wednesday evening testimony meetings. On this Wednesday evening, June 13, meetings were held in a great many places. The First Reader, William D. McCrackan presided over the largest gathering in the new extension. The new president of The Mother Church, William F. Gross conducted an overflow meeting in the extension vestry. Another overflow meeting in the original Mother Church was conducted by Second Reader Laura C. Conant. The several additional overflow meetings in various other halls were conducted by Judge Hanna, Bicknell Young, Bliss Knapp, Edward A. Kimball, William P. McKenzie, Gilbert C. Carpenter, and Irving C. Tomlinson. The Scientists were asked to name the place they lived before testifying, and as soon as the meetings were opened to the congregation, people jumped up to speak — people from Peoria, St. Louis, Berlin, Des Moines, Glasgow, Cuba, Brooklyn, Liverpool, Australia, California, London, Dublin, Paris, etc. The *Boston Herald* reported: "No more cosmopolitan audience ever sat in Boston." The *Herald* report also stated:

> To hear prosperous, contented men and women, people of substance and of standing, earnestly assure thousands of auditors that they had been cured of blindness, of consumption in its advanced stages, of heart disease, of cancer; that they had felt no pain when having broken bones set; that when wasted unto death they had been made whole, constituted a severe tax upon frail human credulity, yet they were believed. . . .
>
> If an attempt were made to give any account of the marvellous cures narrated at the meetings of the Scientists, or wherever two or more of them are met together, it would be impossible to convey a conception of the fervor of belief with which each tells his or her experience. These are tales of people of standing and of substance, professional men, hard-headed shrewd business men. Yet they all have the same stories of their conversion, either through a cure to themselves or to one near and dear to them.

Evidently a good many of the thousands of Scientists who had come to Boston with such enthusiasm either had not read or disregarded the Leader's notice asking them not to come to Pleasant View. Lewis Strang wrote to Hermann Hering, the First Reader of the Concord Church:

> If possible, she would like to have you seek out these thoughtless visitors and bid them spend the time that they are wasting in the worship of personality in careful study of the Church Manual, especially the By-law which positively forbids precisely the thing that they are doing.
>
> Mrs. Eddy desires that you say to them that Pleasant View is neither a watering-place where they may spend their summer nor a hospital where they can steal their healing.

The following letter was written to Mrs. Eddy on June 26, and she had it published in the *Sentinel* of July 7:

> Dear Leader:
>
> Being about to leave the States for South America, to make my home in Ecuador for an indefinite season, I took the liberty of visiting Concord and driving out to your home, some days since.
>
> I just wish to say that the lesson learned during that visit will not soon be forgotten, and I came away with a sense of having intruded upon your much-desired, yea needed, seclusion.

The significance of your words, "time to assimilate myself to God," came to me with renewed force, and I see how, under the guise of loving interest, we might become tedious hindrances to the fulfillment of not only your highest hope, but our own as well. Therefore my next visit to Concord can only be upon special invitation from an authorized source.

From the "genial tropics" my love will go out to you, as it ever has here. In joyous anticipation of future good news to tell you, I am,

Earnestly yours,
Mrs. Nina M. Henderson
Guayaquil, Ecuador

Mrs. Henderson's letter impelled "Personal Contagion" *(My.* 116) from the Leader's pen; which, she wrote to Mr. McLellan, is "one of the most important things of thought I ever expressed." When published in the *Sentinel* Mrs. Eddy's article preceded the letter from Mrs. Henderson and began: "The following letter is so right and requisite, that I hereby endorse it for the readers." In her words to her editor regarding "Personal Contagion," she also said:

> Does it cost me no cross to write this? If you could look into my consciousness you could see it does, even a human rebellion thereto.

In the same issue of the *Sentinel* (July 7) the Leader published the letter written to her by James J. Rome *(My.* 60-62) telling about his night watching work for the church. She also wrote to the directors about Mr. Rome on July 2:

> Mr. Rome's article is rendering honor to whom honor is due, in the great work that is just accomplished. I could not say it in my Message and not comment on the officers in all the leading departments; and the Message was too short for this, and to make it long enough therefor would have occupied in reading too much time for that great occasion of the Dedication.
>
> Mr. Rome I know little of, but I like him, and he has now shown himself. Let us not forget him.

In the summer of 1906 most Christian Scientists were in a state of euphoria which put a greater burden on the Leader as her letter to John Lathrop at that time implies:

> Press on; you are in the line of light, thine to realize the glory of strife. Seeking is not sufficient whereby to enter the Kingdom of Harmony. I sorrow over the ease of Christian Scientists. They are not at ease in the pains of sense, but are at ease in its pleasures. Which drives out quickest the tenant you wish to get out of your house, the pleasant hours he enjoys in it or its unpleasantness? I hope the

teachers of Christian Science will awake to do their duty towards getting out tenants from ease and pleasure in substance and life in matter. I am worn with doing the work alone.

The serpent of envy which had used her promising young student Richard Kennedy, to strike at the Woman in 1871, had become the great Red Dragon of international proportions. An intricate plot had been laid to give extensive news coverage to lies and defamation of character, which had been planned to coincide with the completion of The Mother Church extension, in an effort to destroy the Woman and her cause. But the Woman had been warned of God and had insisted that the extension be completed a year earlier than planned. To mortal sense this was an impossibility; and those who were accomplishing this "impossibility" kept a sacred silence. Even the field did not know the date of completion until it was publicly announced just a few weeks prior to dedication day. And within the next few weeks the news coverage was extensive, fair, incredulous, — full of praise and astonishment. "And the dragon was wroth with the woman, and went to make war . . ." The woman needed the help of her students *now* more than she ever had before, and they were all asleep, — lulled by the wonderful praise and popularity. Even her darling Augusta, who was usually such a help to her, was somewhat nullified. The Leader informed her of this change, in her letter of July 3:

Do you in the least realize the change that has taken place in your kindness to me in caring for my clothes? Mrs. Leonard charged you for me to have that . . . silk made plainly, instead you had it made so I cannot wear it, and depended on it for my dress now, therefore need it to make me comfortable this season. I am working for you and all students *continually* and so have no time to care for my wardrobe. Would not the world expect that the students who say they owe so much to their Leader could do for me what I so much need? while I am doing thus for them? In haste —

Lovingly yours, ever your teacher
and leader to Heaven, health, immortality!

This letter wakened Augusta to a degree from the general state of euphoria engulfing the field. In response to her answering letter the Leader wrote her again on July 7:

My precious Student:

Your dear letter of the 7th inst. is just received. It comforts me. Now let me say — that mental malpractice must be met daily by all the Students, met by your mental protest that breaks the so-called law of a lie, or you are liable to be affected by this lie *all unconscious-*

ly. Dear one, *remember this.* Our Master said,

"Had the good man of the house watched, his house would not have been broken open."

I am thankful for your reassurance of loving me, and pray God to enable me to do you good continually.

Ever lovingly yours,
Mary Baker Eddy

N.B. Your kindness to me has been an example for others, and I shall not forget it nor cease to speak of it as the great cause of your prosperity.

But the glamor in the field, which none but the Leader was aware of, was so pleasantly mesmeric that even her sturdy Augusta was greatly affected and only partially awakened, as Mrs. Eddy knew. So she wrote her "precious Student" again the next day, July 8:

I cannot see you glamoured without an effort to save you. Remember what I have through God already done for you and *wake* to a *true* sense of this, such as you used to have.

Now, darling, I do not want you to attend to my clothes if it hinders your advancement in Christian Science. But you have told me that it did not, and *proved* it so. You have prospered in your growth and field of labor beyond other students, and I have seen that it was because you were so kind to me. If *in any way* I have wronged you, tell me of it, for I would not do it knowingly. I should feel better to pay you a salary that you will name for helping me as you have done. O, my darling student, do not let this spell of *m.a.m. separate us.* You have been strong on this point and often said it *never could do this.* Rouse yourself to saying and realizing this *now. Be strong.* Tell me if you have anything to complain of me, and I will watch and pray that [I] do to you as I would be done by.

The grave danger facing her church was that it would discard the Leader, — the Discoverer and Founder, — for the praise, popularity, and prosperity of the world. If she could not awaken her Augusta from this enticing dream, there was little probability that she could waken anyone. The dear directors were asleep with the rest of the field. They knew that they had helped their Leader to foil a demon scheme, and they thought that they had won the war. All in Boston were rejoicing in victory when they were alerted to another attack.

In May Alfred Farlow and Cornell Wilson had visited McClure's editorial offices in an unsuccessful endeavor to have an interview with S. S. McClure. Following the dedication, a keen writer from *McClure's Magazine* questioned William Lyman Johnson at great length. Midst all the acclaim from other reporters, William Lyman *sensed* that this journalist was not friendly, and after consulting with his father he wrote as much to Mrs. Eddy. But a letter of July 10 to John Willis from a student in Chicago, Mrs. Augusta B. Bensley, revealed the plot more fully. One of Mrs. Bensley's daughters was a freelance journalist in New York, and she had written to her mother:

> By the way, I have something of interest to say to you, which I think you will probably not be very pleased to hear. Mr. McClure, who is the owner and editor of McClure's Magazine and of McClure Syndicates ... has been here a good deal lately; and among other things he has told me that McClure's Magazine is going to start a crusade against Christian Science. They have been at this for some two or three years and have collected as he put it "a whole trunkful of documents," including ... many letters, some of them originals of Mrs. Eddy's and some of them certified copies, and they have watched the whole course of things for some time with great care. They had people at the convention in Boston a few weeks ago, one of whom I know quite well. As far as I can find out, the first of these articles is to be published in January and they are going on through a large part of the year. They are going to take up every phase of development of Christian Science and do what they can to ridicule and destroy it. This information is authentic. I had it from Mr. McClure's own lips. ... I do not know that there is anything that can be done by any of your people to stop it or interfere with his plans, but sometimes it is worth while knowing these things beforehand.

Surely this letter helped to waken her lieutenants in Boston to the Leader's words in Science and Health: "The serpent is perpetually close upon the heel of harmony. From the beginning to the end, the serpent pursues with hatred the spiritual idea. ... when nearing its doom, this evil increases and becomes the great red dragon ... inflamed with war against spirituality ..."

The Leader's next step *for* spirituality was a by-law amendment for her church which had an implication none saw at that time. The change published in the *Sentinel* of July 14 read:

> The general Communion of this Church shall be observed triennially in Boston, Mass., on the second Sunday in June.

But because the Leader had to take her followers one small step at a time, this amendment included a second sentence:

> Its local Communion service shall be held annually at the same date.

Mary Godfrey Parker had known Asa Gilbert Eddy when she was a very small child and had been healed by Mrs. Glover before the latter became Mrs. Eddy; but she was totally uncomprehending when her husband announced one day: "I shall never go to another Communion. If we always have Christ with us, why go to Communion?" But Danforth P. W. Parker was the exception rather than the rule.

A happy note appeared in the last *Sentinel* in July. Under the caption "Prophecy by Longfellow" in this July 28 issue was this note and poem: "The following interesting prophecy by the poet Longfellow appeared in the first number of the *Atlantic Monthly.* — Editor"

> Where'er a noble deed is wrought,
> Where'er is spoken a noble thought,
> Our heart in glad surprise
> To higher levels rise;
> Honor to those whose words and deeds
> Thus help us in our daily needs.
> And by their overflow
> Raise us from what is low.
> A lady with a lamp shall stand
> In the great history of our land,
> A noble type of good
> Heroic womanhood.

When Mrs. Eddy read the July 28 *Sentinel* she penned by the torch design on the right-hand side of the front cover: "What if you put here the figure of a woman with a lamp in her hand? This would illustrate Longfellow's lines in verse. See page 763." On the left-hand side of the cover she wrote: "The same on this side." She also penciled the last four lines of Longfellow's poem on page 763, and sent this marked copy of the *Sentinel* to Editor McLellan. Three days later, on July 31, Mrs. Eddy wrote McLellan again:

> Beloved Student:
> You will accept my thanks for your kind acceptance of my proposition for the Sentinel.

This was the beginning of the new cover design for the *Sentinel* soon to appear.

CHAPTER XXXII

I HAVE RISEN

Thus He teaches mortals to lay down their fleshliness and gain spirituality. — MARY BAKER EDDY

1906

A LENGTHY letter from Mrs. Stetson brought a response from the Leader on July 14 which stated in part:

> I want you to write me a letter containing your statement of the case of cancer that you cured — also copy some other portions of your last *most excellent* letter to me. Make the letter short enough to be published in our periodicals. . . .

On August 3, before the publication of Mrs. Stetson's abbreviated letter the Leader wrote her again:

> Since writing you on the subject of giving testimony on disease, God has shown me that error of any sort is no help to Truth.
>
> Therefore, I shall publish your dear letter to me, but not the testimony on disease which I requested of you.

It would appear that the dragon's intensified warfare against spirituality following the world-wide favorable publicity, gave Mrs. Eddy a great deal to meet. By the first of August the defending and upholding of her spirituality against the deadly attacks demanded her every thought every moment. Even the disease mentioned in a beautiful testimony of healing was "no help to Truth." But she did find help in a letter from Calvin C. Hill, and wrote to him on August 2:

> Mother's darling:
>
> Your dear letter strengthens me. I am having much of the experience that you name but on an opposite basis utterly. "When first I learned my Lord" I was so sure of Truth, my faith so strong in

Christian Science as I then discovered it I had no struggle to meet; but stood on the height of its glory a crowned monarch triumphant over sin and death. But behold me now washing that spiritual understanding with my tears; learning little by little the *allness* of omnipotent Mind; and the nothingness of matter, yea the absolute nothingness of *nothing* and the infinite somethingness of *All*. O bear with me, loved one, till I accomplish the height, the depth, the Horeb light of divine Life, — divine Love, divine health, holiness and immortality. The way seems not only long but very straight and narrow.

Loving in Christ Yours ever,
Mary Baker Eddy

The enemy's deadly blows were forcing the Leader up higher. She must rise or perish; and in this supreme effort to rise beyond the reach of the enemy's shafts she turned to the workers in her household for help. But, alas! she received very little help. Not that they did not try, but no one understood her position. They did not know that she was the one target for the hatred and lust of the whole world. She alone knew the meaning of the words she had written to General Bates more than a decade earlier: "You could not take my place and hold your phenomenon of human life."

Now when she sought aid in holding her "phenomenon of human life" the thoughts of her students were either so material that they chafed, or so fearful that they were an added burden. But even harder for her to bear was a lack of understanding and appreciation of the Leader's position which at times caused some in her household to think that she made much ado about things of little consequence.

But there was one loyal, faithful student who was a strong, earnest worker, who never questioned her Leader and always obeyed instantly. Mrs. Eddy called Calvin Hill to Pleasant View and asked him to deliver this letter to Mrs. Stetson in New York:

August 7, 1906

My beloved Student:

I would love to have you come to me and stop a few days with me in my home.

Do not let anyone know that you are coming here.

With my deepest love,
M. B. Eddy

N.B. If you can do as I ask, please tell Mr. Hill to telegraph "Yes" and the date, from Boston on his immediate return from N.Y.

Again thine,
M. B. E.

There is no doubt that Mr. Hill telegraphed "Yes" immediately upon his return from New York and that Augusta arrived as soon after August 7 as was possible.

There were many times when Augusta Stetson did not understand Mrs. Eddy, but many years earlier Mind had revealed to Mrs. Stetson that Mary Baker Eddy was the manifestation of the Second Coming of the Christ. For that reason she was able to follow implicitly and to accept unhesitatingly whatever the Leader said, whether she understood it or not and regardless of how much the human mind might rebel. However, the world was not ready for the revelation that had come to Augusta, and the Leader had had to caution her in this regard. Although the revelation was true, Augusta's comprehension had to grow up to that truth, for she did not always properly distinguish between corporeality and spirituality. Nearly six years earlier the Leader had written:

> Darling Augusta, my precious child:
>
> I will have you come to me and try to set you just right on this question once more. M.a.m. is darkening the thought on this in two ways, 1st, to make all students turn from taking my advice and strike out blindly on their own from judgment of spiritual things.
>
> The 2nd is to make them believe and say *I am the Christ.* Now dearest one, I have denied this privately and publicly and charged you not to say it so many times. . . . I love you for your faithful work in the field. But darling, you injure the cause and disobey me in thinking that I am Christ or saying such a thing. And m.a.m. is causing you to do this. Read my books on this subject and you will find I always explain Christ as the *invisible* and never corporeal. Jesus was a man corporeal. Christ was, is, and forever will be the Holy Ghost, or in scientific phrase, the spiritual idea of God.
>
> I am corporeal to the senses even as Paul was. But God has anointed me to do His work, to reveal His Word, to lead His people. And your faithful adherence to my directions and love for me, has caused you to prosper in the field even as you have. Now never again, I implore you, get the Trinity wrong in what you teach. Jesus was the man that was a prophet and the best and greatest man that ever has appeared on earth, but Jesus was not Christ, for Christ is the spiritual individual that the eye cannot see. Jesus was called Christ only in the sense that you say, a Godlike man. I am only a Godlike woman, God-anointed, and I have done a work that none others could do. As Paul was not understood, and Jesus was not understood at the time they taught and demonstrated, so I am not. As following them and obeying them blessed all who did thus — so obeying me and following faithfully blesses all who do this.
>
> Now, darling, never again misinterpret Christ or the *visible.*

When Jesus said, "Why callest thou me good? there is none good but one, that is God;" he was endeavoring to keep his followers from deifying personality. Mrs. Eddy was doing exactly the same thing in this letter. It did cause Augusta to change her teaching and her talking on the subject, but it did not change her thought. That had been a revelation from Love which nothing could change.

When Augusta arrived at Pleasant View she found those closest to the Leader quite concerned and Mrs. Eddy struggling with suggestions of physical problems, though maintaining her regular daily routine. Augusta recorded a little of what transpired while she was there. Some of the Leader's words during their first interview were:

> This is what they have done to me. If I had taken the time to take care of myself it would not be so. Take care of yourself.
>
> . . . You have fear. You see an error and you walk right up to it but you don't always put your foot on it. . . .
>
> Do you think of me when you are treating? People heal through the book. Heal them yourself, through your own reflection.
>
> I have risen! Don't look for me in matter. I have risen.
>
> You worship this (pointing to herself). Yes, you do.
>
> Mrs. Stetson: You say I do. I do not *think* I do!
>
> Mrs. Eddy: You worship me — (abhorrence of personality). Turn your thought away from me. Go to God for *everything*. Open the Bible and S&H. These two are your guide. In your trouble you have come to me.
>
> Mrs. S.: When I've gone to God he has always sent *you*.
>
> Mrs. E.: He always will send me.
>
> Mrs. S.: If you have risen, this is the first resurrection; and your resurrection must be my *resurrection*.

Before their interview ended the Leader called Mr. Strang in and said she wanted him to hear what she had told Augusta. So Mrs. Stetson said to Mr. Strang:

> I must not look to idea but to God. I must, however, acknowledge the idea when God sends it.

During the days Augusta spent in Concord Mrs. Eddy asked her to treat her for specific claims, but failed to receive the instantaneous help that others received from her. However, the rest of the household, feeling abused, overworked and unappreciated, experienced relief from Augusta's presence and work.

On August 12 the Leader said to Caroline Foss:

> It comes to me in my prayer to tell you that disobedience and self-justification are the cause of your not mastering m.a.m. I have begged of you to quit telling me why you did a thing wrongly, but you have not obeyed me. I have told you it is like the sick excusing sickness — tell *why they are sick,* and you do know that this would tend to make

it real and to *justify sickness.*

Augusta Stetson had come closer to overcoming disobedience and self-justification than had any other of Mrs. Eddy's students. For that reason she benefited more from the rebukes, and could bear up under them with far less reaction than most of the others experienced. Her example was helpful to those who could see. It may have been during this trying period that Caroline Foss was sent home, for her service terminated in August. It was also in August that Clara Knox McKee came to Pleasant View to serve the Leader

One day following her daily drive the Leader sent for Augusta who came quickly, sat by her, and admired her bonnet. Mrs. Eddy was pleasant and chatty, and Augusta recorded their conversation:

> Mrs. S.: Where is your pretty coat? your pretty gown?
> Mrs. E.: Is a pimple on the face any more real than a boil?
> Mrs. S.: Is a pretty new dress any more real than an old homely one?
> Mrs. E.: No, only that a pretty gown holds my thought to my body.
> Mrs. S.: The homely old one would hold my thought to my body.

The next morning Mrs. Eddy's bell summoned all to her study, and she said sternly: "You asked me yesterday why I did not wear my pretty gowns. I *have to* work for you, while you dress in your pretty gowns." Augusta opened her Bible to Mark 1:13 and read: "And he was there in the wilderness forty days, tempted of Satan; and was with the wild beasts; and the angels ministered unto him."

"What are angels?" said Mrs. Eddy. "God's thoughts," Augusta responded. "That's just it!" said the Leader, and dismissed them all.

Mrs. Eddy opened her Bible and her eyes fell on the parable in Matthew 12:43. She called Augusta back and said to her: "See what I've opened to. Would you go into a frenzy if I should read this to you?" Augusta answered, "Not at all, no matter what you say to me." Then Mrs.Eddy read from her Bible:

> When the unclean spirit is gone out of a man, he walketh through dry places, seeking rest, and findeth none. Then he saith, I will return into my house from whence I came out; and when he is come he findeth it empty, swept, and garnished.

A year earlier in August of 1905, Mrs. Eddy had told this to her household in a very gentle manner. They were all working diligently to cleanse their house (consciousness) and it was swept and garnished — but empty. On that occasion the Leader had told them that the moral atmosphere at Pleasant View was perfect, but that there was a lack. They had not filled their cleansed and empty house with spirituality.

On this occasion in August of 1906 she was not so gentle with Augusta, and read the next verse:

> Then goeth he, and taketh with himself seven other spirits more wicked than himself, and they enter in and dwell there: and the last state of that man is worse than the first. Even so shall it be also unto this wicked generation.

The Leader said to Augusta, relative to her treating: "You hurt me. You use will power. Don't touch me. Leave me alone." But she also said: "If you can heal that man of cancer why can't you heal my bowels?" Augusta probably asked herself that question many, many times. And the answer was most likely the same as it is for all students today — a lack of spirituality. Cleansing the house (consciousness) is not sufficient. It *must* be filled with Spirit if we would not have our problems multiply.

On the eighteenth of August Mrs. Eddy sent Augusta home. The next day this earnest worker wrote a lengthy, helpful letter to a student of hers who was serving the Leader at Pleasant View, probably Miss Jessie T. Colton who went to Pleasant View in July, 1906:

> August 19, 1906
>
> My beloved Student:
>
> I know that God will give you wisdom, strength, and divine love to minister to our beloved Leader in this and every hour that she may need you. Every moment you can claim of your time declare for God's allness, presence, and power, and the nothingness of a so-called claim to another power. Read your Bible and Science and Health every spare moment and this will keep your thought clear to reflect God.
>
> You know that God is with you, and that every member of the dear household is reflecting Love divine to our darling Leader. God is her life, and you know that He will manifest, through her, His mighty power to mankind. Christ Jesus is her example. She will have "twelve legions of angels" to watch with her, and the dear loving ones who do all they *can* to go as far as possible with her. God will "feed" her "famished affections" (Science and Health, p. 17). I am obeying her, and keeping my mind fixed on Christ. I pray to God without ceasing that I may dwell in the secret of His presence every moment.
>
> I have suffered out of the flesh far enough to know, that the will of the flesh has no power but to destroy itself. God's will is my will. There is no other, and I live in Him. There is a great distance between us and our precious Leader. She is rising Christward, and we are trying to help her as a child who has just learned to stand alone tries to follow the mother. But if we obey the Sermon on the Mount,

and her teachings in Science and Health, and cling to God, knowing that all evil is unreal, when we meet it with truth and love, we shall be saved.

Sin, sickness, and death will yield to Life, Love, and Truth.

Be obedient to God's law, and do not fail to pray that you may serve our beloved acceptably. I am writing this to you, dear, because she told me to help you, and I know of no better way than to write you and let you know that I am unable to go further with you personally, as she wants me to rise with her, and leave all work in the home to those who are there. She told me yesterday that she had risen, and that if I held only to God and His idea, not thinking of her corporeality, that I would always be spiritually with her as idea. And so I look to God, and to His spiritual idea, my Leader and Teacher, and I find her in Mind.

I believe we have both come to the hour when, as she has said, "Where God is we can meet, and where God is we can never part:" *[My.* 131:20]. I am peaceful and strong. I have declared the Truth in love as I read it in Science and Health. My love for her is deathless, because I do not look for her in matter. My Father will not disregard His promises to me — to guide, and guard, and save me, if I endure to the end of all belief of life, truth, intelligence, and substance in matter.

God will move you to do what is right. Do not fear; fear is the absence of love — a lie, for Love is God, and God is never absent. Fear incapacitates you, and would prevent you from helping her as you would. Handle the lie of aggressive mental suggestion with the Word of God. Know the voice of Truth and obey our Leader. Do as far as you can just what she asks you to do. God will supply you with strength. Give my love to dear Mrs. L., and tell her to work faithfully for our beloved Leader. Give my endless love to Laura, and Mr. Frye and Mrs. Leonard.

Thank Mr. Lewis C. Strang for his kind letter just received, commending me for the work I did for the Leader while in her home. He says that every member of the household is grateful to me for what I did for her while there. Thank God the flesh-veiled eyes are all opening, and we are not looking into the grave — the matter body — to find each other in God's image. We are now, ever were, and ever will be Life, Love, and Truth reflected.

Always your loving, faithful teacher,
Augusta E. Stetson

While Augusta was writing this letter in New York, Lewis Strang was working at Pleasant View with the following watch which the Leader gave to him that same day:

Your Mother in Israel calls upon you this day — rejoice with her in sense spiritual — *know* there is One Mind, Truth, Love and all will be met. Behold I make all things new is the promise Christ-like. Do you, dear Lewis, understand this? Then *rise up* — defeat the enemy without our gates that defileth and maketh a lie. No night, no darkness, all is Mind. All is God, good. *Hold to this* until I say change.

The suffering and struggling this August which were forcing the Leader up higher did not stop her work for her church, but caused her to take it up higher, too. She wrote to all three editors on August 4:

> One other improvement I beg to have made in our periodicals, namely: Keep out of them all descriptions of shocking suffering and the symptoms of disease.
>
> Rehearsing error is not scientific. I know that you agree with me in this statement and therefore will adopt what I herewith suggest.
>
> Publish as usual the testimonies on healing. Give due authority therefor, and sometimes state the opinions of the M.D.'s on disease, but do this in a way that will not offend them.
>
> You can introduce this change to your contributors in a wise way and request them to conform to it strictly.

After the next *Sentinel* came out the Leader wrote to McLellan further on this issue:

> The testimonials are better but are not right yet, not stated so as to prevent an *image* of disease from getting into thought.
>
> This is the way to keep out a *distinct* form in thought of disease. If the disease is called "floating kidney," you should write it fatal or dangerous, etc., disease of the kidneys.
>
> Do not give the special name of a disease or of a complaint, but state the disease in general terms. If this is not enough to suit the author of the articles, keep it all out.

A new by-law was published in the next issue of the *Sentinel* on August 18. This by-law, entitled "Testimonials," was essentially the same as the present Article VIII, Sect. 24 *(Man.* 47):

> . . . Testimony in regard to healing of the sick is highly important. . . . This testimony, however, shall not include a description of symptoms or of suffering . . .

There had been a good deal of correspondence with Mrs. Stetson regarding her testimonial letter as this change in "testimonials" was developing. Finally, on August 10 Mrs. Eddy wrote to her editor:

> I have now got Mrs. Stetson's article to you for the last time. Pardon the trouble I may have occasioned you. All my part in it has

> been to shorten it and remove her too much praise of me. Let it appear in both Sentinel and Journal and in our next issues.
> N.B. Keep this as quiet as possible till it is published.

In the *Sentinel* of August 18 — the day that Mrs. Stetson returned to New York from Pleasant View — Mr. McLellan published "A Helpful Letter to Mrs. Eddy from one of her students whose work in Christian Science has done much for the advancement of our Cause":

> My Precious Leader and Teacher:
> ... I am ever searching my inmost consciousness and praying earnestly and continually for God to open my spiritual eyes that I may behold wondrous things, as you, His chosen messenger, reveal His law and unfailing love. ...
> As I behold this First Church of Christ, Scientist, of New York City, a tribute of love and gratitude to you, beloved, our prayer in Concord granite, which my students and members of this church have reared to you, I praise God for this evidence of His love.
> Every day I see proofs of your unselfed watch-care and love for your students, including me and mine. How often during the church services I wish you could see the great congregation and hear the testimonies of wonderful deliverance from sin, sickness, sorrow, and death, and their appreciation of your great works and your book Science and Health. ...
> You thank me for getting you wearing apparel and feel indebted to me for the favor. ... I am indebted to you for perfect physical health and almost unlimited strength, for a large body of loving, loyal students and church members, for a large church edifice which shelters multitudes who come to learn through Christian Science the way to eternal life.
> I am indebted to you for the understanding of God's power to heal through man, which recently enabled me to destroy a cancer in the mouth and throat in one treatment — all evidence having disappeared after the second treatment. This was nine weeks ago. ...
> Ever your loving student,
> Augusta E. Stetson

Before the end of August the Leader gave a statement to Mr. Strang to deliver to one of her directors along with this message:

> The enclosed statement hand to Mr. Armstrong Friday. Tell him, *do not come* to Pleasant View until *I say so* and hold no more such Board meetings as this last reported to me here, or I shall not be responsible for results. This Cause depends upon healing, healing and *wisdom.* If these are not added, the salt will lose his savor and this Cause drop down into darkness of oblivion of centuries again.

The Leader did not say that healing and wisdom must be *retained,* but that they must be *added* to uphold her Cause.

Mrs. Eddy received numerous letters in response to her article "Personal Contagion." A number of them were published in the *Sentinel* including this one from Chicago:

> Beloved Teacher:
> . . . You have many times explained to me how in many ways the students have burdened your every day for years and years. Last night I shed many a tear when I thought of the unspeakable burdens that have been laid upon you by us all, and of the continuous sacrifice in which your association with us has involved you; and although it may be of no consolation to you, I want you to know that for any weight of care or sorrow that has ever been laid upon you by me, I am from the depths of my heart's affection sorry beyond description.
>
> Lovingly your student,
> Edward A. Kimball

There were also a great many letters thanking the Leader for the new by-law regarding testimonials, one of which was from the faithful Mrs. Nixon:

> Beloved Leader:
> The new by-law on "testimonials" has already accomplished wonders in thought, although this is the first Wednesday since its publication. Your marvelous wisdom is again seen, and the song "What a Leader! What a Leader!" sings itself in my heart continually. We long to understand and obey you, and I believe this new command falls on listening ears and longing, loyal hearts. I thank God, and feel with others a new life and impulse for our dear Wednesday evening testimonial meetings. God bless you dear Leader and Teacher.
>
> With deepest love, your student,
> Helen A. Nixon

Many of the letters the Leader received touched her heart, and there were many that cost her a tear. She was moved to reply to one letter in the summer of 1906 with these words: "Your perceptions are like 'apples of gold in pictures of silver.'" The letter to Mrs. Eddy that elicited this response was from Mrs. Fannie B. Hunt, a practitioner in Chicago who wrote:

> I am indeed grateful for all that you have done and are still doing for mankind. I am showing this gratitude to you by devoting all my time to healing the sick (so-called), reforming the sinner (so-called), and uplifting the sorrowful (so-called); but I would be much more grateful for that quality of human consciousness which could pro-

gress through an individual understanding of what you are teaching in word and deed, instead of compelling you to make By-laws to rectify mistakes that are purely the result of a false concept of what Christian Science really is. It certainly takes time to write By-laws as well as to read telegrams. I am jealous of your time, and am praying for the day and hour when you will be permitted to spend your time and thought on Mind and its activities instead of matter and its errors.

Mrs. Hunt saw that it was the shortcomings of the students and their lack of scientific understanding that constantly required additional by-laws. But she was mistakenly hoping for understanding in "human consciousness." The uplifting moral qualities of the second degree are requisite, but understanding *must* be spiritual to be on a firm foundation and to be termed reality.

Also in August, on the tenth of the month, Mrs. Eddy was signing the certificates for the Board of Education class just completed. Three days earlier Lewis Strang had written to the Board of Trustees regarding the new cover for the *Sentinel:*

I return the sketch for the cover of the Sentinel. Mrs. Eddy has examined it and endorses it. The only suggestion that she made is a different style of head-dress for the woman.

On August 10 Strang wrote the Trustees again:

Mrs. Eddy approves of the new arrangement of the head-dress. The only change that she suggests in the last design submitted is the omission of the C.S. seal — the cross and crown with "Heal the sick, raise the dead," etc. She thinks that the effect without this will be more artistic. In fact, she is very much pleased with it.

The Christian Science seal, the cross and crown encircled by the words "Heal the sick — Raise the dead — Cleanse the lepers —

Cast out demons," had been on the top of the first page of Volume I when it was first issued, without a cover, as the *Christian Science Weekly.* It was January 19, 1899, when Mrs. Eddy renamed the paper *Sentinel* and gave it the motto, "What I say unto you, I say unto all, *Watch."* Both title and motto appeared for the first time on the front page of the next issue. that of January 26, 1899. The seal continued to be included on the front of each copy. The first cover design, which included the C. S. seal and the motto, had begun with Volume II in September, 1899 and had been used for seven years. This original cover had a torch on each side of the contents.

Now, in 1906, the first issue of Volume IX of the *Christian Science Sentinel* appeared on September 1 with a very significant change.

The poet had seen that —

A lady with a lamp shall stand
In the great history of our land,
A noble type of good, —
Heroic womanhood.

The Discoverer had presented her discovery to the world. The Founder had established this discovery upon a firm foundation which the world could neither ignore nor destroy. And now the time had come for the Leader, the "Lady with a Lamp," to stand forth. Her loyal students had always looked upon her as the Leader, but now the fact of her leadership is being proclaimed to all the field. Every move the Leader made held great significance. The paper is still a *Sentinel* on guard, and the motto remains "Watch." But why is the seal removed? The Leader often said something to silence or to satisfy mortal mind. In this case she said: "the effect without this will be more artistic." That satisfied; but we *know* that the Forever Leader *never* did anything simply because it would be more artistic. Surely that was not her *reason* for removing the Christian Science seal from the *Sentinel.* What was her reason?

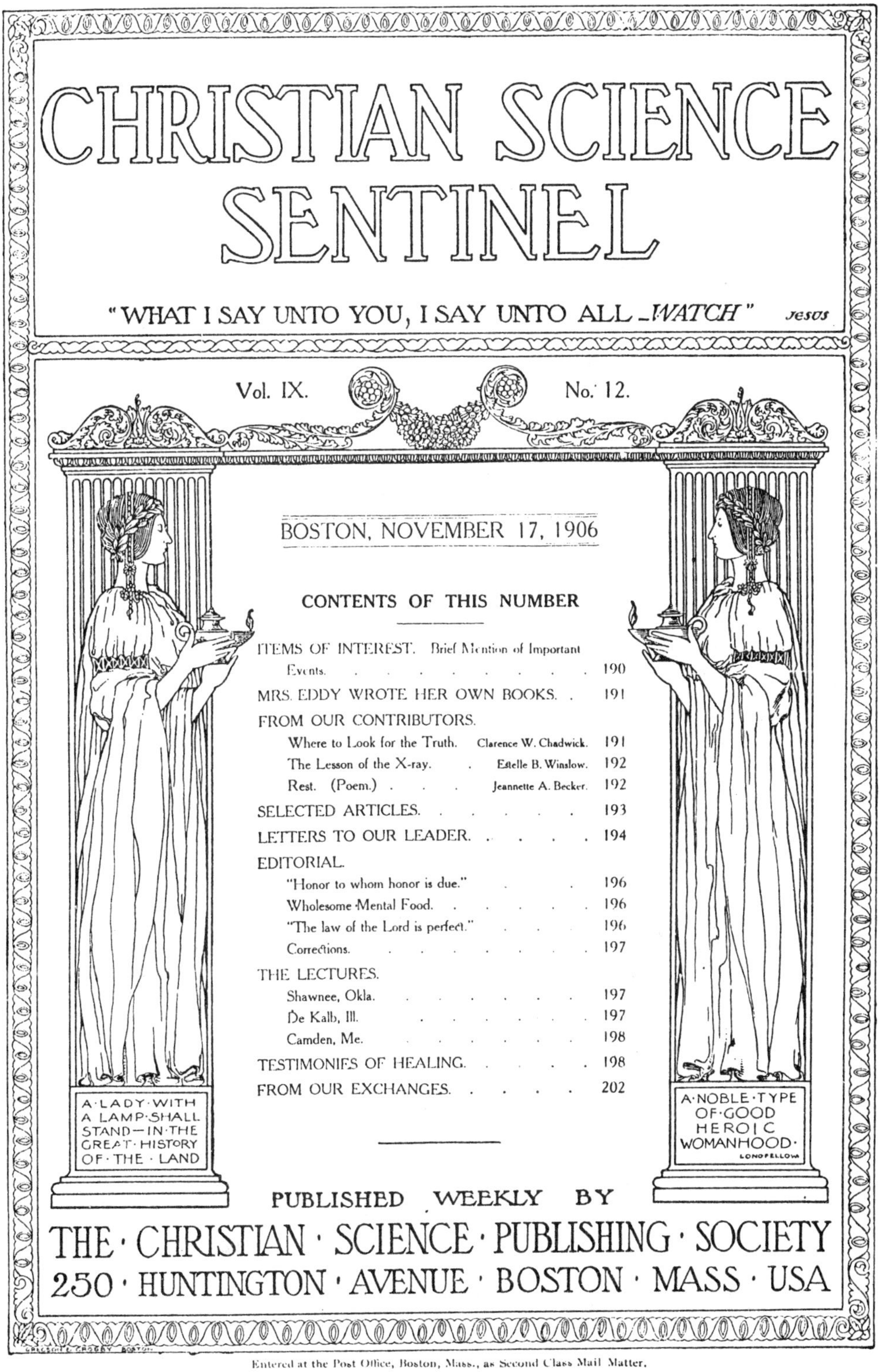

CHRISTIAN SCIENCE SENTINEL

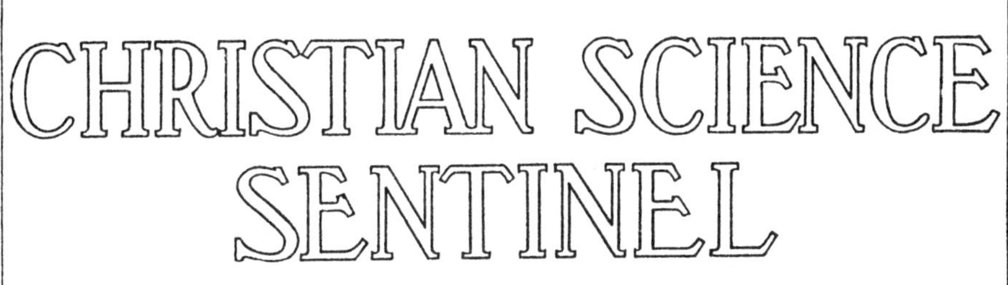

"WHAT I SAY UNTO YOU, I SAY UNTO ALL—WATCH" JESUS

Vol. IX. No. 12.

BOSTON, NOVEMBER 17, 1906

CONTENTS OF THIS NUMBER

A·LADY·WITH A·LAMP·SHALL STAND—IN·THE GREAT·HISTORY OF·THE·LAND

A·NOBLE·TYPE OF·GOOD HEROIC WOMANHOOD· LONGFELLOW

PUBLISHED WEEKLY BY
THE·CHRISTIAN·SCIENCE·PUBLISHING·SOCIETY
250·HUNTINGTON·AVENUE·BOSTON·MASS·USA

Entered at the Post Office, Boston, Mass., as Second Class Mail Matter.

NEW COVER DESIGN
First appeared on Vol. IX, No. 1, September 1, 1906

CHAPTER XXXIII

"THE DRAGON WAS WROTH"

From the beginning to the end the serpent pursues with hatred the spiritual idea. — MARY BAKER EDDY

1906

RIGHT after Communion week, on the twentieth of June, Mrs. Eddy had written "Greetings" *(My.* 175) "to the good folk of Concord." This letter published in the *Concord Evening Monitor* and the *Concord Daily Patriot* began: "I am pleased to see Professor Kent's homestead freshly thriving and to have its occupants again for neighbors." Professor John F. Kent's house was clearly visible from Pleasant View being just across Pleasant Street, and it had been quite well known for a number of years that Prof. Kent was perhaps Mrs. Eddy's bitterest enemy in all of Concord, though that had not always been the case. In a letter to Irving Tomlinson in 1899 the Leader had said: "Animals we please by stroking them the way the hair grows, but stroking it the way we want it to grow will convince *never* a Prof. Kent! I got him once where he loved to hear me talk Science (at least he said so) and I like his frankness, but others have manipulated him out of it — at least his wife has and so has m.a.m." But the import of her greetings to Concordians in June of 1906 was in these two sentences:

> ... May I ask in behalf of the public this favor of our city government; namely, to macademize a portion of Warren Street and to macademize North State Street throughout? ...
>
> I am sure that the counterfeit letters in circulation, purporting to have my signature must fail to influence the minds of this dear people to conclusions the very opposite of my real sentiments.

The card Mrs. Eddy published in the *Sentinel* of July 14 may bear relationship to her request for paving the streets:

Card

We lose the sense of personality when describing love, and so base the behests of praise on worth akin to unworldliness, on goodness shorn of self, and on charity governed by God influencing the acts of men — even as charity which "suffereth long and is kind."

Mrs. Mary Beecher Longyear's charity is of the sort that letteth not the left hand know what the right hand doeth, that giveth unspoken to the needy and is felt more than heard in a wide field of benefactions. Seldom have I seen such individual, impartial giving as this. Therefore I hasten to praise it and turn upon it the lens of spiritual faith and love, which enforce the giving liberally to all men and the upbraiding of none.

Begging her pardon for the presumption of my pen, if such it be to "render unto Caesar the things that are Caesar's," I hope that I have neither grieved her meekness, nor overrated her generosity thereby.

Mary Baker Eddy

The Concord city government called a special meeting on Tuesday evening, August 7, at which time they voted to expend five thousand dollars to improve State Street. If Mrs. Longyear's recent charity had been a contribution to the Concord street fund, it was but the first of many. Contributions accompanied by letters of appreciation poured into Concord and Pleasant View. A number of them were published in the *Sentinel* including one from Emma Thompson whose church in Minneapolis sent five hundred dollars to help "to smooth a little of the way over which you pass on your daily drives." On October 19 Mrs. Eddy wrote a notice "To One and All" thanking them for their lavish giving, but closing the Concord Street Fund.

The second item that Mrs. Eddy addressed in her "Greetings" to Concordians, that of counterfeit letters, was enlarged upon early in September. For several years prior to 1906 every issue of the *Sentinel* had contained this notice:

MRS. EDDY TAKES NO PATIENTS

The author of the Christian Science text-book takes no patients, does not consult on disease, nor read letters referring to these subjects.

In the second *Sentinel* of Volume IX, September 8, 1906, this notice kept the same title but was changed to read as follows:

The author of the Christian Science text-book does not consult nor read letters on disease. Writing to Mrs. Eddy is *not* Personal Contagion. Take no notice of startling reports about Mrs. Eddy. Our Publication Committee will be reliable on this subject. *Beware of counterfeit letters.*

This enlarged notice continued to appear in subsequent issues with the second sentence changed to read: "Writing to Mrs. Eddy *is not* prohibited." There is little doubt that the Leader knew what was coming. The hatred endeavoring to destroy her "phenomenon of human life" had given her a great deal to meet. But she had met it and she had risen, as she said to her faithful Augusta on August 18. Now she was preparing her followers to meet what would soon be seen by all the world. She was warning them to "beware of counterfeit letters" as well as the wicked intent of such letters. She was also warning them to be prepared for *whatever* the enemy would endeavor to do to their Leader, when she wrote: "Take no notice of startling reports about Mrs. Eddy." This notice was preparing her followers for what was soon to break like a storm in the fall of 1906, but it was not for that time alone. It was a notice to her followers for all time, else she would not have continued its publication week after week for all the ensuing years.

The Leader had risen above the enemy's deadly attack in the summer of 1906, and all those in her household at Pleasant View had come through the ordeal unscathed, though probably unaware of the protection their Leader's work gave to them, as well as the danger they were exposed to as her soldiers. However, one of her officials in Boston did not survive the attack. Joseph B. Clark, one of the three trustees of the Christian Science Publishing Society, passed away early in September.

ALLISON V. STEWART

ALLISON V. Stewart had been in the Normal Class of the Board of Education taught by Mr. Kimball in 1901. He had been listed in the *Journal* as a practitioner in Chicago together with Mrs. Stewart. Both were Normal course graduates, and in addition to their practitioners' cards, advertised their "Garden City Institute of Christian Science." In 1906 Allison was also Publication Committee for Illinois when the trustees asked him to come to Boston. He had written letters on business matters to Mrs. Eddy's secretary Lewis Strang prior to Mrs. Eddy's letter of September 14 written in her own handwriting to her two remaining trustees:

> Beloved Students:
>
> I am not so situated as to be informed of the points requisite as you are — hence I leave it to the Trustees to decide who shall fill the vacancy.
>
> Mr. Neal I wish to remain on the Com. on Business and I cannot

see that he can fill his position as a healer and have added to his labor aught of what belongs to another office than that he has already.

Mr. McKenzie wrote at great length both for himself and Mr. Hatten, responding to this letter. Part of McKenzie's letter to the Leader said:

> In accordance with the message in your letter of Sept. 14th the remaining Trustees have given their thought to the problem of filling the vacancy left by the going away of our dear brother Joseph B. Clark, and are unanimous in proposing the name of Mr. A. V. Stewart of Chicago at present Publication Committee for Illinois. Some time ago he relieved himself from all business cares, and has given his whole time devotedly to Christian Science work since then, so that if he should be approved by you, and accept the appointment, there need be no delay in having his assistance here.

The Leader gave her approval on September 19, typewritten, to McKenzie and Hatten:

> You will please accept my thanks for your long loving *wise* letter. I am satisfied with your description, and heartily recommend your election of Mr. A. V. Stewart to fill the responsible office now vacant. Our late loved and lamented Mr. Clark has gone to his reward of "well done." May the God of all grace ever guide and bless you and yours.

On September 25 Allison V. Stewart officially succeeded Joseph B. Clark as trustee of the Publishing Society. Two days later he wrote this letter to Mrs. Eddy:

> Beloved Leader and Teacher:
>
> I wish to tell you how deeply grateful I am for the confidence made manifest in my selection to fill the vacancy on the Board of Trustees of The Christian Science Publishing Society which was caused by the passing away of our faithful, loving, and loved brother Joseph B. Clark. My earnest desire is to do my utmost in the work of the great Cause of Christian Science wherever I am placed, and I am praying for guidance and wisdom in this most sacred trust. When the call came, I arranged to come here without delay, but I must say I came with some misgivings regarding my fitness for the place; however, the welcome accorded me by all of the splendid staff of workers here at headquarters was most hearty and kind, and I am encouraged to press forward, to live and work with the understanding I have gained of your teachings, believing that my shortcomings will be dealt with in a loving manner.
>
> I wish to assure you, my dear Mrs. Eddy, if there is any way whereby I can in the least degree contribute to your comfort and

pleasure, it will be a great joy for me to do so.

Again thanking you, I am

Sincerely and gratefully your student,
Allison V. Stewart

A few days earlier, on the eighteenth of September, Hermann Hering had written the Leader regarding his appointment to lecture in The Mother Church. He said in his letter:

> . . . I thank you deeply for the honor thus conferred and pray that I may be a channel for Truth and Love on that occasion. It will be the first lecture delivered in The Mother Church Extension. If you have any suggestions to make, I will be most happy to receive and adopt them.

Professor Hering also told her (as the First Reader) of progress in the Concord Church; and of contributions he had received for the Concord Street Fund. He included one of the latter in his letter:

FOR THE STREET FUND

Solomon said of Wisdom
  That she giveth true increase;
"Her ways are ways of pleasantness,
  And all her paths are peace."
So to the Leader's wisdom,
  Which imparteth truth today,
I send a tiny tribute
  To make pleasanter the way.

Gertrude Ring

While Scientists were interested in the Concord Street Fund, the general public was being entertained in September by rumors of a wild ride Mrs. Eddy had had behind the prize horses which had been sent to her two or three years earlier. The story was entirely false and was duly denied by Alfred Farlow, Calvin Frye, her coachman, and all others concerned. The fact was that she had never even ridden behind those horses, but the truth did not deter the calumniators.

Another letter Mrs. Eddy received in September was from an early student who had not remained faithful, as had Samuel Bancroft. No doubt it rejoiced the Leader's heart to send this letter to the *Sentinel* for publication:

My Beloved Leader and Teacher:

I want to tell you what a joy I had in visiting First Church of Christ, Scientist, in Concord, N. H., Aug. 30, 1906, of the great pleasure I had in attending the Wednesday evening meeting there, of the delight in seeing the lovely gifts in your room at the church, and hearing the fine organ and the chimes, all of which tell us the story of your faithful love-service to God and man. My heart goes out in boundless gratitude to you for so many blessings. I find no words to number or express them. I know, dear Mrs. Eddy, you will appreciate my fulness of joy and love.

Yours most sincerely,
Clara E. Choate

Late in September Mrs. Eddy received a letter from a German student, Bertha Reinke, who had come to Boston for the dedication of The Mother Church Extension in June. The writer first expressed "praise and gladness" for Christian Science and the Leader, and then told of a book she had been enjoying during her summer in America. The book, the *Apocryphal New Testament,* published in German in 1904, was a compilation of translations by fifteen or sixteen German scholars from original manuscripts in Latin, Greek, Syrian, Ethiopian, and Coptic. Miss Reinke's letter included passages from this book which she had translated into English. Her letter was the leader in the *Sentinel* of October 6, and stated in part:

"The last things. Beliar. The Rule of a Woman. The End of the World and the Second Coming of Christ." "Then the world, ruled by the hands of a woman entirely — shall rest in obedience." "Then, when the royal widow shall thus rule over the whole world — all gold and silver, iron and brass she shall cast into the salt-flood, into the sea, — all the elements of the world shall be forsaken — when God, dwelling in the ether, unfolds the heavens like a scroll of a book. And the whole firmament shall fall upon the earth and into the sea." Then it gives a description of the changes of the seasons similar to what Science and Health says in regard to them: "O ye rushing waves — and the entire foundation of the earth. Now the sun rises which never is to set — and all shall be in obedience again to Him who returns once more into this world."

. . . I shall soon leave these shores to go back to my country, and there endeavor to heal the sick and lead to the truth those who are seeking the Lord with all their hearts. They all love you, are grateful to you, and are waiting patiently the day when your great wisdom will see fit to give them your books in their own tongue. The German nation is ready for the truth as you have given it to the world.

MRS. EDDY'S COMMENT

The above letter from Miss Bertha S. Reinke is deeply interesting, but I will say that the important matter of publishing in the German language my works on Christian Science is not within my jurisdiction, except as I voluntarily assume it.

I have put aside the matter of translating my writings into German since receiving the courteous approval of my thoughts upon this subject from the Countess von Moltke. The Trustees of The Christian Science Publishing Society are the proper *authorities* to settle this question.

Mary Baker G. Eddy

All the Leader's actions were directed by God, even as all the hairs of her head were numbered. In the fall of 1906 her major God-directed project was a major revision of Science and Health in English. Clara McKee, who came in August to serve at Pleasant View, said of this project:

> She had a copy of the three dollar edition taken apart in sections; this was placed right side up in the left-hand side of her desk drawer. She would take off one section at a time and go through it. Then that one was placed upside down in the right-hand side of the drawer. When she had finished going over every page of the entire book, it was in perfect order.

Professor Hering's lecture in The Mother Church was scheduled for Tuesday, October 16, and the Concord church had asked him to deliver the same lecture in their edifice on October 28. On the thirteenth of October the Concord lecture committee wrote to Mrs. Eddy:

> Beloved Leader: — In making the arrangements for the lecture on Christian Science to be delivered in this city by Professor Hermann S. Hering, C.S.B., on Sunday, October 28, the committee have thought of inviting the Mayor, Judge Charles R. Corning, to introduce the speaker, if this choice meets with your approval. Judge Corning performed this courtesy most acceptably last year, on the occasion of Judge Ewing's lecture. . . .

MRS. EDDY'S REPLY

> Beloved Brethren: — I am in receipt of your letter and hasten to say our Mayor, Judge Charles R. Corning, is the very man for the hour and for this introduction. His history armors him with moral mail.
>
> Mary Baker Eddy

On the day of this letter regarding Mayor Corning, Lewis Strang was returning to Pleasant View from a walk in the direction of St. Paul's school when he was stopped a little west of the Pleasant View cottage by a man who asked him if all the property near there belonged to Mrs. Eddy. Mr. Strang told the man the extent of Mrs. Eddy's estate.

About half an hour later Lewis Strang was sitting in his room which looked out upon Pleasant Street and saw this same man together with a second man coming out of Professor Kent's house directly across the street. He watched as they got into a hack and drove toward Concord.

The next day, Sunday, October 14, two men came to the door of Pleasant View where Mrs. Sargent spoke with them. They said that Fred N. Ladd had sent them, gave not their names, but asked to see Mr. Frye. Calvin came to the door and made an appointment to speak with them at three o'clock. After he had shown them out he called Mr. Strang to look at them, and Strang recognized the same men he had seen the previous day. About one P.M. Mr. Strang went to see Mr. Ladd who was a reputable citizen of Concord, treasurer of the Loan and Trust Savings Bank. He was also Mrs. Eddy's cousin and her banker. Fred Ladd told Mr. Strang that the men were reporters from the *New York World* who had questioned him until late the night before with many foolish questions about Mrs. Eddy, refusing to credit anything he said about her being alive.

Mr. Frye asked Lewis Strang to remain in the room during the interview when the men returned at 3 P.M. This is from Mr. Strang's account:

> Mr. Slaght said that he and his companion, Mr. Lithchild, represented the *New York World.* He said that the *World* had received many letters declaring that Mrs. Eddy was dead; that Mr. Frye was the real head of the Christian Science movement, and that money was being received — in short, that a fraud was being conducted.
>
> Mr. Slaght continued that these letters had interested Mr. Pulitzer [owner of the *N.Y. World]* to the extent of sending them here to find out definitely whether or not Mrs. Eddy was alive. They were not after a story. . . .
>
> He said it was not Mr. Pulitzer's purpose to use the material they had collected, provided they could satisfy themselves that Mrs. Eddy was alive. . . .

The reporters rejected Strang's and Frye's assurances that Mrs. Eddy could be seen daily upon her drive, as interested testimony, saying they had been informed that the person in the carriage was not Mrs. Eddy but a dummy. They said they would be satisfied if Professor Kent would identify Mrs. Eddy in their presence. Mr. Frye said he would bring this to Mrs. Eddy's attention and let them know the next day.

Calvin did not notify Mrs. Eddy right away, but waited until the following day, Monday, October 15, after she had returned from her daily drive. Immediately she sent John Salchow to make arrangements with Professor Kent and August Mann to the Eagle Hotel after the reporters, who arrived about 3 P.M. Strang received them and talked with them while awaiting the arrival of Prof. Kent. He also recorded their interview with Mrs. Eddy:

> As soon as Professor Kent arrived the three men and myself went at once upstairs to Mrs. Eddy's office. She arose and stepped to the middle of the floor to meet them. She spoke to Professor Kent, saying that she was sorry he had lost the principalship of the Concord High School and that she hoped he would be re-appointed. I introduced Mr. Slaght first. She shook hands with him, and he said that he was very glad to see her. I then introduced Mr. Lithchild [whose] name escaped me for a moment, and he was obliged to prompt me. Mrs. Eddy shook hands with him. She explained in a few words that her duties made it impossible for her to receive visitors and that this accounted for her seclusion. She signified that this ended the visit, though I believe that she shook hands again with Professor Kent before he left the room. I know that Messrs. Slaght and Lithchild preceded me out of the room and went downstairs. Mrs. Eddy remained standing during the entire visit, and as the men left, turned and walked back to her desk in the bay window.
>
> When we were going down the stairs Mr. Lithchild said to me, with apparent conviction: "She is certainly a well preserved woman for her years." Mr. Slaght also gave me to understand that he was thoroughly satisfied as to the soundness of Mrs. Eddy's physical and mental condition. They furthermore led Mr. Mann, who drove them back to the hotel, to understand that they purposed leaving town that afternoon . . .

But those reporters did not leave Concord. They and several others had been haunting the area since September, interrogating local citizens and spreading evil reports.

One upstanding Concordian who was perturbed by this invasion was Josiah E. Fernald, president of the National State Capital Bank. On October 2 Mr. Fernald had written to Cornell Wilson:

> Now I have known Mrs. Eddy for a number of years and have had business relations with her since she came to Concord and made her home at Pleasant View, which relations extend up to the present time. I have also visited her in her home so that I can state from personal knowledge that it is Mrs. Eddy and no other person, whom I see riding in her carriage. I will also state that she stands high in this community. I do not find those who speak evil of her in this her home city, and I believe those who come here with evil reports come with malicious intentions.
>
> I am not a follower of the Christian Science faith but make this statement as a citizen of Concord who wishes to see the things that are true, the things that are honest, and the things that are just prevail.

Mr. Fernald was a Baptist, but at one time Mrs. Eddy said to him:

"Mr. Fernald, you are a better Christian Scientist than many of my students, because you are a better Christian."

An honored and trusted official of Concord, after answering a number of questions, said to his interrogator: "There is little to gain by continuing this conversation; you are not after what I know; you desire that I should approve guesses. It is clear to me that your purpose is to write Mrs. Eddy down regardless of what her neighbors and those who know her best may say."

What was Mrs. Eddy doing while her enemies were spreading lies? She approved the republication of the following from Volume XVI of the *Christian Science Journal,* March 1899.

(Republished by Request)
WHAT OUR LEADER SAYS

Beloved Christian Scientists: — Keep your minds so filled with Truth and Love that sin, disease, and death cannot enter them. It is plain that nothing can be added to the mind already full. There is no door through which evil can enter, and no space for evil to fill in a mind filled with goodness. Good thoughts are an impervious armor: clad therewith you are completely shielded from the attacks of error of every sort. And not only yourself are safe, but all whom your thoughts rest upon are thereby benefited.

It is the evil thinker who injures himself with what he would have harm others. Goodness involuntarily resists evil. The evil thinker is the evil talker and doer. The right thinker abides under the shadow of the Almighty. His thoughts can only reflect peace, good will towards men, health and holiness.

Mary Baker Eddy

Then to Mr. McLellan she wrote: "You may publish this quarterly if agreeable."

Four days after the *World* reporters were at Pleasant View Mrs. Eddy wrote to the editor of the *Boston Herald:*

Dear Sir:

Another report that I am dead is widely circulated. I am in usual good health, and go out in my carriage every day.

Truly yours,
Mary Baker G. Eddy

McLellan wrote to Mrs. Eddy on October 20:

I like the fac-simile reproduction of your letter in the Herald, and should like to publish it in the same form in the Sentinel and Journal if you approve. . . .

Mrs. Eddy approved, for the fac-simile reproduction of her

letter appeared in the *Sentinel* of October 27, and in the November, 1906 *Journal.*

Another upstanding Concordian who resented the aspersions cast upon their town's leading citizen was the Roman Catholic editor and manager of the *Concord Patriot,* Mr. Michael Meehan. On October 26 Mr. Meehan wrote a personal letter to Joseph Pulitzer which stated:

> Few, if any women living have done as much to pass their names to posterity as has the Rev. Mary Baker G. Eddy of this city and State, and we of Concord, regardless of religious belief, have a great respect for this woman, and we resent any indignity aimed at her or passed upon her, and every decent man and woman in our city experiences a sense of shame on realizing that a great newspaper like the *World,* through the overzeal of its representatives, would annoy her or cause her discomfort by appealing to low natures or those given to gossip or envy to secure guesses and opinions unworthy of the *World,* unworthy of Mrs. Eddy, and unworthy of the intelligence, integrity, and manhood and womanhood of New Hampshire's capital city.
>
> I have met and talked with Mrs. Eddy more than once. I know her, she knows me; have been in her home, in her private room, within a few months and discussed with her many things. I have bowed to her carriage within forty-eight hours and my salutation has been returned by her.
>
> If the intent of the *World's* representative to Concord be carried out in its columns, the *World* will say in substance that Mrs. Eddy is dead and that a dummy or a substitute and not she is in the carriage each day when it passes through the main streets of our city and its occupant is greeted by our people, or it will say that Mrs. Eddy is enfeebled and decrepit and that those brilliant faculties that in the past made her wonderful accomplishments possible have departed.
>
> To every such a statement, or even insinuation, I, as one who knows, say, "It is not true in whole or in part, but, on the contrary, is unqualifiedly false."

Mr. Meehan did not *understand* the enemy's intent nor wickedness, but he did see that it was shameful and totally false. If Mr. Slaght had endeavored to enlist Michael Meehan and the *Concord Patriot* in the *World's* campaign against the Revelator to this age, his effort was a total failure.

CHAPTER XXXIV

BILLOWS OF PUBLIC OPINION

The serpent is perpetually close upon the heel of harmony.
— MARY BAKER EDDY

1906

IT was in October that Joseph Armstrong, Mrs. Eddy's publisher, telephoned Edward Everett Norwood and asked him to come to see him at the Arlington Hotel (Washington, D.C.). The Leader had been working diligently on her revision of Science and Health which would become the last copyrighted edition, and she now was ready for the making of the plates. Mr. Armstrong informed Mr. Norwood that Mrs. Eddy had selected him as a good Christian Scientist to have charge of this work.

On the twenty-third of October Judge Ewing was in San Francisco on his lecture tour, from which city he wrote as follows to Mrs. Eddy:

> I have been in this western country for something over a month now, and early in the trip had a most interesting experience that I intended to write you about.
>
> Your grandsons acted as ushers at the lecture at Lead, South Dakota, and your granddaughter seemed to be the executive head of the enterprise. The young people I met several years ago at St. Joseph, Mo., but this was my first meeting with your son; still, I think I should have recognized him almost anywhere, from his striking facial resemblance to you and the wonderful similarity of your voices.
>
> Mr. Glover came to me after the lecture and expressed his pleasure and the profit received from the meeting. I had quite a conversation with him and his children, and was very greatly pleased with his general attitude respecting your great work. One of the ladies of the audience told me that he said to her with a tear in his voice: "I want to have a part in the wealth of love that is going from so many thousands of people to my mother." I feel that you would like to

GEORGE WASHINGTON GLOVER

MRS. EDDY'S ONLY SON

FROM *McCLURE'S* MAGAZINE

> know this, and am sure it will be a great comfort to you to know that your grandchildren are so active in their devotion to the great Cause that you have brought from its hiding and given to the world. . . .

In those days before airmail Mrs. Eddy had probably not yet received this letter on Sunday, October 28, when the *New York World* launched its diabolical attack on God's Revelator to this age, with blaring headlines proclaiming that Mrs. Eddy was dying.

Mr. Slaght had been very adroit in gaining entrance to Pleasant View and audience with Mrs. Eddy. In fact, he had almost convinced some in the Leader's household that he was sincere in his mission. But the *World* of October 28 made it obvious to all that his ingratiating behaviour had been for the sole purpose of gaining this entrance. Every feature of the interview had been distorted. Mrs. Eddy was pictured as a helpless invalid dying of cancer surrounded by designing students who were controlling both her and her fortune.

The whole country was stirred by this distortion of facts, and all the good folk of Concord were indignant. The telephone and telegraph lines in all of Concord were buzzing all day long, and many prominent Concordians gave press statements that day, including Hon. Charles R. Corning, Probate Judge for Merrimack County and Mayor of Concord; Gen. Frank S. Streeter, prominent attorney; Michael Meehan, editor of the *Concord Daily Patriot;* George H. Moses, editor of the *Concord Evening Monitor;* J. Wesley Plummer, deputy state treasurer; Josiah E. Fernald, president of the National State Capital Bank; plus prominent Christian Scientists including Calvin Frye, Lewis Strang, Hermann Hering, and Pamelia Leonard.

About four o'clock in the afternoon Gen. Streeter took Mayor Corning to Pleasant View and sent a note to Mrs. Eddy requesting that they might see her. She saw them almost immediately and greeted them cordially. Gen. Streeter remarked, "You have a cosey corner here, I see, Mrs. Eddy;" to which Mrs. Eddy responded quickly: "Yes, and some people would like to see me in a closer corner."

That evening when Mayor Corning introduced Prof. Hering at the Christian Science lecture he was probably digressing from his planned introduction when he stated:

> Thus far I have spoken to you as one who by his official position assumed the right to tell you whether or not Concord owes anything to Christian Science. I now want to say something which a good citizen is bound always to say when the intelligence of Concord people is questioned and ridiculed. I am sure you have heard of the muck-rakers. I wish I might use a better and more euphonious term;

JUDGE CHARLES R. CORNING
Mayor of Concord, New Hampshire

but, following the great names of John Bunyan and Theodore Roosevelt, I justify my use of it and speak of muck-raking. More than once I have received letters from many places asking me if I could inform the writers as to whether or not Mrs. Eddy was alive. I have always replied as an honest citizen who wished the truth to be known, but no reply and no assurance seemed to have effect or to satisfy those in search of the sensational and untrue.

Recently there have been in Concord, representatives of one of the great metropolitan dailies, alleging that Mrs. Eddy was no more. Ladies and gentlemen, this is to me a painful and difficult subject. I have seen Mrs. Eddy day after day, year after year, riding through our streets, and more recently I have seen the lady riding past my house, and yet strangers come here, foes to this religion, to assert that Concord does not know its own eyes and has lost its own senses. This afternoon, less than four hours ago, for the first time in my life, I stood face to face with Mrs. Eddy for a half hour. I listened to as bright, as vigorous, and as sprightly a conversation as I have ever listened to in my life, and I wish here to bear my testimony to this cruel, bitter falsehood directed against not only you who belong to this church, loving and devoted friends of the lady and Leader, but it is a stigma on Concord which is a sorrow and pain to one of the best and most generous friends the city of Concord ever had.

Two days later Mrs. Eddy wrote to McLellan: "Please publish Prof. Hering's lecture entire. Also briefly comment and as you know on Mayor Corning's superb introduction." Hermann Hering's excellent lecture entitled, "Christian Science: Humanity's Helper" was the leader in the November *Journal.* It may be that the Leader learned something new from this lecture, for she published "An Amended By-law" in the next issue of the *Sentinel:*

NO LECTURES BY READERS — Sect. 5. No lectures shall be given by a Reader during his term of readership. The duties alone of a Reader are ample.

She also wrote to Prof. Hering that she should like to publish his lecture in pamphlet form to which he responded:

My precious Leader:

Your sweet letter regarding my lecture is just received, and brought some tears. I am embarrassed by your repeated words of approbation of the lecture! but my heart only responds in gratitude to God that I have been able to serve you and your blessed Cause acceptably in some ways. I am very conscious of my shortcomings since coming to Concord and of not doing well the mental and physical work that I see ought to be done in this field, but I am becoming "acclimated" and hope to do better. If proper mental work had been done I feel sure that you would not have been annoyed by the disobedient at

Communion time, nor "investigated" by reporters recently, and the State Street paving would have been completed promptly. These happenings have grieved me, but spurred me on to better endeavor. Perhaps I expect too much but I know the possibilities of divine Mind even though I have demonstrated but little.

Dear Leader, this lecture is yours, to do with as you please. There is nothing in it of good but what I have learned from you, — the mouthpiece of Truth to this age, the discoverer of this wonderful Science. You alone have brought the light of Truth to me. My eighteen years of academic and technical education, although useful in many ways, did not teach me one word of reality. Neither did my religious training give me any correct knowledge of the true God and His Word. All that I am that is really good, and spiritual, all that I know that is true and real, all that I possesss that is lasting has come to me through your teachings and ministrations. You alone have supplied me with the key that opened the doors of heaven and brought absolute Truth and good to my consciousness. Can I do less than give you at all times all credit and offer you all that I have? It is a giving that does not impoverish, for the earth is the Lord's and the fullness thereof. I know that of mine own self I have done nothing, it was the Father who did the works, and you have shown me the true Father.

Please do with the lecture whatever you desire, and I will most cheerfully cooperate and assist. Mr. Meehan published the lecture in full in the Patriot, in a special edition, of which Mr. Farlow circulated nearly 30,000 copies through the Committee on Publication, and the lecture also appears in the November Journal. I hope the violets reached you in good condition. They are such favorites of mine.

With deepest love and gratitude, in which Mrs. Hering heartily joins, I beg to remain,

Your devoted student,
Hermann S. Hering

The "muck-rakers" had spent many weeks securing affidavits. They had gone first to business and professional men of Concord and found not one they could persuade to their predetermined suggestions of idle and sadly distorted gossip. So, according to Michael Meehan, "by adroit interrogations among the more ignorant, intolerant, and prejudicial succeeded in obtaining guesses and prejudiced opinions more to their liking."

Beginning on Monday, October 29, many reputable citizens of Concord began giving affidavits to refute the blatant lies published the day before. What is more important, Christian Scientists around the world were roused to vigorous defence of their Leader. Perhaps some became aware of her foresight, in recalling the words which had been published in the *Sentinel* regularly for several weeks: "Take no notice of startling reports about Mrs. Eddy."

PROFESSOR HERMANN S. HERING

Whether they saw this or not, they were stirred to their depths, and an avalanche of appreciative, supportive letters began pouring into Pleasant View. For forty years the entire weight of the whole movement had been upon the overburdened shoulders of the Leader. Now, for the first time, the field was roused to hold up her hands. It is little wonder that Lewis Strang wrote to Hermann Hering on October 29 that Mrs. Eddy was in splendid shape and that he had rarely seen her more active and alert in all the time he had been there. That same day Calvin Frye recorded in his diary that when she talked with the household "this morning Mrs. Eddy was in unusually happy spirits."

The Leader's secretaries as well as Alfred Farlow, who was considered the spokesman for Christian Science, were besieged with requests and demands for proof that Mrs. Eddy was alive and well. The most persistent reporters were besieging the front doors of Pleasant View, and Mr. Farlow asked Sibyl Wilbur to go to Mrs. Eddy and ask her to receive these men and to let Miss Wilbur speak for her. The Leader agreed to see them the next day just before her daily drive.

Miss Wilbur met the news men and women at the Eagle Hotel in Concord, formulated their questions reducing them to three or four, before they went out to Pleasant View on this Tuesday afternoon, October 30. At Pleasant View H. Cornell Wilson, who had come from New York, would handle the interview. The representatives from fourteen leading newspapers and press associations had agreed that Miss Wilbur of the *Boston Herald* should put the few crucial questions to Mrs. Eddy. Miss Wilbur wrote of the occasion:

> The dainty rose drawing room was quite filled with an official-looking assemblage, . . . about fifteen newspaper men and women . . . her banker, her lawyer, the mayor, and a few men prominent in the Mother Church . . . and many of the faces were intense with expectation of what they were about to behold. When Mrs. Eddy came down her own stairway and stood for a moment in the entrance, confronting the cynical and skeptical world, a world which refused to believe in disinterested virtue, she caught for a moment at the portiere and an expression of pained comprehension slowly swept her face, a crimson stain burned her cheeks, and her eyes flashed a look of reproach over the assemblage.
>
> Professor H. S. Hering, first reader of the Concord church, courteously and briefly stated the purpose of the gathering. Mrs. Eddy bowed. To the first question, "Are you in perfect bodily health?" she replied clearly and firmly, "I am." When the second question was put, "Have you any physician beside God?" Mrs. Eddy loosed her grasp upon the portiere, took a step forward, and stretching out both hands in a sweeping open gesture, declared solemnly and with mag-

nificent energy, her voice thrilling all who heard her, "Indeed, I have not! His everlasting arms are around me and support me, and that is enough."

There may have been some in that assemblage who had not ears to hear, but her stirring words went round the world to all who did have ears to hear. A few weeks later a letter from Frankfurt, Germany said that the *Sentinel* article telling of this interview including the Leader's inspiring words was read at a Wednesday evening meeting and:

> A few nights later, a young German lady, who belongs to the little band of Frankfurt Scientists, whilst passing through a dark, unfrequented street, on her way home from a concert, was startled by a man emerging suddenly from the shadow and thrusting himself on her path. Instantly there rose to her consciousness — checking the tremor of fear — your words, "His everlasting arms are round about me. That is enough." And so complete was the resulting realization of the Divine presence and protection, that the intruder drew back and she was left to pursue her way unmolested. Measureless love and gratitude go out to you, not alone from the happy young Scientist who made this demonstration, but from all who listened to the telling of it. May we listen ever more attentively to God's voice speaking to us through your words and your life.

Back to Pleasant View on October 30, Miss Wilbur asked the third question which was, "Do you take a daily drive?" Mrs. Eddy answered, "I do." And then she abruptly terminated the interview, turned and walked to her carriage which was waiting under the porte-cochiere. The news people crowded the windows and doorway to watch her, and Mrs. Eddy nodded an adieu to them as she drove away. In Sibyl Wilbur's words:

> . . . When her carriage disappeared, they asked to be shown the house, and were escorted over it. They entered the quiet study on the second floor, looked at the pictures on the walls, the books in the cases, stood where she so often did to survey the broad valley. They went through the simple little bedroom adjoining and surveyed the plain austerity of its furnishing with frank curiosity. The women reporters asked to see her wardrobe, and were shown the orderly clothes-room where her garments hung. In the dining room they saw where she sat at table, the chocolate service she used, and inquired who sat on her right and left. They saw the library, her special chair, the table where books of reference were consulted. They examined the rugs and hangings of the drawing-room, the souvenirs, certificates of honor, the paintings. They did not ask to see her account-books . . .

That afternoon while waiting for the Boston train a prominent writer with several books to his credit casually told Miss Wilbur that his magazine was going to open the whole life of Mrs. Eddy. He was an editor of *McClure's Magazine,* and told her that they had had Georgine Milmine working for three years gathering a vast amount of gossip and facts. He also said that Miss Milmine was not literary and that her vast accumulation was a mess of confusion, but that Willa Cather had been hired to put it into readable form, and its publication promised to be a sensation.

Once again Miss Wilbur was stirred to the depths by this malicious attack on womanhood. On the train on the way back from Concord the inspiration came to her that she was the one to do something about it.

While Miss Wilbur was troubled by what she had just heard from the *McClure's* editor, some at Pleasant View were troubled by the interview of that afternoon. Though the pressmen were satisfied, and their reports definitely refuted the *World's* lurid story, those closest to Mrs. Eddy were not altogether pleased with the interview. Lewis Strang wrote to Alfred Farlow the next day:

> The interview yesterday afternoon seemed to be fairly treated as far as the Boston papers were concerned with the exception of the Globe. The position was a very difficult one for our Leader, and although I told her to step right into the room and face the newspaper people there squarely, the mental blast seemed to beat her back momentarily when she reached the door, and so the effect was not quite so positive as we could have wished. At the last moment, too, Mrs. Eddy ordered from the top of the stairs that the portiere of the door be drawn while she came down, which from my personal standpoint as a newspaper man seemed to me a mistake. The [Globe] statement that I was anywhere near Mrs. Eddy during the interview . . . was false, for I was outside the house with the carriage.

Mr. Strang and Calvin Frye both felt that Mrs. Eddy's appearance under the strain of the situation was not representative. Without consulting the Leader they invited the newsmen from the two Concord dailies to come again to observe Mrs. Eddy's departure for her daily drive as it occurred under normal circumstances. The *Concord Monitor* report stated:

> The city editor of the *Monitor* visited Pleasant View again at noon today [Nov. 1], without the knowledge of Mrs. Mary Baker Eddy but upon the invitation of members of her household.
>
> He was accompanied by M. Meehan, editor of the *Daily Patriot,* and the two newspaper men stood in the hallway where they could see very plainly Mrs. Eddy as she descended the stairs . . . but where

she could not see them and was unaware of their presence.

At the usual time, a few minutes before one o'clock, Mrs. Eddy came down the long flight of eighteen stairs. She was unaccompanied and unaided in any way during the descent. The ladies of the household remained on the first floor, and Mr. Frye and Mr. Strang . . . stood at the bottom of the stairs.

Mrs. Eddy passed through the opened door and was assisted into the carriage and the robes tucked in by Mr. Strang. The newspaper men had by this time advanced to the windows on either side of the door and looked at Mrs. Eddy who was still unaware of their presence.

Mrs. Eddy talked vivaciously with Mr. Frye and Mr. Strang and smiled and bowed a good-by to those of the household left behind as her carriage drove away.

The impression made upon the *Monitor* representative today by Mrs. Eddy's appearance was even deeper as to her strength, health, and complete possession of all her faculties than on Tuesday.

As the two men stood looking out the window after Mrs. Eddy, the *Monitor* man remarked to Mr. Meehan: "Mrs. Eddy looks twenty-five percent better than she did when all the reporters were out here." Mr. Strang said that no doubt this was due to the excitement under which she labored at the time; that she was usually more or less embarrassed by strangers.

Even without this second observation of Mrs. Eddy's appearance, the consensus of press opinion was more or less summarized in this brief statement from a paper in Illinois: "The damaging story started by a New York newspaper affecting Mrs. Mary Baker G. Eddy, head of the Christian Scientists, seems to be a gross falsehood worked up for sensational purposes." A more specific report in a publication which had had a representative at Pleasant View stated:

We hold no brief for Christian Science or its Founder, but we cannot forbear remarking, in passing comment on a newspaper story, that the *New York World's* expose of last week has exposed only the *World.* There were three counts in its allegation — first, that Mrs. Eddy was physically unable to take her daily drive and that a Mrs. Leonard of Brooklyn, made up to resemble her, was masquerading in her stead; that Mrs. Eddy was suffering from a cancer and was being treated by a cancer specialist; and that her immediate attendants were taking advantage of her physical and mental infirmities to their own pecuniary benefit. The first count was answered by the appearance of Mrs. Eddy in her carriage, and by the affidavits of many respectable citizens of Concord, who know her well, that she and not Mrs. Leonard was the occupant of the carriage. The second was disposed of in the same way, for the *World* could not, or at least did not, produce the alleged specialist treating Mrs. Eddy for cancer, and there was no evidence that she was suffering visible to any of the reporters who interviewed her. As to the third count, it was based on nothing more substantial than insinuation. If Mrs. Eddy is a charlatan and Christian Science a delusion it will require something more than such a cheap chapter in yellow journalism to prove it.

Pamelia J. Leonard was one of the first to give an affidavit stating that she had never set foot in Mrs. Eddy's carriage. She was also present at the press interview and several interviewers wrote somewhat as did this one regarding her similarity to Mrs. Eddy:

> ... The contrast between the two women was so great that it was at once apparent that one could not possibly attempt to pose for the other without detection. There was but one similarity to be noted and that was the abundance of snow-white hair which adorned the heads of both women. At that point the resemblance ceased.

There was an affidavit given a few weeks later which related to the lie about a cancer specialist, but it was not what the *World* had been seeking:

> I, Ernest Gosselin of Amesbury, Mass., a Licensed Chauffeur of Massachusetts, do hereby certify that on Nov. 2 and 3, 1906, three men came to me, whom I afterwards learned to be detectives for the New York World, and tried to have me say that I had taken Dr. Herman Cooper, of this Town, to some place for the purpose of performing an operation on Mrs. Mary Baker G. Eddy. Failing in their purpose on both these occasions, they came again on Nov. 4, 1906 and said if I would take them to the same place that I had taken Dr. Cooper, in an automobile at midnight, to perform said operation on Mrs. Eddy, that money would be no object to them, that they would pay me any amount I would name for my time and labor. And I hereby certify that, as I did not take Dr. Cooper on any such errand, said proposition was refused.

With all this subterfuge going on Mrs. Eddy continued working as usual. On October 31 she wrote to her trustees:

> Please color the cover of our Sentinel. It looks cheap without this and yet with such fine designs on the cover.
>
> I propose a shade of blue. What say you?

It had been mid-October when Joseph Armstrong had given into Edward Everett Norwood's hands the six hundred pages of Science and Health mounted on larger sheets with margins, with the changes in Lewis Strang's handwriting. Mr. Norwood had let the contract for making the new plates to the largest printing house in Washington, D.C., with Mr. Armstrong's approval, before the latter had returned to Boston with the message that the project was to take two weeks.

Mr. Norwood and the assistant he had selected, who was an earnest Christian Scientist and an expert proof-reader, gave themselves entirely to this project, but they soon learned that working for the Leader was no simple task. At the end of two weeks little had been accomplished. At the end of three weeks a special messenger, Mary Tomlinson, came from Concord with this letter for Mr. Norwood extending his work considerably:

Nov. 3, 1906

Beloved Student:

I hope that Mr. Armstrong has not interrupted the harmony of my business arrangements with you regarding the plates for the revised edition of Science and Health. Please read carefully all the testimonials in the copy and select those which you consider the best and place the most attractive testimonials at the commencement of the chapter of FRUITAGE. The number of pages in this chapter can be accommodated to the testimonials even if this should make my book exceed a little the seven hundred pages of the present edition.

N.B. The great point to attain was the *time* it should take to make the plates. Two weeks was agreed upon and now it is three weeks, and the need of my plates is *imperative now.* Please hasten this delay if possible.

Lovingly yours,
Mary Baker Eddy

Mary Tomlinson was not the only courier to carry messages and materials to Mr. Norwood for this revision of Science and Health. The Leader dared not trust ordinary means of communication. She was God's Revelator to this age and her work was to break the despotic control of the serpent, the prince of this world, and set God's people free. So the serpent was ever at her heel, watching her every move and endeavoring to destroy her work. For that reason her messengers were given explicit instructions and were inspired to regard their mission as a divine commission.

When William Lyman Johnson carrried some copy from Pleasant View to Mr. Norwood in Washington, D. C. Mrs. Eddy instructed him to buy a ticket to New London and spend the night there. Then to go the next day to Washington. She also told him that all during the trip, even while sleeping, to keep the precious package tied to his arm. The Leader had had many treasured and guarded valuables disappear when Richard Kennedy was experimenting with black magic, and had learned to exercise every precaution. She also knew that her messengers were special targets of the enemy. Her secretiveness was as much for their safety and protection as for that of the valuable messages they carried. This became sadly obvious in a later experience of Mary Tomlinson.

Mr. Norwood wrote in retrospect that "it did seem that m.a.m. was on hand and active every minute." By this time he and Mr. Campbell had learned that their work had been sublet to the Globe Printing Company where the two men went every day to expedite this project, sometimes correcting one paragraph as many as thirty times.

While Mr. Norwood was working twelve or more hours every day and also working metaphysically to complete his assignment with dispatch, a peculiar phenomenon occcurred. His watch, which was a very good one, began gaining every day until it was as much as three hours fast and useless to him. Six weeks later when the work was finished, his watch resumed its normal condition. When he recounted this experience to Mr. Armstrong, Joseph said that he had had the same experience during the building of The Mother Church with the exception that he had taken his timepiece to a jeweler for repair. Finally the jeweler had said to him: "It is *you,* not the watch."

CHAPTER XXXV

ARISE AND THRESH

The Science of Christianity comes with fan in hand to separate the chaff from the wheat. — MARY BAKER EDDY

1906

SIBYL Wilbur called on Alfred Farlow to tell him of her conversation with the *McClure's* editor. She was greatly perturbed by all of the malicious gossip that Georgine Milmine had been collecting for three years and told Mr. Farlow that she intended to collect information to refute all the lies.

"You can't do it, Miss Wilbur," he said. "Even I couldn't do it. People refuse me information, sneer at me, falsify, tell long imaginary stories. They hate Mrs. Eddy because they once knew her in humbler circumstances. They envy and despise her work. No, you cannot do it."

To this Miss Wilbur replied: "You mean you cannot, nor any other Christian Scientist. But I can because I am a trained reporter and interviewer, and can truthfully say I am not a member of her church. I will find some magazine to finance me, some poor little magazine that will be glad to give me a stipend to go on. You will see, I will get the truth, and the truth will be better than gossip in the end."

Miss Wilbur did follow through on this proposed action, but almost before she had begun, and before *McClure's* published their first derogatory article, the *New York World* came out with a second attack. This was a two part article published on November 4 and 5 entitled "How Rev. Wiggin Rewrote Mrs. Eddy's Book."

James Henry Wiggin had passed away six years earlier, but numerous letters from people who had known and talked with him began arriving in Boston and at Pleasant View refuting these new lies. Alfred Farlow also wrote a refutation which was published in the *New York American*, but Mrs. Eddy immediately wrote a letter to that publication correcting Mr. Farlow:

> Mr. Alfred Farlow's flimsy article in the *New York American* needs correction. It was a great mistake to say that I employed Rev. Henry Wiggin to correct my diction. It was for no such purpose. I engaged Mr. Wiggin so as to avail myself of his criticisms of my statement of Christian Science, which criticisms would enable me to explain more clearly the points that might seem ambiguous to the reader.

This letter was a jolt to Mr. Farlow, and when he read it he wrote to the Leader:

> The affair may reflect on my reputation for being able to state facts about our beloved Leader, but that is more than compensated by the fact that this letter emphatically shows who is conducting the Christian Science church.

Farlow had been named by the *New York World* as one of the designing Christian Scientists controlling Mrs. Eddy and her money, along with Calvin Frye, Lewis Strang and several others. On the day Farlow wrote to Mrs. Eddy, he also wrote to Lewis Strang:

> You can imagine my surprise and chagrin to find our beloved Leader's letter in the N.Y. American. . . . I have thought all the while that Wiggin actually undertook to help her diction. I believe now that she should see all of Wright's article so she can see just what they are claiming.

It may be that she did read all of what Livingston Wright had written for the *New York World* before her refutation appeared in both *Sentinel* and *Journal* in December *(My.* 317). But the Leader did more than write this correction in this hour of persecution. On November 5 she wrote to Henrietta Chanfrau:

> Have six of your best students loyal and truthful take up every day with you, work mental to sustain the Cause and do their *duty* to their Leader and Mother.

Enclosed with this letter was an "Argument for Transgressors" which began: "One Mind; Truth controls all. You are set free in the Love of God and you cannot make nor believe a lie." This "Argument" ended with: "Divine Mind governs every hour and evil is powerless."

The Leader also amended a by-law which appeared in the *Sentinel* of November 10. This amendment added to what is now Article XXIV, Sect. 9, Committee on Business *(Man.* 79), these two sentences:

> There shall be a Committee on Business, of one or more members, wherever Mrs. Eddy resides. The members of these Committees shall be paid from the Church fund.

She then appointed Rev. Tomlinson and his sister Mary, who lived together in their own house in Concord, as her local Committee on Business.

In 1881 in an hour of anguish and exaltation God had spoken to Mary Baker Eddy in these words:

> And I will give to thee, daughter of Zion, a new heritage and a new people.
>
> Oh blessed daughter of Zion, I am with thee. And none shall take my words out of thy lips. Thou art my chosen, to bear my Truth to the nations, and I will not suffer another messenger to go before thee. . . .
>
> And I will lift thee up Oh daughter of Zion. And I will make of thee a new nation for thy praise.

In 1898 a verse which for fifty years had been forgotten was suggested to the Leader's thought, and she had it inscribed over the entrance to Christian Science Hall.

> Daughter of Zion, awake from thy sadness;
> Awake! for thy foes shall oppress thee no more!
> Bright o'er thy hills dawns the daystar of gladness,
> Arise! for the night of thy sorrow is o'er.

It would appear that following the vicious attacks of the *World* in the fall of 1906 that God spoke to Mrs. Eddy through Micah:

> 4:11 Now also many nations are gathered against thee, that say, Let her be defiled, and let our eye look upon Zion.
>
> 12 But they know not the thoughts of the Lord, neither understand they his counsel: for he shall gather them as the sheaves into the floor.
>
> 13 Arise and thresh, O daughter of Zion for I will make thine horn iron, and I will make thy hoofs brass: and thou shalt beat in pieces many people: and I will consecrate their gain unto the Lord, and their substance unto the Lord of the whole earth.

On November 12 the "daughter of Zion" wrote a letter with an accompanying article entitled "Harvest" to the *Independent* in New York which was published with this editorial comment:

> In response to a request by *The Independent,* following the unfounded statements as to her illness, Mrs. Eddy has been good

> enough to send us this article, which we received in her own handwriting, and which shows none of the tremulous unevenness which often appears in the chirography of a person of her age, she being in her eighty-sixth year. We herewith reprint her accompanying letter, reproduced about one-third. This is the first statement which Mrs. Eddy has made as to recent events, and it is probably the only one she will make. — EDITOR

Then followed Mrs. Eddy's article "Harvest" *(My.* 269) which states in part:

> God hath thrust in the sickle, and He is separating the tares from the wheat. This hour is molten in the furnace of Soul. Its harvest song is world-wide, world-known, world-great. The vine is bringing forth its fruit; the beams of right have healing in their light. The windows of heaven are sending forth their rays of reality — even Christian Science, pouring out blessing for cursing, and rehearsing: "I will rebuke the devourer for your sakes, and he shall not destroy the fruits of your ground." . . .
>
> The lie and the liar are self-destroyed. . . . Let error rage and imagine a vain thing. Mary Baker Eddy is not dead and the words of those who say that she is are the father of their *wish.* . . .
>
> Those words of our dear, departing Saviour, breathing love for his enemies, fill my heart: "Father, forgive them; for they know not what they do." . . .
>
> What we love determines what we are. I love the prosperity of Zion, be it promoted by Catholic, Protestant or by Christian Science. . . .

This message from the Leader went round the world and healed and elevated many, many people — Christian Scientists and non-Christian Scientists alike. And it continues to heal and elevate people today. The Leader was returning good for evil, blessing for cursing, as she always did, but she also knew the deadliness of the enemy in its wicked intent to destroy her, and the necessity for defence. Bliss Knapp was on a lecture tour lecturing as far south and west as Los Angeles, California which he had done in September. In November Mrs. Eddy wrote to Bliss' father Ira Knapp:

> Write to Bliss to make no more engagements to lecture at present, but to return and remain in Massachusetts till our next annual meeting in June. There is a great need of such as he is in Christian Science to be in Boston.

As soon as Bliss arrived in Boston a little later in November, Mrs. Eddy wrote to him:

Beloved Bliss:
I am especially engaged now hence cannot have the great pleasure of seeing you today. Will let you know when I can have this pleasure. I am glad that you are near us. You are needed here more than elsewhere. Boston and Concord are the garrisons which need to be armored and defended. In about two weeks I hope to be with less on hand so that I can make an appointment with you to visit me in P.V.

Most tenderly, lovingly yours,
Mary Baker Eddy

On the day she wrote to Bliss Knapp she also wrote to Lewis Strang giving him an additional assignment:

Can you take up strong, true, ceaseless till Mother says *stop* those *sinning ones* in our Cause who will not listen to the voice and the word of their Leader and Mother in Israel? They and they *only* give us all at Pleasant View to meet them much work. Thank Him, dear student, and pray for our enemies. Do you know this means we have no enemies? Matt. 16:4. Say nothing to Frye about this letter but all this work add to what he gives you to do from me. Mother asks this added burden from her dear one, knowing, trusting in his *faithfulness.*

Several days later, on December 3, she wrote to Mr. Strang again:

Stop the work now. Pleasant View is *safe* — as safe as any place in this world of sinning sense can be and survive. But Mother asks when will faithful students *waken* to the hour, hear His voice and recognize the trials of this Cause?

But a good deal more had transpired before she sent this second message to Lewis to stop his extra work. On November 15 another attack on Christian Science was published in a privately printed pamphlet entitled *The Anarchy of Christian Science.* The author was the Rector of St. John's Episcopal Church in Northampton, Massachusetts, Lyman P. Powell. In his pamphlet Mr. Powell advised "every minister to make a serious study of Christian Science and thus armed fight it to the death, by public and by private words." This attack was considerably different from the others, for Powell was an earnest clergyman who was misled by the lies.

The originators of the lies plus a great many other newsmen were seeking statements from all who had ever known Mrs. Eddy as well as some of those nearest her. In addition to the malicious gossip, which was as invented, encouraged, and untrue as the cancer story, there were a great many truthful, supportive statements including a great many from non-Christian Scientists. One in this category was a letter of November 15 which Calvin Frye received from his cousin Judge N. P. Frye of Lawrence, Massachusetts. *New York World* reporters had sought Judge Frye to support their lies about his cousin, but he wrote Calvin:

> I told them of your good character, that I had known you ever since we were children and played together in good old Andover, that I had never caught you in a mean act, and that I did not believe you would do a wrong thing in your present position, and I am satisfied I told them correctly. . . . Stand by Mrs. Eddy until the end for she is a worthy woman.

One point of interest during this hour of trial is that the representative from the *Concord Monitor* is the city editor Harlan C. Pearson (also the local Associated Press representative), rather than the editor, Mrs. Eddy's friend of many years, George H. Moses. Mr. Moses had issued a lengthy statement to the press refuting the lies of the *World* and telling the truth about Mrs. Eddy. But Mr. Moses' employer, the owner of the *Concord Monitor* was ex-Senator William E. Chandler. By mid-November, if not earlier, the *New York World* had employed Senator Chandler to institute a suit at law against the Revelator to this age and her Cause.

The most famous person residing in Concord, New Hampshire was Mary Baker Eddy, and the second best known resident of that area was William Eaton Chandler. Senator Chandler had exerted a wide influence in political affairs. Michael Meehan wrote of him:

> Mr. Chandler was known as an able lawyer; his power of sarcasm in the United States Senate has been rarely paralleled, never surpassed; . . . he had proven his ability as a debater and pleader; he was adroit and tactful; he was rich in resources, and in the past he had won notoriety, if not fame, along political lines by converting absolute defeat into victory.

The powers of this world were aiming a deadly blow at God's chosen witness, and the weapon of their warfare was the god of this world — money. Money of itself is inert, but the lust for money perverts the morally weak. A number of people had already been told that money was no object — to name their price. And some had succumbed. In his book *Mrs. Eddy and the Late Suit in Equity,* Michael Meehan says that "it is easy to believe that *The World* was the real party in interest; that it employed the counsel . . . and that it was *The World's* money that paid all bills . . ." Mr. Meehan meant of course the *New York World,* but there is a broader connotation to his words.

Both James Slaght and William Chandler were adroit, persuasive, and cunning, and now they were working together to draw others into the web they were weaving to destroy Mary Baker Eddy. On the night of November 22 James Slaght left New York City for Lead City, South Dakota bearing two letters from Senator Chandler.

By Wednesday, November 28, James Slaght had probably changed trains more than once on his way to Lead, South Dakota. On that day Mrs. Eddy had asked one member of her household, Lewis Strang, to do additional work "strong, true, ceaseless till Mother says *stop.*" The next day, Thanksgiving Day, Mr. Slaght disembarked at the railway depot in Lead and went directly to the George Glover house. After introducing himself and ascertaining that Mr. Glover was well aware of and favorably impressed by the well-known ex-senator from New Hampshire, he presented this letter:

> Washington, D.C., Nov. 22, 1906
>
> My dear Mr. Glover: — I have consented to act as legal counsel concerning certain questions which arise in connection with Mrs. Mary Baker G. Eddy. They are stated in a letter from me to Mr. Slaght, who will call upon you and can show you my letter to him.
>
> It is important for public and private interests that these questions should be investigated and met and fairly and justly disposed of as questions involving doubts which from large and commendable motives all good citizens, and especially all relatives of Mrs. Eddy, should help to solve and settle. Therefore please be sure and give Mr. Slaght a full hearing and possess yourself fully of all the facts which he will be able to give you.
>
> Very respectfully,
> William E. Chandler

Probably George retired to another room to "study" this letter as was his custom, for he was illiterate. His daughter Mary acted as his secretary.

The second letter Slaght had brought was designed for Mr. Glover's consumption, though cleverly not written *to* him:

> My dear Mr. Slaght: — I consent to act as counsel concerning certain questions which arise in connection with Mrs. Mary Baker G. Eddy. It seems clear that there are several doubts about several points.
>
> 1. Mrs. Eddy may be detained in the custody of strangers against her will.
>
> 2. She may be so nearly worn out in body and mind as a confirmed invalid that she is incapable of deciding any questions whatever, according to any will or pleasure of her own, and necessarily, therefore, incapable of managing her business and property affairs.

3. Being thus restrained or incapable, or without relatives near her, she may be surrounded by designing men who either have already sought or may hereafter seek, to wrongfully possess themselves of her large property, or induce her to make a disposition of it contrary to what would be her sane and deliberate intentions if she were in perfect possession of her liberty and mental faculties.

These doubts have arisen in connection with investigations recently made. Beyond all questions, steps should be taken to solve the doubts, to correct the wrong, if it exists, and to establish the right in every respect.

This new work should be done, if possible, in cooperation with Mrs. Eddy's son, or any other relative who may be impressed with his duties in this regard; and if the relatives do not move, it should be done by such right-minded citizens as are in sympathy with the commendable movement.

Yours truly,
William E. Chandler

Chandler had carefully said "may be;" for he as well as all of Concord *knew* these allegations were not true. Evil always claims that its actions are "to correct the wrong . . . and to establish the right in every respect." The *World* reported that an agent placed before Glover "his legal opportunity." It had also reported Mrs. Eddy's property at fifteen million dollars, — fifteen times its actual value. But it took more than this persuasion to enlist George Glover in their camp.

If Slaght had expected to find a disaffected or estranged son he was surprised, for George Glover was fiercely loyal to both his mother and Christian Science, although he had little understanding of either. The youngest child, George III who was seventeen years old in 1906, was locked out of "much vigorous argument behind closed doors" which went on for several days.

For many years George Glover had retained the services of an upstanding attorney, James P. Wilson, but Mr. Wilson had moved to Denver three years earlier, and Mary Glover had become advisor to her father as well as his secretary. Mrs. Eddy knew that her son was extremely suggestible and easily persuaded. A neighbor who knew the Glover family well stated in later years that both Mr. Glover and his daughter were gullible, but she believed that Mary was even more gullible than her father.

Slaght found that George had long been antagonistic to Calvin Frye, feeling that he kept him from his mother — which he may well have done in line of duty. So Frye became the villian leading a group of unscrupulous power-hungry, money-hungry men surrounding his mother, and Chandler was the knight in shining armor who would rescue her. When Slaght left Lead, the Glovers were totally deceived and remained so for the rest of their days.

On Thanksgiving Day when James Slaght was calling on the Glovers, Mrs. Eddy was calling her household metaphysical workers together for her usual daily talk with them. This day before finishing she asked each what he had to be thankful for. Frye recorded in his diary that Lewis Strang had answered "for the sense of suffering." Then he recorded the Leader's commendation of this answer: "she told him his answer was the nearest right of any we gave, for mortal sense in all its phases is a lie and the sense of suffering is the nearest out of mortal sense."

One more item of note occurred in November, 1906, and that was the 419th edition of Science and Health. This is *not* the revised edition the Leader is working on, but it is noteworthy because it is the first unnumbered edition. The last numbered editions were the 417th in cloth and the 418th in limp leather.

Mr. Norwood had received further word from Mrs. Eddy regarding the testimonials he was selecting, titling, and arranging for this revision of Fruitage:

> *Another word to you*
> Mr. Norwood, C.S.D.
> *Beloved:*
> If there is not enough new Testimonials of the new ones to make out the 700 pages of Science and Health you can retain some of the old testimonials that are now in this book. Be sure to have 700 pages in this edition and if it over runs this a little in the make-up, no matter. But the original number must not be lessened.

Instead of two weeks, Mr. Norwood worked for six weeks to complete this task. When the time had come to send proofs to Pleasant View, he received a sacredly confidential letter from the Leader with explicit directions as to how this was to be done. In retrospect Mr. Norwood wrote:

> This letter was a most remarkable proof of her wonderful understanding of God — and of the illusion of mortal mind, and its so-called activities. In the letter she said, "Let no one see this but your own dear self," and when I read it, I had such a glimpse of ineffable good and the supreme spiritual height that our God-crowned Leader had attained, it was transcendental! *God bless her!*

When the proofs arrived another student began on his appointed task as final proof-reader. That was the scholarly William D. McCrackan. By the end of November the plates, too, had been sent and Mr. Norwood's mission was accomplished. The Leader wrote to him on December 1:

My beloved Student:

Words are weak to express my gratitude for your strict demonstration and success in *conveyance.* Also, your fidelity in all entrusted to you. I was not mistaken in my man if I were in some men.

My prayer is for all that learn through suffering, and for all who learn by enjoying, to enter into the rest of rightness; for every experience human is met, compensated or punished by *divine Love.* Dear one, learn with me to have but one God, to know of no other Mind, for this will bring peace and spare us the sorrow and agony that so-called mortal mind has in store.

One Mind, and loving others as we would be loved is the panacea for all our wrongs, trouble and strife.

I hope sometime to reward you for your dear heart, and your helping hand in my behalf.

Give my love to Mrs. Norwood.

Lovingly, gratefully yours,
Mary Baker Eddy

CHAPTER XXXVI

BRUTAL ABUSE

It is wise to protect as far as possible a Leader, instead of putting her to the front in every battle. — MARY BAKER EDDY

1906

M*cCLURE'S* advertised their forthcoming series as a "true, full, unbiased story of Mary Baker G. Eddy and of the Christian Science movement" in *Ridgeway's* weekly. In response Archibald McLellan wrote to Mr. McClure: "From the nature of the advertisement I assume that the half-tone cut is intended to be a portrait of Mrs. Eddy ... The cut is not a portrait of Mrs. Eddy and does not resemble her in feature, outline or expression." Even though the advertisement stated that *McClure's* staff had worked "to make this history absolutely fair and accurate," this letter was neither responded to nor heeded. So a seven page Introduction to their extensive "accurate history" appeared in *McClure's* December issue with a genuine signature of Mrs. Eddy under a full-page picture purporting to be Mrs. Eddy, which was not. It was a photograph of a Mrs. Sarah C. Chevaillier. This brought a great many letters of astonishment, ridicule, and correction. One correction included an affidavit from Charles F. Chevaillier in Texas who produced his copy of the same picture together with the assertion that it was a picture of his mother.

This December introduction, professing to be unbiased, presented a very biased account of the orderly crowds waiting to see the Mother's Room when thousands were in Boston for the dedication of The Mother Church Extension. Any reporter may have been astounded to see no unruly boisterousness among so many, but Miss Milmine's description made the Scientists appear as ridiculous simpletons. This "unbiased" account also stated: "To the normal, average mind, *Science and Health,* written as it is in a cheaply symbolic style, seems hazy and obscure."

The article in the January issue, which appeared in December, had no more validity than did the picture of Charles Chevaillier's mother purporting to be that of Mrs. Eddy in the December issue. The Leader expressed her first reaction in these words to Alfred Farlow: "What you send me from McClure's Magazine is too much of lies to have given a thought to." But it did cause her more than one thought and she wrote him again: "Do not reply to this last brutal abuse till the abusers bring out their next threatened article. Then answer both in one article from the Committee."

Sibyl Wilbur had not been inactive since talking with Mr. Farlow. She found an obscure little struggling magazine called *Human Life* which was willing to give her enough to live on while doing her research. So for the next year Miss Wilbur followed in Georgine Milmine's footsteps with an opposite intent, — that of discovering the truth and publishing it to alleviate the "brutal abuse" of the malicious gossip *McClure's* had collected and often helped to invent.

One of the lurid lies which they had encouraged came from Horace Wentworth. Horace had ridiculed Mrs. Glover and her work behind her back when she was living with his parents which had been after the young man was married and no longer living at home. His fabrication was published in a later issue, and subsequently refuted by his younger brother and sister who had been in their teens at the time that Mrs. Glover had lived with the Wentworth family. But correspondence relating to Horace's "story" took place in December, 1906. A letter dated December 19 from Horace Wentworth to S. S. McClure stated:

> Yours of the 17th received. Thank you very much for the check. It came in the right time. I have had bad luck, and it seems like a Christmas present. Shall be glad to assist you what I can, in this work of exposing Eddyism.

Ten years after the publication of these lies, Horace's teen-age granddaughter came to live with her grandparents for several years. In later years she described her grandfather as a bitter, foul-mouthed man who was generous and good-hearted underneath. But most astonishing was his Sunday morning ritual of assembling the family before breakfast and reading to them from "Mary Baker Eddy's book." The Revelator to this age affected every life she touched, even that of the scoffer and liar.

One acknowledged historian of that time wrote of Miss Milmine's work that "most of the statements are readily recognizable as gossip or slander." Many people, however, are not averse to reading gossip and slander, and *McClure's* was slandering the most newsworthy person who ever trod this globe. All the world was eager to read about Mary Baker Eddy. When Miss Wilbur's articles began appearing in *Human Life* in January, 1907 that magazine profited enormously. The circulation which had been approximately 20,000 shot up to nearly 100,000 within three months, and remained high during the year of Sibyl Wilbur's research and writing. At the end of that time the little magazine fell back to normal circulation and subsequently disappeared. A great many experiences in Miss Wilbur's year of research have never been told. In her words:

> There are many stories about how I wrote this Life, how I waited weeks to overcome someone's prejudice, how I traced down gossip and refuted it. But all that is a story written within my own heart.

A letter Helen Nixon had written to the "Beloved Leader" had been published in the *Sentinel* in November. It said in part:

> I am so happy and thankful for my first, as I believe, truly spiritual glimpse of the spiritual interpretation of the pictures in *Christ and Christmas.* . . . It came to me suddenly that the picture "Christian Science Healing" means this: The figure in the background is mortal self, — no longer clamoring, but obeying the injunction, "Be still and know that I am God." (I used to think it was the man's wife.) The figure in the foreground is the "unselfed better self" portrayed in your last message "Choose Ye." Oh, how good God is to us! And, dear Leader, what can we do for you?

Helen Nixon was ever faithful to the Leader, but, sad to say, when her talented young husband left Mrs. Eddy's employ, he soon left Christian Science. By 1906 he had left his wife for Laura May Fulmer of Philadelphia, but he had not prospered financially. As the year drew to a close he saw an opportunity to make some money, and he did not spend the Christmas holidays in Philadelphia with Miss Fulmer. Instead, on Christmas Day he dined (probably in New York City) with S. S. McClure.

Before the end of December Mrs. Eddy had decided to refute the *McClure's* lies herself rather than leaving it to Mr. Farlow. She also wrote to her directors on December 28:

> Please watch the movement of the last *Literary Digest* that has called the attention of its readers to *McClure's* articles on me, and after *McClure's* next article appears, or even before it does, request in our periodicals that every Christian Scientist who has subscribed for the *Literary Digest* or *McClure's Magazine* discontinue his subscription.

Three days later the directors answered this letter saying they had conferred with Mr. Farlow and tended to agree with his opinion that:

> it would not be the best thing to do as it might appear to the public to be a boycott of these magazines, and also many others which have advertised McClure's article, and in that way might secure public sympathy for McClure's.

Mrs. Eddy returned this letter with this note penned on it:

> Beloved Board:
> I agree with Mr. Farlow and with you that some other means would be better.
> Lovingly,
> Mary B. G. Eddy

All this related to the world's attack on its destroyer. While meeting these attacks the Leader's work for her Cause continued unabated. On December 1 she had written to Bliss Knapp:

> My beloved Student:
> I call you *mine* conscientiously for God has given you to me and sometime the world will know this better than it now does. Lecture in the places that call for you now, and whenever called for to those that are within a day's distance of travel from your home. So soon as I have the time given me by God, I shall see you *here* and then can explain many things which I should not by mail.
> Lovingly yours,
> Mary Baker Eddy

God had truly given Bliss to the Leader, His chosen witness. Though many Christian Scientists of that day *said* that Mrs. Eddy was the woman of the Apocalypse, Bliss and his father were two of the very few who really *knew* it.

On December 5 the Leader wrote to her disciple, Calvin Hill:

> Please remove your thoughts utterly away from *me.* Through the weakness of some students who have been here and report what I say, it is known that I have great faith in you, and so the enemy argues that you make me suffer. To meet this, take it up that you can't make any one suffer and no one can make you suffer. But do not *think of me.* Only break the law of the lie. You and the Committee on Business keep *me* out of your thoughts. My great struggle is with so many turning to my personality for one thing or another. But that's a lie, so banish it all into oblivion, for God is All and there is no other Mind.

In a letter to Irving Tomlinson on the tenth of December, Mrs. Eddy wrote: "I *find* the way by *experience,* hence I am a Christian Science weather vane, constantly veering with the winds of Truth." And she knew she was finding *the way,* the one way that is straight and narrow and leadeth unto Life.

When Edward Norwood had completed his assignment on the 1906 revision of Science and Health, Joseph Armstrong told him to send a bill to Mrs. Eddy for the work he had done. Mr. Norwood protested that he could never do enough for her to repay what she had done for him, to which Mr. Armstrong replied: "Well, if you wish to send her a receipted bill, do so, but send it, and name your own terms." So Norwood figured his six weeks time at the same rate of pay for workers at Pleasant View, and early in December sent Mrs. Eddy a bill for $150 which he had marked "Paid." On December 13 Calvin Frye wrote to Norwood:

> Our beloved Leader sent to you yesterday by Am. Ex. a small box containing $100 in gold, and she desires to thank you for your receipted bill for services in connection with work done on Science and Health.

Arthur R. Vosburgh of the Board of Lectureship had accomplished a first for Christian Science in Europe. Several had preceded him in lecturing in the British Isles, but on November 17 he had delivered the first lecture in Holland to an audience of four hundred at The Hague, and on November 21, 1906, Vosburgh had delivered a lecture to an audience of over seven hundred in Berlin, Germany. By December 15 he was back home in Rochester, New York and wrote of his tour to Mrs. Eddy:

> My Dearest Leader:
>
> I write you this to report my return, that you may know where to reach me if for any reason you wish to do so. The work abroad is flourishing, and this is encouraging. There are over seventy places in Great Britain where services are now held. There is a fine loyalty to Science and to you as its ordained Leader, and good work in healing is carrying on the Cause. In my lecture in Edinburgh, early in the lecture I read your letter as published in the *Boston Herald,* stating you were alive and attending to your active duties, etc., and this was met by what a Scotch audience is very slow to give; viz., a round of spontaneous applause, which did not start with the Scientists. This occurred several times in other places. In my last lecture in London, almost at its close I referred to you as the one whom the world knows today as having wrought the work of giving Christian Science to the world, and to my surprise I was completely interrupted by vigorous, hearty applause. The earth is today helping the woman; and the

sturdy sense of justice, and the admiration of real courage and integrity, of the English people, are appealed to by your patient and loving heroism.

With earnest desire to follow closely the way of Life and Love that you have marked out for us,

In sincere love and loyalty,

Faithfully in the Truth,
Arthur R. Vosburgh

Two days after this letter was written Lord Dunmore visited Mrs. Eddy at Pleasant View. The next day, December 18, he gave this statement to the press which was published in the Boston papers:

I was immensely struck with Mrs. Eddy's personal appearance and with the activity with which she got out of her carriage unaided and stepped into the hall. When I was ushered into her presence I could not help remarking to her that she was looking much better and younger than when I saw her last, and during the whole of our interview, which lasted for upwards of three quarters of an hour, I was struck with the remarkable vigor of her mind and the extraordinary memory which she displayed for events which had taken place when I first had the privilege of seeing her about seven years ago. She showed wonderful interest in everything which pertains to the Christian Science movement in Europe and was most interested to hear how well the lectures were attended and received by the English people.

A letter from Augusta Stetson dated December 22 tells of one more of the Leader's activities in December:

My precious Leader, Teacher, Guide and Mother in Israel:

My gratitude fails to find expression in language. . . . I wonder if it is really true that this magnificent jeweled heart, right from God's holy messenger, Love's chosen love, is mine, or if I am dreaming. . . .

The treasure is most exquisite, but the dearest of all the world to me . . . is the picture of the dear Mother and Leader within the heart. . . .

I shall always wear this treasure as a reminder of the long years of your tireless care, your patient forbearance and love, your prayers and tears and toils for humanity and for me . . .

The Leader wrote Augusta on December 28:

Thanks for your letters. The one before it sent to our press. It should be out in the Sentinel. So much is on the tapis — all may not go as we wish; but God reigns and I love Him supremely and I try to love my enemies.

Be strong, be wiser than serpents. Watch, pray, work, and God will work with you and make the evil *less than before.*

Every trial of our faith should make us stronger, purer. Give my love to your dear students — comfort and support them.

It had been on the thirty-first of October that Mrs. Eddy had written her trustees that she would like the *Sentinel* cover to be colored, but this had proved to be more difficult than it sounded. It was not accomplished until the issue of December 22 which her trustees sent to her on December 21 with this letter:

Beloved Leader:

We are pleased to send you herewith two copies of the current issue of the Christian Science Sentinel, the first number with the color cover page.

We trust this will meet your expectations and if so we will ask our printers to arrange to do the work in the most economical way. This however will necessitate the putting in of an expensive rotary color press and they will gladly do so if we assure them that the color cover page will be used permanently.

Obediently and affectionately yours,

The Board of Trustees
of the Christian Science Publishing Society
By Allison V. Stewart

This first color cover was not entirely satisfactory as they had left a white border. Mrs. Eddy wrote on the bottom of their letter: "Be sure to extend the color all over the page and leave no white margin. M. B. Eddy" The next issue had no white margins, but was followed by this letter from the Leader to Mr. McLellan:

I thank you. I had no idea that your specimen to me of one side of our Sentinel in blue meant to leave the other side *uncolored.* Be sure to have both sides of the cover blue.

It was January, 1907, before both front and back covers were a light shade of blue, but the major changes appeared on December 22, 1906. The cover for that issue had been redesigned.

The original "lady with a lamp," with eyes closed, had appeared on each side of the Sentinel cover in September. The new design presents a more mature type of womanhood with eyes open. The pedestals (bearing Longfellow's poem) on which the lady stands, are in turn standing on a solid foundation labeled THE CHRISTIAN SCIENCE PUBLISHING SOCIETY.

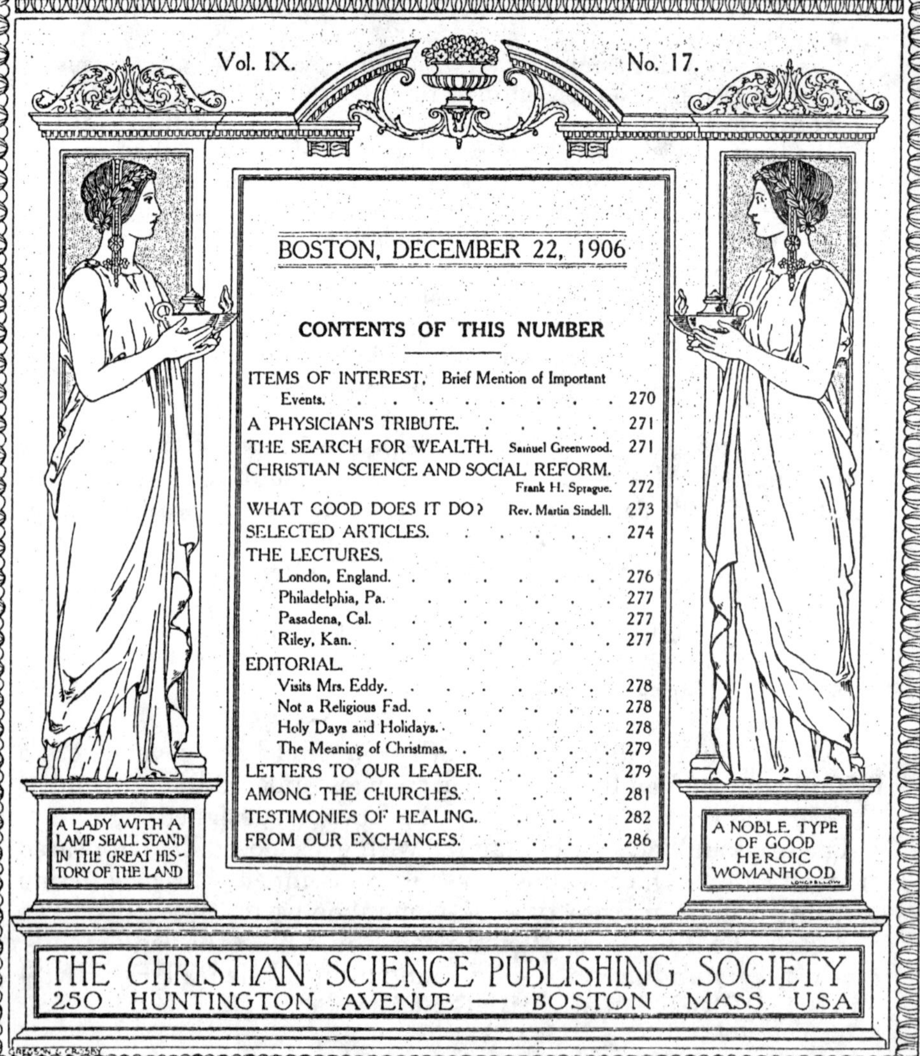

CHRISTIAN SCIENCE SENTINEL

"WHAT I SAY UNTO YOU, I SAY UNTO ALL — *WATCH*" JESUS

Vol. IX. No. 17.

BOSTON, DECEMBER 22, 1906

CONTENTS OF THIS NUMBER

A LADY WITH A LAMP SHALL STAND IN THE GREAT HISTORY OF THE LAND

A NOBLE TYPE OF GOOD HEROIC WOMANHOOD
LONGFELLOW

THE CHRISTIAN SCIENCE PUBLISHING SOCIETY
250 HUNTINGTON AVENUE — BOSTON MASS USA

NEW SENTINEL COVER DESIGN
December 22, 1906

Early in the 1880's Mrs. Eddy placed the Christian Science seal on the cover of Science and Health.

CHRISTIAN SCIENCE SEAL

The original design and size of the Christian Science seal at its first appearance on Science and Health in the early 1880's.

When her *Journal of Christian Science,* "an independent family paper" founded in 1883, was renamed the *Christian Science Journal* and given a cover in April, 1885, the cross and crown seal was the central emblem of the cover design. And it continued to be prominently displayed on the *Journal* cover as long as Mrs. Eddy was here.

This significant emblem also appeared on the front of the first issue of the *Christian Science Weekly* in September, 1898; and when the *Weekly* became the *Sentinel* the Christian Science seal continued to appear on the cover every week through August, 1906.

Mary Baker Eddy had had a resurrective experience in 1866 which had taught her how to "Heal the Sick — Raise the Dead — Cleanse the Lepers — Cast out Demons." The way was the cross glorified by the crown. She had taught this Way to all her students that they might go and do likewise; and she had epitomized this resurrective way in her Christian Science seal which she placed upon all her periodicals and all her writings with the exception of the *Manual.*

But Mary Baker Eddy was more than the Discoverer of Christian Science. Her discovery of Christian Science led her to the discovery and understanding of her own identity. She was God's chosen witness, the embodiment of the motherhood of God as Jesus was the embodiment of God's fatherhood. God's "two witnesses," "the two olive trees," "the two candlesticks," were Jesus and Mary

Baker Eddy exemplifying the manhood and womanhood of God.

> Rev. 11:3 And I will give power unto my two witnesses, and they shall prophesy a thousand two hundred and three score days, clothed in sackcloth.
>
> 7 And when they shall have finished their testimony, the beast that ascendeth out of the bottomless pit shall make war against them, and kill them.
>
> 10 And they that dwell upon the earth shall rejoice over them, and make merry, and shall send gifts one to another; because these two prophets tormented them that dwelt on the earth.
>
> 11 And after three days and an half the Spirit of life from God entered into them, and they stood upon their feet; and great fear fell upon them which saw them.
>
> 12 And they heard a great voice from heaven saying unto them, Come up hither. And they ascended up to heaven in a cloud . . .

Jesus' disciples knew his identity no more than did the disciples of Mary Baker Eddy know hers. Following his resurrection Jesus talked at great length with two of his disciples on the road to Emmaus, "and beginning at Moses and all the prophets, he expounded unto them in all the scriptures the things concerning himself" (Luke 24:27). He gave us a verbal picture of his identity. Mrs. Eddy, through her artist at the easel, James F. Gilman, gave us a visual picture of her identity.

Jesus gave to the world the resurrection. But in the ascension he was out of their sight, even the sight of his own disciples. Mary Baker Eddy's mission began where Jesus' left off. From the time of her discovery her whole experience was resurrective. By the time of the dedication of The Mother Church Extension in the summer of 1906 the Woman had spent forty years in the wilderness, literally, from 1866 to 1906, and the resurrection which Jesus had inaugurated had been proclaimed and heard around the world. That marked the completion of her wilderness experience and of the resurrection era. The ascension era was beginning. Would her disciples be able to see her?

In August of 1906 Mrs. Eddy had announced to the closest of her disciples, Augusta Stetson: "I have risen." She is the Forever Leader to be followed, and she proclaimed this fact to those who have eyes to see, those who would be the "watchmen on the walls of Zion." Once again she has given us a visual picture. The resurrective symbol, the Christian Science seal, was *removed* from her *Sentinel* and replaced by the "Lady with a Lamp," the symbol of the Forever Leader. Is not the message clear that the *Way* beyond the resurrection into the ascension is to follow the Leader? There is one more message that would keep the true follower close to his Leader.

PAINTING BY JAMES F. GILMAN

When she asked her Trustees to remove the cross and crown from the new *Sentinel* cover in August, 1906, she wrote the following and had it hand delivered:

> STATEMENT — To the Christian Science Board of Directors: No student of Christian Science shall occupy a position of trust or confidence in this Cause who does not *daily* declare the truth at least three times in his prayers for the well-being of his Leader, the Discoverer and Founder of Christian Science, the Rev. Mary Baker G. Eddy.
>
> (Can the above be made a by-law in our Manual?)

How many of those who profess to be the Woman's followers today *daily* declare the truth about their Leader? Is this for her well-being or our own? Death will never be overcome until we rise above the resurrection era to the ascension era, and there is only one Way. "He that . . . climbeth up some other way, the same is a thief and a robber" (John 10:1).

Augusta Stetson knew not the cost, but she was ready and willing in 1906 to follow her Leader into the Ascension era. This is a vital decision and a moment important for Truth. Are we ready and willing today to make this momentous decision and to heed our Leader's words?

> The Christian Scientist who is faithful to this Cause and its Leader will reap rewards spiritual, and blessedness beyond the power of human thought to conceive. Will you join your Leader in this, refusing sensuality, animality, lust in any of its forms? Oh, dear ones, I know the cost and I know the joy. Will you, can you, rise in this moment important for Truth?

CHAPTER XXXVII

FORT BESIEGED

Our cause needs defence and its principal fort needs fortification. I now call soldiers to supply this need, defend this fort, and the officer working within it for her Church, the field, and the world.
— MARY BAKER EDDY

1907

MRS. Eddy's lengthy reply to *McClure's Magazine (My.* 308) was published in the January *Journal* and in the January 5 *Sentinel.* It was also republished in part or *in toto* throughout the country along with many criticisms of *McClure's* and their methods.

The Arena magazine came forth with an article in its January issue entitled "The Recent Reckless and Irresponsible Attacks on Christian Science and its Founder, with a Survey of the Christian Science Movement," which caused Mrs. Eddy to publish in the *Sentinel* a "Card" of appreciation *(My.* 316). She also wrote to her Editor-in-chief:

> Please reply to this in our Sentinel this last paragraph of Mr. Flower's letter — for me. Sign your name to it.
> Return letter to me.

The Arena was the magazine which, a few years earlier, had published Josephine Woodbury's attacks upon Mrs. Eddy. McLellan explained in a January *Sentinel:*

> THE ARENA
>
> Several years ago, after Mr. B. O. Flower had been forced out of *The Arena* and it was in the hands of persons hostile to him and, as he says, to "all the interests that had founded the magazine," there appeared some articles in it against Christian Science and its distinguished Leader, therefore it is possible that some Christian Scientists are under the impression that the management of *The Arena* is the

> same at the present time as it was when the articles referred to were published, and it is proper to state to our readers that this is not so.
>
> Mr. Flower returned to *The Arena* subsequent to the publication of these articles, and we are informed that "no one today who is in the least interested in *The Arena* had any hand whatever in the publication or circulation of the papers in question." We take pleasure in making this statement, in order that the present editor and managers of *The Arena* may be relieved from blame which should in no wise attach to them. Mr. Flower is conducting the magazine upon the lines of clean, high-class journalism and we wish him the success which he deserves.
>
> Archibald McLellan

Before this was published Chandler and Slaght had brought George Glover and his daughter Mary to Washington, D.C. where they also provided for all their needs. They were posing as the Glovers' best friends and thoroughly convinced George, as well as his daughter, that they were sincerely concerned about his mother and Christian Science. It is not improbable that some of their accomplices were practising the mental malpractice or black magic they accused the Revelator of practising. By the time an interview with Mrs. Eddy at Pleasant View had been arranged for the Glovers on January 2, George and Mary were so mesmerized that they "saw" exactly what Chandler and Slaght had told them they would see — rather than seeing Mrs. Eddy as she really was.

In August of 1899, a few days after Josephine Woodbury had filed a libel suit against Mrs. Eddy, Calvin Frye had recorded in his diary:

> After a night of agony, struggling with the sense of desertion ... from her students and her church, at this hour of persecution and prosecution by Woodbury, — this morning, Aug. 6, '99 Mrs. Eddy while she was on her swing on the rear piazza at Pleasant View heard these words as distinctly as if audibly spoken to her: "Thou art Mine, saith the Lord of Hosts. In the day when I make up my jewels, I will spare thee, as a man spareth his own son that serveth him."

The Woodbury suit had dragged on and on, and several months later Calvin recorded in his diary that Mrs. Eddy had called him, Laura and Clara:

> and prophesied to us saying "After we get through this Court, the next will be that 'their horses will wade to their bellies in blood.'"

Most likely the Leader had opened her Bible that morning to Revelation 14 beginning at verse 16: "And he that sat on the cloud thrust in his sickle on the earth; and the earth was reaped." The Woodbury case was not that harvest, but Mrs. Eddy foresaw that the next trial would be. This is verified in her response to the initial attack, in November, 1906, which response she entitled "Harvest," with the opening sentence, "God hath thrust in the sickle, and He is separating the tares from the wheat."

The Leader had prophesied this trial seven years before it began. She knew it would be severe, and by January of 1907 she had called a number of tried and true workers to Pleasant View, or back to Pleasant View to meet this attack. Lewis Strang was still there, and George Kinter, Joseph Mann, and Gilbert Carpenter were some who were called back to do mental work during this trying time.

On January 7 James P. Wilson, an attorney in Denver, Colorado wrote to Mrs. Eddy:

> After reading the McClure article and your reply I take the liberty of addressing this letter to you. *I think I see breakers ahead.*
>
> You perhaps remember me as the atty for your son George. I came here three years ago and since then have not been your son's advisor, and we closed our business relations, but we are still very friendly and I think much of him as he has many attributes that command respect. He does not know I'm writing this and has made no request of me to write you, but I write you believing I am doing the proper thing.
>
> Your son, Mr. Glover, has many letters from you in his possession — he has kept a copy of all letters written you and has all your replies.
>
> You should have all those or many of those letters returned — I need not tell you why but there is a reason why. You are making history — you need some of those letters.
>
> Your son is in want, his family is in want, unless you have done something for him lately. You built him a fine home — but he had no money to maintain it. You have done much for him but we can't count the cost in dealing with our children. I need not tell you George has made mistakes — my boys make mistakes, but I do want you to get back many of your letters.
>
> Your son usually followed my advice — when he did he made no mistakes. He sometimes did not take my advice and made some costly mistakes, but I think he will listen to me.
>
> Your work should not be interfered with and no misunderstanding SHOULD ARISE IN THE FUTURE over matters which you can adjust now.
>
> If this is worthy of attention I am pleased to be of some service to you, if not, you can consign this to the waste basket.

Immediately the Leader had Alfred Farlow and also Irving Tomlinson endeavor to retrieve her letters from George who at first promised to return them. But George Glover was already totally under Chandler's influence, so the letters were given instead into Chandler's hands.

The Revelation of Jesus to John states:

> Rev. 10:7 But in the days of the voice of the seventh angel, when he shall begin to sound, the mystery of God should be finished . . .
> Rev. 11:15 And the seventh angel sounded; and there were great voices in heaven, saying, The kingdoms of this world are become the kingdoms of our Lord, and of his Christ; and he shall reign for ever and ever.

After the seventh angel sounded, "there appeared a great wonder in heaven; a woman clothed with the sun," followed by the dragon endeavoring to devour the Woman's child. Then the beast rose "up out of the sea" (elementary latent error, S&H 559:5), and next the false prophet, both claiming to do great wonders that would equal or eclipse the great good brought forth by the Womanhood of God. All this prophecy had seen fulfillment. All the earth knew of the Woman and her work. Some had followed her, some had rejected her, and many had done nothing at all. But all knew of her, and "the time is come . . . to reap; for the harvest of the earth is ripe."

> Rev. 15:19 And the angel thrust in his sickle into the earth, and gathered the vine of the earth, and cast it into the great winepress of the wrath of God.
> 20 And the winepress was trodden without the city, and blood came out of the winepress, even unto the horse bridles . . .

Mrs. Eddy knew the crucial hour that was upon the earth, and particularly upon all Christian Scientists, and was constantly at work to guide her followers through this trial that they might emerge from it elevated and purified. But no one else saw the imperativeness of the hour. On the twelfth of January she gave this message to Lewis Strang:

> If your Mother and your best earthly friend directs work to be done in sense and Science spiritual in the Cause of Christ, why can't, won't you and other students before this faithful always in His sight, do it? The calling of Soul is man's highest example, this I know forty years. Dear one, Mother rejoices at your growth in His cause and that is why she seeks always the chastening rod of His Spirit for you. Do you understand this? Kinter and Mann will take the watch this night. Be you at work; if Mother calls you, you will be ready. One Mind; Love over all, Truth *reigns.*

It was her very best students who most often received the Mother's rebukes and "the chastening rod of His Spirit." The Leader once wrote to Irving Tomlinson that she had rebuked poor Stetson more than any other student.

Mrs. Stetson met every day with twenty-five of her students, all of whom were practitioners in her church. At these meetings they discussed "metaphysical points relating to Christian Science practice," and the teacher constantly impressed her students with the Leader's spirituality and the great importance of following their Leader. Mrs. Eddy received a great many letters of support as the newspaper attacks continued, but none was more appreciative than this letter of January 15 from First Church, New York:

> Beloved and Revered Leader:
>
> The world does not yet know you, but your steadfast, loyal, and watchful followers, the members of this church, together with your loving students and followers throughout the world, do know you. We are continually praising God for Christian Science, His great gift to us through you, its Discoverer and Founder.
>
> At this annual meeting of First Church of Christ, Scientist, New York City, we beg to lay our treasures and our honors at your feet. We delight in striving to emulate your holy example and teaching, through "evil as well as good report;" ever trusting Truth and Love to enable us to follow you up the rugged heights of Christian Science, beyond the clouds and the thunderings of personal sense, into the calm, pure atmosphere of Mind, the sunlight of Love's presence. We have much reason to be humbly grateful for the prosperity in Truth which has attended our flock during the past year. Christian Science Mind-healing has been demonstrated over all manner of sin and sickness, and many new members, who at our last annual meeting knew nothing of Christian Science, are rising to call you blessed. Jesus fed the hungry multitude. He blessed and broke the bread, and gave to his disciples to give to the hungry, which they did. Dearly beloved Leader, have you not prepared and broken the bread of God, and given to your disciples, and have you not bidden them distribute to the multitude? We have been fed with the bread which you have broken with your own dear hands and given to us through your disciple.
>
> You tell us that this is the harvest hour. Indeed, so it seems to us. Blessings innumerable have been bestowed upon us as a church. Not one of the promises of the Bible has failed us, when we have followed your teachings in Science and Health with Key to the Scriptures, and your other writings. The beauty and affluence of the divine Mind is manifest in Health, and in the unity of the good and the true. Love for God and our brother man must increase, as we near the white Christ. Who will be able to gather and care for the bountiful harvest which God had prepared for His anointed and her followers? "The

harvest truly is plenteous, but the laborers are few."

We rejoice in the triumph of Truth over the late attacks made upon you. Our Master said, "If it be possible, let this cup pass from me; nevertheless not as I will, but as thou wilt." In this century the call to meet the enemy of Christ has been met by you, and throughout the world the cry has rung out, "Mary Baker Eddy lives, and loves, and conquers hate and the haters, with 'Father, forgive them; for they know not what they do.'" We bow in humble acknowledgment of your Christian spirit and your divine power to reflect omnipotent Love, which shuts the lion's mouth, and is enabling you to pass through the furnace seven times heated, with no evidence of the experience, save a purer love, exalting you to Horeb heights of spiritual supremacy over the material world, the flesh, and all the claims of evil. We are mute before such unparalleled meekness and might, and rejoicingly follow, with devoted obedience and love, one whom we delight to serve and honor as God's chosen Messenger to draw us to "Immanuel, or God with us;" to reveal to us the invisible Christ, who is "Lord of lords, and King of kings."

Lovingly and faithfully,

First Church of Christ, Scientist, New York City
E. F. Hatfield, *First Reader*

These New York students truly appreciated their Leader and accepted all she said, but their understanding of "the harvest hour" differed greatly from that which the Leader saw and foresaw. She had said in Science and Health: "the higher Truth lifts her voice, the louder will error scream," and her voice was the voice of Truth and had been lifted *higher* beginning in August, 1906 at the beginning of the ascension era. She had also written in Science and Health that the "talking serpent typifies mortal mind" "when nearing its doom, this evil increases and becomes the great red dragon, swollen with sin, inflamed with war against spirituality . . . " Her soldiers needed training for this warfare else they would all become casualties on the battlefield.

Many were called to Pleasant View in 1907 for this training, but, sad to say, some were not responsive. Susie Lang had been in one of Mrs. Eddy's earliest classes in 1882, and she had been a member of the Leader's second normal class in 1885, but she appreciated not the opportunity to serve the Leader. When Mrs. Eddy asked her to come to Pleasant View in 1907, Miss Lang began outlining the great needs of the field in Lawrence. Finally Mrs. Eddy said, "The Lawrence field needs you more than I do." When Susie said, "Do you need me, Mother?" the Leader replied: "I need only what God sends me. I need you but I need you somewhere else than here."

Adelaide Still wanted very much to come to Pleasant View, but perhaps it was only human desire. If God had sent her, the Leader would not have rejected her. As it was, at their first interview, she merely asked Miss Still how the sleighing was in Massachusetts and how long she had been a practitioner, before dismissing her. Miss Still's disappointment may have helped to fit her to serve the Leader, for later, in the spring of 1907, she accepted a menial position in the Pleasant View household.

The Leader increased the mental work as well as the mental workers at Pleasant View. And she directed the work of each, beginning at 5 A.M., as this watch given to Lewis Strang on January 22 indicates:

> Hold the ground: Life, Truth, Love reign this and every hour. No fear, no night dreams, no day dream. M.A.M. is not power. Only reality; God, and His will *is done* on this earth and at Pleasant View. Keep the line; hold your aim, thought externalized is the guide.
>
> Please receive from Mr. Carpenter the texts for thinking and I will name the hour in the morning beginning 5 A.M. The above named watch is uniform.
>
> I do not ask you to treat anyone. I only show you what is in belief and man's daily duty to God.

The February *McClure's* featured another attack on Mrs. Eddy. Many of those who joined in the persecution of God's chosen witness truly knew not what they were doing, but they had put money in God's place in their lives. Hiram Crafts, Mrs. Eddy's first student, had written a statement about his pupilage for Mrs. Eddy's *Footprints Fadeless* in 1901, but Hiram had died in 1906. His wife had been approached by *McClure's* and possibly *New York World* reporters, and she wrote on February 2:

> Dear Mrs. Eddy:
>
> Now Hiram has gone the people want me to tell them your history while you lived with us, the one that will pay me the most money if you will pay me the most I will keep still keep my mouth closed you can have your first choise I want you to be quick about it, not to delay for I don't want to be teased to death.
>
> With regards
> Mary W. Crafts

It is not hard to imagine the kind of stories Mary Crafts "sold" to the press. It has been said that Mark Twain saw an opportunity to make some money, and once again he joined the persecutors with an article in the Sunday *Herald,* February 3.

The *New York World* employed Josephine Woodbury's attorney, Frederick Peabody to assist Chandler. On February 18 Peabody attacked Christian Science with a drastic bill in the Massachusetts legislature to regulate Christian Science practice.

Mrs. Eddy was thinking of her son in Washington, D.C. and of his being influenced against her. On February 6 she wrote to Edward Everett Norwood of that city:

> Beloved Student:
>
> My son is not a Christian Scientist. He, Mr. George W. Glover, is said to be in Washington. I wish he would return to his home in Lead, Dakota. The m.a.m.'s are at work to prevent it. I am giving him a large sum to help him at his home in Lead, Dakota.
>
> To meet the lies let me inform you. After his father passed on I went immediately to my paternal home.
>
> After I thought of such a thing — I asked my father to help me to get some of my husband's property, for I had not anything of it and would not sell his slaves.
>
> My father went to a man in Bow who had done business of that kind in the South and asked him how he should accomplish getting me what belonged to me as his wife.
>
> The man said to him, "Under the present laws of the South she can recover none of his property; it would take eight years to even get out an execution." So father dropped the matter and I never received any means to help me in that way.
>
> Please assert this if it becomes necessary.
>
> Lovingly yours,
> Mary Baker Eddy

Edward Norwood called on the Glovers at their hotel, and they returned the call, but the meetings were to no avail. Mr. Norwood said that he "could plainly see that the poor old man was being worked."

The large sum Mrs. Eddy was giving to her son was one hundred twenty-five thousand dollars and was being set up as a trust fund* giving George and his wife an annual income for the rest of their lives. No doubt Attorney Wilson's letter had caused her to see the necessity for this.

The Leader was also giving thought to all of her financial affairs. On the morning of February 12 she said to Laura Sargent: "Laura, I am going to put business out of my mind. I cannot go on being pulled one way and the other by material and spiritual matters. I am going with God." Two days later Calvin Frye wrote her a memorandum commending her suggestion to transfer her property to a "Christian Science Association of Home and Foreign Missions" from which she could draw what money she needed. Within two or three weeks she made a final decision on another plan for her property.

The most important event in February of 1907 was announced in

*See Appendix D.

the *Sentinel* of February 2:

> THE CHRISTIAN SCIENCE TEXTBOOK
>
> An edition of "Science and Health with Key to the Scriptures" printed from new plates has just been issued. This edition contains many important changes and additions by the author.

The Leader received a great many letters thanking her for this new revision, but perhaps none was more appreciative than this letter of February 2 from her final proof-reader, William D. McCrackan:

> Consecrated Leader and Teacher:
>
> Again you have put the world under obligation in a notable way by your recent revision of Science and Health, the book which heals and reclaims. While efforts were being made to identify Christian Science with the prince of this world, you were lovingly and patiently at work blessing your enemies by this revision. I see in this action of yours a new example of the right way of returning good for evil. A life like yours, filled with such acts of charity, must be instinct with happiness and supreme joy. The little glimpses I get of God as Life, assure me that you have found the secret of perennial gladness.

Although this revised edition of Science and Health was not issued until February of 1907, it was copyrighted in 1906. It would appear that after the Leader had entered the ascension era she took her child (Science and Health) with her, for this is the last copyrighted edition of her textbook. She made many more changes and additions from 1907 through 1910, but never again applied for a copyright. The Book had risen above human law and was free, protected by God's law.

The Leader was trying every day to open the eyes of her students. On February 15 she said to them to "Not arrange things and then go to God, but go to God first." Then she opened her Bible and read Luke 24:1-16.

> Luke 24:2 And they found the stone rolled away from the sepulchre.
>
> 3 And they entered in and found not the body of Jesus.
>
> 6 He is not here but is risen: . . .
>
> 10 It was Mary Magdalene . . . and other women . . . which told these things unto the apostles.
>
> 11 And their words seemed to them as idle tales, and they believed them not.
>
> 15 . . . Jesus himself drew near, and went with them.
>
> 16 But their eyes were holden that they should not know him.

When the Leader stopped reading she said: "Those things are occurring again. My words seem as 'idle tales' to you; but I speak truth." But her disciples' eyes were holden, and they did not know her.

Her lesson for her household workers two days later, February 17, was:

> There are no lies. All is Mind and governs. What is matter? Nothing. Mortal mind is matter; it cannot talk. Then hold to Mind, and the rest will take care of itself — the rest is nothing; this (material) is all nothing.
>
> Life is divine, immortal, and there is no other life. That is all the Life there is and is ours.

On February 23 the Leader said to her household: "Stand with God and you will stand with Mother; stand with Mother and you will stand with God." And on February 26 she gave them this lesson:

> There is but one way through, and only one way through; and that is to unself.
>
> It is my unselfed love that has made a success of this Cause for the world.
>
> Can you get rid of a lie and not get rid of it? No. Is it a lie that there is life, substance and intelligence in matter? Yes. Then unself it. Everyone must do this. There is too much looking out for self instead of others. This is the trouble with the teaching of today, and why there is so much erroneous teaching being done; not unselfed enough.
>
> You cannot *teach* Christian Science in that way. You can say over the words, but unless you prove it you are not *teaching* (imparting). Prove it in healing the sick and casting out sin.
>
> I pray and watch in the little details; someone must, as good is expressed in the minutiae of things.

The Leader had risen above matter, and she was doing all in her power to teach "the way" to her dedicated disciples. But nearly half a century elapsed before this was seen and understood. It was in 1953 that an earnest student, Herbert W. Eustace, wrote and published: "Mrs. Eddy did everything she could to drive it home to you and me, that we are not in the Christian Era, the Era of matter but that we are in the Christian Science Era, the Era of Mind. We are in the Ascension Era."

CHAPTER XXXVIII

WITHIN THREE YEARS

I have more of earth now, than I desire, and less of heaven.
— MARY BAKER EDDY

1907

BY the end of February many of the workers who had been called to Pleasant View had returned to their homes, though others had been called, one of whom was Lida Fitzpatrick. On March 1 Mrs. Eddy asked Henry Baker to come to Pleasant View to see her. Hon. Henry M. Baker was a distinguished lawyer, an ex-member of Congress, and a present member of the New Hampshire legislature. He was a resident of Bow, New Hampshire, and he was also related to Mrs. Eddy, — she and Henry's father were cousins.

Henry Baker had been to Pleasant View many times over the years, and on several occasions Mrs. Eddy had consulted him on legal points. On March 1 she wanted his opinion on a letter she had just received.

The letter was from Washington, D.C., was dated February 25, 1907, and was signed by George W. Glover, but Mrs. Eddy said to her cousin: "George could not write that letter. That letter was written by an educated man skilled in the use of language." She asked Henry what it meant, and his response was that "unquestionably some hostile action was contemplated."

The next day the hostile action was obvious to all. Headlines in the *New York World* proclaimed:

RELATIVES SUE TO WREST MOTHER EDDY'S
FORTUNE FROM CONTROL OF CLIQUE

Chandler had come up with a diabolical plan. On March 1 he had filed in the Superior Court for the county of Merrimack, N. H., a petition wherein Mary Baker Eddy as plaintiff was suing *against*

HENRY M. BAKER
The trustee Mrs. Eddy appointed as sole administrator of her estate

Calvin A. Frye, Alfred Farlow, Irving C. Tomlinson, Ira O. Knapp, William B. Johnson, Stephen A. Chase, Joseph Armstrong, Edward A. Kimball, Hermann S. Hering, and Lewis C. Strang, and requesting that a receiver be appointed to take possession of all her property including copyrights. The petition as well as extensive, lurid newspaper articles stated that Mrs. Eddy was incompetent to handle her own affairs and her vast fortune (which was greatly exaggerated), so her son, granddaughter, and nephew, George W. Glover, Mary Baker Glover, and George W. Baker respectively, were acting on her behalf to wrest her and her property from the despotic control of the ten defendants.

Through smooth-tongued villany all the Glovers were deceived into believing that this was true. The nephew, too, was totally misled, and Chandler very adroitly kept George Baker and the Glovers from meeting. In a letter to his cousin Mary, written in 1909, George said:

> I do wish, Mary, that I could have met you, when you have been East. I proposed such a meeting to Mr. Chandler, but, while he heartily "wished it might be" . . . he never arranged to let me know of the visit of your father and yourself in such a way as to allow of a meeting. Sometimes I've wondered why.

Perhaps William Dana Orcutt's reaction to this bombshell dropped by the *New York World* and the *Boston Herald* on the second of March was typical of all who knew Mrs. Eddy. He wrote in later years:

> I doubt if anyone associated with Mrs. Eddy at that time was more distinctly shocked than those of us at the University Press. We had become familiar, through the years, with Mrs. Eddy's indefatigable energy and continuing activity in connection with the revision of each new edition of Science and Health. The shock was intensified by our definite knowledge of the malicious nature of the attack. Within the period when the citation charged Mrs. Eddy with being mentally incompetent to conduct her business affairs, we had received . . . communications and alterations written in her unforgettable hand which in themselves should have been sufficient evidence to dismiss the suit.

This fantastic falsehood, — that Mrs. Eddy was *non compos mentis* and controlled by others, — from the moment of its publication, spread like wildfire all over America. Pleasant View was flooded with telegrams and letters of support, and Concord was once again invaded by reporters. A letter dated March 3 from George and Elizabeth Kinter from their home in Chicago ended with: "In behalf of Mrs. Kinter as well as myself, I remain ready for instant service anywhere." Within a very few days George Kinter was back serving at Pleasant View.

EBENEZER J. FOSTER EDDY

A letter of March 4 was received by Laura Sargent and was from Ebenezer Foster Eddy in Waterbury, Vermont. "Benny" had written Mrs. Eddy a supportive letter during the Woodbury trial, and now he wrote once more supporting his adopted mother in this latest diabolical plot to separate her from her closest students and from her money. Benny's letter to Laura stated: "I believe her perfect demonstration will be of more value to the world than all the money in it."

Foster Eddy's statement was the absolute truth, but though he could voice it he seemed unable to uphold the truth he had stated. *The World* did not offer him "all the money" in the world, but whatever the smooth-tongue of James Slaght did offer a day or two later was accepted and turned Benny against his mother. This son could not have been as misled as was George Glover, for Benny had had charge of Mrs. Eddy's business account books (otherwise kept by Calvin Frye) for about two years, and his name had appeared on the title page of Science and Health as publisher for a great many editions over a period of several years.

Foster Eddy was not the only relative approached. A second cousin, Fred W. Baker, was enlisted in support of Chandler's action. On March 11 petitions were filed wherein Ebenezer J. Foster Eddy and Fred W. Baker joined in the bill filed by the three other relatives.

Fred's sister, Mrs. Joseph P. Edmond, was astounded by her brother's action. When she was interviewed by the *Boston Post* she stated that Chandler had spent an entire evening trying to persuade her to join in, but it was clear to her that all those involved were "actuated by revenge or mercenary motives" which could not influence her. She stated: "I know nothing about Mrs. Eddy's personal affairs, nor her money matters, and care less." Within the next two months her brother Fred Baker withdrew from the case.

The *New York World* led the public to believe that George Glover was the instigator of this suit, and this deception was perpetuated by transferring Chandler's attacks to the front pages of the *Boston Herald.* If Joseph Pulitzer did not own controlling interest in the *Herald,* there must have been collusion between the two newspapers, because it became obvious to the astute observer that this case was being tried in the newspapers, most particularly the *Boston Herald,* rather than in the courtroom.

When General Streeter gave a press interview early in March he stated that he had sent a copy of the bill in equity as published, to Mrs. Eddy early Saturday morning, March 2, but as far as he had been informed it had not yet been served on any of the defendants. Streeter was very discreet in his statements but he did give a good deal of accurate information including:

> In common with her many friends she [Mrs. Eddy] believes that the initiative in these proceedings was not taken by her son or other relatives . . .
>
> The amount of Mrs. Eddy's property has been grossly multiplied by rumor and unfounded report. She is not possessed of large wealth,

as this term is used.

... With my partner, Mr. Allen Hollis, I am counsel for Mrs. Eddy alone.

... So far as this case can be considered a legitimate proceeding in equity, it seems to be an attempt to have the personal rights and privileges of a citizen adjudicated in a way unprecedented in New Hampshire ...

On Monday, March 4 Mrs. Eddy sent a message to her cousin Henry Baker asking him to come to Pleasant View. She explained to him that she wanted to be relieved of the care of her property and asked if he would be willing to be one of her trustees to handle it for her.

On the afternoon of March 6 he and the two other trustees, Archibald McLellan and Josiah E. Fernald met at Pleasant View with Mrs. Eddy, Mr. Streeter, and Fred N. Ladd. George Kinter and Calvin Frye were also present during at least a part of the interview. Mr. Streeter had drawn up the Deed of Trust* and Mrs. Eddy read one copy aloud while General Baker followed in the second copy. She stopped several times to make comments such as, "That is just what I want." Fred Ladd recalled that once she stopped and said: "You will note that I am reading this without glasses, and I do not have to hold it way off either." This is of special interest to those who know that Mrs. Eddy had had many pairs of reading glasses in earlier years. According to a statement by Josiah Fernald, when she came to the end she said in substance:

"I understand that I am giving up the control of all my property, but I want to sign this deed," and asked Mr. Streeter where she should sign. He pointed out the place on the paper, and she signed each of the two originals, remarking as she did so something to the effect that her hand was not quite so steady today as usual. ... After General Baker signed the acceptance her attention was called to his signature, and she joked him because he could not write so well as she could.

General Baker also stated that some fun was made of his signature in which she laughingly joined. But her next order of business that afternoon was the following for Mr. Ladd:

I hereby appoint Fred N. Ladd my attorney to take all papers and all the contents of my safe boxes at First National Bank in Concord, New Hampshire, and transfer them to the trustees that I have today selected ...

Probably Calvin Frye was very pleased to turn over all his books and papers as well as responsibility in their regard to the trustees.

*Deed of Trust in Appendix E.

JOSIAH E. FERNALD
One of the three men Mrs. Eddy selected to manage her property

One of the first things the trustees did was to have a reputable accounting firm audit Mrs. Eddy's cash account books for the fourteen years prior to March 6, 1907. Their report verified that on that date $871,861.46 in bonds, cash, etc. had been transferred to the trustees. This firm (Harvey Chase and Company) also affirmed that Calvin Frye was an honest agent but not a very good accountant, that he had made more errors against himself than against Mrs. Eddy and that the trustees owed him close to seven hundred dollars.

Most likely the attorneys for all the defendants (including Mrs. Eddy) advised this audit for the "Next Friends'" suit. Mrs. Eddy of course was the main defendant though falsely listed as plaintiff.

Mrs. Eddy had refused to see any of the army of newsmen in Concord and appointed Irving C. Tomlinson to be her messenger in this area. He was dealing with a belligerent group of calloused reporters who were looking for a scandal, and some of whom were determined to see Mrs. Eddy. Mr. Tomlinson dealt graciously with their boorish behaviour, and one of them told him later:

> We hoped that something of a sensational nature would be uncovered. . . . If ever anyone has a right to hate someone surely the Christian Scientists had a right to hate us. We were there to villify Mrs. Eddy if we could. We had no reverance and no decency. We did not believe anything but the worst about anybody, and we wanted if possible to hold Mrs. Eddy up to scorn and ridicule, to expose and denounce her.

Once again the Leader set an example of blessing those who "despitefully use you and persecute you." She asked Mr. Tomlinson to call these men on the telephone and tell them it was impossible for her to see them. She also instructed him to speak only to the head man, and gave him a further message for this man.

The chief man was a steady drinker and a particularly hard-boiled reporter from a big New York newspaper who had been for some years afflicted with a cancerous growth of the throat which was at times extremely painful and overwhelming. He was suffering greatly and unable to speak a word on the evening that Mr. Tomlinson phoned.

All the men were gathered in his room at the Eagle Hotel smoking, drinking and bored, when the phone rang, and Mr. Tomlinson asked to speak to the leading man. The reporter who answered said he was too ill to come to the phone and couldn't talk anyway:

> Remembering Mrs. Eddy's instructions I said, "Tell him to come to the telephone; he can hear what I say even if he can't talk."

Accordingly the suffering newspaper man came to the telephone, showing decided anger (as I was later informed). He listened for a few moments. Those in the room, of course, could not hear what was being said, but when this man turned away from the telephone, he not only could speak perfectly, but was healed.

The healing stirred these men. They sat around, looking at each other, unable to comprehend what had happened and more startled by it than anything else. They had of course heard that Christian Scientists claim to heal the sick, and they knew their comrade had been healed.

. . . These men had believed Mrs. Eddy to be only a humbug, and the reputed healings of Christian Science to be a great hoax. Their whole position was overthrown by this proof offered before their very eyes. They packed their bags and left.

Many years later a nephew of this reporter called at Mr. Tomlinson's office in Boston and said that he had a message for him from his uncle: "My uncle requested me to see you and to tell you that in his last days he turned to Christian Science, and he knew that he owed a debt of gratitude to Mrs. Eddy for his healing in Concord."

The trial in the 1902 edition of Science and Health states: "Materia Medica, Anatomy, Physiology, and Hypnotism are the pretended friends of Man." Following the filing of the Next Friends suit in 1907 Mrs. Eddy changed "pretended friends" in Science and Health to "Next Friends." After the trial was over she changed "Next Friends" in the trial in Science and Health to "Envy, Greed and Ingratitude" (S&H 430:23-24).

On March 7 the lesson the Leader gave her household included:

What is the one evil? Animal magnetism? Yes. Is it person? No. Is it anything? No. Then we cannot be harmed by it. That is what I mean by the one evil.

That same day she wrote two letters to Mrs. Stetson in New York. Her first letter said:

My dear Student:

I cannot believe that you are forgetting your duty to your teacher and leader, so I write to you myself to learn of *you why* my three recent requests that you would send to me a Spring bonnet — have not been even *noticed?* Please answer this my letter, and put on the envelope *personal* then none but myself need see it. (Do *not allow* the *evil one* in your midst to turn you away from me in this hour of crucifixion, or history will repeat itself, and Christian Science will once more be lost as aforetime.) The leading students must not allow this attempt of the enemy to overcome them, and *you* yield to it! The lies that are told about me or what I say of you are not worth your notice nor mine. "Awake! arise from the dead and God will give you life."

As ever, lovingly, your teacher, friend, helper,

The Leader knew the tendency of her students as well as everyone else to personalize evil, so later the same day she wrote Augusta again:

Beloved:

By the "evil one," I by no means refer to a personality, but to the *one evil,* viz. hypnotism or m.a.m.

In haste, your loving teacher,

But the "evil one" was *using* many personalities in this all-out war to overcome the Woman. Every day the *Boston Herald* carried front page stories — lies about Mrs. Eddy and her history. *McClure's* February and March issues revived the Quimby myth while discrediting God's chosen messenger. William Nixon had presented his bitter accounts of Mrs. Eddy and Christian Science to Georgine Milmine and Willa Cather, and on March 9 Nixon wrote to Laura Fulmer that Frederick Peabody had offered him a chance "to make some money with the people he is working for and with in the anti-Eddy litigation." A publisher had suggested that Lyman Powell write a book answering the questions he had raised in his pamphlet: *The Anarchy of Christian Science,* and the rector was getting much of his information from Mrs. Eddy's enemies including Georgine Milmine. "The heathen raged;" and Mrs. Eddy said to her household on March 8:

God gives us the victory. His plan is made long before we know anything about it; then we have to carry it out. The human heart requires many scourgings sometimes before it falls in line, but it must come. . . .

We must not feel too much encouraged over a victory, for everything in mortal mind must be overcome. If you fail in one iota, like an example in mathematics, every figure right but one, the example is incorrect; so it is with our problem. All little things must be overcome. Then we rise above substance matter; and that includes sin, sickness, and death.

Even those nearest the Leader had little idea how far she had already risen above substance matter. She was working out the problem of being not for herself alone, but as the example and the Way for all to follow in all time to come. If Jesus' disciples had held up the hands of God's masculine idea, the Science he practised would not have been lost for centuries; but the world was too much with them. Now God's feminine idea was endeavoring to elevate her disciples above the world. She said to them on March 9:

> What is a way-shower? There is a human and a divine meaning. A way-shower is that which shows the way; it must be some *thing* or some *one.* Jesus was the Way-shower, the Christ with him, and if he had not been, where would we be? He showed the way as the masculine idea of Principle, then woman took it up at that point — the ascending thought in the scale — and is showing the way, thus representing the male and female Principle (the male and female of God's creating).
>
> Is there anything in the world of more importance than holding up the hands of the way-shower? No. If they had all done that with Jesus, we would be in the millenium. We must become unselfed.

The next day, March 10, Calvin Frye recorded: "While Mrs. Eddy was troubled today at the lawsuit just instituted by her next friends (Glover and Baker) she prayed God for direction and opened her Bible to Is. 16:12, 13, 14. This gave her renewed courage." The Leader said to her students: "From the beginning and all the way along, I got my leading from God, through the Bible. . . . Today he is speaking to me again." Then she read to them from Isaiah 16:

> 14 But now the Lord hath spoken, saying, Within *three years,* as the years of an hireling, and the glory of Moab shall be contemned, with all that great multitude; and the remnant shall be very small and feeble.

The Leader added: "I am sure this will be fulfilled, but don't tell anyone about it." Perhaps no one but Mrs. Eddy had any idea what this meant. But God had spoken to her, especially in Isaiah 16:12

> 12 And it shall come to pass, when it is seen that Moab is weary on the high place, that he shall come to his sanctuary to pray; but he shall not prevail.

The Leader had come to her sanctuary often and often to pray for her followers, her children, her church. She had constantly stood before them "on the high place," and she had entreated them in every way she knew to come *up.* But it seemed that she had to go *down* to them. It is not easy to go down to the level of others and still stay "on the high place." Little wonder that she was "weary on the high place." All of her followers had been riding along on her demonstration, and she was ever praying to bring them up to where she was. But on March 10, 1907, God told her that this prayer "shall not prevail." You can help others, but you cannot do their work for them. From that day the Leader knew that her glory was to be removed from them, "and the remnant shall be very small and feeble" when they no longer have her to lean upon.

To help the feeble remnant the mother gave her children an explanation of what would appear to them as a "seeming decease." At that time the chapter "Science, Theology, Medicine" in Science and Health ended with line 16 on page 164. In the third edition of 1907 Mrs. Eddy added the paragraph which began:

> If you or I should appear to die, we should not be dead, and this seeming decease caused by a majority of human beliefs that we must die, would not in the least disprove Christian Science; . . .

and which ends the chapter with Paul's declaration: "Death is swallowed up in victory."

At this time "Christian Science Practice" in Science and Health ended with the sentence: "Christ, Truth, gives mortals temporary food and clothing until the material, transformed with the ideal, disappears, and man is clothed and fed spiritually." For many, many years Mrs. Eddy had been the teacher, guide, wayshower urging her students to greater endeavors in this necessary transformation. In three more years they would be on their own. She had given them the "little book" from the hand of the angel, but they would have the Mother no longer to instruct, direct, correct them. They would have to work out their own salvation. In the fifth edition in 1907 of the textbook the Leader added lines 16-29 to the end of "Christian Science Practice" on page 442, which included Paul's admonition. But she was still the Mother tempering Paul's "fear and trembling" with Jesus' gentle promise:

> St. Paul says, "Work out your own salvation with fear and trembling:" Jesus said, "Fear not, little flock; for it is your Father's good pleasure to give you the kingdom." This truth is Christian Science.

CHAPTER XXXIX

THE ASCENSION ERA

[Jesus] showed the way as the masculine idea of Principle, then woman took it up at that point — the ascending thought in the scale — and is showing the way, thus representing the male and female Principle (the male and female of God's creating).

— MARY BAKER EDDY

1907

FIVE outstanding men were employed as counsel for Mrs. Eddy, Christian Science, and the ten men named as defendants. Foremost among these five was Mrs. Eddy's attorney General Frank S. Streeter of whom Michael Meehan wrote:

> As a lawyer Mr. Streeter is in a class by himself in New Hampshire. He embodies much of that robust spirit in some way attributed to the past. He is big physically and mentally, and he is big of heart. He knows the law and the rights of the citizen under the law, and having taken a stand he has the courage to maintain it, even though he stand alone. He fights in the open and with recognized rightful weapons. Mr. Streeter represents the best in New England legal practice, and when he talks he has the undivided attention of the court he addresses. His presence is commanding, his voice full, his perception quick, his understanding clear, his grasp of his subject firm; he can sit in silence under castigation and wait with patience his opportunity to hit back; he is imperturbable and it is this imperturbability coupled with his knowledge of every detail of his case that makes him so formidable an opponent.

Mr. Streeter and his partner Allen Hollis were representing Mrs. Eddy; Edwin G. Eastman was engaged to represent the New Hampshire defendants; Samuel J. Elder and William H. Morse of Boston were representing the Massachusetts defendants as well as Edward A. Kimball of Chicago.

The first step Mrs. Eddy's attorneys took in this case was to prepare a petition for the substitution of her trustees in place of the "next friends" as plaintiff. On March 22 the Leader wrote to William D. McCrackan, First Reader of The Mother Church, informing him that she had appointed trustees to take care of her property for her. McCrackan asked permission to read the letter *(My.* 135) at a Wednesday evening meeting, which permission was granted, and the proceedings were reported in the *Concord Monitor.* A Card *(My.* 136) on the same subject was published in the *Concord Daily Patriot.*

Though no court proceedings had begun in March, the newspapers continued nearly every day with front page articles against Mrs. Eddy. And *McClure's* April issue came out with pages of "history" of Mrs. Eddy's early years of teaching Christian Science as told by Mary Crafts and others of that ilk. One of the many falsehoods in this issue of *McClure's* was Mary Crafts' assertion that Mrs. Eddy did not heal. On March 12 the Leader said to her household students:

> Do you believe what the book says about chemicalization, that "the higher Truth lifts her voice, the louder will error scream"? . . . I was just thinking how I am being abused (Glover case and newspaper articles) and I could feel the tears starting to come, when suddenly I thought of two cases of healing I had and then joy took the place of sorrow.

She then told them of two hopeless cripples she had healed — one across from the Allen's house in Lynn, and the other at Mrs. Slade's residence in Chelsea — both immediate healings. When she finished she said: "The papers are writing up my history; the history of my ancestry; writing lies. My history is a holy one. . . .

"In writing my history they can say nothing against me, so they begin to tell lies. It will do the same to *you.* Your truth produces the chemical until all is worked out."

On March 16 the Leader said to her students:

> This hour — is the acme of hate against Love, and Love alone can meet it. God *demands* God. Truth destroys error.

The Leader was rising daily to meet this hour of the acme of hate against Love, and we are fortunate indeed to have some of the lessons she gave to her students at that time. The field, too, felt the Leader's ascending thought as is evident in this letter from Atlanta, Georgia which the Leader received in mid-March:

Beloved Leader and Teacher:

Sunday morning I had such an uplifted sense of the splendor of your present position, of the moral courage that inspires and sustains you, that it gave me the very baptismal of Spirit. I saw how it paled all other heroism, in standing for human rights. I saw you on the Rock, — the spiritual sense of man as the Son of God, — and for that divine inheritance you are holding aloft the banner of Life — harmony and immortality. Below you were the important seeming forces of the loosened occultism of the human mind, that has ever tried to drown the spiritual idea, but "the Lord on high is mightier than the noise of many waters, yea, than the mighty waves of the sea." About you was the cloud of witnesses, chanting hymns of praise and gratitude for blessings received; around encamped the heavenly hosts, the angels of His presence; arching the radiance above you was the rainbow of promise — speedy deliverance from the seeming powers of evil. I beheld "the lion of the tribe of Judah," — the moral courage that stands high and firm for the spiritual freedom and divine heritage of man. I saw, as never before, the woman, and the earth helping the woman. ... This seems to me the most marvelous hour of history; God is with you, and our grateful and loving hearts bless you every moment.

In tenderest love, your devoted student,

Sue Mims

A little later in March the Leader received a letter from William Lloyd in Colorado Springs, part of which said:

> ... I am only a plain middle-aged business man; but I owe literally all I have and am, spiritually and materially, to your teachings. May I say, I know you are entirely competent; never so competent. I know this because of the present uproar all over these United States. Had you stood still during the past year, error would be satisfied and silent. You must have reached heights unknown to us, that this seeming turmoil seeks to overwhelm. You have God about you, and hundreds of thousands of loyal followers at your side, — undismayed, — of whom I humbly and gratefully subscribe myself one.

It was true that the Leader had "reached heights unknown to" her followers and she was continuing to do so daily. She was also giving some of the footsteps to her household. On March 17 she said to them:

> We must give up *all* for Christ, Truth ... Error cannot get into the kingdom, so we must divest ourselves of it. We must hold with God alone.

On March 22 she included this in their lesson:

Take the side with God, and put *all* of the balance *there.* This is what is needed. Hold with your Leader and with God.

... Now let us have God without the "crucifixion" ... but resurrected to the living man of God, — the spiritualized sense.

On March 24 she told her students:

I have no child. The kingdom of heaven is in our midst. Heaven is harmony, and harmony is peace, love, joy. We must see health and our relations in the spiritual.

The belief of a material child was persecuting Mrs. Eddy, but she was far more closely related to her humble, grateful followers. George Glover wanted her money, but many loyal followers truly wanted the spirituality she had to give to them. If the "remnant" would follow in her footsteps these faithful followers must learn more about these footsteps now. On March 24 the Leader wrote to Calvin C. Hill:

My beloved Student:

I beg that you will come to me March 26 or 27 to watch with me one or two weeks as the case may require.

This hour is going to test Christian Scientists and the fate of our Cause and they must not be found wanting. They must forget self and remember only their God and their Wayshower and their duty to have one God and love their neighbor as themselves. I see this clearly that the prosperity of our Cause hangs in this balance. May God open your eyes to see this and to come to her who has borne for you the burden in the heat of the day.

In a lesson to her household a few days earlier the Leader had said: "All there is of us, is what there is of us under the fire of mesmerism. ... — the test." She knew how severe "the fire of mesmerism" could be and how few were ready for this test. And she also knew now that all her followers would have to meet this test without their Leader at their side. All needed to learn to unself. A great many were totally absorbed with *my* work, *my* church, *my* reading room, *my* practice, *my* lectures, *my* teaching, *my* patients, *my* students, — thinking they were doing God's bidding. But when God's Chosen One called them to work in His-Her vineyard, they were too busy. And so she wrote to Calvin Hill: "May God open your eyes to see this and to come ... "

Calvin did come and so did several others that she called, until according to Calvin Hill she had twelve students doing special work. Some of those who were there in addition to Calvin Hill, George Kinter, and Lewis Strang, were H. Cornell Wilson, John

Lathrop and Joseph Mann.

On Wednesday, March 27, the Leader told her disciples at Pleasant View:

> The disciples followed Jesus up to a certain point, and then deserted him, and darkness followed. Follow the wayshower and you will follow the divine idea; turn away from the wayshower and you turn away from the divine idea; like turning away from the windowpane, you turn away from the light.

The Wayshower was endeavoring to teach her students that in all time to come if a student turns away from Mary Baker Eddy as the Wayshower, he is turning away from the light. It is not possible to climb up some other way. Those who think they can, are already judged by Jesus' words: "If therefore the light that is in thee be darkness, how great is that darkness!" On March 29 the Leader's lesson included:

> Eating, drinking, sleeping, being clothed, are only a human concept; these and the belief of life, substance, and intelligence in matter, must all be given up for the immortal. The Christ takes us out of the discord of not eating, sleeping, etc., and gives us the pleasurable side of it; takes us out of the pain and gives us the pleasure, then replaces *that* with the spiritual. . . . We must come to see we do not depend upon eating, sleeping, etc., for life and health, but depend on Mind. . . .
>
> Jesus did not make the demonstration over death, but yielded to it — because of the desertion of his disciples. If they had stood by him we should now be in the millenium.
>
> That demonstration must be made or the world will again be left in darkness. The students must hold up the hands of the wayshower.

If they do, they shall be able to meet the fire of mesmerism when they are tried. And many were sincerely trying to hold up the wayshower's hands while the world was displaying a grotesque caricature of the wayshower and buffeting this misconseption unmercifully. These lies were even being translated and spread in Germany.

But another interesting development was taking place. A number of churches, reading rooms, and individual Scientists were writing about the remarkable increase in interest in Christian Science, the literature, and meetings because of the undue publicity. McLellan wrote in a letter to Mrs. Eddy:

> I wish that the growth of interest in Christian Science which is now so manifest, might have come in some way other than through at-

> tacks on you, but the increased interest in your teachings amounts almost to a "boom." The Publishing Society is hard pressed to provide room for all the extra clerks necessary to attend to the wonderful increase in the demand for Christian Science literature. God is making the wrath of man to praise Him.

A letter from Toledo, Ohio, came from one of Mrs. Eddy's early students. Sarah J. Clark had first studied in Mrs. Eddy's Primary class in September, 1885, and had been active in the field for a score of years. She told in her letter of the inspiration she had received from the Leader's article "Harvest." Miss Clark began and ended her letter of March 29 as follows:

> My Very Dear Teacher:
>
> By reason of the flagrant falsehoods concerning you in recent publications, many persons have been led to inquire what is the truth about this matter, and are now eagerly reading the revelations of Truth in your immortal book . . .
>
> If in any way I can do anything for you, do not forget to call on me.

One more disciple was volunteering, was turning to the light, and by June Sarah J. Clark was with the other workers at Pleasant View.

Another reaction to "the flagrant falsehoods" took place before the end of March. Mrs. Eddy's neighbor, Professor John F. Kent, who had aided Slaght, Chandler and Peabody, changed sides according to the *Boston Evening Record* of March 30:

> KENT GOES OVER TO MRS. EDDY
>
> Says Plaintiff Used Him Falsely
>
> . . . "I could not go as far as the enemies of Mrs. Eddy desired that I should. . . . What little information I did give was distorted and magnified." . . .
>
> Finding himself placed in what he considered a false position, Mr. Kent has decided to side henceforth with the defendants.

The next day, March 31, was Easter Sunday, and the Leader's lesson that morning was:

> RESURRECTION. We must be resurrected; must put off the old man and put on the new.
>
> . . . you must put on the whole of the new man — the spiritual idea.
>
> . . . The resurrection is seeing the real man that was never in matter . . . That is the way I did the healing. I never saw the material man before me, but the real man, perfect, and this healed instantaneously, and no relapse. This is the way Jesus healed. . . . This is the resurrection.

On Monday morning, April 1, George Kinter wrote in a letter to McLellan:

> . . . I wish that you and every worker in the field of Christian Science, and indeed the whole world, might have such an opportunity as I am now having; namely, a visit to our dear Leader's home, in order that you might see, as I am seeing, with what equanimity and serene calmness she is passing through what to almost anybody else would be a great and trying ordeal; whereas she, on this the very eve of the trial, is as sweetly content to let God rule as if there were nothing to disturb the waters, as in reality there is not. But one needs to be at her side to realize how great is her spiritual understanding, for she literally trusts God, and this is the secret of her wonderful career.
>
> We shall all appreciate her better, "when these clouds have rolled away," and the scenes now being enacted will serve to send Christianity farther along the way, as Christians of the present epoch note how good a God our God is by their observation of a remarkable instance of entire reliance upon His goodness to His children. A signal feature of the hour is that she has no word of hate or unkindness for those among the people who would do her injustice, but is demonstrating what she teaches, and has ever taught, namely, that Love alone overcomes evil with good, that hate, revenge, or malice have no place in Christian Science.
>
> This home is as quiet and as lacking in any sort of excitement as a church service.

CHAPTER XL

MALICE UNLEASHED

This malicious animal instinct, of which the dragon is the type, incites mortals to kill morally and physically even their fellow-mortals, and worse still, to charge the innocent with the crime.
— MARY BAKER EDDY

1907

THE Concord Daily Patriot published an action filed by Streeter and Hollis on April 2, in its entirety, the essence of which was:

STATE OF NEW HAMPSHIRE
SUPERIOR COURT

Merrimack, ss. April Term, 1907

- - - -

Mary Baker G. Eddy By her next friends, George W. Glover Mary Baker Glover George W. Baker	*vs.*	Calvin A. Frye Alfred Farlow Irving C. Tomlinson Ira O. Knapp William B. Johnson Stephen A. Chase Joseph Armstrong Edward A. Kimball Hermann S. Hering Lewis C. Strang

Motion for Leave to Intervene and be Substituted as Plaintiff in Place of said "Next Friends."

. . .

Wherefore the said Henry M. Baker, Archibald McLellan, and Josiah E. Fernald, as said Trustees, pray that they may be substituted as "next friends" or as plaintiffs in lieu of the "next friends" now of record, and that they be permitted, under the supervision and advice of the court, to prosecute said suit according to its merits and as the protection of the trust property and estate may seem to require.

Streeter and Hollis, Solicitors.	Henry M. Baker Archibald McLellan Josiah E. Fernald

On the same day, April 2, Mrs. Eddy wrote to her church *(My.* 135):

> . . . "Fret not thyself because of evildoers;" . . .
> At this period my demonstration of Christian Science cannot be fully understood, theoretically . . .

The Leader's footsteps at this period were so far beyond the comprehension of the field that she could only direct them to the study of "Atonement." Much more than a decade earlier when Mrs. Eddy went to Pleasant View she told the students who were with her then that she was receiving revelations every day which she could not tell them because they could not bear it yet. From that time on she had gone higher each day. Many students had gone higher too, over the years, but none was even near the Leader's demonstration. If even one had been, perhaps her prayer might have prevailed. The best she could do for them was to call as many advanced Scientists as were willing to come to her that they may gain a little more spirituality from her teaching and her example, and that they might develop greater strength to meet the fire of mesmerism. These dedicated students all thought that they were there to help the Leader. They had little comprehension that *she* was working for *them* in order that they and her great Cause might free the world from its enslavement to materialism, and that her dear students might be able to *stand* in the hour of trial. Protection was emphasized in her lesson of April 5:

> . . . hold your thought in Truth, Life, Love; while doing so can you be touched? No. Then hold there. This will destroy all evil. *This is the period in which it must be done.**
> I live with the Bible; I have not another thing on earth to be one with but the Bible and Science and Health. I, the Bible, and Science and Health, the trinity, three in one.

In her lesson of April 6 she said: "It is all summed up in a few words. Love, Life, Truth, God, is all there is."

On April 6 Chandler, to counteract Streeter's petition of April 2, filed a supplemental bill for the five "next friends" (now including Fred W. Baker and Ebenezer J. Foster Eddy) against Mrs. Eddy's three trustees, Baker, McLellan, and Fernald, making thirteen defendants in place of the original ten — not counting Mrs. Eddy herself, who was of course the one main defendant in the case. This

*Emphasis added.

supplemental bill also asked:

> 2. That the said defendants Baker, McLellan, and Fernald be required to transfer and deliver to the receiver or receivers . . . all the property of the said Mary Baker G. Eddy taken possession of or received by them under the provisions of said deed signed March 6, 1907 . . .

On April 15 the trustees filed their answer with the court. While this was going on, the events of spiritual import were Mrs. Eddy's lessons to those in her home. On April 8 she may have sensed a tendency to give up, for she told them to want to die to get out of this constant struggle was of no use, "for if you should do so, you would still have to keep at it until accomplished." She also said to Lida Fitzpatrick on that day: "Lida, you have done beautifully since you have been here; have helped me *so much."* On April 9 she told her students:

> When we *realize* the allness of God, that He is Life, Truth, Love, omnipotent, omnipresent, infinite Principle, all will be accomplished.

The Leader's lesson of April 11 included:

> "I and the Father are one" . . . in its spiritual sense means one with the divine Principle, God, the only I. Not materially through the personality of Jesus, asking in his name, but spiritually — *yes;* the oneness with the Father; the true individuality. As you rise to spiritually understand that, you lose your sense as an "I" in matter, and gain your true selfhood in Spirit. This brings the divine health, which is not dependent on the body, but is of the Father, forever the same.

The students at Pleasant View were gaining ground spiritually each day, and the enemy continued to attack their Leader and her teachings, most especially her teachings regarding malicious animal magnetism. Chandler and Peabody maintained an upper room at the Parker House in Boston where those opposing Mrs. Eddy were encouraged and often paid to give vent to their hatred and lies against her.

At the same time loyal Christian Scientists continued with letters of love and support to their Leader such as this of April 14 from Mary Tomlinson:

> The first paragraph of your *Miscellaneous Writings* has been very precious to me. Today it comes to me as applying to you. In the

> present "storm and tempest" of error you are "safely sheltered in the strong tower of hope, faith, and Love." You are God's nestling, and "He will hide you in His feathers till the storm has passed."

Her dear students felt sure their Leader would be protected from the storm, but they needed to learn more about defending and protecting *themselves* from the wickedness that was attacking their Leader. Sue Harper Mims had seen "the important seeming forces of the loosened occultism of the human mind," but Irving C. Tomlinson was soon to have a very severe lesson in that regard. A very few days after his sister's letter of April 14 to Mrs. Eddy, Mary Tomlinson was mesmerically drawn to the Parker House in Boston where she committed suicide by throwing herself out of a window from a room directly beneath the one in which Chandler, Peabody and associates were conferring. In the Leader's lesson of April 18 she included:

> If there was an assassin which could overpower you, it would be better for you to know what he was doing, so as to be better prepared to meet it.

When Calvin Hill recalled in later years the work the Leader had had him do for the lawsuit he wrote: "Mrs. Eddy pointed out the need for specifically handling hypnotism in this case."

Edwin G. Eastman was representing the New Hampshire defendants, — Calvin A. Frye, Irving C. Tomlinson, Hermann S. Hering, and Lewis C. Strang. Eastman was also attorney-general for New Hampshire and an associate of the firm of Eastman, Scammon and Gardiner. When interviewed early in the case he made the following press statement:

> Our clients have been charged with a very serious breach of confidence, in connection with their alleged relations with Mrs. Eddy, and among other things that they have misappropriated funds and wrongfully diverted moneys from her estate for their own benefit. We have no reason to doubt that these charges are wholly without foundation, and the defendants will ask and demand that these charges shall be fully investigated by the court, and to that end we shall do what we reasonably can to bring about that result at the earliest practicable time.

On April 17 Eastman filed with the court the answers of the four New Hampshire defendants. But as the case was not consummated in the April term of court, Eastman became associated with Streeter and Hollis representing Mrs. Eddy. Hon. Oliver Branch replaced Eastman in representing the New Hampshire defendants.

The answers of the other defendants were also filed on April 17. On April 20 Mrs. Eddy wrote to the one student she felt would be able to stand under the fire of mesmerism, Augusta Stetson:

> Your dear letter and love encourage me. I cannot thank you enough for this, but do know that your life is blessed and blessing others because of it. This comforts me and best expresses my gratitude therefor.
>
> O may you be spared "His cup" if thus it can be and fulfill His righteousness! So far He has spared you and mine may suffice for this period. . . .
>
> P.S. Pardon haste and brevity. I have much to think of and little that I can write at present.

Mrs. Stetson had written Mrs. Eddy earlier in April about the Peace Congress, scheduled to be held in New York City April 14 through 17, which had requested all the churches to send representatives. But she may not have known that Mrs.Eddy had already asked William D. McCrackan to attend the conference as representative for the Christian Science periodicals. The Congress' Executive Committee had also asked all New York churches to hold meetings on April 14 to explain the purpose of the Association for International Conciliation, which Mrs. Stetson planned to do with the Leader's approval. Mrs. Eddy did even more than approve. She authorized a Peace Meeting at The Mother Church. On the evening of April 14 every seat in the Extension was filled and over a thousand stood to hear the addresses of John D. Long, ex-Governor of Massachusetts, William Lloyd Garrison, and ex-Secretary of the Navy, John L. Bates.

But the real progress for the only true peace for the world was going on at Pleasant View. On April 18 the Leader said to her disciples:

> The wayshower must explore the way. You learn that way by that experience. You are learning now from my experience. . . .
>
> If the work had been done in the time of Jesus, it would not have to be done now; but the disciples did not do their part; they were not obedient to him; they questioned what he was doing; did not understand, and it was not done. So it must be done now.
>
> We can enter into immortality here on earth, and now, and overcome death. We must do it. . . .

The Leader knew this *could* have been done in Jesus' time if his disciples could have understood and supported him. She knew, too, that she could do it now if her disciples could understand and support her. And on March 10 God had told her that that would not be the case; that her disciples, too, would be left alone. Nonetheless, she kept telling them what could be done and what *must* be done. And the work she was doing was encircling the globe. Letters of support were coming not only from every State in the Union and from Europe, but from as far away as South Africa, South America, and Australia. Surely this letter of April 18 from Sydney, Australia cheered the Mother's heart:

> . . . I have lately passed through deep waters of mortal belief, and seem to see clearer than before the God-inspired work you have achieved for suffering humanity. It is so far above our comprehension at present, so high and holy, that it is only by small degrees we catch faint glimpses of the wonders of your revelation, of your sacrifices, cross-bearing, and wondrous pilgrimage for us. But you are now able to wear the crown, so we may rejoice exceedingly, and humbly strive to follow your dear footsteps and thank God for you.

CHAPTER XLI

GETHSEMANE

Could ye not watch with me one hour? — JESUS

1907

THE *Broadway Magazine* published a "History of Christian Science in New York City" which Mrs. Stetson sent to the Leader with the statement: "We are not pleased with this story, because it says too much in praise of *our* church and of me, and for this reason we do not think it wise to circulate it." Evidently Mrs. Eddy did not feel that way, for the article was the leader in the *Sentinel* of May 4.

About this time Mark Twain and Lyman Powell both came out with books which were bitter attacks against *Christian Science: The Faith and its Founder,* as Powell titled his assault. The *Cosmopolitan Magazine* for May published an article entitled "Mark Twain, Mrs. Eddy, and Christian Science,"* the first part of which was quotations from Twain's volume. Edward A. Kimball had been asked by the editors to write an answer which stated in part:

> It almost seemed as though everyone who cared to cast a stone at Christian Science or was willing to wound the leader had already put his hand to such endeavor, when lo! there appeared a new and unexpected participant to re-enforce the efforts of those who are intent upon detraction and ruin.
>
> A man whose wit had been the object of a nation's admiration . . . comes with deliberate offensiveness to denominate Mrs. Eddy a liar and a fraud.
>
> It matters not that hundreds of thousands of grateful hearts hold her in high esteem for what she has done for them and for the world. . . .
>
> Christian Science . . . is surrounded by every conceivable form of antagonism and will continue to abide, if need be, in the storm, until the ingenuity of hostility shall have exhausted itself, until the persecution shall have done its utmost, and until mortals learn of the

**Lectures and Articles on Christian Science* by Edward A. Kimball, pp. 361-378.

consummate beneficence of Christian Science and of its limitless value to all men.

DANIEL HARRISON SPOFFORD IN 1907

McClure's Magazine for May continued with its biased history, painting glowing pictures of Richard Kennedy and others who opposed their teacher, while belittling Mrs. Eddy with misrepresentation of facts as well as blatant lies. Again attributing Christian Science to Quimby, Miss Milmine quotes an affidavit of Daniel H. Spofford. She does however, make this one true statement: "Mr.

Spofford still says that no price could be put upon what Mrs. Glover gave her students, and that the mere manuscripts which he had formerly studied were, compared to her expounding of them, as the printed page of a musical score compared to its interpretation by a master." The affidavit quoted caused Sibyl Wilbur to visit Mr. Spofford in his home near Amesbury. Miss Wilbur wrote of this visit:

> I went for the express purpose of asking him to explain the discrepancy between his statements of Mrs. Eddy's teachings, the one in his affidavit printed in *McClure's Magazine* for May, 1907, and the one in the resolution he helped to draw up in 1875.
>
> Mr. Spofford is today a man about sixty-five, slightly bent in carriage, with clear blue eyes and whitened hair. His manner is very gentle and courteous, and his personality sensitive and I should say, idealistic. Mr. Spofford made no immediate reply to my question as to the disparity. After some hesitation he turned from the question by saying, "I believe Mrs. Eddy is the sole author of Science and Health and I believe it is the greatest book in the world outside the Bible. . . . I don't wish it to be understood that I have said Christian Science is Quimbyism. I said that Mrs. Eddy taught some of the Quimby doctrine when I first knew her in 1870. Mrs. Eddy developed her own ideas and wrote her own book, Science and Health, and I was the publisher of the first edition and I know that book thoroughly. I don't confuse in my own mind the work of Quimby and of Mrs. Eddy. I don't see why the world should do so. It is clear to me that Mrs. Eddy at first taught some of the ideas of Quimby; that later she abandoned those ideas entirely for her own, incorporating her own system of religious interpretation in her book."

Mrs. Eddy kept her students working metaphysically and endeavored to impress upon them the importance of keeping their thoughts spiritually elevated so they were ready to meet quickly whatever presented itself. Mr. Carpenter has said that if one in the household had a physical claim and needed help —

> she would look the household over and select the one whose thought was highest. She would then give from fifteen to twenty minutes for this work. If one was unsuccessful, she would select one who could quickly lift his thought to the required healing level, until the results were obtained.

She also regularly assigned specific work to advanced and dependable students outside the home thus causing them to elevate their own thought. If a student is working to *help* a director, lecturer, architect, builder, etc. as the case may be, he is far less apt to indulge in gossip, speculation, criticism, — which amounts to mental malpractice. On May 20 Mrs. Eddy wrote to Henrietta Chanfrau:

> You are to take up work for Miss Wilbur as Mother said when you were last here.

It is possible that others, too, were helping Miss Wilbur, but whether or no, she wrote Mrs. Eddy on May 22:

> It is a remarkable experience which I am passing through, following in your footsteps, observing the impressions which your acts made upon others and their acts upon your life. . . . I don't know how it is done. I don't know what force or power accomplishes it, but every one of your so-called enemies receives me, answers my questions, and in some way confuses himself in his own falsehoods, or, with amazing frankness, tells the truth. Of these witnesses there are those who have sworn to other statements, and when I have addressed them on certain matters they have allowed the truth to escape, as it were, inadvertently. . . . "Atonement and Eucharist" and "Footsteps of Truth" and "Pond and Purpose" were not written by the woman painted in dyes of deception with a brain teeming with worldly design. It is my intent and desire to make the whole world outside your church realize this.

One of Mrs. Eddy's letters that has been often copied and quoted was written to Mrs. Stetson on May 1:

> My darling Student:
>
> Yours read and *understood.* Now let me forewarn you to make no more investigations at the White House, and send no more of my publications nor those of other Scientists there — till the new President is elected, whoever he be, and not then. Remember this that I charge you, viz., avoid being identified pro or con in politics. If you do otherwise, it will hinder our cause, remember this. Keep out of the *reach* of such subjects. Give all your attention to the moral and spiritual status of the race. God alone is capable of government; you are not, I am not, but God has governed through His anointed and appointed one in the way of divine Science, — not politics nor the making or breaking of national laws or institutions. He, God, *alone* is capable of this.

On the seventh of May the Leader told the mental workers in her home something that should cause every serious student to study and ponder all he can find about her instruction at Pleasant View. That is:

> There is one thing needed all over the field and which is only

supplied here, and might not be supplied in the field in centuries; that is, to have but one God, divine Principle and its *demonstration.*

She also told them that day that everyone wants to get rid of death and there is only one way — by *realizing* the sense of Life. "You may die a thousand deaths until you realize this, for it is the only way."

On May 9 the Leader opened her Bible to Matthew 26. She said to her disciples: "History repeats itself, but in different forms; now without the crucifixion." Did any of the students who heard her say this ever know that *her* story as it was unfolding in May of 1907 could be read in the twenty-sixth chapter of Matthew?

> Matt. 26:3 Then assembled together the chief priests, and the scribes . . .
> 4 And consulted that they might take Jesus by subtilty . . .
> 18 . . . The Master saith, My time is at hand; . . .
> 26 And as they were eating, Jesus took bread, and blessed it, and brake it, and gave it to the disciples, and said, Take, eat; this is my body.
> 27 And he took the cup, and gave thanks, and gave it to them, saying, Drink ye all of it;
> 28 For this is my blood of the new testament, which is shed for many for the remission of sins.
> 31 Then saith Jesus unto them, All ye shall be offended because of me this night; for it is written, I will smite the shepherd, and the sheep of the flock shall be scattered abroad.

It is written, "Within three years, as the years of an hireling, and the glory of Moab shall be contemned, with all that great multitude; and the remnant shall be very small and feeble." Jesus' next experience in Matthew 26 was his night of agony in the Garden of Gethsemane when he asked his closest disciples to watch with him, — and they did not.

Some of Mrs. Eddy's statements which have been recorded are: "Stand alone. Never allow anyone to help you: as sure as you do, you cripple yourself; you weaken your power. . . . when you have all you can bear, and even more than you think you can bear, go and say, 'Watch with me one hour,' and then once more take your stand." And again: "never ask for help except you come to the agony of the garden."

The Mother in Israel had been ministering to her children for forty years. Now she had come to the garden and was asking some of them to watch with her. She said to her students as recorded by Calvin Frye: "If you are faithful and watch with me in my Gethsemane you will learn your way through." She was enduring "the agony of the garden" for the benefit of her dear children for all time to come, not for herself, and at least one of those children saw this fact. A grateful letter from a student in Los Angeles, Mrs. Mary E. Backus, to her "Beloved Leader" said in part:

> I enclose in this letter an extract from *Tent Life in Siberia* by George Kennan which tells of a wonderful phenomenon February 26, 1866. . . . Siberia typifies to me the "long cold night of discord," and the heavens divinely illumined told of the light coming to the world again. The two arches mentioned by Mr. Kennan signified to me the first and second appearing of Truth. For years I have wondered if some physical phenomenon which we had been too much asleep to appreciate had not heralded this second appearing of Truth. I have been loth to trespass upon your time, and have waited nearly two years before telling you this, but now more than ever before my heart goes out to you in this hour of trial. I know you are enduring this because of your great love for humanity, for you yourself do not need the fiery baptism. Enoch and Elijah walked with God and departed, but Jesus, whose teachings you are emphasizing, demonstrated the way of life for the world.

Surely this letter of appreciation and recognition touched the Leader's heart. She sent it to her editor for publication, and when it appeared in the *Sentinel* of May 11, "Arctic Aurora" also appeared as the leader in the same issue.

Part of the Leader's lesson on May 14 was:

> God has worked through one in this age because He could. The light will come through the window because it will let it, while the wall will not; it would shine through the wall if it could. God is no respecter of persons. Then would you say the wall can let in the light the same as the window? No. Then does one person let in as much light as another? No. Can the one who lets in the light see what is best for the others better than one who does not? Yes. That is the trouble with those outside (the wall); they think they can run things just as well and a little better than I can (the windowpane).

On May 16 the Leader told her students that if they have to argue to be very careful *what* they argue. But on that day she also defined the standard for a Christian Scientist: "If you are a Christian Scientist and can speak the Word and it is *done,* all right."

On May 19 she told them: "You can heal ignorant sin, but wilful sin must be suffered out."

During this time she was meeting often with her lawyers at Pleasant View. On May 16 she wrote out her affidavit for the trial, which was in the form of a personal letter to Judge Chamberlin *(My.* 137) in her own handwriting, which was very firm and distinctive.

This letter alone which was filed on May 18, should have been sufficient to end this action, but the enemy was continuing to try the Woman with false evidence in the newspapers. William Nixon had written to Laura Fulmer near the end of April that Chandler was making a "real picnic" out of the case, and more than one front page story by Nixon against Christian Science and Mrs. Eddy appeared in the *Boston Herald* in May. In a lecture in Manchester, New Hampshire in May, the Hon. Clarence A. Buskirk said:

> ... the evidence has become incontestable ... that [Christian Science] is truly healing all manner of sickness and all manner of disease. Now its opponents ... are turning their attention to procuring yellow journalism to attack its Founder and Leader, the Rev. Mary Baker G. Eddy. They have left the field of fair argument and are appealing to prejudice with, *ad captandum* [for the sake of pleasing(the crowd)], personal attacks.
>
> ... They now theorize that because, as they say, she is over eighty-five years old, she must, therefore, be incapable of managing her own business affairs, and are petitioning the courts to be allowed to manage her property for her. They are daily filling the papers with artful, insinuative gossip and mendacious inventions. They are trying their case through the newspapers by means of anonymous evidence and fabricated facts;
>
> ... Mrs. Eddy stands today the foremost woman and public benefactor of our age, because she has furnished to the world what all its gold and silver could never buy. During long years, misunderstood, misrepresented, too often falsely maligned and reviled, she has been sustained by the high consciousness that she is working for God and for humanity.

Comparatively few had heard Buskirk's honest facts in refutation of the enemy's "mendacious inventions" by May 23 when there was a hearing for the trustees' motion in Judge Chamberlin's courtroom. Little wonder the Leader had recently said that you cannot heal wilful sin — it must be suffered out. Chandler was surely lending himself a willing tool to malicious mind when he said of God's chosen witness: "The poor woman is crazy." He also stated to the court that because of "the incompetency of this aged, palsied woman" she was unable to do anything of her own free will and that Calvin Frye and the other defendants were "prepared to inflict any torture on Mrs. Eddy to make her do what they want." He was a little less critical of Baker, Fernald, and McLellan when he described them as "the three most capable trustees to take care of a lunatic that ever were."

Such blatant falsehoods were totally unrelated to God's Messenger, and she knew it. But they did reach her in an indirect way, through the thoughts of her students. She was constantly having to write to one or another of those closest to her: "Do not think of me," or "Keep me out of your thoughts." She had written this to Calvin Hill in earlier years, and once again in 1907 she wrote him: "Again I have to write, do *not think of me.* Your tender thought reaches me — *costs me much.* Leave me in God alone. He loves us both. I love all — friends and enemies."

The students had no understanding that it was *their* thoughts that caused the Leader to suffer. And so many thought of her so often that she did not always immediately pinpoint the erroneous thought that was reaching her and causing her suffering. Mr. Hill loved the Leader dearly and often let his tenderest thoughts rest upon her, but he had not been able to love his or her enemies as she taught and practised. When he was discussing the lawsuit with her one day he said that he would like to go wring the necks of those who were responsible for this outrage against an innocent and good woman. Immediately Mrs. Eddy answered: "Now you've helped me." She saw instantly that he was letting the enemy use him as a channel to reach her instead of meeting this evil and overcoming it in his own thought.

The students were such babes in their comprehension of *how to work* for their Leader and for the cause. At one time when Mrs. Eddy was giving them vital instruction in this regard, she said to Laura Sargent, "Go write it, go write it." Laura returned with this:

> She said when we take up our watch, we do not help *her with our* thought; we simply clear our own thought of its belief of evil, and this is getting rid of *our* thought and getting out of God's way so the light can shine through, and this blessed light helps us and all in its shining. This is the blessed, blessed way from sense to Soul.

Mrs. Eddy read what Laura had written and then wrote upon the page, "Well done, — Mother."

On May 24 Mrs. Eddy said to her metaphysical workers:

> There are three things to keep before us continually: to have one God — one Mind; to love our neighbor as ourselves; and do unto others as we would have others do unto us. To have one Mind means for all to work alike; — not you work in your work and I in my work, but work together. It is time for us today to be Christian Scientists and keep these points before us, by asking ourselves these questions every time before doing anything.

While the Leader was meeting the malice of the world at Pleasant View the Cause prospered in the world as never before. A May *Sentinel* told of phenomenal sucess in London. Bicknell Young had lectured to an audience of ninety-nine hundred. The Leader may well have asked What of the healing? Perhaps there had been some, for that was not uncommon at lectures, but the letter from London did not mention it.

One student from London, after studying Christian Science, had come to America for the express purpose of serving the Leader. But when Mrs. McKenzie had taken Adelaide Still to meet Mrs. Eddy the interview was short, and the Leader did not accept Miss Still's service. However, this English woman did have a true desire to serve the Leader, and when a position to help in the kitchen was offered her in May, she accepted it and moved to Pleasant View. In this position she did not meet with Mrs. Eddy and was not included in the morning lessons for the mental workers. On May 25 part of the Leader's lesson was:

> God is All. To have God is to have all — harmony. Discord comes from looking away from all, thinking there is something else.

The next day her lesson included:

> What I am reaching is the spiritual; the material fights it and I fight the material; it will do it to you; the more spiritual the thought, the more will you be fought. That which takes the place of God and creates men and women, and sees everything material, will fight the spiritual. We must see everything spiritual.
>
> To sense I am on the cross. Am I? No. What makes me on the cross? The belief that I am there. . . . See me (and others) all right, as a spiritual idea, and not on the cross; then you will see me as I am.

The Leader's lesson of May 30 dealt with reversal and true law. She said:

> God's laws are eternal; they cannot be reversed; they *stand.* In your work you declare the Truth about things; know those declarations *cannot* be reversed. I have for forty years stood with God through all this effort to reverse my work. If I had allowed the devil to reverse my work where would it have been? No. I have stood and carried this Cause in spite of it and all of you can do the same.
>
> Are the laws of health to be relied upon? No. They are material. Are the laws of husbands, wives, sons, etc. to be relied upon? No. . . .
>
> God is infinite; is there anything else? No. He is the only lawgiver. Hold to it. There is but one law and that is the law of Love, Life.

CHAPTER XLII

FROM CROSS TO CROWN

For the wisdom of this world is foolishness with God. For it is written, He taketh the wise in their own craftiness. — PAUL

1907

CHANDLER and the New York World probed all the county records regarding Mrs. Eddy's property and made much of a fact they uncovered. Mrs. Eddy had not paid her taxes in full!

The prosperity of Concord was largely due to Mrs. Eddy's residence there. She was undoubtedly the city's most generous donor to every worthy cause, but when, because of her wealth and fame, the city fathers elected to mulct her by overtaxing Pleasant View, she made a silent protest. She had the money with which to pay this excessive tax, but it was God and not the city fathers that dictated *all* her acts. So the Leader of Christian Science paid what she felt was just and right, and the city did not press her for the unpaid balance. Gilbert Carpenter said of this:

> This country belongs to its citizens, and the government of country, state and city functions solely for the benefit of the common citizen. When she found . . . the city fathers [embracing] the opportunity to mulct her, when it came to taxes, she protested in the only way at her command, and that was to refuse to pay them in full. And her attitude is an example for her followers. Whereas they should be willing to do all that is right to support their country in every way, they should never sit back and submit to injustice without a protest . . .

The injustice to and persecution of Mrs. Eddy continued daily in the newspapers with no apparent progress on the case. On June 5 Streeter and Hollis filed a motion for Mrs. Eddy requesting an immediate investigation and speedy decision. On the same day,

June 5, Judge Chamberlin denied the trustees' motion to replace the "next friends."

Two days later, June 7, Chandler filed an amendment requesting a jury trial and, according to Michael Meehan, "contended long and earnestly" for same.

Mrs. Eddy had many conferences with her lawyers at Pleasant View, and it was probably about this time that God told her the steps to take which differed from their learned opinions. The attorneys were all in agreement as to the proper course of action, but they could not convince Mrs. Eddy with all their arguments. In her *Life of Samuel J. Elder,* biography of her father, Elder's daughter wrote of this interview at Pleasant View:

> They made no impression. Mrs. Eddy was obdurate. The opposite position was the only one which could be sustained. She spoke quietly and reasonably but imperiously. Her brilliant black eyes shone with determination. The lawyers were very patient with her. She was an old woman, nearly as old, my father recalled, as his mother. Her person commanded deference, but clearly her legal opinion was valueless. The conference had reached this *impasse* when the hour came for Mrs. Eddy's drive. She dismissed her lawyers who adjourned to Mr. Streeter's office to continue their discussion.

A very short time later a negro boy, who was a servant in Mrs. Eddy's household, appeared at Mr. Streeter's office door saying that Mrs. Eddy was outside in her carriage and wished to speak to Mr. Elder. He went out immediately, and when he came to her carriage she reached out her hand and quietly laid it upon his arm:

> "Mr. Elder," she said with great impressiveness, looking steadily at him, "you are wrong in this matter which we have been discussing. I wish that you would return to the other gentlemen and ask them to reconsider it. Will you do that?" He assented reluctantly. Then she repeated, "Mr. Elder, you are wrong." Her carriage drove off and Mr. Elder slowly remounted the steps to the office. The situation was awkward, but having given his assent, Mr. Elder could do no less. He returned to the conference, told of Mrs. Eddy's request and insisted that they reconsider their decision, all the time regarding the matter in the same light as did his colleagues. So they went over all their arguments again. The result was that they reversed their decision, followed the lines insisted upon by Mrs. Eddy, and during the trial it became indubitably clear that she had been right.

"The children of this world are in their generation wiser than the children of light." But their day is past. It was the wisdom of this world that was seeking to overcome the Woman, and she saw the subtilty of their plan and foiled it.

It is doubtful that her attorneys agreed with the course she insisted upon, but they acquiesced. On Monday morning, June 10, at 11 A.M. their motion of June 5 was to be heard, but to the surprise of all present Mr. Streeter "announced that he would not at that time press upon the court for consideration the motion then pending, and asked to have a hearing on the consideration of it suspended for the time being."

The world and the *World* were caught off guard. This was not what they had expected nor planned. Chandler immediately filed a motion demanding that a hearing for the motion be ordered. He also filed requesting the court to allot from Mrs. Eddy's estate funds to pay for the "next friends" action. This latter motion and that for trial by jury were both denied about the same time that Fred W. Baker withdrew from the case.

Mrs. Eddy in the meantime was pursuing a new course. She granted an interview at Pleasant View to one of America's foremost journalists. Arthur Brisbane had been Sunday editor for Pulitzer's *New York World* before he became managing editor of Hearst's *New York Evening Journal.* His was one of the first newspaper columns to become syndicated, and by the 1920's he was the highest paid journalist in the United States if not in the world. But he will be remembered by future generations for his interview on the eighth of June in 1907.

On that Saturday afternoon at about two o'clock he approached what he described as "extremely simple and unpretentious, a plain little frame dwelling, situated rather close to a country roadway on the side of a most beautiful New Hampshire valley." That was the journalist's impression of Pleasant View. He said the house was furnished very plainly and scrupulously neat, and also that those who called it "A House of Mystery" were "writers of strong imagination":

> As a matter of fact, the house is about as mysterious as the average little New England home. . . . All the doors, downstairs and upstairs, are open.

General Streeter who was also present on this afternoon had talked with Mr. Brisbane prior to the interview. The writer was deeply impressed by Mrs. Eddy's beauty and youthful appearance, and her spirituality caused him to write, "nobody could see this beautiful and venerable woman and ever again speak of her except in terms of affectionate reverence and sympathy." He regretted that he could not report what Mrs. Eddy wore, because "with Mrs. Eddy you see only the face, the very earnest eyes, and the beautiful quiet expression . . .":

> When she was asked to discuss the lawsuit affecting her, and other matters now in the public mind, she became very earnest, absolutely concentrated in expression, voice, and choice of words. She spoke sometimes leaning back in her chair, with her eyes turned upward, sometimes leaning forward, replying to questions with great intensity. She said to one of her friends, "Please close the door," and then talked freely on all the business matters that affect her. . . .
>
> Asked why the lawsuit had been started, seeking to take away from her control of her money and of her actions, Mrs. Eddy replied in a deep, earnest voice that could easily have been heard all over the biggest of her churches:
>
> "Greed of gold, young man. They are not interested in me, I am sorry to say, but in my money, and in the desire to control that. They say they want to help me. They never tried to help me when I was working hard years ago and when help would have been so welcome. . . ."

Streeter had impressed upon Brisbane before the interview his desire that the writer ascertain positively for himself Mrs. Eddy's business competence. So for at least half an hour he asked detailed questions "with an insistence that in the case of a woman of Mrs. Eddy's age would be most unusual and unnecessary."

> Mrs. Eddy's mind on all points brought out was perfectly clear, and her answers were instantaneous. . . .

She explained clearly her reasons for entrusting her property to trustees, and described the character of each:

> In praising her cousin, a former congressman and at present a member of the legislature, Mrs. Eddy laughingly described him as a very good man "and as honest as any lawyer can be." She laughed more like a young girl than a woman of eighty-six as she said this, looking quizzically at her thoroughly trusted lawyer, General Streeter.

Brisbane tested the Leader's ability in reading and writing during the interview which became three separate talks during the course of the afternoon. She read aloud and wrote a note at his request. She also wrote her name upon a photograph of herself, which had not before been seen, and gave Mr. Brisbane permission to publish it. His lengthy interview appeared in the *Cosmopolitan Magazine* for August, wherein the author stated that he was "not a believer in Christian Science, but a believer in material science, in non-sectarian government, and in the absolute right of Christian Scientists to

MARY BAKER EDDY
Photograph given to Arthur Brisbane on June 8, 1907

believe whatever they choose." Brisbane's impressions could be summed up in these words:

> The lawyers who oppose her would like to show that Mrs. Eddy is not fit, mentally or physically, to take care of herself or of her fortune, which is considerable. They would like to remove her from her present surroundings, and make her physically subject to the will of others appointed to control her. Success in this effort, in the opinion of the writer, would be shameful, a degradation to all womanhood and old age.
>
> Mrs. Eddy said in her interview, "Young man, I made my money with my pen, just as you do, and I have a right to it." Mrs. Eddy not only has a right to it, but she has the mind to control it.

On the day Arthur Brisbane was at Pleasant View the Executive Members meeting in the original Mother Church sent a message of appreciation to the Leader. The next day, June 9, was Communion

Sunday at The Mother Church. The auditorium was well filled, but there was not the general attendance from all over the world because of the recent by-law inviting members to attend only triennially. Mrs. Stetson attended both meetings, and there must have been something against her in the Boston papers that Sunday, for she wrote Mrs. Eddy from the Hotel Touraine where she was staying:

June 9, 1907

My precious Leader:

I am glad I know that I am in the hands of God, not of men. These reports are only the revival of a lie which I have not heard for a long time. It is a renewed attack upon me and my loyal students, to turn me from following in the footsteps of Christ, by making another attempt to dishearten me, and make me weary of the struggle to demonstrate my trust in God to deliver me from the "accuser of our brethren." It is a diabolical attempt to separate me from you, as my Leader and Teacher, and thus deprive *you* of your faithful student and her faithful students, who are living, as far as they can demonstrate, according to your teachings in Science and Health. We are striving to emulate your holy life, and to trust in God, as you do, in every hour of sorrow or joy.

My disloyal students and others are determined to destroy me and my work. Their efforts to prevent me from loving and obeying you, as Leader and Teacher, are futile to terrify me. I shall follow your example of trust in God, so far as I can, and God will never forsake me, nor any who puts his trust in Him.

Oh, dearest, it is such a lie! No one who knows us can believe this. It is vicarious atonement. Has the enemy no more argument to use, that it has to go back to this? It is exhausting its resources and I hope the end is near. You know my love for you, beloved; and my students love you as their Leader and Teacher; they follow your teachings and lean on the "sustaining infinite." They put their trust in God, and recognize you as the messenger who brings to them the message of salvation from sin, sickness, and death, through making their atonement with the creator, the one God, who is the source and supply of every need.

They who refuse to accept you as God's messenger, or ignore the message which you bring, will not get up by some other way, but will come short of salvation. I see the subtle suggestion of the enemy and am not afraid. My trust is in God. I know, and my students know that we must work out our own problems as you work out yours — but we shall follow your teachings and strive to emulate your example, and love you as our Leader. *Your* Father is *our* Father. He will protect *us* as He *has* and *ever will* protect *you.* We have much to do to stand in this hour, but we trust in God.

Dearly beloved, we are not ascending out of sense as fast as we desire, but we are trusting in God and are putting off false mentality

> and putting on the Mind of Christ. This lie cannot disturb you nor me. I love you, my students love you, and we never send out such thoughts as are mentioned.
>
> Your loving child,
> Augusta

Augusta was experiencing the very thing the Leader had described in a lesson to her household workers a few days earlier: "What I am reaching is the spiritual; the material fights it . . . it will do it to you; the more spiritual the thought, the more will you be fought." Mrs. Eddy did not need this letter to know that Mrs. Stetson was sincere and dedicated and that the stories were lies, but the field did; so she had it published in full in the *Sentinel* of June 22.

The Leader was well aware of Augusta's steadfastness as well as of the envy and jealousy this devoted disciple aroused in others. Mr. Carpenter said:

> Mrs. Stetson had the finest church in the Field, she had the wealthiest and most socially prominent students in New York among her congregation and association. These students would give her anything she wanted, and they did give her much. Her students who were business men advised her in her investments so that she might be prosperous and live in elegance. All this served to inflame the envy of others who were not as wealthy or prominent as she was. . . .
>
> I can recall that Mrs. Stetson's errors formed the chief topic of conversation among many careless students. The gossip about her was equal to that in an old people's home! Yet she was a brilliant woman with a recognized ability and understanding of leadership far greater than any other student I ever knew outside of our Leader. The latter knew about the envy and jealousy aimed at Mrs. Stetson and perceived that the whole thing was animal magnetism.

Perhaps Sarah J. Clark was at Pleasant View by June 2 when Mrs. Eddy said to her mental workers:

> When Christian Scientists come to Pleasant View, I demand of them that they leave their belongings and take up the cross. You cannot win the crown without bearing the cross.

The Leader had *so much* to give to her disciples, and she knew how soon this great privilege of sitting at her feet was to be removed from them. She yearned to give them more in the passage from sense to Soul "in which," she told them, "we must each take part," but so few were willing to leave "their belongings and take up the cross."

Clara Shannon came from England for a visit in 1907, very

possibly to attend Communion in The Mother Church plus the annual meeting on Tuesday, June 11. When Miss Shannon visited Pleasant View, Mrs. Eddy hoped that she would remain with her, but she told Clara if she felt she must return to England she should begin teaching there. If Clara had known that the golden opportunity she was passing by would soon be unavailable she probably would have remained with the Leader, but she did not. She returned to England and held her first class there in 1907. In later years Miss Shannon titled her memoirs "Golden Memories by One who is grateful to be able to testify to the truth about our beloved and revered Leader."

On June 15 Mrs. Eddy granted a second press interview. This time the fortunate journalist was Edwin J. Park of the *Boston Globe.* When he was ushered into Mrs. Eddy's study at 2 P.M. that Saturday, the Leader arose, stepping forward, and welcomed him with a firm handshake and the words:

> Mr. Park, I am very glad to see you. I am glad to welcome you here, for I am aware of the fairness with which you and the *Boston Globe* have treated me.*

In his brief description of Mrs. Eddy's attire Mr. Park noted that she "was dressed in a black silk dress, with white lace about her throat and wrists, that her lace collar was caught at the throat with a diamond sunburst of great beauty and undoubted value." Mr. Park had no idea of the significance of Mrs. Eddy's diamond brooch.

For some time Mrs. Eddy had had a crown of diamonds breast pin which had been given to her by a devoted student. This pin was "of great beauty and undoubted value." Could it have been what Mr. Park described as a sunburst?

In public appearances in the past the Leader had *always* worn her *cross* of diamonds. On June 8, one week earlier, Arthur Brisbane had noted that she wore "no jewelry of any kind." She had removed the cross, but on that date General Streeter had not yet asked the court to suspend the hearing. Now the tide has turned. This is the Ascension Era and she has risen! It is most probable that she is now wearing her diamond crown.

When Mr. Park asked Mrs. Eddy to tell him something about the "next friends" litigation, she replied immediately with the trace of a smile: "You mean the 'next friends' *alias* 'next enemies' do you not?"

Later in the interview Mrs. Eddy "summoned the Bohemian housekeeper to the study." This was probably Anna Machacek whom Park described as:

*Interview in Appendix F.

> A young woman who had been recommended to Mrs. Eddy by a Western Christian Scientist and who is greatly appreciated by Mrs. Eddy.
>
> The housekeeper was plainly flustered at her unexpected summons before the head of the house, and she started in to apologize for her appearance, although there was nothing about it that required an apology. She was a neat, wholesome-looking young woman in the attire in which she had been at her duties about the house.

Everyone loved Anna beginning with the Western practitioner who had first found the lonely girl in a Czech colony in Cedar Rapids, Iowa. Shy Anna had fled from her European farm home to escape the marriage her prosperous father had arranged and was lonely in this New World. Her new friend taught her to read and write English coordinating Anna's Bohemian Bible with the English Bible and Science and Health; and she soon recommended the willing, cheerful girl as a laundress at Pleasant View. Anna's fine qualities were not unappreciated and it was not long before she was promoted to housekeeper. When she left Pleasant View everyone missed her.

Mr. Park probably saw Anna after she had returned at Mrs. Eddy's request to serve again at Pleasant View. William B. Johnson wrote to her:

> Our dear Anna:
>
> I am so glad to know that you are again with our beloved Leader. She loves you and I know you love her and your willingness to leave all to serve her will be rewarded.

Anna's willingness was rewarded. By 1909 this sweet, eager young woman was a successful Christian Science practitioner in Cedar Rapids.

On June 16 when Edwin Park's interview appeared in the *Globe,* Hermann Hering induced the Leader to give another interview of an entirely different sort. One Christian Scientist visiting the Concord church in June was Eva Thompson from Burlington, Iowa. Eva was also a good friend of the George Glover family in Lead, South Dakota and felt that she might be able to afford a reconciliation between Mrs. Eddy and her son. During their interview Mrs. Eddy wrote a short note which she asked Miss Thompson to deliver to her son.

George Glover and his daughter were back in Lead in the summer of 1907, and when Miss Thompson arrived at their home her reception was less cordial than usual. She wrote in her reminiscences:

> I, however made nothing of it, and delivered to Mr. Glover the

letter which his mother had written. He retired with other members of the family to read the message and left me with Mrs. Glover. On his return, Mr. Glover asked me if Mr. Frye hadn't gotten hold of me. I assured him that I hadn't even seen Mr. Frye, but that through Mr. Hering, had obtained an interview with his mother, that all the advances had been made by me, and that unsolicited, I had gone to Concord seeking ways and means of reaching his mother in order to get help for him. But Mr. Glover did not believe a word I said.

After a short conversation, the situation began to ease a little. . . . After that there seemed to be a kind, receptive thought, and I spent a very pleasant and profitable two weeks.

I would like to mention the physical conditions I found there. Mr. Glover was in a very dazed condition all the time, constantly falling asleep during a conversation, and later going sound asleep during the church services. Mary manifested a very angry eruption on her face. After a few days of reading the Lesson morning and evening and lovingly correcting the suspicions and misconceptions in regard to his mother, these physical errors gradually disappeared. . . .

During all the time I was in the home, every day and part of the evenings, a young man from New York would visit them. He said that he represented a group of wealthy people in New York who wished to help Mr. Glover develop his mine. However, with all this talk, he took no steps toward that end. . . . He seemed to have convinced Mr. Glover that he was his friend and was there to help him. . . . I recognized him as being a regular detective and agent [hypnotist?] of Mrs. Eddy's enemies, and told Mr. Glover so in no uncertain terms. The thought I held to all the time was, "Mental malpractice cannot put man to sleep to his best interests." After that Mr. Glover was wide awake both mentally and physically, and would listen to what I had to say without falling asleep.

On the last day of Eva Thompson's visit the Glovers brought Mrs. Eddy's letter, which Miss Thompson had delivered to them, to the breakfast table and read it aloud. Mrs. Eddy had written to her son on June 16:

I love you, my only child. Why do you allow yourself to be used to bring this grief and trouble on your own aged mother?

As ever affectionately,
Mary B. G. Eddy

Eva burst into tears, and before long the whole family was crying. Before she left that day George Glover told her that he would do all in his power to end the suit. A few days later he left for the East for that purpose, but that is another episode.

The day after Mrs. Eddy saw Eva Thompson and wrote the note to her son, an attorney in Baltimore, Maryland, John Henry Keene, wrote an appreciative letter to the Leader. A non-Christian Scientist, Keene had come to the defence of Mrs. Eddy and her cause in 1902 with a pamphlet titled *Christian Science and Its Enemies* which action Mrs. Eddy had acknowledged and appreciated. However, Keene was fighting fire with fire which method Mrs. Eddy could not endorse, much to Keene's disappointment. His letter of June 17, 1907 indicates that he may have begun to appreciate the Leader's pacific methods:

> Reverend and Most Revered Leader:
>
> Deeply discerning and serene in her meekness, calm in this insolent hour of shamelessness and serpentine craft, bowing her anointed head to the axe of persecution, the unexampled Founder of Christian Science is making one of the holiest demonstrations of Christ.
>
> Your wonderful course is enlightening mortal thought throughout America, Europe, and in the far-off islands of the seas. Towering above the highest in spiritual power and grandeur, what canonized saint since the days of Christ, has been the pioneer of so vast, so fundamental a revelation, and so religious a reformation as Christian Science? Made a spectacle unto the world, your grand struggle with the crisis of error constrains the heartfelt sympathy for you of enlightened Christendom.
>
> The sons and daughters of Christian Science behold in their sacred Leader the restorer of an uncompromising high spiritual discipline, not less than the loving mother strengthening the weak hands, confirming the feeble knees; full of sympathy, full of sweetness, full of gentleness, full of patience, full of allowances, full of longsuffering, and of that goodness which is the fruit of the Spirit.
>
> The watch of your night is far spent.
> The new-born day will right soon be upon us,
> Fair as the new-born star that gilds the morn.
>
> Reverently,
> John Henry Keene

On June 27, "in this insolent hour of . . . serpentine craft," Judge Chamberlin appointed a Master and ordered an investigation to determine "whether said Mary Baker G. Eddy is competent to intelligently manage, control, and conduct her financial affairs and property rights."

The next day, June 28, Mrs. Eddy granted a third press interview, — this time to the very well-known foreign correspondent for the Chicago *Record-Herald,* William E. Curtis, who was spending several days in Concord and other parts of New Hampshire. On his return to Chicago his article in the *Record-Herald* was headlined:

MRS. EDDY, MARVEL IN MENTAL ACTIVITY
Vitality Wonderful in Woman of Eighty-six Years,
Who Still Seems in Perfect Health

Mr. Curtis had recently returned from China, and Michael Meehan, who accompanied him to this interview, recalled in later years that Curtis:

> made a statement about affairs in China, touching which Mrs. Eddy asked for more detailed and definite information, and quite unconsciously, seemingly, she took the topic entirely out of his grasp, and . . . dwelt on the details of the Chinese situation, with such a wonderful insight and with such intimate knowledge of its social, political and economic conditions, as to quite confound the man. . . .
>
> As we drove from Pleasant View, Mr. Curtis marveled how a woman who so completely excluded the world could possibly know so much about the world's affairs, and particularly how she could have acquired such accurate and comprehensive acquaintance with the history and national habits of the Chinese, a people so little known, and with the court customs and the unpublished intrigues of its rulers. As we parted, he said, "Just one more surprise, one more instance of where we came to preach, and remained to pray."

In his article in the *Record-Herald* on July 19 Curtis said:

> Every one who has come to Concord impressed with the belief that there was some reason or justification for the lawsuit instituted by the so-called "next friends," and who has had opportunities to talk with this remarkable woman, has gone away with the well-defined conviction that among sane people Mrs. Eddy is one of the most sane, that among responsible people she is one of the most responsible, and that among competent and successful business men and women she is one of the most competent and most successful.

Michael Meehan editorialized in the Concord *Daily Patriot* that Curtis' words about Mrs. Eddy "will be read by millions of Americans and will be believed by them." Meehan also quoted Curtis' words in describing their visit:

> There was no difficulty in securing an interview with Mrs. Eddy. As soon as Mr. Meehan, editor of the *Concord Patriot,* notified her household, I received an invitation to call at Pleasant View at two o'clock and he went with me. . . .
>
> As we entered her study, Mrs. Eddy arose from an easy chair in which she had been sitting beside a desk covered with correspondence and books and gave me a hearty greeting. Her hand is thin and almost transparent. . . . She was dressed simply in a white shirtwaist,

> trimmed with a good deal of lace, and a black skirt. A gauze scarf was thrown over her shoulders and a brooch of diamonds with delicate settings in the shape of a coronet was fastened at her neck. Her hair is abundant and perfectly white, and is dressed low on her forehead with graceful waves. . . . Her eyes are full, clear, and bright. Her grasp is quite strong and indicates considerable physical vitality. Indeed, I have never seen a woman eighty-six years of age with greater physical or mental vigor.
>
> As we stood for a few moments exchanging greetings, my companion slipped his hand under her arm. She drew away impatiently, inquiring:
>
> "Why do you take hold of my arm?"
>
> "To support you," was the reply.
>
> "I need no support," said Mrs. Eddy, rather independently, "but I think it is better that we all sit down."
>
> She indicated a chair beside her table for me and another for my friend, and resumed her seat in a large easy chair upholstered in red velvet, which she had been occupying before we came into the room. I watched her very closely — every motion that she made — because her physical and mental condition is now the subject of litigation; but during the interview, which lasted about twenty minutes, I did not see the slightest sign of the "senile debility," "mental infirmity," or "physical incapacity" which has been alleged as the basis of a suit to deprive her of the care of her property.

Probably most readers of this interview were interested in or amused by the rebuff to Mr. Meehan's solicitous action. But Mr. Curtis' account carried a far more important message to the Christian Scientist, if there was one at that time who could read symbols. There is no doubt that the brooch Mrs. Eddy was wearing fastened at her neck was her *crown* of diamonds.

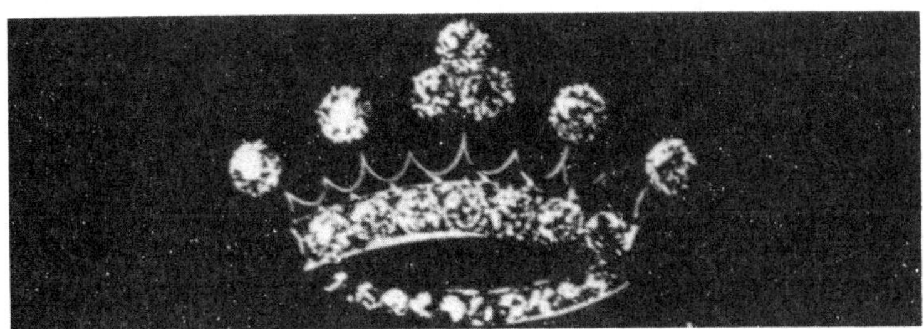

MARY BAKER EDDY'S CROWN OF DIAMONDS

CHAPTER XLIII

SUBDUING THE STORMS

When it looks like thunder and lightning, handle it; . . . You can do this, . . . When you have the first indication — forestall it.

— MARY BAKER EDDY

1907

THE Leader had risen, and on a few significant occasions replaced her diamond *cross* with her *crown* of diamonds. She also continued her recent policy of making herself available and on several occasions invited students to Pleasant View for a visit and instruction. Recent callers included the Hannas, Bicknell Young, and Annie Knott. Early in July she invited members of The Mother Church to visit her at Pleasant View on Independence Day.

One morning shortly after the July 4 visit Mrs. Eddy opened the swinging door from the dining room to enter the kitchen just as a housekeeper's assistant she had not seen before was coming out. The Leader put her hand on the girl's arm as she said, "Good morning," and looked into her face very searchingly as if reading her character. She kept her hand on her arm as she spoke to each one in the kitchen. Then Mrs. Eddy went into the library and called Laura Sargent to ask the name of the new assistant. She learned that Miss Minnie Adelaide Still had been there several weeks but this was the first time they had seen one another.

An amended By-law in the July 6 *Sentinel* abolished the General Association of Teachers in the Leader's gradual method of first making their meetings triennial.

As Mrs. Eddy had risen, Truth's voice was lifted higher throughout the world, and "the higher Truth lifts her voice, the louder will error scream." All Christian Scientists need to learn how to meet these fearful-appearing, shrill outbursts of evil, and for this purpose the Leader called many to Pleasant View and to Concord.

One of those who came to help at this time was Victoria Sargent, Laura's sister. During the several weeks that Mrs. Sargent was working in Concord, she was also called to Pleasant View a number of times. On one of these occasions she said to the Leader:

> My students recognize you to be God's witness and mouthpiece. They are convinced that God is guiding you in this work which you are carrying on for the Cause of Christian Science. They feel that you fulfill the prophecies of the Scriptures — that you represent the God-woman mentioned in the Apocalypse.

Mrs. Eddy responded immediately pointing her finger upward and saying, "That is from above." Victoria was often inspired "from above," and she was also greatly appreciated by the Mother in Israel. At one time when Victoria was at home in Wisconsin, Laura, who was in Concord with the Leader wrote to her sister:

> I wish you could have heard the loving word that Mother said of you today. She told me to forget self and be self-sacrificing as you are, and then she said of you, "She is God's anointed child." I knew these words would cheer your dear heart and give you strength to do whatever God requires.

The students working in Concord as well as those at Pleasant View all felt that they were working for the Leader. None knew that it was just the opposite, that she was working for all of them. She longed to take them farther, faster, but few were truly ready to devote their lives to Christ's cause. At the end of one year's service almost all who came were still in the primary department in the Leader's eyes, but they were very eager to return to their homes and their own interests. But while there, they were all learning a great deal. The malice hurled at Christian Science, Mrs. Eddy, and Pleasant View caused the Leader to keep her mental workers working on every aspect of error as it presented itself. One day early in July it appeared as a cyclone. Clara McKee recorded later:

> During this trial it seemed that every phase of evil presented itself to be met and destroyed. One day Mrs. Eddy called her students into her study and pointed to a very black cloud, shaped like a cornucopia, coming toward the house in direct line with her front study window. She asked each one to go to a window and face it, and to realize that there were no destructive elements in God's creation. Although appearing to whirl straight toward Pleasant View, a mile or so away the cyclone changed its course and went around Concord into the mountains, doing very little damage.

Shortly thereafter Mrs. McKee, who was Mrs. Eddy's personal maid, reminded the Leader that her year was nearly up and she desired to return to her home and office. How the Leader yearned for students who chose to stay with her and learn Christ's way, but she graciously let them return to the world.

On Friday, July 12, after the Leader had taken her morning walk through the downstairs rooms she asked Clara McKee to send Miss Still to her. The cook's name was Minnie Weygandt, so Minnie Adelaide Still was called Adelaide. Mrs. Eddy asked Adelaide a few questions about Christian Science and her teacher, and then said, "Did you see the storm last week?" The storm was so severe that it had seemed to Adelaide as if the house would be taken off its foundations, and she assured Mrs. Eddy that she had seen it. The Leader said, "You know it was divine Love that saved us, don't you?"

"Yes, Mrs. Eddy," answered Adelaide.

"Will you be my maid?" was Mrs. Eddy's next question. Miss Still told her that she would very much like to, but she had never done work of that kind. Mrs. Eddy responded, "I know, dear, but I will teach you. Now go back to your work and say nothing to anyone about it, and when I'm ready I will send for you." Just as Adelaide was leaving she added, "I have been asking God to send me the right one and I believe He has."

Judge Chamberlin had appointed Hon. Edgar Aldrich as Master to determine Mrs. Eddy's competence, and on July 5 he appointed two co-masters to assist Judge Aldrich, one of whom was an expert alienist. Streeter filed an exception to this action on Mrs. Eddy's behalf on July 11. The defence also took independent action on this issue by requesting an expert, critical report from an alienist of their choosing, Dr. Edward French, Superintendant of the Massachusetts Hospital for the Insane at Medfield.

The alienist examined Mrs. Eddy on July 10, and in his report* stated that "there was not the least evidence of mental weakness or incompetence." During the course of the examination Dr. French asked Mrs. Eddy to write a letter in his presence. Part of what she wrote for him stated:

> I rise at about 6 o'clock A.M. eat my breakfast at about 7 A.M. Open my Bible and read whatever I open to with a mental invocation that the divine Love give me grace, meekness, understanding and wisdom for each hour of this day. . . .
>
> I daily look into the rooms of my house to see that neatness and order are preserved and afternoons I take my daily drive.

Mrs. Emilie B. Hulin of Brooklyn, New York, had been called to Pleasant View on several occasions, and she was one of the mental workers there in the summer of 1907. One day in Mrs. Hulin's

*Dr. French's Report in Appendix G.

presence Mrs. Eddy was looking rather depressed, and, as if thinking aloud, said, "I don't know, perhaps they will have their way." Mrs. Hulin responded, "Mother, they will not. We love you. You will win." And she felt that the Leader was cheered.

Mrs. Eddy loved Pleasant View. At one time when Henrietta Chanfrau was there Mrs. Eddy had said to her: "Henrietta, if I ever go away from here to another house it will be to be delivered up to my enemies." Sibyl Wilbur said that she was non-suited for the enemy "in this dream home, so simple and altogether lovely. The spacious and handsome home of Chestnut Hill was then devised and planned by others." In mid-July, although her household knew it not, Alfred Farlow and Archibald McLellan were seeking to find a suitable property for Mrs. Eddy near Boston.

Mid-July was a very important time for Adelaide Still, for it was July 14 when Mrs. Eddy asked her to begin as her personal maid. Adelaide was younger in years and experience than the mental workers in the home, and though she was a practitioner she had not been taught by the Leader as had most of her workers or watchers as they were often called. Adelaide was not one of the metaphysical workers, but she was well aware of their function and described it as follows:

> The Watchers' duties were to take turns in working impersonally for the home day and night, for the protection of our Leader and the house, and to handle specific questions and problems which might come up for the home or the Cause. During the Next Friends' Suit, the Watchers watched continually.

But the lessons and instructions for the metaphysical workers were only a part of the daily routine. There were also lessons which included the other workers. Mrs. Eddy began her morning lessons by opening her Bible (and Science and Health) and reading aloud the message God gave her. On the morning of Monday, July 15 she opened to Romans 14:22, "Hast thou faith? Have it to thyself before God. Happy is he that condemneth not himself in that thing which he alloweth." The Leader said, as Miss Still recalled:

> We should allow nothing which we cannot justify. He who sees sin and condemns it not will suffer for it. Can we work out a problem correctly if one figure is not in accord with the principle of mathematics? Can I enter the kingdom of heaven if I allow one sin? Will not that destroy the whole problem?

One devoted disciple endeavoring to follow the Leader's teachings, wrote her on this same Monday:

> Your wonderful letter reached me ... I rose into newness of life with the baptism which came from your loving words and watch-care.
>
> ... I shall continue my earnest endeavor to follow and obey the "Star of Concord," whom I have loved and followed so long ...
>
> I find that I need more and more the Mind of Christ to enable me to demonstrate over the higher and subtler claims of error ... The law of Love must be fulfilled in me if I am to continue to be a worthy disciple of my Leader and Teacher. Love alone will deliver from malice, hatred, and envy, which seem today to be aroused to destroy the Christian Science soldier.
>
> ... I am strong in faith that I shall endure unto the end of the belief of a power opposed to good.
>
> ... I sometimes feel that I am the least of all the flock, but I know in whom I believe, and I stand firmly clasping my Father's hand, trustingly awaiting divine guidance in hours which seem darkest. A rift in the cloud always reveals my faithful Leader and Teacher beckoning me to come up higher ...
>
> I shall not faint in the race, dearest. ... With unfailing faith in Love and Her chosen messenger, I am, as ever,
>
> Your grateful, loving child,
> Augusta

This faithful student had also adopted the Leader's practice and method of turning to God, for she said in her post script: "When I had finished my letter to you, I asked God to speak to me. I opened my Bible to II Thes. 3:3-5 and was comforted."

Almost immediately Mrs. Stetson received a rebuke (as did students in the household repeatedly), and on July 18 she wrote:

> When I received your loving warning and rebuke to error I was *aroused* ... I was *awakened.*
>
> ... I should have been fortified and have escaped the snare. However, I am awake, and will profit by the reproof and rise ...

The Leader was always cheered when a student did not react to a rebuke, but profited from it. She wrote to her darling Augusta on July 20:

> Your dear letter assuring me of your compliance with the strict demand — "Come out from the world and be ye separate" — in the sense of Science — comforts me.
>
> O, for a closer, clearer, nearer view of the divine Science of being that we all may be perfect even as our Father the Principle thereof is perfect. This we must be in order to be Christian Scientists.

She was ever endeavoring to turn her students to the spiritual, *here* and *now.* She had said to her household workers the day before, "Life understood spiritually is heaven here." If she could only waken them to this fact they need not lose the guidance nor the presence of their Mother in Israel.

A few days later in the Friday morning lesson, July 26, Mrs. Eddy opened Science and Health, even as she did her Bible, and read to her students the message from God on pages 38:21-39:30

> Jesus experienced few of the pleasures of the physical senses, but his sufferings were the fruits of other people's sins, not of his own. The eternal Christ, his spiritual selfhood, never suffered. Jesus mapped out the path for others. . . .
>
> Meekly our Master met the mockery of his unrecognized grandeur. . . .
>
> The educated belief that Soul is in the body causes mortals to regard death as a friend, as a stepping-stone out of mortality into immortality and bliss. The Bible calls death an enemy, and Jesus overcame death and the grave instead of yielding to them. He was "the Way." To him, therefore, death was not the threshold over which he must pass into living glory.
>
> *"Now,"* cried the apostle, "is the accepted time;" . . . Now is the time for so-called material pain and material pleasures to pass away . . . To break this earthly spell, mortals must get the true idea and divine Principle of all that really exists and governs the universe harmoniously.

Every word she read applied to Christ Mary as well as to Christ Jesus. While the Leader was daily endeavoring to open her students' eyes and take them up higher, the serpent was ever at her heel. *McClure's* magazine article for July was largely a whitewash of Richard Kennedy, ridicule of Mrs. Eddy, and a recount of the Salem witchcraft trial instituted by Arens. Miss Milmine, however, by-passed Arens and called it "Mrs. Eddy's attempt to revive the witch horror." The August issue continued this false "history" of malicious gossip, while the Boston papers continued with hostile headlines such as the one on July 30 asking for the arrest of Mrs. Eddy's secretaries, Calvin Frye and H. Cornell Wilson.

The editor of the *Grand Rapids* (Mich.) *Evening Press* addressed a question to "this aged woman of world-wide renown" "requesting the courtesy of a reply." His question was: "What is nearest and dearest to your heart today?" Mrs. Eddy did give him the courtesy of a reply *(My.* 271) stating in her brief response: "what is 'nearest and dearest' to my heart is an honest man or woman . . . Goodness is greatness . . ."

Senator Chandler's ability was exceptional. Had goodness been his motivation he could have risen to greatness, but he was doing his utmost to have "this aged woman," Mrs. Eddy, dragged into court by physical force, although he did *not* want the Glovers in the courtroom to hear the other side of the story he had told them. Very possibly the young man from New York who visited the family every day that Miss Thompson was there was employed to keep the Glovers asleep and satisfied in Lead. So Chandler was not happy when George Glover appeared with the letter his mother had written him on June 16 and the story of Eva Thompson's visit. But he had convinced Glover that he had his mother's interests at heart, and he exploited the episode with a good deal of elaboration.

Large headlines in the Sunday *Boston Herald* announced: "Says Glover will drop case. Persuaded by Miss Thompson of Boston." On Monday the headline read: "Glover turns down offer of Mrs. Eddy (through Miss Thompson) to drop suit." The stories went on to say that Eva Thompson *of Boston* was a close friend of Mrs. Eddy and had consulted with her and her attorney Streeter for several days. Of course when Farlow was approached he very naturally said that he knew no Eva Thompson and that she was not a close friend of Mrs. Eddy. In less than a week's time the headlines stated: "Glover gets to home city full of fight." So the issue was dropped.

But Chandler had become a father figure to George Glover and his daughter. He presented them with many gifts, especially jewelry and furs for Mary and her mother, and his letters in which he always spoke kindly of Christian Science and Mrs. Eddy were those of a family friend. George Glover passed away in 1915 unaware of the hostile things Chandler had written to others and said and done in his crusade *against* his mother and Christian Science.

While George Glover and Chandler were discussing Eva Thompson, Sibyl Wilbur was taking a very serious step forward. When Mrs. Eddy had answered the questions Miss Wilbur had first propounded in 1905, she also said: "If you require further teaching, my student Alfred Farlow is a good teacher." In the summer of 1907 while still researching Mrs. Eddy's history and writing a truthful chapter for *Human Life* each month, she also attended Alfred Farlow's Christian Science class.

Mr. Farlow may have been interrupted in the middle of his class, for the attorneys for the plaintiff began taking the depositions of Christian Scientists on Thursday, August 1. General Streeter who was present for these sessions at the Parker House wrote Mrs. Eddy on August 3:

> As you know, depositions were begun here on Thursday afternoon. Most of the day yesterday was taken up with the cross-examination of Mr. Farlow on the general subject of malicious animal magnetism. I think I ought to say to you that Mr. Farlow's statements on this

> subject were clear, sane and convincing. Everyone present, including Mr. Elder, Mr. Morse, Mr. Eastman, and myself, felt that Mr. Farlow had added a splendid contribution to the literature on that subject.

That Saturday, August 3, was very hot and humid in Concord. The sky was cloudy and overcast, and about 4:30 P.M. the day grew dark as the heavy clouds became very black. It looked as if they were going to have a severe thunderstorm. Adelaide Still went into Mrs. Eddy's study to see if she needed her:

> Mrs. Eddy sat in her chair . . . watching the clouds with a smile and a rapt expression on her face. It seemed to me that she saw beyond the storm and her present surroundings and I do not think that she was conscious of my presence. In a few moments the clouds broke and flecked and the storm was dissolved into its native nothingness.

This was the first time that Miss Still was a witness to Mrs. Eddy's subduing of a storm, and it made a vivid impression upon her. About half an hour later she had occasion to go to Mrs. Eddy's room again, and the Leader said to her, "Adelaide, did you see the sky?" "Yes, Mrs. Eddy," Adelaide replied. "It never was;" said the Leader. "God's face was never clouded."

DR. ALLAN McLANE HAMILTON

CHAPTER XLIV

SIX DAYS OF HEARINGS

For now we see through a glass, darkly; — PAUL

1907

DR. Allan McLane Hamilton had the reputation of being the very best alienist this country affords. Despite the fact that he had testified against practitioners of Christian Science in the Brush will case in New York City in 1901, Mr. Streeter felt that Dr. Hamilton's character and honesty were such that he was the one to make a thorough study of Mrs. Eddy in this case, for his report would stand unquestioned. So the noted alienist spent a month in Concord in mid-summer studying Mrs. Eddy as well as a good deal of her correspondence.

It was Monday, August 12, that Dr. Hamilton called at Pleasant View in company with Mr. Streeter. It is *possible* that Mrs. Eddy was wearing her crown of diamonds on that day. Dr. Hamilton merely said: "She was simply attired in a dark dress and light sacque, relieved by a simple ornament, a diamond brooch." At one point in their discussion Mrs. Eddy said that she had no doubt she was going to win in this matter; and as the doctor recorded, "that her followers had done much to help her, and that she would like to have me on her side."

The next day, Tuesday, August 13, was the first day of the hearing before the Masters. By recognized court usage the counsel for the plaintiff were to have opening and closing, so Chandler took almost all the first day. Near the close of the session Judge Aldrich said: "I do not ask that the question be answered now, Mr. Streeter, but sometime I shall ask you whether we are to be permitted to hear the statement of Mrs. Eddy in respect to her business affairs." With a good deal of judicial procedure and over Chandler's objections it was submitted that Mrs. Eddy would be pleased to have them come to Pleasant View the next day at 2 P.M.

Mrs. Eddy was apprised of the events of the day's hearing very quickly, for one of the several Christian Scientists in the courtroom was Calvin Hill who carried word from General Streeter each day to Mrs. Eddy at Pleasant View:

> She always received me at once, apparently waiting for me to come from the courtroom. I have a vivid picture of her, sitting quietly and listening to what I had to report. She reminded me of a gray gull riding calmly, serenely, on a storm-tossed sea. She had full confidence in the triumph of Truth in this trial. As I recall she once said to me, "You cannot hurt anyone by telling the truth, and no one can hurt you by telling a lie."

The courtroom was full of lies the next morning as counsel for the "next friends" attacked Christian Science and Mrs. Eddy's sanity. After a morning of argument, it was decided that only Chandler, Streeter, and a court stenographer would accompany the three masters to Pleasant View at 2 P.M., and that none but the masters was to do any questioning.

A few days before, Adelaide Still had heard Mrs. Eddy say to Mr. Frye, "Calvin, are you sure they can't come and take me away without my consent?" She also wrote to her lawyer:

> If you let this case remain as it now is could the "next friends" take possession of my person? If they could not then is it not better to let this suit stand as *it is?* I fear if you press it they will get Judge — to decide it against me and give my person to my enemies (called "next friends") and they will take me away from my real friends, students, and thus *get rid* of me by such means, then fight over my last will.

Many times the Leader dictated letters that were never sent, and this one to her lawyer was one of those unsent letters. Sometimes she was restrained by God, sometimes she had further thoughts on the matter, and it is very probable that there were times that her main purpose for the letter was to inform her secretaries and mental workers in the home on an issue. This was an indirect way of instruction that got information to mortal mind without the usual reaction and resistance, and the Leader used every conceivable means to accomplish this. She knew that her life and her person were in God's hands alone, but if her students feared losing her they might be roused to resist the enemy with vigor which all must learn to do sooner or later.

On Wednesday, August 14, Adelaide Still helped the Leader dress for the occasion of the Masters' visit which meeting was held in her study:

> As I looked at her sitting in her chair in the tower window of her study waiting for them to be ushered into her presence, her face was uplifted and looked clear, calm and confident. Only the three alienists [masters] and the two lawyers [plus a court stenographer] were actually in the room with her, but the doors were open and we heard all that was said.

At one point during the interview* Mrs. Eddy called Miss Still to get something for her, and as Miss Still recalled:

> I have forgotten what she asked me to give her; but, because the alienists were sitting in front of her, I went behind her chair and handed the paper to her over her shoulder. As I looked up, I caught the disgruntled look on the opposing lawyer's face, and I knew that he realized that he had lost his case.

It has also been recorded that Chandler was later overheard to say, "That woman is smarter than a steel trap."

Mrs. Eddy had been interrupted in the middle of telling the masters about her discovery of Christian Science, and after they had left the room she sent Adelaide to ask them to return. Mr. Frye brought them back and asked them to be seated, and to Miss Still's amusement "they had to listen to a brief account of her discovery of Christian Science."

The balance of the afternoon in the courtroom was a vicious attack on Mrs. Eddy's sanity by Chandler's colleagues. For three more days this continued as largely an attack on Christian Science with introduction of all the damaging evidence they could produce from such witnesses as Richard Kennedy, Arthur Buswell and others who had renounced Mrs. Eddy and Christian Science. Chandler repeatedly requested that they be allowed to have alienists examine Mrs. Eddy. Though it is no part of the court record, Mrs. Eddy did give an interview to an alienist employed by the next friends, Dr. Henry R. Hopkins of Buffalo, New York. Perhaps Dr. Hopkins' report to Chandler influenced his next move, for the Leader made a deep impression upon the doctor. In fact the impression was so deep and lasting that the doctor's daughter became a lifelong student of Mrs. Eddy's writings.

Practically all of the depositions the next friends presented were ruled out by the court, and after five days they had presented little of consequence and had exhausted their subject. It was now time for the defence to be heard.

On the sixth day of the hearing, Wednesday morning, August 21, Senator Chandler was again the first to speak. He said:

*See Appendix H.

> May it please the court, it will doubtless be a relief to the Masters to be informed that the counsel for the "next friends" have this day filed with the clerk of the court a motion for the dismissal of the pending suit, and that they hereby withdraw their appearance before the Masters without asking from them any finding upon the questions submitted to them by Judge Chamberlin.

As soon as Chandler had resumed his seat Mr. Streeter arose and delivered an impressive and memorable address* asking the Masters to proceed with the hearing. But the judge stated that the petition for dismissal left nothing for them to decide.

The numerous reporters in the courtroom quickly spread the news that Mrs. Eddy had won. But Mr. Streeter was not the only one perturbed by the lack of testimony on Mrs. Eddy's behalf. Dr. Hamilton was interviewed by a good many of the reporters in attendance at the trial and he gave them a very interesting and detailed statement** regarding Mrs. Eddy's competency and unusual executive ability.

Mrs. Eddy had directed the work of her mental workers in connection with the lawsuit which was to be handled with absolute metaphysics. Calvin Hill recorded that he "was not to outline what the verdict would be but to know that Truth would prevail." One of her lessons at this time was from Genesis, "Shall not the Judge of all the earth do right?" As Calvin rushed to Pleasant View with the good news on August 21 he felt that divine Mind had directed the verdict which he was eager to impart to the Leader:

> Of course I remember best of all the eventful day when I hurried out to Pleasant View and told her that the legal battle was ended — and that she had won. When she heard this she raised her hands from the arms of her chair and dropped them again, she lifted her head — a movement which had become familiar to all of us when she was doing metaphysical work or when she was deeply moved. Her eyes had a far-off look as if she were seeing the very heart of heaven.

The next thing she did greatly impressed Mr. Hill and caused him to think of Jesus' words, "Father, forgive them; for they know not what they do." She turned at once to her desk and wrote a letter of overflowing forgiveness to one in whose name the suit had been brought — most likely her son, George Glover.

The *import* of her next step seemed to have gone unnoticed at that time, but it had obviously been planned in advance awaiting the moment for implementation. The Leader released a new edition of Science and Health with a frontispiece of her portrait and signature facing the title page.

*See Appendix I — General Streeter's Address, August 21, 1907.

**See Appendix J — Dr. Hamilton's Report to Newsmen.

MARY BAKER EDDY
Frontispiece in 1907 Science and Health

This picture appears to be the same one she had given to Arthur Brisbane in June except with a *dark* background and the addition of her diamond *cross.* There must be significance to the fact that she placed this portrait upon a very dark background. Perhaps that bears relationship to the unjust persecution she has been enduring. Or it could represent the thought of Christendom as to her mission and her message; or even the understanding of Christian Scientists regarding her identity and spirituality. Most of her closest students were almost totally blind (very dark?) in this area else Gilbert Carpenter would not have written in later years as previously quoted: "It is an interesting commentary on human blindness that any of Mrs. Eddy's household should have felt that, although they had a great love for her and an appreciation of what was unquestionably good in her life and teaching, it required more or less tolerance on their part to overlook Mrs. Eddy's own impatience and to ignore her lack of appreciation and even criticism of what was done for her through their love and effort."

The Leader knew these students' thoughts and their total lack of comprehension, but a mother cannot explain herself or her actions to her children when they are not yet beyond babyhood. Perhaps this dark picture is an explanation.

Two weeks later the *Sentinel* for September 7 contained this notice:

A NEW EDITION OF SCIENCE AND HEALTH

There is now on sale by the publisher a thoroughly revised edition of Science and Health with Key to the Scriptures, upon which the author has expended much care and labor during the past six months. In making this revision Mrs. Eddy has, for the first time, read her book consecutively from cover to cover, "in order," as she writes in the Preface, "to elucidate her idealism." This revised edition contains a fine photogravure portrait of Mrs. Eddy, together with a facsimile of her signature.

After the collapse of the lawsuit the Leader sent copies of this new edition to a few selected recipients, but probably not before the avalanche of telegrams and letters of congratulation began pouring upon Pleasant View from all corners of the earth. One from England said simply:

Frimley, Aug. 22, 1907

Mrs. Eddy, Pleasant View, Concord, N. H.

Sincere congratulations.

Dunmore

Lord Dunmore and his family had been very active in Christian

Science for many years. When the Next Friends' suit was inaugurated he had made a trip to America to ask Mrs. Eddy how he could be of help to her. No one rejoiced more than did he at this victory, and he once again gave public testimony of his wonderful healing in Christian Science. And malicious mind struck back. In less than a week the *London Weekly Times* published: "We regret to announce that Lord Dunmore died very suddenly early on Tuesday morning at the Manor-house, Frimley, near Camberley." A cablegram from Pleasant View dated August 31 read:

> Countess of Dunmore and family,
> Divine Love is your ever-present help. You, I, and mankind have cause to lament the demise of Lord Dunmore; but as the Christian Scientist, the servant of God and man, he still lives, loves, labors.
> Mary Baker G. Eddy

The issue of the *Sentinel* which published Mrs. Eddy's cablegram to Lord Dunmore's family also published:

> A NEW BY-LAW
> SUDDEN DECEASE — Sect. 2 [Now Article IX] If a member of The Mother Church shall decease suddenly, without previous injury or illness, and the cause thereof be unknown, an autopsy shall be made by qualified experts.

At midnight of September 25 the Leader was reading what she had so recently added to page 164 of Science and Health on death:

> If you or I should appear to die, we should not be dead, and this seeming decease, caused by a majority of human beliefs that we must die, would not in the least disprove Christian Science.

As she read, she made the following changes in and additions to these four lines replacing the subjunctive mood with the indicative [changes italicized]:

> If you or I should appear to die, we should not be dead. The seeming decease, caused by a majority of human beliefs that *man* must die, *or produced by mental assassins, does* not in the least disprove Christian Science ...

"The seeming decease ... *does* not in the least disprove Christian Science."

CHAPTER XLV

NOBILITY OF CHARACTER

Whatever envy, hatred, revenge — the most remorseless motives that govern mortal mind — whatever these try to do, shall "work together for good to them that love God." — MARY BAKER EDDY

1907

COUNSEL for "Next Friends" did not dismiss the suit graciously. The next morning, August 22, their statement to the press included:

> Taking a larger view of the matter and considering its bearing upon Mrs. Eddy's alleged religion, which I have long conceived to be utterly nonsensical where it is not distinctly harmful, it is to be regretted that circumstances did not permit of a full hearing and determination upon the merits. . . . Speaking for myself, I shall never cease to regret that so-called Christian Science could not, by judicial decree, have been shown to be the creation of a discordant mind.

Little wonder that the Revelator to this age put a very dark picture of herself in the "little book."

Next Friends' counsel also endeavored to imply in the press that they had not asked for dismissal, but that there had been a compromise. The editor of the *Concord Patriot,* Michael Meehan, was very perturbed by this insinuation of a compromise and wrote: "If a doubt still lingers, let it be dispelled by the positive statement of the author (and he knows): 'There was no compromise.'"

The following letter which came from New York City was written August 24:

> My Dear Mrs. Eddy:
>
> Upon my return to the city I found the autographed copy of the new edition of Science and Health, containing the new picture, for which I thank you. I shall prize it greatly because of the inscription. I am well pleased with the quality of the reproduction. Again thanking

you, and with best wishes, I am

Cordially yours,

B. Frank Puffer

Beneath the new picture in Science and Health, above the facsimile of Mrs. Eddy's signature are the words: "Copyright 1907 by B. Frank Puffer, N. Y."

Augusta Stetson had probably acted as liason between Mr. Puffer and Mrs. Eddy, and she, too, was the recipient of a copy of the new edition right after the lawsuit collapsed. Her letter of August 25 to the Leader included: "I have just opened another new edition of Science and Health with Key to the Scriptures. I cannot express my exceeding great joy as I beheld within its covers your dear face . . ."

Mrs. Eddy greatly enjoyed conversation with a real thinker, and Adelaide Still recalled a visit she had with her astute cousin, probably after dismissal of the lawsuit. Henry M. Baker was not a Scientist, and according to Miss Still, Mrs. Eddy asked him —

> some questions about matter and Mind which he had to admit that he could not answer; then she said something which made him laugh and kept him good humored so that when he left he was smiling and happy and evidently felt that he had had a good time with her. After he had left the room, however, Mrs. Eddy looked up at me with a smile on her face and said, "I have given Henry a dose of Truth that he will not get rid of for a long time."

But Henry Baker's visit on August 25 was of a different nature. He brought with him to Pleasant View, W. T. McIntyre of the *New York American,* though he was doubtful as to whether Mrs. Eddy would or should grant an interview* which, however, she did.

> "Persecution cannot last forever. There is always a reaction. But I hold no enmity. Those who have attempted to injure me have gained nothing."
>
> Mrs. Mary Baker G. Eddy uttered this sentiment of Christian forbearance to me today in the first interview she has granted since the collapse of the suit brought by her "next friends."
>
> No one who has talked with Mrs. Eddy can doubt her deep spiritual nature. No one who has met her can fail to be profoundly impressed by her nobility of character.

The Leader proved that she held no enmity by writing to her adopted son a few days later addressing him as Benny as she had fondly called him in happier days. In her letter she said she would "be pleased to see your dear face once more for a chat with you after the old way." But Foster Eddy's sense of guilt kept him from

*Interview with W. T. McIntyre in Appendix K.

accepting this invitation.

On the day that Mr. McIntyre was at Pleasant View, Dr. Hamilton, another real thinker, was back home in New York giving an interview about Mrs. Eddy* to the *New York Times* in which he stated:

> the sensational stories which have been disseminated about her have no foundation in fact — although they can be very easily traced to a spirit of religious persecution that has at last quite overreached itself.

An interesting post script to Dr. Hamilton's month in Concord and investigation and examination of Mrs. Eddy is this letter the Leader wrote to Allan Hamilton:

> I am in receipt of your kind letter and it would give me great pleasure to comply with your request that I sit for a photograph, were it not for the fact that latterly I have failed to obtain a satisfying picture of myself, and have so given up the effort. The solution of this failure may lie in this, that Christian Science depicts the real man or woman spiritually and not materially; hence the difficulty for me to obtain a photograph of that which is not real ... understanding as you do human nature, you may see the consistency of the above explanation of the failure to depict that which we deny as the actual and eternal.

The progress gained by the dismissal of the lawsuit was somewhat overshadowed by the desertion of the Leader by the students who felt that the crisis was past, and who were eager to return to their own (worldly?) interests and endeavors. The Business Committee gave Calvin Hill some names of new prospects for help at Pleasant View, and he wrote Mrs. Eddy on August 27 that he would start investigating them the next day. She wrote on the back of his letter:

> Darling, I thank you. Please wait till I get breath over Mr. Wilson leaving me. I have now to watch and to qualify a new Sec. The persecution of your leader is far from being over.

Mrs. Eddy wanted a secretary who would remain with her for the next three years. Irving C. Tomlinson had been a member of her last class in 1898, following which she had had him move to Concord. For the past nine years she had worked closely with Mr. Tomlinson; he had often been to Pleasant View and had done some secretarial work for her for short periods. Now that his sister was no longer with him he was eager to become a permanent member of Mrs. Eddy's household. But Mrs. Eddy knew Irving far better than

*See Appendix L — Dr. Hamilton's Statement to *New York Times.*

he knew himself. She also knew that the animal magnetism that had so hypnotized his dear sister would not overlook Irving as he became more useful to the Leader.

Many a student had been blinded to her Christliness and thus turned away from the Truth. Malicious mind endeavored to *destroy* those who could not be blinded nor turned aside, which was so evident in Mary Tomlinson's case. Such occurrences caused the Leader to tell her students:

> I have told you that evil has no power, yet I have told you to handle evil as though it had power. This is because of your place in growth spiritual. When the Allness of God is seen, the nothingness of evil is evident — hold to that.

Handling evil impersonally for another or knowing theoretically that it has no power is but the first step. *Standing* under fire is the test. The Leader saw that Mr. Tomlinson needed something more to fortify him and to strengthen his resistence to the attacks of malicious animal magnetism. Before he moved to Pleasant View as her secretary she had Mr. Streeter draw up a contract which bound him in the minutest details. This agreement stated exactly what she would furnish him and what Mr. Tomlinson was expected to furnish her in return. Should he lose his desire to stay and serve the Leader, he was bound to remain with her until the contract was fulfilled.

But a new secretary was only one of the items demanding the Leader's attention. The issue that was foremost in her thought was leaving New Hampshire. Much as she loved her native state, in New Hampshire her personal appearance in court could be compelled, — which she had been informed was not the case in Massachusetts. She needed a larger house than Pleasant View for her ever-enlarging household, but she did *not* want anything pretentious; and, she wrote to Alfred Farlow, "I want a window in my room like the one here. It relieves my *lonely hours.*"

Above all she wanted absolute secrecy on the move until it was an accomplished fact, so only the few directly concerned knew anything about it. One of those concerned few was Calvin C. Hill whose commission was to have exact duplicates made of the furniture in her sitting room and bedroom, the only difference being that the reproductions were to be mahogany in place of oak.

On September 10 after she had greeted the metaphysical workers gathered in her room for the morning lesson, she opened her Bible as was her custom and read:

> Rom. 15:23 But now having no more place in these parts, and

having a great desire these many years to come unto you;
24 Whensoever I take my journey into Spain, I will come to you: for
I trust to see you in my journey ...

Mr. Tomlinson recorded in his diary that day:

> She said in substance that she could not tell us the import of the words, that they were in perfect harmony with what she had been dwelling upon the entire morning. I asked what was meant by "Spain" and she only smiled.

She may have been thinking of moving in "sacred secrecy" when she wrote in her notebook on September 17, 1907, "Let my church buy the house and rent it to me." Or she may have been thinking of not owning property that could be attached by lawsuits, — or perhaps it was both.

In the *Sentinel* for September 21 the advertisement for Science and Health included: "This edition contains a fine photogravure portrait of Mrs. Eddy, together with a facsimile of her signature." This advertisement mentioning her portrait continued every week as long as Mrs. Eddy was here with us. When later editions of the textbook included textual changes, this sentence in the advertisement for Science and Health was changed to read: "This work contains important changes and additions by the author, also a photogravure portrait of Mrs. Eddy, together with a facsimile of her signature."

September 30 was the date set for final dismissal of the "next friends" suit in Judge Chamberlin's courtroom. The Masters' report was read and accepted, and then Mr. Chandler made extended remarks and "in a negative way left the impression that he expected the suit to continue," stating that Mr. Streeter had objected to dismissal. Mr. Streeter arose and said that he had no objection to granting Mr. Chandler's request for dismissal, but Chandler asked for delay.

> Judge Chamberlin: This is a motion to dismiss, is it not?
> Mr. Chandler: Yes.
> Judge Chamberlin: What necessity is there for argument?

Nonetheless, Chandler continued to argue a number of points, one being that Mrs. Eddy should pay all costs of the suit. Mr. Streeter left this determination with the court, stating, "The Masters' fees have to be paid, but I object to an order compelling Mrs. Eddy to pay them, while I would not object to an order against Mrs. Eddy's trustees under the trust deed of March 6, for the purpose of bringing them in as parties to the proceeding."

Before this issue was settled Chandler sought to submit a brief of his objections to the rulings of the Masters. Finally Judge Chamberlin held:

1. That the brief could not be filed.
2. That the motion of "next friends" to dismiss the bill be granted.
3. That the report of the Masters be affirmed.
4. That the trustees under the deed of trust . . . be allowed to come in and be heard on the question of costs.
5. That "next friends" have until October 10 to file a brief on the question of costs.
6. That counsel for trustees have until October 15 to reply.
7. That arguments on the question of costs be submitted on October 15.

The point Mrs. Eddy had sought to establish in the first place was at last acknowledged, — that issues involving her property should be handled by her trustees.

After Chandler had first filed for dismissal on August 21 the Leader's heart had overflowed with forgiveness to all those who had oppressed her. She had written forgiving letters to "next friends" and she had even mentioned inviting Mr. Chandler to visit her at Pleasant View. However, right after this court session on September 30 Mr. Streeter wrote to her:

> I think I thoroughly know W. E. Chandler. I have carefully observed his attitude of mind with reference to yourself personally and this case. The objection to your plan is that he strongly disbelieves in you and in your system of healing and in your religion. He has convinced himself that the claims of yourself and your followers are arrant humbuggery. . . .
>
> The differences between you and Chandler are fundamental. His only purpose in going to your house would be to get some advantage over you. He would not meet you with the same spirit with which you would receive him. . . .

The one thing Mr. Streeter did not know about Mr. Chandler which Mrs. Eddy understood so well was that he was the tool of animal magnetism. But Mr. Streeter was probably right in his assessment that Chandler would merely use the visit as an opportunity to gain some advantage against Mrs. Eddy even as had Mr. Slaght.

In the *Sentinel* for October 12 was an announcement that the time had arrived for the erection of a suitable building to house the Christian Science Publishing Society and inviting contributions for this purpose.

Earlier in 1907 Mrs. Eddy had purchased the house next door to her Commonwealth Avenue house. By October 12 a suitable residence had not been decided upon and Mrs. Eddy was considering occupying her two houses. In a letter to Mr. McLellan on that day she said:

> Buy all that is needed on Commonwealth Ave. in Boston, so that my carriage may come to my door and be shielded from too near neighbors. I shall need a stall for 2 horses. There is needed also a door into my house now occupied by Mr. Armstrong, and one of the large rooms should be made into two rooms.
>
> There must be nine sleeping rooms for my household. What I shall need, if I can have it, is an addition to my house, also a stable in the rear with rooms for my driver and his family. Elevators would add to convenience.

Commonwealth Avenue had been built up considerably plus becoming an artery for traffic since Mrs. Eddy had been there, so this plan was not practical. Mr. McLellan acted upon her further statement which was:

> I would, however, like to purchase the right place in Brookline. It may be possible that you can purchase of the madam in Newton. Do it if you can but have her make no mention about it.

The twenty-five room house on Beacon Street in Newton on approximately twelve acres of land, partly wooded, could better accommodate Mrs. Eddy's large household. So Mr. McLellan arranged the purchase. The stone carriage house and stable were already there, but extensive alterations to the house, plus decorating, were necessary before it would be ready for Mrs. Eddy. In October the estate was purchased by Robert P. Walker, a wealthy Chicago real estate dealer and well-known Christian Scientist. The extensive remodeling was begun with orders for the greatest possible speed. Mrs. Eddy wrote in her notebook, "My home on Beacon St., Brookline cost $207,061.36."

The question came up at this time as to the advisability of sponsoring lectures in areas where there was no Christian Science activity. Mrs. Eddy answered this question for all time, although indirectly through her editor in the *Sentinel* of October 12:

> The lecturers are doing a magnificent work in their line of endeavor, but this work would be practically useless as a means of enhancing the growth of Christian Science were it not for the "signs following." The true basis of the establishment of Christian Science in any community must be the healing of the sick and the deliverance of the

> sinful, and this must precede every other form of work or organization. . . . To heal the sick is the eternal mandate of divine Love, and Christian Science churches cannot be established and maintained on any other basis.

On October 15 the Leader had Irving Tomlinson write to the Trustees:

> Because of important duties here, and after consultation with our beloved Leader, she has suggested that I ask you to find a substitute to act for me, while I am temporarily absent from the meetings of the Bible Lesson Committee.

John Lathrop was called to Pleasant View once again for a few months of service, either to assist or to replace Mr.Tomlinson. Irving Tomlinson loved both Christian Science and Mrs. Eddy dearly, and endeavored to devote himself to her service. All newcomers to Pleasant View were startled by the severe rebukes to shock them "out of a mesmeric influence," and few if any understood such treatment in the slightest degree. Those who did not profit from this stern treatment by becoming chastened, receptive and teachable, and thus going up higher, were soon sent away. Tomlinson was not a newcomer, but perhaps the Leader had not rebuked him severely in the past. When she did, on more than one occasion he reacted to the rebukes, and more than once he was sent away. October 19 was one day that Mr. Tomlinson reacted to the chastening rod. Mr. Frye did not say whether he was dismissed at that time, but he did record in his diary the next day: "Last evening under the influence of m.a.m. Mr. Tomlinson told Mrs. Eddy she was ungrateful and a tyrant."

The Leader did not express gratitude or much appreciation when things were done for her in a human way, that is by mortal mind. But her gratitude was lavish whenever a student turned to God in his efforts to help her. Often the Leader was very patient with the slowness and dullness of her disciples, although she did say, "I feel like telling my students to hurry up." There was not one speck of animosity in her rebukes. They were wholly from Mind and she was only the spokesman. Adelaide Still recorded:

> Occasionally when smarting under a mortal mind sense of resentment after some such rebuke I have gone into her room in answer to her call and found that she had completely forgotten the circumstances and she would look at me in astonishment and say, "What are you crying for, Adelaide?"

There were few students who could not profit from severe rebukes and thus grow Spiritward. In fact, there may have been only one humble enough to escape this chastening treatment, — the conscientious John Salchow. But even John learned the intended lesson by witnessing the rebukes of others. Laura Sargent was severely reprimanded one day when John was working in Mrs. Eddy's study, and when Laura was called to the study again she was in tears. John recorded the Leader's surprise and gentle words: "Why Laura, I was not speaking to you; I was speaking to the error. You should not take it to yourself."

The Leader so longed for students whose *only* desire was to progress spiritually. She knew they could make half a century of progress in one year in her home, which a great many did. Half a century was no where near enough, but none seemed to want the continued discipline demanded by spiritual advancement. She had sensed that Miss Still truly had this desire when she had said to her: "I have been asking God to send me the right one, and I believe that He has." But there were times when mortal mind tempted Adelaide to leave, and sensing this too, Mrs. Eddy would say, "You won't leave me, will you Adelaide? You will stay with me as long as I am here?" Miss Still said:

> At such times one would feel such a sense of love in her thought that all sense of hurt or resentment was wiped out and I would say, "Yes Mother dear, I will stay with you as long as you need me."

Mrs. Eddy did not need Adelaide as much as Adelaide needed the Leader, but Mrs. Eddy was far more aware of this than was Miss Still. The Leader also knew what Adelaide did not, — that she had but three short years for the Divinity Course in her home. Before the end of 1907 Mrs. Eddy amended the by-law in the *Manual,* "Opportunity for Serving the Leader," which had required twelve consecutive months of service. It now read, "It shall be the duty of the member thus notified to remain with Mrs. Eddy three years consecutively." Obviously she felt there would be a greater blessing for mankind from one individual with three years of the Divinity Course than from three individuals with one year each. Some said she was getting old and didn't like change which was their own human opinion. All of the Revelator's decisions were God-directed.

One of the letters Mr. Tomlinson had written for Mrs. Eddy recently was to Dr. Hamilton in New York, who responded on October 25:

> My Dear Mrs. Eddy:
>
> I received the most interesting history of the Congregational church at Concord, read it, and hasten to return it, as Mr. Tomlinson

MICHAEL MEEHAN

requested. It reflects, as Mr. Tomlinson says, the kindly feeling toward you in your community. In my opinion it does more, for it is the admission of respect of one church for another, and the recognition of your own sincerity and purity of your life.

With the hope that when I next go to Concord I may have the pleasure of seeing you, and with congratulations upon your continued good health.

I am sincerely your friend,
Allan McLane Hamilton

On October 15 the final hearing regarding costs for the next friends suit was postponed by mutual consent till November 12, but this was not Chandler's final action against Mrs. Eddy. On October 25 he began further negotiations supposedly on behalf of George Glover to get a portion of Mrs. Eddy's million dollar estate.

Most people thought the litigation was ended on August 21 when the next friends had filed to dismiss the suit. The official end was on November 12 when the court ordered:

1. That by consent the trustees pay the Masters' fees, but as an offset to this said trustees have a judgment against "next friends" for $3000.
2. The defendants in this suit have judgment against "next friends" for their costs.
3. The regular court costs are taxed up against "next friends."

There was one person who was not finished with this suit. Michael Meehan had followed every aspect of this persecution of Mrs. Eddy since it first began with the invasion of Concord by hostile and aggressive reporters more than a year earlier. On more than one occasion the unmanly lies had aroused righteous indignation in him, and he had decided to write the truth of the whole story in a book. The masters and attorneys had all gone over the complete transcript of the hearing and "each made such alterations therein as conformed to the requirements of good usage and the elucidation of his thought and eliminated therefrom ambiguous and redundant expressions." Mr. Meehan felt that Mrs. Eddy should have the same privilege. Her appreciative, handwritten response to Mr. Meehan so pleased him that he published it in facsimile in his book:

Nov. 16, 1907

Mr. M. Meehan
Beloved Student:

I am glad to have had opportunity to read and revise my interview with the Masters for your book — the history of the court trial. I fancy I have not exceeded my privilege. I have added nothing; have not changed the thought, but have erased some unnecessary statements and repetitions in both the questions and answers, — also I have corrected some errors in rhetoric and grammar that must have resulted from inability on the part of the stenographer to distinctly hear what was said.

Affectionately and gratefully,
Mary Baker G. Eddy

Sue Harper Mims who was in Concord to deliver a lecture at the Concord church, was invited to visit the Leader at Pleasant View. Mrs. Mims wrote before leaving Concord:

Beloved Leader:

Words cannot thank you sufficiently for the joy and uplifting from my visit to you, beloved of the Lord. I see the cordon of angelic hosts that encircles Pleasant View, and nothing evil can pierce those walls of salvation nor come nigh thy dwelling.

The lecture was a success; a choice and most attentive audience greeted me, and I felt that the truth was received. It will interest you to know that General and Mrs. Streeter were there, and that after the lecture they both came to congratulate me and to say how much they enjoyed the lecture. I had met Mrs. Streeter in Atlanta, at a luncheon given by my daughter, and she said she had often thought of me and my work in Christian Science, that she would love to entertain me were I remaining longer, and many other pleasant things. In greeting General Streeter, I said, "You know, dear General Streeter, we all love you for your magnificent defense of our beloved Mrs. Eddy," and Mr. Hering said he seemed much pleased and touched. . . . The lecture, however, seems but an incident — the cherished event is my short but glorious visit with you, beloved one, God's anointed chosen one, whom He ever guards and protects.

I am enjoying a visit with my dear friends, your devoted, loving, and loyal students Mr. and Mrs. Hering.

With fondest love,

Your devoted student,
Sue Mims

CHAPTER XLVI

HUMAN TEACHERS

Unless there is less teaching, less church making, and better ***healing,*** *and more of it — our denomination will sink into the slough of past sects in having a religion of the letter without the spirit — of doctrine without demonstration.* — MARY BAKER EDDY

1907

THE persecution of 1907 brought great growth and prosperity to the Christian Science movement, and all publications were eager for news about Mrs. Eddy. When she contributed "Youth and Young Manhood" *(My.* 272) to the *Cosmopolitan,* that magazine published a facsimile of the manuscript just as it was received with the interlineated corrections in Mrs. Eddy's handwriting. For two months in advance, the *Ladies' Home Journal* advertised that they would have an article by Mrs. Eddy in their December issue.

A change in the *Manual* in 1907 eliminated primary classes under the Board of Education and stated that Normal classes will be held triennially beginning in 1907. The Leader chose Judge Hanna to be the teacher of the class which was to convene December 4, the first Wednesday in December.

Mr. Kimball had been *the one* normal teacher for the first four years of the Board of Education. His understanding of metaphysics was far beyond that of most students at the turn of the century. Mr. Kimball was in New England in the fall, and it is possible that the Leader suggested that he might give Judge Hanna some ideas which would be helpful to him in teaching. Mr. Kimball wrote the judge a lengthy letter on November 29 congratulating him on the fact that he had been selected to teach the 1907 Normal Class, and then going into detail on points that had been misinterpreted:

> I do not know that Dr. Baker ever taught anything in the College classes, but by way of general refutation. I know that everything that

was supposed to have been taught irregularly, was laid at my door before they got through with it. The nearest I ever heard after this fashion, was that the doctor in disposing of error, matter, simply wiped out everything and presented a philosophy which seemed to have annihilation for its ultimate.

Mrs. Eddy spoke with me about this propensity or let me say incompleteness. She said: "I said to Dr. Baker, Jesus said 'stretch forth thy hand,' but all you have got to say is, 'you haven't got any hand.' " She also spoke of a patient who passed away in Concord and of her inquiry as to the treatment which disposed of the whole matter or was supposed to, by saying, "There isn't any case." She denounced that sort of negation and said that the patient got nothing curative.

She said to me, "Declare, 'I have a perfect liver,' — and let the spiritual import of this declaration destroy the false concept about liver."

Later Mrs. Kimball told Mrs. Eddy that she had explained this to Mrs. Webster and that it had healed her of a claim of long continuance. Mrs. Eddy said, "Yes! You may declare I have a perfect liver — or there is no liver provided the thought back of these declarations is right." After talk with her she expressed her conviction that I was absolutely right in my interpretation of her utterance.

Feeling constrained by this conversation and instruction I went into the class and repeated her exact words and with much amplification, led up to and completed the line of explanation.

I have heard of the healing of hundreds of cases through the appreciation of this particular phase of practice.

I am under the impression that nearly all the students I taught got a fairly correct appreciation of it but on the contrary, by the time it got out into the field, — without the metaphysical analysis and the preliminary explanation, — the ones who got it second hand, or third or fourth or fifth hand, landed on the supposition, . . . that Mr. Kimball was teaching that we had spiritual organs . . .

Thousands have in a similar manner misconstrued Mrs. Eddy's teaching . . . enemies . . . said that my teaching was defective because I spiritualized matter or the body. Mrs. Eddy told me that she never believed these things about it because she knew where I stood in the matter.

I . . . will say briefly by way of outline: Being is *One* and being infinite it is not composed of duplicates. This One or infinity is primarily *Mind* (noumenon) — secondarily *Ideas* (phenomena) — Hence the statement, there is one *Mind.*

. . . That which seems to be the material universe, man and body, is not what it seems to be . . .

Followed to the end it appears that every normal thing in matter is a lie about a spiritual fact or idea and the spiritual thing is all right. As Mrs. Eddy also said "Perfect in God."

Now what is the remedy, — is it annihilation or transformation?

If there were no opposite affirmation to the concept "my liver is imperfect" then the ultimate would be a belief of disaster, instead of transformation.

What is the opposite affirmation? It is something like this. Body is spiritual; it consists of spiritual ideas. Every idea is perfect, the idea of which liver is a false concept is perfect, in Good, or finally getting down to an immediate offset, "I have a perfect liver in God."

Mrs. Eddy used to have an equivalent in Science and Health like this — "Realize the presence of health and the harmonious action of organs," etc. I do not know that I quote this correctly.

There was a good deal more in this letter which was undoubtedly very helpful to Mr. Hanna. At the completion of the class he wrote to Mrs. Eddy:

December 14, 1907

Beloved Teacher:

The class in the Board of Education closed last Wednesday. Including Miss Eaton and Miss Campbell there were thirty-two in the class. I think the class was a good one in its make-up. I hope it will prove to have been well selected. It was as well instructed as I knew how to have it, and I hope for right results. I made the examination as thorough as I could, and I think all are fairly entitled to the certificates. These I shall have prepared very soon. The class — with the exception of Misses Eaton and Campbell — was selected from primary students of the Board. It seemed to us this was in fair and logical order under the amended By-law. It no doubt disappointed many, but many would have been disappointed under any circumstances. I am grateful for the opportunity to have conducted the class. I learned much, and was greatly helped. I enclose a copy of the names, etc.

We unite in deepest love to you.

Sincerely your student,
Septimus J. Hanna

Judge Hanna may not have been the most gifted teacher nor the most outstanding metaphysician, but he did have one thing that put him beyond almost all others in the field. Mind had revealed to him in 1898 the identity of the Discoverer and Founder as the Second Coming of the Christ, — a revelation which never left him. Only part of the editorial he had written on that subject at the time was published, and he wrote of this in his reminiscences in later years:

Although the last letter [from Mrs. Eddy] indicated permission to proceed with the publication of the entire article . . . I concluded it best to publish only that of Mr. Spring and the more general part of what I said of the prophecy of Isaiah, deferring the other until a

> future time and make it a separate article. After this, events in connection with the work and the Woodbury suit came so thick and fast that there seemed no opportune time to again bring the matter to Mrs. Eddy's attention (which I felt I must do before publishing it), and there it rested. My own conception of the whole matter, however, has not changed and I see it today just as I saw it then . . .

Perhaps this normal class was the "future time" for the dissemination of Judge Hanna's revelation to thirty-two selected students rather than to the field at large. At least one of those students (and perhaps more) received the revelation as if it was his own, and it never left him. That one was Bliss Knapp.

Before the close of the normal class the directors sent a sad note to the Leader which began: "It is with deep regret that we notify you of the passing on of our beloved friend and associate, Joseph Armstrong, C.S.D." Mrs. Eddy's immediate response *(My.* 296) was published in the *Sentinel* of December 14:

> "HEAR, O ISRAEL"
>
> The late lamented Christian Science brother and the publisher of my books, Joseph Armstrong, C.S.D., is not dead, neither does he sleep nor rest from his labors in divine Science; and his works do follow him. Evil has no power to harm, to hinder, or to destroy the real spiritual man. He is wiser today, healthier and happier, than yesterday. The mortal dream of life, substance, or mind in matter, has been lessened, and the reward of good and punishment of evil and the working out of this Adam dream of evil will end in harmony, — evil powerless, and God, good, omnipotent and infinite.
>
> Mary Baker Eddy
>
> Pleasant View, Concord, N. H., Dec. 10, 1907

The next day, December 11, Calvin Frye wrote to the trustees of the Publishing Society:

> In reply to your letter of yesterday received by our beloved Leader, I am requested to say she does not recommend that the Publishing House be closed at the hour of the funeral services tomorrow. She does not approve of recognizing these claims of mortal mind by acknowledging the reality of sin, disease and death to any unnecessary extent.
>
> She was deeply grieved at the announcement of the decease of our dear Brother Armstrong as all were at Pleasant View . . .

Mrs. Eddy's message to the world in the December *Ladies' Home Journal* is destined to elevate all Christendom, and it comforted the mourners at that time:

WHAT CHRISTMAS MEANS TO ME *(My.* 261)

To me Christmas involves an open secret, understood by few — or by none . . .

God creates man perfect and eternal in His own image. Hence man is the image, idea, or likeness of perfection — an ideal which cannot fall from its inherent unity with divine Love, from its spotless purity and original perfection.

. . . Christmas to me is the reminder of God's great gift, — His spiritual idea, man and the universe, — a gift which so transcends mortal, material, sensual giving that the merriment, mad ambition, rivalry, and ritual of our common Christmas seem a human mockery in mimicry of the real worship in commemoration of Christ's coming. . . .

The splendor of this nativity of Christ reveals infinite meanings and gives manifold blessings. Material gifts and pastimes tend to obliterate the spiritual idea in consciousness, leaving one alone and without His glory.

On December 20 Dr. Hamilton wrote to Mrs.Eddy again:

My Dear Mrs. Eddy:

I send you a little Christmas remembrance and hope you will enjoy the book that I send with my best wishes. The past year has been full of annoyance for you from the "nexters" and other designing people, but I am sure you have already cast aside your annoyances. It is the lot of every one who is in earnest in this life to have rivals and sometimes calumniators, and you have certainly had your share. May 1908 be full of peace for you.

Very sincerely your friend,
Allan McLane Hamilton

"The 'nexters' and other designing people" had not ceased annoying the Leader. McLellan wrote Mrs. Eddy on December 19 (regarding the action begun on October 25) that the trustees had agreed upon a settlement of $140,000 with the "nexters" including Foster Eddy. The necessary papers were drawn up by Streeter and Chandler and were to be signed by all parties on December 23. But for reasons known only to himself Chandler did not have George Glover and Foster Eddy in Concord to sign the papers on the date set. And, because they had not been completed in the specified time, Mrs, Eddy declined to consummate the agreement, writing her counsel that she refused to change the conditions relative to her heirs.

Chandler referred more than once to the fact that they had "uncovered" Mrs. Eddy's million dollars, and he never ceased urging his "clients" (Glover and Foster Eddy) to get as much of it as they could. But Mrs. Eddy counteracted this acquisitiveness in an interesting way. On December 14 she wrote to one of the trustees of her personal property, Archibald McLellan, and her letter was published in the next issue of the *Sentinel* on December 21:

My Dear Trustee:
I desire to commence immediately to found a Christian Science institution for the special benefit of the poor and the general good of all mankind. The founding and endowment of this institution will cost at least one million of dollars.
Please come to me at your earliest opportunity, and I will give you further details.

Most truly yours,
Mary Baker Eddy

Both Pleasant View and the Publishing House were inundated with joyful response as well as contributions, causing the announcement that this was Mary Baker Eddy's charity and contributions were *not* requested. Further letters requested the *privilege* of participating. Whether Mrs. Eddy's intention at the end of 1907 was to pursue this project is a question, for the organizational part was never set up. But the announcement made on December 21 was widely copied by the daily press, and as 1907 was turning to 1908 there was a great deal of favorable editorial comment regarding Mrs. Eddy's proposed project.

To the sincere student who will go back and reread Mrs. Eddy's letter of December 14 with thoughtful consideration, it is easy to see that it is the story of her life. She is describing her every thought and action for the past forty-one years, — "to found a Christian Science institution for the special benefit of the poor and the genral good of all mankind. The founding and endowment of this institution will cost at least one million of dollars." It had cost the Discoverer, Founder, and Leader a great deal more than "one million of dollars!"

CHAPTER XLVII

400 BEACON STREET

Henrietta, if I ever go away from here to another house it will be to be delivered up to my enemies. — MARY BAKER EDDY

1908

IRVING Tomlinson was banished from Pleasant View on January 1, 1908, and he wrote to the trustees of the Publishing Society on the same day:

> This is to let you know that I expect to resume my work upon the Bible Lesson Committee on Saturday next.
>
> I return to this labor of love with the approval of our beloved Leader.

The Leader may not have been quite so beloved in Irving's eyes on that New Year's Day, but he was seeing more clearly when he wrote her a few days later. This was not the first time Mr. Tomlinson had been exiled, but on this occasion the Leader called Arthur Vosburgh to Pleasant View to replace him. In her answer to Tomlinson on January 11 she said:

> Your suggestion to return to me seemed nothing but a lack of faith in what I had before tenderly and honestly as usual *explained* . . . and you agreed with me afterwards and said so. Now the tempter turns you back to your old temptation to doubt either the honesty or the spiritual understanding of [Mrs. Eddy]. . . . If I should have you return to me I should disobey God for I know what He teaches me and you do not know it and even disbelieve me when I tell you.

While this was going on the Leader had called Allison V. Stewart and talked with him in regard to his succeeding Joseph Armstrong as her publisher. It is possible that she did not mention the directorship to him during the interview. Stewart wrote to her on January 8:

Beloved Leader,

Again I come to you with love and gratitude, and I sincerely thank you for the additional duties you have assigned to me in connection with the great Cause of Christian Science. I also thank you for the further expression of confidence which you have vouchsafed me. My election as a member of The Christian Science Board of Directors of your church The First Church of Christ, Scientist, in Boston impresses me deeply, as I regard this office as a sacred trust and feel that it is a great honor to serve you and the Cause in this capacity.

It is my prayer that I may ever keep in mind these your recent words of loving admonition to me: "Lean on Him [God], trust Him, understand Him, and He will give you foresight, wisdom, and capacity to execute His will and benefit His Cause."

Lovingly yours,
Allison V. Stewart

The day before Mr. Stewart wrote this letter there had been another casualty in the wake of the battle of the "next friends." Pamelia Leonard died at her home in Brooklyn. Many of those who had served at Pleasant View knew Mrs. Leonard well, for she had come there many times to serve the Leader. On January 12 Mrs. Eddy wrote to George Kinter:

Life is the law of health, and you are the manifestation, the embodiment of this law. Know this, *feel* it. The ways of God are often hard to determine, but Love is preparing us all for a great work.

Though very few people knew about it, the date for Mrs. Eddy's move to Chestnut Hill had been set for Sunday, January 26; however, she wrote Mr. McLellan a week earlier:

Beloved:

I am sorry to say I must go sooner than Sunday next if *possible.* It seems more than I have power to meet with all the . . . Make the date earlier if you can. If all the work is not finished in the house it can be completed after I am there. Work was done in this house while I was in it. Name an earlier time if possible.

Lovingly yours,
M. B. Eddy

We hope that there was truly an effort toward an earlier date for her move. God's chosen witness complained not of the heavy and sometimes changing demands placed upon her, but bowed her head in meek submission. The same cannot be said for her less than humble followers. Many times they considered their human opinions and plans superior to the Leader's requests. Had they been as obedient as she, she would be with us here today leading all the world to spiritual understanding. And had she not thundered at them at times to force them to obey God's behests, she would not have accomplished as much as she did for all mankind. If they did try to comply with her request of January 19, it was not possible.

Sunday morning, January 26 the routine at Pleasant View began as usual. The mental workers gathered in Mrs. Eddy's study and she opened her Bible to I Corinthians 9:10-14 which she read to them:

> I Cor. 9:12 . . . Nevertheless we have not used this power; but suffer all things, lest we should hinder the gospel of Christ.
>
> 13 Do ye not know that they which minister about holy things live of the things of the temple? and they which wait at the altar are partakers with the altar?
>
> 14 Even so hath the Lord ordained that they which preach the gospel should live of the gospel.

This inspired what John Lathrop described as a "grand talk."

About the time the household was having their noon meal, a special train consisting of a locomotive, a baggage car, a private car, and a regular passenger car was made up and backed into the Concord station while the railroad yard men knew not its purpose. About one o'clock according to Adelaide Still:

> Mrs. Eddy started out as if for her drive at the usual time. Then hacks came up one after another until all the household were on their way. Mrs. Eddy's carriage went around a longer way, so that when she reached the station, we were all on the special train . . . and as soon as she was seated, we started on our journey.

Archibald McLellan who had been responsible for all the arrangements was also present on this journey with Mrs. Eddy and her household. According to the next day's newspapers, "The departure by special train at two o'clock was witnessed by only a chance handful of station loiterers." The *Boston Globe* said on January 27:

> Every precaution to safeguard Mrs. Eddy was taken, the special train being preceded by a pilot engine to see that there were no obstructions, while another locomotive followed the special at a distance of half a mile to guard against the possibility of a rear-end collision. The special train had the right of way . . . [and after several line transfers, was] transferred to the Newton Circuit line, over which it was taken to the Chestnut Hill station.

One of Mrs. Eddy's carriages was waiting for her at the station as well as taxis and hacks for the rest of the party. Miss Still and the others in the taxis arrived first and were at the door of 400 Beacon Street when Mrs. Eddy arrived. A group of reporters was also there awaiting her arrival. John Salchow, riding in the last hack, saw them, jumped down and ran to Mrs. Eddy's carriage just as she was ready to step out. "John, can you get me into the house?" she asked, and John responded, "I surely can."

John swept her up in his strong arms, pressed through the startled newsmen straight into the house, where he bore her upstairs and set her down in her chair in her study. She clapped her hands and her joyous laugh rang through the hall. All the newspapers had to say of the episode the next day was: "A huge Swede grabbed Mrs. Eddy and ran off with her."

In the statement Alfred Farlow gave to the press that evening he said:

> The Lawrence estate, which has been remodeled . . . has been quietly furnished for Mrs. Eddy and her household, and she occupied it at 4:45 this afternoon. . . .
>
> They left Concord at 2 P.M. on a special train . . . Here everything was found in full equipment and supper was served at the usual hour. Except for the three hours required to make the trip, there was no break in the usual routine of the family.

Anyone who has ever moved knows what a feat that was! The Leader truly demonstrated her words recorded in *Divinity Course and General Collectanea:*

> Malicious animal magnetism cannot through any claim of business necessity or policy move me either internally or externally. It cannot change my habitation, for I inhabit infinity, eternity. I dwell in the realm of unending bliss, in a house not made with hands high in the heavens of Life, Truth, and Love. I live in the atmosphere of purity, peace and plenty, and in the sunshine of Love and joy. My home has an everlasting foundation. There is no limit to its beauty and pleasantness, and infinite Love conducts my home. There is but one home-maker; one home beautiful; one builder; one habitation. "For in Him we live and move and have our being."

Mrs. Eddy's spiritual sense of beauty and pleasantness had permeated every part of Pleasant View. Her followers had done their utmost *humanly* to prepare her new home for her, but to the Leader the dark gray stone mansion was austere and repelling. She later dictated to Adam Dickey: "When . . . I looked on the house . . . I was shocked, and went to my room and wept." As she looked around that first afternoon she said, "Oh! splendid misery!" And on

CHESTNUT HILL
As it looked in January, 1908

further inspection the next morning, according to Adelaide Still's reminiscences, she said: "A great barn of a place!"

On the day Mrs. Eddy moved to Chestnut Hill William B. Johnson wrote to Adam Dickey in Kansas City. Both Mr. and Mrs. Dickey were active practitioners and Mr. Dickey was a teacher as well as First Reader in their church in Kansas City, Missouri. The Pleasant View Committee had called on Mr. Dickey several times during the past year and asked his assistance in finding suitable help for Mrs. Eddy's home. Mr. Dickey knew many who would have jumped at the opportunity but none who could meet the qualifications. He had imagined that Mrs. Eddy lived in quiet, comfortable luxury:

> I had no idea that she was constantly besieged by all the forces of evil and that she had to be in the front line of battle, day and night, throughout all the years of her leadership. . . . and that those serving in any capacity in her home came under a line of malpractice that existed nowhere else on earth.

It became clear to Mr. Dickey that only experienced practitioners could qualify for working in the Leader's home, but he did not know that he was being considered for such work until he visited The

Mother Church in June of 1907. At that time a committee of three had questioned him rather closely. When asked about his willingness to serve, he said he would immediately drop everything to go even to shovel snow off her sidewalk. He was laughingly assurred that finding help to shovel snow was no problem. It was work of a different nature that concerned them.

Mr. Johnson's letter of January 26 extended a call to Mr. Dickey to serve in the Leader's home. Mr. Dickey received the letter on Wednesday, January 29 and was on his way to Boston the following Monday.

Before Mr. Dickey arrived Mrs. Eddy had decided to do some remodeling. Her study, with a rose patterned carpet, was far too large. She said that she could not wait for her secretary to come to her across all those roses.

While Mrs. Eddy had a good deal of adjustment to make, so did the city of Concord which was in a state of shock. Irving Tomlinson, who had accompanied the household on the train, wrote to the Leader from Concord on Tuesday, January 28:

> Dearly Beloved Leader:
>
> I have been home but a short time, but long enough to learn of the universal regret in Concord because of the departure of our beloved Leader. My progress down town this morning was slow, because so many stopped me to express their sorrow for their great loss. . . .
>
> The following are a few of the sincere expressions of regret spoken to me in the few hours that I have been at home. I give only a few words from each one.
>
> I met in Boston, while going to the Union Station, your old friend, Mr. Amos Blanchard, who, you know, is now spending the winter in Boston. Mr. Blanchard testified to the great loss to Concord in your departure, and said: "I found people very much disturbed. Concord feels badly about it."
>
> On the train I saw General Streeter, who said: "There is a general feeling of regret. I certainly hope she will return."
>
> Since my arrival here the telephone has been busy with regrets, some of which I will give you, as well as a few from those I have met upon the street.
>
> Mr. Josiah E. Fernald: "Concord has received a great surprise. From a large number of people I have heard nice things said of Mrs. Eddy. I shall write her about it."
>
> Mr. Isaac Hill, the grandson of Governor Hill, the friend of your brother Albert, said: "I deeply regret the outcome. Those people will awaken to the loss to Concord. Our foremost citizen has gone from us."
>
> Mr. Corser, the express agent: "I can't tell you how badly I feel. Those who have failed to appreciate Mrs. Eddy will find out what a loss Concord has suffered."

Mrs. Haskings: "It is hard to lose those we love. It is the greatest calamity that ever overtook Concord. Neighbors all express regret. Mr. Dunlap, the druggist, told me that Concord had lost its best citizen."

Mr. J. Wesley Plummer: "I have had a very blue day. I feel that a great blow has fallen upon Concord."

Mrs. Putnam: "The whole town is in mourning. Regret is expressed on all sides."

Mr. W. W. Hill who called in to see me, said: "Wherever you go people are downcast. They realize now how much Mrs. Eddy has been to Concord. Mrs. Hill feels very badly."

Mrs. M. Meehan: "I felt as if someone near and dear to me had gone. I wished when reading of the Brookline residence that Concord could have built the same suitable house for her here."

Dr. Worthen telephoned his sincere regret, and said that he was to call a church meeting to allow the people to express their sorrow for their loss.

Lovingly yours,
Irving C. Tomlinson

Dr. Worthen did call a meeting of the Concord Christian Science church the next day at which time the members adopted a letter of regret and appreciation to Mrs. Eddy. John Worthen also made a trip to Brookline on Thursday, January 30 to present Mrs. Eddy with a handsome jeweled insignia, containing five rubies and seventy-five diamonds, together with another letter from her Concord church:

Beloved Leader and Teacher:

The resident members of First Church of Christ, Scientist, Concord, N. H., have secured from France the jeweled insignia which you are entitled to wear by reason of the honorary decoration of *Officier d' Academie* which has been bestowed upon you for valuable and distinguished services.

It is a great joy to us and to all your followers that a great nation has recognized you as an author of excellence, whose works are of unusual merit. We fully realize that no worldly honor that can be bestowed begins to measure the wonderful good that you have brought and are bringing to all mankind.

The local members of this church joyfully embrace this opportunity of proving to you in a degree our appreciation of the good we have received directly and indirectly from you and your writings. We present to you with our deepest gratitude and love this insignia of the *Officier* which the French Government has recently conferred upon you.

John H. Worthen — Josiah E. Dwight
Joseph A. Moore — William A. Thompson
J. Wesley Plummer

Concord, N. H., January 28, 1908

CHAPTER XLVIII

CELESTIAL OR TERRESTRIAL?

Follow the wayshower and you will follow the divine idea; turn away from the wayshower and you turn away from the divine idea; like turning away from the windowpane, you turn away from the light. — MARY BAKER EDDY

1908

WHETHER Rev. Vosburgh lasted only a few weeks as Mrs. Eddy's secretary, or merely departed from his lecturing temporarily to help until a permanent secretary was found, he left Chestnut Hill on February 5, the day Adam Dickey was scheduled to begin. Snowstorms across several states, however, had delayed the trains and Mr. Dickey was a day later than expected. Mr. Vosburgh wrote the Leader the next day:

> Dearest Leader:
> I have come up this morning to instruct Mr. Dickey regarding one or two points that I omitted in the note I left for him last night. I regretted extremely, when I learned he did not arrive until this morning that I did not remain with you over the night. I am grateful for the infinite patience, and for the divine impatience with which you deal with your workers' shortcomings, and long-goings, — with which you have dealt with mine; and I am going, with renewed consecration and resolution, to work for the ideal that is given in Christ Jesus, and that your teaching is making practical, demonstrable to us, as it was to his early followers.
> Lovingly, faithfully,
> Arthur Reeves Vosburgh

Although several others seemed to know what was expected of Mr. Dickey, he had no idea when he arrived early on Thursday morning, February 6. He had first been introduced to Calvin Frye, and at breakfast met Laura Sargent, John Lathrop, and one or two others. He knew nothing about the household routine and was surprised at the reticence of the others to enlighten him. Later he understood and wrote:

> I was a comparative stranger, little known to any of them. They knew I had been sent for on Mrs. Eddy's call. They also were aware that I would have to pass the customary examination, through which every one passed who was brought to Mrs. Eddy's home with the expectation of serving her. None of them knew whether I would remain after the interview long enough to unpack my valise, or whether I would remain for three years. Many of the people who came to our Leader's home scarcely crossed the threshold, while others were interviewed by Mrs. Eddy and remained perhaps a day or two, and when she saw their services were not to be desired, they were allowed to depart and return home.

John Lathrop took Mr. Dickey under his wing and began teaching him about the household routine and secretarial duties. Mr. Frye was one of the most valued household members, and Adam felt that John spoke volumes when he whispered to him: "If I were you, I would cultivate Frye." Mrs. Eddy was obviously pleased with Mr. Dickey, for after much questioning during their first interview that morning:

> She then gave me a brief outline of some of the duties she would expect of me, and asked me if I would like to come and live in her household and become a member of it, and enter her service as a mental worker. I told her I would be most happy if she would employ me in any capacity whatever.

In a very short time Mr. Dickey was employed in two totally unexpected capacities. All mental workers were asked to do mental work for the Leader, as Mr. Carpenter told us, after they had been there about three weeks. But that was in 1905. In 1908 she did not wait three weeks before beginning this training and probing of the student's thought. Mr. Dickey had just returned to his room on this first morning and had not even learned that his signal was four bells, when the four-bell signal rang. As soon as he had learned what it meant, he went quickly to Mrs. Eddy and was given the startling assignment of working for the Leader as well as explanations of how to do this work and why it was necessary.

The second unexpected assignment was of an entirely different nature. Three days later, on Sunday morning, February 9, someone had occasion to go to the barn and reported that the horses had not been cared for. It was nearly noon before it was discovered that Burt, the coachman who had been there only one week, had died in the night. This drastic example surely proved to Mr. Dickey that all of Mrs. Eddy's help must be working Christian Scientists. When Mrs. Eddy called her household together she said: "There is a snake in the East that only attacks when a person is asleep." She talked with them about the subtle claims of malicious mental malpractice. She also gave a good deal more thought to this occurrence. The coachman had died of heart failure, and in talking with Mr. Dickey about it later Mrs. Eddy opened Science and Health to 187:13, "The valves of the heart, opening and closing for the passage of the blood, obey the mandate of mortal mind as directly as does the hand, admittedly moved by the will." Then she impressed upon Mr. Dickey that Science and Health is like a tool box for the metaphysician when she said:

> . . . when I turn to this book, I am like a mechanic who turns to his tools and picks up the one he wants. This reference on page 187 has a direct bearing on the case. When it occurred I knew where it came from, for it presented itself clearly to me in thought.

When Calvin Frye came into Adam Dickey's room after dinner that first Sunday afternoon and said how disappointed Mrs. Eddy was at not being able to take her drive, the following conversation ensued:

> Adam: Why can't she take her drive?
> Calvin: There is nobody to drive her.
> Adam: Can't you?
> Calvin: No, I never have driven a horse attached to a sleigh, and Mother is not willing for me to undertake it.
> Adam: Would you like me to drive?
> Calvin: Can you do it?
> Adam: Yes, I have been accustomed to horses all my life.

Mrs. Eddy questioned Mr. Dickey, with the result that he acted as her coachman for the next few days, — very pleased that such a slight service meant so much to her. But before the arrival of the new coachman on Thursday, February 13, another new member was added to the household.

MARTHA W. WILCOX

MARTHA Wilcox had grown up on a farm near Ottawa, Kansas and taught in schools near her home prior to marrying in 1895. Within six months of her marriage her young husband was drowned while on a business trip and the bereaved young widow returned to teaching.

In 1899 Martha married Dwight D. Wilcox, the father of one of her young pupils, which marriage gave her two step-sons, although the older boy was soon self-supporting. When Mr. Wilcox became seriously ill in 1902 the physician advised that he be taken to Kansas City for specialized treatment, and it was there that Martha was first introduced to Christian Science. Mrs. Wilcox devoured the "little book" and almost immediately began devoting part of each day to healing work. Many severe cases were healed in her first years of practice, but her dear husband passed away before the end of 1904. From that time Martha devoted her entire thought to the understanding of Christian Science.

Early in February of 1908 Mrs. Wilcox received a call from James A. Neal to come to Boston to serve Mrs. Eddy at Chestnut Hill where she arrived on Monday, February 10. As soon as she had removed her wraps Laura Sargent took her into Mrs. Eddy's study and introduced her saying, "This is Mrs. Wilcox from Kansas City." Mrs. Eddy said, "Good morning, Mrs. Wilcox, I felt your sweet presence in the house." During this first interview she asked Martha what she could do and what she was willing to do. When Martha replied that she was willing to do anything Mrs. Eddy wanted, the Leader replied, "My housekeeper has had to go home because of the illness of her father, and I should like to have you take her place for the time being."

Martha was very young in Science and not yet ready for the lessons given to the experienced mental workers each morning, but the Leader began her first lesson that morning on the subject of mental malpractice:

> Sometimes a sense of a personality arises before your thought and leads you to believe that a personality is something outside and separate from your thought that can harm you. She showed me that the real danger was never this threatened attack from outside my thought . . . but that the real danger was always within my thought. . . .
>
> Mrs. Eddy no doubt realized that at my stage of growth, I thought of creation — that is, all things, — as separated into two groups, one group spiritual and the other group material, and that somehow I must get rid of the group I called material. But during this lesson I caught my first glimpse of the fact that all right, useful things — which I had been calling "the unrighteous mammon" — were mental and represented spiritual ideas.

When Mrs. Eddy had finished this first lesson she said: "Now take your young child down into Egypt and let it grow up until it is strong enough to stand alone." And Martha did just that, — pondered it silently. Years later she could summarize this first lesson briefly: 1) to handle mental malpractice within my own consciousness, and 2) there are not two groups of creation, just one.

Following the lesson Mrs. Eddy said, "I should like to have you make a pudding for my dinner today — an apple Betty pudding. No one seems to get pudding to taste as it used to taste when I lived at Lynn." Martha did glimpse the importance of mental work for everything, even pudding, and she did her best. However, she was almost overwhelmed with all she had learned in less than half a day. After dinner Mrs. Eddy said to her maid: "Tell Martha that the pudding was very good, but no better than Mrs. Scott made yesterday," which made Martha realize that everyone in the house was being trained individually.

What Mr. Dickey had at first thought was a crude system of bell ringing in Mrs. Eddy's home soon appeared to him as a very effective, ingenious institution which he thought Calvin Frye must have improvised. Different numbers of bells rang in different areas of the house depending upon which student was being summoned. He had not been in the household long when he heard the bells ringing all over the house one morning, and before long Mr. Frye opened his door and said, "That means everybody." When all the mental workers had presented themselves in her study Mrs. Eddy opened her Bible and read to them:

> James 1:21 Wherefore lay apart all filthiness and superfluity of naughtiness, and receive with meekness the engrafted word, which is able to save your souls.
>
> 22 But be ye doers of the word and not hearers only, deceiving your own selves.
>
> 23 For if any be a hearer of the word, and not a doer, he is like unto a man, beholding his natural face in a glass:
>
> 24 For he beholdeth himself, and goeth his way, and straightway forgetteth what manner of man he was.
>
> 25 But whoso looketh into the perfect law of liberty, and continueth therein, he being not a forgetful hearer, but a doer of the work, this man shall be blessed in his deed.

When Mrs. Eddy expounded this passage to them, Mr. Dickey saw his own true being more clearly than he had ever seen it before. After inspiring them, she exhorted them to greater efforts with this reprimand:

> You are not doing your work as you should and I shall not instruct you further until you have demonstrated something more of what has been taught. It would be a poor teacher that would take students up into the higher branches of mathematics before they had proved

addition, subtraction, multiplication, and division. Therefore, until you demonstrate in better fashion what you have already been taught, I shall teach you no more.

The Leader was a natural teacher teaching every minute of every day in all she said and did, but all of her students needed nudging most of the time to force them toward spiritual accomplishment.

Further instruction for all the field was published in the *Sentinel* of February 15:

A NEW BY-LAW
Article XXVIII (Now Art. XXIII)

Requirements for Organizing Branch Churches. Sect. 8. A branch church of The First Church of Christ, Scientist, Boston, Mass., shall not be organized with less than sixteen loyal Christian Scientists, four of whom are members of The Mother Church. This membership shall include at least one active practitioner whose card is published in the list of practitioners in *The Christian Science Journal.*

About this same time, and when she had been at Chestnut Hill but a short time, Mrs. Wilcox was called by Mrs. Eddy to be her personal maid for a month. In the first few days Martha learned a great lesson watching Mrs. Eddy work:

She wrote almost constantly for three days. She consulted the dictionary, the grammar, studied synonyms and antonyms, and when she had finished, she had . . . two lines to add to Science and Health. I marvelled at her perseverance . . . But she had worked out a scientific statement for Christian Science students that would stand through the ages.

This statement occasioned by the sudden, fatal attack on her coachman was introduced as follows in the *Sentinel* of February 29:

Take Notice

I request the Christian Scientists universally to read the paragraph beginning at line 30 on page 442 in the edition of Science and Health which will be issued February 29. I consider the information there given to be of great importance at this stage of the workings of animal magnetism, and it will greatly aid the students in their individual experiences. . . .

Mary Baker G. Eddy

The paragraph of two lines plus one word added to page 442 in the February 29, 1908 edition of Science and Health read: "Christian Scientists, be a law to yourselves that mental malpractice can harm you neither when asleep nor when awake." Numerous letters of appreciation for this instruction were published in the *Sentinel.* One student correlated this latest addition with the passage in *Miscellaneous Writings* (258:12-15): "In the spiritual Genesis of creation, all law was vested in the Lawgiver, who was a law to Himself. In divine Science, God is One and All; and governing Himself, He governs the universe."

Another notice in the February 29 *Sentinel* stated that the new Publishing House building was "being pushed as rapidly as possible" and asked the branch churches to help keep the treasurer supplied with necessary funds.

Martha Wilcox was working as diligently as she knew how. With no training in such work, the Leader had given her seven finely written pages of things to be done which "necessitated continuity of action without false moves or forgetting." Another student was very happy to receive the letter Mrs. Eddy wrote to him on February 20 telling him to come to Chestnut Hill for four weeks:

> Do not fail to come and then if you and God and I think best you can arrange perhaps to remain here.

So Irving C. Tomlinson returned to Mrs. Eddy's household about the same time that John Lathrop returned to his work in New York City. After the four week trial Mr. Tomlinson continued at Chestnut Hill and remained with Mrs. Eddy through 1910.

The remodeling that Mrs. Eddy wanted for her rooms necessitated her moving temporarily to Miss Eveleth's rooms on the third floor. The architect said it was impossible to install a second elevator where Mrs. Eddy wanted it, but she insisted and it was done along with reducing the size of the rooms in her apartment and lowering the windows for a better view. A day shift and a night shift of workmen helped to expedite the project, but also made the housekeeping quite difficult. It was the second week in March when Mr. Dickey joyfully carried the news up to Mrs. Eddy that she could return to her own apartment on the following Saturday, which pleased her greatly. There was still a good deal to be done and, in addition to the workmen, all the household worked eagerly to complete the project. Following her drive on Saturday, March 14, she moved back into her own suite of rooms. Everything was finished except her pink parlor, and the work on that continued.

A few days later carpet layers from Boston were scheduled to lay the carpet in her pink parlor while she was out on her daily drive, but the room was not ready for them. The floor was covered with fresh plaster, etc. John Salchow who usually took care of such jobs was away that morning, and Martha Wilcox said:

> So I cleaned the floor and the carpet paper and laid it and had the room ready for the men to lay the carpet — but I myself was a sight to behold. The men were through and gone by the time the carriage returned, and I had a few minutes to freshen myself.

Martha was barely presentable when Laura Sargent came to her and said, "Martha, Mother wants you."

> When I entered, the mental workers were all standing about the room. I went to her and said, "What do you want, Mother?" With tears rolling down her cheeks, she replied, "I have been praying for God to send someone who will stand, no matter what comes up, and he has told me to call you. Now come in every day with the mental workers and have your lessons and do your mental work."

The Leader had also discovered in Mr. Dickey a most desireable quality that few, other than her darling Augusta, had, — and that was obedience. Mr. Dickey had heard before coming to Chestnut Hill that the Leader had great difficulty in finding workers who would *follow* her orders implicitly, and he laid the obligation upon himself before he began in Mrs. Eddy's employ, of absolute obedience without questioning:

> It did not take Mrs. Eddy long to discover this quality of obedience in my thought and she at once evidenced a pleasure in having me do things for her, so that when she moved into her new room and settled it, I was privileged to stand at her hand and place everything where she wished it. She herself named the spot on the mantel where each ornament should rest, while I, overjoyed at this rare privilege, moved things back and forth at her command until everything was placed as she desired it.

Mrs. Eddy also supervised the hanging of all the pictures in the house and most especially those in her study and bedroom. On the day Mr. Dickey helped her with this he particularly noted a remarkably well-executed painting, entitled "The Return from the Crucifixion":

> It showed the beloved disciple ascending the steps of his home, sustaining the drooping form of the mother of Jesus . . . The faces of the group . . . with the exception of Jesus' mother, were anxiously turned toward a hill beyond the walls of Jerusalem, where silhouetted against the sky appeared the three crosses, which stood as mute witnesses of the dreadful day's experience.

A very few minutes after Mr. Dickey had completed the picture hanging and returned to his room he was recalled to Mrs. Eddy's study:

> pointing with one hand to the picture just described and placing the other on her breast, she said in a voice deep and earnest in its subdued tones, "Mr. Dickey, I think you had better remove that picture. It suggests too much for me. Won't you kindly put another in its place?" This I did . . .

Another type of "remodeling" was going on at this same time. William Lyman Johnson had made an interesting discovery in pursuing his study of heraldry and related topics. He wrote Mrs. Eddy soon after she had moved to Chestnut Hill that the crown in the Christian Science seal was a ducal coronet with strawberry leaves, whereas he felt that it should be the Christian's crown of five stars. Many times the Leader had bowed to man's opinion, and she did so once again.

On February 14 Adam Dickey returned the five new seal designs (on one of which Mrs. Eddy had written "Eddy") to William D. McCrackan who had replaced Allison V. Stewart on the Board of Trustees. The letter from Dickey to McCrackan enclosed with the seal designs may indicate that Mrs. Eddy did *not* select the new design that Mr. McCrackan had recommended:

> In reply to your letter to our Leader under date of February 13th, enclosing new designs to be used on Christian Science books, I have to report that she has selected the enclosed, detached, design which bears her signature.
>
> I also enclose the unapproved designs.

The letter Mr. Dickey wrote to Archibald McLellan on March 10 is probably in reference to the new crown in the new seal design:

> I enclose herewith Mr. William Lyman Johnson's letter to our Leader, which explains itself. It seems that she wishes the matter referred to you, and I have written Mr. Johnson to that effect, and asking him to take the matter up with you.

The Leader did have an interview with Mr. McLellan and Stephen A. Chase at Chestnut Hill on March 16, but that could have been in relation to the new building for the Publishing Society which was under construction and closely related to another project she had in mind but had not yet voiced. God had spoken to her one day when she opened her Bible to Isaiah 62:

> 10 Go through, go through the gates; prepare ye the way of the people; cast up, cast up the highway; gather out the stones; lift up a standard for the people.

A letter from the trustees of the Publishing Society dated March 18 stated:

> Beloved Leader and Teacher:
>
> Knowing the kindly interest which you take in the progressive work of the Christian Science Publishing Society, I take pleasure, in behalf of the Trustees, in sending you a copy of the new cover for The Christian Science Journal. It will appear with the April number. We have bound this cover over the March number, in this instance, that you might have a clearer impression of the appearance of the new cover. We hope that it will be considered by you as an improvement. The new seal is being used in connection with this cover, showing a celestial crown, or a Christian's crown, combined with the cross.

Whenever a student accomplished anything by turning to Mind to guide him Mrs. Eddy was lavish in her praise and appreciation, even if the accomplishment seemed insignificant. Mr. Carpenter said:

> Mrs. Eddy was most punctilious in sending letters of appreciation for services performed. She took her valuable time that was needed in other directions, and sent letters to those of her students who performed faithful service. She never failed to express appreciation for work that was done by demonstration. . . .
>
> On one occasion, when I made a demonstration for her in a minor matter, it seemed strange to have Mrs. Eddy so appreciative about it; but she thereby indicated how little demonstration she received, so that when one did work according to divine Mind, her appreciation seemed almost extravagant.

Contrariwise, when a student's efforts were directed by the human mind, and he did not turn to Mind, God, for guidance (which was far more often the case), there was little or no appreciation and sometimes criticism or rebuke from the Leader. Knowing this, causes one to ponder the response to the trustees regarding the new seal. Did she consider *this* "progressive work of the Christian Science Publishing Society" as an improvement? Or did she submit to *man's* idea of a "celestial crown" as she had to her mansion in Brookline? Mr. Dickey wrote to Mr. McCrackan the next day, March 19:

> In reply to your letter of the 18th inst., addressed to our Leader, accompanied by a copy of the new cover for the Christian Science Journal. Mrs. Eddy was busily engaged on another matter when I presented your book, and without making any special comment, she requested me to ask the Trustees to "Keep on the outside of our Periodicals, the emblem of the Celestial and not the terrestrial."

I take it by this, that the new design was acceptable to our Leader, and that you may proceed with that understanding.

Many a student in Mrs. Eddy's household was offended when his *human* efforts were criticized or, in his eyes, unappreciated. Mayhap Mr. McCrackan was offended by the Leader's seeming indifference to their "celestial crown improvement," for two or three weeks later he tendered his resignation with what McKenzie and Hatten (the other trustees) felt was insufficient reason, and a few months later left Boston and removed to Switzerland. Only three months earlier Mr. McCrackan had written to "Beloved Leader and Teacher":

> . . . Let me as the first act of my Trusteeship, thank you for this added mark of your confidence. I welcome the duties of this new office as a further opportunity of serving God and mankind by helping to disseminate your teachings over the broad receptive earth.
>
> With renewed expression of my profound gratitude I have the honor of signing myself
>
> Your faithful follower,

This Publishing Society trustee was an example of just how receptive "the broad receptive earth" was to Mrs. Eddy's teachings. If this "faithful follower" felt that *his* ideas "of serving God and mankind" were better than Mrs. Eddy's, he was not the first one. There were many students who had caused Mrs. Eddy to say, "they think they can run things just as well and a little better than I can."

Jesus had answered the disciples' question Who is greatest in the kingdom of heaven?

> Matt. 18:3 . . . Except ye be converted, and become as little children, ye shall not enter into the kingdom of heaven.
>
> 4 Whosoever therefore shall humble himself as this little child, the same is greatest in the kingdom of heaven.

The Mother spent all her years in teaching her children *how* to "become as little children." But lessons in humility are difficult for all capable people and doubly so for the accomplished and talented individual who needs it most of all. At one time Mrs. Eddy said:

> The human sense of leadership creates a poison, the virus of which is more deadly than the bite of the moccasin, and from which the victim cannot heal himself or be healed, but must suffer. This is the sin against the Holy Ghost, because it sets up a mind and mental activity separate from God and His idea. In other words, substitutes itself and its sense for Principle and its reflection, and thereby

becomes a belief of another god and reflection — though sensual instead of spiritual — all error.

Alfred Farlow had written the Leader an interesting letter on March 9 regarding another issue on which she had bowed to the claims of men:

Dear Teacher:

You remember that a few years ago critics affirmed that your first husband, George W. Glover, was not entitled to be called Colonel, and that some of the North Carolina students claimed to have discovered that he could properly be called Major but not Colonel. During the past winter I took up that question again, and I have learned, upon good authority, that Mr. Glover's position as a member of the governor's staff made him a member of the staff militia, the governor of the State being commander-in-chief of the State militia, and that it was a custom all over the South to apply the title "Colonel" to one who had occupied that position. Thus you may note that you were correct in referring to your husband as Colonel George W. Glover, and in saying that he was sometimes called Colonel and at other times called Captain.

Most likely Mrs. Eddy had never doubted that she was correct, but she had acquiesced to the demands of men.

When Gilbert Carpenter had heard early in February that Mrs. Eddy was in need of a coachman he had recommended one of his patients who had been a minister, Mr. Adolph Stevenson. Mr. Stevenson came to Chestnut Hill on February 13 and served Mrs. Eddy well at her new house in Newton. But this house was not like her Pleasant View which she loved so dearly. All of the world and most of her students felt that her spacious new home was a great step in advancement. Henrietta Chanfrau may have recorded the Leader's words in her heart on the day that she had told her if she ever left Pleasant View it would be to be delivered up to her enemies. But probably only Mrs. Eddy had any idea what that meant. Mr. Stevenson may have suggested a beautification project for her new estate, for she wrote him a letter on March 17, part of which said:

I hereby tell you that no garden or flowers shall be cultivated on my place. Make no road for one to see such things on this place; the road to heaven is not one of flowers, but it is straight and narrow; it is bearing the cross, and turning away from things that lure the material senses, denying them and finding all in Spirit, in God, in good and doing good.

Mrs. Eddy wrote letters to all of her employees, and she wrote to Mr. Stevenson again on March 19:

> My dear Mr. Stevenson:
>
> If you treat either of our horses for the fear of an automobile it will help them just as it heals the sick, by destroying their fear. Horses are nearly as receptive of the effect from C.S. treatment as human beings are. In haste.
>
> Affectionately,
> M. B. G. Eddy

As always her interest extended to everyone and everything, but for quite a long time, — ever since God had spoken to her through Isaiah 62:10, — she had been considering another major undertaking which would spread around the world. She had even decided upon a name for this new project, though she had not yet breathed one word of it to anyone. But the Mind that was unfolding this new step in her thought was also nudging the receptive thought of others. On March 12 she received a letter from one of her followers in Boston, John L. Wright, deploring the disappearance of the "stable, sane, patriotic newspaper" and outlining a great many of the features she had been considering as desirable in a daily newspaper, with one important exception. His letter stated:

> I am not thinking of a daily official Christian Science paper, or one containing in its title the words Christian Science . . .

That was exactly what the Leader *was* thinking of, and she wrote on the back of Mr. Wright's letter:

> Beloved Student:
>
> I have had this newspaper scheme in my thought for quite a while and herein send my name for our daily newspaper
>
> The Christian Science Monitor
>
> This title only classifies the paper and it should have departments for what else is requisite.

There is no record that this response was ever sent to Mr. Wright, but in a very few months he was one of the newspapermen employed to bring forth *The Christian Science Monitor,* and he was its first city editor.

CHAPTER XLIX

"AND THE GLORY OF MOAB SHALL BE CONTEMNED"

Mortals must take up the cross if they would follow Christ, and worship the Father "in spirit and in truth."

— MARY BAKER EDDY

1908

On March 30 Adam Dickey wrote to Allison V. Stewart:

> I return herewith the samples you sent to Mrs. Eddy of the new seal to be used on the covers of the different bindings of Science and Health.
>
> Our Leader wishes me to thank you for your kindness, and to say that she approves of the samples sent. You may go ahead and use them.

The new seal made its first appearance on the cover of the *Journal.* The April, 1908 issue began Volume XXVI of the *Christian Science Journal* with a new cover design which included the newly designed Christian Science seal.

Mrs. Eddy had known for over a year that the movement was not to have her personal guidance much longer. She also knew that the glory God had given to her Cause would be contemned when she was no longer there listening for God's voice to direct every step. Her students had questioned every progressive step she had taken and constantly tried to have her make her revelations and directions from God conform to the opinions and usages of men. It was her absolute obedience to God alone that made the Way glorious, but she had complied with the opinions of men at many times and on many points. Whether the "celestial crown" was one of those points is a question. But the new seal design seems to lack the glory

PUBLISHED MONTHLY · PRICE $2.00 PER ANNUM · SINGLE COPIES 20 CENTS

VOLUME 26 ✿ APRIL 1908 ✿ NUMBER 1

THE CHRISTIAN SCIENCE JOURNAL

FOUNDED APRIL, 1883, BY MARY BAKER G. EDDY
AUTHOR OF THE CHRISTIAN SCIENCE TEXT BOOK
"SCIENCE AND HEALTH WITH KEY TO THE SCRIPTURES"

OFFICIAL ORGAN OF THE FIRST CHURCH OF CHRIST, SCIENTIST, IN BOSTON · MASSACHUSETTS

ARCHIBALD McLELLAN
EDITOR
JOHN B. WILLIS · ANNIE M. KNOTT · ASSOCIATE EDITORS

PUBLISHED BY
THE · CHRISTIAN · SCIENCE · PUBLISHING · SOCIETY
250 · HUNTINGTON · AVENUE · BOSTON · MASSACHUSETTS · U · S · A

Entered at the Post Office, Boston, Mass., as Second-class Matter.

NEW COVER DESIGN BEGINNING APRIL, 1908

of the previous seal. A great many students compared the two designs, and inquiries began pouring in asking if there was significance to the new design which made the cross appear so much larger.

NEW

CHRISTIAN SCIENCE SEAL

CHRISTIAN SCIENCE SEAL

The cross in the new seal design is slightly larger, the crown is considerably smaller, and the imperative demands are reduced in size. The significance of these points was left for the student to figure out for himself. Mrs. Eddy answered all the inquiries in these words through Archibald McLellan's article entitled "The Cross and Crown" which was published in the *Sentinel* of May 30:

> To those of our readers who have been searching for some hidden significance in the larger cross, we may say for their reassurance that the cross we are called upon to bear as Christian Scientists is no larger or heavier than heretofore. What we most need to impress upon our thought is that the crown has been brought nearer than ever through the ministry of Mrs. Eddy.

The significance of the cross' appearing to be larger could very well be the fact that Christian Scientists would soon have to start bearing the cross that the Leader had been bearing for them all these years.

At the time the Christian Scientists in Boston were working on the new seal Michael Meehan completed and copyrighted his volume *Mrs. Eddy and the Late Suit in Equity.* Following his recital of all the court proceedings he included over forty pages of editorial comment, "because," as he wrote, "with the exception of very few papers in the entire world, they held, even in the light of their limited knowledge of the facts, that the proceedings instituted by 'next friends' were without precedent in law, equity, morals, or civic responsibility." Meehan continues:

> These unbiased utterances of wide-awake men go to show that as yet there is a widespread regard for the Constitution of the United States, wherein it guarantees to all religious liberty. They go to show that the civic ideals that urge reverence for age and womanhood must be maintained.

Following are brief excerpts from one editorial Mr. Meehan included which was from the *Daily News,* Pasadena, California:

> The widely heralded attack on the leader of the Christian Scientists has collapsed. Insincere movements are peculiarly subject to sudden collapse. For a long time it was persistently rumored that Mrs. Eddy was dead and . . . was being impersonated . . .
>
> When this very senseless piece of foolishness was exploded and it was proven conclusively . . . that Mrs. Eddy not only lived but was in a remarkable state of preservation, alert, capable, and incisive . . . the malice which had inspired these silly stories turned elsewhere for means to embarrass her and her very remarkable following. Unfriendly newspapers bent to the work with a will, circulating all manner of evil reports, none of which seems to have been authentic, as has since been abundantly shown. *McClure's Magazine* lent itself to the task and has been feeding its readers with fiction on the subject in serial form ever since. *McClure's* even presented what purported to be a picture of the revered Leader of the Christian Scientists, which was not a picture of Mrs. Eddy at all, but a spurious reproduction of the photograph of another woman, which was fully proven. . . .
>
> These "next friends" have simply been used. The real attack has been against Christian Science. It has ignominiously failed . . . This remarkable movement will stand or fall on its merits.

The first copy of Michael Meehan's book (of the five thousand published in the spring of 1908) was sent to Mrs. Eddy who read it immediately. The next day she wrote to Mr. Meehan that she wished the book withheld from sale and circulation, adding:

> You will render me a statement of all expenses to which you have been put. Make liberal allowance for those who have aided you in the work. Put a value upon your own time and service while engaged on it, and when you have done this, double the value you have placed on your own work, and double it again, and then send me the bill.

This had been a costly book to publish, and in regard to Mrs. Eddy's instructions Mr. Meehan wrote:

I did this, and as soon as a complete bill was rendered, she wrote out a check in full of account, amounting to many thousands of dollars.

Early in April the *Sentinel* announced a "New Concordance to Science and Health," stating that "A *Complete Concordance* . . . revised from the latest edition of Science and Health is now on the press and will be ready for delivery in a few days." When those few days had expired Mrs. Eddy received the following letter dated April 17:

Beloved Leader:
Will you kindly accept the enclosed copy of the new Concordance as a slight token of love and gratitude from the Christian Scientists who have had the privilege and pleasure of compiling, proof-reading, editing, and publishing it.

Emma T. Houtz	Ruth L. Ingalls
N. Florence Mellen	Louise C. Souther
Laura C. Conant	Amanda A. Carey
Albert F. Conant	Allison V. Stewart

Later issues of the *Sentinel* and *Journal* said of the new Concordance:

Mrs. Eddy has said, "I have revised Science and Health only to give a clearer and fuller expression of its original meaning" (S&H p.361); and an eloquent testimony to the time and thought our Leader has devoted to this labor of love is found in the fact that out of the five thousand references added to the Concordance nearly sixteen hundred were required for new words, changes from the original text accounting for the balance.

On the second of April the president of the United States, Theodore Roosevelt, had addressed the North Carolina Peace Society commending their aims and also their stance for equipping "the country with vessels and munitions of war to make splendid defense in case of attack." President Roosevelt said in his short speech:

. . . for peace societies merely jeopardize the national welfare, and are profoundly hostile to American national life, if they obstruct the Government in providing ample military and naval power to meet conditions in the actual world of today.

Mrs. Eddy's brief statement entitled "War" *(My.* 286) in the next issue of the *Sentinel* supported the president in its closing paragraph. But she did not leave the issue there. In all the history of the world no one had ever founded a greater peace movement than had the Discoverer and Founder of Christian Science. If those who called themselves Christians would follow the guidance of God's two witnesses on this planet, they could manifest peace on earth. The time had come for the Leader to point this out to Christian Scientists which she did with a by-law amendment:

> THE PROMOTION OF PEACE. Sect. 14. — It shall be the duty of the members of The Mother Church and of its branch churches to promote peace on earth and good will toward men; but to do this it is not *needful* to form *organizations.* Members of The Mother Church shall not hereafter become members of other societies except those specified in the Church Manual, but they shall strive to promote the welfare of all mankind by demonstrating the rules of divine Love.

A short time later this by-law became what is now Section 16 of Article VIII *(Man.* 45).

Augusta Stetson wrote on April 8, and both her letter and Mrs. Eddy's response were published in the *Sentinel:*

> My Precious Leader and Teacher:
>
> Since you have moved into your new home, I have greatly desired to send you an expression of my love, but I have been unable to find anything which I thought would be pure and perfect enough to offer to my precious Leader. Nothing I ever could get would express my deep love and loyalty, and my ever-increasing gratitude to you, so I ceased my search and settled upon this flower holder, which I send to you dearest, as a reminder of my affection for you, and of nearly twenty-four years of your patient, unselfed watch care of me and mine. I trust it will speak to you of my constant appreciation of your Christly love for me and mine and all mankind, and of my earnest endeavor to continue to follow and obey your consecrated life and sublime teachings. My heart is overflowing with gratitude to God for such a Leader, and Teacher, and Guide to eternal Life.
>
> Ever your loving child,
> Augusta E. Stetson
>
> - - - - -
>
> My Beloved Student:
>
> Your gift to me — a "flower holder" — is a dream of beauty. I thank you. God give you and your students the beauty of love in the highest, peace and good will to men.
>
> Lovingly,
> Mary B. G. Eddy

The Leader's "watch care" of this "beloved student" was expressed the next week in this letter:

> Darling:
> A temptation is upon you, viz. to have a quarrel with Anne Dodge. I shall not take your side nor her side in this quarrel, but only God's side, namely, to love your friends and enemies. I shall not help nor hinder her forming a church and you must not hinder if God is directing her, and if He is not, she will not prosper in whatever she does. The old m.a.m. is trying to make discord between you and Miss Dodge — *disappoint it* — now. Be strong in your trust in God and all will be well with you. . . . Let me know if you get this letter. . . .
> N.B. You prosper best by keeping your thoughts and your students' thoughts *away from me* for then God fills my mind and shows me how to help you all.

The Leader wrote two more short letters to Augusta on that same day, April 15. The first one said:

> My darling Student: — Come and see me some time. Let me know when. I want you to see your presents to me and how I have had them placed.
>
> With love unbounded, yours

The other letter was addressed to Mrs. Stetson and her Students and said:

> Darlings: — Do not send me another thought or thing material. My treasures are spiritual and laid up in Heaven.

Shortly thereafter she wrote to all Christian Scientists in this regard, but she did it in a new manner. Instead of publishing her note of thanks to "the dear Christian Scientists" *(My.* 274) in the *Sentinel,* she sent it to the *Boston Herald* for publication. It was then republished in the *Sentinel* of April 25.

Mrs. Eddy's *nota bene* on her April 15 letter to Augusta Stetson was a point she had to remind her students of again and again. She was constantly at work shutting out the world's thoughts about her, but her students' thoughts reached her and robbed her of God's thoughts. She wrote to Calvin Hill on April 24: "Please keep your thoughts *apart* from me, and accept my forever gratitude." This was a very difficult point for the students to grasp. They could not understand how or why she should suffer from their tender, loving thoughts. Those tender thoughts were the expression of *good mortal mind.* The students saw only the *good.* The Leader *felt* the *mortal mind.* Good mortal thought can be likened to pleasure in matter which is far more likely to keep one from spirituality than is pain in matter.

On April 26 the Leader wrote to her coachman:

Mr. Stevenson
My dear Student:

You do all that you do so well I need not request anything further — But I noticed today that the spirit of Dolly so increased that it may give me some anxiety for I rest on her to guard against Princess' spirits. So please keep Dolly calm and all will go on as it has done — well.

Affectionately,
Eddy

On the day that Mrs. Eddy and Adolph Stevenson were concerned about Dolly in Boston, Edward A. Kimball was delivering a lecture to "a large and appreciative audience" in Southampton, England. Most likely Mr. Kimball had visited Mrs. Eddy at her new home before he left on his European lecture tour, for he carried a message from the Leader to the family of the late Earl of Dunmore.

Mr. Kimball had lectured in Paris, France on April 3, Zurich, Switzerland on the seventh, and then at The Hague, Holland three days later. The report of his lecture in London on April 13 said:

> Edward A. Kimball of Chicago delivered a lecture ... at Queen's Hall on April 13. The hall has a seating capacity of about three thousand and the lecture was announced for eight o'clock. The doors were opened at a quarter past seven, and in fifteen minutes nearly every seat was occupied. Half an hour later the nine entrances had to be closed, and a crowd of many hundreds turned away in spite of their punctual arrival, as not a seat was to be had in any part of the vast hall. Such an attendance in this, the most populace concert hall in London, is without precedent ...

One day in the spring of 1908 when Mr. Kimball was lecturing to appreciative audiences in England and Scotland Mrs. Eddy called Mr. McLellan to Chestnut Hill. She said to her editor that she would like to have a daily newspaper started. Mr. McLellan objected to her idea and said that it could not be done, so the Leader turned away and said no more. The date could have been May 3, for on that day she wrote a letter to Archibald McLellan and Allison V. Stewart in which she said:

> The time has come when we must have a daily paper entitled Christian Science Monitor. Allow no hesitation or delay in this movement. I will loan you all the money I can raise to help do it. When I proposed having the weekly Sentinel students held back at first; they may hold back this time but I in the name of God direct you to do this. Answer me immediately.

McLellan and Stewart did not answer her immediately because

this was one of the many letters which Mrs. Eddy wrote but did not send. Mrs. Eddy was meeting the same resistance in Boston that she had encountered with every new step, but on the other side of the Atlantic Mr. Kimball encountered a resistance to truth that was new to him.

Mrs. Eddy published a letter in the *Sentinel* of May 2 from a Christian Scientist in Pilot View, Dalkey, Ireland who had taught Sunday school in branch churches in both Belfast and Dublin. She went on to say: "Though the Christian Scientists are not a very numerous body here as yet, they are very earnest in their wish to follow, even if but slowly, where you lead, knowing that you 'follow Christ.'"

On Sunday afternoon, the tenth of May, Mr. Kimball delivered a lecture in Dublin, Ireland which was reported as follows in the *Daily Express* of May 11:

> Yesterday afternoon Mr. Edward A. Kimball delivered an interesting address in the large hall of the Ancient Concert Rooms on the subject of Christian Science. There was a large attendance. Mr. Walter Wilding, M.R.C.S.,M.R.C.P.,presided, and, in introducing the lecturer, said the study and practice of medicine practically absorbed his time until he heard of Christian Science and actually witnessed the healing of several cases of organic diseases amongst his patients. One was the case of a cripple, and the surgeon in the infirmary advised that nothing would save the leg from amputation but an operation on the knee. The Christian Science treatment was tried and the patient was healed. He had examined the limb the day before and the day after the cure and he could not doubt that a miracle had been performed, as no material power could have produced the result. This and other equally wonderful works — the result of prayer — convinced him of the efficacy of Christian Science, and there was only one outcome of that conviction — that was to cease practising medicine.

The next evening, Monday, May 11, Mr. Kimball lectured at Belfast, Ireland, which was reported in the *Boston Globe* of May 13:

> Belfast, (Ireland). Edward Kimball of Boston, a Christian Scientist, lectured tonight in Exhibition Hall. A howling mob was present, largely composed of Queen's College (medical) students, who rushed the doors. By the use of drums, tin pans, and toy trumpets they did their utmost to disturb the lecture. On being expelled from the building, they threw stones. Windows were smashed and the platform was littered with missiles. Eventually quiet was restored and the lecture delivered.

Three years later in the same location Bliss Knapp had a similar experience before Belfast peaceably accepted Christian Science.

Mr. Kimball delivered several more well attended lectures in Scotland and England in May of 1908 before returning to the continent where he lectured on May 26 to the largest audience ever assembled in Berlin, Germany to hear a Christian Science lecture. The day before his last lecture in England he wrote to Mrs. Eddy:

Manchester, England, May 21, 1908

Beloved Teacher:

I have hesitated to take any of your time, but it seems to me that you will be glad to hear what I can tell you about the status of the Christian Science movement in Great Britain. I had no idea it had taken on such large proportions and was so well known and so largely discussed; moreover, I did not suppose the work was being so favorably presented and maintained by the Christian Scientists, as I find to be the case. The characteristic sturdiness and earnestness and stability of the better class of people in these islands serve a very large purpose when these people become Christian Scientists. As a rule they have a high and dignified appreciation of Science itself and of what constitutes legitimate and effective practice. They have accomplished much over here, and the present situation and activity of our Cause are full of great promise.

The lectures are largely attended, — sometimes crowds of people are unable to gain entrance, — and they have received quite as much and as respectful attention from the press as is given them in America. One of the great London religious papers has announced its intention to publish the lecture which I am to give in London tomorrow night, in order that the readers of that paper and the people of that denomination (the Congregational) may have a statement of Christian Science from its advocate rather than from its opponent. The editor has stipulated that I am to speak of certain phases of the subject which he has named, and particularly that I shall tell them "something about Mrs. Eddy."

I think that this is the first instance of the kind in our history. No religious paper in America, other than our own, has ever published the full text of a Christian Science lecture. In this case it is opportune, because there is to be a great meeting in June of the Church of England, and at that meeting the delegates are to discuss Christian Science. A Congregational minister said to me, "Mrs. Eddy has presented the only perfectly concatenated religious system in existence. If one accepts the premise, he must accept the conclusion. I am ready to accept the premise, because Christian Science is the only religion that gets God into the world as or through His spiritual idea, instead of as a man."

Tomorrow, at St. James Chapel in London, we shall attend the christening of the grandson of the late Earl of Dunmore. This ceremony in behalf of a future peer of England, or rather Scotland, is of such importance that the King is to be present.

With many good wishes for you, I am, as ever, lovingly yours in the kinship of immortal Life.

Edward A. Kimball

Mrs. Eddy had Mr. Kimball's letter published in the *Sentinel* of June 6 followed by:

MRS. EDDY'S COMMENT

Forty years ago I said to a student, "I can introduce Christian Science in England more readily than I can in America."

Mary B. G. Eddy

* * *

CHRISTIAN SCIENCE BIBLE LESSONS

Vol. XIX. JULY, AUGUST, SEPTEMBER. No. 2.

July 5, 1908.

Subject: GOD.

Golden Text: "Thou art good, and doest good; teach me thy statutes." Psalm 119 : 68.

NEW SEAL IN *CHRISTIAN SCIENCE QUARTERLY*

CHAPTER L

THE PRECIOUS VOLUME

That which when sown bears immortal fruit, enriches mankind only when it is understood, — hence the many readings given the Scriptures, and the requisite revisions of SCIENCE AND HEALTH WITH KEY TO THE SCRIPTURES. — MARY BAKER EDDY

1908

THE adjustment from Pleasant View to Chestnut Hill was not an easy one for Mrs. Eddy. One day she said to John Salchow, "This is not my home. Pleasant View will always be my home." The quieter countryside was the horses' home, too. They were disturbed by the automobile traffic in Newton, and Mrs. Eddy no longer enjoyed her daily drive. What had once been a pleasant diversion became a chore.

Calvin Frye found the adjustment as difficult as did Mrs. Eddy. His responsibilities and burdens were increased with the larger house and household. His every thought was to help the Leader, but she also took "watch care" of him, as is evident from this note she wrote Mr. Dickey when they had been at Chestnut Hill only a few weeks:

> Mr. Frye needs *encouragement* — despondency is his belief and the dear man has shared my deprivations many years hoping they would cease and so give him release as well as myself. Encourage him to find all happiness in *divine Love* life spiritual here and now.
>
> You are able to depict this, for you seem to realize it.

At Pleasant View Mrs. Eddy had started calling Adelaide Still Ada because there had been another Adelaide in the home. At Chestnut Hill the Leader reverted to Adelaide, but many others continued calling her Ada. Miss Still was aware of how difficult the adjustment from Pleasant View to Chestnut Hill was for Mrs. Eddy, and she put forth every effort to help her. But the effort was no help to Mrs. Eddy because it was human and not divine. Tender loving *human* care was a great weight and burden upon the Leader which none seemed able to understand. And the harder Adelaide tried humanly, the more difficult it seemed to be to please Mrs. Eddy, — until one day Archibald McLellan broke the mesmerism for this student.

Mr. McLellan was often at Chestnut Hill on business of one kind or another, but he was not at all familiar with the household routine. As Mrs. Eddy left on her daily drive on this afternoon, Mr. McLellan turned to Miss Still who was standing beside him and asked what she did while Mrs. Eddy was away. Miss Still replied that she had dinner:

> Mr. McLellan: And how long is the drive?
> Miss Still: Not more than half an hour these days.
> Mr. McLellan: That means a pretty hurried meal, doesn't it?

To this Miss Still burst out, "Oh, I wouldn't mind if I never had my dinner, if only I could do things right, if only I could please her!"

Mr. McLellan looked at Adelaide for a moment and then said quietly, *"You can,* Ada. *You can."* In that brief moment Ada dropped her anxious human effort; and the Leader's response was immediate. By the time she returned from her drive she expressed loving appreciation for all that Adelaide did for her.

This incident marked a great step in progress for Miss Still. A short time later the Leader told her to be present when she gave instruction to the metaphysical workers. From that time when the students were called to the Leader's study for their morning lesson, Adelaide was there, though she did not stand up with them. Sometimes afterward Mrs. Eddy would ask her, "Did you hear what I said to my students this morning?" Miss Still would respond, "Yes, Mrs. Eddy, thank you," to which the Leader would reply, "That's right dear, you always be present when I teach my students."

Another student, Calvin Hill, had received helpful statements from Mrs. Eddy on several occasions because of a latent fear she detected in his thought. Once again in the spring of 1908 when he had sent her some especially fine strawberries she said in her letter of thanks: "May, O may the Love divine feed you and fill you with a strong sense of *liberty,* of waking from the dream of life in lungs — the Infinite in the finite — and show you just how a lie destroys itself by saying I am real!"

This dedicated student looked upon Mrs. Eddy as his adopted mother, and he loved her dearly, but he was one of the many who could not understand how his tender loving (human) thoughts could cause her suffering. It was probably the *human* thoughts of her own followers that caused her more suffering than any other one thing. The malicious intent of the wicked to destroy her life and her work was something her advanced students could understand and they were willing workers under her direction to meet these insidious attacks. But all were misled in varying degrees by *good* mortal mind, thinking because it appeared as good that it was right, and therefore spiritual. The way of spiritual reality is very straight and narrow. The Leader was finding every step of this way, often through suffering, and endeavoring to teach it to the students nearest to her. She well knew that they profited most and progressed fastest from rebukes, and those in whom she had the greatest hope were rebuked more than any others, "For whom the Lord loveth he chasteneth, and scourgeth every son whom he receiveth." Some of those who were rebuked went up higher, and some turned away from their Leader and walked no more with her.

Her rebuke to William McCrackan had been indirect and comparatively mild. Nonetheless he had turned away from the Leader, separating the revelation from the revelator in his own thought. And now another dear student failed the test. Calvin Hill had devoted himself to serving Mrs. Eddy for nearly ten years and during this time had given up business to devote all his time to the practice of Christian Science together with performing many services for the Leader. One day when he called at Chestnut Hill he found her suffering distressfully and breathing with great difficulty. His tender sympathy was an added burden upon her and she rebuked him sharply saying he must remove his thought from her. He could not see how his highest sense of human devotion could cause her to suffer. He reacted to her rebuke and left in anger, walking no more with his Leader. Wounded pride and self-justification caused him to burn some of her precious letters to him, though he did so in tears, and he never saw the Leader again. It was another twenty-five years before he was able to understand her letter to him:

> Beloved in Christ:
> Again I have to write, *do not think of me.* Your tender thought reaches me — *costs me much.* Leave me in God alone. He loves us both. I love all — friends and enemies.

On May 1 the Leader wired a response to a request from the editor of the *Daily News* in Minneapolis, Minnesota:

> Editor Daily News — Christian Science can and does produce Universal Fellowship. *[My.* 275] As the sequence of divine Love it ex-

plains love, it lives love, it demonstrates love. The human, material, so-called senses do not perceive this fact until they are controlled by divine Love; hence the Scripture, "Be still, and know that I am God."

Mary Baker G. Eddy

The editor wrote appreciatively to Mrs. Eddy on May 7:

Dear Madam:

Permit me on behalf of the *Daily News* to extend to you my sincere thanks for your gracious telegraphic response to my request. Your communication was printed in our Fellowship edition of last Saturday, of which it gives me pleasure to forward you two copies.

Again thanking you for your courtesy, I remain

Sincerely yours,
John Burgess
Editor *Daily News*

Whenever the Leader suffered from an attack she called upon one or another of her mental workers to work for her, for this was a very important part of their metaphysical training. If they could see, understand to some degree, and help to meet the attacks upon the Leader they were meeting the same error for themselves and for all mankind. But this advanced work was a part of the Divinity Course and not for the neophyte. It is important that the beginner focus upon the perfection of being and not the errors in the path.

One of the errors that had been attacking the Leader for years was malicious reports and rumors of her death or ill health. These reports had been sporadic for many years until 1906 when they became almost constant, world wide, and increasingly wicked, culminating in the "next friends" suit and the dedicated work of many students to meet it. Now, once again, on Saturday the ninth of May a New York newspaper reported that the Discoverer and Founder of Christian Science was seriously ill at her handsome new home, and suffering so severely that she had been unable to go out for her daily drive for two weeks.

This, of course, was picked up by all the other newspapers, and the following Tuesday, May 12, Edwin Park from the *Boston Globe* went out to Chestnut Hill to see for himself. He said in the next day's *Globe:*

Yesterday I went to Chestnut Hill on the 12:20 P.M. train to see Mrs. Eddy take her drive, and I entered the grounds of her estate at 12:55. As I approached the house I saw her carriage drawn up before the house. The door of the house opened, and Mrs. Eddy, walking alone and with a vigorous step, emerged from the door and approached the carriage through the porte-cochere. Calvin Frye was holding the door

> of the carriage open, and Mrs. Sargent walked behind Mrs. Eddy with her sunshade and some light wraps. I stopped one hundred feet from the carriage, and as Mrs. Eddy stepped out from the house she stopped and looked around at the flowers and budding trees. I came within her range of vision and she bowed and smiled.

Mr. Dickey went over to Mr. Park, and as the carriage drove past Mrs. Eddy leaned forward and gave him another bow and smile. He was invited indoors and entertained by Mr. Dickey, Mrs. Sargent, and Rev. Irving Tomlinson, who told him that Mrs. Eddy had missed her drive only twice since moving to Chestnut Hill, both times in consideration for the horses in heavy, freezing weather. They also denied seriatim the other statements in the false report stating that no inquiry had been made at the house. They of course, did not know whether the Leader would see him upon her return, but she did call him up to her study for a brief but gracious greeting. He wrote in his article:

> . . . the writer . . . certifies that she is apparently stronger physically and quite as alert mentally as she was eleven months ago . . . when I visited with her for forty minutes on the afternoon of June 15 at . . . Pleasant View . . . If there has been any change in Mrs. Eddy's physical condition during the past eleven months it has been for the better. . . .
>
> As Mrs. Sargent and I entered the commodius room Mrs. Eddy rose from her chair, and quickly taking the three or four steps which covered the distance between her chair and the end of the desk, advanced to meet me, with right hand outstretched in greeting. She looked me straight in the eyes, and as she took and shook my hand with a strong grasp, she said, "Mr. Park, I am very glad to see you again." It was then that I remarked that she was looking wonderfully well and asked her if she were well, and she replied, "Why, of course."
>
> Still holding my hand Mrs. Eddy again said, "I am glad you called. I would ask you to sit down, but this is my time for work. It is a work of eternity. The hours do not give me time enough."

Following Mr. Park's visit the Leader sent two notices for publication in the next *Sentinel,* the first, a word of advice "To Whom It May Concern" *(My.* 276) that they "be composed and resigned to the shocking fact that she [Mrs. Eddy] is minding her own business, and recommends this surprising privilege to all her dear friends and enemies."

The second *"Nota Bene" (My.* 139) because of "the recent rumors" was reassurance for her students at that time and for all time:

> Rest assured that your Leader is living, loving, acting, enjoying.

She is neither dead nor plucked up by the roots, but she is keenly alive to the reality of living . . .

The day before these notices were published Mrs. Eddy dictated to Mr. Dickey one more statement regarding this recent rumor — a letter to the *New York Herald (My.* 275). This letter of May 15 brought the following response of May 18 from the Committee on Publication in New York City, Mr. John V. Dittemore:

Dear Mrs. Eddy:
Your splendid letter to the editor of the *New York Herald* was published yesterday. I enclose clipping in order that you may see by the prominence they gave it how highly it was appreciated. The broad-minded charity, love, and tolerance you have expressed will add to the rapidly increasing recognition by the whole world of its debt to you.

In my talk with you last week you said, "Everything must come out right when we trust in God." This statement has been with me constantly, and a realization in some small measure of what *you* know it means has brought me a clearer understanding of the omnipotence of God and of His present availability than I have ever before known. I shall not try to express in words my gratitude to you but rather may my "works" bear witness. I hope I shall never be "found wanting" when any opportunity arises for serving you and our beloved Cause.

Most sincerely,
J. V. Dittemore

The spring and summer of 1908 were marked by unusually severe thunderstorms in Newton. For many years Mrs. Eddy had taught the students in her household that they were not Christian Scientists until they handled the weather. In one of her lessons at Chestnut Hill she said:

mesmerists claim they can do what they want to the weather — as they claim they can do as they will with sickness. You all know you can control a headache or a belief of dyspepsia and you are not afraid of it.

Sickness is a belief of mortal mind. Now what is a storm? Is it not a false claim of material law? Is there any such thing as material law? Then if bad weather or lightning is an erroneous concept of mortal law, can't you break it up? Now I want you to prepare yourselves to do this. I remember once when we were having a terrific storm and the lightning was around the house like chains, the students were with me and I declared to them that there was no surplus electricity and in a few minutes the whole storm disappeared. Now you know there are no thunderstorms in divine Mind. No lightning in heaven

— so prepare to break up these violent storms. There is no need for them.

Adam Dickey recorded that after all the workers had repaired to their several rooms to work following the Leader's instructions regarding weather, the bells started ringing calling them all back to her study. After they had lined up in front of the Teacher she pointed her finger at the first student and said, "Mr. Dickey, can a Christian Scientist control the weather?" "Yes, Mother," he responded. She put the same question to each, with the same answer. Then with a look of scorn she said emphatically, much to everyone's surprise, "They can't and they don't!" Then she explained to them:

> They can't, but God can and does. Now I want you to see the point I am making. A Christian Scientist has no business attempting to control or govern the weather any more than he has a right to attempt to control or govern sickness, but he does know, and must know, that God governs the weather and no other influence can be brought to bear upon it. When we destroy mortal mind's belief that it is a creator, and that it produces all sorts of weather, good as well as bad, we shall then realize God's perfect weather and be the recipients of His bounty in that respect. God's weather is always right. A certain amount of rain and sunshine is natural and normal, and we have no right to interfere with the stately operations of divine Wisdom in regulating meteorological conditions. Now I called you back because I felt you did not get my former instructions correctly and I want you to remember that the weather belongs to God, and when we destroy the operations of mortal mind and leave the question of regulating the weather to God, we shall have weather conditions as they should be.

A letter was published in the *Sentinel* of May 30 which Mrs. Eddy had received a week or two earlier from a student in Lawrence, Massachusetts:

> Dear Leader:
>
> In the first edition of your remarkable book, Science and Health, we read, "Life is the forming and governing Principle of all things." This statement makes plain the meaning of Jesus' words, "I am come that they might have life, and that they might have it more abundantly." With grateful heart I thank you for the spiritual help received through obtaining and reading, from time to time, the new revisions of this, our textbook, which so illumines the Bible, thus leading thought to clearer views of God's universe of Spirit, Mind. As I have gained some realizing sense of the great amount of work you have put into Science and Health, the price paid for each book seems

a very meagre return for your loving labor. Faithful Leader! No words can better express your love for all mankind, it seems to me, than those given in the striking tribute you have paid to the memory of your earthly mother, and chiseled on stone in the pretty "Park Cemetery" at Tilton, N. H. —

Her life the grand realities impart
That fix their records deeply in the heart.

Lovingly yours,
Lewis Prescott

Did this letter cause the Leader to think about that precious first edition and the many revisions that had followed in the ensuing thirty-three years? She says of this stupendous work: "I have revised Science and Health only to give a clearer and fuller expression of its original meaning. ... That which when sown bears immortal fruit, enriches mankind only when it is understood, — hence ... the requisite revisions of Science and Health with Key to the Scriptures" (S&H 361). In *Retrospection and Introspection* she calls the first edition The Precious Volume "containing the complete statement of Christian Science." A comparative study of the changes and additions is enlightening and rewarding, and a study the Leader recommended in the much publicized review of the fiftieth edition of Science and Health which stated in part:

> A practical suggestion or two regarding study of the new edition: In the first place, *do not attempt to dispose of the earlier editions.* ... Fortunate is he who has all former revisions, together with the original edition of 1875! ... Keep them all; they will prove a *"treasure trove."* ... Let the new volume be studied *in connection with earlier editions.*

Of course the latest edition is necessary for the weekly lessons in the *Christian Science Quarterly,* but the lesson is only the beginning of the student's study. Perhaps Mrs. Eddy began thinking once more of encouraging the student to comparative study of the revisions of their textbook. *Miscellaneous Writings* had seen many editions in the eleven years since it was first published. At least seventy-nine editions, and perhaps more, had been published when in 1908 she added footnotes on several pages. All of these footnotes refer the reader to earlier editions of Science and Health. Some of the footnotes have been changed since 1910, but this listing is as Mrs. Eddy left them:

p. 35 See editions prior to that of January, 1886.
p. 83 See the revised edition of 1886.
p. 309 See the revised edition of 1890.

MARY BAKER G. EDDY
The Discoverer and Founder of Christian Science

Frontispiece in *Miscellaneous Writings* from 1896 through 1910

p. 379 See Science and Health, p. 47, revised edition of 1890.
p. 401 Page 292 of the revised edition of 1890.
p. 415 Page 234, revised edition of 1890.

The major editions prior to 1886 were the first edition (1875), the third edition (1881), and the sixth edition (1883). The revised edition of 1886 was the sixteenth edition, and that of 1890 was the fiftieth edition. Not one of these editions was available in the reading rooms in 1908 when Mrs. Eddy had these six footnotes added to *Miscellaneous Writings.* What could her purpose have been other than to turn the student to a comparative study of earlier editions of the textbook?

The portrait and caption on page 459 also appeared in the 1908 edition of *Miscellaneous Writings.* This picture was one of several of Mrs. Eddy taken about 1886. Another in the series was used as a frontispiece for Science and Health in some of the early editions about that time. This picture was the frontispiece in *Miscellaneous Writings* from its first edition copyrighted in 1896 and first off the press early in 1897. And this portrait of Mrs. Eddy continued as the frontispiece in *Miscellaneous Writings* as long as the Leader was here. However, no artist or photographer was able to portray Mrs. Eddy as she was, for their thought was so far from where hers was. So she was never satisfied with their pictures. It is recorded in *Collectanea* that she once commented about the picture in *Miscellaneous Writings:* "It is too confoundedly pleasant." Her sweetness was heavenly serious.

CHAPTER LI

THE LAST COMMUNION

Our Eucharist is spiritual communion with the one God.
— MARY BAKER EDDY

1908

THE Executive Members were gathered in Boston on Saturday, June 13 for their annual meeting on the day before Communion Sunday in The Mother Church. But in the *Sentinel* of that day was a by-law amendment stating that "There shall be no annual meetings of the Executive Members." On the same day Mrs. Eddy's "Word to the Wise" *(My.* 139) appeared in the *Boston Globe.* Perhaps Augusta Stetson was the first to respond to this surprise. She wrote the Leader immediately from the Hotel Touraine, stating in part:

> I have just read your message, "A Word to the Wise." . . . I indeed rejoice and am unspeakably grateful that the impersonal idea, through your teachings, has brought us to this hour. . . .
>
> Beloved, the "purpose of your requests" has always been "sacred." You have ever striven to turn us from the contemplation of *finite* personality to the worship of one God and the *spiritual* personality or divine individuality. . . .

It is interesting to note that the Leader's messages are no longer sent to the members of the Christian Science organization. Her "Word" given on June 13 to "My Beloved Brethren" embraced all the world and was given to the world through the secular press. Her mission was to all mankind and was not to be limited to the organization that she had built up for its protection and promotion.

The next day, June 14, was Communion Sunday in The Mother Church. The students nearest the Leader at Chestnut Hill were aware that she had been suffering for several days and was restless and unsettled. She called her mental workers to her again and again directing their work, but still did not get relief. Adelaide Still recorded:

> Then she turned to Laura Sargent and said, "What is it, Laura? I have always suffered for what was wrong with my church." Laura could not answer her question, so Mrs. Eddy turned away and we knew from her attitude that she was praying and working over it.

A little later when she called Adam Dickey to her study she was lying on the lounge still "wrestling with a malicious attack of unusual severity," but she dictated to him a new by-law for her church. Mr. Dickey took it to his room, transcribed it, and:

> I returned with it immediately to her room and was overjoyed to find her seated at her desk, wreathed in smiles, and pursuing her regular work with her usual vigor.

This was a new experience for a newcomer to the home such as Mr. Dickey, but he learned later from Mr. Frye that a great many progressive steps for her church had been brought forth through the Mother's sore travail. The new by-law read:

> Communion Service. — Sect. 16 [Now Article XVIII, Sect. 1] The Mother Church of Christ, Scientist shall observe no more Communion seasons.

Mrs. Eddy kept the students in her home busy working metaphysically all of the time. Martha Wilcox said, "There were many demonstrations we made and many that we did not make." But working metaphysically and talking metaphysics were not the same. The latter was not allowed. Mrs. Wilcox recorded:

> The members of her household were not supposed to talk or discuss Christian Science at the table or among themselves. We were to live Christian Science, and not just talk the letter. This was one place in the world where the chatter about Christian Science was not heard.

But Mrs. Eddy knew that this chatter was heard throughout the field, and on June 14 she wrote to her directors:

> Faith without works is the most subtle lie apparent. It satisfies the students with a lie, it gives them peace in error, and they never can be Christian Scientists without that faith which is known and proved by works. Words are often impositions, and faith without works is dead and plucked up by the roots. It is not faith, but a deceiving lie lulling the conscience, and preventing demonstration. A satisfied sinner is

the most hardened sinner.

A little later in the month she made this assertion again in a "Take Notice" *(My.* 351:22) in which she refused to endorse a Christian Scientist's book which was philosophy in place of practice.

The Leader showed the new communion season by-law to the students in her household before sending it to the directors, and it may have been Reverend Tomlinson who remonstrated with her saying it was a mistake. This troubled Laura Sargent, and while Mrs. Eddy was out for her drive Laura turned to Mind and opened *Message for 1902* to page 19:21-25.

> Are earth's pleasures, its ties and its treasures, taken away from you? It is divine Love that doeth it, and sayeth, "Ye have need of all these things." A danger besets thy path? — a spiritual behest, in reversion, awaits you.

Laura showed this to the Leader when she returned, and she in turn showed it to the objector saying, "There, see that." But she had yet to conciliate her church and the world to this radical step. Before doing that, however, she sent another new by-law which is now Article XXXI, Section 5 *(Man.* 94), together with several by-law amendments. One, which is now Article XIII, Sect. 1 *(Man.* 56), required none but officers to be present at annual meetings. Another was titled "No Malpractice" and is presently Article VIII, Sect. 8 *(Man.* 42).

But abolishing "a material form of communion" was another message for all her children for all time to come; so, even though her letter of June 21 *(My.* 140) was addressed to "Beloved Christian Scientists" it was sent to the *Boston Globe.* Everything the Leader did has meaning for her followers. When she gave vital messages to Christian Scientists through the secular press, could this not symbolize that all her children on this planet are Christian Scientists whether they know it or not, and that she is their Mother in Israel leading the way? Do not her actions correspond with Jesus' words? "Other sheep I have that are not of this fold."

Alfred Farlow gave a press statement that evening to the *Boston Globe,* "Communion Season is Abolished" *(My.* 141) which appeared in the *Globe* of June 22.

Judge Clifford P. Smith had moved to Boston from Iowa to replace William D. McCrackan both as the new First Reader for The Mother Church and as a trustee of the Publishing Society. The new Second Reader was Mrs. Carol Hoyt Powers of Boston. The names of sixteen lecturers were announced for the Board of Lectureship for the year July 1, 1908 through June 30, 1909, as follows:

Mrs. Mary Brookins	Bliss Knapp
Hon. Clarence A. Buskirk	Frank H. Leonard
Clarence C. Eaton	Rev. William P. McKenzie
Judge William G. Ewing	William N. Miller
F. J. Fluno	Mrs. Sue Harper Mims
Judge Septimus J. Hanna	Rev. Irving C. Tomlinson
Prof. Hermann S. Hering	Rev. Arthur R. Vosburgh
Edward A. Kimball	Bicknell Young

Some of these lecturers attended the annual meeting in Boston on June 16, and others were in distant places. In June Mr. Kimball was lecturing in Geneva, Switzerland, and Bicknell Young was embarking upon another first for the Christian Science movement. Mr. Young had recently left our Pacific shores on the first round the world Christian Science lecture tour. His first lecture in Australia was in Sydney on Sunday, June 21 to an audience of twenty-five hundred. The following Monday, June 29, he spoke again in Sydney to another audience of twenty-five hundred.

Meanwhile back at Chestnut Hill the daily work was going on as usual. There was much talk about drought in Boston in the summer of 1908, and this could have been the time that Mrs. Eddy called Martha Wilcox to her study one hot, sultry day and said, "Now, Martha, you go upstairs and write out a treatment for rain. We need rain." Martha had barely seated herself when her number rang. She went quickly to Mrs. Eddy, who said, "Well, give me the treatment." Martha responded, "Mother, I did not have time to write it out;" and Mrs. Eddy said, "Well, just tell it to me."

Martha began, but hadn't gotten far when the Leader stopped her and said, "Now, Martha, come down from sailing around up there. It's rain we need. Let's have rain." Humbly and in tears Mrs. Wilcox said, "Mother, I can't do it." The Leader replied: "It took Calvin Frye and Laura a long time to do it, but you can see that it must be done, and learn somewhat of how to do it." Then she gave Martha a lesson on weather which she wrote down as soon as she returned to her room:

> God does not make sultry weather, and if we through belief make sultry weather, we must unmake it. God governs the weather. He governs the elements and there are no destructive winds or lightning. Love always looks out from the clouds. Beliefs about the weather are easier healed than sickness.

Laura Sargent was regularly assigned the duty to work on the weather, and on June 26 Laura opened her Bible at random to Genesis 2:5 and showed it to Mrs. Eddy. According to Adelaide Still Mrs. Eddy immediately took the work out of Laura's hands and wrote the following letter to her Board of Directors:

> *Confidential*
> Beloved:
> Have several Christian Scientists who are best adapted to it, take up the weather and know that "God sendeth the rain upon the just and the unjust," hence the latter, *it is raining.* Continue this prayer till the result follows it. Let none know, that will tell it, what is being done.

There was gossip and grumbling about the abolition of communion season, but there were also letters of appreciation such as this one from a practitioner in Washington, D.C.:

> Beloved Leader:
> From the point of view of the practitioner, the wisdom of abolishing the Communion seasons at The Mother Church is manifest. It has seldom occurred in my practice that I felt justified in leaving my local work to go to Boston. . . .
> The bustle of a big crowd, even of our orderly members, is less conducive to spiritual communion with the one Mind than "the quiet sanctuary of earnest longings" (S&H, p.5).
> Faithfully yours,
> William Holman Jennings

Another student welcomed another new by-law in an interesting manner as expressed in this letter of June 29 from Springfield, Massachusetts:

> Beloved Leader:
> When I arose this morning my first act was to open my Bible. Before me was the 21st chapter of I Chronicles. This I carefully studied until I realized somewhat the momentous lesson therein contained. Later in the day I read in the *Sentinel* of June 27 the new By-law under the caption "Numbering the People." This chapter in Chronicles brought to consciousness as never before a sense of your wonderful spiritual discernment, its insight and foresight, coupled with integrity of purpose and moral courage, culminating in implicit obedience to God. Then I thanked God that it was my privilege to be your follower; that a life-long desire to know something not subject to chance or change was satisfied in your teachings, and that I could realize that the teachings and author must of necessity be inseparable in character.
> In deepest gratitude for unmeasured blessings flowing from your

life-work of love, I am

Sincerely yours,
Guy S. Perkins

It is possible that the Leader had envisioned leading her movement until the whole world was wakened and lifted out of its sinning sense, but after God spoke to her in March of 1907 she knew that that was not to be the case. She had never *excluded* the world, for she well knew her mission was to all mankind, but more and more in 1908 she was reaching out to include all. Near the end of June there was a manifestation of the effectiveness of her life's work. A receptive thought saw in vision what the Leader had so long envisioned and labored for. The eminent American author of "The Battle Hymn of the Republic," Julia Ward Howe, had a vision which she was induced to give to the public. The following was published in the *Boston Sunday American* of June 28, 1908:

> One night recently I experienced a sudden awakening. I had a vision of a new era which is to dawn for mankind and in which men and women are battling, equally, unitedly, for the uplifting and emancipation of the race from evil. I saw men and women of every clime, working like bees to unwrap the evils of society, and to discover the whole web of vice and misery, and to apply the remedies and also to find the influences that should best counteract evil and its attending suffering.
>
> There seemed to be a new, a wondrous, ever-permeating light, the glory of which I cannot attempt to put in human words — the light of the new-born hope and sympathy blazing. The source of this light was born of human endeavor, immortal purpose of countless thousands of men and women who were equally doing their part in the world-wide battle with evil, and whose energy was bended to tear the mask from error, crime, superstition, greed, and to discover and apply the remedy.
>
> I saw the men and the women, standing side by side, shoulder to shoulder, a common, lofty, and indomitable purpose lighting every face with a glory not of this earth. All, all were advancing with one end in view, one foe to trample, one everlasting good to gain. I saw them advancing like a mighty army, laden with the fruits of their research, their study, their endeavor, in this battle with the powers of darkness and ready to tear vice from the earth, to strip away all of selfishness, of greed, of rapine. Then I seemed to see them stoop down to their fellows and to lift them higher, higher, and yet higher. Men and women, a vast host whom none could number, working unitedly, equally, with superhuman energy, all for the extirpation of the blackness of vice and for the weal of the race.
>
> And then I saw the victory!
>
> All, all of evil was gone from the earth. Misery was blotted out.

> Mankind was emancipated and ready to march forward in a new era of human understanding, all-encompassing sympathy, and ever-present help. The era of perfect love, of peace passing understanding.

Julia Ward Howe may not have known what she saw in her vision, but serious students of Christian Science did. Already they had made a mighty advance "with the fruits of their research, their study, their endeavor." All had healed the sick, and they were working to "raise the dead, cleanse the lepers, cast out demons." The Leader had taught "men and women of every clime ... to discover the whole web of vice and misery, and to apply the remedies." She had given them the little book from the hand of the angel wherein they could "find the influences that should best counteract evil and its attending suffering."

Another had glimpsed the glorious reality of the fulfillment of Christian Science whether she knew it or not. This glorious reality looks away from the crucifixion to the resurrection, and to the glorified being of the ascension. A new paragraph was added to page 200 in the fourth revision of Science and Health in 1908:

> St. Paul said: "For I determined not to know anything among you, save Jesus Christ, and him crucified." (I Cor. ii.2.) Christian Science says: I am determined not to know anything among you, save Jesus Christ, and him glorified.

CHAPTER LII

LIFT UP A STANDARD

Go through, go through the gates; prepare ye the way of the people; cast up, cast up the highway; gather out the stones; lift up a standard for the people. — ISAIAH

1908

FOR several weeks "The Publishing House Building Fund" notice in the *Sentinel* had said, "as it is expected that the building will be finished early in July there is but little time to spare in completing this fund."

Mrs. Eddy wrote a very important letter "early in July," July 3 to be exact. The letter was handwritten to her publisher, Allison V. Stewart, and said:

> I am impressed to write what must not be named before the debt of our Publishing House is paid — and it is this:
>
> We should have a daily newspaper . It is very important to our cause and the bulk of this cause demands it.
>
> I hereby state that so soon as said debt is paid I will head a subscription list for this purpose with $100 subscribed and I ask that you entitle this newspaper The Christian Science Monitor. Please keep silent on this matter till our Church debts are paid. I want to name it to you and hear from you on this subject.

It was exactly two months since she had written her first letter on this subject to Stewart and McLellan, and as with that letter of May 3, this one of July 3 was not sent.

A short editorial by Archibald McLellan in the *Sentinel* of July 4 began:

> ALLEGED EARLY MANUSCRIPTS
>
> We have been asked about certain unpublished manuscripts said to have been written by Mrs. Eddy in the early years of her discovery of Christian Science. All we can say is, that if these manuscripts are

> genuine, they are probably what she refers to in the Preface of Science and Health. . . .

The rest of this article quoted from Science and Health — the last paragraph on page viii and the last paragraph on page ix. There has been an interesting change in that second paragraph since this July 4, 1908 editorial. What at that time said: "These efforts show her ignorance . . ." now says, "her comparative ignorance."

Immediately above McLellan's "Alleged Early Manuscripts" is a "Take Notice" by Mary Baker Eddy *(My.* 237:4) which begins, "What I wrote on Christian Science some twenty-five years ago I do not consider a precedent for a present student of this Science."

This statement has been used to turn students away from the earlier editions of Science and Health, but at the same time it was issued she added the footnotes to *Miscellaneous Writings* turning the students *to* the earlier editions. Her latest edition is most adapted to the thought of the age, so it should come first, that is, take precedence. But should it not also turn the student to an interest in the Revelator's footsteps and in her more incisive declarations?

This notice ends: "Hence, it were wise to accept only my teachings that I know to be correct and adapted to the present demand." Did she write for that time only, or for all time? What is the *present* demand? Did the Leader ever teach anything that she did not "know to be correct"? The story in Science and Health (184:27) of the woman she cured of consumption, occurred in 1864, two years prior to her discovery of Christian Science. If her work at that time had not been correct, would she have left it in our textbook? The one thing she taught (or allowed) to her earliest students and very soon repudiated, was Dr. Quimby's method of manipulation. This was, however, merely a crutch, as she told those students, and a procedure *she* never used. All of this took place prior to the first edition of Science and Health in which she wrote:

> Since witnessing the evil one student did in the name of science, we have utterly objected to students rubbing the head. . . .
>
> We knew of no harm that could result from rubbing the head, until we learned it of this mal-practice, and never since have permitted a student, with our consent, to manipulate.

Advanced students today who are not healing as they know they should be, need to study the final chapter in the first edition of Science and Health, "Healing the Sick."

A letter written on July 2 and published in the *Sentinel* of July 18 was a bit of history that no doubt thrilled the field and rejoiced the

Mother's heart:

Leominster, Mass., July 2, 1908

Dear Leader:

I had an uncle by marriage who was a helpless cripple and who was deformed. All his limbs were withered, and on very pleasant mornings a special policeman would wheel him out on Boston Common in his wheel chair. One morning a number of years ago, he sat there in his wheel chair as you were passing through the Common, and you stopped and spoke to him, telling him that man is God's perfect child, and a few other words. Later, after you had left him, he declared you had helped him. The next morning he looked and looked for you in the same place, and morning after morning continued to do so, until one day you came. Again you repeated to him what you had said before, and this time he was healed and made perfect, — every whit whole; and after that he was able to go into business for himself and provide his own living. No doubt you will remember the whole circumstance. His bones had hardened so that when sitting or lying down his knees were drawn up and rigid, his brother having to carry him up and down stairs, and feed him and care for him all the time; but after he was healed through your spoken word, he was able to be as active as other men and earned his own living; and whereas before he could not even brush a fly from his face, he regained the use of his hands, and became more than an ordinary penman.

It was you, dear Leader, who spoke to him of the healing Christ and set him free, when you met him so long ago on Boston Common, and many times I have desired to tell you about it, and to express to you my gratitude for the many benefits I also have received from Christian Science. Words can never express it.

With deepest love, in which my husband joins me,

Your loving student,

Mrs. Charlotte F. Lyon

All the students at Chestnut Hill, and particularly the new students, were learning a great deal every day in endeavoring to help the Leader and to follow her instructions. One sentence in the first edition of Science and Health (p. 370) gives a slight indication of what this teaching cost her: "Healing in science has its reward even here, but the task of teaching the science of being is quite another thing." She also said, "those in health and at ease in their possessions are reluctant to change masters, hence the more thankless and toilsome task of teaching, compared with healing." In a note to Calvin Frye on July 2 the Leader said in part:

> Beloved, If you knew with what I am beset continually . . .
>
> Mr. Dickey yields to m.a.m. to such an extent he affords me very little help in anything. I have to correct him continually.

This was true of all the students as well as Mr. Dickey who recorded Mrs. Eddy's words to the students one day: "Where all students have failed is in not knowing how to handle animal magnetism. If we don't break the belief that mesmerism has power, we are still the victims of mesmerism and it is handling us. Now then, the main point is to keep your watch." Mr. Dickey had by this time learned a good deal about the importance of keeping watch and the work of the watchers. The one thing that none of them seemed to realize was that *every* student must learn to watch all of the time "that mental malpractice cannot harm you [or your universe] either when asleep or when awake." Mrs. Eddy did this, and if her students had done more in this area her work and suffering would have been lessened. But in 1908 she had to direct all their "watching" because, in Mr. Dickey's words, "She seemed to be the only one who was able to discern the course that error was pursuing."

Chestnut Hill was Truth's garrison in a world of sin and mental malpractice and needed to be guarded at all times. The Leader was doing her utmost to train these guards to "watch," to detect the enemy's maneuvers, and to meet the attacks. Four mental workers were each assigned two hour watches from 9 P.M. till 5 A.M., but the Leader was *always* on guard. Adam Dickey wrote:

> When a watch was kept . . . she always knew it and the one keeping his watch was commended the next day. If the watch was not kept, and they were far more frequently not kept than kept, a corresponding rebuke was administered to the one who failed.

What would an Army have done to such soldiers who were on guard duty in time of war? Every advanced step Christian Science had made in this world had increased the intensity of the warfare the Leader had first described many years earlier:

> The powers of evil are leagued together in secret conspiracy against the Lord and against His Christ, as expressed and operative in Christian Science. Large numbers, in desperate malice, are engaged day and night in organizing action against us. Their feeling and purpose are deadly, and they have sworn enmity against the lives of our standard-bearers.

There were many times when the mental workers at Chestnut Hill did meet some specific attack against their Leader or her Cause, but there were many more times when they did not. As a consequence very often they were all called into the Leader's study and admonished for their failure.

The *Sentinel* for July 11 contained another new by-law, Article

VIII, No Monopoly — Sect. 30 *(Man.* 49). It also contained this Notice:

> Article V of the Church By-laws, creating Executive Members, has been repealed. There being no further necessity for this organization, it is therefore disbanded.

On the day that these two changes were published Martha Wilcox left Chestnut Hill. She had received word of the death of her younger step-son and went immediately to Kansas City.

A few days later Mrs. Eddy suffered a very serious attack of intense pain and did not go out for her daily drive on Tuesday, July 14. Calvin Frye said she was confined to her bed with little help from the mental workers. Evidently, in their failure to relieve her, some of them wanted her to call an M.D., but Calvin records that she would not consent to this.

Though she continued her work and her daily routine, she suffered a great deal for the next week or two. During this time a letter she received caused her to send it and her answer to the *Boston Transcript.* Once again her message is to all the world, as reprinted from the *Transcript:*

> A LETTER FROM MRS. EDDY
>
> Mrs. Mary Baker Eddy, Leader of the Christian Science movement, will hereafter abandon her much-talked-of "daily" drives, and instead will drive out only when her work makes no urgent demand on her time. This announcement comes through a response to a letter written to Mrs. Eddy by Mrs. Ella E. Williams, formerly Second Reader of The First Church of Christ, Scientist, in this city, and now a resident of Chestnut Hill. Mrs. Williams wrote as follows: —
>
> Beloved Leader: — I have been pleased to see you drive out in your carriage every day, also to know that you can take time from your work to enjoy this daily drive. It brightens the day for me when I see you in your carriage.
>
> Very lovingly your student,
> Ella E. Williams
>
> Chestnut Hill, July 24
>
> In reply Mrs. Eddy wrote: —
>
> Box G, Brookline, Mass., July 25, 1908
>
> Beloved Student: — I enjoy brightening your day, but the divine Principle and not a personality should illumine the life of a Christian Scientist; therefore, I repeat, turn your thought away from matter to Spirit. I have so much that is of more importance to attend to than a daily drive that hereafter I shall go out only when the demands on my time at home are not imperative, and if I remain at home, I hope you will be influenced by a higher thought than a peep at my personality, and know that I love you.
>
> Mary Baker G. Eddy

In the first edition of Science and Health Mrs. Eddy had written:

> Observation and experience teach us, those scorning to swerve from a direct line of duty, or vainly to stoop to personal aggrandizement at the sacrifice of conscience, and make popularity paramount to Truth, are traduced by many whom that line of duty touches. . . .
>
> The humanitarian is above the arrows in the quiver of ignorance, envy, or malice; they fly beneath his feet, until spent of their fury, they fall to the ground.

The arrows of ignorance, envy, and malice had been aimed at the Revelator before she penned those words. In the thirty-three years since their publication the arrows that had first been from the quiver of one malpractitioner had increased until the strongholds of all the evil on this earth were aiming their shafts at the Revelator. The students in her home who thought they were helping her, knew very little about the evil they were battling. During one severe siege she said to them: "You don't any of you realize what is going on. This is a dark hour for the Cause and you do not seem to be awake to it. I am now working on a plane that would mean instantaneous death to any of you."

The attacks of malice had kept Mrs. Eddy on the lounge in her study or in bed most of the time for nearly a week until the evening of July 27 when Calvin Frye said "she despaired of living until morning." It was almost midnight when the editor of the *Boston Herald* telephoned Mr. Dickey at Chestnut Hill and asked him at what hour Mrs. Eddy had died. He said that the rumor on the street was that Mrs. Eddy was dead. Suddenly the practitioners in the home were able to see that this was attempted mental murder and were able to do some effective mental work.

The very next morning Mrs. Eddy sent this note to William B. Johnson:

> *Notice* So soon as the Pub. House debt is paid I request the C. S. Board of Directors to start a daily newspaper called *Christian Science Monitor.* This must be *done* without fail.
>
> M. B. G. Eddy

It was probably that same day, July 28, that she called Archibald McLellan to Chestnut Hill and told him that she wanted him to start a daily newspaper the next week. Adelaide Still said:

> This was a bomb shell! They had just finished paying for the Publishing House, and sent out a notification that no more money was needed. He told her they would have to get the tenants out of the buildings, take them down and build an extension to the new Pub-

lishing House, get correspondents all over the world, procure presses, etc. She said, "Well, how soon can you do it?"

So Mr. McLellan went back to Boston with plenty of work to do. On August 3 Mrs. Eddy sent some further instructions to her editor in these words: "Have on the cover of the Christian Science Monitor, 'First the blade, then the ear, after that the full corn in the ear,' and have that illustrated with a pretty design." But she sensed that she did not have his whole-hearted cooperation. Two days later on August 5 she had Mr. Dickey write to her editor-in-chief:

Dear Mr. McLellan:

Our Leader wishes you would have some thoroughly responsible outside person, write an article to the *Sentinel* setting forth Mrs. Eddy's unexampled leadership in the interests of Christian Science. Let the article be entitled COMPETENCE, and have it point out the fact that from the inception of this movement, until the present time, not one false step had marred the long line of successful efforts put forth by her in support of her religion.

From the time when stones were thrown through the windows and Church doors were closed against her, until today when Christian Science Churches are encircling the globe, the wisdom of her every act has been abundantly sustained by the complete success that had followed every new move she has made.

No special attention need be given to the above wording, the object being to impress thought with our Leader's unerring wisdom and entire COMPETENCY in every branch of life's work she has undertaken. Let the article be *strong,* and carry with it complete conviction as to her ability to lead under divine guidance.

Sincerely yours,
Adam H. Dickey

The object, of course, was to impress Mr. McLellan's thought "with our Leader's unerring wisdom and entire COMPETENCY," and the Leader's next step in leavening the thought of her editor was a second letter to him from Mr. Dickey later that same day:

Since writing the attached letter, our Leader has thought it would be better to have *you* write the article referred to as an *editorial,* for as she stated, no one is more competent to do this than you. She further said that the article should make it clear that every move that has been made in the line of demonstration for the Cause of Christian Science has originated with her.

You will understand that the article is preparatory to making public her intention of starting a daily newspaper. Mrs. Eddy does not care whether it appears in this week's Sentinel or next.

She allowed McLellan two days for preparing this *strong* editorial on her competency "preparatory to making public her intention of starting a daily newspaper." Then on August 7 she had Calvin Frye write to him:

> Dear Bro McLellan:
> Mother says Do not publish that article on Competence in this week's Sentinel.

While this was going on the directors were hedging and discussing the situation. They felt that the trustees were the ones to undertake this project and suggested that an order should go to them from Mrs. Eddy. So the Leader complied, with this letter of August 8 to the Christian Science Board of Trustees which she entrusted to Mr. McLellan to deliver to them:

> Beloved Students:
> It is my request that you start a daily newspaper at once, and call it the Christian Science Monitor. Let there be no delay. The Cause demands that it be issued now.
> You may consult with the Board of Directors. I have notified them of my intention.
> Lovingly yours,
> Mary B. G. Eddy

The trustees had just begun to relax after working for nearly a year on the new publishing house. The *Sentinel* of August 8 announced "The Publishing House Building Fund Completed." It also stated, "It is expected that the *Sentinel* of August 15 will be issued from the new building." On August 4, after the foregoing announcement was assured, Trustee McKenzie and his wife had left Boston for a vacation on the summer farm of the Metcalfs in Dublin, N. H.

The directors had kept Mrs. Eddy's new project to themselves for ten days, but on August 9 Mr. McKenzie received a telegram saying business of great importance had arisen and to take the first train to Boston. At four o'clock the next morning he walked three miles to flag down the first train and was in Boston for a meeting of the trustees at 10:30 A.M. on August 10, at which meeting Mr. McLellan delivered Mrs. Eddy's letter to them. Their work began from that moment.

Trustees and directors met the next morning and recorded in their minutes: "It was agreed between the two boards that the Directors are charged with the duty of providing the building or place for the publication of the Monitor and that the Trustees are charged with the duty of organizing and starting the new paper . . ." The same day the trustees wrote Mrs. Eddy:

> Your letter of August 8 was delivered to us yesterday. . . .
> As soon as we received your letter we immediately began the work of starting the new Daily and we shall proceed with it without delay. Today we consulted with the Board of Directors. Tomorrow and next day we will confer with two practical newspaper men from Pittsburgh and Chicago whom Mr. McLellan has called here as advisors.

Two days later the trustees sent the Leader a lengthy, detailed letter outlining requirements and expenses. The following day, August 14, Adam Dickey sent this response:

> Your letter of the 13th instant addressed to Mrs. Eddy comprising the report of your plans for starting a Christian Science daily paper is at hand. After reading this report our Leader expressed surprise at the amount of capital that would be required. Her original thought on the subject was, that you should proceed to get out a small paper of about eight pages and with a circulation of about fifty or sixty thousand copies, at a much less outlay than the amount stated in your letter. Her intention was not to branch out at once into metropolitan greatness, but rather to begin in a comparatively small way and grow into bigger things with the progress of time. However she does not wish to hamper your movements by placing restrictions on the amount you shall spend, but wishes you to go ahead with wisdom and economy as your guides.
> Our Leader hopes you will not find it necessary to consult with her with regard to details, but proceed with the work in your own way doing the best you can.

Mrs. Eddy was exceedingly interested in the issuance of the *Christian Science Monitor,* but there was one great departure in this new venture. In every other forward step she had encouraged her lieutenants to make decisions, but had watched every detail most carefully and usually had to make all the decisions herself, ofttimes reversing theirs. This time she was leaving the details and the decisions to her trustees and directors, with the instruction through Mr. Dickey to "proceed with the work in your own way doing the best you can."

Many people have mentioned that Mrs. Eddy was always interested in new inventions. Martha Wilcox said that all the rooms at Chestnut Hill were carpeted and had to be cleaned with brooms until the vacuum cleaner was manufactured, when they had one of the first ones. Mrs. Eddy loved her horses and carriage, but Calvin Frye recorded early in August that "Mrs. Eddy took an half hour's ride in her limousine today." Calvin also recorded on August 16,

"Today completes 26 years continuous service in Mrs. Eddy's employ."

The workers in Mrs. Eddy's home were learning more about Christian Science than any others in the world, and she offered this sacred privilege to a great many. Few, however, were capable of receiving this training. Some of those few at Chestnut Hill were Mrs. Minnie Scott, Mrs. Minnie McDonald (Victoria Sargent's daughter), and Mrs. Ella Hoag of Toledo, Ohio.

Mrs. Minnie Scott was at Chestnut Hill in the summer of 1908 and was Mrs. Eddy's maid for a time as Martha Wilcox had been. On August 10 Calvin Frye recorded in his diary that Mrs. Scott's niece had been playing with some Roman Catholic children and one of them had said that old Mrs. Eddy has got to die and there are sixty Bishops praying for it. Mrs. Eddy said one day to her maid, "Minnie, if you knew that someone was trying to get into your home to bother you, would you just know that Love was your protection and that no harm could come to you?" Mrs. Scott answered, "Yes, Mother, that is what I would know; but at the same time I would see to it that the doors and windows were all tightly locked." Mrs. Eddy replied: "There, you have given me both the Spirit and the letter, and there is nothing more to be said."

Her mental workers, too, needed strengthening. Adam Dickey recorded this Watch on August 16: "There is no psychology and no Roman Catholic prayers frightening us in this house. There is no *sin,* and no *fear* of *sin.* Christian Scientists love the psychologists and the Roman Catholics and they love us. *Good* is all *power* and the *only* power."

Again and again in her talks to her students the Leader quoted Jesus' words: "Could ye not watch with me one hour?" And oft she quoted his words in Matthew 24, "If the goodman of the house had known in what watch the thief would come, he would have watched." One morning after she had talked with them at length, admonished them, and dismissed them to do their work, she called them back and said: "Now what is the great necessity I have been impressing on you?" Mr. Dickey replied, "Demonstration." Several others gave other answers, and she said: "No, you are all wrong. You have missed the importance of the lesson I have just given you. I felt it and called you back to show you your ignorance. The lesson is this — keep your watch." Once again they were dismissed, but very shortly she called them back once more. This time she said:

> What I have to meet, you will all have to meet, now or again. Therefore, know that the mesmerist cannot afflict either you or me, with erroneous beliefs.
>
> If you will keep your watch, I shall be a well woman. If you stay

> here until you learn to handle animal magnetism, I will make healers out of you. I had to do it, and did it for forty years, and you must do it. You must rise to the point where you can destroy the belief in mesmerism, or you will have no Cause, It tried to overcome me for forty years and I withstood it all. Now it has gotten to the point where the students must take up this work and meet animal magnetism. I cannot do it for you. You must do it for yourselves, and unless it is done, the Cause will perish and we will go along another 1900 years with the world sunk into the blackest night. Now will you rouse yourselves? You have all the power of God with you to conquer this lie of mesmerism. The workers in the field are not healing because they are not meeting animal magnetism which says they cannot heal.

Then the Leader asked each in turn, "Will you keep your watch?" After each had answered in the affirmative she said, "To keep your watch doesn't only mean to be awake at that hour and be working mentally. It means to do the work and succeed in breaking the mesmerism for the two hours assigned. If you don't succeed you haven't kept your watch."

The look the Leader gave to Mr. Dickey and the extra pressure she gave to his hand as she held it in both of hers when he promised to keep his watch caused him to redouble his efforts. She followed this promise with a further assignment to Adam Dickey, that students of the future may learn from his record what is to be met and how to meet it.

Most often when Mrs. Eddy returned from her daily drive she would lie down to rest for an hour before beginning the afternoon's work, usually resting on the lounge in her study. On the afternoon of Tuesday, August 25, she was still lying there when she summoned Mr. Dickey. When he arrived she requested the three students who were present, Calvin Frye, Laura Sargent, and probably Adelaide Still, to leave the room. Then, according to Mr. Dickey:

> she beckoned me to approach. She extended her hand to me, took mine in both of hers, and asked in a deep, earnest voice, "Mr. Dickey, I want you to promise me something, will you?"
>
> I said, "Yes, Mother, I certainly will." "Well," she continued, "if I should ever leave here — do you know what I mean by that?"
>
> "Yes, Mother."
>
> "If I should ever leave here," she repeated, "will you promise me that you will write a history of what has transpired in your experiences with me, and say that I was mentally murdered?"
>
> I answered, "Yes, Mother, I will."
>
> "Now, Mr. Dickey, do not let anything interfere with your keeping this promise. Will you swear to me before God that you will not fail to carry out my wish?"

I raised my right hand and said, "Mother, I swear before God that I will do what you request of me, namely write a history of what I have seen, and heard from your lips, concerning your life."

"That will do, dear. I know now that you will not fail me."

Her whole demeanor was one of solemn intensity, and there was an eagerness in her voice and manner such as I seldom saw.

I returned to my room and pondered deeply over what she had said. In a few minutes one of the workers and Mrs. Sargent brought me a sealed envelope. In it was a penciled note reiterating the statement that she had made in our conversation of a short time before.

Mrs. Eddy knew on that summer afternoon that she would soon be leaving them, but Mr. Dickey had no idea in August of 1908 how difficult an assignment it was to "not let anything interfere with your keeping this promise." Because "the powers of evil are leagued together in secret conspiracy against the Lord and against His Christ as expressed and operative in Christian Science," *everything* interfered with his fulfilling this obligation after the Leader was mentally murdered. It took Mr. Dickey fourteen years to break the mesmerism and keep his promise.

Before the end of August Mrs. Eddy had Mr. Dickey write a letter of great import to all the field for all time, though he did not realize its importance at that time. It was also a thrilling letter for Mr. Gaspard of East Aurora, New York to receive as is evident from his response on August 29:

Beloved Leader:

Through Mr. Dickey I have just received notice of your favorable judgment of my drawing, and the request for permission to use the portrait in Science and Health. Surely this is a splendid crown for my effort, and I am at a loss how to express my satisfaction in this unlooked-for result of my work.

Although the drawing was not made with this end in view, you have recognized in it a labor of love. The desire and purpose to make as good a portrait as I could, have indeed been mine ever since my recognition of the truth and beauty of Christian Science and of its bounty and benefit to me so that, in a small measure at least, this drawing testifies to my gratitude and love.

Devotedly yours,
Jules Maurice Gaspard

CHAPTER LIII

FROM DARKNESS TO LIGHT

Ye were sometimes darkness, but now are ye light in the Lord: walk as children of light. — PAUL

1908

THE last paragraph of the attack upon Mrs. Eddy and Christian Science by Georgine Milmine and *McClure's Magazine* began: "On the theoretical side, Mrs. Eddy's contribution to mental healing has been, in the main, fallacious, pseudodoxal, and absurd." Though this series included some authentic historical material and purported to be the story of Mrs. Eddy's life and the history of Christian Science, it was motivated by malice and instigated by "the powers of evil . . . leagued together in secret conspiracy against the Lord and against His Christ . . . in Christian Science." That fact is what impelled Sibyl Wilbur to pursue and present the truth with an opposite motive.

Throughout 1907 Miss Wilbur's articles had appeared in *Human Life* magazine, and since that time she had been working diligently on her *Life of Mary Baker Eddy.* During the writing Miss Wilbur took her questions to Alfred Farlow who, in turn, sent them to Mrs. Eddy. Miss Wilbur said, "Her dictated replies came to me from her secretary with occasional handwritten notes of encouragement from the Leader." As the writing progressed Miss Wilbur read her manuscript, a few chapters at a time, to Mr. Farlow who occasionally advised an omission where Miss Wilbur waxed too bitter in refuting the malice. During this time she also had a few letters from Mrs. Eddy and a few visits with her both at Pleasant View and Chestnut Hill. She knelt beside Mrs. Eddy's chair in a last interview at Chestnut Hill and the Leader said to her: "I am an old woman, my dear, and I have never found it wise to argue with a lie. You are doing what I cannot do for myself; do it wisely."

By the time the last installment of *McClure's* fourteen part series appeared in June of 1908, Sibyl Wilbur's biography was nearing completion. John V. Dittemore from Indiana, who had resigned from the business world to give full time to Christian Science, had recently been made Committee on Publication for New York. He, together with two partners, organized the Concord Publishing Company to publish Miss Wilbur's book. The volume was printed, bound, and ready for issuance on August 29 when Mrs. Eddy called Alfred Farlow and directed him to stop the circulation of the book.

On that Saturday Mr. Frye wrote in his diary:

> Mrs. Eddy told me Aug. 29, 1908 that she told Rev. I. C. Tomlinson that he was not broad enough to write her history, but that she would sometime get the right one to write it for her.
>
> Calvin A. Frye

Adam Dickey wrote in his book in regard to Mrs. Eddy's history:

> I knew ... that on several occasions the proposition had been made to her by others to write a history of her life and experiences, all of which she firmly declined to consider. Her reply to proposals of this kind was, "The time has not yet come for my history to be written. The person to whom this important work should be intrusted is not here yet and I will not give my consent to its being done at this time." This was the nature of the reply she invariably made whenever some of her loving students proposed to her that her life history should be written.

The Leader's encouragement of Sibyl Wilbur in her project may have been merely for Miss Wilbur's own progress Spiritward. Be that as it may, on Sunday morning, August 30, Mr. Farlow called on Miss Wilbur and delivered a letter to her from Mrs. Eddy. Miss Wilbur was devastated as she read the letter with trembling hands and blanched face. She wrote of this moment:

> How could I know what counseled delay. But Alfred Farlow knew and stood watching me. "Does this mean never?" I asked. "It may mean never," he said. "What message shall I take from you to Mrs. Eddy."
>
> After a pause I faltered, "Tell her," I said, "Divine Love governs."
>
> "I will tell her what you say and that you are a good soldier." It was characteristic of him that he gave me no encouragement, and left me with his usual cheerfulness and equanimity ...

Mrs. Eddy wrote Miss Wilbur a letter of thanks that same day, but the latter was cast into the depths of despair and anguished for the next month.

John Dittemore wrote on September 10 to one of his partners in

Box G, Brookline, Mass.

Aug. 30, 1908

Miss Wilbur,

My Beloved Student:-

Please to accept my thanks for your goodness and wisdom in acting so promptly and cheerfully relative to publishing my personal history. I remember your heroism shown in Concord New Hampshire and that same honesty and divine purpose are governing your life.

Lovingly yours;
Mary B. G. Eddy
N. B. Please send to me two of the aforesaid book and your bill Eddy

Letter to Sibyl Wilbur, August 30, 1908

this publishing venture, William R. Brown:

> Miss Wilbur has consulted Mr. Elder and he is going to undertake to find out for her whether the suppression of the book can be withdrawn. Miss W. seems pretty much worked up and has numerous theories as to "why" things are as they are.

Whether they were contemplating legal action or merely hoping that Mr. Elder could influence Mrs. Eddy to withdraw her objection is not clear. In a note of September 24 Adam Dickey wrote: "As a choice of two evils, do you not think it would be better to waive objection to the circulation of the book, and let them go ahead without your endorsement?" Mrs. Eddy withdrew her objection, and the Concord Publishing Company was one of the first to apply for an advertisement in the *Christian Science Monitor* when it was first announced in the *Sentinel* of October 17.

A *Christian Science Monitor* dated September 15, 1908 was printed as a sample to show to Mrs. Eddy, but it was not sold, and few were even aware of its publication.

On September 19, little more than a month after the announcement that the Publishing House had been paid for, a new appeal for contributions to enlarge the Publishing House was published, with no explanation. This announcement probably caused a good deal of speculation throughout the field and doubly so in Boston where the demolition of the buildings had begun which were on the site on which the addition to the publishing house was to be erected.

Before the announcement of the daily paper on October 17 Mr. Kimball had returned from his European lecture tour and spent two days with Mrs. Eddy at Chestnut Hill. There was a good deal of talk in the field about Mr. Kimball's teaching, and it had not escaped his ears. The general thought about Christian Science in 1908 could be expressed as the *physical* healing of a *material* body. Mr. Kimball taught that there is no material body, that "All is infinite Mind and its infinite manifestation," including the body. But the right thing at the wrong time is no longer right, and many other teachers in the field began saying that Mr. Kimball was spiritualizing matter. Many years later another teacher said, "What else are you going to do with it?" But in 1908 the thought was not sufficiently leavened to comprehend one perfect spiritual being. Most students had two creations, a false material one that must be denied and overcome, and a true spiritual creation which must be brought forth and demonstrated. Gilbert Carpenter who was there in 1908, analyzed the controversy:

> Edward A. Kimball was a giant in a metaphysical sense and one of Mrs. Eddy's outstanding students. Yet he taught many things that seem questionable to the present student of Science and Health. A statement from his pen to illustrate this point is, "Every organ or function of the body is an idea of God," ... Apparently he had authority from [Mrs. Eddy] for it, since she told him at one time that it was permissable for him to state Christian Science in this way. Her words were, "Declare, 'I have a perfect liver in God,' and let the spiritual import of this declaration destroy the false concept about liver. You may declare, 'I have perfect liver,' or 'there is no liver,' provided the thought back of these declarations is right."
>
> If Mr. Kimball's statement ... had Mrs. Eddy's authority, then why in the manuscript which he sent her ... did she draw a pencil line around it, and write in the margin A LIE? ...
>
> Mrs. Eddy corrected some of Mr. Kimball's statements ... not because they were necessarily wrong, but because he was planning to give them to the public, who could not possibly distinguish between the real which as yet has not appeared, and the unreal which seems to be with us always.

If the first edition of Science and Health in 1875 contained the "complete statement of Christian Science" *(Ret.* 37), then the author's subsequent changes were not metaphysical corrections but accommodations to the thought of the age she was addressing. Mr. Carpenter has said of her revisions and revising:

> Mrs. Eddy revised Science and Health, not because there was anything untrue about the first edition, but because it did not present Christian Science in a form sufficiently adapted to the needs of the world . . . No one will ever know the spiritual thought and effort Mrs. Eddy expended in order to step down and accommodate revelation as it came to her, so that it could be comprehended by the beginner . . . In fact she once remarked that she had brought Science and Health or Christian Science down just as far as she could, without losing it.

Mr. Kimball's grandson wrote that his grandfather's two day interview with Mrs. Eddy at Chestnut Hill in the fall of 1908 was in regard to teaching "body." This undoubtedly led to a part of his Association Address of 1908 in which he stated:

> As against the statement frequently made by Scientists — "Well, I suppose we must all pass through the belief of death in order to get rid of this material body," we are warranted in this statement: There is no "this material body" to get rid of. The very statement itself, so often made by Scientists, is a death sentence in itself. Moreover, a mortal cannot die out of the belief that body is material. He has to live out of it. There is no way out of the belief of death but to live. Life is Love, Spirit, and if we would overcome the false material sense of life in matter, we must love our way out. He who loves not, lives not, for Love is Life. In order to get the body that manifests life, we must begin to declare for it, and gradually, or rapidly, come into our own — namely eternal body.
>
> In your treatment of the sick, be sure to declare the facts about body. Some of the physicians show a more correct sense of body than do some Christian Scientists. Dr. W. A. Hammond, former Surgeon-General of the United States, has recently said that there is no physiological reason why the body of a human being should die. He refers to the capacity of the body to renew its tissues and to continue its functions and says that this [could] go on indefinitely . . .

It is altogether possible that it was during this two day interview when they were going so thoroughly into the teaching of "body" that Mr. Kimball asked Mrs. Eddy what would happen to the Christian Science Movement if she should pass on:

> She replied: "It would degenerate into material prosperity." He then asked what would happen if she ascended. She hesitated, before

answering with a beatific smile, "The Mother Church would be dissolved."

Mrs. Eddy had a unique gold ring, a gift from her son George W. Glover, which was made from several colors of gold from the Dakota Black Hills. In the summer of 1908 she had had inscribed on the inner band "M.A.S., August, 1908 from M.B.E." and presented this ring to her maid, Minnie Adelaide Still. In the year that Miss Still had been with her a good many students had been called to Mrs. Eddy's home. Some had remained a few days, some a few weeks, and some had not stayed at all, but all felt blessed by their brief meeting with the Leader. Mrs. Eddy, however, said one day to Mr. Dickey, "This matter of students coming here for a few days and then going away and proclaiming what wonderful things they have learned is a menace to the Cause. When they learn anything, they stay here. They are not sent away. When they are sent away and give out the idea that they know so much, they are over-reaching themselves, and deceiving others." In the fall one more student came who did stay and become a member of the household.

William R. Rathvon, a Colorado business man, first learned of Christian Science in 1893 while living temporarily in Chicago. At that time he and his wife Ella both had class instruction with a pioneer student of Mrs. Eddy, Mrs. Mary W. Adams. Ten years later the Rathvons were members of the Primary class of the Board of Education taught by Mr. Kimball in 1903. Mr. Rathvon also attended Judge Hanna's Normal class in 1907. Ella continued her Christian Science practice in Boulder, Colorado when William was called to Chestnut Hill in the fall of 1908.

The new students in the home such as Mr. Rathvon and Mr. Dickey were dedicated Christian Scientists, but there was one great difference between them and Calvin Frye. Their loyalty was divided between the Leader and her organization, whereas Calvin saw the Leader and her organization as one. After he had been there for a time Rathvon described this difference in his diary:

> It came to me that CF is different from the rest of us, among other things, in this. We have two aims in our work here: first, to protect our Leader; and second, to protect the Cause. CF has shown his are: first, to protect our Leader; and second, to protect our Leader.

Mrs. Eddy needed the youthful, fearless, buoyant enthusiasm of the newcomers to carry out her instructions for the progress of the Cause, but none could ever know what Calvin Frye meant to her. To Calvin, Mrs. Eddy *was* the Cause, and he had stood by her side through twenty-six years of malicious persecution. At times he had basked in her praise and appreciation, and very often he had suffered severe rebukes. The other students had little understanding of the importance of Calvin's role, but one student who did have great appreciation for Mr. Frye was Alfred Farlow.

Mr. Farlow had been on another front line as Committee on Publication for a good many years. On May 31 he had been called to Chestnut Hill where he planned to spend the nights while maintaining his office as COP in Boston from 9 to 5 each day. But Mrs. Eddy worked night and day, and assisting the Leader at Chestnut Hill was much more of a full time position than most students ever imagined. The schedule was more than Alfred could maintain, and he left Chestnut Hill on June 2. In a letter he wrote on August 3, Mr. Farlow said to Calvin Frye:

> Knowing as much as I do about what you have to contend with constantly I am in a position to appreciate your excellent service. For that reason I would be glad to take off my shoes and give them to you any time and walk home bare foot, so please get rid of your exceeding modesty on this subject.

A letter from the new First Reader, Clifford P. Smith, indicates that Mrs. Eddy may have changed her mind about flowers at Chestnut Hill. Judge Smith wrote on Sunday, September 13:

> Beloved Leader:
> I wish to thank you, in behalf of the congregation as well as myself, for the beautiful roses which you so thoughtfully and lovingly provided for today's services in The Mother Church. Announcements were made to both congregations that the flowers were your gift; and I am sure that all enjoyed them as flowers and appreciated them as your gift. I certainly did. . . .

Mrs. Eddy enquired every day about the progress of the *Monitor* which may have prompted the September 15 sample they had made for her, and which undoubtedly kept everyone working diligently. All who knew the Leader, however, knew that none worked as diligently and unceasingly as did she, and she was their ensample. A week before an editorial by Archibald McLellan announced the forthcoming *Christian Science Monitor,* another item of interest and import appeared in the *Sentinel* of October 10. It was the letter that Mrs. Eddy had received in August from Jules Maurice Gaspard. If Mr. Gaspard had not already done so, Mrs. Eddy had him copyright his portrait of her, and this new portrait including "Copyright 1908 by Jules Maurice Gaspard" became the frontispiece in the fifth revision of Science and Health in 1908.

This portrait appeared above the facsimile of her signature begin-

MARY BAKER EDDY
Frontispiece in Science and Health beginning in the Fifth Revision of 1908

ning in 1908 and continued to appear in each edition of Science and Health throughout 1909 and 1910. She is wearing her diamond cross in this picture, but the *dark* background has been removed.

In this edition which replaced the dark portrait with a light one there was another significant change. Ever since the first edition each succeeding edition had presented the greatest obstacle the Founder had had to meet and the greatest stumbling block to all students. It was depicted on the page following the title page in the words:

> I, I, I, I, itself I.
> The inside and outside, the what and the why,
> The when and the where, the low and the high,
> All I, I, I, I, itself I.

This anonymous poem was removed along with the dark picture and replaced with the Leader's words:

> Oh! Thou hast heard my prayer;
> And I am blest!
> This is Thy high behest; —
> Thou here, and *everywhere.*
> — MARY BAKER G. EDDY

CHAPTER LIV

TO BLESS ALL MANKIND

Has Mrs. Eddy lost her power to heal?
Has the sun forgotten to shine, and the planets to revolve around it? . . . Who is it that discovered, demonstrated, and teaches Christian Science? That one, whoever it be, does understand something of what cannot be lost. — MARY BAKER EDDY

1908

LETTER from Adam Dickey to Archibald McLellan at the end of September had stated in part:

> Her object in saying what she did in the Boston Post was to make it plain that Christian Scientists were not seeking an opportunity for self-aggrandizement, but were doing this through a purely Christian motive.
>
> In line with your suggestion, Mrs. Eddy does not wish her Boston Post article to appear in our periodicals.

But her statement to the *Boston Post* on "Politics" *(My.* 276) early in November did appear in the periodicals, first in the *Sentinel* of November 7. Christian Scientists who tended to be overzealous in this area may have been turned to a higher power by the Leader's brief answer to the question What are your politics? "I have none in reality, other than to help support a righteous government; to love God supremely, and my neighbor as myself."

While the country at large was involved with the presidential election of 1908, the Leader's mission for all mankind continued at Chestnut Hill. Practically all of the students felt that her great Christian Science organization was to redeem the whole world, while the Leader knew that nothing but the student's own spiritual understanding could even begin to maintain what she had discovered and founded. So she worked night and day to impart this understanding by precept and example to the students in her home.

An example on the night of Monday, November 9 was one never to be forgotten by the three students involved. Not long after Mrs. Eddy had retired for the night (which was usually about 9 P.M.) a greatly agitated Laura Sargent came to Mr. Dickey's door for help. Laura had found Calvin Frye unconscious on the lounge in his room and had been unable to rouse him. The two returned quickly to Calvin's room and Mr. Dickey —

> found Mr. Frye stretched on the lounge in a most uncomfortable attitude, speechless and eyes closed, apparently breathless and with no pulse or indication of life whatever. We continued our efforts to arouse him but with no success. We called him, shook him, and used every means at our command.

At this point Irving Tomlinson arrived on the scene and the three, with redoubled efforts, endeavored to restore Mr. Frye, but in Tomlinson's words, "he appeared to have passed on."

They had hesitated notifying Mrs. Eddy until they felt defeated. Then Laura hurried to tell her of the situation. Mrs. Eddy rang immediately for her maid and began to rise to dress, but dropped back into bed and said: "I cannot wait to dress. Bring him to me." Laura protested that he was unconscious, but Mrs. Eddy said: "Bring him to me at once."

Tomlinson lifted the unconscious Frye into a low rocking chair which they dragged through the hall, through Mrs. Eddy's study, into her bedroom, and right beside her bed where she was sitting with a shawl about her shoulders. The workers watched, and Mr. Dickey later recorded:

> Our Leader reached out her hand and placed it upon Mr. Frye's shoulder and addressed him in a loud voice, "Calvin, Calvin, wake up. It is Mother who is calling you. Wake up, Calvin, this Cause needs you, Mother needs you, and you must not leave. Calvin, Calvin, wake up. Disappoint your enemies. You shall not go. I need you here. Disappoint your enemies, Calvin, and awake." All this time Mr. Frye's head was hanging limp on his shoulder. I had hold of the back of the rocking chair in which we had placed him to steady him. I placed my hand on his head to lift it up. Mrs. Eddy instantly stopped me, and said, "Do not touch him. Leave him entirely to me." Again she repeated her calls to him to arouse himself and remain with her. It was now something like half an hour since Calvin had first been found, and ... the time seemed to pass without any appreciable response to her work. This did not discourage her. She redoubled her efforts and fairly shouted to Mr. Frye her commands that he awake. In a moment he raised his head and drew a long, deep breath. After this his respiration became regular and he was restored to conscious-

ness. The first words he uttered were, "I don't want to stay. I want to go." Mrs. Eddy paused in her efforts and turning her gaze to the workers around the room said, "Just listen to that." She again turned to Mr. Frye and in her commanding tones insisted that he awake and remain here.

Mr. Tomlinson recorded that she commanded: "Say that you do want to stay and help me;" and Mr. Frye responded, "Yes, I will stay." Mrs. Eddy then told him to work for himself, and Calvin said, "Yes, I will come back." Shortly he was recovered and walked back to his room unaided, though another student remained with him through the night. Calvin was at the breakfast table the next morning and about his accustomed duties as usual. The occurrence was never mentioned to Mr. Frye, but it was recorded by those who witnessed it. Mr. Dickey wrote:

> I had heard of similar occasions when rumors had reached the workers in the field that at different times our Leader had restored prominent students to life after experiences of this kind, but of this incident I was an eye-witness and from the very first my attention was not diverted for one second from what was going on, and I am simply relating this event exactly as it occurred.

Mr. Tomlinson's concluding words about the incident were:

> It is most inspiring to recall that throughout the entire experience Mrs. Eddy manifested tremendous spiritual strength and poise. Those of us who were present on that occasion can testify that this remarkable woman had lost none of her healing power in her eighty-eighth year. She spoke in strong, clear tones. There was no fear, no doubt, no discouragement; only absolute confidence, only perfect assurance of the victory of Truth. The following morning Mrs. Eddy was up at the usual hour, and at nine o'clock when I entered her study, I found her busily occupied in reading her Bible. She called my attention to verses 7 and 8 of Psalms 138 which she marked in pencil:
>
> Though I walk in the midst of trouble, thou wilt revive me: thou shalt stretch forth thine hand against the wrath of mine enemies, and thy right hand shall save me. The Lord will perfect that which concerneth me: thy mercy, O Lord, endureth for ever: forsake not the works of thine own hands.

In the next issue of the *Sentinel* on November 14 there was a change in the announcement at the top of the editorial page. This announcement entitled "Mrs. Eddy Takes No Patients" which appeared in each issue, was changed to read:

The author of the Christian Science textbook takes no patients, and reads no letters on disease, distress, or error of any kind. Reliable news concerning Mrs. Eddy will be found in the Christian Science publications.

The *Sentinel* of November 21 contained two more new by-laws, one of which was Article VIII, Christian Science Nurse. Sect. 31. *(Man.* 49) The other read:

Article XXII. CLOSED TO VISITORS. Sect. 14 [Now 17]. The room in The Mother Church formerly known as "Mother's Room," shall hereafter be closed to visitors.

[There is nothing in this room now of any special interest. "Let the dead bury their dead," and the spiritual have all place and power.]

Mary Baker Eddy

The Christian Science Monitor had been announced in the *Sentinel* of October 17 and work was being pursued with diligence at the Publishing House for its issuance. Mrs. Eddy's approval had been sought on many points and Mr. McLellan had conferred with her frequently, but on more than one occasion her answer through a secretary contained such messages as "she wished you would make this appointment on your own judgment" or "proceed with the work in your own way doing the best you can." She was training her officers to make their own decisions, but her letter of November 18 to Mr. McLellan was also a warning to proceed in this area with the utmost care:

Beloved Student:

I hereby forewarn you and demand of you to guard carefully the old landmarks that heretofore have been fought over, and gained their precedence and authority from your leader and the leading Christian Scientists.

I trust that with you "forewarned" will result in being"forearmed," to be faithful in history, true to your leader and her precedents that have been justified by forty years of success.

Lovingly yours,
M. B. G. Eddy

One decision regarding the new newspaper Mrs. Eddy did *not* leave to her officials was the name. Mr. McLellan had objected from the outset to the words Christian Science in the name of a daily newspaper and had tried to convince Mrs. Eddy that it was a handicap and a mistake. Many agreed with him including Alexander Dodds, the managing editor, also the manager of the Publishing Society, and even some of the members of Mrs. Eddy's own household. Irving Tomlinson describes the final attempt to delete the words Christian Science:

> As a last resort an interview was secured with Mrs. Eddy, at which time the editor-in-chief and the manager of the Publishing Society endeavored to win her to this view. The members of the household were on tiptoes, waiting outside the door of Mrs. Eddy's room, while the final decision was being made. . . . A moment or so and the editor emerged. Said he, "Mrs. Eddy is firm, and her answer is, 'God gave me this name and it remains.' "

John J. Flinn, one of the first newspaper men called in to help found the *Monitor,* said:

> The impression that we all received of Mrs. Eddy's attitude toward the name of the newspaper was: That since the Monitor was to represent Christian Science in journalism, the only thing, because the right thing to do, was to stamp it at once with its proper designation.

All seem to have missed the real point. They were concerned with the establishment of a successful daily newspaper in the world. Mary Baker Eddy was concerned with the establishment of Christian Science in this world, and the newspaper was one more God-directed vehicle to this end.

A letter from Mr. Dickey to Mr. McLellan on November 24 said:

> I have submitted to Mrs. Eddy the sample copies of "The Christian Science Monitor" which you and Mr. Dodds left with me last evening.
>
> Our Leader prefers the heavy style of type shown in the title of the paper which I enclose herewith, but insists that the article "The" properly belongs in the title and wishes it placed there. This will necessitate making another design that can be as easily read as the one enclosed.
>
> The placing of the motto beneath the title on the editorial page is satisfactory for Mrs. Eddy, and in other respects she is well pleased with the appearance of the newspaper.

The next day, Wednesday, November 25 (the day before Thanksgiving), dawned so murky and dark that ships were unable to dock in New York and Boston harbors, but it was the great day at the Publishing House. The first issue of *The Christian Science Monitor* off the press was sent immediately to Mrs. Eddy, — a practice continued every day, with the religious articles and each editorial rubber-stamped with the name of the writer. Mr. Tomlinson wrote in his diary:

At nine o'clock on the date of the Monitor's first issue all the workers were called by Mrs. Eddy to her study. Present — Frye, Sargent, Miss Alice Peck, Adam Dickey, Mr. Rathvon and I.C.T. The morning dark and foggy. Mrs. Eddy asked if it were a dark morning. "Yes," replied one, "a heavy fog makes it darker than usual." Mr. Frye said that according to sense it was dark. Mrs. Eddy replied: "Yes, but only according to sense. We know the reverse of error is true. This, in Truth, is the lightest day of all days. This is the day when our daily paper goes forth to lighten mankind . . ."

Frank Bell, a newspaper man in Pennsylvania, had written a letter to Mrs. Eddy on November 2 which brought forth from her pen an article which she sent along with Mr. Bell's letter to her editor for publication. Following this, on November 11 she wrote to Mr. McLellan: "Please have my article last sent to you appear in the first issue of the Christian Science Monitor." So the first editorial in the first issue was:

SOMETHING IN A NAME
By Mary Baker G. Eddy

The gentleman, Mr. Frank Bell, has caught my thunder; therefore, he will not object to the lightning which accompanies it.

I have given the name to all the Christian Science periodicals. The first was The Christian Science Journal, designed to put on record the divine Science of Truth; the second I entitled Sentinel, intended to hold guard over Truth, Life and Love; the third Der Herold der Christian Science, to proclaim the universal activity and availability of Truth; the next I named Monitor, to spread undivided the Science that operates unspent. The object of The Monitor is to injure no man, but to bless all mankind.

- - - - - - - - - - - - -

Harrisburg, Pa., Nov. 2, 1908

Rev. Mary Baker G. Eddy, Brookline, Mass.

Dear Leader: — As a newspaper man I thank you for The Christian Science Monitor in prospect, and I feel sure that such will be the sentiment of hundreds of newspaper workers all over the land when The Monitor in fact shall have demonstrated the feasibility of clean journalism.

A definition of "monitor" is "One who advises," and I foresee that when this Christian Science Monitor shall have proved that there is such a thing as newspaper success along non-sensational lines, there will follow a widespread readjustment of news policies, for which I am sure none will be more truly thankful than an army of honest, conscientious toilers in the ranks of newspaperdom.

Gratefully yours,
Frank Bell
Managing Editor, Harrisburg Telegraph

Mrs. Eddy recorded in her private notebook on November 25 that one hundred sixty thousand copies of the *Monitor* were sold on the day it came out and that the Publishing House could not fill all the orders! But she also recorded: "When I first proposed to the Christian Scientists to have this newspaper and gave it its name, I had not much encouragement from them that it would be a success."

Five days later an article in a New York newspaper turned the thoughts of many Scientists in another direction.

CHAPTER LV

THE CARRIAGE CONVERSATION

When my dear brethren in New York desire to build higher, — to enlarge their phylacteries and demonstrate Christian Science to a higher extent, — they must begin on a wholly spiritual foundation, — than which there is no other, and proportionably estimate their success and glory of achievement only as they build upon the rock of Christ, the spiritual foundation. — MARY BAKER EDDY

1908

EARLY in 1884 when Augusta Emma Stetson saw Mary Baker Eddy for the first time she felt an attraction which she little understood or heeded on that spring day. But the Founder of Christian Science understood it, and she said to Mrs. Stetson: "I want you to come and see me. You are going to do a great work in Christian Science."

When Augusta was very young in Science, Mrs. Eddy gave her a demanding test at Reading, Massachusetts and afterward stated, "You stood, Augusta. You stood, you did not run." Almost every time they met, the Leader reminded her of this experience and reiterated, "You stood, Augusta, you did not run."

In a letter to Augusta in 1891 Mrs. Eddy said: "Your prompt obedience to me shows a wisdom that will crown your life with success. You evidently have learned this from God . . ." In another letter two years later the Leader wrote to Augusta:

> I am fixed and more and more in my confidence in your strength to stand and "having done all to stand." . . .
>
> Oh, dearest, precious child, how much you have done and will yet do for our cause none knows but me.

Augusta's obedience did crown her life with phenomenal success; but what was she to do for the cause that none but the Leader knew?

Over a twenty-five year period hundreds of letters passed between Mrs. Eddy and Mrs. Stetson. In reading this correspondence alongside other correspondence of the period it sometimes seems that the Leader was intentionally separating Mrs. Stetson from other Christian Scientists.

Augusta was a gifted leader, second only to Mrs. Eddy. Her financial success, the beautiful temple she built (First Church, New York), her success in healing, preaching, teaching, all fanned the flames of envy and rivalry throughout the field and most especially in Boston. Mrs. Eddy was aware of the tide of malicious gossip against Mrs. Stetson, and had on occasion mentioned it to her, but it does not appear that the Leader endeavored to stem this tide. Is it possible that she was training Augusta to stand alone, as she herself had done, before a hostile world?

In 1908 First Church in New York City was so over-crowded at every service that they had been holding overflow meetings of two or three hundred in their Reading Room, as well as discussing at their board meetings what to do about the situation. Then Mrs. Eddy wrote a new by-law which appeared in the 74th edition of the *Manual* in 1908:

> **Overflow Meetings.** Sect. 4. A church of Christ, Scientist, shall not hold two or more Sunday services at the same hour.

This caused them to think seriously in terms of another branch church. A desirable site was available and they took an option on it. A New York newspaper reported on November 30 that First Church of Christ, Scientist of New York was starting a branch church and that "It was proposed to have a church edifice, rivaling in beauty of architecture any other religious structure in America. . . . It was learned last night that Christian Scientists here have aspired to build another and more splendid edifice, ever since the Boston Christian Scientists erected the $2,000,000 Mother Church." Very naturally this news item brought more condemnation upon Mrs. Stetson.

Mr. McLellan's editorial for the next (Dec. 5) *Sentinel,* according to Mr. Carpenter, was dictated to him by Mrs. Eddy:

> CONSISTENCY
>
> Is matter real?
>
> No; there is no matter. God is All, and God is Spirit; therefore they that worship Him, worship him in spirit and in truth.
>
> Is God Spirit?
>
> He is.
>
> Then, do you make God, who is real, supreme in your affections, or are you making matter, which you admit is not real, supreme?
>
> Are you striving, in Christian Science, to be the best Christian on

earth, or are you striving to have the most costly edifice on earth?

Are you striving to make the most possible of matter which you admit is unreal, or are you striving to make most of Spirit, which you admit is All and that there is none beside Spirit?

Let every Christian Scientist answer honestly to his God the above questions, then obey the command, "Choose you this day whom ye will serve." If it be Spirit, let it be Spirit; and if it be matter, let him acknowledge it, and remove his name from the list of Christian Scientists. This he must do, and will do if he is honest.

The more modest and less imposing material superstructures indicate a spiritual state of thought; and *vice versa.*

The house Mrs. Eddy now occupies is larger than she needs, because she could not find exactly what she wanted; but it is a plain house, and its furnishings are not extravagant. Mrs. Eddy has continued to declare against the display of material things, and has said that the less we have of them the better. Since God has taught her that matter is unreal and Spirit is the only reality, any other position would be unscientific.

McLellan wrote another article for the December 5 *Sentinel* quoting the New York news item and criticizing First Church, New York. The next day a New York newspaper carried a correction from First Church stating that the new church would be Seventh Church of New York and its only connection with First Church would be that the latter would help to finance its building project.

Mrs. Eddy wrote to Mrs. Stetson on December 7:

My beloved Student:

I have tried and hoped all through the past season to have you come to me and take a drive with me around the Chestnut Hill Reservoir but have failed hitherto. Is it too late for you to enjoy it? If not, appoint a day and the hour when you will be here and I will be on hand.

My present hour for driving is between 1 and 2 p.m.

Lovingly yours,
M. B. G. Eddy

The next day upon receipt of this letter, Augusta caught the midnight train for Boston. The following morning, Wednesday, December 9, she notified Calvin Frye that she was in the city and received a note from Mrs. Eddy saying: "Please be here at 1 p.m. today and take a short drive with me."

When Mrs. Stetson arrived at Chestnut Hill, Adam Dickey told her that Mrs. Eddy was in the carriage awaiting her at the door. They had carefully tucked a white lamb's wool robe snugly around her as protection against the cold, with a warm carriage rug on top. In Mrs. Stetson's words:

When I entered, Mrs. Eddy took both my hands in hers and kissed me and expressed herself as greatly pleased to see me. One of the attendants, after I was seated, drew over me the dark carriage rug, when Mrs. Eddy said, "Remove that and put Augusta under the white robe with me." Noticing that they had so carefully and lovingly protected her from the cold, and fearing that she might not be so protected by this change, I exclaimed, "The carriage rug is sufficient for me; please let the lamb's wool remain." She again said, "No, I want you to share this with me." They acceded to her request and we drove away.

There was significance to everything Mrs. Eddy did at this last meeting with her beloved Augusta. Her words, "Put Augusta under the white robe with me," were never to be forgotten. Though Augusta knew it not on that cold December day she was being elevated to equality with her Leader and that elevation would cost an awful price. When that terrible price was exacted of her, Augusta would often recall this day and her Leader's words. Many years later Mrs. Stetson wrote:

Repeatedly during these hours, days, and months of severe test of my faith and understanding of divine metaphysics, I have heard her words as she sat in her carriage that day: "You did not run, did you Augusta?" And for the first time she added most emphatically, "And you *never will.*"

Mrs. Eddy asked Mrs. Stetson not to speak of their conversation that afternoon, so it was long a point of speculation and conjecture. However, the following, which Mrs. Stetson wrote upon returning to her hotel in Boston after the drive, was found among her papers:

December 9, 1908

Carriage Conversation

S. — Entered carriage with Mrs. Eddy at 1 P.M. After personal salutation I said we have been having quite a little work in New York.

E. — Said, yes, when you get home write and tell me all about it.

S. — I have a paper here. Reporters have made mistakes. We have made only one payment on the land to hold it. We have not begun to build yet.

E. — Why are you going to build?

S. — I said, why, because of the overflow. We cannot accommodate our people. We have been worshipping upstairs to avoid the congestion in the auditorium. We would have continued to worship upstairs but you made the by-law that two services could not be held in one building at the same time. From this I thought you wanted us to build another church.

E. — Oh, darling, do you remember Mother's experience; she

thought she could do or demonstrate for everybody and do everybody's work and started to build a church to help them build. I gave them my money and how they turned upon me and rent me. Never give your students money, give them of your spiritual help and let them make their own demonstration. What did I do for you, Augusta? I put you out in New York City and let you make your demonstration or fall. What have you done? You have made the biggest demonstration and have done the most good and are still doing good. Just as sure as you give money to people — the overflow — you will have the same experience as Mother had. They must make their own demonstration.

S. — But, I said, they will need the strong support of the old, advanced students. The overflow are all young students, they do not know much.

E. — But, never mind that, let them go out and demonstrate.

S. — They have not the means perhaps to build a church.

E. — How did you get your money? I did not give you any. How did you build your church? Look at your demonstration; if they haven't the means to build they will find it by struggling and your people can loan them money but not give it to them. You are having the same experience that Mother had and she loved her people so she thought she could put them in a place. That was human love, and, oh, how I suffered for it. Now I know that divine Love trusts them to God and if they are good and if they hold on to God and my teaching, as you have done, God will do as much for them as he has done for you.

Mrs. Eddy said, look at my aged face.

S. — I answered, the author of Science and Health said, "never record ages." Mrs. Eddy laughed. She was only testing me to see what my concept was. I said, now we are going to demonstrate over the world, the flesh, and the devil.

E. — Yes, and death, and then we shall know there is no death.

S. — I said, there is no separation, all one body we.

E. — Answered, we have no material body.

S. — I said, no, we are the embodiment of Spirit.

E. — Answered, the material body is not anything and we must not believe it is.

E. — You are my very best beloved student but I have to be so careful to hide it from others.

Mr. Dickey and most likely Mr. Rathvon were waiting for them when the carriage returned to Chestnut Hill about three-quarters of an hour later. This may have been Mrs. Stetson's first visit to Chestnut Hill for Mr. Dickey showed her about the house, pointing out different things and most especially the onyx table Mrs. Eddy had bought to put Augusta's flower vase on. In a few minutes Mrs. Eddy sent for her and remarked as she approached: "How healthy and strong you are. You look years younger than when I saw you last." Then:

E. — Now, when you go back, do you know just what to do?

S. — I don't know, I think I am very sure.

E. — I will tell you. Don't tell any one, not any one. Now when you go back, don't shock your students — have your three services — and you just give that money back as quickly as you can. Do it, God will show you how. God will show you some wise way to cover it.

S. — The payment will have to be made.

E. — God will take care of that — this will be just and easy. The overflow will take care of the matter.

E. — This was only pressure and grand overflowing love. Don't deprive any one of his experience.

S. — They are so young in Science.

E. — They need not do it. When they are jammed let them go where they will.

E. — You have but to make one demonstration — that is overflowing love — But this is divine Love that makes *them* do it.

S. — When will they go out and start another branch?

E. — What do you care, let them do it when they get ready. How I have suffered for helping people and preventing them from making their own demonstration.

S. — Oh, Dear, I think how hard I made it for you when we built that first church, whenever I had burdens I rested on you.

E. — Well, wasn't that right?

S. — I don't care what mortal mind says. I am not afraid, all I want to do is the will of God.

E. — Oh, thank God, you dear, dear child.

Augusta bade the Leader good-bye and went downstairs, but before she went out to her carriage Mr. Dickey came to tell her that Mrs. Eddy wanted to see her again. They went back upstairs, met Laura Sargent in the upper hall, and Mr. Dickey opened the door of Mrs. Eddy's room for Augusta to enter. The chair Augusta had been occupying had been removed, and almost involuntarily she knelt beside Mrs. Eddy's chair. The Leader took Augusta's face in her hands and said, "O my beloved Augusta, God bless you forever and forever and forever." After a moment of impressive silence she added, "This is the happiest hour of my life — the very happiest hour of my life, on earth." Then, "If you have anything to say or ask, I want you to say —"

Augusta responded, "I can only say, I love you."

Mrs. Eddy waved her hand for Augusta to go, and the latter was very surprised when she arose and turned toward the door to see Mr. Dickey and Mrs. Sargent standing inside the room as witnesses. Mr. Dickey opened the door and the three of them left. A few minutes later when Augusta was in the drawing-room waiting for her carriage Mr. Dickey brought her a sealed letter from Mrs. Eddy which Augusta said she "later learned was an added evidence of her faithful protection of me."

Later that same day, December 9, Mrs. Eddy followed this visit with another letter to Augusta:

> Darling:
>
> I charge you not to have your students think that it is I personally that changes your actions and thoughts, for it is *not I*. It is God, and has moved the world in this way. If you plant this change on a person, it will not prosper, but if you know and say the Divine Principle is doing it, all will end well.
>
> Again, lovingly,
> M. B. G. Eddy

At that time Augusta may have felt that the purpose of this meeting had been for the handling of the overflow situation in her church, but the Leader knew differently. Nearly twenty years earlier she had written in a letter to Augusta: "Your *devotion* is beyond that of Ruth's, it is like the women at the cross. Oh, child of my heart, God is ripening you for His hour." Augusta was ripened; and His hour was almost upon them.

MARY — WOMAN OF PROPHECY

Pen and Ink Drawing by Edythe Rekstad

CHAPTER LVI

MOTIVE

Time tells all stories true. — MARY BAKER EDDY

1909

MR. Dickey had not kept abreast of all of the by-law changes, and when he had left Kansas City to serve in Mrs. Eddy's home had thought it was for a period of one year. Before his arrival at Chestnut Hill he had read the latest *Manual* stipulating a three-year term of service; nonetheless, as he began his twelfth month, according to Adelaide Still "he begged to go back to Kansas." So on January 14 Mr. Dickey returned to Kansas City, but he was no doubt well aware of the new by-law in the *Sentinel* of January 2:

> A NEW BY-LAW
> Article XXII
>
> AGREEMENT REQUIRED. — Sect. 13. When the Christian Science Board of Directors call a student, in accordance with Article XXII, Sect. 11 of our Church Manual, to the home of their Leader, Mrs. Eddy, said student shall come under a signed agreement to remain with Mrs. Eddy during the time specified in the Church Manual.

One interesting change Mr. Dickey took care of in January of 1909 before leaving for Kansas City was a notification sent to Mrs. Eddy's editor. Mr. McLellan's reply to Mr. Dickey on January 7 stated:

> I am in receipt of your letter of the 6th inst., instructing me that our Leader wishes her name to appear hereafter, wherever practical and legal, as Mary Baker Eddy, leaving out the initial "G" ...
>
> The "G" has been... and will be taken out... with the possible exception of the copyright notice ...

About the time Mr. Dickey left Chestnut Hill another dedicated student returned to serve the Leader — that was Martha Wilcox. But Martha and many others in the household were babes in the metaphysical realm. The Leader's editorial in the *Sentinel* of January 16 was for the advanced metaphysician and most especially for her veteran soldier in New York City.

In 1875 the Revelator to this age had published in the first edition of Science and Health, page 166: "We have no need of creeds and church organizations to sustain or explain a demonstrable platform that defines itself in healing the sick and casting out error." But her mission was to *lead* the Children of Israel out of the land of bondage. She had to begin where she found them, and they were not yet ready nor able to give up church organizations. So she helped them to establish one saying, "suffer it to be so now." This transitional step, however, was allowed no place in the sacred pages of the "little book" from the hand of the angel, save brief mention in the preface.

Before the organization had an edifice or the guiding *Manual,* the Leader had written: "When students have fulfilled all the good ends of organization, and are convinced that by leaving the material forms thereof a higher spiritual unity is won, then is the time to follow the example of the *Alma Mater.* Material organization is requisite in the beginning; but when it has done its work, the purely Christly method of teaching and preaching must be adopted." *(Mis.* 358)

Mrs. Stetson was not convinced that she should leave the material organization. In fact, she had probably never thought about it; but evidently her Leader felt that she had "fulfilled all the good ends of organization" and was ready for a higher step. Pursuant to her conversation with Mrs. Stetson on December 9 Mrs. Eddy wrote an editorial outlining this higher step, but before its appearance, she wrote to Augusta on January 14 softening its demands:

> My Darling Student:
>
> When you read my article in our periodicals, I beg you to know that I am not referring to one student only but to every one who needs my instruction.
>
> God gives me His instructions wherewith to instruct the students and I should be an unfaithful servant if I did not impart what He gives to me to others and to all mankind.
>
> In haste, ever lovingly yours,
> Mary Baker Eddy

Despite this letter, her January 16 editorial "The Way of Wisdom" *(My.* 356), which is speaking today to every one who is ready for this step, did speak directly to Mrs. Stetson and her students in 1909:

> materiality is wholly apart from Christian Science, and is only a "Suffer it to be so now" ... matter is the absolute opposite of spiritual means, manifestation, and demonstration. The only incentive of a mistaken sense is malicious animal magnetism, — the name of all evil, — and this must be understood.
>
> ... When my dear brethren in New York desire to build higher, — to enlarge their phylacteries and demonstrate Christian Science to a higher extent, — they must begin on a wholly spiritual foundation ...

The New York students little understood the import and implications of this message from the Leader, but they accepted the challenge and responded immediately. Mrs. Eddy published their letter of January 17 in the next (Jan. 23) *Sentinel* under the title "Where Shall Wisdom Be Found":

> Beloved Leader:
>
> When searching for the answer to Job's question, "Where shall wisdom be found? and where is the place of understanding?" we found it in you, our beloved Leader, who are wisdom's mouthpiece to this age.
>
> The demonstration of our church is the direct result of your instructions obeyed, and we shall continue to follow as you forever lead on in "the way of wisdom." You are continually pouring into our lamps the oil of consecration, and we are drinking of the wine of inspiration which you provide. The word has gone forth, "Hurt not the oil and the wine."
>
> In grateful acknowledgment of the redemption of the first-born, mindful of the ever-present protection of divine Love, we will enlarge our spiritual phylacteries, binding them as frontlets between our eyes, that we may "demonstrate Christian Science to a higher extent." Having completed our demonstration of the church militant, we will strive more earnestly to attain the higher understanding which will reveal the church triumphant, where "Spirit is infinite; therefore *Spirit is all;*" no mistaken sense whose incentive is malicious animal magnetism can prevent this unfolding.
>
> The "spiritual modesty" with which you have "crowned The Mother Church building" has been and ever will be our abiding inspiration in building upon "a wholly spiritual foundation." Glorious, indeed, is it to have the horizon of our spiritual vision thus widened by virtue of your vigils on the watch-tower of Zion.
>
> Loyally yours,
>
> The Board of Trustees of First Church of Christ, Scientist, of New York City
>
> E. F. Hatfield, *Chairman*
> John D. Higgins, *Clerk*

Glorious indeed was the enlarged horizon of their spiritual vision, but little did these students dream, in January of 1909, of the Red Sea in their pathway.

Before the end of January Mr. Dickey returned to Boston bringing Mrs. Dickey with him. He was hoping that both he and Mrs. Dickey could serve at Chestnut Hill, but the Leader knew that at their stage of metaphysical development this would have been a divisive rather than a unifying influence. She was still on the battle front continually and knew that she had more than a year of intensive labor ahead of her. She needed soldiers willing to give up all in this war for religious freedom. Mr. Dickey agreed to stay for the "duration," and Mrs. Dickey moved her residence from Kansas City to Brookline, Massachusetts.

Adam picked up his secretarial duties where he had left off two weeks earlier. In answering a letter of January 29 from the trustees, he penciled at the bottom: "Call me up about this. A.H.D." This note did not relate to the text of the letter but to the added penciled comment by Mrs. Eddy: "Hitherto I have been pleased with the articles contributed by Prof. J. R. Mosley to our periodicals, but I am surprised and disappointed with his article "The True Orthodoxy" in our C. S. Sentinel of January 30, 1909. Will Prof. Mosley and our readers peruse the scripture according to Jeremiah 6:14, 15, 19, 20, 21, on this subject . . ."

> Jer. 6:14 They have healed also the hurt of the daughter of my people slightly, saying, Peace, peace; when there is no peace.
>
> 15 Were they ashamed when they had committed abomination? nay, they were not at all ashamed, neither could they blush: therefore they shall fall among them that fall: at the time that I visit them they shall be cast down, saith the Lord.
>
> 19 Hear, O earth: behold, I will bring evil upon this people, even the fruit of their thoughts, because they have not hearkened unto my words, nor to my law, but rejected it.
>
> 20 To what purpose cometh there to me incense from Sheba, and the sweet cane from a far country? your burnt offerings are not acceptable, nor your sacrifices sweet unto me.
>
> 21 Therefore thus saith the Lord, Behold, I will lay stumblingblocks before this people, and the fathers and the sons together shall fall upon them; the neighbor and his friend shall perish.

There is no doubt that Mrs. Eddy's departure from Concord, New Hampshire a year earlier had depleted the revenue in that metropolis, and it may have brought another situation to light. The Concord church was in debt! Mrs. Eddy had *given* the land and one hundred thousand dollars to build this church. Additional gifts had poured in, and it would appear that those who should have been responsible had not exercised wisdom and economy. Now in January of 1909 the men at headquarters in Boston were endeavoring to help pay off this debt as is evident in Mrs. Stetson's January 27 response to their appeal:

> Dear Mr. Farlow:
>
> Your letter requesting me to assist in raising money to pay a debt of the First Church of Christ, Scientist, at Concord, was received this morning. It appears that this fact is of such a character that it would have prevented the dedication of that church until the matter was properly met.
>
> Neither the *original,* nor the *continued concealment* of this condition, from those entitled to know it, could have come from aught but error. Participation in the *concealment* of this fact is unwarranted in Christian Science, which is a law reading, "There is nothing covered, that shall not be revealed" (Luke xii, 2). This law reveals things that are false and evil, and things that are true and good.
>
> It is impossible, therefore, for me to contribute *sub-rosa* to the cancellation of a debt upon the church, which existed when the edifice was dedicated. Taking any other course than this, regarding an error, whether manifested through an individual or through a church-body, is contrary to the principles of Christian Science, and constitutes disobedience to our Leader, and to the Cause which she is commissioned by God to carry to a complete, scientific, and *universal* triumph.
>
> It was, and ever will be a joy to contribute of our love expressed in money to any Christian Science church, in the hour, and "The Way of Wisdom," but for me to ask my students or church-members to aid in the way you suggest, would violate my teachings and practice among them.
>
> . . . Again I must repeat, that it would be pleasant, and an easy thing to do, to send the money to the church; but in this case "I must be cruel only to be kind."
>
> You mistake, dear Mr. Farlow, when you call our church a wealthy body. We are rich in love for God, for our beloved Leader and for all who do the will of our Father, but we are not rich in material possessions. I believe that each church, rich in love and in the understanding of Truth, can prove the promises, and find God able to supply all human needs. . . .
>
> I trust that all will end in strict accordance with Principle.
>
> Sincerely yours,
> Augusta E. Stetson

Jesus' words: "There is nothing covered, that shall not be revealed; neither hid that shall not be known," correlate with Mrs. Eddy's words: "Time tells all stories true." Nonetheless, Mrs. Stetson's refusal to aid in concealing this situation from the Leader did not endear her to those who were already hypercritical of everything she said or did.

They did manage to raise the money elsewhere to pay off this debt, but it is improbable that it was *concealed* from Mrs. Eddy, for it was in their thoughts, and reading the conscious thought of their students to both Mrs. Eddy and to Jesus was like reading the open pages of a book.

It was the thoughts of her students, — often latent or unconscious, — that caused the Leader more physical suffering than any other one thing. But she endured this suffering in order to learn the thought of the Children of Israel that needed to be remedied and elevated. Mr. Dickey's record of one such occurrence verifies this conclusion:

> . . . when she was wrestling with what seemed to be a physical disturbance, I was trying to help her and in talking over the situation with her, I said, "Mother, you can't be made to feel the effect of mortal mind thoughts and mortal mind cannot make you feel its argument." At the time she was lying down with closed eyes, but as soon as I made the statement that "mortal mind cannot make you feel its argument," she looked up, and raising her hand in warning said, "Don't say that, Mr. Dickey." Then she went on in her loving and quiet way to explain that when she was able to feel what mortal mind had in thought, it enabled her to do that thing which was most helpful to the Cause of Christian Science.

Very often such struggles ended with a new by-law, message, or edict from the Leader's pen, following which her recovery from the physical attack was instantaneous.

In the 1940's the author was told by an employee of the Christian Science Publishing Society that a man had been sent over from England to take control of *The Christian Science Monitor* when it was first started; that Mrs. Eddy sent him back to England two or three months later, but that he was back not long after she was gone. The only person that comes near fitting this description is Frederick Dixon of London.

Mr. Dixon was a literary man of great talent and insight who became interested in Christian Science near the end of the century and joined The Mother Church in 1900. He soon became Committee on Publication for London, and his excellent articles were often in the *Sentinel.* Dixon's letter of June 5, 1908 was published in the *Sentinel:*

> Beloved Leader:
>
> I want to take a minute of your time to tell you of the happiness with which I have heard the news of my appointment, by the Directors, as District Manager of the Publication Committee in Great

Britain and Ireland . . .

I find it impossible to express in any adequate way what I think I perceive of "the vast design and purpose" of the publication work, and of the wisdom which instituted it. Eight years ago, when I was appointed Publication Committee for London, for the first time, I had no conception of what the work meant or was intended to mean. Only very gradually as I have come to understand better the teaching of Science and Health, has your wisdom in foreseeing the necessities of the work, and providing for them, become at all clear to me; and I begin to see that to become more ready to obey, by listening more alertly to hear Truth speak, is not the least of the ways in which we can show our gratitude to you, in proving that we are at last beginning to understand, something of the true meaning of Love.

Your loving follower,
Frederick Dixon

Archibald McLellan was the editor of the newly established newspaper, and on November 27, two days after the first *Monitor* was issued, Mr. Dickey had written to Mr. McLellan:

> Mrs. Eddy wishes me to say to you, that taking entire control of the editorials in our daily newspaper in addition to your regular duties, is more than should be put upon you, and in order to relieve you of some responsibility our Leader wishes you to send for Mr. Frederick Dixon of London, England, to take charge of the editorial page of The Christian Science Monitor.

Mr. Dixon arrived in Boston just two weeks later, on December 11, to take up his duties there. In January, before Mr. Dickey had returned from Kansas City Mrs. Eddy had written to Mr. McLellan:

> We have called Mr. Dixon from England to America: he was our star in England and he should be promoted to some office in America. He would make a splendid Editor but we do not want to change our present chief Editor. Please consider this matter and act wisely and justly.

For about three months three names appeared in the paper's masthead — Archibald McLellan, Editor; Alexander Dodds, Managing Editor; and Frederick Dixon, Associate Editor.

Martha Wilcox, who spent 1909 and 1910 at Chestnut Hill, tells us that Frederick Dixon was one of the many Scientists Mrs. Eddy had out for interviews and for dinner. On April 11 Mrs. Eddy wrote a letter to Mr. Dixon explaining why she wanted him to return to England. This letter, as had been the case with many others, was never sent. Perhaps it was *to* Mr. Dixon, but not intended *for* him.

It may have been to prepare the thought of her secretary, who would send the basic message to Mr. Dixon less than two weeks later, and to answer the cloud of speculation that would arise in Boston at such a sudden and unexpected move. Five days later, on April 16, 1909, Mrs. Eddy wrote:

MOTIVE

We think before we speak, then if our thought is right our words will be as nearly right as our thoughts; but if our thoughts are wrong and our words are right, the result will follow the wrong direction. We may deceive man but we cannot deceive God. He searcheth the heart and rewards or punishes the motive until the act follows in the right direction. Oh! Thou eternal Love, I leave my adopted children — and Thy children — to Thee who art wisdom, unfailing and unfaltering wisdom and Love, to guard them in this hour of the attempted reign of M.A.M., the reign and rule of all that is selfish, debased and unjust.

My beloved students: Enter into the closet of divine Love and there in humility ask this ever-present power to shield and to defend you from the enemies of your souls and bodies, to defend you and guard you and guide you in the paths of righteousness, pleasantness and truth.

Be not deceived; "God is not mocked: for whatsoever a man soweth that shall he also reap." God knows your motive and will reward it or punish it according to His wisdom and justice, not yours. Not the so-called human, but the divine wisdom shall reign despite your mistaken human hopes, motives or acts. Examine your motives; ask if selfish desire governs them; or if in obedience to the divine command you are taking up your cross and following Him. Self-seeking will never result in Soul-finding — in finding divine wisdom and Love apart from self, and self swallowed up in a victory of Soul. There is but one way of salvation from sin, disease and death, and this way is to take up the cross in order to follow Christ; then God, who knows your motive, will reward your act according to that motive and not according to your words. Hear O Israel! You cannot succeed with a wrong motive for it will result in a wrong act. Cleanse your hearts, ye doubleminded and keep your account with God, for ye shall be judged according to the Book of Life that registers motives, and records the impulses of Mind, not matter. Let thy tongue and thy pen be employed in the execution of right motives, then shall thy reward come from heaven, that overcometh the powers of earth and wherein and whereby man deals justly, walks humbly.

On April 24 Mrs. Eddy had her secretary write to Mr. Dixon sending him back to England. Part of the letter said: "your opportunities for doing good are greater in your native land than they have been here. Our Leader trusts you will understand that this step is for your good, as well as for the advancement of our mutually beloved Cause." His name was removed from the masthead of the *Monitor* on May 1.

FREDERICK DIXON

After Mr. Dixon returned to England he organized a London *Monitor* office with funds privately raised where a staff of sixteen or more collected and edited overseas news and forwarded it to Boston.

Mr. Dixon was back in Boston in 1914 when the directors elected to appoint him editor of the *Monitor,* even though Mr. McLellan felt some concern about resigning. On June 8, 1914, at a meeting of the Board of Directors and various staff members to announce Mr. Dixon's appointment Mr. Dodds made an outspoken protest against it. Mr. Dodds had been the first man called upon to help found the *Monitor* and had also been managing editor from the start. At this point he resigned. Mr. Dixon assumed the editorship immediately, and then departed at once for Europe where "he wished to take a swing around the diplomatic circuit," leaving the *Monitor* with no editor or managing editor for several weeks at this crucial time. Erwin Canham has written of Mr. Dixon's "tireless and shrewd involvement in diplomacy" and his "extensive, continuous, and intimate contact with leading world statesmen." He also says that he was:

> on intimate terms with Colonel Edward M. House, President Wilson's confidential assistant. Mr. Dixon appears in Colonel House's papers and letters as a kind of unofficial intermediary between the British and the American governments. When frank but delicate information needed to be obtained Mr. Dixon could readily get it from British sources and provide it to Colonel House or President Wilson direct.

In the spring of 1909, when Mrs. Eddy sent Mr. Dixon back to England, she made an interesting change in a periodical which may have been noticed by few.

CHAPTER LVII

ANIMAL MAGNETISM

Where all students have failed is in not knowing how to handle animal magnetism. — MARY BAKER EDDY

1909

ON March 10, 1909, it had been two years since God had spoken to Mrs. Eddy through Isaiah (16:14), "But now the Lord hath spoken, saying, Within three years, as the years of an hireling, and the glory of Moab shall be contemned, with all that great multitude: and the remnant shall be very small and feeble."

For two years she had been working to strengthen, guard, guide, direct and protect the remnant with new and amended by-laws, and she would continue to do this for another year. At the same time she delegated more and more responsibility to her officers in Boston; nonetheless, Adelaide Still has testified that she conferred with Mr. McLellan almost daily, often giving him the subject matter and sometimes even the wording for his editorials. Mr. McLellan was one of the two younger members on the Board of Directors, and her letter the previous November had demanded that he "guard carefully the old landmarks," and had *forewarned* him "to be faithful in history, true to your leader and her precedents."

The three veterans on the Board of Directors who had faithfully aided the Leader in establishing "landmarks" and "precedents" did not have to be exhorted to guard them carefully, but the younger workers had not their experience nor their knowledge of the battles that had been fought to establish Truth in this world. The younger generation was a part of "that great multitude" that had been enlightened and blessed. They saw the success of Christian Science encircling the earth and were sure that it would simply continue and increase unto ultimate glory. They did not *know* that every aspect of the success they were beholding was entirely due to God's chosen witness, Mary Baker Eddy, and to her alone. She alone

ARCHIBALD McLELLAN

knew that "the remnant shall be very small and feeble." In 1909 none but God's witness could foresee what the aftermath would be when "the glory of Moab shall be contemned, with all that great multitude."

Eager young workers frequently had ideas for enlarging and expanding the cause of Christian Science in the world. It is not improbable that the two younger directors, McLellan and Stewart, were often in agreement with such plans; but the three veterans, William B. Johnson, Ira O. Knapp, and Stephen A. Chase, were quite immovable unless directed by spiritual guidance from their Leader. Is it not likely that every innovation was more or less stymied by a three to two opinion?

It would not be surprising if, as has been said, Mr. McLellan approached Mrs. Eddy with the suggestion that the successful businessman from Indiana, John V. Dittemore, (who had left business for Christian Science) replace Mr. Johnson on the Board of Directors and as clerk of The Mother Church. It was probably Mr. Dickey who told Mr. Johnson's son in later years that Mrs. Eddy twice rejected this proposition, but late in May when McLellan once again petitioned for Dittemore's election she answered: "If you want him, take him and all that goes with him." So Mr. Johnson was handed a letter from Mrs. Eddy asking him to resign, to which he responded on May 31:

> Beloved Leader and Teacher:
>
> My dearest earthly friend, I hereby lovingly inform you that I have this day tendered to the Christian Science Board of Directors of your dear church my resignation as Clerk, also as a member of that honorable body.
>
> As I look backward through nineteen years in which I have served in those capacities, and through memory recall sweet associations connected with the duties of those offices, — most especially the opportunities which these duties gave me to see you and talk with you, and to receive from you the priceless instruction, the counsels and the blessings, my lips are mute. The heart only can know its gratitude to you, dear one.
>
> It is now twenty-five years since you taught me the way of Life. I shall now devote all my time to the practice of what you have taught me.
>
> With tenderest affection,
Your loving student,
William B. Johnson

Mrs. Eddy published Mr. Johnson's letter in the *Sentinel* of June 5, following which he received hundreds of letters from all over the field expressing regret that he would no longer be in the post he had

WILLIAM B. JOHNSON

occupied for so long. But the one letter that was a balm to his aching heart was the one Mrs. Eddy wrote to him on June 1:

> My beloved student:
> I thank you deeply for your dear, loving letter. I think it is for your good you have taken the step you name. Having no office work to meet in a business way will give you a better chance to attend to yourself, and all of us must do this sometime or the weeds will choke the growing grain.
> One of the happiest moments of my life would be to have more hours in which to help myself and for others to give more time in helping themselves. You have named to me in confidence certain needs of your own. Now dear one, attend persistently to them and you will conquer and be blessed in all ways.
> As ever, lovingly yours,
> Mary Baker Eddy

Numerous applicants for class instruction plus more patients than he could care for kept Mr. Johnson very busy following his retirement.

Though the Leader longed for her students "to give more time in helping themselves," she never ceased helping them. On April 29 she made a change in *Unity of Good* which appeared in the June *Journal* with the caption "A Clearer Understanding." The editor stated that the rewording would "help Christian Scientists to a clearer and better understanding of this well-known . . . passage of Scripture." The new wording *(Un.* 55) followed:

> Job's faith and hope gained him the assurance that the so-called sufferings of the flesh are unreal. We shall learn how false are the pleasures and pains of material sense, and behold the truth of being, as expressed in his conviction, "Yet in my flesh shall I see God," that is, Now and here shall I behold God, divine Love.

Previously this paragraph had read: "Job's faith and hope gained him the assurance that by the sufferings of the flesh he should learn how false are the pleasures and pains of material sense, and behold the Truth of Being, as expressed in his conviction, 'Yet in my flesh shall I see GOD' — not *without my flesh,* but *in my flesh."*

The Leader was finding the way out of "the so-called sufferings of the flesh" for our sake. "Jesus could have withdrawn himself from his enemies" (S&H 51). He endured the cross "for the salvation of us all." If the masculine appearing of the Christ "had power to lay down a human sense of life for his spiritual identity," is it not probable that Christ's feminine appearing had that same power?

She endured the cross for forty years "for the salvation of us all." But perhaps that cross was growing a little lighter by 1909.

All the field was aware of the change in the design of the cross and crown in the Christian Science seal in 1908, but the change in 1909 was possibly noticed by few. The new seal had appeared on and in the *Christian Science Quarterly* for the first time in July, 1908, when the seal in the center of the cover for that issue had the new celestial crown around a black cross. The title heading design on page 1 also included the same seal in reduced size.

The change in the seal design in the *Quarterly* in 1909, which practically went unnoticed, was a lightening of the black cross. A shaded cross took place of the *black* one, which continued to lighten through 1909. The cross in the seal on the cover of the *Journal* also appeared lighter during 1909.

Perhaps the cross was a little lighter, but the world did not stop its malicious attacks upon the Woman. Mr. Dickey who was at Chestnut Hill through 1910, wrote:

> In the later years of her Leadership there was no cessation or even diminution of these mental attacks upon her, but they continued with ever-increasing volume in the attempt to destroy her life and obliterate her work.

So Mrs. Eddy still had much to meet along with the necessity for teaching the workers in her home what caused "the so-called sufferings" and *how* to meet it. One example was her pleasant daily drive which had become an irksome duty and at times a severe task. One afternoon when it was nearly time for her drive the bell rang summoning Mr. Dickey to the Leader's room. When he entered Mrs. Eddy was sitting in a chair dressed for her drive, painfully drawing on her gloves, and she said to him: "Mr. Dickey, I want you to know that it does me good to go on this drive." In answer to the question in his thought she continued: "I do not mean that the physical going for a drive does me good, but the enemy has made a law that it hurts me to go on this drive, and they are trying to enforce it, while I want you to take the opposite stand with God and know that every act I perform in His service does me good. I do not take this drive for recreation, but because I want to establish my dominion over mortal mind's antagonistic beliefs." In Mr. Dickey's words:

> I at once saw the point she was making and replied to her with encouraging statements of Truth from her own book and in a few moments every trace of the attack had disappeared and she was . . . ready to make her departure.

But before she left there was more to be added to Mr. Dickey's lesson. Banishing the suffering was only the first part. She said to him:

> Mr. Dickey, I want you to see what we have done. We have routed the enemy and broken the belief that it injured me to go on this drive. Now take this lesson to yourself, and whenever anything happens to you of an unfortunate nature, do not admit anything on the wrong side, but instantly declare that the experience does you good. Even if you should fall down and break your leg, get up and say, "I am the better for this experience." This is the Truth as God would declare it, for every attempt of evil, when surmounted and destroyed, helps the one who is attacked, and your quick and right declaration to the effect that instead of harming you, it has done you good, breaks the claim of evil, and you become a law to yourself that evil cannot harm you.

Communion in The Mother Church had been abolished in 1908 because it "might in time lose its sacredness and merge into a meeting for greetings." So in 1909 the directors invited Mrs. Eddy to attend the Annual Meeting. She said in her response on June 5 *(My.* 142), "I will attend the meeting, but not *in propria persona."* The one added sentence in her message is an everlasting precept: "Watch and pray that God directs your meetings and your lives, and your Leader will then be sure that they are blessed in their results."

Once again the newspapers were reporting malicious lies about Mrs. Eddy. This may have coincided with the publication of Georgine Milmine's book which was the *McClure Magazine* attack in book form. On June 7 Mrs. Eddy sent a message to the Concord church *(My.* 144) saying: "Give yourselves no fear and spare not a moment's thought to lies afloat . . ." On the same day she issued one more refutation of the lies *(My.* 143) which included: "Above all the fustian of either denying or asserting the personality and presence of Mary Baker Eddy, stands the eternal fact of Christian Science and the honest history of its Discoverer and Founder."

The *New York Evening Journal* sent her a kindly message to which she responded on June 8: "I can assure you that I am in my usual health and prosperity, and that God is blessing me because of Christian Science." That paper published a facsimile of her letter on June 10 together with a truthful editorial which said in part:

> Feeling that some friends of Mrs. Eddy may have been disturbed by the false and malicious stories recently published concerning her, we here publish, with very great pleasure, a letter just received from Mrs. Eddy . . . signed in her own handwriting. . . . Christian Scien-

tists may rest assured that they have in their Leader an actual, living person, energetic, determined, and marvelous in her apparent defiance of great age.

She was marvelous in her defiance, but not of age. Her defiance was of animal magnetism. Of age she has said:

> If the heart stays young, old age can never become anything but enobled thereby. Years do not make one grow old if one grows in grace. Decay does not belong to matter so much as to mind. . . .

And again:

> Overcoming age is not resuming our youth; it is thought going into new paths which history has never recorded.

The Leader was constantly endeavoring to teach her students that it was never age or disease or accident or death that needed to be met. It was *always* animal magnetism. She had said that teaching students "without teaching them how to handle animal magnetism, is like sending soldiers into battle with brass buttons and braid but with no ammunition for their muskets." Of mental malpractice she said:

> This is a mental age. Malpractice would dominate, and unless Christian Scientists are awake to it and alert, it would hold back Christian Science for centuries.

In one more effort to waken Christian Scientists to the malpractice that was again striking maliciously at her in June of 1909 (and would strike at all of them), she published in the *Sentinel* of June 12:

> TAKE NOTICE
>
> *To Christian Scientists:* See Science and Health, page 442, line 30, and give daily attention thereto.

The *Sentinel* of June 26 contained the republication of "A Correction" *(My.* 217) by Mrs. Eddy which had originally appeared in 1899. The next day, June 27, one of the students in the home recorded that while Mrs. Eddy was reading the articles and testimonies in the latest *Sentinel she* —

> commented upon someone getting results from declaring his divine sonship, etc. Then she said: "No such experiences ever come to me. I reach the results without intermediate steps. If anyone was said to be

ill in the next room, I wouldn't have to treat, I would just *know* the Truth about them and they would seem to be no more sick or dead than you are. I cannot tell you how I do it, but I have none of the experiences recorded by others, though I enjoy reading them."

The students' experiences were *because* of the Woman's work in this world. Their healings were due to the Truth presented in Science and Health. If they follow in the Leader's footsteps they will learn to *know* this Truth as she did. Then they, too, will have immediate "results without intermediate steps." But she could not tell them *how* to do this. Each student must learn for himself by *practising* Christian Science every minute of every hour of every day. She did, however, direct their footsteps with another new by-law which appeared in the *Sentinel* of July 3. This by-law, Article XXVII, Class Teaching. Sect. 5, then as now ended with "(Retrospection and Introspection, page 84.)" This page in *Ret.* begins:

> Centuries will intervene before the statement of the inexhaustible topics of Science and Health is sufficiently understood to be fully demonstrated.
>
> The teacher himself should continue to study this textbook, and to spiritualize his own thoughts and human life from this open fount of Truth and Love.

CHAPTER LVIII

FEED MY SHEEP

Material organization is requisite in the beginning; but when it has done its work, the purely Christly method of teaching and preaching must be adopted. — MARY BAKER EDDY

1909

MRS. Stetson entered into whatever she did with her whole heart and soul. This may have been the quality that Mrs. Eddy had perceived at their first meeting when she said: "You are going to do a great work in Christian Science." Augusta had been reluctant to enter into this "great work," but once she did, she gave to it a dedication far beyond that of the average student. This brought phenomenal healing, devoted patients, and devout students. Her experience, however, was not unlike that of Jesus and Mrs. Eddy in that nine out of ten of those healed and taught went their own way. Nevertheless she had a large number of consecrated students in the public practice of Christian Science.

At the end of the nineteenth century a good many of the Reading Rooms included a practitioner's office, which practice First Church of New York expanded. Their magnificent edifice was designed to include an ample Reading Room together with offices for twenty-five practitioners.

Mrs. Stetson imitated Mrs. Eddy in everything she did. Mrs. Eddy "mothered" her cause and her church, and Mrs. Stetson endeavored to do the same. She met daily with the twenty-five practitioners in her church and taught, directed, and exhorted them very much as Mrs. Eddy did the students in her home. They were, as a result, exceptionally devoted, devout, and unified in their work. Mrs. Stetson had just written a lengthy letter to Mrs. Eddy on the twenty-third of May in which she said: "For twenty consecutive years we have never had a divided vote nor a dissenting voice at any of our annual or church meetings."

But the day for mothering was over. Mrs. Eddy had closed the

Mother's Room. God's hour had arrived. The import of the Leader's words: "Oh, child of my heart, God is ripening you for His hour," was to see fulfillment. Augusta's devotion and steadfastness were to be tested to the utmost.

On the morning of July 10 Mrs. Stetson's twenty-five chosen practitioners surprised her with a gift of letters of appreciation from each of them together with a box of gold. Augusta immediately wrote the following letter to Mrs. Eddy:

July 10, 1909

My precious Leader:

I have just this morning received these letters and the box from twenty-five practitioners in our church Reading Room. They were a great surprise to me, and were written hurriedly at the suggestion of one student. No one knew what the others had written. I have had Mr. Higgins copy these letters and the students have signed them. Thus you may read them more readily. They make a letter which you will appreciate as demonstration of the one Mind; all of "one accord in one place." They were sent to me as expressions of loving gratitude the day before our Communion service. I feel they belong to you, dearest, and are your fruit; for without your divine instruction and Christly guidance I should not have had them, so I send this copy of the dear letters to you, with the type of the gold of human character which is fast melting into spiritual understanding in each of these students.

You asked me years ago this question, "Augusta, lovest thou me?" I answered, "Yes, beloved Leader, I love you." Again you repeated the query, "Lovest thou me?" and again I replied, "Yes, I love you, my Leader, Teacher, and Guide to eternal Life." Then you said, "Feed my sheep." I have earnestly and prayerfully endeavored to do this. These are thine, Holy One; I trust they are all strong in Christ, and are armored with spiritual understanding and love to meet the tests that are before them in this crucial hour. They are daily going forth to battle with the beast and the false prophet, confident that Christ goes before them to destroy the claim of lust and hypocrisy, and to reveal God and His body — the spiritual universe. May none fall away! They desire to honor you, our great forever Leader; they have come up out of great tribulation, and have washed their robes. I feel that my prayers and my alms are come up before God. We are observing your advice in the *Manual,* Article XXX, Section 7, and are rejoicing that "the devils are subject unto us through thy name." These are evidences of the preparation made in the "large upper room," where the last supper may be eaten, when we are ready to receive the ascended One coming to his-her own never to depart. During our Communion service tomorrow we shall look for the "reappearing" of our Lord, and shall silently "commune with the divine Principle, Love" (Science and Health, p. 35). Precious Leader, my love for you is inexpressible. God grant my constant prayer that I may be worthy to be called

Your faithful, obedient, loving child,
Augusta

Mrs. Eddy received this letter together with the twenty-five letters of appreciation and the box of gold on July 11, and she answered the next day:

July 12, 1909

Beloved Student:

I have just finished reading your interesting letter. I thank you for acknowledging me as your Leader, and I know that every true follower of Christian Science abides by the definite rules which demonstrate the true following of their Leader; therefore, if you are sincere in your protestations and are doing as you say you are, you will be blessed in your obedience.

The Scriptures say, "Watch and pray, that ye enter not into temptation." You are aware that animal magnetism is the opposite of divine Science, and that this opponent is the means whereby the conflict against Truth is engendered and developed. Beloved! you need to watch and pray that the enemy of good cannot separate you from your Leader and best earthly friend.

You have been duly informed by me that, however much I desire to read all that you send to me, I have not the time to do so. The Christian Science Publishing Society will settle the question whether or not they shall publish your poems. It is part of their duties to relieve me of so much labor.

I thank you for the money you send me which was given you by your students. I shall devote it to a worthy and charitable purpose.

Mr. Adam Dickey is my secretary, through whom all my business is transacted.

Give my best wishes and love to your dear students and church.

Lovingly your teacher and Leader,
Mary Baker Eddy

The Leader sent this letter with its strengthening admonitions to her disciple with an overflowing sense of love; but to those who believed that Mrs. Stetson was malpractising, this letter appeared very cold and critical. Mrs. Eddy knew that in the very near future Augusta was going to need her admonition: "Beloved! you need to watch and pray that the enemy of good cannot separate you from your Leader and best earthly friend." Mr. Carpenter has stated that the church would have excommunicated Mrs. Stetson ten or fifteen years earlier if Mrs. Eddy had not been there to restrain them, and now the Leader was about to step aside. The malicious gossip about Mrs. Stetson had grown to such proportions that even some in Mrs. Eddy's own household had at times endeavored to apprise her of

Mrs. Stetson's errors, and were upset when she would permit nothing to be done about it. In order to quiet their thought on the issue she had written:

> Never notice publicly an error if it can be avoided. Never rejoice in victory over it nor lament. It gives power where it does not belong. Evil is not *something.* Then wherefore give it the honor of noticing it further than to remove it? Then let the dead bury their dead. Have no funeral knell or trumpet blast over nothing; otherwise you will make it something and consistency is especially desirable in dealing with nothingness. To talk of evil is as inconsistent as to talk of sickness, unless it be to untalk it and get it out of mind forever.

Mortal mind's reaction to Mrs. Eddy's Christly endeavors had torn her church to shreds in 1881 and again in 1888 forcing the Leader to disorganize and build her Church on a wholly spiritual foundation.

Mrs. Stetson's successes had also brought forth a good deal of reaction from mortal mind which had often forced her up higher. She was unaware, however, of the great tide of animosity that the Leader had restrained for many years. Mrs. Eddy had done her utmost to prepare this disciple and to teach her what animal magnetism is and how to meet it. The time had come for Augusta to stand or fall by her own efforts. So Mrs. Eddy sent Augusta's letters from her students to the Board of Directors with the words: "Act, and act quickly. Handle the letters according to Science and Health, and The Mother Church Manual." In later years Mrs. Stetson wrote of this moment and this message as follows: "When Jesus' hour of exaltation or further development of spiritual power came, he used about the same language; 'That thou doest, do quickly.'"

Mrs. Eddy's letter of July 12 *(My.* 357) was published in the *Sentinel* of July 17. Six days later she wrote to Mrs. Stetson again:

> July 23, 1909
>
> My Dear Student:
>
> Awake and arise from this temptation produced by animal magnetism upon yourself allowing your students to deify you and me. Treat yourself for it and get your students to help you rise out of it. It will be your destruction if you do not do this.
>
> Answer this letter immediately,
>
> As ever,
>
> Lovingly your Teacher,
> Mary Baker Eddy

Augusta did answer immediately. Her lengthy letter of July 24* stated in part:

*See Appendix M — Augusta E. Stetson letter to Mary Baker Eddy, July 24, 1909.

The sensuous world refused, and continues to refuse, to follow and obey the impersonal Christ which Jesus and you, my beloved Leader, have declared. They held him in the bonds of personal sense. The wise see you today as the Messiah, or the Anointed of God to this age, fulfilling the law of Love. They do not deify your *human* personality, but will not lose sight of your *spiritual individuality,* or God with us. Although all of my students have been taught this, doubtless some have not assimilated it. . . .

I have always taught my students to love and reverence you as the one whom God has appointed to voice His Word to this Age.

My students know that I am endeavoring to obey your teaching and demonstrate Christ, and for this reason they, in turn, have confidence in me as a teacher and demonstrator of Christian Science. For twenty-five years "the enemy of good" has been using every subtle suggestion to separate me from the Christ which you represent, and are demonstrating, but it has signally and utterly failed. If my students have shown more zeal than wisdom in expressing their love for their Leader, and their teacher, I will try still further to warn them of the danger of deifying *physical* personality. . . .

Beloved Leader, you are ever speaking to my heart, "Awake!" and I reply,

I will listen for Thy voice,
  Lest my footstep stray;
I will follow and rejoice
  All the rugged way.

More than a month later, on August 30, Mrs. Eddy wrote a final letter to Mrs. Stetson:

My Dear Student:

Your kind letter was duly received. You know that I love you and you know that God has made, and is making His ways and works manifest through Divine Science. I trust He will direct your path in the footsteps of His flock. The Holy Bible, Science and Health and The Mother Church Manual are your safe guides, follow them.

I have not the time to think of the Students in all their varied duties of life, but I have the faith to leave them in the hands of God, who giveth to all men liberally and upbraideth none.

As ever yours in Christ,
Mary Baker Eddy

A great deal had transpired prior to this letter of August 30. In July Herbert W. Eustace was asked to come to Boston, which he did, to discuss the advisability of his moving to New York to teach — a plan which was later abandoned. Also in July Mrs. Stetson had been called to appear before the Board of Directors where she was confronted by a witness against her, Mrs. Maude Kissam Babcock. Mrs. Babcock was examined by the directors in Mrs. Stetson's presence and then cross-examined by Mrs. Stetson. Mrs. Babcock had been a student of Mrs. Stetson who had turned to theosophy. She had been renounced by her teacher because she had denounced the Leader. When Mrs. Stetson returned to New York she found Mrs. Babcock's letter to her denouncing Mrs. Eddy and sent it to the directors. The result was a telegram from the directors to Mrs. Stetson on August 3 signed by Mr. Dittemore and stating: "Charges against you dismissed. Will write more fully later."

At the same time an editorial by Archibald McLellan entitled "None Good but One" appeared in the *Sentinel* of July 31 quoting many of the more effusive passages from the letters Mrs. Stetson's students had written to their teacher. McLellan criticized the letters, the teacher and her teaching stating, "This is emphatically not Christian Science."

A new by-law was also published in the July 31 *Sentinel,* — Article XXIII:

> **Teachers' and Practitioners' Offices.** Sect. 11. Teachers and practitioners of Christian Science shall not have their offices or rooms in the branch churches, in the Reading Rooms, nor in rooms connected therewith.

No one was more affected by this new by-law than were Mrs. Stetson and her twenty-five practitioners; but the new rules from the Leader's pen were for all mankind for all time. Was not this new by-law one more step separating the practice of Christian Science from organization and turning thought to her original statement that "we have no need of creeds and church organizations to sustain or explain a demonstrable platform, that defines itself in healing the sick, and casting out error"?

The Leader had set the wheels in motion for Augusta, and all who "desire to build higher," to "begin on a wholly spiritual foundation." But few in the field were ready for such a step.

The wonderful organization which Mrs. Eddy had developed for the founding of Christian Science had encircled the earth. Under her spiritual leadership every step had advanced Christian Science in the world, and the new *Christian Science Monitor* was adding recognition and prestige. The Leader knew well that those in charge of this marvelously flourishing organization would have her spiritual direction to guide them for only a few more months. With the thought of directing their efforts toward a worthwhile activity without her physical presence she wrote a new by-law for them. She sent this by-law to her directors on July 27 along with the following letter:

Beloved Brethren:

Please vote on the adoption of the following by-law, and if adopted publish it in our periodicals and in the Church Manual.

Mary Baker Eddy

The by-law was adopted, followed by correspondence between Mrs. Eddy and the directors regarding the project it proposed. The new by-law read:

> The Mother Church shall establish and maintain a Christian Science resort for the so-called sick.

This new by-law was not for all mankind for all time, and it had no place in the spiritual guidebook for Mary Baker Eddy's Church, *The Mother Church Manual.* No one knew this better than did Mrs. Eddy. She was not giving a rule for all her children for all time to come. She was giving her directors a project and some guidelines for using the great wealth her organization had engendered and would continue to produce. By August 11 she had accomplished this purpose, which the directors announced in 1916 was "to be known as The Christian Science Benevolent Association." But on August 11 in 1909 Mr. Dickey wrote to the directors that the Leader is willing "to let this matter rest for the present and suggests that you vote on the repeal of the by-law providing for the same."

But this was far from all that was demanding the Leader's attention that August.

CHAPTER LIX

MISCELLANY

In Science, individual good derived from God, the infinite All-in-all, may flow from the departed to mortals; but evil is neither communicable nor scientific. — MARY BAKER EDDY

1909

WILLIAM Dana Orcutt had given considerable time and thought to what he had hoped would be his masterpiece —a sumptuous edition of Science and Health. He had approached Mrs. Eddy on the subject on several different occasions over the years and had received some encouragement. Early in March, 1908, Orcutt had sent her samples, set in the early, elegant Bodoni type, together with detailed plans and specifications. In April he had received word from the directors that it was not deemed expedient to go on with this project at this time, which was a bitter disappointment to him and caused him to drop the project entirely from his thought.

One day, after the *Monitor* was a daily reality, Mr. Orcutt was lunching with Mr. McLellan who enquired "as to the extent to which Mrs. Eddy entered into the details in the manufacture of her books." Mrs. Eddy's ability to plan and follow through in every detail had never ceased to amaze Mr. Orcutt, and he surmised that Mr. McLellan had had a similar experience in his work with the Leader. McLellan concurred, remarking with a smile: "She has left us nothing to conceive or originate — simply to carry on and to execute."

The editions of Mrs. Eddy's various titles were succeeding each other with increasing regularity, and though largely routine by 1909, nothing beyond routine was done without Mrs. Eddy's full knowledge and approval. Such matters, however, were handled most efficiently by Mr. Stewart, and as all Mr. Orcutt's conferences were with Mr. Stewart, he expected he would not see Mrs. Eddy again.

During 1909 Mr. Orcutt was offered the opportunity to become associated with the Plimpton Press at Norwood, Massachusetts, which had a much larger and more modern plant than did the University Press. Before making the move he discussed the matter with a few of his clients one of whom was Allison V. Stewart. Mr. Stewart thought it a wise move, but added: "There is one matter that needs to be taken up. I have among my standing orders an old letter from Mrs. Eddy, dating back, I think to Dr. Foster-Eddy, instructing the publisher always to leave the manufacture of her books in John Wilson's hands. As you were his successor at the University Press, I have never had occasion to raise any question. If you leave the University Press, are you or is the University Press John Wilson's successor?"

Two days later, after talking with Mrs. Eddy, Mr. Stewart telephoned Orcutt to tell him that the shift was all right, and added the welcome news that Mrs. Eddy wanted to see him. It had been five years since Mr. Orcutt had seen Mrs. Eddy — years including the "Next Friends" suit, the move to Chestnut Hill, and unceasing newspaper harrassment — and he was expecting to see considerable change as he entered her study:

> There was but one change I noted — it was the first time she had ever received me sitting down. But the clear voice that greeted me, the bright eyes, and the keen expression of interest belied any thought that her sitting posture was enforced. During our conversation she rose with ease — before I could anticipate her — to reach an object on the table. There was another change — in addition to all other personal attributes which were always present there was an added tranquility — perhaps serenity is the better word — that crowned them all. . . . Our conversation started as if there had been no long interruption.

Mrs. Eddy assured Mr. Orcutt of her support with the words: "When John Wilson placed his mantle upon your shoulders, he himself made you his successor wherever you might be. My old friend put far more than type and printer's ink into the volumes he made, and the lessons you assimilated from him are what I always wish to have incorporated in my books." She then proceeded to amaze Mr. Orcutt by asking the most astute business questions about the Plimpton Press. In explanation she said: "I am thinking of the future. This change may mean that the Plimpton Press will make my books for many years to come. Mr. Fernald used a financial expression the last time I saw him which I had never heard before, and I like it. 'Now is the time,' Mr. Fernald said, 'to consolidate your gains.' That is what I am doing — consolidating my gains, while I keep on with the building."

When they had covered the situation Mr. Orcutt rose to leave, but Mrs. Eddy motioned for him to reseat himself, and to his astonishment and delight said:

> I want you to know how sorry I was to have you disappointed about that grand edition of Science and Health you had in mind. We gave it careful thought. The idea pleased me. If and when it is right for this edition to be made, it will be made.

It was 1939 before the time arrived for the elegant edition of Science and Health, but Mrs. Eddy's parting statement to Mr. Orcutt on that day in 1909 guided him in a new direction on his long-cherished dream. "By the way," she said as he was leaving, "I like *your* Humanistic type much better than Mr. Bodoni's!"

* * *

IN late winter or early spring of 1909 Edward A. Kimball had gone to Marion, Alabama where he had a lumber company. After taking care of personal business there, he returned to Europe to complete the lecture tour begun the previous year. On his return to the United States in midsummer, Mrs. Eddy sent two of her church directors to meet him in New York and ask him to teach the next Normal Class of the Board of Education which was to be held in December, 1910. Mr. Kimball accepted this appointment, but he was not to teach that class.

Mr. and Mrs. Edward Merritt of Chagrin Falls, Ohio, had long been friends of the Kimballs. On his way from New York to Chicago Mr. Kimball became ill and left the train at Chagrin Falls to recuperate at the home of these friends. The Merritts had sad news to telegraph to Boston on August 13, — Mr. Kimball had passed away at their home.

This news was one more blow to the workers at Chestnut Hill who had had much to meet during the past month and had not always been successful. Mr. Frye had recorded in his diary on July 13:

> Two of Mrs. Eddy's horses were under strange beliefs and the veterinary surgeon did not know what to call the disease — it was unlike anything known about horses. Dolly was shot today.

On the night of August 2 Mrs. Eddy had suffered intense pain and received no help from any of her mental workers, so they had called Dr. Bertram to administer a hypodermic pain reliever. W. H. Bertram was one of Mrs. Eddy's students who had left her and Christian Science in the rebellion of 1888. After nearly twenty years of studying and practising *materia medica* he had begun longing for Christian Science in 1907 and had written the Leader of his continuing gratitude to her.

The following Monday night, August 9, according to Calvin Frye's diary, Mrs. Eddy had awakened about ten P.M. "in a severe belief and called for help but all seemed so dazed they were unsuccessful." A day or two later Calvin recorded: "This morning I received a bitter letter from George W. Baker which he wrote August 9th."

On Sunday morning, August 15, Mrs. Eddy called her household students to her and told them that she had discovered the way to destroy animal magnetism — it is to *love* your enemies. "Turn your thought to the operator with a sense of love and that will destroy the belief of hate." Then I John 4:

> 20 If a man say, I love God, and hateth his brother, he is a liar; for he that loveth not his brother whom he hath seen, how can he love God whom he hath not seen?

In the *Sentinel* of August 21 the field was notified of Mr. Kimball's decease in Mr. McLellan's editorial "Edward A. Kimball, C.S.D." Mrs. Eddy's oft-quoted notice *(My.* 297) was published two weeks later:

> THERE IS NO DEATH
>
> A suppositional gust of evil in this evil world is the dark hour that precedes the dawn. This gust blows away the baubles of belief, for there is in reality no evil, no disease, no death; and the Christian Scientist who believes that he dies, gains a rich blessing of disbelief in death, and a higher realization of heaven.
>
> My beloved Edward A. Kimball, whose clear, correct teaching of Christian Science has been and is an inspiration to the whole field, is here now as veritably as when he visited me a year ago. If we would awaken to this recognition, we should see him here and realize that he never died; thus demonstrating the truth of Christian Science.
>
> Mary Baker Eddy

Mrs. Eddy was very aware of the malicious gossip and criticism of Mr. Kimball's teaching that permeated the field; and she was also aware of the persecution that would be heaped upon Mr. Kimball and his teaching when she no longer restrained it. Many an earnest student was enabled to endure this persecution without faltering because of the Leader's words; "My beloved Edward A. Kimball, whose clear, correct teaching of Christian Science . . . " etc.

But the Leader did even more. In her sermon *Christian Healing,* delivered at Boston in the early days, she had said: "I have never yet had a student who has reached this ability to teach; it includes more than they understand." This sermon "by Mrs. Glover Eddy" was copyrighted and printed in pamphlet form at an early date. The second edition bears the date 1881, and the fourth edition, 1889. It continued to be available from the Christian Science Publishing Society in the twentieth century, was listed each week in the *Sentinel* advertisement for 21 cents each, and had seen more than thirty editions with the sentence about "ability to teach" unchanged. But as further protection for the one student whose teaching she designated as "clear, correct teaching," the Leader changed that sentence to read as it reads today: "I waited many years for a student to reach the ability to teach; it included more than they understood."

Mr. Kimball's students were grateful for the Leader's words. One appreciative letter was published in the *Sentinel* followed by Mrs. Eddy's comment:

September 6, 1909

Dear Leader:

We hasten to express gratitude for your forceful and helpful lines — "There Is No Death" — published in this issue of the *Sentinel.*

We who are Mr. Kimball's students appreciate the "clear, correct teaching" we received; and also his precept and example of unfaltering and unwavering loyalty and obedience to you. In loving and grateful appreciation for these lines we will continue to follow implicitly your every request, as he taught us to; and in humility consecrate our lives anew, that we may become better demonstrators of the truth and more worthy of the blessings we have received through him from you.

Ever yours in love,
Chauncey J. Guthrie
Alice E. Guthrie

Mrs. Eddy's comment:

The above tribute to our beloved brother is *just,* and my soul sends forth its echo.

Mary Baker Eddy

At Chestnut Hill, after talking with Mrs. Eddy, Adam Dickey recorded:

When we can awaken ourselves out of the belief that all must die, we will then have reached a point where death means nothing to us, and we will then be able to bring back all that death claimed to have taken away from us. In other words, we will be able to reproduce the

> presence of those who thought they died, whether it was ten minutes ago or ten years ago. However, when that time comes, death will not appear to us what it now seems to be, and it is hard to predict even in the light of Science just how things will appear to us under changed conditions. On page 72 (Science and Health) the author is trying to explain the impossibility of evil being communicated from the departed to mortals, and incidentally remarks that good may come to us in this way. Thought on the other side of the grave is not different from thought on this side. Edward Kimball is not dead, and has not stopped his Christian Science work. In fact, he knows he has not died and he still teaches and holds Association meetings. Good, therefore, may flow from him to his students through the efficacy of enlightened thought. That evil can flow from the departed to mortals is the false belief. That good may thus flow is the spiritual fact.

Perhaps Mrs. Sargent recalled at this time a vision Mrs. Eddy had once told to her, — a vision in which she could see, across the river, a glittering and grand city from which her mother came to her in a small frail boat. She and her mother were on the beautiful green bank which led down to the river:

> There was a soft clear light over everything, but it was not like either sunlight or moonlight. They walked together down to the river, which was very clear, and pure white pebbles could be seen at the bottom of it . . . [Her mother] said, "Get into the boat, Mary;" but Mrs. Eddy said, "Why I should tip it over if I stepped in." Her mother said, "No, you would not. Look there on the sand." Mrs. Eddy said she looked down at the side of where she stood and there lay her own corpse. "Now get into the boat," said her mother, and she stepped in at once and the boat glided across the river. She said she seemed to realize then that the boat was not substance. When they reached the other side her mother took her into one of the buildings. There were different apartments. Her mother had one apartment where little children were and was teaching them; then in another room was her brother Albert and he was teaching adults. His thought seemed to be so occupied he did not seem to see her. In another room she saw Dr. Quimby and he was so glad to see her. In his room she saw Shakespeare and Dr. Quimby said to her, "I can not teach him, but you can."

Mrs. Eddy accepted Quimby's invitation and "stepped up on the platform and commenced teaching Science." Mrs. Sargent said Mrs. Eddy told her that this vision was later a proof to her that what she had written in Science and Health was the truth about the belief of death.

In August of 1909 the Leader took one more decisive step. Three years earlier, following the dedication of The Mother Church Extension, she had asked her directors to compile the history of that event as an addition to *Pulpit and Press.* A letter she had written to them on August 1, 1906, said in part:

> I thank you for giving me this great help on perpetuating the history of The Mother Church.
>
> I have amended the Church By-law ... But it should not be published in the Sentinel until history is grafted into Pulpit and Press.
>
> ... You can have the history written and ready whenever you have time to do it.

For whatever reason, this was never done, and Mrs. Eddy herself collected and compiled the articles concerning this history of The Mother Church to add to her collection of articles from her pen since the publication of *Miscellaneous Writings.* Eight days after Mr. Kimball passed away in Chagrin Falls, Mrs. Eddy sealed up this package of prepared articles on August 21, and wrote on the wrapper: "Nobody shall open this or read its contents during my lifetime without my written consent."

CHAPTER LX

FOLLOW THE EXAMPLE OF THE *ALMA MATER*

In the dark hours, wise Christian Scientists stand firmer than ever in their allegiance to God. Wisdom is wedded to their love, and their hearts are not troubled. — MARY BAKER EDDY

Whenever they are equal to the march triumphant, God will give to all His soldiers . . . the proper command, and . . . we all shall take step and march on in spiritual organization.
— MARY BAKER EDDY

1909

MRS. Ella Hoag, who had been healed by Christian Science in 1887 and taught by Mrs. Eddy in 1888, served several times in Mrs. Eddy's home between 1908 and 1910. Early in September of 1909 she returned to her work in Toledo, Ohio, and was replaced by another Ella. William Rathvon's wife had moved from Boulder, Colorado to Newton, Massachusetts earlier in 1909. On September 3 when Mrs. Hoag left Chestnut Hill, Ella S. Rathvon began serving Mrs. Eddy there, and she remained with Mrs. Eddy through 1910.

Many a Christian Scientist has penned a note in the front of his textbook which reads: "Laura Sargent said Mrs. Eddy's favorite paragraph is 188:11-17." This paragraph begins, "Mortal existence is a dream . . . " On the twentieth of September Mrs. Eddy enlarged on this subject with a short article that was not published:

DREAMS

Is mortal life a dream? Yes! Then you admit the necessity of dreams so long as you entertain the belief of mortal life. Suppose you reverse this statement and begin your logic logically, so that one wrong statement will not include another one; and you must abandon the first to avoid the last. Admitting that mortal life is a dream is admitting that it is something, when the fact remains that it is nothing, since there is no mortal life. God, Truth, is the only Life and

> a dream is not Truth. The dream and the dreamer are one, even the supposition that nothing is something. Eschew that statement of life unscientific — state it scientifically and commence your solution of the problem called life on fact and not fable. Then you begin with Truth, not error; with God, not man; with Principle, not idea; and solve Life as having no beginning and no ending, the eternal now and forever.

For forty-three years the Woman had been working to waken mankind from the dream that existence is mortal and to "Break earth's stupid rest." And the dragon's persecution of the Woman had never ceased.

On Saturday, September 25, the *Sentinel* announced that arrangements had been made with Mr. Bicknell Young to have him move permanently to London to teach and lecture. On that same day the Boston newspapers published a statement by Chandler that the "Next Friends" suit was to be revived. The household discussed it, and Laura Sargent advised Adam Dickey to tell Mrs. Eddy about it. A repetition of the ordeal of 1906-1907 was a disheartening prospect, and Mrs. Eddy prayed Mr. Dickey to prevent it. He replied: "There will be no suit. All the next friends want is money — to compromise." She told Mr. Dickey to get a settlement, but she also called her mental workers to her room. When Calvin Frye, Laura Sargent, Adam Dickey, Mr. and Mrs. Rathvon, and Irving Tomlinson had all assembled she requested each to raise his right hand and promise that he would not leave her but stand by her until this revival of the next friends was met.

About six weeks later, on November 10, the Boston newspapers carried Chandler's words that the terms were entirely satisfactory to him, announcing the settlement in headlines such as those in the *Boston Traveler:* "Sons Get $290,000 from Mrs. Eddy. Head of Christian Science Church, in Agreement Announced Today, Pays Geo. W. Glover $245,000 and Ebenezer J. Foster Eddy $45,000 to Release All Their Claims."

This was called the "Final Chapter in 'Next Friends' Suit," but perhaps the final chapter was a letter Mrs. Eddy received a month later from George Glover (written by his daughter) in which he said, "you will hereafter have nothing to complain of against me or my children. . . . and I do not think there ought longer to be a cloud between you and me and my family." Mrs. Eddy had ever endeavored to dissipate that cloud, but, sad to say, George did not even honor this final agreement he signed in the fall of 1909. Later events would indicate that the man who helped him to get a quarter of a million dollars of his mother's hard earned money, got most of it away from him in further litigation against her estate.

During these weeks that Mrs. Eddy was once again confronted with the next friends suit, Augusta Stetson was meeting a "next friends suit" in her experience. In September the Board of Directors in Boston began summoning members of First Church, New York, to Boston for questioning, and on September 24 summoned the Readers and Board of Trustees (excepting Mrs. Stetson) to a conference where Mr. McLellan told them that an investigation was in progress "because of the widespread impression ... through the Field that there is something wrong with the teachings and practices" in their church. Two days later when Mrs. Stetson received notification of the findings against her, the removal of her card from the *Journal,* and the revocation of her license to teach, she sent a telegram to Mrs. Eddy:

> My precious Leader:
>
> "For I am persuaded that neither death, nor life, nor angels, nor principalities, nor powers, nor things present, nor things to come, nor height, nor depth, nor any other creature, shall be able to separate us [me] from the love of God, which is in Christ Jesus our Lord" — and Mary Baker Eddy, my "best earthly friend."
>
> With ever increasing love, and unspeakable gratitude for your precious gift of Christian Science, I am
>
> Your child,
> Augusta

The Leader did not answer. In her last letter to her "child" she had said: "The Holy Bible, Science and Health and The Mother Church Manual are your guides, follow them." Augusta also had a collection of over four hundred letters received from her Leader over the past twenty-five years with many comforting messages such as this one:

> I love you as words can never tell on paper. I love you because you love good and are loyal to its pioneer ... Take courage, dear heart, God loves you, Mother loves you, and evil has no more power than you give it. ... I cannot sufficiently thank you for what you are doing. Oh, what a child you are to watch and work so faithfully for Mother!

Before Mrs. Eddy's discovery of the Science of Being, she, together with all of the Children of Israel, was asleep in the dream of the reality of sin, disease and death. Now the Mother in Israel was awake, and thousands of her children were daily denying the reality of all evil. But they were not awake! They were asleep in the dream of health, success, affluence, and prosperity in matter. None had been more successful in this dream of *good* matter than had Mrs.

AUGUSTA E. STETSON

Stetson. Thousands were willing to waken from the painful dream and reject it, but who was willing to be wakened from the pleasurable, lulling illusions of animal magnetism? Not one. So for forty years the Mother had been working all alone in a direction often opposite to that of her children. The words she had written to Augusta on December 11, 1898, were just as applicable in the fall of 1909:

> All are far from seeing or understanding what I am at work all the time, and in every direction, to destroy; and so I am met by all in a certain sense, with antagonism. It is the errors that my students do not see, either in themselves or others, that I am constantly confronting and at war with. If they and the world did see these errors which I do, they would take up arms against them, and I could lay down mine.

Mrs. Stetson had been forging ahead "to build higher . . . on a wholly spiritual foundation" as her Leader had directed in "The Way of Wisdom" *(My.* 357), but she did not know that she must forsake the landmarks outgrown. Instead, valiant warrior that she was, she redoubled her efforts to defend them; and it almost appeared as if there would be a battle between the directors of The Mother Church and the trustees of the New York church. Augusta had been so occupied with building her organization that she had not had the time to trace her Leader's footsteps in that area nor to ponder her words in *Retrospection and Introspection:*

> Despite the prosperity of my church, it was learned that material organization has its value and peril, and that organization is requisite only in the earliest periods in Christian history. After this material form of cohesion and fellowship has accomplished its end, continued organization retards spiritual growth, and should be laid off, —

Augusta had demonstrated the *value* of material organization, but she had not seen its *peril.* If we do not *see* a point we shall learn it by experience, and the Leader knew that Augusta was ready for this experience. She wrote to Mr. McLellan on October 12:

> Beloved Student:
>
> Learn at once if The Mother Church can be prosecuted for suspending a student, or even expelling them, who is giving us so much trouble as Mrs. Stetson does, and if it can be done safely drop Mrs. Stetson's connection with The Mother Church.
>
> Let no one know what I have written you on this subject.
>
> Lovingly yours,
Mary Baker Eddy

No one knew what the Leader had written until this letter was published by John Dittemore in 1926. In November of 1909 Mrs. Stetson was dropped from membership in The Mother Church. Mrs. Stetson's affairs had often made headlines over the years and once when the Associated Press had asked Mrs. Eddy for a statement regarding her she had responded:

> Your letter to my secretary received. In it you request that an answer be made from Pleasant View in regard to an alleged charge that too much authority is assumed by Mrs. Stetson in New York City. To this charge I wish to state that Mrs. Stetson is one of my respectable students. Not being familiar with facts relative to said charge, I find I cannot answer you. Mrs. Stetson's students bravely protect her, and such action on their part is a virtue!

This virtue in Mrs. Stetson's students was expressed in bravely defending their teacher in 1909, and sixteen of them were also dropped from Mother Church membership. This trying period was an anguishing ordeal for Mrs. Stetson which she did not understand at the time, but she never wavered in her loyalty to her Leader. During her "trial" by the directors in mid-November a copy of Mrs. Eddy's message of November 13 to First Church, New York *(My.* 360) reached her and caused her to state to the press: "My Leader's letter induces me to believe that I may have been wrong where I felt that I was absolutely right."

A few days later when Mrs. Stetson received notice of her dismissal she resigned from her own church and wrote to Mr. Dittemore, Secretary of the Board of Directors in Boston, on November 22:

> Dear Sir:
>
> I have received your favor of the 18th instant, advising me that my name has been dropped from the roll of membership of The Mother Church. I note with due appreciation the hope expressed in the concluding words, "that your future course of action may show your desire to again become eligible for membership in this Church."
>
> I assure you that I shall not neglect any opportunity to draw nearer to God, and to follow my Leader, Mary Baker Eddy, into the "full understanding of the divine Principle which triumphs over death" (Science and Health, p. 31).
>
> Kindly convey to each of the Directors my sincere wish that we may all assist and rejoice her, by rising to this height of realization and demonstration. In such case there will be no possibility of continual separation. The "unity of good" will have destroyed the error that has occasioned the present action.
>
> Meanwhile I wish for each member of the Board of Directors a continual increase of fidelity and fruitful service to our beloved

Leader, and to the Cause of Christian Science, of which she is the Discoverer, Founder, and perpetual Head.

Very sincerely yours,
Augusta E. Stetson

Two years later in answering a letter from an inquirer Mrs. Stetson said:

> You ask me if I am in favor with the Board of Directors. I remain in the same attitude as when they dropped my name from membership in The Mother Church. I cannot change my method of teaching and practice. I stand for absolute Christian Science, a *present* immortality. I teach this, always have taught it, and shall continue to teach it as I was taught by Mary Baker Eddy. I demonstrate it as fast as I can, and teach all to do the same. I speak to impersonal error and its mouthpieces whenever I hear it voiced by persons. I have from the beginning done this. I meet every argument of the "enemy of good" with spiritual love — the only power which dissolves the adamant of suppositional hatred, malice, envy, jealousy, and revenge — nothingness.
>
> ... I have spoken publicly during the past two years only when I have been accused of being disloyal to my Leader, Mrs. Eddy, or as not teaching Christian Science according to the textbook.
>
> ... I was exonerated by my own church, but later I resigned, lest my personal presence might cause the opposers to disturb the peace, and I faintly apprehended that I was ready to leave material organization ...
>
> Hundreds of my students have stood with me during all these tests. ...
>
> I have not been moved by influence or money to take my large body of students, and those who follow my teaching of Spirit as all, and form another church, ... but I have taught the Truth, and am demonstrating love, which must convince all that I am a Christian Scientist. I have always stood against false statements in regard to our beloved Leader, no matter who voiced these charges.

As Mrs. Stetson said in this letter, she "faintly apprehended that" she "was ready to leave material organization," when she was dismissed in November, 1909. But as the years went on and she continued the constant study and practice of Mrs. Eddy's writings, the Leader's words in *Miscellaneous Writings* grew clearer and dearer to her:

> When students have fulfilled all the good ends of organization, and are convinced that by leaving the material forms thereof a higher spiritual unity is won, then is the time to follow the example of the *Alma Mater.*

If, in the fall of 1909, Mrs. Eddy forced Augusta to take this step which no one then understood (but which a future age would need to study and ponder for the survival and continuance of her great Cause), the words she had once written to Augusta could well apply again: "Accept, dear one, thanks from the depths of a lone, loving heart, whom the world hath not yet half known, but which you value and seek to comfort."

The Leader's letter of December 11 to Mrs. Marion E. Stephens, one of Mrs. Stetson's questioning students, was also for students of a future generation: "I do not presume to give you personal instruction as to your relations with other students. All I say is stated in Christian Science to be used as a model. Please find it there, and do not bring your Leader into a personal conflict." Was she not endeavoring to lead Mrs. Stephens, and all students, to an understanding of her words in her *Message for 1901,* "The Christian Scientist is alone with his own being and with the reality of things," when she wrote:

> God is above your teacher, your healer, or any earthly friend. Follow the directions of God as simplified in Christian Science, and though it be through deserts He will direct you into the paths of peace.

CHAPTER LXI

"NEVER ABANDON THE BY—LAWS"

The Holy Bible, Science and Health and The Mother Church Manual are your safe guides, follow them. — MARY BAKER EDDY

1909

MRS. Eddy had often sent out an angel thought in the form of a new by-law only to have it return battered and bruised and to have to take it in and cherish it for another season. Unknowingly Mrs. Stetson had performed a wonderful service. For several months a stream of new by-laws and by-law amendments had poured from the Leader's pen which would guide and protect her children and her Cause in ages to come. Mortal thought, which might have battered and bruised these angel guides under other circumstances, embraced them willingly thinking they were intended to restrain Mrs. Stetson, rather than mortal thought. "Thou knowest best what we need most ... Truth is strong with destiny; it takes life profoundly; it measures the infinite against the finite." These words of the Leader first published in 1903 were sent out to the field once again in mid-December when Mrs. Eddy had "Mental Digestion" *(My.* 229) republished in the *Sentinel* of December 18. Christian Scientists were reminded that "eternity awaits our Church Manual," every rule and by-law of which "will increase the spirituality of him who obeys it" and will invigorate his capacity to heal, to comfort and to awaken. A student wrote a few weeks later:

> I wish to thank you for the Manual of The Mother Church as it stands today. Clothed in its revisions and additions, it is unquestionably the richest gift and greatest blessing the world has received in the year nineteen hundred and nine ...

Following this letter was Mrs. Eddy's comment:

Wise as a serpent and harmless as a dove.
Mary Baker Eddy

On December 11 the directors wrote requesting Mrs. Eddy's final approval for one of their projects. Shortly after the completion of The Mother Church Extension they had elected to place a marble statue of a woman kneeling, on a pedestal above the organ, and had obtained her consent. They had also financed the sculptor to a year's study in Paris under St. Gaudens. The Leader encouraged and assisted a great many projects for the progress and development of those concerned (or, as in this case, to make an indelible point on the issue involved) only to withdraw her approval or consent when completed. This was one such project. The beautiful marble statue of a woman kneeling with her right hand on her heart and her left hand holding a book was ready to be installed. The Leader had known from the beginning what her final word on this project would be, and the time had arrived for that final word. She wrote such letters with the utmost care. In Mr. Dickey's words:

> She was unusually careful in her choice of words and would many times hold a letter for hours, refusing to allow it to go out until she had found the exact word to express her meaning. Sometimes two or three different dictionaries would be consulted, and then after the letter had been changed several times she would recall it and make still another change. On these occasions, which were numerous, she would apologize to her secretary and say, "Mr. Dickey, won't you forgive me if I ask you to bring that letter to me again?" I always assured her that I was perfectly delighted to make every change she suggested, for I always saw the improvement in what she was giving out. It was no task for me to write a letter for her, and the mere circumstance of coming into her room in response to her bell was always a joy to me.

The letter regarding the statue was one of those that was rephrased a number of times. And the lesson intended by that letter was also given orally to her household. Mr. Tomlinson recorded Mrs. Eddy's words in his diary on December 13:

> Insofar as one personalizes thought he limits his spiritual growth. We grow in understanding, and if I have ever permitted any personality I have outgrown it.

That same evening Mr. Rathvon recorded in his diary:

> A Minnesota woman has been at work on this and now notifies the Directors that it is ready for placing. This brought out a strong

countermand from our Leader and was the subject of several talks this PM on the necessity of impersonalization of thought. Among other things she said, "You will bear testimony that I have of late repudiated the elevating of graven images of personality."

On December 14, after her letter to the directors had been finished and signed, she called Mr. Dickey once more and said: "Mr. Dickey, I must apologize to you for calling you so frequently, and troubling you so much, but won't you kindly bring that letter back to me." Mr. Dickey hastened to do so, and as she glanced over the letter she drew a line through one word replacing it with another. Handing it back to him she said, "There, that is exactly what I want to say." But before he had turned to go, she took the letter from his hand once again and wrote across the top: "Remember that the so-called human mind is expected to increase in wisdom until it disappears and Divine Mind is seen to be the only Mind." "There, you may have that," she said as she handed it back to him. The letter to the directors in its final form read:

> No picture of a female in attitude of prayer or in any other attitude shall be made or put into our Church, or any of our buildings, with my consent. This is now my request and demand: Do nothing in statuary, in writing, or in action, to perpetuate or immortalize the thought of personal being; but do and illustrate, teach and practice, all that will impersonalize God and His idea man and woman. Whatever I have said in the past relative to impersonation of thought or in figure I have fully recalled, and my Church cannot contradict me in this statement.

Adam Dickey became Mrs. Eddy's secretary when he first came to Chestnut Hill, but changes in her writings, and most especially in Science and Health, were still handled by Mr. Frye. In time Mr. Dickey was entrusted with this important work and has described the procedure:

> Our Leader would first make the change in lead pencil in her book; then a letter was prepared to Mr. Stewart, her publisher, requesting that the change be made. This letter was signed by Mrs. Eddy, as her publisher would under no circumstances make any alteration in her books except in response to a direct request from her. The proposed change was then sent to the printer and a proof sheet made, which was in turn sent to our Leader for her approval. After this was obtained the order was put through for a change in the plates, and when this was done Mrs. Eddy was notified that the final arrangements were completed, and then the editions containing the change were issued. I am giving this detail in order that the reader may know how much care was exercised whenever a change was to be made in

Science and Health.

Alice Orgain has said that the last textual change in Science and Health was made in 1909 on page 265. Lines 20-22 which had read: "The truth of being is perennial, and the error is seen only when we look from wrong points of observation," was changed to read:

> The truth of being is perennial, and the error is unreal and obsolete.

All the field thought that Mrs. Eddy had denied and renounced Mrs. Stetson, which she had been most careful not to do. Her household felt that she was anguishing and suffering because of Mrs. Stetson's situation. She may well have been, for none knew as well as the Mother what her Augusta was going through. But was not the Mother "the faithful and true witness" who says "as many as I love I rebuke and chasten"? In her own words:

> There is a flower whose language is "I wound to heal." There is a physician who loves those whom He chastens. There is a woman who chastens most those whom she loves. Why? Because like a surgeon she makes her incisions on the tender spot to remove the cold lead that is dangerous there.

No one had been more rebuked than had Augusta Stetson, who was indeed being chastened. Augusta wrote in January to some of her faithful students referring them to Romans 8:31-39, and also said in her letter:

> I rejoice that you are all standing firm in faith and understanding which Christian Science has given you, and that you never yield to the aggressive mental argument of so-called malicious animal magnetism, namely a power opposed to God. . . .
>
> Our beloved Leader, Mrs. Eddy, says, "Divine Love always has met and always will meet every human need." . . . I am so free, so peaceful, so confident that Love will deliver me and mine, that I am strong and happy in the midst of "the fiery darts of the wicked," which I know are only illusions. Oh! dear ones, follow our blessed Leader into this spiritual consciousness which is heaven here and now.

Though anguishing in her heart Augusta stood; she did not run. Her Leader's words on their last visit, "And you never will," helped to sustain her now. Sometime later in another letter to her students she referred to her "experience of the past two years" saying: "I have had to wait and trust, and apparently stand alone with God, to make my own demonstration of what my beloved Leader has taught me for many years."

Christmas Day in 1909 was a beautiful day, clear and cold, and Mrs. Eddy was up earlier than usual. She called her household to her early and greeted them cheerily with, "A cheery, Holy Christ Mass to you all." All were impressed with her undiminished vigor so apparent on that morning as well as her loving graciousness. Mr. Rathvon recorded in his diary on December 25:

> Mrs. Eddy was in her study earlier than usual and a few minutes afterwards called us to her side. ... Never did she appear more vigorous physically and mentally, nor was her manner ever more gracious and loving. ...

This was the third Christmas, and it would soon be three years since God had spoken to Mrs. Eddy through Isaiah saying, "Within three years, as the years of an hireling, and the glory of Moab shall be contemned." On that Christmas morning she said to her students very impressively: "By another Christmas there will be great changes. See that you make them for the better." She may have known at that time the date she would leave her students, for a pamphlet she left open on her desk the following December 3 left no doubt that she knew in advance.

Later in the morning a letter was sent to Mrs. Eddy, — a Christmas message from all the workers in her home. The Leader responded right away and before noon called them all to her study once more where Mrs. Sargent read to them the lines just penned:

> *My Household*
> Beloved:
> A word to the wise is sufficient. Mother wishes you all a *happy Christmas;* a feast of Soul and a famine of sense.
> Lovingly thine,
> Mary Baker Eddy

The Leader's happy mood was still very much in evidence a week later on New Year's morning. She had opened her Bible to John 14 and then called her entire household to her study to talk to them about it:

> 1 Let not your heart be troubled: ye believe in God, believe also in me.
> 2 ... I go to prepare a place for you.
> 4 And whither I go ye know, and the way ye know.
> 12 Verily, verily, I say unto you, He that believeth on me, the works that I do shall he do also ...
> 13 And whatsoever ye shall ask in my name, that will I do, that the Father may be glorified ...

14 If ye shall ask anything in my name, I will do it.
15 If ye love me, keep my commandments [by-laws].
18 I will not leave you comfortless: I will come to you.
19 Yet a little while, and the world seeth me no more; but ye see
me: because I live, ye shall live also.
21 He that hath my commandments, and keepeth them, he it is
that loveth me: and he that loveth me shall be loved of my Father,
and I will love him, and will manifest myself to him.
29 And now I have told you before it come to pass, that, when it is
come to pass, ye might believe.

On that New Year's Day her students had little comprehension that Jesus' words applied equally to Christ's Second Coming in its feminine appearing. A very few minutes after the Leader had dismissed her household she called them all back again to hear the postlude to the words from John, which Adelaide Still had watched her compose in the intervening ten minutes:

I

O blessings infinite!
  O glad New Year!
Sweet sign and substance
  Of God's presence here.

II

Give us not only angels' songs,
  But Science vast, to which belongs
The tongue of angels
  And the song of songs.

CHAPTER LXII

KEY TO THE SCRIPTURES

Go and take the little book which is open in the hand of the angel which standeth upon the sea and upon the earth.

— REVELATION

1910

VERY early in the new year Mrs. Eddy received an interesting letter from San Jose, California. The previous July Mr. Eustace had visited in Boston and along with forty or fifty other visitors had been invited to Chestnut Hill by Mrs. Eddy who had graciously said she wished to see them. The day after Christmas Mr. Eustace had written the following letter:

Dear Mrs. Eddy:

I believe it will please you to know that First Church of Christ, Scientist, San Jose, Cal., has forwarded to the treasurer of The Mother Church a check for two thousand two hundred and thirty five dollars and seventy cents, of which amount the Sunday School contributed one hundred and thirty dollars, for the enlarging of the publishing house. It will interest you also, I am sure, to hear that this was the spontaneous result of reports given at the annual meeting of this church in October by a number of its members who had been in Boston during the past summer, to the effect that it was plainly evident that there was both an immediate and a growing need for much larger accommodations at the publishing house in order that our Christian Science publications, especially our great world-metropolitan daily newspaper The Christian Science Monitor, be not hampered by lack of space or facilities. On hearing this, the church unanimously ordered a committee appointed to arrange for a contribution, which was promptly and joyously responded to.

Beloved Leader, our hearts will never cease to thank you for urging us all to be more and more impersonal; to look to divine Principle, and not to person; and to work for our Cause and not for locality.

Faithfully yours,
Herbert W. Eustace

The Leader had Mr. Rathvon send Mr. Eustace's letter together with the following letter to Mr. McLellan for publication in the *Journal:*

January 2, 1910

Dear Mr. McLellan:

Mrs. Eddy has just read the enclosed letter from Mr. Eustace, advising her of the subscription ($2,235.70) of First Church of Christ, Scientist, San Jose, Cal., for enlargement of the publishing house.

Our Leader was much impressed by the fact that the gift was spontaneous, and that no solicitation of funds for this purpose has been made at any time. Understanding that the new building is already crowded, and that more room will soon be necessary to take care of the growing business, she has decided to make a personal subscription of twenty-two hundred and fifty dollars for building an extension, and directs me so to inform you.

Mr. Eustace's reference to Mrs. Eddy's great "world-metropolitan daily newspaper" surely touched her heart. In later years more than one member of her household recalled having heard her say: "When I established *The Christian Science Monitor,* I took the greatest step forward since I gave Science and Health to the world."

In January one of her helpers in Boston wrote describing the *Monitor* as "a most genial persuader of men." As Mrs. Eddy read his letter she exclaimed: "That is the spirit I have enjoined upon them from the start!" and had her secretary convey her "loving thanks" to the writer.

Another letter on the subject received a few weeks later pleased the Leader greatly. She sent it to Mr. McLellan for publication in the *Sentinel* along with this Introductory Note:

Dear Reader: — The following letter is a gem of the first water, that should receive the best setting and the most prominent place on the walls of society.

MARY BAKER EDDY

Dear Mrs. Eddy:

The *Monitor* is meeting one of the greatest possible needs, and to have in our family a clean, newsy newspaper has filled a long felt want, as this has been a matter I have thought of for the last thirty years. . . . I now feel that I should do more than this, and I am taking great pleasure in sending you a check for five hundred dollars, to be used in connection with the *Monitor* in increasing its circulation, or sending papers to institutions, or for further extension of buildings, or for any purpose which in your wise judgment seems best fitted. . . .

I also want to express heartfelt gratitude for all of the Christian Science publications, and especially for the textbook, which has been

> such a healer and help in every line of work. I truly confess that until I received this book, which is indeed a "Key to the Scriptures," I was not able to read the Bible with any interest or understanding. . . .
>
> Yours in truth,
>
> Clarence H. Howard

Perhaps the last sentence is the gem that should receive "the most prominent place on the walls of society." The child in the seventh picture in *Christ and Christmas* is reading "Science and Health Key to Scriptures." Had the time come to publish this title more prominently? This could have been the time of which Mr. Dickey wrote:

> On one occasion Mrs. Eddy called me into her room and I found her considering a change in the title of her book Science and Health. Instead of having it "Science and Health with Key to the Scriptures," she proposed making it read, "Science and Health, Key to the Scriptures."
>
> She asked me what I thought of the idea and if I understood the import of it. I told her that I did indeed, and that I thought it would be a splendid change as it would at once convey to people the thought that her whole book was the "key" which unlocked the Scriptures, and not [just] chapters 15, 16 and 17 . . .
>
> Mrs. Eddy . . . talked it over with her publisher and explained that she would like to make this change in the title . . . provided it did not conflict in any way with her copyrights.

Mr. Stewart conferred with her Boston attorneys and word came back from them that they would not advise it as it might affect the copyrights. Mr. Dickey regretted that this proposal which would have enlarged thought regarding Science and Health was abandoned, and said, "I shall always look on the whole book as 'Key to the Scriptures,' as I am sure she desired Christian Scientists should do." In April a Sunday School teacher wrote that she had asked her primary class, "What does Key to the Scriptures mean?" A little girl answered, "To unlock our unbelief and open our understanding." Mrs. Eddy's comment was: "Out of the mouth of babes and sucklings thou hast perfected praise."

The description of Jesus in Science and Health, "His rebuke is fearful," applied as well to his feminine counterpart. "There is a woman who chastens most those whom she loves," but most often this chastening was resisted and misunderstood. One day after Laura Sargent had been rebuked and left the room Mrs. Eddy said to Adelalide Still, "That woman hasn't a scrap of gratitude for all that I've done for her." Obviously Laura was entertaining false beliefs, but Adelaide's sympathies were with Laura and she defended her saying, "You know that isn't so, Mrs. Eddy, it's just animal magnentism that makes you say things like that." Pointing to a chair Mrs. Eddy replied sternly, "Sit down, Adelaide." Then:

> "Am I the Discoverer of Christian Science or are you?" I said, "You are, Mother." Then she said, "Did I uncover animal magnetism or did you?" and again I said, "You did, Mother." "And do you know more about handling animal magnetism or do I?" "You do, Mother." Again she said, "Do I know Laura Sargent or do you?" I answered, "You do, Mother."

Then the "woman who chastens" those she loves said mildly, "Thank you, Adelaide," and dismissed her. Once Gilbert Carpenter had fathomed such occurrences he was able to write:

> How fortunate students would be today, if the slightest effort they made under the human mind would bring them a sharp rebuke. Mrs. Eddy stood ready to rebuke the slightest deviation from the demonstration of God's wisdom, protection and care. The dangerous attitude for a student was for him to feel that he could function under his own mind, and still believe that he could do the thing Mrs. Eddy asked him to do in a satisfactory manner. Such a fancy betrayed the error that suggested that in many instances one could get along without God, as well as he could with Him. Mrs. Eddy characterised it as self-justification, in her endeavor to awaken students to its serious nature.

Mrs. Eddy often quoted to the workers in her home, "Trifles make perfection, but perfection is no trifle." And in her lessons to her mental workers over and over she said such things as, "I pray and watch in the little details," or "If you fail in one iota . . . the example is incorrect." The Leader did not fail in one iota. Those who thought she did never really knew her. But they did see manifestations of her perfectness (exactness) in the minutia of things. The poet's words, "Order is heaven's first law," was a truism no more obvious in astronomy than in Mrs. Eddy's everyday life. Martha Wilcox wrote of this:

> She showed forth to an unusual degree the exactness and divine order of God — her Mind — and she required perfection of thought and action from those of her household. She, herself, never made a false movement. Even the different lengths of pins had their respective corners in her pin cushion, and she took out the pin she needed without taking out and putting back the different lengths. . . . Mrs. Eddy believed that if one's thought was not orderly and exact in the things that make up present consciousness, that that same thought would not be exact to give a treatment or use as exact Science.

Mrs. Eddy's sense of order was so exact that the least little thing out of place was as obvious to her as a picture hanging crookedly on the wall is to others. The hardest work for the five women (all working Christian Scientists) who cared for the thirty rooms and ten bathrooms, was replacing every item in its proper spot. Three of them worked rapidly during the time Mrs. Eddy was out on her daily drive each day to keep her apartment clean and sparkling. But often they failed to replace the furniture at its proper angle until Mrs. Wilcox placed tacks in the carpet for a guide. Martha knew this was not demonstration, but she gave thanks that Mrs. Eddy "had taught us in Science and Health that God, our Mind, guides us into the right use of temporary as well as eternal means." Sad to say, there were times when the Leader's discriminating sense of order was not appreciated, and a reproved helper would say she was overly-exacting, fussy, and impossible to please. Self-justification together with criticism of the Leader's demand for perfect order moved such a student farther from "heaven's first law," for if something is not appreciated, it is depreciated.

Often Mrs. Eddy called her mental workers to her study, and at times she called her whole household. But most often of all she called only one worker, for she worked individually with each one in her home. Each was on a different rung of the ladder of Christian Science. Of one of her first lessons Martha Wilcox wrote that "she taught me that the Mind I then had was God, and that I was to show forth God — my own Mind — in order and exactness and perfection." After each lesson the Leader wanted immediate application and demonstration. Some, who had no comprehension of the Divinity Course they were being taught in the details of daily experience, thought that the Teacher created problems for them unnecessarily. Of course she did! Practising the Truth they were learning in solving problems *was the* Divinity Course.

But the Divinity Course was not to continue much longer. March 10, 1910, may have come and gone unmarked by any at Chestnut Hill save the mistress of the house. Several who had been with her at Pleasant View three years earlier had recorded her words on that earlier date but had been unaware of their import. She had said then, "Today He [God] is speaking to me again . . . 'Within three years . . . and the glory of Moab shall be contemned . . . ' "March 10 marked three years from the date of that message. Essentially the Woman's mission was completed. She could say in Paul's words: "I have fought a good fight, I have finished my course, I have kept the faith."

CHAPTER LXIII

"I HAVE FINISHED MY COURSE"

As Mary Baker Eddy, I am the weakest of mortals, but as the discoverer and founder of Christian Science I am the bone and sinew of the world. — MARY BAKER EDDY

1910

THE *Sentinel* of March 12 published a statement by Mrs. Eddy entitled "Mrs. Eddy's History" *(My.* 297) in which she said, "I briefly declare that nothing has occurred in my life's experience which, if correctly narrated and understood, could injure me." The rest of the statement is more an appreciation than an endorsement of Sibyl Wilbur's book, *The Life of Mary Baker Eddy,* but it does grant "permission to publish and circulate this work." Those in the field who missed reading this message in the *Sentinel* may have read it in the April *Journal* or in a future edition of Miss Wilbur's biography. But another message from the Leader published in April may have been noticed by few.

A year earlier the black cross on the cover of the *Quarterly* had begun to grow gradually lighter, as had the smaller cross in the title heading on page 1. In April, 1910, the Christian Science seal inside the *Quarterly* on page 1 was reduced in size, and this smaller cross was no longer shaded. It was white. By July this white cross and seal were larger than they had previously been.

There was a change at Chestnut Hill after March 10. God's Chosen Witness who had mothered the whole world, knew that she had completed her mission, and, probably for the first time since 1866, felt free to do something for herself. One thing she did was to collect some of her poems, — a few of which dated back to her girlhood, — and ask her publisher, to arrange for a small edition for private distribution.

When Allison Stewart handed the manuscript to William Dana Orcutt it was a very unusual assignment. In the past Mrs. Eddy had been concerned about every smallest detail of all the work Mr.

CHRISTIAN SCIENCE BIBLE LESSONS

Vol. XXI. APRIL, MAY, JUNE. No. 1.

April 3, 1910.

Subject: UNREALITY.

Golden Text: "How shall I pardon thee for this? thy

SMALL WHITE CROSS
Inside the *Christian Science Quarterly* of April, 1910

Orcutt did for her. This time as Mr. Stewart gave him Mrs. Eddy's poems he said: "She wishes to have them put into book form — just a small edition for private distribution. I am instructed to hand the manuscript over to you with no further comment than that she would like to have you design the volume for her. I presume you will prepare a dummy to submit for her approval. Let me know when it is ready and I will arrange for you to show it to her."

Mr. Orcutt remembered Mrs. Eddy's fondness for pink roses and had his artist include these in a cover design. He selected the typeface himself and had a few of her poems typeset for samples. Then he bound the volume in vellum and was ready for another visit to Chestnut Hill; — but he was surprised to find a different Mrs. Eddy.

> Instead of her customary poise, she showed a shyness about the publication of her poems quite unlike her usual self-confidence. When I handed her the dummy volume, her face lighted, and she exclaimed with obvious pleasure, "Oh you have put my pink roses on my poems." She held the dummy in her hands for some minutes before glancing inside.
>
> "These are poems," she said, "which I have written from time to time, ever since I was a girl. Ideas have come to me which I seemed to be able to express better in verse than in prose. I am not sure that

CHRISTIAN SCIENCE
BIBLE LESSONS

Vol. XXI. JULY, AUGUST, SEPTEMBER. No. 2.

July 3, 1910.

Subject: GOD.

Golden Text: "Know therefore that the Lord thy

LARGER WHITE CROSS
Inside the *Christian Science Quarterly* of July, 1910

they ought to be given the dignity of book publication. I am planning to issue them privately for a few friends."

Mrs. Eddy opened the volume and became deeply absorbed. "How much better this looks in type than in manuscript," she said. Then she slowly read aloud the first sample he had printed which was "'Autumn' — Written in childhood in a maple grove." As she read she returned to the days of its writing, oblivious of all around her. At the end she read the descriptive line once again and said, "I think the word *girlhood* would be better than *childhood.*" She reached for a pencil and made the change in the dummy. Then she read the first stanza aloud once more:

What though earth's jewels disappear;
  The turf whereon I tread,
Ere autumn blanch another year,
  May rest above my head.

After a thoughtful moment she said, "I don't like that first line." Then she drew a pencil line through the first two words and substituted *Quickly.* Turning to the second poem he had typeset she read aloud:

Joy for thee happy friend! thy bark is past
The dangerous sea, and safely moored at last —
Beyond rough foam.
Soft gales celestial, in sweet music bore —
Mortal emancipate for this far shore —
Thee to thy home.

Then she read it through a second time emphasizing the penultimate line. After a moment's silence she said, *"Mortal* is not the right word." She crossed out *mortal* and replaced it with *Spirit.* Then:

> Still with her pencil in hand, she turned to the inside cover and wrote her name in a firm hand, giving the dummy her approval. Handing it back to me, she remarked: "Mr. Stewart is urging me to print also an edition for general distribution. But I am hesitating. Somehow poems seem more personal than prose."
>
> "I hope that you will yield to his persuasion," I remarked.

It was several months before this little volume was ready to go to press, but this was Mr. Orcutt's last visit with its author. The autographed dummy volume became to him a symbol of this meeting, and he kept it among his treasured souvenirs. Even though Orcutt had never embraced Christian Science, the following December when he heard that Mrs. Eddy had departed, his reaction was absolute incredulity. And frequently after that when he heard her referred to in the past tense he would take the little dummy volume from the shelf and *feel* her presence.

Another step Mrs. Eddy initiated in March or April of 1910 was the diminishing of her instruction to the mental workers in her home. It was no longer a daily affair, but no less vital when given. On the morning of April 9 Archibald McLellan arrived just as she was beginning a lesson to her household and he was included with the other students. William Rathvon wrote in his diary that day:

> As all hands . . . were assembling in the Pink Room, AMcL arrived and joined us. Then for forty minutes our Leader held forth in most remarkable fashion at her very best. She took high ground and held it; she thrust and parried and had everybody on the run, yet it was all straight Science.

Martha Wilcox never ceased to marvel how Mrs. Eddy could hold her Bible between her hands letting it open where it would, and how the first words her eyes fell upon were always the right lesson for that moment.

In April William McKenzie made a parting call on household

members at Chestnut Hill before departing on a European lecture tour. He was delightedly surprised when Mrs. Eddy called him to her study. Much had transpired since he had seen her last:

> She appeared as one who had been through conflict, showing evidence thereof, yet remaining victor. Her first question was, "Did you know me? . . . " [After discussing his lecture tour and the Publishing Society]
>
> There must have been a silence for a time. I seemed in that quiet to newly discern her purpose that all of us . . . should be actually manifesting an obedience to God similar to her own. . . .
>
> I know that as I sat quietly in Mrs. Eddy's presence for the last time, I gained a new sense of the word patience . . . In the sixteen years of our friendship she had revealed to me the Christianly patience of the mother guiding the child . . . rebuking mistakes with a clarity which produced not resentment but enlightenment.

Some in Mrs. Eddy's household did not perceive the Mother's patience. In his diary Mr. Rathvon even implied that she lacked grace and righteousness, although he also said: "I can well understand how she could sway those whose service or support she needed, for a more lovable person could not be found in the pages of history or in the hearts of men." Neither could a more gracious, righteous, or patient individual be found in the pages of history; but that righteousness and patience were greater than the students in 1910 could comprehend. Those in her household often thought that her severe rebukes were due to impatience.

That was the case one morning in April when the Leader missed Laura and asked Adelaide where she was. It was not the fact that Mrs. Sargent was indisposed and still in bed that brought an outburst, but rather the acceptance of mortal mind's reasoning about the situation. Miss Still thought Laura was exhausted from her service, ill in consequence, and needing a rest. The students in the Leader's home, above all others, should have been turning to God's words in Science and Health: "The struggle for Truth makes one strong instead of weak, resting instead of wearying one." "The consciousness of Truth rests us more than hours of repose in unconsciousness." "The highest and sweetest rest, even from a human standpoint, is in holy work." Instead of helping Laura, they were sympathizing with her problem, accepting and embracing the suggestions of mortal mind; which caused the Leader to denounce vigorously the animal magnetism that was blinding them. After the whole household was stirred to its depths she sat quietly in her armchair. Then she called Adelaide to her and dictated the truth of the situation which was published in the *Sentinel* of April 23 as "A Paean of Praise" *(My.* 355), which said in part:

> The Christian Scientists at Mrs. Eddy's home are the happiest group on earth. . . . their footsteps are not weary . . .
>
> When will mankind awake . . . and praise and love the spot where God dwells most conspicuously in His reflection of love and leadership? When will the world waken to the privilege of knowing God . . .

Her words to her disciples were not unlike those of her brother to his disciple: "Have I been so long time with you, and yet hast thou not known me, Philip? he that hath seen me hath seen the Father." Some of the Leader's words to her household recorded by Irving Tomlinson could have been at this time:

> You must examine yourself and learn what are your temptations and errors, then rest not until you take up arms against them. Put all under your feet that is not worthy to be called Truth, wisdom, and Love. Practise this when alone. Do not think it wearies you to practise the truth by which you heal the sick, and that to turn away from this to lightness and frivolity rests you. This is error and belief — not Science.
>
> "My yoke is easy, and my burden is light," were the words of him who taught and demonstrated the Science of God.

When, oh when, would her students waken to her identity and to their own potential? For years and years she had been telling them and showing them these things, yet on the eve of her departure they were still as dull as Philip had been. Fortunately a few of the things she said and did to waken them have been recorded.

More than twenty years earlier when Mrs. Eddy was teaching in her second story classroom on Columbus Avenue, she said to her class one day: "Were it not for the minds around me, I could step out of this window, and not fall to the ground." In other words her thought, which included her body, was totally leavened by Spirit which could not fall to the ground. It was only the unleavened thought of those around her that prevented their *seeing* this demonstration.

There were also times when she did give her students something to *see.* One day when Ella Peck Sweet was with her Mrs. Eddy laid her hand on Ella's arm. Mrs. Sweet "saw" Mrs. Eddy's hand disappear. When her hand later became visible the Leader said: "Ella, I am showing you things I could not tell you."

After three years of teaching, on the eve of Jesus' departure from his disciples, there was strife among them as to which of them should be accounted the greatest. According to Luke Jesus said: "He that is greatest among you, let him be as the younger; and he that is chief, as he that doth serve. . . . I am among you as he that serveth." But John recorded more than the Master's words. He described the dramatic, unmistakable example Jesus gave to bring this lesson home, — by washing the disciples' feet. He set an example for all Christians in all the centuries to come.

Mrs. Eddy also gave an example for all Christian Scientists in all the centuries to come. Some had thought that she would attend The Mother Church after moving to Boston. Many had hoped that she would make an appearance and perhaps address them there. And perhaps all had expected that she would visit her magnificent temple, — but she did not. Adam Dickey recorded:

> It was a long drive from her home to The Mother Church, and only once during her residence at Chestnut Hill did she take the time to drive to Falmouth and St. Paul Streets, and then she did not alight, but had her first view of The Mother Church from her carriage.

But she did more than this. She set an example which she knew could not be forgotten. One day she announced to her household that she would visit the beautiful Extension. This caused a good deal of excitement for all knew she had not entered the edifice and they were eager to have her see it. Her helpers were stimulated in their preparations for her all morning. When the time came for her departure, Laura held her shawl for her just as she was leaving, and then with the rest accompanied her to the front door. But that is as far as the Leader went. At the front door she turned back, returned her shawl to Laura, and said: "That was Mary wanting to go." One of Sarah Farlow's reminiscences of Mary Baker Eddy on another occasion stated: "She placed her finger to her lips and said, 'That was Mary talking, now let God talk.' "

Perhaps the household at Chestnut Hill saw no significance to the white cross inside the *Quarterly* in April nor in the larger white cross in the next issue in July, but they had noticed a great change in their Leader. The malicious attacks on her life had not ceased, and at times all the mental workers were called upon to meet them. Her watch to her mental workers on May 4 was:

> There are no thoughts sent here but the divine Mind. There is no malicious mesmerism nor hypnotism, no evil thoughts in this house, or that can be sent here. All is God, divine Love. Divine Love is infinite and there are no other minds. One Mind and this Mind is Love divine, immortal Life, Health and Holiness right here in this house. No malicious thought coming here. All is divine Love and its manifestation health, holiness and immortality.

A few days later, at four o'clock on the afternoon of May 10, she called all her mental workers to her study and said to them: "God is numbering his people. Stand by God and His anointed and appointed Leader." Mr. Dickey responded, "We will; to whom else shall we go?" and the Leader reminded him that the Scripture adds, "Thou hast the words of eternal life."

In the *Sentinel* of June 4 was a "Take Notice" signed by Adam Dickey, Secretary, which stated: "Mrs. Eddy has requested that as a rule no more letters to her shall be published in our periodicals." The Leader was devoting more of her thought to eternal Life and less to the demands of the cause. In May or June she said to a student: "I feel I am just really beginning to understand Science and Health."

For many years Mrs. Eddy had been making such statements as: "Is it necessary that one eat and sleep? No. Then do not talk about eating and sleeping being a normal condition." The students in her home had accepted such utterances, but only theoretically. Probably the Leader could have demonstrated her words, even as she could have stepped out of a second-story window without falling to the ground, if her students could have supported her. But they neither understood nor believed much of the Science they had theoretically accepted. Members of Mrs. Eddy's household had often worried because she ate so little. Now she ate practically nothing, not enough "to support a kitten," Mr. Rathvon recorded in his diary on June 13. Neither Mr. Rathvon nor anyone else in the house knew why the change had been so great since the tenth of March, but they were all aware of it. Rathvon wrote in his diary on the sixth of July:

> The most marked change of any since my coming here has been taking place in the past three months. It portends a metamorphosis of some extraordinary nature and which I must believe is for the good. There is a general softening and broadening. The nights are quieter than for years and years, I am told, and the days are full of rest and quiet. I would like to see more vigor mentally and physically, and more interest in things that were once the center of thought, but these may be incidental in the working out of the problem that I feel is under way. There is little or no physical ailment, the many things that we have had daily to struggle with having all disappeared into their native nothingness.

God's "anointed and appointed Leader" had received the promised Comforter and presented it to the world. Then followed her six days (forty-four years) of labor in founding God's Science on this planet. Now her founding work was well done, and she was entering into her seventh day of rest. If Mr. Rathvon could have understood this he would not have desired to have her return to work completed and evince "more interest in things that were once the center of thought."

Mr. Rathvon's words "working out of the problem that I feel is under way," was probably his way of stating what many of her helpers were thinking, — that Mrs. Eddy is very old and will pass away very soon. The truth of the situation is expressed in these words from Mrs. Eddy: "The first revelation that came to me was that I could not die. I saw Life, and that it was impossible for me to die." Since that first revelation forty-four years earlier the Leader had been endeavoring to teach this truth of Life to her followers. In their practise of Christian Science many had healed dying patients, and some had brought back those who had thought they had died, but none had wakened to see that *this* is Life eternal here and now. They were still asleep in the dream that *this* life is material and all must die out of it sooner or later. The Leader never ceased trying to waken them to present immortality. One day she touched Adam Dickey's hand with her finger and asked him, "What is this?" He replied, "Matter," and she said, "It is *not;* it is Spirit." At another time she looked at him and said, "You are Spirit." Adam replied, "No, Mother, I am spiritual." She repeated in a very emphatic way, "You are Spirit." And he said, "Mother, I do not see that." She stated a third time, "You are Spirit." Adam still could not understand and discussed it with other members of the household.

In July of 1910 she knew all her students were still mesmerized to believe that Spirit was elsewhere and *present* reality was mortally material. And she probably read Mr. Rathvon's thought about her which he recorded in his diary on July 6: "I would like to see more vigor mentally." Two days later he recorded in his diary that Mrs. Eddy had called all hands in for an especially long session and "kept us all busy answering questions." He wrote that she was at her very best in "poise, acumen, and graciousness" throughout this long session, and concluded his account: "I never saw a better or more wonderful exhibition of clear skill."

She knew her students could not see the spiritual path she was taking. They thought it was leading her *away* from them. She knew it was taking her beyond their present vision and comprehension. On July 13 one of her students recorded her words: "Not wearing out, you mean wearing in." And the advice she gave another student on the twenty-first of August was what she herself was doing every minute of every day: "Keep hold of the hand of God."

ADAM H. DICKEY
Photograph taken outside Chestnut Hill

CHAPTER LXIV

IGNORANT MALPRACTICE

Watch, too, that you keep the ***commandments*** *that experience has compelled to be written for your guidance and the safety of Christian Science in our Church Manual.* — MARY BAKER EDDY

1910

YOUNG Mr. and Mrs. Clark from Montana were both devoted students of Christian Science. Mr. Clark was also a mining engineer, and, accompanied by his wife, he had gone deep into a great forest to examine a mine. On the day of their arrival at their proposed camp they found themselves surrounded by a forest fire which grew to huge proportions, with no way of escape. Together with the five miners they battled the flames, at times beating out the fire on one another's clothing or going down to the ground for a breath of air. All this time the Clarks were doing their best to declare the power of God to save them.

At a terrifying crisis, after they had been battling the flames for more than seven hours, Mrs. Clark called to her husband: "Oh, let's despise the danger; God never made it! This would have to destroy God before it could destroy His reflection." This was the turning point. And soon what seemed a miracle appeared, — a long green unburned path which the fire had passed around and along which all seven found their way to safety.

Readers of the *Sentinel* were thrilled to read the Clark's testimony, and their teacher could not help being proud of this demonstration of his fine young students. Their teacher had moved to Boston in 1908, and when the Clarks later visited Boston they arranged to have an interview with him.

So it was that Mr. and Mrs. Clark were in the library at Chestnut Hill visiting with their teacher, Adam Dickey. But they did not know what the youngest member of their family was doing during this interview. Martha Wilcox had taken charge of their one-year-old son, and when Mrs. Eddy heard that there was a baby in the house she sent word to have Martha bring him to her room. So Baby Clark had an interview denied to almost everyone else in the world, which impressed him not at all. He was much more interested in Mrs. Eddy's silver stamp box than he was in its famous owner. And when he left he carried it away held tightly in his chubby little fist. No doubt he heard the story of his treasured souvenir many times as he was growing up.

Ex-senator Chandler had not forgotten George Glover nor his two hundred forty-five thousand dollars, and in the summer of 1910 the lawyer invited the two youngest Glovers to spend their vacation at his home in New Hampshire. Twenty-one year old George III and his younger brother Andrew did not have particularly happy recollections of that visit. George complained that Chandler kept them working on his boats most of the summer. But there was one bright spot. On July 16 the two boys visited their grandmother at Chestnut Hill. This visit did not escape the notice of the press, and George and Andrew Glover were photographed outside Mrs. Eddy's home by a news photographer.

Mrs. Eddy was very happy to see her grandsons and asked at once about their father. George handed her a little gift from his father which she opened eagerly. And she exclaimed with pleasure as she lifted the delicate gold pin from its box to the palm of her hand.

Martha Wilcox said the boys did ample justice to a good supply of homemade cake and ice cream. Adelaide Still recorded that Andrew did most of the talking while George just sat quietly and smiled at his grandmother. Many, many years later when asked about this interview, George recalled that Andrew did most of the talking and told her about the farm and the store, etc. When asked what he was thinking while Andrew was talking, tears came to his eyes as he recalled the scene and answered quietly, "Why — I thought she loved me!"

Mrs. Eddy was very pleased with George who was reader in his little home church, and she invited both boys to stay at Chestnut Hill. George replied, "Grandmother, we would like to stay, but we are needed on the farm." Before they left she gave each a copy of Science and Health inscribed with his name followed by, "Lovingly Grandmother Mary Baker Eddy."

Mrs. Eddy was "Grandmother" to George Glover's children, but she was "Mother" to all mankind. Public ridicule of this fact had caused her to change this appellative to Leader in 1903 *(Man.* 64); however, she continued to be Mother to those in her household. But the time had come when her children in her own household must, on their own, begin to follow their Forever Leader rather than

GEORGE AND ANDREW GLOVER

George Washington Glover III and Andrew Jackson Glover photographed by a news photographer outside Chestnut Hill, July 16, 1910.

having the watchful eye of the Mother guide their every footstep. Irving Tomlinson recorded in his diary on July 16 that she called the household together and asked them to discontinue calling her Mother saying it would be "better and more scientific."

As Mrs. Eddy withdrew from her household her daily drive again became more enjoyable to her. These outings which had been reduced to barely half an hour now often extended to an hour once more. She also spent more time alone, sometimes not calling her workers to her for days on end. Though she always had her place at the table, her meals were usually served privately in her room, and many days she was never seen by her household except at the time of her daily drive.

Often the Leader spent the whole day alone in her rooms attended only by Adelaide Still, and there were times when even Adelaide was excluded. Perhaps Miss Still enjoyed a respite, for she sometimes felt overburdened by being constantly on call. But Laura Sargent and Martha Wilcox at times grew concerned on days when Mrs. Eddy was long alone.

One day when the Leader asked to be left alone and not to be disturbed, they both listened attentively for a summoning bell, but none rang. After several hours had elapsed and she had not come out nor called for anyone Laura and Martha began to worry that something had happened. Finally, after a good deal of deliberation, they decided to go in. As they listened at the door they heard voices, and as they opened the door to see if everything was all right, Mrs. Eddy said: "Girls, why did you disturb me? I was talking with Jesus." Did Laura and Martha share this with the household or ponder it in their hearts? Perhaps it was the latter.

Fewer and fewer demands were placed upon the Leader's two long-time faithful helpers, Laura Sargent and Calvin Frye. Adelaide Still gave almost constant service throughout 1910, and her confidential secretary Adam Dickey was called upon fairly frequently. Even though Mr. Dickey could not always comprehend the lesson Mrs. Eddy was endeavoring to teach him, she acknowledged his merit and understanding in August by conferring upon him the degree C.S.D.

"Letters to Our Leader" which had been a focal point in the periodicals for quite some time were discontinued following the Notice from Mr. Dickey in the June 4 *Sentinel.* However, another letter and Mrs. Eddy's response were sent to the editor for publication at the end of August. The question raised in that student's letter was a basic issue greatly disputed at that time, so "Instruction by Mrs. Eddy" *(My.* 342) was published in the *Sentinel* of September 3 and also in the October *Journal.* Mrs. Eddy's reply begins: "You are scientifically correct . . . You can never demonstrate spirituality until you declare yourself to be immortal and understand that you are so."

By September when Mr. Orcutt was ready to print Mrs. Eddy's poems she had yielded to persuasion and decided to issue it in two styles. She also asked Mr. Dickey to write a Preface for the volume. One hundred copies were bound in full vellum for the Presentation issue, and two thousand bound in white cloth for general distribution. Both editions had pink roses stamped on the cover.

When the Presentation edition arrived at Chestnut Hill Adam Dickey opened the box and immediately took a copy in for Mrs. Eddy to see. At once she asked him to read something from it, and he opened to the poem titled "Constancy." When he finished reading he looked up and saw tears streaming down Mrs. Eddy's cheeks. "Mr. Dickey, that was written when I lost my husband," she said with much feeling. Then she numbered the copy "1", autographed it, and gave it to Mr. Dickey.

On the twenty-fourth of January in 1896 Calvin Frye had recorded Mrs. Eddy's words in his diary:

> 1) David saw corruption. The body was buried and decayed.
> 2) Jesus died in belief but the body did not see corruption but was raised again.
> 3) The demonstration for me is that it shall not be death, even, but a body transformed "by the renewing of Mind" — spiritualization.

On March 10, 1907 the Leader knew that her students would not see that demonstration. From that day in 1907 when God had told her she would be personally guiding her church only three more years she had worked constantly to strengthen the one that was to continue protecting and guiding her cause and the Children of Israel in this world. That one was her *Manual* which had seen more than twenty editions in the last three years. It was nearly completed by the end of 1909, but there had been a few more amended bylaws causing new editions in 1910. The eighty-fifth edition was announced in the *Sentinel* of February 5, the eighty-sixth edition on April 9, and the eighty-seventh on April 23. In September Mrs. Eddy made one last amendment, and her last edition of the *Manual,* the eighty-eighth, was announced in the *Sentinel* of September 17.

General Frank S. Streeter, who was one of the ablest lawyers in New England, perhaps even in the United States, once asserted, according to his son's testimony, that Mrs. Eddy knew more law than he did. Most probably Mrs. Eddy would have said that it was God who knew all law and it was He that told her what to do. But some of her Boston officials felt that they knew better. A good deal of "mental murder" was going on among her directors and other officers by the last quarter of 1910. That is, they were thinking and discussing their belief that Mrs. Eddy will pass away before long. Some of them were also discussing how the organization would function without her controlling hand.

Archibald McLellan was the lawyer on the Board of Directors and pehaps the one most concerned about some of the by-laws in the *Manual.* He was well aware, as he had once told Mr. Orcutt, that Mrs. Eddy "has left us nothing to conceive or originate — simply to carry on and to execute."

There were even a number of things which they could not carry on if they adhered to the by-laws in the *Manual* because Mrs. Eddy's approval was required, often *in writing.* So a campaign began to induce Mrs. Eddy to change some of the by-laws that restricted the directors. Adelaide Still was present on one occasion when one of the directors (probably Mr. McLellan) tried to get Mrs. Eddy to remove these restrictions from the *Manual,* but she refused.

It may have been after this interview that she said to Mr. Dickey, in a voice filled with earnestness and pathos, that if she could find one individual, who was spiritually equipped, she would immediately place him at the head of her church government. After she had said this she asked Mr. Dickey to take a pencil, and then dictated very slowly so that he would not miss one word:

> I prayed God day and night to show me how to form my Church, and how to go on with it. I understand that He showed me, just as I understand He showed me Christian Science, and no human being ever showed me Christian Science. Then I have no right or desire to change what God had directed me to do, and it remains for the Church to obey it. What has prospered this Church for thirty years will continue to keep it.

While Mrs. Eddy was talking with Adam Dickey, Mr. McLellan was explaining the dilemma he foresaw to William Rathvon. None of her students had wakened themselves in accordance with the short paragraph on page 75 in their textbook:

> When you can waken yourself or others out of the belief that all must die, you can then exercise Jesus' spiritual power to reproduce the presence of those who have thought they died, — but not otherwise.

Jesus was awake and was endeavoring to waken Peter, James, and John "out of the belief that all must die" when he "bringeth them up into an high mountain apart" and reproduced the presence of

Moses and Elias. Mrs. Eddy had been endeavoring for forty years to waken her students "out of the belief that all must die," and now knew that they would have to waken themselves and others. But she was awake and was on "an high mountain apart" at Chestnut Hill when she was talking with Jesus. While the Leader was totally awake to Life, her helpers in Boston as well as in her home were asleep in the dream that all must die, and in this dream were malpractising upon their Leader constantly, — believing that she was growing physically frailer day by day and would not be with them much longer. The students saw the manifestation of their own thought, and the Leader suffered from it. This was mental murder, but she knew they could not understand that incisive terminology at this time. That is why she had charged Adam Dickey to put it in writing for a future generation that could comprehend.

One of her last efforts to waken the mental workers in her home was on Monday, September 26. She called Calvin Frye, Laura Sargent, Irving Tomlinson, Adam Dickey, and Ella and Willliam Rathvon and demanded that they heal her. She said she was tired of going on this way, enumerating the false beliefs of age that they were holding over her. According to Calvin Frye's diary:

> She added that she would give any one of us $1000 to heal her. A.H.D. said he would give $1000 to be able to heal her. . . . So said the others in substance. I did not reply for some time for I felt quite confused and discouraged, but finally said, "Well all we can do is to keep up our courage and work on up to our highest understanding." She replied, "Has it come to this!"

What do her words mean? Do they not imply that her students who had fearlessly faced all forms of sickness and disease as well as the sin of malicious mental attacks upon their Leader, were accepting with non-resistance the false claim of death? They had not wakened, and still considered death as inevitable. So the Leader said: "If you all feel like that, turn your minds away from me and know that I am well."

These faithful workers did not know that they were failing to practise the Principle they had accepted. The Leader knew they must waken to see this else lose the Science they were proclaiming to practise. In September she dictated a short article to Adam Dickey entitled:

> PRINCIPLE AND PRACTICE
>
> The nature and position of mortal mind are the opposite of immortal Mind. The so-called mortal mind is belief and not understanding. Christian Science requires understanding instead of belief; it is based on a fixed eternal and divine Principle, wholly apart from mortal

conjecture; and it must be understood, otherwise it cannot be correctly accepted and demonstrated.

The inclination of mortal mind is to receive Christian Science through a belief instead of the understanding, and this inclination prevails like an epidemic on the body; it inflames mortal mind and weakens the intellect, but this so-called mortal mind is wholly ignorant of this fact, and so cherishes its mere faith in Christian Science.

The sick, like drowning men, catch at whatever drifts toward them. The sick are told by a faith-Scientist, "I can heal you, for God is all, and you are well, since God creates neither sin, sickness, nor death." Such statements result in the sick either being healed by their faith in what you tell them — which heals only as a drug would heal, through belief — or in no effect whatever. If the faith healer succeeds in *securing* (kindling) the belief of the patient in his own recovery, the practitioner will have performed a faith-cure which he mistakenly pronounces Christian Science.

In this very manner some students of Christian Science have accepted through faith, a divine Principle, God, as their savior, but they have not understood this Principle sufficiently well to fulfill the Scriptural commands, "Go ye into all the world, and preach the gospel." "Heal the sick." It is the healer's understanding of the operation of the divine Principle, and his application thereof, which heals the sick, just as it is one's understanding of the principle of mathematics which enables him to demonstrate its rules.

Christian Science is not a faith-cure, and unless human faith be distinguished from scientific healing, Christian Science will again be lost from the practice of religion as it was soon after the period of our great Master's scientific teaching and practice. Preaching without practice of the divine Principle of man's being has not, in nineteen hundred years, resulted in demonstrating this Principle. Preaching without the truthful and consistent practice of your statements will destroy the success of Christian Science.

While pointing the way in Science, the Leader did not lose touch with, nor interest in, the manifestations of progress in the world. When the Wright brothers gave an exhibition of flying at an aviation meet near Boston in September, Mrs. Eddy was desirous that members of her household should go to see it. Martha Wilcox said that usually she did not want her "family" to be away, but on this occasion she was most insistent that Martha along with several others should attend this meet. She also showed the keenest interest in hearing every detail of the exhibition after they returned home. Perhaps she wanted to be sure that her students understood her words in Science and Health:

We welcome the increase of knowledge and the end of error, because even human invention must have its day and we want that day to be succeeded by Christian Science, by divine reality.

It was important that students of Science should differentiate between material progress and "divine reality." The excitement over flying bespoke a tendency for mistaking material flying for spiritual progress. This could become even greater as human invention overcame time and space. Though she showed the liveliest interest in every detail the students discussed, she did not share their enthusiasm. Instead she dictated to Mr. Dickey:

SOARING

To fly materially is animal, to fly spirituallly is divine. . . . Flying materially is a sport that may become engrossing. . . . The elevation worth obtaining or possible to obtain in Science is spiritual ascent, thought soaring above matter. . . . Oh when will the age plant its discoveries on spiritual cause and effect, on that which is not only capable of going up but is ascending physically, mentally and spiritually. Almost one century of experience has caused me to say, How long, O Lord, how long.

MARY — WOMAN OF PROPHECY

CHAPTER LXV

SOARING AND ASCENDING

*Do **not allow** the **evil one** in your midst to turn you away from me in this hour of crucifixion, or history will repeat itself, and Christian Science will once more be lost as aforetime.*

— MARY BAKER EDDY

1910

"TO fly spiritually is divine." Is this not what Jesus was doing when his disciples saw him "walking on the sea, and drawing nigh unto the ship . . . Then they willingly received him into the ship: and immediately the ship was at the land whither they went" (John vi.19,21)?

One day when Mrs. Eddy had dismissed Adelaide Still and asked not to be disturbed, Laura Sargent and Martha Wilcox grew concerned after quite some time elapsed with no word from the Leader. After waiting longer and discussing it further, they finally decided to enter her room. They listened first at her door but heard nothing. And when they entered they found nothing. Mrs. Eddy was not there!

Laura and Martha searched the whole house and the entire household was alerted. Returning to Mrs. Eddy's room following some six or eight hours of searching and consternation, they found her there. After calming the household the Leader asked to see Martha and Laura alone.

When the others were gone and the door was closed, Mrs. Eddy said, "Girls, come here and put your arms around me." As they did so Mrs. Eddy disappeared and was standing on the other side of the room looking at them. She then cautioned them about relating this experience to those metaphysically unprepared for it and told them not to put it in writing.

Many years later during the day of her annual Association meeting Martha Wilcox asked two or three of her students to remain after the meeting as she would like to talk with them. This was not long before Mrs. Wilcox passed away in July, 1948. When she and these chosen students were alone she told them of this experience and also of the time that she and Laura Sargent had heard Mrs. Eddy talking with Jesus. One of these students chosen to hear Mrs. Wilcox tell her personal experience lived in California, and in the 1950's she related it, just as she had heard it from Mrs. Wilcox, to a friend in Oakland, California. Through that friend it came to the author.

For many years I pondered this in my heart and, obeying Mrs. Eddy's instruction to Martha and Laura, did not put it in writing. In 1966 feeling constrained to make these experiences known, an effort was made to contact Mrs. Wilcox's student through whom they had come, only to learn that she had just passed away. At that time, lest they be lost, I wrote down the episodes as they had been told to me. For twenty-four years that writing has been in my file seen and read by no one, but it appears today that Mrs. Eddy's instruction to Martha and Laura was for that day and no longer applies in the latter part of the twentieth century in the church age of the Laodiceans.

In October of 1910 the Leader was satisfied that her work for mankind was finished. At one time she felt that her nineteenth century mission was to be completed by the end of the century, which probably induced her writing and publishing of "Satisfied" in January, 1900. More than a decade had passed since that time and before the republishing of this poem as the final selection in her book of poems. "Satisfied" not only appeared in her new book in the fall of 1910, but it was also republished in the October, 1910 *Journal* with form and punctuation changed since its first appearance, as this last stanza shows:

January, 1900: The centuries break!
The earthbound wake!
God's glorified;
Who doth His will,
His likeness still,
Is satisfied.

October, 1910:
The centuries break, the earth-bound wake,
God's glorified!
Who doth His will — His likeness still —
Is satisfied.

One more symbol was published in October. The white cross on the inside of the last two *Quarterlies* now also appeared on the cover of the last *Quarterly* in 1910.

COVER OF OCTOBER, 1910 *CHRISTIAN SCIENCE QUARTERLY*

Adam Dickey was called home to Kansas City on personal business and George Kinter came to Chestnut Hill in October to substitute for him while he was away. Mr. Kinter found an entirely different routine from that which he had known before in Mrs. Eddy's home and wrote of this to his friend John Lathrop with whom he had served at Pleasant View. The members of the household now saw little of the Leader, and George's letter of October 13 to John tells how they occupied their time:

> . . . Now as to matters here, in which I am sure you are always mightily interested. Things have changed perceptibly and perhaps as much as in any other particular our dear friends own manner of spending the days. But little reading and scarce any writing, a quieter and more peaceful day by all odds than ever before, with far greater serenity, and contented reliance upon others to do, at least, as well as may be. All but one may and usually do retire in the evening and are seldom ever called during the night now. [Mrs. Eddy] does not breakfast nearly so early as of yore, and the drive comes at one or as soon thereafter as convenient, generally before half past, but sometimes lasts a full hour, oftener about three-quarters. Musicals comprise a frequent means of divertissement and entertainment, sometimes we are all asked to join, but oftenest it is a solo or more by one of the ladies who sings and plays well; the victrola is now in the pink parlor and is frequently brought into requisition. . . .
>
> Perhaps as great as the sort of thing I have related is the increasing release of pressure upon those in attendance; Calvin is quite another person, having as you doubtless know, much less to do, he is very much more affable, and tractable, more communicative, and far less querulous. Then the folks disport themselves in manners and fashions unknown in days of yore. For example right after breakfast we usually go into the library and look over the daily Boston papers until about 8 o'clock, then each goes his own way, or sometimes two or more go together, one day recently several of us found ourselves in the woods opposite on a chestnut hunt, again Irving took me out to a golf club some miles away with the Ford Runabout, and we spent an hour very agreeably on the links, returning to the house about half past nine.
>
> The Rathvons take the Ford one noon hour and Irving the next; and they all go to the neighborhood libraries, and I am now appropriating the new horse Nellie for a drive either morning between half past seven and 9:30 or at noon. . . .

While the members of her household were thus occupied the Leader was usually thinking alone in her room with Adelaide Still generally nearby. One October day she called Adelaide to her and dictated the following:

> The deepest hallowed intoned thought is the leader of our lives,

> and when it is found out people know us in reality and not until then. The surface of the sweetest nut is often a burr, and the thought that guides our life and expresses our being is unseen, except in the outward expression and actions thereof. Hence the folly of declaring obstinately who is who and what is what, unless we have tested and proven the who and what. The wisdom of the wise is not as much expressed by their lips as by their lives.
>
> I sit quietly alone in my room conversing with the world, and the people thereof answer me intelligibly, the good in man comforts me, affords me pleasure and gives me no displeasure, and our communings are sincere and sacred. All this has its fulfillment, without a sign dishonest, insincere, ungrateful, unjust. But the opposite of this experience claims as much feasibility and reality as the experience itself. Here learn a lesson of the parable of the sower, both sprang up and bore fruit, the good fruit was productive and the evil fruit produced nothing, for good is real and evil is unreal.
>
> The wisdom of this hour and the proper labor of this hour is to know of a certainty the quality of the seed which takes root in our thought . . . in short, the moral life's history is, Be good, do good, speak good, and God, infinite good, cares for all that is and seems to be. . . . Who believes what I have written? He who has the most experience of Good. Who disbelieves it? He who has the most fear of evil. What is the remedy for this belief? It is experience, for every moment, hour and day of mortal existence brings each one of us nearer the understanding of the nothingness of evil in proportion to our understanding of the allness of good.

The cooks and housekeepers and gardeners at Chestnut Hill had work to keep them busy, but it would appear that, despite their months or years of training, the mental workers had not the self-discipline, desire, or ability to keep at their work without the Leader's constant instruction and direction. They had not yet wakened! They would all have worked eagerly and diligently to meet and overcome any false claim of evil, — sickness, accident, storm, calamity, etc. But they were earth-bound in their blindness to the necessity for meeting and overcoming the false claims of material good. In other words they wanted God to be their only Mind when things went wrong, but not when everything was pleasant and enjoyable. So, as soon as the Leader ceased stirring things up to keep them working, they ceased working. Instead of turning to God as the One Mind, they were letting mortal mind direct them. Though they would not have put it into words, one of the directions mortal mind was giving them daily was that they were just waiting for Mrs. Eddy to die.

Calvin Frye's allegiance had always been devoted one hundred per cent to the Leader, but William Rathvon's had been divided all along between the Leader and her organization. Now he was greatly concerned about the *Manual* provisions which would restrict the functions of the organization when Mrs. Eddy was no longer here. He consulted with two lawyers in Boston, Judge Septimus J. Hanna and the First Reader of The Mother Church, Judge Clifford P. Smith. The three of them came up with a plan for the formation of an advisory council to act in Mrs. Eddy's place if she were unable to give her signature. But Mrs. Eddy's confidential secretary, Mr. Dickey, would not present their plan to her. Had he not recorded her dictated words: "I have no right or desire to change what God has directed me to do, and it remains for the Church to obey it"?

Mrs. Eddy's astute cousin and trustee, Henry M. Baker, was a lawyer of reknown. One day when he was at Chestnut Hill Mr. Rathvon asked to have a word with him:

> "General Baker," inquired Rathvon, "for some time I have been quite concerned about how certain parts of our *Manual* would function if Mrs. Eddy could not supply her assent or signature as it requires. I thought best to ask you as a lawyer and one in whom Mrs. Eddy has every confidence."

General Baker assured Mr. Rathvon that he need not worry. "It is a matter of common law," he said, "in a case of this kind where it is physically impossible to carry out specified conditions by the one named, that the next in authority assume that jurisdiction."

Mrs. Eddy had not the slightest doubt in 1910 that the Board of Directors would physically assume her position and usurp her authority. But her position and her authority were both given of God and they were not physical. They were spiritual. If her disciples had seen this, they would have known her by now. But she could not be known (understood) physically, — only spiritually. When an individual wakened to reality and was ready to forsake materiality for spirituality, he would also comprehend and obey the by-laws in the *Manual* as God gave them. Then he would understand and know the Forever Leader.

There were few students in Boston or in the entire field who were anywhere near this metaphysical awakening. Mrs. Eddy's students had always felt that she was frequently wrong and that they could run things just as well as and perhaps a little better than she could. It is improbable that Stephen A. Chase was the originator of the document pointing out the weaknesses in Mrs. Eddy's organization and outlining what should be done, but he still had it in his file. The document was headed "The Following Scheme of Church Government Is Suggested for Christian Scientists;" and some of its provisions stated:

> 1. Large cities should represent large districts. . . .
> 2. The First Church of each district should be built by general subscription from the whole United States in the largest city in the district.
> 3. These churches would be built when ordered by The Mother Church. . . .
> 6. The Board of directors of every first church shall be named by the Mother Church. . . .
> 12. It would be desirable to call in learned and experienced Roman Catholics to advise concerning the details of the scheme as they know more about organization than all the rest of christendom. . . .
> 14. The Mother Church must own all the First Church edifices and all other societies must be tributary and subordinate to them.
> 15. This constitutional basis should be adopted during Mrs. Eddy's life time. Her authority is now sufficient to procure its unquestioned adoption. If delayed till after her death no extensive organization will ever be possible and the sect will be split into an hundred heads.

When one sees the kind of "help" the men in Boston endeavored to give the Woman, her accomplishments are seen as well nigh miraculous. Though the above plan had been thwarted by Mrs. Eddy, a few of its provisions were still cherished by some prominent men in Mrs. Eddy's organization. They were very much concerned that the authority so soon to fall into their hands might "be split into an hundred heads." McLellan, Rathvon, Hanna, and Smith had all endeavored to have Mrs. Eddy make changes in the *Manual,* to no avail. So, according to McLellan, the directors felt impelled to consult their lawyers.

Whether changes in the *Manual* prior to Mrs. Eddy's departure (which they felt was imminent) were suggested by their lawyers or originated with the directors is not known. But two very basic changes were planned. It is very probable that Ira O. Knapp would not agree to such a step. Ever since his eyes had been opened to Mrs. Eddy's spiritual identity as he sat in her class in the fall of 1885, he had known the Leader to be the "woman clothed with the sun, and the moon under her feet." But very suddenly, on the eleventh of November Mr. Knapp passed away.

On November 13 someone recorded these words from Mrs. Eddy: "Manna must fall from your lips every day to help some mortal mind for time and eternity."

Very soon thereafter the directors had new plates made for three pages in the *Manual,* pages 21, 120, and 127. The change on page 21 deleted "Rev. Mary Baker Eddy, Pastor Emeritus." The change on the other two pages was the addition of the words "and Branch Churches," which, in those three little words extended a centralized control from Boston, unknown before, all over the world. This general official control was in violation of the by-law on page 70 of the *Manual* which states: "The Mother Church of Christ, Scientist, shall assume no general official control of other churches . . ." The reason for making this change in the *Manual* at this time may have been stated in No. 15 of the "Scheme of Church Government" — "This . . . should be adopted during Mrs. Eddy's life time. Her authority is now sufficient to procure its unquestioned adoption. If delayed till after her death no extensive organization will ever be possible . . ."

The *Manual* with these changes was issued as the 89th edition and went on sale in January of 1911. The following pages are taken from an 88th edition of 1910 and an 89th edition of 1914.

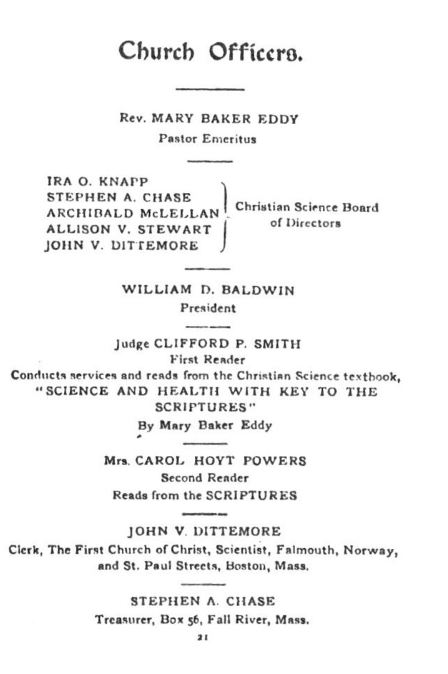

Church Officers.

Rev. MARY BAKER EDDY
Pastor Emeritus

IRA O. KNAPP
STEPHEN A. CHASE
ARCHIBALD McLELLAN
ALLISON V. STEWART
JOHN V. DITTEMORE
Christian Science Board of Directors

WILLIAM D. BALDWIN
President

Judge CLIFFORD P. SMITH
First Reader
Conducts services and reads from the Christian Science textbook, "SCIENCE AND HEALTH WITH KEY TO THE SCRIPTURES"
By Mary Baker Eddy

Mrs. CAROL HOYT POWERS
Second Reader
Reads from the SCRIPTURES

JOHN V. DITTEMORE
Clerk, The First Church of Christ, Scientist, Falmouth, Norway, and St. Paul Streets, Boston, Mass.

STEPHEN A. CHASE
Treasurer, Box 56, Fall River, Mass.

21

Manual — 88th Edition, page 21

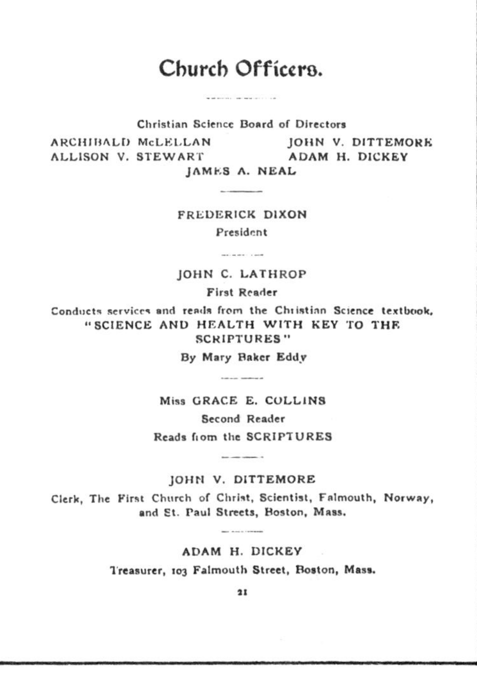

Church Officers.

Christian Science Board of Directors
ARCHIBALD McLELLAN JOHN V. DITTEMORE
ALLISON V. STEWART ADAM H. DICKEY
JAMES A. NEAL

FREDERICK DIXON
President

JOHN C. LATHROP
First Reader
Conducts services and reads from the Christian Science textbook, "SCIENCE AND HEALTH WITH KEY TO THE SCRIPTURES"
By Mary Baker Eddy

Miss GRACE E. COLLINS
Second Reader
Reads from the SCRIPTURES

JOHN V. DITTEMORE
Clerk, The First Church of Christ, Scientist, Falmouth, Norway, and St. Paul Streets, Boston, Mass.

ADAM H. DICKEY
Treasurer, 103 Falmouth Street, Boston, Mass.

21

Manual — 89th Edition, page 21

The field seemed not to notice the changes on pages 120 and 127, but there was considerable reaction to the removal of Mrs. Eddy's name as Pastor Emeritus from her *Manual.* This discontent increased until "Rev. Mary Baker Eddy, Pastor Emeritus" was replaced in 1924 at the top of the page headed Church Officers. It has also been recorded that Mrs. Annie C. Bill had "discovered" Mrs. Eddy's plan of spiritual leadership in her *Manual.* Mrs. Bill came

120 APPENDIX

Present Order of Services in The Mother Church.

Republished from the *Sentinel.*

SUNDAY SERVICES.

1. Hymn.
2. Reading a Scriptural Selection.
3. Silent Prayer, followed by the audible repetition of the Lord's Prayer with its spiritual interpretation.
4. Hymn.
5. Announcing necessary notices.
6. Solo.
7. Reading the explanatory note on first leaf of *Quarterly*.
8. Announcing the subject of the Lesson-Sermon, and reading the Golden Text.
9. Reading the Scriptural selection, entitled "Responsive Reading," alternately by the First Reader and the congregation.
10. Reading the Lesson-Sermon. (After the Second Reader reads the BIBLE references of

Manual — 88th Edition, page 120

120 APPENDIX

Present Order of Services in The Mother Church and Branch Churches.

Republished from the *Sentinel.*

SUNDAY SERVICES.

1. Hymn.
2. Reading a Scriptural Selection.
3. Silent Prayer, followed by the audible repetition of the Lord's Prayer with its spiritual interpretation.
4. Hymn.
5. Announcing necessary notices.
6. Solo.
7. Reading the explanatory note on first leaf of *Quarterly*.
8. Announcing the subject of the Lesson-Sermon, and reading the Golden Text.
9. Reading the Scriptural selection, entitled "Responsive Reading," alternately by the First Reader and the congregation.
10. Reading the Lesson-Sermon. (After the Second Reader reads the BIBLE references of

Manual — 89th Edition, page 120

ORDER OF EXERCISES 127

Order of Exercises for the Sunday School of the Mother Church.

1. Call to order by the Superintendent.
2. Hymn.
3. Subject of the lesson announced; Golden Text repeated by the children; Responsive Reading.
4. Silent prayer, followed by the audible repetition of the Lord's Prayer in unison.
5. Instruction in classes, in accordance with Sections 2 and 3 of Article XX of the Manual of The Mother Church.
6. Entire school reassembles.
7. Hymn.
8. Scientific Statement of Being read by the Superintendent.
9. School dismissed.

Manual — 88th Edition, page 127

ORDER OF EXERCISES 127

Order of Exercises for the Sunday School of the Mother Church and Branch Churches.[1]

1. Call to order by the Superintendent.
2. Hymn.
3. Subject of the lesson announced; Golden Text repeated by the children; Responsive Reading.
4. Silent prayer, followed by the audible repetition of the Lord's Prayer in unison.
5. Instruction in classes, in accordance with Sections 2 and 3 of Article XX of the Manual of The Mother Church.
6. Entire school reassembles.
7. Hymn.
8. Scientific Statement of Being read by the Superintendent.
9. School dismissed.

[1] If a collection is taken, it should be taken in the classes before they reassemble.

Manual — 89th Edition, page 127

from England to Boston in 1921 and presented her "discovery" to officials of The Mother Church. However, instead of seeing Mary Baker Eddy as the Forever Leader, Mrs. Bill interpreted the bylaws as a plan of spiritual evolution and felt that she was to become the spiritual leader of Mrs. Eddy's organization. Mrs. Bill's followers felt that replacing Mary Baker Eddy as Pastor Emeritus in her *Church Manual* was merely to thwart Mrs. Bill and this "evolution" of leadership.

Later the field began to become aware of other changes that had been made in Mrs. Eddy's writings. To stem a tide of unending criticism the Board of Directors issued "An Important Statement" on pages 92 and 93 of the February, 1955 *Christian Science Journal.* This statement, too, was so roundly criticized that those two pages were replaced with different reading matter in many of the Reading Room copies. The original statement did contain the following sentences relating to actions in November of 1910:

> The words "and Branch Churches" were added to the titles on pages 120 and 127 of the Manual. This printing went to press in Mrs. Eddy's lifetime.

Were the officials in Boston so eager to remove the Pastor Emeritus from the pages of her *Manual* that this first printing of the 89th edition "went to press in Mrs. Eddy's lifetime"? If so, that may be why she called Laura Sargent to her on November 28 and dictated: "It took a combination of sinners that was fast to harm me." Was this not a repetition of Jesus' experience? Seven years earlier she had said to her students: "It was not the material cross that killed Jesus, but it was the desertion of his students that killed him."

Going to press with a new edition of the Manual may not have been the only thing that caused her to make that statement. Every edition of her *Miscellaneous Writings* beginning with the first edition in 1897 through the last edition of 1910 had had Mrs. Eddy's portrait as a frontispiece. A similar portrait had been in an early edition of Science and Health, but Mrs. Eddy had removed it. Following the Next Friends Suit in 1907 she had once again placed her portrait in Science and Health where it had continued as the frontispiece in every edition since then. The Leader's portraits were removed from both of her books beginning in 1911.

The new books without the Leader's portrait and the changed *Manual* without the Pastor Emeritus were all issued very quietly with no announcement of any kind and no explanation of the changes. But there was an attempt to make these changes during Mrs. Eddy's lifetime.

The Publisher's Announcement for Science and Health which

appeared each week in the *Sentinel* had, since 1907, included the sentence: "This work contains important changes and additions by the author, also a photogravure portrait of Mrs. Eddy, together with a facsimile of her signature." This announcement remained unchanged through November, 1910. Officials in Boston were in close touch with members of the Chestnut Hill household who felt that Mrs. Eddy would leave them very shortly and who were aware that she no longer read each periodical as it was issued and also that she had read practically nothing for the past several weeks. In the *Sentinel* of December 3 the above sentence ended with the word author. The last fourteen words were deleted.

The *Sentinel* of Saturday, November 26 included in the advertisement for Science and Health the "photogravure portrait of Mrs. Eddy together with a facsimile of her signature." There had to be some planning right after November 26 in order to have those words removed from the same advertisement (unchanged in other respects) just one week later. It may have been their first order of business the following Monday morning, November 28. Mrs. Eddy's statement to Mrs. Seal in 1902: "I know always what my children are doing," was just as true in 1910. Little wonder that she had called her faithful Laura Sargent on November 28 and dictated: "It took a combination of sinners that was fast to harm me." And after Laura had written and dated that message of November 28, Mrs. Eddy signed it.

It took a com-
bination of sinners
that was fast
to harm me.
Mary Baker Eddy
Nov, 28 1910.

Facsimile of statement dictated to Laura Sargent, November 28, 1910, and signed by Mary Baker Eddy.

CHAPTER LXVI

SEEMING DECEASE

We can enter into immortality here on earth, and now, and overcome death. — MARY BAKER EDDY

1910

MRS. Eddy was not deceived. She knew the eagerness of leaders in her organization to assume control and to promote Christian Science the way they thought it should be done. It was this very ambition of mortal mind that blinded their eyes to the eternality of Life, and consequently would mentally murder their forever Leader. But as always she was patient with their blindness. Experience would open blind eyes and she knew as she had written: "Time tells all stories true." Thirty or more years later Gilbert Carpenter began to awake, and he wrote:

> [Mrs. Eddy] knew that the success of her Cause depended upon her being given the most important place in it; that the moment interest in and love for her as the Revelator and Demonstrator began to lessen, at the same time the spirituality in the Cause would begin to diminish. When students begin to believe that their obligation toward their Leader is fulfilled merely by acknowledging her as the Revelator, and studying her writings, they are committing an error that is far more serious than appears on the surface. The tendency to ignore her life, — her demonstration of her own teachings, — is an error that would eat at the very heart of her Movement, and seek to rule out of it its spiritual vitality . . .
>
> Mrs. Eddy considered impersonally and spiritually, is the heart of Christian Science. When the heart weakens, the whole body is affected. Medical law rules that under such circumstances the body may become fat. The Cause of Christian Science may increase size and wealth, and yet that may not be a spiritually healthy condition. Certainly it may be said to have heart trouble, when error succeeds in pushing the Leader out of her place as the heart of the Cause.

In November of 1910 animal magnetism was using some of her best workers to push "the Leader out of her place." Sooner or later they, and all sincere Christian Scientists, must waken to see this. To aid in opening blind eyes she made a statement in the latter part of November that she wanted all her students to hear. She called her devoted Calvin Frye and extracted from him a promise, even as she had done from Adam Dickey some time earlier. Calvin wrote in his diary:

> Some week or more before our beloved Leader passed from us she called me to her and asked me to promise her that I would tell her students it was malicious animal magnetism that was overcoming her and not a natural result from the beliefs incident to old age and its claims of limitation.

Whether Calvin endeavored to impart this message to others or kept it in his heart is a question, but he fulfilled his promise to his Leader in 1917. That year Calvin A. Frye was president of The Mother Church, and he stunned some of his audience at the time of the Annual Meeting. On that day, without consulting the directors, Calvin gave Mrs. Eddy's message from the platform of The Mother Church to the students that had gathered from far and wide. Shortly thereafter on August 24, his seventy-second birthday, Calvin Frye passed away. But before that time Bliss Knapp invited Mr. Frye to dine at his home and begged him to repeat the message from Mrs. Eddy. Calvin repeated her words:

> Calvin, I want you to promise me that you will tell my followers that I am not under the claim of old age, — it is not old age or being worn out that is affecting me. Tell my followers that this is not a normal condition, but this is the work of malicious animal magnetism that I do not seem to be able to overcome.

The Leader had overcome the work of malicious animal magnetism for herself, but she could not do it for her followers. Each must do it for himself. She probably could have disappeared from their midst even as she had done on at least one day at Chestnut Hill. Jesus let them crucify his body that his teaching be not lost. Even so, Mary Baker Eddy let them watch her body die to keep her teaching alive in their hearts. Twenty-four years later one student, Herbert W. Eustace, was able to write:

> Why did Mrs. Eddy pass on? Why, with her clear understanding of the Science of being, should she not have demonstrated continuity of life here?
>
> One, with even a slight grasp of Christian Science, has no doubt of

> Mrs. Eddy's understanding of Life, for he knows that Christian Science could not have been discovered and promulgated had a single link been missing in the spirituality of the discoverer.
>
> Then Mrs. Eddy's death involves a deeper and more far-reaching reason than that of an ordinary death.
>
> ... the human mind, in its present phase of materiality, insists upon knowing, not only when the mortal appears, or is born, but more important to that mind, when and how the mortal dies or disappears.
>
> Had Mrs. Eddy disappeared in any way other than in the traditionally accepted manner called death, the human mind would have been stirred to its depths in opposition to Christian Science. It would have declared Christian Science to be a fake, and Christian Scientists frauds, for saying that Mrs. Eddy had miraculously disappeared. ...
>
> Mrs. Eddy had to leave to the world an interpretation of her disappearance that human belief could admit was proper and legitimate.
>
> She did this by appearing to die and be buried.
>
> However, the fact remains that Mrs. Eddy gave up her sense of life, as it is called, because of the demand of the hour, which was the ignorance of her followers, as well as the rest of mankind. ...
>
> Through a clearer understanding of Christian Science, it is now seen that Jesus never actually gave up his sense of life, and it will eventually be seen that Mrs. Eddy did not die. The willingness to believe that she did die is purely hypnotic illusion, and is the mesmerism that encourages the one who believes she did, to do likewise.

While Mrs. Eddy was willingly letting her household watch her body die, many were merely waiting for what they considered inevitable to take place. But there were at least three in the household who constantly were doing their utmost to practise the Science they had been taught and to uphold their understanding of life for their Leader. Two of those three were the devoted and faithful Calvin Frye and Laura Sargent. Gilbert Carpenter heard a good deal of criticism of and gossip about Mrs. Eddy, her demands and her rebukes, both when he was in her home and for years and years afterward in Boston. But he said of Laura Sargent:

> Never was she known to criticize her [Mrs. Eddy] to a single individual either inside or outside of the home. Once Mrs. Eddy said of Laura, that she had been with her under more trying conditions, than any other student.

The third student that was doing her very best every day was Martha Wilcox. It was about the eighteenth of November, when the afternoon was growing dark, that Mrs. Eddy rang for Martha. In Martha's own words:

> About two weeks before she left us she called me into her study about five o'clock in the evening. She was resting on her couch, as she usually did before her evening meal. I wish you might have heard her expressions of gratitude for her home and her gratitude to those who were caring for her home. She commented on how clean and beautiful we were keeping it and what it meant to her to have such a place in which to do her work and carry out the Movement of Christian Science. She said, "You girls are so good to do this for me." Then she said, "Martha, is there any reason why you should not stay with me forever?" I replied, "Mother, I will stay with you as long as you need me to stay."

Had Martha understood the great import of the Leader's question, her reply would have been a little different. But Martha was a very young student and replied from her present standpoint of understanding, which satisfied Mrs. Eddy. She patted Martha's arm and said, "Oh Martha, I do not like you to be fat." Then after a minute she added, "Well, I once weighed one hundred and forty pounds."

After Mr. Kimball had passed away in 1909 Mrs. Eddy had asked Bicknell Young to teach the Normal Class which was to be held in 1910. Mr. Young had returned from England for that purpose and was now in Boston.

In the late weeks of fall in 1910 Mrs. Eddy had fewer dinner guests than usual at Chestnut Hill, but Mr. Young was invited to dinner not many days before the Normal Class was to convene on December 7. After the meal Mr. Young said to Mrs. Eddy: "That was the best dinner that I ever ate," and according to Martha Wilcox Mrs. Eddy expressed just as much pleasure at his remark as any other woman would have. Following the twelve o'clock dinner Mrs. Eddy had an interview with Bicknell Young regarding the class he would be conducting soon. She probably told him that afternoon that Martha Wilcox would be one of the pupils in his class, although Martha did not yet know it.

Not long thereafter Mr. Frye told Martha that Mrs. Eddy had decided that she was to receive Normal Class instruction at the Metaphysical College. The Leader had also arranged to have Martha return to Kansas City for a short visit prior to the class. Following the class Martha was expecting to return to Chestnut Hill to serve Mrs. Eddy. She did not know that Mrs. Eddy wanted her away from Chestnut Hill on December 3. Martha's next assignment for serving her Leader was a much larger one than she then realized.

A few days after the decease of Ira O. Knapp on November 11, the remaining directors sent to Mrs. Eddy through her secretary, Mr. Dickey, their nomination of William P. McKenzie to fill the vacancy, but they did not receive the customary acknowledgement from the Leader. It has been written that Mrs. Eddy offered the directorship to Calvin Frye, but that he refused it. On November 21 the directors received a brief undated note from Mrs. Eddy stating:

The Board of Directors
Beloved Students:
Please appoint Mr. Adam H. Dickey member of the Board of Directors.

Lovingly yours,
Mary Baker Eddy

Mr. Dickey was very eager to begin his new duties and was present at the beginning of the regular meeting of the board on Friday, November 25. Most of the mental workers at Chestnut Hill had been doing as they pleased much of the time for several weeks, but Mrs. Eddy did not intend that Mr. Dickey should begin his duties as a director just yet. He was still her secretary, and she had Calvin Frye telephone the secretary of the Board recalling Mr. Dickey to Chestnut Hill. His letter to the directors the following Wednesday may have been the last one he wrote for the Leader:

Nov. 30, 1910

Dear Brethren:
Your letter of the 23rd instant to Mrs. Eddy recommending the appointment of Mr. Lewis C. Strang as Mr. Knapp's successor on the Bible Lesson Committee has been received by her. Her reply is that she has no special request to make, but that you may elect the one whom you think best fitted for the position.

Sincerely yours,
Adam H. Dickey, Secretary

Lewis C. Strang had been one of the Leader's finest helpers at Pleasant View. He and his wife Martha were both dedicated practitioners in Boston, and Lewis was also listed as a teacher. Both of their listings were still in the *Journal* in 1918, but some time after that he disagreed with some of the officials and left the church organization. Nonetheless his words regarding the Leader in his article "Lest We Forget" written in 1906 are immortalized as the Preface to *First Church of Christ, Scientist, and Miscellany.*

The next day, Thursday, December 1, Mrs. Eddy's helpers thought she was suffering from a cold. When it came time for her drive they said to her, "Don't you think it would be wise, Mother, to stay at home today?" Mrs. Eddy answered as she had for many years when her students voiced the lying suggestion instead of the scientific reality of being: "That's right, talk with the devil!" Mrs.

Sargent opened her Bible and, after silently reading the passage she had opened to, she thought, "I wish I might ask Mother what this means." As Mrs. Eddy was arranging her bonnet she said, "Laura, do not bring your questions to me, take them to God. You lose your answer if you take them to me."

Laura Sargent accompanied her on her drive that day, and recorded one of the Leader's last messages for her followers. During the drive Mrs. Eddy appeared to be thinking deeply and said aloud: "Oh! if the students had only done what I had told them to do, I should live and carry on the Cause."

When they returned from the drive Mrs. Eddy appeared very weak, to those in her household. She asked for a pad which Ella Rathvon brought to her, and on it she wrote her last written message: "God is my Life." Later that evening she ate her supper as usual.

The next day, December 2, Mrs. Eddy did not dress, but she insisted on getting up and going to the couch in her study. And a little later she dressed her hair. Once again she had her mental workers keeping a watch.

On Saturday morning December 3, Mrs. Eddy stayed in bed, but she was alert and sent messages to her mental workers. In the afternoon when she was sitting up in bed, Miss Still felt she was working for herself. Most likely she was dwelling on words very similar to those of her brother in John 17:

> This is life eternal, that they might know thee the only true God, and Mary Baker Eddy, whom thou hast sent.
>
> I have glorified thee on the earth: I have finished the work which thou gavest me to do.

The Leader's next message to her mental workers was: "Drop the argument, and leave me with Divine Love, that is all I need." Miss Still reported that she was very happy and ate her supper. Everyone felt that a demonstration had been made and the claim of illness had been met. But they did not yet know the message that Mrs. Eddy would leave on her desk before that day was over.

The great pyramid has been called "The Bible in Stone." Mrs. Eddy referred in *Christian Healing* to "the great pyramid of Egypt, — a miracle in stone." She also left a pamphlet on her desk on December 3, 1910 which was entitled *The Latter Days: with Evidence from The Great Pyramid.* This pamphlet was left open on Mrs. Eddy's desk. It was opened to page 32. One of the sentences on page 32 read: "By the same standard of interpretation, the termination of The Grand Gallery 1,910 inches, gives the 3rd of December, 1910, as the end of the present era, which we accept as an approximation only, though possibly a very close one."

Following the service at The Mother Church on Sunday morning, December 4, First Reader Clifford P. Smith read a portion of Mrs. Eddy's letter of June 3, 1891 *(Mis.* 135). After reading the sentence: "You can well afford to give me up, since you have in my last revised edition of Science and Health your teacher and guide," Judge Smith paused. Then he continued:

> Although these lines were written years ago, they are true today, and will continue to be true. But it has now become my duty to announce that Mrs. Eddy passed from our sight last night at 10:45 o'clock at her home at Chestnut Hill.

Committees on Publication had been notified and this message was given that Sunday morning in branch churches around the world.

Earlier that morning the medical examiner for Newton Center, Dr. George L. West, had been called to Chestnut Hill to issue a death certificate. After the usual investigation Dr. West pronounced death due to natural causes and issued the customary certificate. But all the world wanted to know more. The following was published the next day in the *New York Herald* of December 5:

> The request to Dr. West that he go to the magnificent home of Mrs. Eddy of Chestnut Hill and view the body with the idea of granting a certificate of death was received about nine o'clock in the morning from Edward F. Woods, an alderman of Newton Centre, and Dr. West departed at once for the house in Brookline. On reaching there, Dr. West was ushered at once into an upper front room in which on the bed, and clad in a heavy white robe, was the body of the Leader of the Christian Science cult. There were several persons in the room at the time, and several others were observed moving about other parts of the house by Dr. West as he entered and as he left. They were members of the Christian Science faith.
>
> "To me it merely was the performance of a perfunctory duty," said Dr. West in comment. "Although, had I realized at the moment that I was in the presence of the body of a woman who had ruled thousands for many years, I might have been impressed with the importance of the official service I was performing. What struck me most as I looked into the dead face was its extraordinary beauty. She must have been a beautiful child, a beautiful maiden, and extraordinarily beautiful when in the full flower of womanhood. There still were substantial traces of beauty left in the white face reposing on the pillow. Time indeed had laid its hand lightly on her all through the years. Wrinkles were there, of course, but they were not the wrinkles that come with age, after a life fraught with the cares of a home, of the bringing up of children, or of a thousand and one other things

that arise in the life of the ordinary woman to furrow her brow. The wrinkles that she bore looked more as if some one had been playing a little prank, and as if they might be brushed away with the gentle smoothing of a hand. They did not seem to belong amid those features. The entire countenance bore a placid, serene expression, which could not have been sweeter had the woman fallen away in sleep in the midst of pleasant thoughts. I do not recall ever seeing in death before a face which bore such a beautifully tranquil expression."

The next day the undertakers who had also been called on Sunday morning voluntarily issued the following statement:

December 6, 1910

To Whom It May Concern:

We were called to the residence of Mrs. Mary Baker Eddy in Chestnut Hill, Mass. at 8:15 A.M., Sunday December 4, 1910, to care for her body. We found it in an excellent state of preservation when first called, and also fifty-eight hours after death. No preserving compounds were used until that time. The tissues were remarkably normal; the skin was well preserved, soft, pliable, smooth and healthy. I do not remember having found the body of a person of such advanced age in so good a physical condition. The walls of the arteries were unusually firm and in as healthy a state as might be expected in the body of a young person. The usual accompaniments of age were lacking, and no outward appearance of any disease, no lesion or other conditions common to one having died at such an advanced age were noticeable.

In the process of embalming we found the body at sixty hours after death, in as good condition of preservation as we always find at twelve to twenty-four hours after death.

This is our voluntary statement made without solicitation or influence of any kind.

Frank S. Waterman
George A. Pierce
Katherine M. Foote

The undertakers' statement confirmed the Leader's words to Mr. Frye: "I am not under the claim of old age, — it is not old age or being worn out that is affecting me."

Accounts of Mrs. Eddy's last few days and hours in December, 1910 have been told and written many times. But there was another account that was only whispered. It was seventy years before that story was finally put into writing.

CHAPTER LXVII

THE FOREVER LEADER

According to the glorious gospel of the blessed God, which was committed to my trust. — PAUL

Martha, is there any reason why you should not stay with me forever? — MARY BAKER EDDY

1910

CARL Lundstrom was a consecrated and dedicated practitioner of Christian Science to whose care the events of the night of December 3, 1910 were entrusted. About 1954 or 1955 Mr. Lundstrom made a trip to New England from his home in California to visit the historical landmarks of interest to Christian Scientists. It was twenty-five years later, in 1980, that Mr. Lundstrom recorded what he learned on that trip. This is Carl Lundstrom's account:

The message I am about to impart is not only an important message for all Christian Scientists, but in my estimation, it is the most important incident in Mrs. Eddy's experience which proves without any doubt the infallibility of her complete demonstration of the revelation of Christian Science. Before relating this incident, I feel impelled to express my gratitude that this important message was given to me and that through many years of study and growth in Christian Science, I was able to realize how momentous this message is and bring it forth at God's direction. The following account reveals how this message was intrusted to my care.

Twenty-five years ago I had the privilege of visiting all of the historical landmarks pertaining to Mrs. Eddy's revelation of Christian Science. Lasting impressions were gained from my visits to Mrs. Eddy's residences. At 12 Broad Street, Lynn, Massachusetts . . . the attic room was interesting, but I remember most of all the three flights of circular stairs reaching from the basement to the attic. It moved me very much to realize the countless times our Leader must have used those stairs in meeting the needs of her roomers while at the same time persistently going forth with her God-given mission. . . .

The last house I visited was Mrs. Eddy's home at 400 Beacon Street, Chestnut Hill, Mass. It is here that I was to be told the incident about Mrs. Eddy which I am about to relate. This house and the surrounding grounds were beautiful. It was autumn and the driveway was covered with leaves of every hue. When I entered the front hall I was greeted by two very lovely, gracious ladies. I was surprised to find I was the only one there to be guided through the house. After waiting for some time, and it being mid-afternoon, one of the women in charge suggested, as there seemed to be no one else to join us, that she and I would start the tour of the house together. As I look back upon this experience I realize now how important it was to have been the only visitor. I felt free to inquire about many things I would never have asked about were there others present. Likewise she directed pertinent questions my way. For instance, at one point in our conversing together, she inferred that I was a Christian Science teacher, which I assured her I was not . . . As we wandered through this lovely home, I felt the balance, order, and beauty of each niche and corner and the touch of truth and love that only a spiritual seer could have demonstrated. By this time, because of the warmth and friendliness of my guide, I asked many questions which she answered lovingly and interestingly.

Our last stop of this tour was Mrs. Eddy's bedroom. It was not what I expected, for what I had seen of the rest of the house gave forth an atmosphere of regality. This room was homespun and expressed simplicity. The ceiling had been lowered, the guide told me, and although a bathroom had been added, Mrs. Eddy had preferred to use the commode stand with its bowl and water pitcher. I was impressed to see several pictures of Jesus hanging on the walls. It was at this moment that my guide turned to me and said that she felt impelled to tell me what happened to Mrs. Eddy on December 3, 1910. She went to the door of the bedroom to see if we were alone and then proceeded to tell me the following incident, which was told to her by Miss Adelaide Still, one of the three persons watching with Mrs. Eddy in the final hours of her human experience. She told me that Miss Still had requested her not to repeat what she was about to tell me because she had promised those in authority at the Boston headquarters of the Christian Science church never to speak of this experience to anyone. I can assure you that by this time I was not only awed but more than moved by what she was relating.

On the night Mrs. Eddy passed, her three valued and beloved workers were with her. They were Miss Adelaide Still, Mrs. Laura Sargent, and Mr. Calvin Frye. On this eventful day in December, 1910 the furnace had ceased to function and a repair man had been summoned to fix it. When he arrived, Mr. Frye and Mrs. Sargent went downstairs to the first floor to admit the repair man. Mr. Frye

> accompanied him to the basement while Mrs. Sargent waited in the front hall. Miss Still was left sitting by Mrs. Eddy's bed. In a short while the furnace was in working order and Mr. Frye and Mrs. Sargent hurried to the second floor to return to their post by Mrs. Eddy's side. As they neared the bedroom they noticed that Miss Still was standing in the doorway. Approaching her side they looked into the bedroom and beheld Mrs. Eddy by the side of the bed smiling at them. Then Mrs. Eddy turned and pointed to the bed where they saw the form of the one they had called mother. As their gaze turned again to Mrs. Eddy she was shaking her head back and forth as if to say, "I am not there; I have risen." Then as these three watched, the vision of their beloved leader gradually faded from their sight. At that moment, as I stood there looking into Mrs. Eddy's bedroom, I felt a wave of insight into the magnitude of Mrs. Eddy's mission I had never felt before. They had witnessed the ascension of their Leader! ... Before we returned to the entrance hall on the main floor, my guide, who had told me her name (which I have forgotten), expressed the importance of what she had related to me. She repeated that she felt impelled to tell me this incident which she had heard from the lips of Miss Adellaide Still — who was her sister. ...

Obviously the students who witnessed this event told it to "those in authority at the Boston headquarters," and it was probably related to a few others in addition to Adelaide Still's sister. Both Laura and Calvin passed away within the next few years, and Miss Still's "official" account differs from the occurrence as she related it to her sister. Perhaps the surprise and disbelief of those in authority was too great to enable them to accept the true account.

Those in authority experienced another surprise, next to disbelief, when they read in Mrs. Eddy's will: "I give and bequeath ... to Mrs. Augusta E. Stetson of New York City, my 'crown of diamonds' breast pin." Those few words brought strength and joy unspeakable to Mrs. Stetson.

Carol Norton's young widow Elizabeth G. Norton was one of the students Mrs. Eddy had selected to attend the Normal Class of 1910 which was scheduled to begin on December 7. The day before the class convened, on Tuesday, December 6 Mrs. Norton and Miss Grace Collins were both at Chestnut Hill. The two women may or may not have thought of the events which transpired on the third day after Jesus' crucifixion:

> Matthew 28:1 In the end of the sabbath, as it began to dawn toward the first day of the week, came Mary Magdalene and the other Mary to see the sepulchre.
>
> 2 And behold there was a great earthquake ...
>
> 5 And the angel ... said unto the women, Fear not ye: for I know that ye seek Jesus, which was crucified.

6 He is not here: for he is risen . . .
7 And go quickly and tell his disciples that he is risen from the dead; . . .
9 And as they went to tell his disciples, behold Jesus met them . . .

This was the third day after Mrs. Eddy's passing and Elizabeth and Grace had come "to see the sepulchre," — that is, they were in the room where the body lay. Calvin Frye and two directors were in the next room. Suddenly there was a great noise, almost like an explosion. The men went to investigate. They went through the house and to the cellar, but found no cause for nor effect from the disturbance.

But the women's experience was entirely different. Immediately following the great noise Mrs. Eddy appeared to Mrs. Norton and Miss Collins. During the Woodbury trial when Mrs. Eddy's attorneys had asked her about the accusation that she considered herself the Woman of the Apocalypse, she had written them that "a white-haired old lady could not be the woman of the Apocalypse." On December 6, 1910 Mrs. Norton and Miss Collins did not see the world's false concept of Mrs. Eddy as "a white-haired old lady." They saw her true being, for the Leader was youthful, dark-haired, beautiful, and radiant. The two women watched as Mrs. Eddy walked across the room and disappeared through the wall. Then Mrs. Norton turned to Miss Collins and said, "Grace, did you see what I saw?" Grace answered, "Yes."

When Elizabeth Norton told the directors what they had seen, they said that it must not be told yet.

Perhaps in 1910 there were not many Christian Scientists who wanted to understand and were willing to follow their Leader. Mrs. Eddy's awareness of this was evident in her words to Mr. McLellan in 1908: "I left house, home, and friends, and I gave up a large salary, as a writer, in order to serve the Cause of Christian Science. I have endured all shame and blame in its behalf, and I have lived these down. This is the experience of your Leader. Are her followers willing to take up their crosses, as she has taken up hers, in order to follow Christ, or do they demand all that they humanly want? Sad, sad thought that money regulates the actions of so many students. Had your Leader been governed thus, Christian Science would be minus today, instead of overcoming all opposition, ruling and reigning."

Dear reader, are you laboring in the Leader's vineyard? If so, then she is speaking to you today the words she spoke to Martha Wilcox in 1910: "Is there any reason why you should not stay with me forever?"

APPENDICES

APPENDICES

APPENDIX A — (Chapter III, page 27) A *Boston Journal* reporter's interview with Edward A. Kimball representing Mary Baker Eddy, published in *The Boston Journal* June 8, 1901, and in the *Christian Science Journal* for July, 1901, Vol. XIX, pages 207-209.

It was for the purpose of making clear the attitude of Rev. Mary Baker Eddy, the Discoverer and Founder of Christian Science, regarding certain points that came out in the testimony submitted by plaintiff in the trial of the Woodbury-Eddy libel case, just finished, that a *Boston Journal* reporter asked Mrs. Eddy for a statement.

Mrs. Eddy referred the matter to Edward A. Kimball of Chicago, who has been on here during the last three months assisting in the preparation of Mrs. Eddy's case in the courts.

Mr. Kimball said: —

"Mrs. Eddy does not wish to make any statement relative to this subject. She has solemnly declared from the first that she did not refer to the plaintiff when writing about the Babylonish woman, and the only dignified and consistent course open to her is to rest peacefully on that declaration, and let others contend if they will."

"What about the statement the Christian Scientists regard her as being infallible?"

"Mrs. Eddy does not believe or teach or want any one else to believe or teach, that she is infallible. She and we believe in the infallibility of God only."

"Does she think that she is the 'woman clothed with the sun' spoken of in Revelation?"

"She does not. She does not teach or want any one to teach that. On the contrary, we do not believe that the word 'woman' means any particular woman, but rather refers to conditions of thought, or the revelations of truth."

"Why did not the witnesses explain what your belief is about Mrs. Eddy?"

"Because there is no formulated belief on the subject. She discovered Christian Science and founded or established 'Christian Science' as a religious belief or faith. It may be said in a general way that Christian Scientists regard her as the one who has perceived this great spiritual science and as one who by reason of her moral and spiritual culture has become the logical, beloved, and well-equipped leader of this denomination. She is generally recognized as being one of the foremost religious teachers of the age. She says that she has never taught, privately or otherwise, any theories concerning generation or any of the phenomena of existence contrary or in addition to those which have been uniformly presented in her classes and stated in her books. In her work *Retrospection and Introspection,* she writes: 'We do not question the authenticity of the Scriptural narrative of the Virgin Mother and Bethlehem babe and the Messianic mission of Christ Jesus, but in our time no Christian Scientist will give chimerical wings to his imagination or advance speculative theories as to the recurrence of such events.'"

"An effort was made to show the exercise of unusual control by her over the affairs of the church. What do you say about that?"

"The by-laws of our church are originated by Mrs. Eddy and adopted, or rejected as may be, by the church. No by-law can be enforced unless the church does enact it. These by-laws do seem to lodge with her considerable discretion or veto power, but this is not for any other purpose than to maintain the integrity of the denomination and its affairs. As a matter of fact, she never exercises any of the privileges provided for, except in the interest of the church; and all our branch churches are independent organizations."

"There is considerable comment about Mrs. Eddy's income and the financial affairs. What are the facts?"

"There are over five hundred church societies in our denomination. None of the usual provisions have been made for the financial support of a central denominational organization, the per capita contributions and pew rent being applied to the immediate expenses of the Mother Church. Other denominations take up quarterly or annual collections for this purpose. We have none. The only money we get for such purposes is derived from the sale of literature, including Mrs. Eddy's works. I think that during the last five years a very large part of her means has been devoted to the advancement of the cause."

"What do you expect to be the result of this verdict?"

"I cannot predict. I am convinced that people generally realize that Mrs. Eddy was ever a tender, loving teacher, intent upon the genuine welfare of her students."

"To whom did your people think the message referred?"

"I do not know. I can only say that I have never yet talked with any one who said he thought it meant a person."

* * *

APPENDIX B — (Chapter VI, page 46) LAST WILL AND TESTAMENT OF MARY BAKER EDDY

Be It Known that I, Mary Baker G. Eddy, of Concord, New Hampshire, being of sound and disposing mind and memory, do make, publish and declare this to be my last will and testament in manner and form following, that is to say;

1. I hereby nominate and appoint Honorable Henry M. Baker, of Bow, New Hampshire, sole executor of this my last will and testament; and having ample confidence in his ability and integrity, I desire that he shall not be required to furnish sureties on his official bond.

2. Having already transferred and given to my son, George W. Glover, of Lead City, South Dakota, four certain mortgage deeds bought of the Farmers Loan and Trust Company, of the state of Kansas, and having already given him a house and lot located in Lead City, South Dakota, and monies at various times, I hereby confirm and ratify said transfers and gifts, and in addition thereto, I give and bequeath to my said son, George W. Glover, the sum of ten thousand dollars.

3. I give and bequeath to George H. Moore of Concord, New Hampshire, the sum of one thousand dollars; to each of the five children of my son, George W. Glover, the sum of ten thousand dollars; to Mrs. Mary A. Baker, of Boston, Massachusetts, widow of my late brother, the sum of five thousand dollars; to Frances A. Baker, of Concord, New Hampshire, the sum of one thousand dollars; to Henrietta E. Chanfrau, of Philadelphia, Penn., the sum of one thousand dollars; to Fred N. Ladd, of Concord, New Hampshire, the sum of three thousand dollars; to my adopted son, Benjamin J. Foster, M.D., the sum of five thousand dollars; to Calvin A. Frye, of Concord, New Hampshire, the sum of ten thousand dollars, provided he continues in my service to the date of my decease; to Pauline Mann, of Concord, New Hampshire, the sum of one thousand dollars, provided she continues in my service to the date of my decease; to Joseph G. Mann, of Concord, New Hampshire, three thousand dollars, provided he continues in my service to the date of my decease; to Laura E. Sargent, of Concord, New Hampshire, three thousand dollars, provided she continues in my service to the date of my decease.

4. I give and bequeath to The Mother Church — First Church of Christ, Scientist, in Boston, Massachusetts, the sum of fifty thousand dollars.

5. I give and devise to Calvin A. Frye and Joseph G. Mann, above named, provided they shall respectively remain in my service to the date of my decease, the right, during the term of their respective natural lives, to occupy and use my homestead and grounds called "Pleasant View," in Concord, New Hampshire, as their residence and home, but the rights hereby conditionally granted to said Frye and Mann shall not be assignable to any other person. Said homestead and grounds connected therewith shall not be leased to, or occupied by, any persons, except as herein provided. No part of said homestead, or lands connected therewith, shall be devoted to any other uses or purposes than those of a home for said Frye and Mann during their respective lives (provided they respectively

remain in my service to the date of my decease) and a home for my grandchildren according to the terms of this will and, after the termination of the rights of said Frye and Mann and my grandchildren as herein provided, as a place for the reception, entertainment, and care of Christian Science visitors and their friends, and to such other purposes looking to the general advancement of the Christian Science religion as may be deemed best by the residuary legatee. All the personal property, except my jewelry, in and about said homestead and lands shall be kept and carefully used on said premises.

In my contract with Edward A. Kimball, of Chicago, dated October 9, 1899, provision is made for the creation of a trust fund for the purpose of procuring an annual revenue or income which shall be used for maintaining in a perpetual state of repair my said homestead. A further provision is also made for that purpose in said contract. If for any reason, sufficient funds for such purposes shall not be provided from the sources named in said contract, then I direct that my residuary legatee shall provide and expend such sums, from time to time, as may be necessary for the purpose of maintaining said homestead and grounds, in a perpetual state of repair and cultivation.

I hereby give and devise to my grandson, George W. Glover, Jr., the right and privilege of living and having a home at Pleasant View and of being supported therein in a reasonable manner at the expense of my estate while he is obtaining his education preparatory to admission to Dartmouth College, providing he shall select and choose to obtain his education at that institution. I also direct my executor to pay all of said George W. Glover, Jr.'s reasonable expenses while at said College, giving him, in the meantime, the privilege of a home at Pleasant View.

I also give and devise to my granddaughters the right and privilege of living and having a home at Pleasant View, and of being supported therein in a reasonable manner at the expense of my estate, while they, or either of them, are obtaining a high school education, provided they, or either of them, desire the advantages of such course.

6. I give and bequeath to the Christian Science Board of Directors of The Mother Church — The First Church of Christ, Scientists, in Boston, Massachusetts — and their successors in office, the sum of one hundred thousand dollars, but nevertheless, in trust for the following purposes, namely; said trustees shall hold, invest, and reinvest the principal of said fund and conservatively manage the same, and shall use the income and such portion of the principal, from time to time, as they may deem best, for the purpose of providing free instruction for indigent, well-educated, worthy Christian Scientists at the Massachusetts Metaphysical College and to aid them thereafter until they can maintain themselves in some department of Christian Science.

I desire that the instruction for which provision is hereby made shall be at the said College, but my said trustees are hereby authorized to provide said instruction elsewhere, if, in the unanimous judgment of all said trustees for the time being, such course shall seem best. The judgment and discretion of said trustees with reference to the person to be aided as herein provided and the amount of aid furnished to each of said persons

The words "in said contract" inserted before signing. — M.B.G. Eddy shall be final and conclusive.

7. I hereby ratify and confirm the following trust agreements and declarations, viz.

(1) The deed of trust dated September 1, 1892, conveying land for church edifice in Boston and on which the building of the First Church of Christ, Scientist, now stands.

(2) The trust agreement dated January 25, 1898, conveying to Edward P. Bates, James A. Neal, and William P. McKenzie, and their successors, the property conveyed to me by the Christian Science Publishing Society, by bill of sale dated January 21, 1898, the said trust being created for the purpose of more effectually promoting and extending the religion of Christian Science as taught by me.

(3) The trust agreement dated February 12, 1898, specifying the objects, purposes, terms, and conditions on which the First Church of Christ, Scientist, in Boston, Massachusetts, shall hold the real estate situated at #385 Commonwealth Avenue, in Boston, Massachusetts, which was conveyed by me to said church on said February 12, 1898.

(4) The trust agreement dated January 31, 1898, whereby certain real estate was conveyed to George H. Moore, Calvin A. Frye, and Ezra M. Buswell, and their successors, and in addition thereto, the sum of one hundred thousand dollars, for the purpose of a Christian Science Church to be erected on said real estate.

(5) The trust agreement dated May 20, 1898, under which the sum of four thousand dollars was transferred to The First Church of Christ, Scientist, in Boston, for the benefit of the children contributors of the Mother's room in said church.

(6) The deed of trust dated December 21, 1895, transferring five hundred dollars to the trustees of Park Cemetery Association, of Tilton, New Hampshire.

8. I give, bequeath and devise all the rest, residue and remainder of my estate, of every kind and description to the Mother Church — The First Church of Christ, Scientist, in Boston, Massachusetts, in trust for the following general purposes; I desire that such portion of the income of my residuary estate as may be necessary shall be used for the purpose of keeping in repair the church building and my former house at #385 Commonwealth Avenue in said Boston, which has been transferred to said Mother Church, and any building or buildings which may be, by necessity or convenience, substituted therefor; and so far as may be necessary, to maintain my said homestead and grounds ("Pleasant View" in Concord, New Hampshire) in a perpetual state of repair and cultivation for the use and purposes heretofore in this will expressed; and I desire that the balance of said income, and such portion of the principal as may be deemed wise, shall be devoted and used by said residuary legatee for the purpose of more effectually promoting and extending the religion of Christian Science as taught by me.

Witness my hand and seal this thirteenth day of September, A.D., 1901.

Mary B. G. Eddy (L.S.)

Signed, sealed and declared by the above named Mary Baker G. Eddy as and for her last will and testament, in the presence of us, who, at her request, in her presence, and in the presence of each other, have subscribed our names as witnesses hereto.

Mary E. Tomlinson
Irving C. Tomlinson
Myron J. Pratt
Alvin B. Cross

BE IT KNOWN that I, Mary Baker G. Eddy, of Concord, New Hampshire, do hereby make, publish and declare a codicil to my last will and testament, originally dated September 13, 1901, a duplicate of said will having been this day re-executed by me upon the discovery of the loss of the original dated September 13, 1901, as aforesaid, in manner following, namely;

1. I hereby revoke the bequest in paragraph numbered 5 of my said will, to Joseph G. Mann, of the right to occupy with Calvin A. Frye my homestead premises known as "Pleasant View," during the lifetime of the said Mann, and I hereby bequeath unto Irving C. Tomlinson, of Concord, New Hampshire, and to his sister Mary E. Tomlinson the right during the term of their respective lives to occupy and use as a home said premises known as "Pleasant View," said occupancy and use by them to be personal to them and not assignable to any other person by them or either of them and shall be exercised with due regard to the rights of other persons named in said will, excepting said Mann, to occupy and enjoy said premises.

2. I give and bequeath to Laura E. Sargent the sum of Five Thousand Dollars ($5,000), this legacy to be in lieu of the legacy provided for her in paragraph numbered 3 of my said will, and to be unconditional.

3. I give, devise and bequeath to the Second Church of Christ, Scientist, in New York City, a sum not exceeding One Hundred and Seventy-five Thousand Dollars ($175,000) sufficient to pay the indebtedness which may exist at the time of my decease upon the church edifice of said Second Church of Christ, Scientist, and direct that said sum of One Hundred and Seventy-five Thousand Dollars ($175,000), or so much thereof as may be necessary for the purpose, shall be applied as soon as may be after my decease to or towards the extinguishment of said indebtedness; if the amount required for this purpose shall not be as much as One Hundred and Seventy-five Thousand Dollars ($175,000), then this legacy shall be limited to the amount actually required.

4. I give and bequeath to Mrs. Pamelia J. Leonard, of Brooklyn, New York, the sum of Three Thousand Dollars ($3,000); to Mrs. Augusta E. Stetson of New York City, my "crown of diamonds" breastpin; to Mrs. Laura Lathrop, of New York City, my diamond cross; to Mrs. Rose Kent, of Jamestown, New York, my gold watch and chain; and to Henry M. Baker, of Bow, New Hampshire, my portrait set in diamonds.

5. Mrs. Mary A. Baker, to whom I have bequeathed Five Thousand Dollars ($5,000), by my will having deceased since the original execution of said will on September 13, 1901, I hereby revoke the legacy therein provided for her.

6. The bequest in my will to Calvin A. Frye is hereby increased to twenty thousand dollars, but subject to the same condition as therein provided.

Paragraph 6 inserted before signing. — Mary Baker G. Eddy

I hereby ratify and reaffirm my will as originally executed on September 13, 1901, and as again executed this day, in all respects except as herein modified.

In witness whereof I have hereunto set my hand and seal at Concord, New Hampshire, this seventh day of November, A.D., 1903.

Mary Baker G. Eddy (L.S.)

Signed, sealed, published and declared by the above named Mary Baker G. Eddy to be a codicil to her last will and testament in presence of us, who at her request, in her presence and in the presence of each other have subscribed our names as witnesses hereto.

Myron J. Pratt
Alvin B. Cross
Calvin C. Hill
34 St. Stephen St., Boston

BE IT KNOWN THAT I, MARY BAKER G. EDDY, of Concord, New Hampshire, do hereby make, publish, and declare this second codicil to my last will and testament originally dated September 15, 1901, a duplicate of said will having been re-executed by me on November 7, 1903, in manner following, namely;

I. I hereby direct and require that the executor of my will shall sell, within three months after his appointment, at public auction or, if he sees fit, at private sale, for such price as he may determine upon and to such purchaser as he may see fit, my real estate in said Concord known as "Pleasant View," consisting of my homestead and the grounds occupied in connection therewith, and I hereby direct that the proceeds of such sale shall be forthwith paid over to the Directors of the First Church of Christ, Scientist, in Boston, Massachusetts, to be used for such purposes in connection with said Church as said Directors may determine. Nothing contained in my will or codicil thereto shall be considered inconsistent with said Church purchasing said real estate, if the Directors may consider it desirable so to do.

I hereby revoke the provision of my will and first codicil providing for the occupancy of said real estate by various persons, the preservation and maintenance thereof at the expense of my estate, and all other provisions of my will and codicil inconsistent with the foregoing direction to my executor to sell said real estate.

II. I hereby give and bequeath to The First Church of Christ, Scientist, in Boston, Massachusetts, all the contents of my said homestead and of the other buildings at "Pleasant View," — except so far as any of the same may be specifically bequeathed in my will and codicils thereto which specific bequests I do not modify by this provision, — the same to be kept or disposed of as may be determined by the Directors of said Church; but I direct that Calvin A. Frye shall have the privilege of selecting from said articles such keepsakes or mementos,not exceeding in intrinsic value the sum of five hundred dollars, as he may desire, and I give and bequeath the same to him when so selected.

III. I hereby direct that said Calvin A. Frye shall be provided with a suitable home in my house at No. 385 Commonwealth Avenue, Boston, if he so desires, he to have the exclusive occupancy of two furnished rooms therein, to be designated by my executor, and to have his board, suitable heat, light, and all other things necessary for his comfortable occupancy of said premises during his natural life, the expense thereof to be provided out of the income from the residue of my estate which I have left to said The First Church of Christ, Scientist, in Boston, Massachusetts.

IV. I give and bequeath to Lydia B. Hall, of Brockton, Massachusetts, the sum of one thousand dollars.

V. I give and bequeath to Irving C. Tomlinson, of said Concord, the note which I hold signed by him, it being my intention hereby to release him from said indebtedness.

In all other respects except as herein specified, I hereby ratify and reaffirm my will and codicil above mentioned.

IN WITNESS WHEREOF I have hereunto set my hand and seal at Concord, New Hampshire, this fourteenth day of May, A.D. 1904.

Mary Baker G. Eddy (L.S.)

Signed, sealed, published and declared by the above named Mary Baker G. Eddy to be a codicil to her last will and testament, in presence of us, who, at her request, in her presence, and in the presence of each other, have subscribed our names as witnesses hereto.

Josiah E. Fernald
Mary E. Thompson
Calvin C. Hill

Suffolk S.S., Dec. 6, 1928
Probate Court
A true copy, attest
John R. Nichols, Asst. Register.

* * *

APPENDIX C — (Chapter XXIV, page 210) AN INTERVIEW WITH REV. MARY BAKER G. EDDY by Sibyl Wilbur in *Boston Herald* of Sunday, June 11, 1905.

I have seen Mrs. Mary Baker G. Eddy. I have conversed with her and secured her answers to a number of questions concerning Christian Science. I have held her hand in mine, felt the touch of her thought, listened to her kindly blessing, and received from her lips a message to the world.

Mrs. Eddy is alive and well, she is in full possession of her mental and physical powers. She has no visible physical malady; she is a beautifully poised woman of advanced years. Her mind is clear and energetic, marvelously alert and delicately attuned. Her eyes are radiant, her voice like a bell. In a word, Mrs. Eddy seems to have reached an adjustment between her physical and spiritual powers which promises to carry her existence through many years to come.

The secret which the world has been trying to wrest from the closely guarded home at Pleasant View, the secret which for several years has been construed to mean illness, physical or mental collapse, and even, by the extremists of worldly-mindedness, the actual dissolution of Mrs. Eddy and the substitution in her place of a representative — this secret has been disclosed, and in its disclosure is a rebuke for all the petty suspicions which have been heaped against a blameless life.

The secret of Pleasant View is no secret at all. It is the plain and simple truth, which any well-ordered mind might readily have fathomed without the necessity of painful intrusion upon the well-earned seclusion of a woman who gave the full measure of her services to humanity before retiring from the theatre of human activities.

At Pleasant View, in Concord, N. H., lives a remarkable woman, over eighty years of age, who is going through the gradual process of completing the spiritualization of her faculties. She is performing the miracle of human life which may be witnessed in any home where dwells a grand old father or mother. She is performing the miracle which the saint-like Leo, the later father of the Catholic Church, performed, when he prolonged his life to a grand old age by isolation from the world, when he had opportunity for the spiritualization of his life by reading, prayer, and contemplation, uttering annually a vigorous and spiritually visioned encyclical.

There is no great palace at Pleasant View, such as is the Vatican at Rome; no house with its hundreds of corridors, its doors opening upon doors, its every passageway guarded with soldiers, to insure quiet and sanctity from intrusion; there is no walled garden extending for miles in which one may walk alone with nature and God, sheltered from the prying eye of vulgar curiosity. There is only a simple cottage home set in a few acres of low-fenced ground. A ring of the front door-bell means that every member of the house is disturbed, and the entrance of a visitor into the cottage hall-way means an actual intrusion upon a family whose chief member is the most influential woman living in the world today.

TRADITIONS SHATTERED BY THE TRUTH

The writer is not a Christian Scientist. It is necessary to confess at the outset that the interview with Mrs. Eddy was desired because Mrs. Eddy had become the object of the most intense curiosity of the public press in America. Every great newspaper in the country has striven within the past few years to get an audience with the head of the Christian Science Church, and, failing in this quest universally, they have built up an office tradition which is as monstrous as it is silly when touched with the dissolvent of truth.

The story which has gradually been built up since Mrs. Eddy retired from active life, over ten years ago, has been that the Christian Science Church was founded on the doctrine of everlasting life on earth; that it has declared that death shall be overcome; that it has not the courage to face the inevitable physical dissolution of its Founder. Therefore, as the world no longer had the privilege of seeing Mrs. Eddy, it was likely, nay, probable that Mrs. Eddy had fallen into physical disability, or had become weak-minded, if indeed she had not already passed away.

There were other stories to the effect that Mrs. Eddy was alive, but that she was daily treated by masseurs and beauty doctors; that the dignity of years was travestied by applications to her person; in a word, that she was tricked out by artificial means to keep up a semblance of youth for the bolstering of the impossible dogma of everlasting youth. A woman's instinct naturally made this point one of especial interest, and, besides, I was determined to be able to give to the world the exact facts.

That the Christian Science Church will not be placed in any predicament for its philosophical teachings in the ultimate demise of its Leader, is made clear by the explanation of the real teaching of Christian Science on this subject of everlasting life, which had been given the writer by an authoritative statement from a member of the Publication Committee. This statement shows the absurdity of the popular misconception of the doctrine.

"We do not claim," said this Christian Scientist, "that it is possible for one to live eternally in the flesh. We accept the Scriptural prophecy that eventually mankind will have attained to such a high degree of spirituality that death will cease to be a phenomenon of human experience. But centuries may pass before such an exalted state is attained by any mortal. Christian Scientists believe, however, that already longevity has increased through their religious teachings, and that it will continue to increase in each successive generation."

This explanation answers effectually the critic who delighted in imagining that the Christian Scientists had got themselves into a corner; and as to the more flippant comment on the artificiality of Mrs. Eddy's personal appearance, it is possible for the writer to assure the loving followers of Mrs. Eddy, that no indignities have been perpetrated against their Leader; that she is surrounded by loving and devoted friends; that she is the mistress of her own house in an undeniable way; that she is growing old as beautifully as any woman ever did.

And after meeting her and her family, I believe that when, in the fulness of time, the curtain of everlasting life is lifted higher, the world will know of it, and that she will pass on to the greater glory with the triumph of Christian faith, and all Christians the world around will be ready to acknowledge that a useful life has closed as fall the cadences of music, as comes the winter solstice after the long glories of autumn closing in upon the harvest of the year. There will be no greater miracle advocated in her behalf by her million of followers than the one great miracle of a good life which comes to each human being out of the womb of time.

SECURING AN INTERVIEW WITH MRS. EDDY

The interview with Mrs. Eddy was not secured without considerable delay, without a long series of arguments with various members of the Governing Board of her Church, without eventually overcoming the opposition of the manager of the Publication Committee, Alfred Farlow, whose offices are in Huntington Chambers, Boston. The attempt to have an interview with Mrs. Eddy was begun in February by *The Boston Herald,* and culminated successfully on Sunday, May 21.

The objection which Mr. Farlow made to giving a letter of introduction to Mrs. Eddy, or her secretaries at Pleasant View, was a very natural one. He said that he had not the authority to make demands on Mrs. Eddy's time, and that he did not like to disturb her with requests which she had repeatedly refused to consider. He said that her days were fully occupied, and that it was his duty to assist in protecting her from intrusion. Nevertheless, Mr. Farlow eventually consented to refer *The Herald's* request to Mrs. Eddy, and endeavor to win her permission for the visit.

The kindly offices of Mr. Farlow resulted in a letter from Mrs. Eddy to *The Herald's* representative. The letter was written on her notepaper, under the embossed seal of her crest, the motto of which is "Vincere aut Mori." The date was March 25, and the letter read: —

"My Dear Madam — You will excuse me, since I must be uniform in declining the honor of calls from newspaper reporters. Christian Science cannot be carried on in certain worldly ways. Accept my thanks and this book. Please read page 464, paragraph 1.

"Sincerely yours, MARY BAKER EDDY."

The letter was written on a typewriter, but the signature was in the clear handwriting of Mrs. Eddy. It is a noticeable fact that it is quite modern in style, and remarkable for one of her years. The letter was accompanied by a copy of Mrs. Eddy's book "Science and Health with Key to the Scriptures," and the paragraph indicated read as follows: — "It has been said to the author: 'The world is benefited by you, but it feels your influence without seeing you. Why do you not make yourself more widely known?' Could her friends know how little time the author has had, in which to make herself outwardly known except through her laborious publications, — and how much time and toil are still required to establish the stately operations of Christian Science, — they would understand why she is so secluded. Others could not take her place, even if willing so to do. She has therefore remained unseen at her post, working for the generations to come, never looking for a present reward."

The message was entirely courteous, but the refusal seemed complete. Yet *The Herald* was not willing to give up its purpose of obtaining some data of interest about Mrs. Eddy.

The proposal was therefore made to Mr. Farlow that *The Herald's* representative be allowed to visit Pleasant View under the guidance of one of the secretaries, go over the house and grounds during Mrs. Eddy's absence on her drives, and, if possible, obtain a glimpse of Mrs. Eddy as she entered or left the carriage.

All during the month of April this request was held in abeyance, and finally it was conditionally denied. The time was not favorable, the secretaries declared, and if a more opportune time did present itself later the request might be granted. Not until the close of May was the matter brought up again, when a reconsideration of certain flippant reports about Mrs. Eddy, and the incomplete and unsatisfactory descriptions of her which had heretofore appeared in print, renewed the interest in *The Herald's* proposed interview on the part of the Publication Committee, while it also increased my own determination in the matter.

When *The Herald's* representative asserted the intention of going to Concord, and seeking what information was obtainable, finding what welcome there might be, the manager of the Publication Committee wrote letters to the secretaries at Pleasant View, and gave the writer of this story a letter of introduction, begging the courtesies of the house and all that the time might warrant, but not including a request for an interview with Mrs. Eddy. With this the writer had to be content.

I have stated the full particulars of these proceedings to show with what jealous care Mrs. Eddy's representatives guard her seclusion, and I now feel that this jealous care is warrantable, and that, even in the face of misunderstandings and also accusation, these representatives do well in so performing their duty and standing to their guns, as it were, in the face of suspicious or unworthy motives. The life of Mrs. Eddy is very precious to the Christian Science Church.

PLEASANT VIEW BUILDINGS AND GROUNDS

The trip to Concord, N. H., from Boston is a pleasant one. The two hours' ride up the valley of the Merrimac River, through the low hills which are as the foothills of the White Mountains, carries one through a rugged farming country and many factory towns to the sober little capital city, with its wide, shaded streets, old-fashioned homes, and many churches. The city lies, as it were in a basin, the rim of which is encircling hills. Old elm trees make roofs of green over the streets, and there is a quiet, sleepy atmosphere about the town.

The public buildings are grouped together in the centre of the city, the capital, the state library, the postoffice, and the city building, with six or eight churches grouped around them. Most of the buildings are of New Hampshire granite, and none are more beautiful than the Christian Science church, which was the gift of Mrs. Eddy to her followers in Concord. This building is built of the virgin stone of a freshly opened quarry, and it is almost as fair as marble in color. It has a great tower, which is plain and four-faced, and recedes from its broad base to a lofty belfry, in which are placed tubular chimes on which old hymns are rung out to the city every Sunday morning.

I arrived in the city Saturday afternoon, and was driven almost immediately out Pleasant Street, past the State Asylum, with its beautiful grounds, past the Odd Fellows' Home, past numerous handsome private homes, until, perhaps a mile from the centre of the city, I reached the grounds of Pleasant View.

The place is to the south and west of the city. One hundred acres slope from the hill road down to the blue river. There is a low granite curbing, surmounted by an ornamental iron fencing. The grounds are laid off like a park, with very careful landscape gardening. There is a sweep of lawn, in the centre of which stands the modest three-storied frame cottage, with its balconies, verandas, and tower effects, giving large window views to the chambers.

There is an ornamental fountain in the foreground, and a circular drive sweeps up to the door from a granite gateway, in which is set a little iron wicket. Beyond the house the lawn slopes to the river, and in various parts of the grounds are large beds of tulips, pansies, hyacinths. Beyond the garden are orchards, which were in full flower at the time of the visit.

From the house a pathway leads toward a miniature lake, on which is built an ornamental boat-house, and here is kept the small skiff in which Mrs. Eddy has sometimes enjoyed drifting about this placid little body of water. The view across the river is beautiful from the windows of Mrs. Eddy's room, and, in fact, from all the rooms on that side of the house. Monadnock rears its purple head some miles away, and directly opposite are the hills of Mrs. Eddy's birthplace.

MR. FRYE, THE FIRST SECRETARY

I dismissed my carriage at the gate and walked across the pebbly walk to the vestibule entrance, over which are stained-glass windows, which give a brightly ornamental effect in the pale green color-scheme of the house. My ring was answered by an elderly lady, who greeted me with a smile, and took my card and letter of introduction to Calvin A. Frye, who is Mrs. Eddy's first secretary. She admitted me and directed me to the parlor, where she left me.

I have spoken of the modest dimensions of the house, but the double parlors, which occupy the eastern half of it on the ground floor, are so arranged as to give an effect of stateliness. They are hung in rose-pink silk brocade, carpeted with white velvet, and curtained with filmy lace at the windows. They are full of sunlight, and contain several handsome paintings, one of which is a three-quarters length portrait of Mrs. Eddy, representing her as standing in the pulpit of her church in Boston.

I had but a moment to observe the exquisite daintiness of the rooms, when Mr. Frye came downstairs and invited me into the library, across the hall. This is a small, square room full of books shut up behind glass doors, with several handsome steel engravings hanging over the cases. The furniture is of leather upholstery, and it is a comfortable, old-fashioned sort of room. Mr. Frye seated himself opposite me, and looked at me thoughtfully for some minutes without speaking. Then he said: —

"I don't want to seem inhospitable to you after your making this trip to Concord, but I cannot do more for you than to let you see our living-rooms, and talk to you for a few minutes. I am busy every day with important work with Mrs. Eddy, and she, of course, cannot be disturbed."

I looked at Mr. Frye in turn, and also remained silent for some time. He is a man of clerical appearance, with hair slightly tinged with gray. He was distinctly disturbed, and perhaps a little annoyed by my visit. He seemed about to frustrate the work of three months by interposing his personal refusal to my quest.

"I want to see the house and the grounds, certainly; all of your home that you can conveniently show me," I replied. "But I also want to see Mrs. Eddy."

"I am not able to command Mrs. Eddy's time. I have told her of your request, and she has not seen fit to grant you an audience," said Mr. Frye. "She is engaged, and does not care to be interrupted."

"Is she engaged with the affairs of the Christian Science Church?"

"She is at present engaged on her own personal affairs, and her secretaries are at work assisting her."

"It was not my intention to inquire as to the exact nature of her business at this moment," I explained. "I merely wished to suggest that the affair upon which I come is of relative importance. I am willing to wait in Concord until such time as Mrs. Eddy will be at leisure to see me. If Mrs. Eddy is ill I will not wait; if Mrs. Eddy is not ill I shall wait with what patience I can find, knowing that you will eventually understand that my business is serious."

Mr. Frye reflected. Presently he said: "As I have told you, I cannot persuade Mrs. Eddy to do anything which she does not wish to do. I will tell her what you say. In the meantime I will have you shown about the place, and I will send you word what Mrs. Eddy decides. I hope the news will be favorable."

At this moment an electric bell rang in the rooms above, and someone came to summon Mr. Frye. I heard a pleasant voice speaking with him, and then the doors closed, and I was left alone to inspect the library if I desired.

After I had looked at two most interesting pictures, the one "Christ or Diana?" the other "Daniel in the Den of Lions," another lady came to see me, a lady whom I afterward found was Mrs. Laura E. Sargent. She had a very pleasant face, and she looked at me with a slightly quizzical smile, as though she were in a mood to tease me about the persistence of all news writers. But she said: —

"If you will come with me I will introduce you to our steward, and he will show you about the grounds and stables."

We passed through the dining-room and kitchen, giving me the opportunity to see that, to the last corner of this house, order, simplicity, and absolute daintiness prevailed. The steward, August Mann, was waiting for us, and he took me in charge.

"Show her all about, everything she wishes to see," said Mrs. Sargent, kindly, and Mr. Mann smiled on me in a large, wholesome way — a smile to dispel the doubts of a Thomas, for he has an open friendly countenance.

APPENDIX C

TOUR MADE WITH THE STEWARD

The stables include a carriage house, horse stables, and cow barns. I was first shown the carriages. Mrs. Eddy's rockaway had just been washed after her daily outing, and I was permitted to sit in it to see how comfortable it was. It is a coupe, hung on especially easy riding springs. It is upholstered in dark green, has silver-mounted lamps, and bears Mrs. Eddy's monogram on the door.

Mrs. Eddy's parasol and a light wrap still lay on the seat. There was a lavender silk knitted handkerchief-bag hanging from the card-case in the front of the carriage, a little clock fixed in the centre of this case, and two crystal bottles set in the wall pockets. These small bottles may have been intended by the makers of the carriage for smelling-salts, perfume, or tiny confectionery, but when I saw them they were empty, and appeared to be merely ornamental fixtures.

The seat of the carriage was especially comfortable, being upholstered with air cushions, and providing a most luxurious and easy resting-place for the back.

"Do you think you could enjoy that in comfort for a long ride?" asked Mr. Mann.

There were several other carriages in the different rooms, an old rockaway which is used on runners in the winter time, but which is far from being a shabby vehicle; a large double-seated surrey for the use of the family, a small runabout, and a top buggy.

On the door leading to the stables there is printed: "Always speak to the horses before entering the stalls."

We entered the stalls, and Mr. Mann duly spoke to each animal, calling each by name. Dolly and Princess are Mrs. Eddy's own carriage horses. They are large, fine-looking animals of seal brown color, but not of any particular blooded stock. There are two other horses — Jerry and Bess, I believe — just ordinary well-fed creatures.

But down at the cow barns we saw two of the daintiest little Jersey heifers that ever browsed on tender grass. They looked like little deer in color and shapeliness, and in beauty of eyes, and came at the call of the steward as though they were great pets.

After fondling the wet noses of the little cows we went up to the greenhouse, and looked at the plants which are being prepared for the gardens, looked at the hotbeds of salads and early garden truck, and then came up across the lawn, which had attained a plushy softness, to investigate a century plant, with its long blue swordlike leaves.

Two or three men were at work grubbing out dandelions from the lawn, and caring for the turf edges of the walks. I had seen two men in the stables, and judge there were several men servants employed about the place. Its careful gardening shows the effects of their work, for the whole place is kept with exquisite care. At a small summer-house in the grounds we stopped, and the steward invited me to pick all the pansies I wanted. Mr. Frye came down to me there, and told the steward to send the carriage to the door to drive me back to the hotel.

"Mrs. Eddy will send you word tomorrow when you may come to see her," he said, and shook me cordially by the hand.

A MESSAGE COMES FROM MRS. EDDY

On Sunday morning I attended service in First Church of Christ, Scientist, in Concord, and after the services, which are unusually brief to one used to a long ritualistic service, I went for a stroll, not yet having received any message.

I was walking in a general way in the direction of Pleasant View, when I saw Mr. Mann driving toward me. He drew up at the curb, and said he was coming to fetch me. Mrs. Eddy had decided to see me for a few minutes at one o'clock. We drove back to the little villa, and this time, as I walked up the driveway, I heard the piano, which someone was playing on softly, and just before my ring a ripple of laughter.

All the foolish fears of a great secret at Pleasant View suddenly dropped from me like a hateful cloak. I perceived the beauty of a happy home life, being lived naturally and agreeably here in this well-ordered, well-kept country residence.

The housekeeper answered my ring on this occasion, and said she would take my card to Mrs. Eddy. I went to the parlor, and there met Mrs. Sargent again and a young man, an under secretary, who has recently gone to Pleasant View. It was he who had been striking the piano keys.

The maid came back to fetch me, and said: "Mrs. Eddy will see you now."

"You are going up with me, are you not?" I asked Mrs. Sargent.

"I will go to the door with you, if you wish it," she replied. "But Mrs. Eddy wishes to see you alone."

"And may I talk with her?"

"Certainly. That is what you are here for," smiled Mrs. Sargent again, with her bit of quizzical playfulness.

We went upstairs to Mrs. Eddy's study, which is in the tower room with the balcony running around the window. Mrs. Sargent left me at the door, and, to my surprise, closed the door after her as she left me. I saw a lady with white hair standing in the window with her back to me. She stood there quietly for a few seconds, and then turned and came toward me. She held out her hand cordially and spoke my name.

She was the rarefied image of that painting in the room below which I had studied so carefully, and every feature was the feature of the photograph which all the world is familiar with as the picture of the Founder of Christian Science. She wore a gown of black silk, with a piece of rare old lace arranged in fichu fashion about her neck. Her hair was perfectly white, and rippled softly away from her face. Her skin had the delicate bloom of a dear old lady's, and, though it was fine and almost transparent, it was in no way artificially touched. The hand which she gave me in greeting was very small and well formed. In stature she must be about five feet, five inches.

"All this fuss to see poor little me," said Mrs. Eddy, looking at me with radiant eyes, and smiling upon me benignantly.

"I feel greatly honored at the privilege granted."

"But why should you, my dear child? Why do so many people wish to see me?"

I could not answer. I felt some way overwhelmed.

"All that I ask of the world now," continued Mrs. Eddy in a voice which had the sweetness of a silver chime about it, "is that it grant me time, time to assimilate myself to God."

Again I was silent, for there was force and decision in every word so gently uttered. The force was like a command from a mind accustomed to be obeyed.

"Are you satisfied, now that you have met me personally, and now that I have acceded to all your requests?"

"I am satisfied," I replied.

"I would that I could satisfy everyone who wishes to see me," went on Mrs. Eddy. "I would that I could entertain them all, take them all to my heart. But I cannot do it. I can only say to those who cherish this ambition, 'Look on Truth and forget my personality.' All that I ask of the world is time."

I lifted Mrs. Eddy's delicate hand to my lips, and bowed in assent to her apparent desire to terminate the interview. She touched my forehead with her fingers, and lifted her hand as though to bless me as I withdrew from the room. My last glimpse of her was as she stood there, erect as youth, dominating in expression, and yet gentle, flowerlike, and very lovable. Her last gesture was a wave of her uplifted hand.

TREASURES IN THE HOUSE

Mr. Frye was waiting down the hall for me, and he took me to the parlor. There I met the assembled family, Mrs. Pamelia J. Leonard, of New York, Mrs. Sargent, and the assistant secretary. Mrs. Eddy had asked them to show me certain of the treasures in the house, and they were waiting to carry out her wishes.

Among these was the gold scroll on which was inscribed the invitation from The Mother Church in Boston for Mrs. Eddy to visit and accept the edifice as a testimonial from the loving hands of four thousand members. This scroll rests in a case upon a table which is covered by a silk embroidered cover, brought from Pekin by Mrs. Conger, wife of the former minister to China, who, as is well known, is a devout Christian Scientist, and who practised her faith among the frightened prisoners at the siege of Pekin during the uprising of the Boxers.

Under this table is a large rug of ostrich tips sent from South America. On another table lies a copy of "Bohemia," done in white vellum, beautifully printed and illuminated, being the second impress of an imperial edition of fifty copies of this work, this number being especially printed for Mrs. Eddy. There is a large tapestry painting on one of the walls, of Jesus as the Good Shepherd, with the inscription, "His banner over me is Love." Another painting which is particularly prized by Mrs. Eddy, having been given her by a student, is "The Angel of the Resurrection."

On the table in the back parlor lie the two silver trowels which were used in laying the cornerstones of the churches of Concord and Boston. The trowel used for the Concord church was given Mrs. Eddy by Lady Victoria Murray, daughter of Lord Dunmore.

In the library is a loving-cup presented by the Executive Members of the Boston Church. This is a beautifully embossed silver urn, in the rim of which are set twelve large pearls. There are also some miniatures in this room of great value and beauty. There are portraits of King Edward and Queen Alexandra of England, and paintings of "The Madonna and Child," and "The Holy Family," done by a pupil of Raphael, and presented to Mrs. Eddy by Lord Abinger. His crest is on the back of the frames, and under this is written, "From Abinger, an admirer, to the Rev. Mary Baker Eddy."

On the wall hangs a Persian rug which was wrought for an empress, and which is valued at $5,000; but no one could quite tell its history. The rug was woven by hand, and required eighteen years in the making. There was an old Bible in this room printed in 1551, and a quaint old clock which seemed to have a history hid away somewhere. There is also a beautiful old clock in the hall, whose silver chimes ring out the quarter hours. It was presented by her Church. Of its kind there are but few in existence.

DAILY LIFE AT "PLEASANT VIEW"

We walked for a few minutes on the rear veranda, while Mrs. Sargent related something of the daily life at "Pleasant View."

"Mrs. Eddy is an early riser," she said. "She has all her meals with great punctuality, coming downstairs for most of them. She is not faddish about her food in any way, has never given up the eating of meat, nor in any way does she show a peculiarity about what she takes for nourishment, though, of course, she has always been very moderate in her appetite. She would like to take more exercise than she does, but there is little seclusion for us in these grounds, as you can see. She can walk here on the veranda, and she takes her daily ride, which is always an hour in length.

"She loves order and regularity above all things, and she likes to have the household affairs move with precision. She also likes to have a family around her, as you see. She sometimes throws aside all other work and writes poetry. Her writing is excellent, and she punctuates each sentence with great care.

"She takes a personal interest in her daily mail, which is voluminous. She answers a great many letters entirely in her own writing, writing rapidly and apparently without effort; but a large number of letters are disposed of by dictation to her secretaries.

"She superintends all the business which is carried on here, supervising all business of her secretaries. Sometimes she spends long periods in contemplation, and she likes to look across the river there to Bow Hill, where she was born. She told a member of the household the other day that she knew every bit of that territory over there, and that she could see seven counties from her window.

"Our life here is very simple, though quite busy. But it is a life consecrated to God, and every day seems to bring a renewed blessing from association with this beautiful life of Mrs. Eddy. She is always gentle, always self-effacing, and only interested in the living of a holy life. We who are spending our days at 'Pleasant View' have the opportunity of growing wonderfully in the tenets of the Christian Science faith."

The carriage was brought around to the door again, and I was driven back to the hotel. The personal interview with Mrs. Eddy has been faithfully described. I left with her secretaries the outline of an interview which Mrs. Eddy agreed to look over at her leisure, and dictate the replies. This included questions which would involve too long a conversation to be held at one time. The questions were later considered, and given to *The Herald* with Mrs. Eddy's comments, as follows: —

QUESTIONS ANSWERED BY MRS. EDDY

Is Christian Science a new religion? Yes, a new old religion and Christianity.

Does it stand in relation to Christianity as Christianity did to Judaism? Somewhat.

Are you, Mrs. Eddy, an interpreter of Jesus' teaching, or have you presented that which is new to his teaching? An interpreter thereof.

Is the textbook of Christian Science the Word of God in the same sense as the Bible is? All Truth is of God, and Christian Science is eternal Truth, demonstrable, based on fixed Principle and rules susceptible of proof.

Is "Science and Health with Key to the Scriptures" a fulfillment of the New Testament promises of a latter-day revelation? It is.

Is Christian Science in antagonism to natural science? No, not to Spiritual Science. There is no material Science.

Does it (Christian Science) discourage the study of it, or any portion of it? It is gained by study and rightness.

Does it (Christian Science) discourage the study of anatomy, physiology, and hygiene? Not of spiritual hygiene.

Does it (Christian Science) deny the existence of disease germs, or merely assert man's superiority over such forces? Denies the existence thereof.

Does Christian Science expect its followers to live immediately as though entirely spiritualized beings? No.

Is it proper for the Christian Scientist to disregard the laws of hygiene, or merely to disregard them if circumstances make it necessary? To disregard all that denies the Allness of God, Spirit, and His laws.

May the Christian Scientist make use of physical culture, use especially nutritive foods, or make use of the fresh-air treatment as aids to physical well-being? No, not necessarily.

Under any conceivable circumstances would the Christian Scientist make use of surgery? Yes, and no.

In the case of infectious disease would the Christian Scientist yield himself to the customary treatment of isolation and disinfection? If the law demands it, yes.

Does Christian Science regard poverty as a manifestation of disease? No.

Is poverty a disease of society or the individual? Of both.

Can the individual, by use of Christian Science, overcome worldly defeat? Yes.

Is there a doctrine taught by Christian Science that evil can be willed against another as well as good? This doctrine is hypnotism. Christian Science can only produce good effects.

Has an evil mind power against a spiritual life? Evil works against all good, if it works at all.

Do you regard death as the great world fear which the human race wills against itself? Yes.

* * *

APPENDIX D — (Chapter XXXVII, page 336) Trust Deed For The Benefit of George W. Glover and Family.

First: I, Mary Baker G. Eddy, of Concord, New Hampshire, do hereby transfer, assign, grant, and convey to Frank S. Streeter, of Concord, New Hampshire, Archibald McLellan, of Boston, Massachusetts, and Irving C. Tomlinson, of Concord, New Hampshire, who are hereby constituted trustees for the purposes herein set forth, the securities enumerated in the schedule hereto annexed, amounting at face value to the sum of one hundred and twenty-five thousand dollars; to hold the above granted and assigned securities, with all the rights and privileges thereto belonging, unto the said Frank S. Streeter, Archibald McLellan and Irving C. Tomlinson, their heirs, successors, and assigns, but, nevertheless, upon the following trusts and conditions, that is to say:

1. I direct my trustees to pay to my son George W. Glover, or for the benefit of my son George and his wife (as in the discretion of my trustees may seem best), the sum of fifteen hundred dollars annually during the lifetime of said George; and, upon his decease, to pay to his said wife, or for her benefit, such an amount annually during the balance of her life as, in the discretion of my said trustees, may seem reasonable for her comfortable support and maintenance; also to pay the taxes and insurance on their homestead in Lead, South Dakota, and keep the buildings thereon in reasonable repair.

2. I direct my trustees to pay to my granddaughter, Mary B. Glover, the sum of five hundred dollars annually until the termination of the trust hereby created or until her decease, if that event shall happen before the termination of the trust.

3. I direct my trustees to pay to my grandson Gershon Glover the sum of five hundred dollars annually during my earthly life.

4. I direct my trustees to pay the reasonable and proper expenses of my grandson George W. Glover in obtaining a liberal college education under the care and supervision of Rev. Irving C. Tomlinson, who shall receive from said trustees a reasonable and proper allowance for his services and expenses in the exercise of such care and supervision; also that my said grandson George W. Glover shall receive from the trustees such an annual allowance as, in their discretion, may seem best, until the termination of the trust hereby created or until his decease if that event shall happen before the termination of the trust.

5. I also direct that my said trustees shall pay the reasonable and proper expenses of my grandson Andrew Jackson Glover in obtaining a thorough school education, not including a college course; also that my said grand-

son Andrew Jackson Glover shall receive from the trustees such an allowance as, in their discretion, may seem best, until the termination of the trust hereby created or until his decease, if that event shall happen before the termination of the trust.

6. I desire that Warren S. Schell, who was the husband of my deceased granddaughter Evelyn T. Glover, shall have a home in said homestead at Lead, South Dakota, so long as he desires and remains unmarried.

Second: I hereby authorize my said trustees, by their unanimous action, to expend such further sums from time to time, as, in their judgment, may seem best, for the benefit of my son George W. Glover, and his wife and their children (my grandchildren), my purpose in making this provision being to provide against unforeseen contingencies and necessities of my son and his wife and my grandchildren which may arise during the continuance of this trust.

Third: This trust shall continue during the life of my son George W. Glover and his wife and at least until my youngest grandchild reaches the age of twenty-one years. Upon the death of my son and his wife and the arrival of the youngest grandchild at the age of twenty-one years, this trust shall terminate and the balance of the trust property then remaining in the hands of my said trustees shall then be paid over to and become the property of my grandchildren, in equal shares, namely, the children of my son George W. Glover and his present wife; *provided,* however, that if any one or more of the beneficiaries under this trust shall directly or indirectly make any contest of opposition to my will or to the disposition of other property by me, all right and interest of such beneficiary or beneficiaries in this trust fund shall thereupon and thereby terminate, and all their interest in this fund shall become a part of my estate and pass to the residuary legatee in my will.

Fourth: I give unto my trustees full power to manage, care for, control, and reinvest said trust property and securities and the income thereof, with all powers necessary or convenient for such purposes, desiring, however, that investments of income and reinvestments of principal shall always be made in bonds or other securities of a conservative character, having regard for the safety of the principal. It is my wish that in the making of investments preference shall be given to state, government, city, and municipal bonds, but I leave this to the judgment and discretion of said trustees, relying on said discretion being conservatively exercised.

Fifth: In case of a vacancy in said board of trustees caused by death, refusal to act, or resignation of any of them or for any other reason, a new trustee or trustees shall be appointed by the chief justice of the Supreme Court of New Hampshire for the time being, preference being given to the nomination of the remaining trustee or trustees.

Sixth: I direct that my trustees shall each be liable only for his own acts in the management of this trust and that no trustee shall be answerable for loss or damage which may happen to the trust property without his own wilful default or misfeasance.

Seventh: I desire said trustees and their successors to furnish a surety bond or bonds and the expense thereof shall be paid from the trust fund.

Eighth: The trustees shall receive five per cent of the income of the trust fund for their personal services as trustees, to be divided between them as they may decide, and shall also be reimbursed for all necessary travelling expenses and all other expenses incurred by them in the management of the trust estate.

In Witness Whereof I have hereunto set my hand and seal this twenty-fifth day of February, 1907.

(Signed) Mary Baker G. Eddy (L.S.)

In the presence of:

HERMANN S. HERING
JOSIAH E. FERNALD

* * *

APPENDIX E — (Chapter XXXVIII, page 344) Deed of Trust for the property of Mary Baker Eddy.

DEED OF TRUST
MARY BAKER G. EDDY TO HENRY M. BAKER,
ARCHIBALD McLELLAN
JOSIAH E. FERNALD.

KNOW ALL MEN BY THESE PRESENTS:

That I, Mary Baker G. Eddy of Concord, New Hampshire, in consideration of one dollar to me paid by Henry M. Baker of Bow, New Hampshire, Archibald McLellan of Boston, Massachusetts, and Josiah E. Fernald of Concord, New Hampshire, who are hereby constituted trustees and attorneys in fact for the purposes hereinafter set forth, do hereby grant, convey, assign, and transfer unto the said Henry M. Baker, Archibald McLellan, and Josiah E. Fernald, their heirs, successors,and assigns all my interest of every kind and description in and to any real estate wherever situated; also all my interest of every kind and description in and to any estate, personal or mixed, which I now own or possess, including stocks, bonds, interests in copyrights, contracts, actions, and causes of action at law or in equity against any person.

TO HAVE AND TO HOLD the above granted and assigned premises, with all the privileges and appurtenances thereto belonging, unto said Henry M. Baker, Archibald McLellan, and Josiah E. Fernald, trustees, to them and their heirs, successors, and assigns; *but, in trust, nevertheless,* for the following purposes and upon the following conditions, viz.:

First: To manage, care for, and control all the above granted real estate and interest therein during my earthly life and, at the termination thereof, to dispose of the same in accordance with the provisions of my last will and the codicils thereto; but I hereby reserve for myself the right of occupancy and use of my homestead, "Pleasant View," in Concord, New Hampshire. I hereby also reserve all household furniture, my printed library, and all horses, carriages, tools, and other articles of use or adornment now being or in use in or about my home premises at "Pleasant View." I hereby also reserve the right to occupy and to rent for my own benefit my two houses at 385 and 387 Commonwealth Avenue, Boston, Mass.

Second: I give unto my trustees full power to manage, care for, control, invest, and reinvest all said trust property and the income thereof with all powers necessary or convenient for such purpose, desiring, however, that investments of income and reinvestments of principal shall always be made in bonds or other securities of a conservative character, having regard for the safety of the principal. It is my wish that, in the making of investments, preference shall be given to the state, government, city, and municipal bonds; but I leave this to the judgment and discretion of said trustees, relying upon said discretion being conservatively exercised.

Third: Said trustees shall pay to me, from time to time, out of the net income of said trust property, (1) such sums as I may need or desire for the purpose of keeping up the homestead "Pleasant View," and paying the expenses thereof and of my household, in the same general way as heretofore; (2) such sums as I may desire for my own personal expenses and for charitable purposes; and (3) such sums as I may personally desire to use for the advancement of the cause and doctrines of Christian Science as taught by me. Said trustees shall also pay and discharge whatever claims and accounts may be outstanding against me at this date.

Fourth: At the termination of my earthly life, this trust shall terminate, and all the personal estate then held by my said trustees shall pass to the executor of my last will and the codicils thereto, to be disposed of in accordance with the provisions thereof.

Fifth: Said trustees are hereby appointed my attorneys in fact and, as such, are hereby vested with full power and authority for me and in my behalf and in behalf of the trust estate hereby created, either in their own names as trustees or in my name, as they shall decide, to bring, appear in, prosecute, defend, and dispose of as in their judgment shall seem best for the protection and preservation of the trust estate, any actions, causes of action, suits at law or in equity, whether now pending or hereafter brought with reference to any matter in which I may be personally interested or the trust estate hereby created in any way affected. And I hereby give to my trustees and attorneys in fact full power and authority to employ attorneys-at-law and other agents in such matters and in all other matters pertaining to the trust estate.

Sixth: In case of a vacancy in said board of trustees, caused by death, refusal to act, or resignation of any of them, or for any reason, a new trustee or trustees shall be appointed by me and, in case I fail to act, said new trustee shall be appointed by the chief justice of the Supreme Court of New Hampshire for the time being, preference being given to the nomination of the remaining trustee or trustees.

Seventh: I direct that my trustees shall be liable only for their own acts in the management of this trust and that no trustee shall be answerable for loss or damage which may happen to the trust property without his own wilful fault or misfeasance.

Eighth: I desire said trustees and their successors to furnish a surety bond or bonds to the amount of five hundred thousand dollars, and the expense thereof shall be paid from the trust funds.

Ninth: The trustees shall receive a reasonable payment from the trust fund for their personal services as such, and shall also be reimbursed for all expenses incurred by them in the management of the trust estate.

Tenth: The trustees shall render to me personally, semi-annual accounts of the trust property and the income and expense thereof.

IN WITNESS WHEREOF, I have hereunto set my hand and seal this sixth day of March, A.D. 1907.

MARY BAKER G. EDDY *[seal]*

Signed and sealed, and delivered in the presence of: FRANK S. STREETER
FRED N. LADD

STATE OF NEW HAMPSHIRE, *ss.*
MERRIMACK

On this sixth day of March, personally appeared the above named Mary Baker G. Eddy and acknowledged the foregoing instrument to be her free act and deed.

Before me: FRANK S. STREETER,
[Notarial seal] Notary Public.

CONCORD, N.H. *March 6, 1907*

We, Henry M. Baker, Archibald McLellan and Josiah E. Fernald, severally accept the foregoing trust and agree to perform the same according to the conditions and terms thereof; but we severally reserve the right to resign said trust.

HENRY M. BAKER,
ARCHIBALD McLELLAN
JOSIAH E. FERNALD,
Trustees.

THE BOND

KNOW ALL MEN BY THESE PRESENTS,

That we, Henry M. Baker of Bow, New Hampshire, Archibald McLellan of Boston, Massachusetts, and Josiah E. Fernald of Concord, New Hampshire, as principals, and the United States Fidelity and Guaranty Company of Baltimore, Maryland, as surety, are held and firmly bound to Mary Baker G. Eddy of Concord, New Hampshire, and her executors in the sum of five hundred thousand dollars to be paid to said Mary Baker G. Eddy or her executors, to the payment whereof we bind ourselves and our heirs, firmly by these presents.

Sealed with our seals and dated the eighteenth day of March, A.D. 1907.

THE CONDITION OF THIS OBLIGATION IS, that

WHEREAS, the said Mary Baker G. Eddy, by deed duly executed and delivered on the sixth day of March, 1907, subject to certain reservations therein named, granted, conveyed, assigned and transferred unto the said Henry M. Baker, Archibald McLellan and Josiah E. Fernald, their heirs, successors and assigns, all the grantor's interest of every kind and description in and to any real estate wherever situated, also all the grantor's interest of every kind and description in and to any estate, personal or mixed, which the grantor then owned or possessed, including stocks, bonds, interest in copyrights, contracts, actions, and causes of action at law or in equity against any person, but, in trust, nevertheless, for the purposes and upon the conditions fully set forth in said trust deed; now, if said Henry M. Baker, Archibald McLellan and Josiah E. Fernald, as such trustees, shall well and truly carry out and perform all the obligations imposed upon them and each of them by and according to the terms, conditions and stipulations set forth in said trust deed, then this obligation shall be void.

HENRY M. BAKER
ARCHIBALD McLELLAN
JOSIAH E. FERNALD
The United States Fidelity
& Guaranty Co.
By Arthur P. Morrill,
Its Attorney-in-Fact

Signed, sealed, and delivered in the presence of:
FRED N. LADD
FRANK S. STREETER

* * *

APPENDIX F — (Chapter XLII, page 380) Edwin J. Park of the *Boston Globe* Interview with Mary Baker Eddy, June 15, 1907 [From *The Boston Globe].*

MRS. EDDY IS KEEN, ALERT.

EDWIN J. PARK

Concord, N.H., June 15. — At her beautiful home, Pleasant View, this afternoon, Mrs. Mary Baker G. Eddy, Discoverer and Founder of Christian Science, for the first time in six years gave a real newspaper interview, and for forty minutes talked not only entertainingly but with animation and keen intelligence on a number of subjects in which she is concerned.

When I make the statement that this was the first real interview Mrs. Eddy has given to a newspaper man in six years, I use the word "real" because I have in mind the fifty-five second meeting which about a dozen — eleven I think was the actual number — of newspaper writers had with Mrs. Eddy at her home on the 30th of October. At that time Mrs. Eddy was in the presence of the reporters for less than a full minute and only a few questions, three or four, as I now recall it, were asked of her. The questions on that occasion were asked by a young woman who had been selected to perform that duty, and while Mrs. Eddy answered them readily, no opportunity was given any of the other writers present to propound any queries of their own or to hear her participate in a sustained conversation.

This afternoon I met Mrs. Eddy under far different and more satisfactory conditions. I was admittted to her study, and sitting in front of and close to her, I had for forty minutes an opportunity for uninterrupted conversation with the famous woman and for observation of her.

MRS. EDDY DID THE TALKING

In the interests of strict accuracy I desire to state at this point that most of the talking was done by Mrs. Eddy, and that my role was principally that of a most interested and earnest listener. The principal part I took in the conversation was occasionally to propound a question. Mrs. Eddy talked fluently and incisively. At no time was she at loss for a word or an idea in conveying her meaning to me. Considering her age — she will be eighty-six years old the 16th day of July — Mrs. Eddy's memory for dates, names, and circumstances seemed to me to be marvelous. In fact her memory in that regard is far superior to mine, as I took occasion to tell her, and I am a great way from being eighty-six years of age.

It is not my purpose to write a brief for Mrs. Eddy nor in her behalf, but to relate with entire truthfulness and as much accuracy as possible what occurred between us at Pleasant View this afternoon. I am not an alienist, and my experience with women eighty-six years of age has been *nil,* but I do desire to say here that if the mental competency of Mrs. Eddy had not been called in question by the "next friends," and if I had met her and talked with her as I did this afternoon, the thought that she was not fully competent mentally would have been the last one that ever would have entered my mind.

It is true that Mrs. Eddy is not robust, physically, and that her hearing is not acute, but her brain is keen and active, and there never is a moment of hesitation in replying to a question nor delay in forming the phraseology in which she answers. The trend of her thoughts remains unbroken, and her alert mind turns instantly from one line of suggested thought to another one put forward to take its place.

QUICK SHIFT OF TOPIC

This afternoon I purposely diverted her mind from one line of thought concerning a question I had asked her in regard to her son, George W. Glover, by suddenly inquiring of her if she personally keeps an oversight of her household and its affairs, and she took up the new idea suggested to her and proceeded to talk upon it with not a moment's delay, her mind grasping the new subject, as dissimilar from the former one as I could think of, almost before I had the question formulated.

Apparently every faculty of Mrs. Eddy, with the single exception of her hearing, is unimpaired. To my mind, one of the most remarkable things she did this afternoon was to read without glasses. When I entered her study she was reading with the naked eyes a typewritten letter from J. R. Mosley of Macon, Ga. It contained a message of sympathy and good cheer and Mrs. Eddy was much pleased by it. She read the letter to me, and later she read to me a selection from her book, Science and Health, printed in small type, as an answer to a question I had propounded to her. Still later, in my presence, she took a copy of Science and Health, which she presented me, and wrote in it my name and "Compliments of the author, Mary Baker G. Eddy." When she came to write my name she took my card in her left hand to make sure of the initial, and read the card without glasses, as she had the typewritten letter and the extract from the printed book.

RECEIVED AT PLEASANT VIEW

I was received at Pleasant View about 1:57 o'clock by Mrs. Laura Sargent, Mrs. Eddy's companion. Mrs. Sargent showed me into the reception room at the easterly side of the hall, the room in which I had seen Mrs. Eddy last October, and in that room I met Archibald McLellan of Boston, one of the three Trustees of Mrs. Eddy's estate. I chatted with Mr. McLellan about two minutes, and then Mrs. Sargent came to the door and said Mrs. Eddy was ready to receive me. Mrs. Sargent showed me to Mrs. Eddy's study at the head of the stairs on the second floor, and I was introduced to Mrs. Eddy. Mrs. Sargent retired.

Mrs. Eddy was sitting in a large easy-chair, in the south-easterly corner of the large room, a writing-desk at either side of her and a magnificent view of the Merrimack valley stretching away to the eastward. When I was presented, Mrs. Eddy arose and stepped forward about three or four feet to meet me, with her right hand outstretched in greeting. Mrs. Eddy grasped my hand firmly and said, —

"Mr. Park, I am very glad to see you. I am glad to welcome you here, for I am aware of the fairness with which you and the *Boston Globe* have treated me."

Mrs. Eddy then stepped back to her own chair, and motioning me to another easy-chair directly in front of her, asked me to be seated. In the brief time the introduction and reception occupied I noticed that Mrs. Eddy, who had only just returned from her daily drive down to the city, was dressed in a black silk dress, with white lace about her throat and wrists, that her lace collar was caught at the throat with a diamond sunburst of great beauty and undoubted value, and that her pose was that of a distinctly self-contained and reliant woman.

READS RAPIDLY AND CLEARLY

When I entered her study Mrs. Eddy was reading a typewritten letter, and she held it in her left hand as she rose to greet me. When she had made me welcome and had resumed her chair, she said, —

"I was just reading a most cheering and comforting letter from Mr. Mosley. I will read it to you," saying which she read me the letter rapidly and clearly. When she had laid the letter aside I remarked that I never had had the pleasure of meeting her personally before, and I said, "You do not appear in public much of late years, Mrs. Eddy. I am sure many people would be glad to see more of you."

"It is quite impossible to do so," she replied.

"Many have wondered that you do not," I ventured.

"The best reason why I do not appear more in public," responded Mrs. Eddy, as she reached out her left hand and took from the desk a well-worn copy of Science and Health, "appears in this book. I will read it to you."

Then, without the aid of glasses and unhesitatingly, she read the following from Science and Health, which I found later in the copy she gave me to be printed on page 464: —

"It has been said to the author, 'The world is benefited by you, but it feels your influence without seeing you. Why do you not make yourself more widely known?' Could her friends know how little time the author has had, in which to make herself outwardly known except through her laborious publications, — and how much time and toil are still required to establish the stately operations of Christian Science, — they would understand why she is so secluded. Others could not take her place, even if willing to do so. She therefore remains unseen patiently at her post, seeking no self-aggrandizement but praying, watching, and working for the redemption of mankind."

"DEAR," IN KIND, MOTHERLY WAY

When she had concluded reading this excerpt Mrs. Eddy laid the copy of her book carefully back on the desk and said, "I shall be glad to present you with a copy of my book. Would you like it?" I replied that I would, and Mrs. Eddy reached for a push-button which hung conveniently at her right hand, and there was an answering ring, three times repeated, in another part of the house. Almost immediately Mrs. Sargent appeared in the doorway and said, "Yes, Mrs. Eddy."

"Please get a copy of Science and Health, dear, for Mr. Park," said Mrs. Eddy, and Mrs. Sargent bowed and disappeared. She returned quickly with the copy of the book, and Mrs. Eddy said, "Thank you, dear." Mrs. Sargent asked if there was anything else Mrs. Eddy wanted, and she replied, "No, dear," and then Mrs. Sargent retired.

"Dear," spoken in a kind, motherly way, appears to be a favorite expression with Mrs. Eddy. At a later time in the afternoon, when she had summoned the Bohemian housekeeper to the study, she called her "Dear," and several times when replying to questions I had asked her, she spoke to me similarly, saying, "Yes, dear," or, "No, dear."

Before I left her this afternoon Mrs. Eddy wrote my name and "Compliments of the author, Mary Baker G. Eddy" on the fly-leaf of the book she gave me. By or on behalf of the "next friends" the authority of Mrs. Eddy's signature to several letters or other documents has been questioned. There can be no question as to her signature in my book. I saw her write it.

TALKS OF HUSBAND'S DEATH

Mrs. Sargent having brought the copy of "Science and Health" which I was to be given, and having retired, I said to Mrs. Eddy:

"You know, of course, of the great interest which has been aroused by the 'next friends' litigation. Won't you tell me something about it? And also something about your son, George W. Glover?"

"You mean the 'next friends' *alias* 'next enemies,' do you not?" she replied, without a moment's hesitation and with a trace of a smile. Then she continued: —

"I was unfortunately situated about the time of the birth of my son. My husband, Maj. George W. Glover, was in business in Charlestown, S.C., where we had gone to live after our marriage. We had not been married quite a year when he went to Wilmington, N.C., on a business trip and I went with him. At Wilmington he was attacked by yellow fever and he died there after nine days.

"The people in Wilmington said that it was unprecedented for a man to live so long with yellow fever, and they attributed his withstanding the disease so long to the prayers of his wife. When my husband died I was in a most distressing predicament, as I was left alone far from my friends. The people there told me that it would be months, perhaps years, before I could get all his affairs settled, and I desired to return to the home of my father at Sanbornton Bridge in this State.

"My husband had been a Mason, and the dear Masons of Wilmington were very kind to me. One of them was chosen to accompany me to my father's house, and he never left me until he had seen me safely inside the door. My son was born at my father's house, but my father married again, and it was not pleasant for me there. You know that old couplet, 'A mother's a mother all the days of her life, but a father's a father until he takes another wife.'

LEAVES FATHER'S HOUSE

"When my son was eight years old I determined to leave my father's house to pursue my literary work, and I selected as the woman best calculated to care for the child, the wife of Simeon Cheney, who was formerly Mahala Sanborn, who had been our nurse and who I knew to be a good girl, kind and tender, and who I knew would take good care of mv boy.

"I was then able to earn fifty dollars a week by my writings, and I had been offered three thousand dollars a year to write for the *Odd Fellows Covenant,* as it was called in those days, published by the United States Lodge of the Odd Fellows. Later the name was changed to the *Odd Fellows Magazine."*

Mrs. Eddy mentioned the names of the different men who were editors of the magazine, and at a point where she paused briefly I remarked: —

"Your memory for names and dates is much better than mine."

Mrs. Eddy leaned forward and said earnestly: —

"You could do it if you tried. It is all a question of the triumph of Mind over matter. You could do it if you tried. I should love to have you for a student."

NEVER FORGOT BOY

Continuing, Mrs. Eddy said: —

"I was very busily engaged in my writings, but I never forgot my boy. He was a very smart boy and the Cheneys grew very fond of him, and they wanted to keep him for their own. I sent them money for his education and support, and I wrote to him many times, but they kept my letters from him, and they told him his mother was dead. The result was that finally, believing me dead and not liking the way in which he was treated at the Cheneys, George ran away. I searched and searched for him, but never could find him, and for a long time I could get no trace of his whereabouts. Finally I heard through a letter from my relative, Mrs. Alexander Tilton of Sanbornton Bridge, that my boy had enlisted in the army and had gone to the front. It was then too late to do anything. George went into the army when he was sixteen and served four years, coming out when he was twenty, and then he went back to the West. I got in communication with him then, and wanted him to come to me, but he preferred the Black Hills. In 1899 I built and furnished him a house in Lead City, S.D., and it is a better house than the one I live in, and I have furnished him money from time to time."

OTHER SUBJECTS INTRODUCED

At a pause in Mrs. Eddy's story concerning her son I suddenly switched the conversation by saying: —

"You have a very beautiful place here, Mrs. Eddy. Do you look after it and personally control your household?"

"No living person," she replied at once, with marked animation, "abridges my rights in this house or governs my actions."

Then I made another abrupt change in the line of thought by saying: "Mrs. Eddy, would you mind telling me what impelled you to place all your property in the hands of your three Trustees at the time you did (March 6)?"

"Certainly not," she said without the slightest hesitation. "I had come to a place where I could not carry on my work of Christian Science and attend to my business affairs. Some nights I had lain awake all night considering my Christian Science work, and then the next day I would be occupied all day with my business affairs, and there had been long growing in my mind the understanding that I must give up one or the other. My mind was too much diverted by business cares to give the thought to Christian Science which that demanded, and finally, a week or a fortnight before I created the trust, I called Laura Sargent into my room and I said: 'Laura, I am going to put my business out of my mind. I cannot go on being pulled one way and the other by material and spiritual matters,' I said, 'I am going with God.' No one but Laura Sargent knew of my decision until I sent for General Streeter and told him what I wanted done.

SELECTION OF TRUSTEES

"I will tell you why I selected each of the Trustees. I selected H. M. Baker because I knew he was a Baker and was honest. I knew him thoroughly and knew that he was capable of my business. I took Archibald McLellan, the editor of my papers, for the next one, because I knew him and that I could trust him. I took Josiah E. Fernald of Concord, who is president of a national bank and who is treasurer of the Old Ladies' Home, and is a man I know personally, for the third one, and I don't believe I could have done better in making my selections. I picked them all out myself and for the reasons I have given you.

"By appointing them Trustees of my estate, I was made safe in my property and was relieved of the burden of caring for my material interests. I was not only relieved of the burden of caring for my business, but I was also relieved of what I call the inconsistency of bearing the burden, for one cannot serve two masters, and I chose the spiritual. I went with God. I have shut out society; I haven't time for it. I have things of more value to my life and to mankind to attend to."

DEVOTED TO HER WORK

"May I ask," I said to Mrs. Eddy, "if you are now at work on additional writings on Christian Science; if you are amplifying what you have already written?"

"Yes, constantly. I am writing and studying, reflecting, all the time. I have dismissed material affairs from my mind wholly and am giving myself altogether to my work."

At this point, although having somewhat abruptly changed the subject of conversation in the same way once or twice before, I said to Mrs. Eddy: —

"Mrs. Eddy, adverting again to the subject of your household, do you wish me to understand that you personally oversee the arrangements and operation of the establishment?"

Inadvertently I had dropped my voice quite low, and Mrs. Eddy did not catch the question offhand. She leaned forward in her chair and said: "What, dear?"

I repeated the question, and she immediately reached for the push-button, which was near her right hand, and I heard the bell ring.

"I will answer you in a few moments," she said smiling.

REFERS TO NEXT FRIENDS' ALLEGATIONS

Pending a response to the bell, and the response was not long in coming,

Mrs. Eddy remarked, referring to the allegations of the next friends that she is not mentally competent, "I think I am *compos mentis,* but I may be mistaken." She smiled when she said this. Then she said: "I look after the house in a general way, and I look after the whole place, too. Why, when they repaired the fountain out there (pointing to the lawn), a short time ago, the men watched my window about all the time to see if I was looking at them, and they found I was. They were very grateful to me for the words of praise I gave them."

When Mrs. Eddy had proceeded thus far there came a response to the call she had sent on the bell, and the response was Mrs. Eddy's housekeeper, a young woman who had been recommended to Mrs. Eddy by a Western Christian Scientist and who is greatly appreciated by Mrs. Eddy.

The housekeeper was plainly flustered at her unexpected summons before the head of the house, and she started in to apologize for her appearance, although there was nothing about it that required an apology. She was a neat, wholesome-looking young woman, in the attire in which she had been at her duties about the house.

"Never mind, dear, you're all right," said Mrs. Eddy, and that quieted the housekeeper somewhat.

DIRECTION OF HOUSEHOLD

Then, as an answer to my question as to whether she really concerns herself, personally, in the matter of looking after the household and the estate at Pleasant View, Mrs. Eddy held this colloquy with the housekeeper: —

Mrs. Eddy — "Are you my housekeeper?"

"Yes, ma'am," affirmed the pleased and radiant girl, bowing and smiling.

"Do I go down stairs and look around every day and see that everything is running smoothly?" asked Mrs. Eddy.

"Yes, ma'am, you surely do," answered the housekeeper.

"Am I careful and observant?" said Mrs. Eddy.

"You surely are, ma'am."

"Have I arranged the furniture and shown just how I wanted it?" pursued Mrs. Eddy.

"Yes, ma'am, you've told me just how everything is to be."

"That will be all, dear," concluded Mrs. Eddy, and the housekeeper bowed herself out.

"My household is very harmonious and very devoted to my interests," continued Mrs. Eddy, after the housekeeper had gone. "Mr. Frye has been with me for twenty-five years, Mrs. Sargent for eighteen, and my cook for fifteen, and they are all most faithful."

As her last act in concluding the interview Mrs. Eddy wrote the inscription in the copy of Science and Health which she presented to me, and as I was leaving her study Mrs. Eddy, showing no signs of fatigue from the interview, which had lasted forty minutes, said: —

"I am very glad to have seen you, Mr. Park."

APPENDIX G — (Chapter XLIII, page 388) Report of Alienist, Dr. Edward French.

Doctor French's visit to Mrs. Eddy was on July 10, 1907, and as a result of his investigation he submitted a brief report. Later, at the request of Mr. Hollis, he furnished this more extended one:

In reply to your favor of July 13 concerning a mental examination made by me of Mrs. Mary Baker G. Eddy on July 10, 1907.

I was given opportunity at Mrs. Mary Baker G. Eddy's home for a full and complete examination into her mental state and responsibility. Her mental application I found good; also concentration. Her memory both for recent and past events was excellent. Her sense of time was excellent. At my request she wrote a letter with my pencil, which was well expressed, logical in construction, and coherent both in language and idea. I asked her many questions concerning personal matters, her business affairs, and received her replies, which in every case I found fully sane and above the average in intelligence and directness. She gave me freely her reasons for appointing trustees, with a personal description of each man selected by her for this trust. I was fully persuaded that there was not the least evidence of mental weakness or inconsistency, and I was impressed with her intelligence and business ability. In my opinion she is mentally capable and competent to manage her own affairs of whatever nature.

* * *

APPENDIX H — (Chapter XLIV, page 397) Interview with Masters at Pleasant View, August 14, 1907.

The visitors were graciously received, and when all were seated Judge Aldrich began the interview by saying in a kindly voice, "Mrs. Eddy, the gentlemen here wish to have an interview with you, and we desire to make this call as comfortable as possible for you, and we want you to let us know if we weary you."

MRS. EDDY: I am very glad to see you and I thank you.

Q. What is your native town?

A. Bow, in New Hampshire. My father's farm lies on the banks of the Merrimack. He did much of his haying in Concord, but the house was in Bow.

Q. How long have you lived in Concord?

A. At this time, do you mean? About twenty years; between eighteen and twenty since I came here, after my marriage and residence in Boston.

Q. Well, the gentlemen present want to ask you some questions, and we all want to make this interview as pleasant for you as possible —

A. Thank you very much.

Q. — and to have regard all the time to your comfort and convenience, and if you feel at all fatigued, we want to have you say so at any time.

A. What?

Q. If you feel fatigued, we want to have you speak of it and let us know.

A. Thank you. I can work hours at my work, day and night, without the slightest fatigue when it is in the line of spiritual labor.

Q. Did you acquire all this property here at the outset, or did you acquire it gradually?

A. I purchased it at the outset and suggested every construction and arrangement of my grounds throughout, and I still attend to it.

Q. How many acres have you?

A. Really, I do not know the number of acres.

Q. Well, that is something that women do not always carry in their minds.

A. This little pond (indicating) was made for me by my friends. It is an artificial pond. I have a little boat down there in the boathouse.

Q. [By DR. JELLY] All this has been done under your direction, has it? The development of this place has all been under your direction, has it?

A. It has. You can ask my foreman, August Mann. He resides in the cottage.

Q. [By DR. JELLY] We shall be glad to take your word for it, Mrs. Eddy, and no one's else.

Q. [By MR. PARKER] Do you raise fruit here on the place? I see you have fruit trees.

A. Yes, sir.

Q. Oh, you do?

A. And there were no trees except pines when I came here. The rest of the trees I have planted, and when I suggested that a large tree be planted they laughed at me, but I said, "Try it and see if it will succeed." Every one of these trees around here [indicating] was planted by myself, — that is, not by myself but by my direction.

Q. [By JUDGE ALDRICH] I have heard now and then that you have taken an interest in public affairs round about Concord and other places in New Hampshire. What about that? I have heard occasionally that you have given money to the city of Concord, and perhaps to other parts of the state, for highways and other institutions. What about that?

A. I have, with great pleasure. When I came here they had no State Fair grounds and very little pavement. A one-horse car moved once an hour. There was very little being done in Concord then compared with what I anticipated when I came. It seemed to be going out, and I admire the apparent vigor and flourishing condition of this dear city now. I had a great desire to build up my native place. Am I talking too much?

Q. No. We are all interested in what you say.

A. They asked me in Boston to remain. Jordan & Marsh, White, and other firms requested me not to leave the city, and they said to me, "Have we not helped you to accumulate money since you have been here?" And I replied, "Have I not helped you?" And they said, "Yes, you have, and that is why we want to have you stay." Then I said, "I want to go home and help my native state a little."

Q. [By DR. JELLY] And that was how long ago, Mrs. Eddy?

A. Between eighteen and twenty years.

Q. Did you go directly to this place then — to this spot?

A. I did, and there was a hut here, a simple hut. I had it moved off and I made what there is here. The house was not built by myself; it was moved from where my cottage is. I built the cottage and moved that house which was then in its place here.

Q. [By MR. PARKER] Did you come direct from Boston here?

A. I did.

Q. To this very place here?

A. Yes, sir. They laughed at me for taking this place, and I said, "You will see, it will be pretty, soon."

Q. Did you live on State Street here in this town? Didn't you live on State Street at a time?

A. I did not at this time, but I have resided on State Street.

Q. When was that, Mrs. Eddy?

A. It was when I — Well, I should think it was about seventeen years ago.

Q. How long did you live there, Mrs. Eddy, on State Street?

A. About two years.

Q. And from State Street you came here?

A. Yes.

Q. Then, when you came from Boston, you came and resided on State Street first, didn't you?

A. I did. I had forgotten that.

Q. And from State Street you moved here?

A. Yes, sir.

Q. [By JUDGE ALDRICH] Some one was telling me that you had given to the public streets, — the improvement of streets in Concord, — is that so?

A. I have, $10,000 at one time.

Q. Where was that expended?

A. It has been expended on this street and on other streets, Main Street and State Street.

Q. Was that done at the suggestion of anybody, or was it your own idea?

A. It was mine. They consulted me with regard to it. My students contributed towards it also and left the decision to me. When I built this church here, I put into it one-half of my property. Mr. Whitcomb, the builder, an honest man, told me it cost over $200,000.

Q. It is a beautiful structure.

A. I think so.

Q. Now about your investments; we will touch on those just a little today, not much. About your investments. You have some income, I suppose, now?

A. Some income, yes.

Q. My life insurance is coming due pretty soon, and I want to make good use of it. What do you consider good investments?

A. I do not put it into life insurance. God insures my life.

Q. I carry a little life insurance and it is coming due, so I am interested, you know. You wouldn't advise my throwing it away, would you? For instance, my life insurance comes due next year.

A. Yes, I respect that. I respect the life insurance; I think it is very valuable to many, but I have not any need of it.

Q. It was not really in that sense that I suggested it. I wanted to get your idea as to what would be a good investment.

A. Yes.

Q. What do you say?

A. Shall I tell you my ideas?

Q. Yes.

A. Trust in God. God is life. God is infinite. Therefore, if we are the image and the likeness of Infinity, we have no beginning and no end, and are His image and likeness; that is my life insurance.

Q. It was not a question of that at all — at least, my thoughts were not running in that particular direction, but, what would be a sound investment of money that comes from life insurance or anything else?

A. Well, I should invest it in the hands, at my age, of trustees that I could vouch for from my own knowledge. And why? Because, when I found my church was gaining over 40,000 members, and the field demanding me all over the world, I could not carry on the letters, make answers to inquiries that were made of me. Then I said, "Which shall I do, carry on this business that belongs to property, or shall I serve God?" And I said — and it came to me from the Bible — "Choose ye this day whom ye will serve. Ye cannot serve God and Mammon." Then I chose, and I said, "So help me God," and I launched out, and I gave my property — I gave $913,000 to the trusteeship, to others for the benefit of my son — no, not for the benefit of my son, but — $913,000 into the trusteeship for myself. For my son I gave $125,000 into trusteeship for himself and for his family.

Q. [By JUDGE ALDRICH] Where did that idea of putting your property into the hands of trustees originate, with yourself or somebody else?

A. Utterly with myself. It came to me in an hour in this room, and I think the first one that I named it to was Laura Sargent, and I said to her, "Do not speak of it, but I feel impressed that it is my duty."

Q. When was that?

A. That was in February, 1907.

Q. Last winter, you mean?

A. I do.

Q. Now this is all interesting and useful, but still I have not quite made myself understood. For instance, without regard to your trusteeship now, if you had a hundred thousand dollars to invest today, and we will lay aside for the purposes of this question the matter of trusteeship, what kind of investments would you consider sound, municipal bonds, or government bonds, or bank stock, or what?

A. I prefer government bonds. I have invested largely in government bonds, and I prefer bonds to stocks. I have not entered into stocks.

Q. Why?

A. Because I did not think it was safe for me. I did not want the trouble of it, that was all. Perhaps I was mistaken, but that is my business sense of it, and the only time I took the advice of a student and went contrary, I lost ten thousand dollars by it.

Q. What was that?

A. That was an investment that was made in property in the West, where the land, they said, was coming up and going to be a great advancement in value, and I lost it, and I never got caught again. I always selected my own investments.

Q. How do you select them now?

A. Now?

Q. Yes.

A. I leave them to my trustees.

Q. Before that?

A. I will tell you. I have books that give definitely the population of the states, and their money values, and I consult these, and when I see they are large enough in population and valuation to warrant an investment I make it.

Q. Well, now, upon what philosophy do you base your calculations upon population? Why do you take population as the standard?

A. Because I think they can sustain their debts and pay them.

Q. Well, I should think that was pretty sound. Would you go West for municipal investments, or would you rather trust yourself in the East, in New England we will say?

A. I would rather trust my trustees now. I do not take those things into consideration.

Q. Dr. Jelly desires that I should ask you, laying aside for the present the matter of trusteeship, what would be your idea, whether there was greater security of investment in Eastern municipalities or Western?

A. The East I should say.

Q. [By DR. JELLY] Mrs. Eddy, are you willing to tell us something about the development of your special religion? Are you willing to tell us about how the matter came about, and how it has existed and developed? It would be interesting to us to know, if you are willing to tell us, about Christian Science. Tell us something about the development of that; are you willing to do it?

A. I would love to do it.

Q. Tell us as fully as you please. I think we would all like to hear it.

A. I was an invalid born in belief, I was always having doctors —

Q. When you say "born in belief," I perhaps do not understand what you mean.

A. I mean born according to human nature, born not of God but of the flesh. That is what I mean. I was an invalid from my birth.

Q. Can you tell us something about the way in which you were an invalid, if you can recollect it?

A. No, I cannot recollect it, only I was considered weak and delicate.

Q. I asked you to tell me something about the development of Christian Science. Will you go on if you please?

A. My father employed M.D.'s of the highest character, and they were estimable men, and they would say — Dr. Renton was one, and he said, and the others said: "Do not doctor your child, she has got too much brains for her body; keep her outdoors. Keep her in exercise, and keep her away from school all you can, and do not give her much medicine." Then it was all allopathy, you know.

Q. Can you tell us how long ago that was, please — about how long? I don't suppose you can tell exactly, but somewhere near.

A. No. I should say I was eighteen years old, perhaps, and it came to me through Dr. Morrill, he was a homeopath, and I had never heard of that before; it was a new subject in New Hampshire, and father said: "I thought he was a fine fellow, but he must have gone mad to have taken up homeopathy." That was the general idea of things then. When Dr. Morrill came to Concord he healed cases that the other M.D.'s did not, and my father employed him, and I got well under his treatment. Then you asked me to tell my footsteps? I said, I will study homeopathy. I did. I was delighted with it. I took a case that a doctress considered hopeless, and I cured the case. It was dropsy; the patient looked like a barrel in the bed, and I cured her. I began to think something about what it was that cured, when the highest attenuation —

Q. What did you say about the highest attenuation?

A. I began with the highest attenuation in which the drug absolutely disappeared, and I sent that attenuation to Dr. Jackson of Boston and asked him if he could discover the origin of that? It was common table salt.

Q. Was it Dr. Charles T. Jackson, the chemist?

A. Yes, sir; and he replied to me, "I cannot find a particle of salt in it."

Q. I knew him personally.

A. Did you?

A. Yes.

A. Then I said, "I will be safe and see if I am deceived," and went to work on a patient. I gave her a high attenuation of medicine, and she took it and recovered rapidly. Then there were symptoms of relapse, and I had been quite interested in homeopathy and thought by giving too much of this diluted, attenuated medicine there might be a crisis produced and difficulty, so I took away the medicine and gave her a single pellet unmedicated, nothing but the sugar pellet, and she went on and gained just the same. At last I said to her, "Now, you need no more medicine; go without it," and she said, "I will." In three days she came to me and said, "I feel some of the old symptoms." I repeated my pellet, not one particle of medicine, and she began to gain again.

That was my first discovery of the Science of Mind. That was a falling apple to me — it made plain to me that mind governed the whole question of her recovery. I was always praying to be kept from sin, and I waited and prayed for God to direct me. The next that I encountered were spiritualists who were claiming to be mediums. I went into their seances to find what they were doing. Shall I go on with this unnecessary detail?

[At this point the Board of Masters stepped out of the room and returned in a few minutes.]

DR. JELLY. I will not trouble you to go into that in any further particulars just now, but Mr. Parker would like to ask you a few questions.

MRS. EDDY. Yes. Shall I continue this subject to show how I entered into the understanding of Christian Science?

DR. JELLY. I will leave that to Mr. Parker.

Q. [By MR. PARKER] I want to talk about every-day affairs. May I?

A. Yes.

Q. If we desire on some other occasion to have a talk with you, we will come again.

A. Thank you.

Q. Mrs. Eddy, you have not travelled much — you have not gone about the state much, have you?

A. No, I have not.

Q. Do you know where I live?

A. No, I do not.

Q. I live in Claremont.

A. In Claremont?

Q. Yes, over on the Connecticut River. We think it is a very beautiful town.

A. Yes, it is, I am told.

Q. In your drives, how far do you drive every day?

A. I am out anywhere from half an hour to an hour.

Q. Do you feel refreshed? Why do you go to drive?

A. Yes, it is a pleasant recreation. It keeps me away from my desk.

Q. Do you feel refreshed when you come back?

A. Yes.

Q. You don't leave your home here; at least you don't go out of town, or out of the city anywhere?

A. No.

Q. Would you have sufficient strength, do you think, to take the train for Boston? Could you do that?

A. I could, but I should not wish to undertake it because I have so much resting upon me here to do.

Q. I see. How many hours in the day do you work in an intellectual way? How many hours in the day do you keep your mind upon your work?

A. Well, I rise in the morning early and have few hours during the day that I am not at work, and I have the care of the house as much as I ever had it.

Q. Now, your intellectual work, or your work in connection with your subject. Do you write? Are you writing? Do you write letters nowadays?

A. I write them or dictate them. Others seldom write letters for me, save through dictation; then I iook them over and see if they are right.

Q. You look them over yourself?

A. Yes, I do.

Q. Is that invariable? Don't you ever let letters go away from you without that?

A. I do not when they pertain to business of my own.

Q. Is that so with regard to your property affairs, that you look over the letters before they are sent away?

A. Yes, unless I know not when they are written.

Q. My attention is called to your last answer. I asked you if you looked over your letters pertaining to your property matters, and you said you did, unless they wrote letters when you didn't know about them.

A. I am answering you there about my action before I constituted the trusteeship.

Q. Yes, but I suppose you have more or less business now, don't you, of a financial character?

A. Yes.

Q. But the large responsibility you put upon your trustees?

A. Yes. Mr. Fernald here is the superintendent of the Old Folks' Home; he is a good man to take care of me, is he not?

Q. Yes, I know him.

A. And I know Henry M. Baker, my cousin, and I certainly know Archibald McLellan, and a better man we do not need to have. Now, I am thinking why cannot we have this all in love and unity and good will to man?

Q. It is. Do you read more or less, Mrs. Eddy?

A. Indeed I do.

Q. You do?

A. Every chance I get, for a rest.

Q. Are you fond of music?

A. I used to be exceedingly, and I have an artificial singer in my house. You know what I mean by that. I will have them show it to you in the vestibule. [Ringing bell for attendant, who responds promptly]

MRS. EDDY. [To the attendant] Tell Mr. Frye to come to me.

THE ATTENDANT. Yes.

MRS. EDDY. It will imitate a voice.

Q. Were you musical in your younger days?

A. Yes. I never was taught, but all the other members of the family were, and yet I would compose music.

[Mr. Frye came in at this point and was introduced to the Board of Masters]

MRS. EDDY. Mr. Frye, I want you to show them my artificial singer.

MR. FRYE. Yes. It is a graphophone, gentlemen.

Q. [By JUDGE ALDRICH] I want to say before going that my mother is still living and she is eighty-seven years of age.

A. Give my love to her.

Q. I will.

A. God bless her. She is not a day older for her eighty-seven years if she is growing in grace.

Q. Well, she feels pretty happy.

A. I have no doubt she is. I mean mere decaying when I say "older." She is rising higher. Decay belongs not to matter but to mortal mind. We do not lose our faculties through matter so much as through mind, do we? Now, my thought is, that if we keep our mind fixed on Truth, God, Life and Love, He will advance us in our years to a higher understanding; He will change our hope into faith, our faith into spiritual understanding, our words into works, and our ultimate into the fruition of entering into the Kingdom.

Q. Well, I will say good afternoon.

A. Pardon my mistakes, if I have made any.

DR. JELLY. Good afternoon, Mrs. Eddy.

MRS. EDDY. Excuse my sitting; come and see me again.

DR. JELLY. We do not want to tire you.

MRS. EDDY. Thank you. [To the stenographer] We have kept you very busy. Thank you for your services.

[After listening to the graphophone a message was brought Judge Aldrich that Mrs. Eddy wanted to see the Board of Masters again, because she thought there was something she had omitted, and thereupon the Masters returned to her room]

MRS. EDDY. I feel that I did not answer you fully; that I dropped my subject before I concluded it with regard to the footsteps to Christian Science. Now, allow me to complete that thought. I got to where I told you I found it was mind instead of the drug that healed —

JUDGE ALDRICH. Let me make one remark. There were two reasons why we suggested we would not pursue that branch of the inquiry any further. One was, that we were a little afraid we might weary you, and the other was that in certain quarters it is suggested that this investigation is an attack on your doctrines, and we did not want to have it appear that we were requiring you to make any statements about it.

MRS. EDDY. Not at all. I shall regard it as a great favor if you will condescend to hear me in this.

JUDGE ALDRICH. If you desire it, we are bound to listen to you — if you desire to express yourself about it.

MRS. EDDY. When I came to the point that it was mind that did the healing, then I wanted to know what mind it was. Was it the Mind which was in Christ Jesus, or was it the human mind and human will?

This led me to investigate spiritualism, mesmerism, and hypnotism, and I failed to find God there; therefore I turned to God in prayer and said, "Just guide me to that mind which is in Christ," and I took the Bible and opened to the words, "Now, go, write it in a book." I can show you where this Scripture is in the Bible.

I then commenced writing my consciousness of what I had seen, and I found that human will was the cause of disease instead of its cure; that neither hypnotism, mesmerism, nor human concepts did heal; they too were the origin of disease instead of its cure; and that the Divine Mind was the Healer; then I found through the Scripture that "He healed all our diseases." Also the command, Go ye into the field, preach the Gospel, heal the sick, and I felt there was my line of labor, and that God did the healing, and that I could no more heal a person by mortal mind, the mind of mortals, or will-power, than by cutting off his head. I know not how to use will-power to hurt the sick.

When people began to talk mesmerism, I doubted it; and I said to a facetious student, "Hanover Smith, you go into another room and see if I can sit here and tell lies enough to make you suffer." He went into another room, and I commenced arguing what they said made folks sick, and I did my best talking it. When he returned to me, I said, "Hanover, do you feel ill?" He replied, "I never felt better in my life than I do now. I feel rested."

A Christian Scientist can no more make a person sick than he can at the same time be a sinner and be a Christian Scientist. He does not knowingly make people suffer or injure them in any way — he has not the power to do it. All the power that Christian Scientists have comes from on High. We have no other power and no faith in any other power.

I thank you for you kindness and attention very much.

* * *

APPENDIX I — (Chapter XLIV, page 398) General Streeter's Address, August 21, 1907.

If your Honors please, in behalf of Mrs. Eddy, my associates, the Attorney-General, Mr. Eastman, and Allen Hollis, join me in presenting the following motion: That the Masters proceed with the hearing, to determine the question submitted, namely, Mrs. Eddy's competency to manage her business affairs March 1, 1907.

Upon this motion I desire to speak briefly, and perhaps more temperately than the circumstances would justify me in speaking.

If we are allowed to proceed we should show you that on February 12 Mrs. Eddy began to arrange for the entire management of her property during her life, and to make liberal provision for her kindred during that time. I will not go into the details of these matters excepting to say to you that if your Honors are not already satisfied we should be able to satisfy you beyond question, not only of Mrs. Eddy's absolute competency to deal with her affairs, but that during the last two weeks of February, the last two weeks before this suit was brought, she was dealing with those questions with sagacity so far as her business matters were concerned, and as a noble Christian woman so far as her next of kin were concerned.

Now, your Honors, neither Mrs. Eddy nor her counsel have the power to prevent her so-called "next friends" from trying to persuade Judge Chamberlin to let them dismiss the bill and get out of court. Neither have we the power to prevent their unconditioned surrender in the middle of this hearing before the Masters.

They volunteered to begin this wretched assault upon the person, property, and religious faith of an aged citizen of New Hampshire, and now, six months later, when their charges have utterly collapsed, they run to cover. This is their legal right, but I speak of the legal right of Mrs. Eddy.

Let me temporarily review the situation. She is an honored citizen of this state, entitled to the protection of its courts. She is the founder and head of a great religious organization, with many hundred thousand devoted followers. On March 1 last, she was living peacefully in her own home, surrounded by faithful friends of her own choice. She was possessed of a large property, acquired almost solely from the sale of her religious writings. It will sometime appear that, after providing liberally for her own kin, she has devoted much of her estate to the promotion of the religious views taught by her. She was a good citizen. She was, and is, entitled to the protection of the law.

On that day, March 1 last, this suit was instituted by a great newspaper which had hired and paid eminent counsel to bring it. It was primarily an attack upon the religious teachings of a great religious leader. A son and an adopted son, inconsiderately loaned the use of their names as "next friends," and the agent of this newspaper who visited the son at Lead City, Dakota, November 29, and the adopted son at Waterbury, Vermont, March 6, and persuaded them to co-operate, is now writing in the presence of your Honors at the reporters' table.

This suit was brought in her name against ten honest men, alleging, first, that she was incompetent to protect her property, and, second, that these ten defendants have wrongfully misappropriated her funds. Not one of these defendants had ever taken a dollar of her money. They have answered under oath. The truth of their answers is admitted. The suit was based on false pretences. The situation was unique in legal history. Mrs. Eddy, in the eye of the law, was not a defendant, although the proceedings were, in fact, being directed solely against her. She was not a plaintiff; the suit was brought against her will. Her trustees, who held and were managing her entire estate under a valid deed, prayed for leave to intervene. Their petition was denied. She personally appealed to the court for protection. She urged that the maintenance of these proceedings by these alleged "next friends" was an abuse of the processes of the court and an unwarranted interference with her constitutional and legal rights, and that she was entitled to speedy relief.

She represented that under the constitution and laws she was of right entitled to a determination of the questions, first, whether her property interests have been and are now fully protected, and whether there is any lawful or just occasion for the maintenance of these proceedings by said "next friends;" and, second, whether the trust deed and the appointment of trustees and attorneys by her was thereby her free and intelligent act and carried out her own wishes; and, third, whether the proceedings were brought in good faith for her personal benefit, and as a citizen she prayed for a speedy determination of these and other questions — all without avail.

These so-called "next friends," her assailants, bitterly opposed her petitions and they were denied. They insisted that her competency should be determined by the court, and their requests were granted against her protests.

You were appointed Masters to pass on the question submitted in your commission.

Knowing that upon the evidence there could be but one outcome of this hearing, she did not hesitate to submit to your decision. She has cooperated with you to obtain a full investigation. She has assented to every suggestion made by the Masters to enable them to arrive at a just decision. She has submitted herself to your personal examination in the presence of counsel for the alleged "next friends," and the stenographic report thereof, inaccurate in many respects, has been given to the world. She has been asked to submit herself to the examination of hostile alienists, and, for the purpose of enabling you to reach a just conclusion in your own way, she has assented to that. Nothing that your Honors thought would aid in the ascertainment of the truth has been objected to by her or her counsel.

This trial has been proceeding five days, and with the exception of her own examination before you, the only evidence submitted is a few letters selected out of thousands written by her, and a few fragments of her other writings. Upon the charge that her money has been misappropriated, that her property was not safeguarded, not one word of testimony has been introduced. The charge that she is incompetent has utterly collapsed, and now these altruists who pretended and represented to the court that they brought this suit as her friends, for her protection and in her interests, have made their public confession to the world.

Under these circumstances, we submit that Mrs. Eddy has a legal right to a finding on the case as it now stands. If you think otherwise, then to a finding upon such further evidence as she may produce.

Any other result will bring reproach, in the eyes of the world, upon the administration of justice here.

I speak, your Honors, not only for Mrs. Eddy, but for every other citizen of this state whose person, property, and religious convictions are now endangered.

In their name, and in the name of this honorable and honored woman, we respectfully demand that a finding of competency be made by your Honors upon this issue, thrust upon her and submitted to your decision by the court.

* * *

APPENDIX J — (Chapter XLIV, page 398) Report of Dr. Allan McLane Hamilton to Newsmen in Concord, New Hampshire.

After the proceedings had been abandoned the following interesting statement was given out by Doctor Hamilton, who was interviewed by a number of the newspaper reporters in attendance at the trial:

I have informed myself in regard to the mental condition of Mrs. Mary Baker G. Eddy, and for this purpose have examined a large number of documents and letters, perhaps one hundred in all, and have examined her at her home, Pleasant View, in this city. I have also read the original bill filed by her "next friends," George W. Glover, *et als.,* and the affidavits presented by them in support of their contention that she is an incompetent. It will appear from the complaint of these people that she is "incapable of so understanding her property rights as to be unable to exercise her free and unbiased will with respect to the same, or to manage her affairs and protect her property with prudence and discretion against the undue influence, control, and fraud of others, and to take charge of and manage the present legal proceedings."

The inspection and examination of autographic letters written by her show inherent evidences of mental vigor. Her mode of expression is logical and connected. Her construction is admirable, and these as well as the typewritten communications emanating from her are the products of an unusually intelligent mind. Not only are their contents responsive, but they show concentration and the exercise of a normal memory. In several of them there are interlineations, corrections, and additions, which convey more fully what she has already said. In her letters to her counsel, which I have read with some care, I find that she has returned to him certain ones with explanatory interlineations, and there has been a promptness and vigor in her replies to his own letters. The handwriting itself is remarkably firm for a person of her age, and there are no mistakes; neither are there omissions. Her words are well formed, and although there is a slight tremor, not uncommon in old people, and possibly because her mind travels faster than her pen, I do not regard this in any way as pathological.

From the large number of letters appended which I have read, there is no mental defect indicated. In those written to Mr. Farlow there is a keen anxiety regarding her copyright, a desire to avoid the violation of the copyright laws, an appreciation of what has been done for her by him, certain directions in regard to the preparation of the literature of the church, and other matters connected with her daily life and her position as the head of the church. I find in the letters addressed to Mr. McLellan the same kind of intellectual good order, and in fact there is no where the remotest suggestion of mental feebleness. My particular interest is with the papers written by her in the period beginning March, 1906, and extending down almost to the present time. These papers, which I understand have been prepared or drafted by her, indicate, either alone or together, a good deal of intellectual strength and consistency, and in this connection I will draw attention to the draft of a trust deed prepared in March, 1906, and another in February, 1907, one of which was the basis for the establishment of a trust for the benefit of George W. Glover and his family.

I have also read the instructions conveyed in the letter of February 12, 1907, which were sent enclosed in a letter written by Mrs.Eddy to her personal counsel, Mr. Streeter, and which led to an extended correspondence. All these things prove that she possessed a continuity of intention and much deliberation, which is, of course, antagonistic to anything impulsive; that she had good and sufficient reasons in the preparation of this trust deed; that there was tenacious purpose in continuing to elaborate and carry out her original idea of providing for her next of kin and in advancing the interests of the Christian Science Church. She showed an ability to direct and criticise others, as to her affairs, and in everything a normal amount of will power, which was exercised in the proper direction. She had the capacity to appreciate details, to correct mistakes, and to see that others were put right, which implied a power of attention that would not exist in an individual of weak mind. She possessed a perfect knowledge of her surroundings and the duties and obligations of those who were serving her.

My visit to her house was made on the afternoon of August 12, at two o'clock. I found her to be an elderly woman of delicate frame, and evidently somewhat affected by the heat. There was, however, no visible indication of any motor symptoms of insanity or nervous disease. Her expression was intelligent and in consonance with what she said and did. She was dignified, though cordial, and possessed a certain sense of humor which led her to perpetrate a joke about the so-called "next friends," to whom she referred as "nexters." There was no tremor, no affectation of speech — I found nothing the matter with her. She fully understood the nature and object of my visit, and was willing to answer my questions. In doing so she did not manifest any excess of feeling, but responded quickly and intelligently in every instance.

The interview was opened by her disavowal of any prejudice against physicians. In fact she said that her cousin was a regular doctor who had become a homeopath, and that her father had believed he was getting crazy because he had adopted this method of practice; but that he, however, had taken care of Mrs. Eddy, who had gotten better, and then she herself commenced a series of experiments, gradually giving more and more feeble medicines, until she gave those with no potency whatever, but her patients got well just the same. She then referred to her exposures of spiritualism, which for a time she became interested in. She said that she had afterwards investigated various religions, at different times criticising the older ministers, and finally adopted the idea that infinite love and salvation were universal; in other words, that she adopted her present faith and that it was the evolution from her earlier experiences.

She referred to the fact that she had done and was performing an enormous amount of work, which I knew to be true. She said that she had no doubt she was going to win in this matter; that her followers had done much to help her, and that she would like to have me on her side. In answer to questions about her affairs, she said that she had put her property into the hands of three trustees, Henry M. Baker, Archibald McLellan, and Mr. Fernald of Concord; that she did this because it was in conformity with her faith, and that no man could serve two masters, God and mammon. She said that she would do this to see that her money would eventually go where she wanted it to go, that is, to the church she had established. She declared that the trustees of the deed were Mr. Baker, Mr. McLellan, and Mr. Fernald; that she had chosen Mr. Baker because he was a good and successful man and to be trusted, and that the others would dispose of her money conscientiously.

She stated that she had taken care of her son, built him a house and furnished it from top to bottom, and had done everything for him; that in February last she had put money in trust for him, and that she had made a trust of one hundred and twenty-five thousand dollars and put it in the hands of "that honest man [pointing to Mr. Streeter] and two others." She referred to the fact that many years before, when her husband died, she asked her son to come home saying, "You are all I have; come and stay with mother, and I will let you have all my property, all my real estate. Here is a home up here, and mother waiting for you, if you will come and live with me." But he refused. She referred to the condition in her trust deed that George Washington Glover and Andrew Jackson were to have different forms of education.

From my knowledge of the case and a careful study of all the letters and documents submitted to me, and from my examination of Mrs. Eddy, I am firmly of the opinion that she is not coerced in any way. In fact, it would appear as if she takes the initiative upon all occasions. The allegations concerning Mrs. Eddy's belief in "malicious animal magnetism" are ridiculous. I am convinced that the words are only used synonymously with "malign influence," "malignant" or "mendacious animal magnetism" and therefore a *facon parler,* as the French say. She certainly has been subject to sufficient annoyance to entertain the fear that she is to be subjected to further disturbance. False reports that she was dead are among these, and her home has been broken into and valuable documents have disappeared.

That she has delusions regarding her son is an absurdity, for only a few days before he brought the suit to have her declared incompetent, she had without suggestion made the trust deed to have him and his family provided for. Mrs. Eddy has no insane delusions, and in print elsewhere simply enunciates the conventional part of her creed which she and eight hundred thousand believe in. No matter how improbable or unacceptable it may prove to be to the community generally, it is no more remarkable than others that have been before or that exist today, and her alleged delusion regarding mesmerism, the non-existence of matter, and the power of healing, form an integral part of very many religious beliefs.

When asked, she said property was mostly in bonds; she said that she could not be tempted to invest in stocks, not even in preferred stocks, and that upon one occasion she had taken the advice of one of her students and had lost ten thousand dollars, and that she has never bought stocks since. When asked if she had been interested in mining stocks, she said, "No, I despise mining stocks." When asked, "Has any one ever tried to make you buy mining stocks?" she replied, "Yes, indeed." When asked who, she replied, "My son." She said that when she bought stocks she always picked out just those she wanted, government or municipal bonds, and that when she selected any, she had a book which she consulted in regard to the population of the chief cities, and that she would find out what the population was before she would take any interest in them, because it was safe to know if the community was responsible. When asked if it made any difference about the size of the cities, she said, "Yes, I found it did," and that she always formed an estimate of their wealth.

Throughout the entire conversation she showed no evidence whatever of mental disease. She did not manifest any delusions, which she probably would have done had she been a paranoiac, as it has been asserted she was, nor did she once refer to malicious animal magnetism, which I understand was alleged to be an evidence of her state of mind. In person she was neat and clean, I am informed is most careful about the condition of her house, quickly noting any changes that may be made in the arrangement of furniture, books, or decoration; that she gives her own orders, manages her own servants, and suggests the selection of food. During my visit I heard the sound of electric bells repeated two or three times, signals evidently being made, and I was informed that this was in accordance with a code she had established for summoning to her the different members of her household. She pays her own bills, sometimes questions the use of provisions, comments upon the change in menu, takes an intelligent interest in the affairs of her native town and the events of the day.

Before leaving, she sent for a copy of her book, "Science and Health," and inscribed her autograph, apologizing for her nervousness in signing her name.

* * *

APPENDIX K — (Chapter XLV, page 403) Interview with W. T. McIntyre of the *New York American,* August 25, 1907.

"I HOLD NO ENMITY," SAYS MRS. EDDY.

Concord, N. H., Aug. 25, — "Persecution cannot last forever. There is always a reaction. But I hold no enmity. Those who have attempted to injure me have gained nothing."

Mrs. Mary Baker G. Eddy uttered this sentiment of Christian forbearance to me today in the first interview she has granted since the collapse of the suits brought by her "next friends."

No one who has talked with Mrs. Eddy can doubt her deep spiritual nature. No one who has met her can fail to be profoundly impressed by her nobility of character.

Mrs. Eddy is old, very old in years and wisdom — yet her heart is still young, for she herself so told me. Indeed she imparted that interesting information with so pretty a smile that youth itself seemed to shine forth from the snow-capped face with the clear blue eyes, and while youth and old age blend in a charming way in the Leader of Christian Science, it is also indisputably true that she is entirely mistress of her mentalities and both physically and mentally a phenomenon. With the exception of a slight deafness she is a woman in full possession of her faculties.

My name as the representative of the *American* was presented to Mrs. Eddy by her cousin and one of her trustees, General Henry M. Baker, who was present during the audience. Some doubt was expressed by General Baker as to the advisability of Mrs. Eddy being interviewed because of her age and the strain which she had undergone. He said, however, that Mrs. Eddy personally desired to see the interviewer save for the thought that she might be considered as showing discrimination and that it was impossible for her to be often interviewed. The matter was finally settled by Mrs. Eddy herself, who informed one of the ladies of her household that she would see me.

I was ushered up the thickly-carpeted stairway of the celebrated "Home of Mystery," which isn't a bit mysterious, but an unusually comfortable New England home, and taken into the apartments of Mrs. Eddy. As I entered the room I saw a white-haired lady of venerable appearance rise smiling from a rocking-chair near a French window, and come forward with outstretched hands, holding herself very straight, and with wonderful light in her eyes she greeted me as follows: —

"I am glad to have you call upon me. Now, won't you sit down here and talk to me." She seated herself beside her literary work table, covered with dozens of letters, a volume of Science and Health, and a book of hymns.

Tears filled her eyes when I told her that there were legions who were not Christian Scientists who rejoiced that the suits against her had collapsed and that her persecution was ended.

In a voice slightly quivering, but of indescribable softness, Mrs. Eddy leaned forward and said: —

"Truth and right will always prevail. Persecution cannot last forever. There is always a reaction. But I hold no enmity. Those who have attempted to injure me have gained nothing.

"But why would they persecute me? All that I ask in the remaining years of my life is peace and quietude. Are not gray hairs sacred? Have I ever injured any one? Am I not to be left alone to pursue that mission in which I am the appointed agent of the divine Being to spread truth and peace and happiness throughout the world?

"I have much work to do and I have consecrated my life to God. That is why I turned my property over to my three trusted trustees. I could not serve both God and mammon. I trust in God, and He will give me strength to accomplish those things which have been marked out for me to do.

"I know that my mission is for all the earth, not alone for my dear devoted followers in Christian Science. I can still do a vast amount of work. All my efforts, all my prayers and tears are for humanity, and the spread of peace and love among mankind.

"There is a tremendous amount of good in the world, and it will not harbor resentments against those who have inflicted ill upon you."

When Mrs. Eddy was told of an old lady of the writer's acquaintance whose reply to a question as to the secret of her youth in old age was that "her heart had never grown old," she smiled and said: —

"Yes, if the heart stays young, old age can never become anything but enobled thereby. Years do not make one grow old if one grows in grace. Decay does not belong to matter so much as to mind. Now I believe that if we kept our mind fixed on God, Truth, Life, and Love, He will advance us in our years to a higher understanding and change our hope into faith and our faith into spiritual understanding, and our words into works, and our ultimate faith into the frution of entering into the kingdom."

Reverting again to the actions brought by her "next friends," Mrs. Eddy failed to mention the name of her son, but she did say that she had received hundreds of letters from her followers denouncing the attack.

"Here is a letter that I have received that I wish you would publish in your great newspapers," Mrs. Eddy said, as she handed me the following from a woman in Chicago. "This letter from my dear friend shows how bitterly grieved are all Christian Scientists over the attack made upon me." The letter follows: —

Mrs. Mary B. Eddy, Concord, N. H. Chicago, Ill., Aug. 20, 1907.

Deeply Revered Leader: — The unmerited persecutions which have been laid upon you during the past few months and your Christly attitude toward them have often called to mind a little incident connected with your presence in Chicago at the association meeting in 1888. A relative of ours, who was not a religious man, had his curiosity aroused by your presentation of the gospel, "with signs following."

He purchased Science and Health and read it with interest, but read it to criticise, and those of his friends who had accepted this new faith dreaded his caustic comments. He early expressed his determination to attend the public lecture which you gave in Central Music Hall, and as he said, to see and hear this "Great I" for himself. He attended and listened very intently. While leaving the hall after your lecture, he turned and said to me in response to a question:

"Do you know, when Mrs. Eddy came on the platform and stood silently before her audience I could not help thinking of that great painting of 'Christ before Pilate.'" Never did he criticise you. He did not unreservedly embrace Christian Science during the few years that he remained on earth, but as far as he knew, always defended it and acknowledged its influence on his life. Again your Christlike bearing of wrongs will win souls. I, too, met you to take your hand, to hear your voice, to look upon your spiritual face.

Humbly and gratefully yours,
Mrs. S. J. FOLLETT

7437 Stewart Avenue.

In commenting upon newspaper attacks made upon her, Mrs. Eddy paid high tribute and thanks to what she characterized as "the eminent sense of fairness of the Hearst newspapers."

As Mrs. Eddy talked on with a singular sweetness of intonation — as her deep, clear eyes brightened with something at once luminous and spiritual — the impression grew of the absurdity of the attempt to discredit her as mentally incompetent.

"Do you not find this a delightful view?" she asked as she waved her hand in the direction of the wide stretch of greenery that rolled undulating to the foothills. "I love to sit here or on the verandas and watch this quiet stretch of countryside. And you know over there at the other end of the valley I was born.

"But you know," Mrs. Eddy continued with a touch of naivete that lends sprightliness to her conversation, "I cannot always sit and dream. I have much work to do — a great correspondence to answer and I am always busy. I rise very early and write many hours of the day. I enjoy driving for a half hour or one hour a day, and then I rest quietly until I begin my work anew."

* * *

APPENDIX L — (Chapter XLV, page 404) Dr. Allan McLane Hamilton's Statement to the *New York Times.*

ADDITIONAL REPORT BY DR. HAMILTON

On his return to New York from Concord, Doctor Hamilton was asked by the "New York Times" for a statement of his views on Mrs. Eddy, and in reply gave out the following:

"There really is no mystery about Mrs. Mary Baker G. Eddy. Her case is a perfectly simple one, and the sensational stories which have been disseminated about her have no foundation in fact — although they can be very easily traced to a spirit of religious persecution that has at last quite overreached itself."

Dr. Allan McLane Hamilton, the expert alienist who has devoted the last month to an exhaustive investigation of the mental condition of the Founder of Christian Science and whose final testimony, given a few days ago, forms an important factor in the withdrawal of the suit against Mrs. Eddy, expresses himself as having no sympathy with the religious teachings of the latter, at the same time that he is emphatic in his belief as to her sanity. Seen yesterday in his picturesque study, forming a long rambling wing in the charming bungalow which he has built for himself amid the Berkshire Hills, one might, it is true, be tempted to take him for a follower of some of the mystic cults of antiquity, whose shadowy influence penetrates various transcendental fads of the day. At the threshold of his home sits a stone idol from India, while in various niches of the room, interspersed with long rows of learned books, are curious relics from Eastern temples, culminating in an ancient statue of the inscrutable Buddha himself. But in spite of these rather suggestive surroundings, mysticism plays no part in the intellectual equipment of the medical expert who has figured in so many famous cases during the last thirty-five years.

"I studied Mrs. Eddy without regard to the peculiar religious system with which she is identified," he said in explanation of the work he has just completed in Concord, "and viewing her in this way, simply as a woman, I have come to the conclusion, as stated in my official report of the case, that she is absolutely normal and possessed of a remarkably clear intellect."

Doctor Hamilton was reminded that other investigators had reached quite a different conclusion regarding Mrs. Eddy, conspicuously the delegation of reporters who interviewed her some months ago in her Concord home and who gathered the impression on that occasion that she was mentally dependent on certain members of her household.

"One journalistic inquisitor," he replied, with a suggestive twinkle of the eye, "is frequently enough to perturb an ordinarily sane person. What can you expect, therefore, when an army of them is suddenly let loose upon you? The placidity of the Buddha yonder might be ruffled by such an invasion — and I am not at all surprised that a lady eighty-six years old was agitated, to say the least, by the ordeal!

"When I met Mrs. Eddy a few weeks ago I had quite a different experience from that reported by many of her interviewers. Remember, I had the experience of the newspaper reporters in my mind and I was thus naturally on the lookout for evidence of the mental weakness in her which they claimed to have discovered.

"I found Mrs. Eddy, on the occasion to which I allude, seated in a comfortable armchair in her study, a large back room on the second floor of her house. She was simply attired in a dark dress and light sacque, relieved by a simple ornament, a diamond brooch. Her white hair was worn in the style made familiar by her pictures. Her face was thin, as was her body. I was immediately impressed with the extraordinary intelligence shown in her eyes. In aged persons the eyes are apt to appear dimmed, contracted, and lacking in expression. With Mrs. Eddy, however, they are large, dark, and at times almost luminous in appearance.

"As she talked to me, or answered my questions, the play of expression on her features evinced unusual intelligence, and was in strict keeping with what she said. Her whole bearing was dignified and reserved, in perfect accord with what one would expect in a woman of education and refinement.

"The day upon which my interview took place was, unhappily for us both, the very hottest of the season. Hence my visit was not prolonged beyond the limit of about half an hour.

"As for our conversation, it covered a wide range of topics. Mrs. Eddy knew, of course, the purpose of my visit, and she very amiably answered all my questions bearing on her mental condition. In her turn she told me about her religious beliefs, giving me a sort of general summary of the Christian Science faith. It was a kindly talk throughout, and my venerable hostess manifested no ill feeling against any of the 'next friends' (to whom she jokingly alluded as 'nexters') who were attacking her in the courts, although she did appear to be hurt by the fact that the granddaughter who was associated in the proceedings against her was nevertheless a member of The Christian Science Church.

"For obvious reasons, arising from the nature of the suit that was brought against her, our conversation dealt largely with business matters in which she was personally interested. On these subjects she showed great shrewdness and a knowledge evidently gained from long experience. Thus, she talked readily about various investments she had made, assuring me, among other things, that nowadays she never buys stocks, because she had once lost the sum of ten thousand dollars through a stock transaction into which she entered at the suggestion of one of her students. But she has a liking for the purchase of bonds — preferably municipal bonds — and to help her in this direction she said that she was in the habit of consulting a little book of hers which furnished her with statistics as to population, real estate values, and other data from the various cities which offered a field for the investment of her capital. As to future investments, she told me that she expected to leave all such operations in the hands of the trustees whom she had appointed to take this burden from her shoulders.

"I must confess that I approached this conference with Mrs. Eddy in a decidedly prejudiced state of mind. I had read the current abuse of her that one finds in the magazines and newspapers, and from this reading had become imbued with a distinctly adverse feeling toward Christian Science and its chief exponent. But when I saw and talked with the latter, and read and analyzed her correspondence, I experienced a complete revulsion of feeling, and this to such an extent that I have now become candidly of the opinion that Mrs. Eddy is not only sincere in all she says and does, but I believe also, that she unselfishly spends her money for the perpetuation of a church which, in her estimation, is destined to play an important part in the betterment of humanity — nor have I found that she is guilty of any extravagant indulgences such as one might look for were her motives less pure.

"In regard to Mrs. Eddy's daily life, the position which she occupies in her own household, there have, of course, been many conflicting rumors, all tending to depreciate her own individuality and variously describing her as a non-entity, a dummy in the hands of others. My investigations, extending over a month in Concord, have convinced me that the real truth is quite the reverse of these rumors. As a matter of fact, Mrs. Eddy's personality is an exceedingly strong one, and she has succeeded in impressing it on all around her.

"Mrs. Eddy lives in a very simple, unpretentious frame house, with a somewhat showy Francis I. tower, in the environs of Concord on the road to St. Paul's School. The grounds, consisting of eight or ten acres, are situated on the crest of a hill overlooking an exquisite landscape, and have been attractively laid out, under her direction. The interior furnishings of the house are costly, but simple and in good taste. The room in which I talked with her was such as one would expect to find, with its carefully selected books and paintings and prettily arranged flowers, presided over by a woman of her dignity and refinement. She herself, I discovered, far from being a mere visionary, is an excellent housekeeper, taking the keenest interest in the disposition of all her affairs and belongings. She is accustomed to give minute directions about all the details of her household. She selects the food for her table; she supervises the work of her retainers. In her study she has a separate set of signals, numbering seven or eight, for each person who lives with her. All of these people are absolutely devoted to her, and she seems to exert a marked influence over them. The idea that this strong-minded woman is ever a victim of coercion is manifestly absurd.

"Her own daily life is run on a thoroughly systematized set of rules. At six o'clock she is up and attending to her household affairs, after which she dictates to her stenographer or writes with her own hand. Every day she takes a drive in a closed carriage, accompanied by one of her household, who sits on the box with the driver.

"In her ordinary conversation she is witty, a bit satirical, but with a great gentleness in her demeanor to those around her. In the town where she lives she has spent a large amount of money in municipal improvements and for the beautifying of the church which was dedicated a short time ago.

"Mrs. Eddy has led, and still leads, a secluded life; but that is in accordance with the religious belief which she has adopted. For a woman of her age I do not hesitate to say that she is physically and mentally phenomenal. In the matter of her longevity some Christian Scientists have gone so far as to assert that she will never die. She herself, however, does not hold to any such ridiculous belief, but refers frequently to the life after death as a state of existence to which she is liable. I fancy that the belief among some of her followers involving the indefinite continuance of her earthly life arises purely from the visible evidence of Mrs. Eddy's great vitality and the absence of any of the usual tokens of mental breakdown natural to one of her great age.

"There is certainly no sign as yet of the coming of this breakdown. Nor can Mrs. Eddy's religious teachings, strange and unreasonable though they may be, be advanced as a pathological evidence of mental debility. After all, her teachings are merely a culmination, a crystallization, of similar systems that have been cropping up during the last half-century under the leadership of such enthusiasts as Noyes, Cullis, Simpson, Boardman, and a score of others who, influenced by a certain phase of idealistic philosophy, have denied the reality of matter and disease. In this country every one is entitled to hold whatever religious belief he or she may choose; and this being so there seems to be a manifest injustice in taxing so excellent and capable a woman as Mrs. Eddy with any form of insanity."

* * *

APPENDIX M — (Chapter LVIII, page 525) Letter to Mary Baker Eddy from Augusta E. Stetson, July 24, 1909.

7 West 96th Street, New York City
July 24, 1909

Reverend MARY BAKER EDDY,
Chestnut Hill, Brookline, Mass.

My precious Leader: —

Your dear letter of to-day is before me. I thank you for your continued watch-care during this perilous passage (through material sense to Soul) from the will of the flesh, or human energy, which embodies itself in physical personality, to the will of God, or divine energy, which dissolves finite personality together with all the phenomena of the carnal mind, and reveals Spirit, God, as the only creator, and man as His image and likeness, the compound idea or divine personality, the reflection of the infinite Person.

In your *Message to The Mother Church for 1901,* page 41, I read:

> Do Christian Scientists believe in personality? They do, but their personality is defined spiritually, not materially — by Mind, not by matter. We do not blot out the material race of Adam, but leave all sin to God's fiat — self-extinction, and to the final manifestation of the real spiritual man and universe. We believe, according to the Scriptures, that God is infinite Spirit or Person, and man is His image and likeness: therefore man reflects Spirit, not matter.

I have always tried to teach my students to differentiate between finite and infinite personality, between the physical personality, which is the image of the beast or so-called mortal mind, specifically named animal magnetism, and the divine personality, which is the image of God — the spiritual idea or Christ. By failing to discern this difference some of my students in the past have lost "the way." "Jesus demonstrated Christ" *(Science and Health,* p. 332). He showed the way by which humanity could escape from the bondage of fleshly personality; he designated the Christ as "the way" when he said, "No man cometh unto the Father, but by me," and "He that hath seen me [the spiritual idea or my individuality] hath seen the Father."

The sensuous world refused, and continues to refuse, to follow and obey the impersonal Christ which Jesus and you, my beloved Leader, have declared. They held him in the bonds of personal sense. The wise see you today as the Messiah, or the Anointed of God to this age, fulfilling the law of Love. They do not deify your *human* personality, but will not lose sight of your *spiritual individuality,* or God with us. Although all of my students have been taught this, doubtless some have not assimilated it.

In your letter to me, which was published in the *Sentinel* of July 17th, you thanked me for acknowledging you as my Leader. I have always delighted to revere, follow, and obey you as my Leader, to whom I pay loving, loyal allegiance. I am abiding by the divine rules laid down in your writings, and am following your Christly example so far as Love reflected in love illumines the way. This sincere endeavor to possess the Mind of

Christ must bring its blessing. Your comforting assurance that I am "aware that animal magnetism is the opposite of divine Science" (Christian Science Journal, vol. xxvii, p. 313) gives me renewed courage to wield the two-edged sword of Truth and Love with intent to decapitate this opponent, the beast and false prophet; for the lie, lust, and hypocrisy, which contend against innocence and truth — the Lamb of Love, shall not continue to engender and develop, for God worketh with us.

Precious Leader, I am watching and praying that "the enemy of good" cannot "separate" me from you, my Leader and Teacher. "For I am persuaded, that neither death, nor life, nor angels, nor principalities, nor powers, nor things present, nor things to come, nor height, nor depth, nor any other creature, shall be able to separate us [me] from the love of God, which is in Christ Jesus our Lord" — and Mary Baker Eddy, my beloved Leader, "and best earthly friend."

I have always taught my students to love and reverence you as the one whom God has appointed to voice His Word to this age.

My students know that I am endeavoring to obey your teaching and demonstrate Christ, and for this reason they, in turn, have confidence in me as a teacher and demonstrator of Christian Science. For twenty-five years, "the enemy of good" has been using every subtle suggestion to separate me from the Christ which you represent, and are demonstrating, but it has signally and utterly failed. If my students have shown more zeal than wisdom in expressing their love for their Leader, and for their teacher, I will try still further to warn them of the danger of deifying *physical* personality. I believe, however, that they are clear on the fact that "none is good, save one, that is, God," and His idea, and that "I can of mine own self [material self] do nothing," "But the Father that dwelleth in me [in my spiritual individuality], He doeth the works."

As you continue to demonstrate the "infinite calculus defining the line, plane, space, and fourth dimension of Spirit" *(Miscellaneous Writings,* p. 22), may wisdom enable me to maintain, through you, God's idea, the consciousness of my unity with Him. This I believe I have always done in the letter, and in an ever increasing degree in the spirit. I have taught my students to look straight at and through the brazen serpent of *false* personality, and to behold the immortal idea, man where the mortal seems to be. Malicious animal magnetism still persists in its efforts, by its indiscriminate denunciation of personality in general, to slay the spiritual idea, Christian Science, to which you have given birth. I understand your teachings to mean that we must judge righteous judgment, and discern between the false and the true, so that, when bidden by the Lord of the harvest, we may bind the tares into bundles to be burned, while we gather the wheat into the garner. No man can serve two masters, but every man must serve one master, Christ.

The Scriptures show us that in every age God has spoken through a person. Abraham, Moses, Samuel, David, Jesus, and Mary Baker Eddy, are some of the human names by which God's chosen representatives have been known in history. You refer to this fact in *Miscellaneous Writings,* page 308, "personal revelators will take their proper place in history, but will not be deified."

THE FOREVER LEADER

Beloved Leader, you are ever speaking to my heart, "Awake!" and I reply,

I will listen for Thy voice,
  Lest my footsteps stray;
I will follow and rejoice
  All the rugged way.

Your loving child,
AUGUSTA

INDEX

INDEX

BIBLIOGRAPHY: *Author Title Publisher Copyright #vol # pages Edition*

Armstrong, Joseph The Mother Church Christian Science Publishing Society 1897 103 second

Baker, Alfred E., M.D., C.S.D. Instruction in Metaphysics Carpenter, Gilbert C., Jr., C.S.B. 45 first

Bancroft, Samuel Putnam Mrs. Eddy As I Knew Her In 1870 Longyear Foundation 1923 127 first

Bates, Edward P. Reminiscences... Construction of The Mother Church ... The Gethsemane Foundation, St. Maries, Idaho pub.-1989 40 second

Bates, Ernest Sutherland, P.H.D. & John V. Dittemore Mary Baker Eddy, The Truth and the Tradition Alfred A. Knopf 1932 512 first

Beals, Ann Crisis in the Christian Science Church Ann Beals, P.O. Box 801143, Santa Clarita, California 91380 1978 145 first

Beasley, Norman, The Continuing SPIRIT, Duell, Sloan&Pierce, N.Y.1956 403 1st

Beasley, Norman The Cross and The Crown Duell, Sloan & Pierce, N.Y. and Little, Brown & Co., Boston 1952 664 first

Beasley, Norman , (© by Meredith Publishing Co.) Mary Baker Eddy Duell, Sloan & Pierce, N.Y. 1963 371 first

Braden, Charles S. Christian Science Today; Power, Policy, Practice Southern Methodist University Press, Dallas 1958 SMU 432 first

Brisbane, Arthur Mary B. G. Eddy, The Ball Publishing Co., Boston 1908 64 first

Brisbane, Arthur What Mrs. Eddy Said to Arthur Brisbane M. E. Paige, Publisher, 33 W. 42nd St., NewYork 1930 64

Brosang, Ernest J. , A Christian Science Library, Ernest J. Brosang 1990 214 first

Byrum, E. E. Miracles and Healing Gospel Trumpet Company 1919 302 first

Caldwell, Sallie Bowman Mary Baker Eddy Christian Science Publishing Society 1936, 1942 20 first

Canham, Erwin D. The Christian Science Monitor: To injure no man, but to bless all mankind. The Newcomen Society in North America, 1954 28 first

Carpenter, Gilbert C., C.S.B., & GCC, Jr., C.S.B. Mary Baker Eddy, Her Spiritual Footsteps Carpenter, Gilbert C., Jr., C.S.B. 1934 432 first

Carpenter, Gilbert C., Jr., C.S.B. On the First Evening in February of 1866 ...The Carpenter Foundation 2 first

Carpenter, Gilbert C., Jr., C.S.B., COP-Rhode Island Questions and Answers on Christian Science, Newport County Sentinel, Tiverton, R.I. 1932 128 first

Carpenter, Gilbert Congdon, C.S.B., G. C. C., Jr., C.S.B. Poems of Spiritual Thought Gilbert C. Carpenter, Jr., C.S.B. 1933 30 first

Carpenter, Jr., Gilbert C., C.S.B. 500 Watching Points for advancing students of Christian Science Gilbert C. Carpenter, Jr., C.S.B. 1942 317 first

Carpenter, Jr., Gilbert C., C.S.B. Address on Christian Science The Newport County Sentinel, Tiverton, Rhode Island 1932 32 first

Chanfrau, Henrietta Remin. of Mary Baker Eddy The Gethsemane Found., St. Maries, Idaho 1994 12, second

Christian Science Publishing Society Editorial Comments on the Life and Work of Mary Baker Eddy CSPS 1911 132 first

Christian Science Publishing Society Landmarks from Bow to Boston Christian Science Publishing Society 1948 N.P. fourth+

Christian Science Publishing Society Mary Baker Eddy Mentioned Them Christian Science Publishing Society 1961 239 first

Christian Science Publishing Society Permanancy of The Mother Church and Its Manual-Revised Edition CSPS 1954 28 Revised

Christian Science Publishing Society We Knew Mary Baker Eddy-Volume I Christian Science Publishing Society 1943 1/4 87 first

Christian Science Publishing Society We Knew Mary Baker Eddy-Volume II Christian Science Publishing Society 1950 2/4 75 first

Christian Science Publishing Society We Knew Mary Baker Eddy-Volume III Christian Science Publishing Society 1953 3/4 96 first

Christian Science Publishing Society We Knew Mary Baker Eddy-Volume IV Christian Science Publishing Society 1972 4/4 110 first

Christian Science Publishing Society - 12 authors Mary Baker Eddy, A centennial appreciation Christian Science Publishing Society 1965 115 first

Compilation from Ladies Home Jour. & C.S. Monitor America's Twelve Great Women Leaders during the Last ... Associated Authors Service, 222 West Adams St., Chicago, IL 1933 55 Century of Prog.

Covington, Benjamin N. A Clarion Call Benjamin N. Covington, Atlanta, Georgia 1985 53 first

d'Humy, Fernand E. Mary Baker Eddy Fulills Prophecy Library Publishers, New York 1953 217 first

d'Humy, Fernand E. Mary Baker Eddy, in a new light Library Publishers, New York 1952 181 first

Dakin, Edwin Franden MRS. EDDY, The Biography of a Virginal Mind Charles Scribner's Sons, N.Y., London 1929 553 first

Dickey, Adam H., C.S.D. Memoirs of Mary Baker Eddy, Lillian S. Dickey, C.S.B., Brookline, Mass. 1927 141 first

Eddy, Mary Baker, Collectanea of Items by and about Mary Baker Eddy Carpenter, Gilbert C., Jr., C.S.B. 193 248 first

Eddy, Mary Baker Essays on Christian Science ascribed to Mary Baker Eddy Carpenter, Gilbert C., Jr. C.S.B. 158 first

Eddy, Mary Baker First Church of Christ, Scientist and Miscellany Allison V. Stewart, Boston, Mass. 1913 364

Eddy, Mary Baker Footprints Fadeless Joseph Armstrong, 95 Falmouth St. (orig.), GCC, Jr. 1902 67 First

Eddy, Mary Baker Fragments Gathered From Unpublished Items Gilbert C. Carpenter, Jr., C.S.B. 1947 208 first

Eddy, Mary Baker Instruction in Metaphysics, Gilbert C. Carpenter, Jr., C.S.B. 45

Eddy, Mary Baker Items by and about Mary Baker Eddy culled from the press Carpenter, Gilbert C., Jr. C.S.B. 1961 116+40 first

Eddy, Mary Baker Notes on the Course in Divinity recorded by Lida Fitzpatrick, 1903,4,7 Carpenter, Gilbert C., Jr. C.S.B. 60 second

Eddy, Mary Baker, Poems, Mary Baker Eddy (priv. printed) 1910 79 Presentation

Eddy, Mary Baker Repaid Pages, Mary Baker Eddy, Concord, N.H. , 1896 First

Eddy, Mary Baker Retrospection and Introspection Trustees under the Will of Mary Baker Eddy 1891, 1892 95

Eddy, Mary Baker Rudimental Divine Science/No and Yes Trustees under the Will of Mary Baker Eddy 1891, 1908 46

Eddy, Mary Baker Science and Health 124th

Eddy, Mary Baker, Science and Health with Key to the Scriptures, Eric William Winston Taylor 1906 700

Eddy, Mary Baker Science and Health with Key to the Scriptures, Allison V. Stewart, Falmouth and St. Paul Streets, Boston, Mass. 1875, 1906 700 1910

Eddy, Mary Baker Stetson Letters Ann Beals, The Bookmark

Eddy, Mary Baker, Unity of Good, Tstees of Will of Mary Baker Eddy 1908 64

Eddy, Mary Baker Visions of Mary Baker Eddy as recorded by her secretary, Calvin A. Frye, Carpenter, Gilbert C., Jr., C.S.B. 1935 89 second

Eddy, Mary Baker What is Nearest and Dearest to My Heart The Harmony Shop, 38 West St., Boston 1907 1 first

Eddy, Mary Baker (many authors about MBE) Misc. Documents relating to Christian Science & Mary Baker Eddy, Carpenter, Gilbert C., Jr. C.S.B. 232 first

Eddy, Mary Baker as prepared by Alfred E. Baker, Notes on Metaphysical Obstetrics, Obstetrics Class of June, 1900, Carpenter, G. C., Jr., C.S.B. 1930 41 first

Eddy, Mary Baker G. Historical Sketch of Metaphysical Healing. Eddy, Mary Baker G. 1885 1 21 first

Eddy, Mary Baker G., Mind-Healing: Historical Sketch. Eddy, Mary Baker G. 1886 1 24 first

Eddy, Mary Baker G. Miscellaneous Writings 1883-1896 Trustees under the Will of Mary Baker Eddy 1896 471

Eddy, Mary Baker G. Retrospection and Introspection Joseph Armstrong, 250, Huntington Ave., Boston, Mass., 1907 1891, 1892 130

Eddy, Mary Baker G. Rudimental Divine Science Joseph Armstrong, CSD, 95 Falmouth St., Boston, Mass., 1897 1891 35 tenth

Eddy, Mary Baker with commentary by GCC, Sr., & Jr. Mary Baker Eddy, Her Spiritual Precepts, volumes I-V Gilbert C. Carpenter, C.S.B., & Gilbert C. Carpenter, Jr., C.S.B. 1942 5 np first

Eddy, Mary Baker, compiled by G. C. Carpenter, Jr. Fragments Gathered from Unpub. Items ascribed to Mrs. Eddy, Carpenter, G. C., Jr., C.S.B. 1947 208 first

Eddy, Mary Baker, compiled by G. C. Carpenter, Jr. Watches • Prayers • Arguments Carpenter, Gilbert C., Jr., C.S.B. 1950 114 final

Eddy, Mary Baker-©James Neal & Thomas Hatten Church Manual of The First Church of Christ, Scientist, in Boston, MA Christian Science Publishing Society, 95 Falmouth St., Boston, Mass. 1897 76

Eddy, Rev. Mary Baker, Christ and Christmas, Mary Baker Eddy 1897 53 third

Eddy, Rev. Mary Baker, Pulpit and Press Mary Baker Eddy 1895 131 first

Ernest Sutherland Bates, Mrs. Eddy's Right-Hand Man, Harper & Bros 1931 162 12

F. A. Moore, ed. Gems for You William H. Fisk, Manchester, NH 1850 312 first

F. E. H. The Latter Days with Evidence from The Great Pyramid London: Robert Banks & Son, Racquet Court, Fleet Street, E.C. 1895 40 first

Fisher, H. A. L. Our New Religion, Jonathan Cape & Harrison Smith, New York 1930 201 first

Flower, B. O. Christian Science as a Religious Belief and a Therapeutic Agent 20th Century Company 1909 158 first

Fosbery, Arthur F., C.S. Healings Done by Mrs. Eddy, Arthur F. Fosbury, C.S.

Frye, Calvin A. Diary Calvin A. Frye n/a n.p. photost

Gilman, James F. Recollections of Mary Baker Eddy Gilbert C. Carpenter, Jr., C.S.B. 1937? 92 second

Glover, Mary Baker, Science and Health, Christian Scientist Pub. Co. 1875 456 first

Glover, Mary Baker Science and Health Asa G. Eddy, Lynn, No. 8 Broad Street 1876 2nd 167 second

Glover, Mary Baker Science and Health 19th

Glover, Mary Baker The Science of Man by which the sick are healed embracing Q's & A's . . . Mary Baker Glover 1870 22 second

Glover, Mary Baker (Mary Baker Eddy) Science and Health Winifred W. Gatling, Mizpah, Jaffa Road, Jerusalem, Israel 1874 456 first

Grekel, Doris Principle and Practice, Science in Education, 1980 353 first
Grekel, Doris The Individual Christian Scientist-vol. 4, no. 4 661 first
Hanna, Septimus J. Christian Science History CSPS 1899 44 first
Hanna, Septimus J. The Christian Science Case Ernest J. Brosang, 4 Glen Rd., Bound Brook, NJ (republished) 21
Hanna, Septimus J.-orig. published by CSPS Healing through Christian Science. Discourses & Editorials, Ernest J. Brosang, Bound Brook, NJ 1902 36
Harper's Magazine vol. 162, 2/31
Hartsook, Andrew Christian Science after 1910 Andrew Hartsook, Zanesville, Ohio 1993 215 first
Hay, Ella H. A Child's Life of Mary Baker Eddy Christian Science Publishing Society, One Norway Street, Boston, Mass. 1942 120
Henry, Edward L. The Birthplace of Mary Baker Eddy-Bow, New Hampshire The Woodbury E. Hunt Company, Concord, New Hampshire 1914 np(12) first
Henty, Doris Dufour, C.S. Addresses and Other Writings on Christian Science, Mulberry Press, Box 461, Carmel, Calif. 93921 1990 346 first
Houpt, Charles Theodore Bliss Knapp, Christian Scientist Charles Theodore Houpt 1976, 1979 417 first
Hufford, Kenneth Mary Baker Eddy: The Stoughton Years Longyear Foundation, 120 Seaver St., Brookline, MA 1963 41+2 first
Irving C. Tomlinson, M.A., C.S.B. Twelve Years with Mary Baker Eddy; Recollections and Experiences CSPS, Boston, Mass., USA 1945 227
Johnson, William Lyman From Hawthorne Hall The Homewood Press, (Dorchester) Boston, Mass. 1922 421
Johnson, William Lyman The History of the Christian Science Movement The Zion Research Foundation 1926 2 958 first
Johnston, Julia Michael Mary Baker Eddy: Her mission and Triumph Christian Science Publishing Society 1946, 1974 195 ?
Jones, Elizabeth Earl Reminiscences of Mary Baker Eddy Elizabeth Earl Jones
Joseph S. Robinson Waymarks . . in the life of Mary Baker Eddy The Pond-Ekberg Company, Springfield, Mass. 1942 108 LimitedDe Luxe
Kathrens, R. D., (compiler) Sidelights on Mary Baker Eddy-Glover-Science Church Trustees Controversy Kathrens, R. D. 1907 88 first
Keene, John Henry Christian Science and its Enemies. W. E. C. Harrison & Sons, Baltimore 1902 49 first
Kimball, Edward A. Lectures and Articles on Christian Science Edna Kimball Wait, Chesterton, Indiana 1921 486 first
Kimball, Edward A.-edited by Frank Baker Smith, Teaching and Addresses of Edward A. Kimball, C.S.D., Metaphysical Science Assoc., Los Angeles, CA 1917 382
Knapp, Bliss Ira Oscar Knapp and Flavia Stickney Knapp: A Biographical Sketch Plimpton Press 1925
Knapp, Bliss The Destiny of The Mother Church Bliss Knapp 1947 234 first
Kratzer, Rev. G.A., Dominion Within, Kratzer, Rev. G.A. 1913 224 first
Kratzer, Rev. G.A. Revelation Interpreted The Central Christian Science Institute, Chicago 1915 396 first
Lambert, Rev. L. A. Christian Science • Before the Bar of Reason Christian Press Association Publishing Company 1908 212
Longyear, Mary Beecher The Genealogy and Life of Asa Gilbert Eddy Mary Beecher Longyear 1922 140 first

Longyear, Mary Beecher The History of a House • Its Founder, Family and Guests The Zion Research Foundation, Brookline, Mass. 1925 69 first

Lord, Myra B. Mary Baker Eddy Davis & Bond, Boston 1918 62 first

Meehan, Michael Mrs. Eddy and the Late Suit in Equity Meehan, Michael 1908 371 Authorized

Milmine, Georgine Mary Baker G. Eddy; The story of her life & the history of C.S., S. S. McClure Co. (and originalholder of copyright) 1906 4

Milmine, Georgine , The Life of Mary Baker G. Eddy and The History of Christian Science, Doubleday, Page & Company, New York 1907 495 first

Norton, Carol The Christian Science Church; Its Organization and Polity Christian Science Publishing Society 1904 38 first

Norton, Carol, NCSA copyright holder The New World Christian Science Publishing Society 1894 np second

Norwood, Edward Everett Remin. of Mary Baker Eddy, Edward Everett Norwood

Nowell, Ames, C.S.B., D.D., Th.D. Mary Baker Eddy, Her Revelation of Divine Egoism Veritas Institute, Inc., New York 1963, 1965 264 first

Oakes, Richard F., C.S., Discerning the Rights of Man, Richard F. Oakes, 1971 42

Oakes, Richard, C.S., compiler Divinity Course and General Collectanea of Items By & About MBE Rare Book Company, 286 second

Oakes, Richard, C.S., compiler Essays and other Footprints, Rare Book Co. 280

Oakes, Richard, C.S., compiler Mary Baker Eddy's Lessons of The Seventh Day Christian Science Research Library, Christian Science Found., 1989 377

Oakes, Richard, C.S., compiler, Mary Baker Eddy's Published Writings-(other than Prose) 1895-1910, Christian Science Research Library, C.S. Found. 1987 535

Oakes, Richard, C.S., compiler Mary Baker Eddy's Six Days of Revelation Christian Science Research Library 1981 561

Oakes, Richard, C.S., compiler The Story of The Chicago Addresses of Mary Baker Eddy Richard Oakes 1988 70 Revised

Orcutt, William Dana Mary Baker Eddy and her books Christian Science Publishing Society 1950 198 first

Orgain, Alice Distinguishing Characteristics of MBE's Progressive Revisions of S & H, Rare Book Company, 99 Nassau Street, New York, NY 1933 80

Orgain, Alice Story of the Christian Science Manual • Proving its immortality Rare Book Company 1934 331 first

Orgain, Alice L. The Detached Branch, The Olive Branch of Peace The Detached Branch, 1931 503 first

Orgain, Alice L., A Loyal Christian Scientist, As It Is, A. L. Orgain, 1929 949 first

Peel, Robert Mary Baker Eddy, The Years of Authority, 1892-1910 Holt, Rhinehart and Winston of Canada 1977 3/3 528 first

Peel, Robert Mary Baker Eddy, The Years of Discovery, 1821-1875 Holt, Rhinehart and Winston of Canada 1966 1/3 370 first

Peel, Robert Mary Baker Eddy: The Years of Trial, 1876-1891 Holt, Rhinehart and Winston of Canada 1971 2/3 391 first

Powell, Lyman P. Mary Baker Eddy: A Life Size Portrait The MacMillan Company, New York, 1930 1930 364 first

Quimby, Phineas P./ ed. by Horatio W. Dresser The Quimby Manuscripts Thomas Y. Crowell Company, New York 1921 462 first

Ramsay, E. Mary Christian Science and its Discoverer Christian Science Publishing Society 1923, 1935cs 118 second

Richard Southall Grant Landmarks for Christian Scientists from Bow to Boston Rand Avery Co., Boston, Mass. 1937 174 third

Salchow, John G. Souvenir Album of the Home of Rev. Mary Baker Eddy, Chestnut Hill,... John G. Salchow 1911 np first
Sargent, Laura and Victoria Reminiscences of Mary Baker Eddy
Sass, Karin with illustrations by Christa Kieffer Mary Baker Eddy: A Special Friend Christian Science Publishing Society 1983 np second
Seal, Frances Thurber Christian Science in Germany Longyear Historical Society, 120 Seaver St., Brookline, MA 02146 1931 83 third
Searle, George M. The Truth about Christian Science Paulist Press, NY 1916 305
Shannon, Clara M. Sainsbury, C.S.D. Golden Memories The Gethsemane Foundation, St. Maries, Idaho pub.-1990 36 second
Shannon, Clara M. Sainsbury, C.S.D. In the Service of Mary Baker Eddy-Remin. by Clara M. Shannon, Longyear Foundation, Brookline, Mass. 1958
Simonsen, Reverend Severin E. From The Methodist Pulpit into Christian Science & How I Demonstrated ... M. Simonsen, Fair Oaks, CA 1928 294 ninth
Smaus, Jewel Spangler Mary Baker Eddy, The Golden Days Christian Science Publishing Society 1966 CSPS 193 first
Smillie, Paul R. Loving Our Leader The Gethsemane Foundation, St. Maries, Idaho 1988 52 first
Smillie, Paul R. Mary Baker Eddy: The Prophetic and Historical Perspective-Vol. I The Gethsemane Foundation, St. Maries, Idaho 1979 333 second
Smillie, Paul R. Our Leader's Demonstration of Generic Man The Gethsemane Foundation, St. Maries, Idaho 1987 12 first
Smith, Clifford P. Historical and Biographical Papers; First Series Christian Science Publishing Society 1934 1/2 103 first
Smith, Clifford P. Historical and Biographical Papers; Second Series Christian Science Publishing Society 1934 268
Smith, Judge Clifford P. Christian Science and Legislation Christian Science Publishing Society 1905,1909 128 second
Smith, Judge Clifford P. Christian Science: Its Legal Status, A Defence of Human Rights, Christian Science Publishing Society 1914 127 first
Smith, Judge Clifford P. Historical and Biographical Papers Christian Science Publishing Society 1934 127 first
Smith, Karl N., and Walter H. Wilson Support for the Christian Science Board of Directors Plainfield Community Church, Plainfield, NJ 1945 np.
Smith, Louise A. Mary Baker Eddy: Discoverer and Founder of Christian Science, Christian Science Publishing Society 1990 198 20th century
Spencer, Ralph B. The Overwhelming Evidence Concerning Spiritual Healings thru MBE Ralph B. Spencer, Seekonk, Mass. 02771 1963, 1976 68 Fourth
Springer, Fleta Campbell According to the Flesh; a biography of Mary Baker Eddy Coward-McCann, Inc., New York 1930 CMcC 497 first
Stetson, Augusta E., C.S.D. Reminiscences, Sermons and Correspondence / 1884-1913 G. P. Putnam's Sons, New York and London 1913 1200 first
Stetson, Augusta E., C.S.D., Sermons Which Spiritually Interpret the Scriptures and Other Writings G. P. Putnam's Sons, New York and London 1924 1277 first
Stewart, Myrtle The 1910 Coup Stewart, Myrtle 1972 58 first
Still, M. Adelaide, Reminiscences of Mary Baker Eddy M. Adelaide Still
Studdert Kennedy, Hugh A. (Anketell) Mrs. Eddy As I Knew Her The Farallon Press, 58 Sutter St., San Francisco, CA 1931 118
Studdert Kennedy, Hugh A. (Anketell) Christian Science and Organized Religion The Farallon Press 1930 335 first

Studdert Kennedy, Hugh A. (Anketell) Mrs. Eddy The Farallon Press, San Francisco 1947 507 first
Swain, Richard L. The Real Key to Christian Science Fleming H. Revell Company 1917 95 fifth
Tomlinson, Rev. Irving C. , M.A., C.S.B. Twelve Years with Mary Baker Eddy: Recollections and Experiences ©1945,1966,renewed 1973, CSPS 227 first
Twain, Mark Christian Science with notes containing corrections to date Harper & Brothers Publishers, New York & London 1899 362
Walter, William W., The Unfoldment William W. Walter 1921 206 first
Wilbur, Sibyl, Cradled Obscurity or The Finding of the Christ,The Bookmark 11
Wilbur, Sibyl The Life of Mary Baker Eddy Christian Science Publishing Society 1907 384 first
Williamson, Margaret The Mother Church Extension Christian Science Publishing Society 1939, 1968 2/2 109
Wright, Helen Mary Baker Eddy: God's Great Scientist-Volume I Helen Wright 1984 1/3 255 first
Wright, Helen Mary Baker Eddy: God's Great Scientist-Volume II Helen Wright 1984 2/3 133 first
Wright, Helen Mary Baker Eddy: God's Great Scientist-Volume III Helen Wright 1987 3/3 265 first
Wright, Helen M. If Mary Baker Eddy's Manual were Obeyed-Enlarged Edition Helen Wright 1986 231 Second, enlarged
Wright, Helen M. Mary Baker Eddy Reveals Your Divinity Hearthstone Book 1991 271 first
Wright, Helen M., Humanity's Divinity, HM Wright Publishing 1994 331 first
Wright, Helen M. Made Whole Through Our Marriage To God HM Wright Publishing 1996 346 first
Wright, Helen M. Mary Baker Eddy's Church Manual and Church Universal Triumphant Helen Wright 1981 319 first
Young, Alan MBE-Her Pleasant View and Infinite Vision The Bookmark 9

To Obtain Additional Books
In this Trilogy by Doris Grekel

Please contact your local bookstore for the following titles:

The Discovery of the Science of Man (Volume I)
The Life of Mary Baker Eddy (1821-1888) 412pp
ISBN: 1-893107-23-X Paperback $16.95

The Founding of Christian Science (Volume II)
The Life of Mary Baker Eddy (1888-1900) 538pp
ISBN: 1-893107-24-8 Paperback $18.95

The Forever Leader (Volume III)
The Life of Mary Baker Eddy (1901-1910) 673pp
ISBN: 0-9645803-8-1 Paperback $22.95

If your local bookstore does not have them in stock, you can order these titles from your bookstore through "Books in Print" or you may contact the publisher, Healing Unlimited, at (800) 962-1464.